THE LIFE MODEL OF
SOCIAL WORK
PRACTICE

ALEX GITTERMAN
CAREL B. GERMAIN

THE LIFE MODEL
OF SOCIAL WORK
PRACTICE

ADVANCES IN THEORY AND PRACTICE

•

THIRD EDITION

COLUMBIA UNIVERSITY PRESS

NEW YORK

Columbia University Press
Publishers Since 1893
New York   Chichester, West Sussex
Copyright © 2008 Columbia University Press
All rights reserved

Library of Congress Cataloging-in-Publication Data

Gitterman, Alex
    The life model of social work practice : advances in theory and practice / Alex
Gitterman and Carel B. Germain.—3rd ed.
        p.   cm.
    Includes bibliographical references and index.
    ISBN 978-0-231-13998-4 (cloth : alk. paper)—ISBN 978-0-231-51153-7 (ebook)
        1. Social case work.   2. Human beings—Effect of environment on.
    1. Germain, Carel B.   II. Title.
    HV43.G47   2008
    361.3'2—dc22   2007053008

This book is dedicated to Professor **Carel Bailey Germain**, who died on August 3, 1995, just as we were editing the final manuscript of the prior edition.

Our collaboration began in 1972 as faculty colleagues developing the first integrated practice course at the Columbia University School of Social Work. This led to a twenty-three-year writing collaboration and close friendship. The effort to develop and express our ideas about practice forged an enduring bond between us.

Professor Germain was internationally recognized for her brilliant scholarship. She drew on numerous academic disciplines to develop ideas about human ecology. Her body of work reflects an uncommon intellect and erudition. She bequeaths a lasting gift to the profession.

Professor Germain held fast to her ideas, never cutting her cloth to suit the fashion of the day. She was graceful, gentle, and gallant. Her understated wit was illuminating and often trenchant.

The epilogue in our second edition ended with "And so our journey continues!" Without Carel the journey has been lonelier, but her originality, powerful ideas, and loyalty have been sources of continuing strength.

Alex Gitterman

CONTENTS

PREFACE

For the authors, the first edition of *The Life Model of Social Work Practice* symbolized a long, adventurous journey. It began in 1972 at the Columbia University School of Social Work when we and another colleague, Mary Funnyé Goldson, were asked by the dean to develop a plan for the first year of social work practice courses. Earlier the faculty had decided to restructure the total curriculum to take into account emerging knowledge, new human needs, and developments occurring in practice itself as agencies sought to meet the challenges of that era. This led to our effort to reconceptualize practice and to develop an integrated social work method. Out of this joint work on a first-year practice curriculum came our further collaboration in workshops, consultations, and writing.

We found that ecological ideas helped us to understand how each of us became a source of learning for the other. Sometimes our different professional traditions, knowledge base, and practice experiences felt like barriers to mutual understanding, but actually facilitated and enriched the development of our ideas. The first edition represented a beginning attempt to work out the dimensions of integrated method practice with individuals, families, groups, social networks, and organizations. Our ideas rested on the assumption that there are many common skills in working with people, no matter on what level people are organized. The first edition also attempted to identify distinctive skills such as those used in forming groups or influencing organizations. The common skills, as well as the distinctive ones, were presented within an ecological perspective that offered a dual, simultaneous focus on people and environments. These skills were presented within the context of underlying diverse theories and knowledge at each level of human organization—individuals, families, groups, bureaucratic systems, social networks, and the physical environment.

In the twenty-seven years since the publication of the first edition of *The Life Model of Social Work Practice*, and in the eleven years since the publication of the second edition, there have been dramatic changes in the profession and in the societal context of new social problems, new populations, and new public attitudes. Social workers today deal with profoundly vulnerable populations, overwhelmed by oppressive daily struggles with poverty, discrimination, and various life circumstances that they are powerless to control. Social workers in the 2000s confront daily the devastating impact of homelessness, substance abuse, chronic mental disorders, child abuse, unemployment, family and community violence, and AIDS and other grave illnesses. While social problems are growing more intractable, resources to mitigate them continue to decrease. In this new edition we respond to these pervasive changes and present a more fully developed life-modeled practice—a practice modeled on natural life processes. While retaining and refining the core of our previous work, we make use of new concepts and new content. We believe this book provides social work practitioners and students with the necessary knowledge base and practice guidelines to deal with the many professional, societal, theoretical, empirical, and ethical issues they face.

We remain committed to our original conceptions and have broadened and deepened them. The *ecological metaphor* continues to provide concepts that illuminate the continuous exchanges between people and their environments. In the second edition, we adopted a *life course* of human development and functioning. In this edition, we continue to develop the life course formulation. In contrast to traditional stage models of development, this formulation takes into account diversity in race, ethnicity, sex, age, socioeconomic status, sexual orientation, and physical/mental challenges, and environmental forces within historical, societal, and cultural contexts. "Life course" is a multidisciplinary formulation (in anthropology, social psychology, social history, biology, psychiatry, and sociology), adapted here for social work. We use "life course" to replace the traditional, linear "life cycle" models and their assumption that emotional and social development proceed in fixed, sequential, universal stages without reference to the diversity of life experience, culture, and environments.

In this edition we further develop an *integrated practice*. We continue to believe that professional specialization should not determine whether a client receives individual, family, group, or community services. Rather, the service should be based on client needs and preferences. Two formulations are particularly helpful in developing an integrated life-modeled practice.*

---

*We use the term *life* model interchangeably with *life-modeled practice* in order to add still more emphasis to the fact that the practice is patterned on natural life processes. We are less concerned with whether the approach is a model in the technical sense and

The first, *degree of client choice*, differentiates common professional methods and skills in the initial phase by how much choice an individual, family, or group has in accepting or rejecting a social work service (i.e., whether the client sought the service or an agency offered or mandated a service) rather than by a particular modality. The second, *life stressors–stress–coping*, supports an integrated practice related to the assessment of and intervention in varied life stressors rather than to an agency's service mode. Life stressors and associated stress include (1) difficult life transitions and traumatic life events; (2) harsh social and physical environments; and (3) dysfunctional interpersonal processes in families and groups, and between workers and clients. Recent research and practice reveal that managing a life stressor of any kind can involve simultaneous changes in (1) social, psychological, and biological functioning; (2) interpersonal processes; and (3) altered environmental processes requiring new responses.

While we realize that any separation of phenomena distorts the reality of simultaneous processes, we think analyzing them separately has distinct advantages. Social work practitioners are overwhelmed by the nature, range, and intractability of life stressors faced by the people they serve. The life stressor–stress–coping paradigm covers an almost limitless variety of human plights and provides a useful schema for specifying, grouping, and organizing data throughout the helping process. The paradigm also provides heuristic guidelines that focus and direct interventions at any point during the helping encounter and links clinical practice with practice in growth-promotion and prevention programs. We caution readers that life stressors often must be managed simultaneously or, at least, any one of them may need to be managed in such a way as to have a positive impact on the others.

The oppression experienced by many of those we serve leaves their families, networks, and communities vulnerable to deprivation and deterioration. These realities have required us to work more intensely on building bridges between the clinical and social reform traditions of the profession. Social workers whose practice is life-modeled must be increasingly engaged in organizational, community, or neighborhood and policy practice. When working with individuals, families, and groups, many life-modeled practitioners expand their practice to populations of similarly affected persons, helping them to undertake social action and develop preventive and growth-promoting programs. We continue to make a determined effort in this book to explore the connections between people's life stressors (private troubles) and community, organizational, and legislative influence and change (public issues).

---

more concerned with ensuring the embodiment of those real-life processes that release human potential and lead to continued growth, empowerment, satisfying biopsychosocial functioning, and effective action to improve environments and contribute to social justice.

The book is divided into three parts. Part 1 offers a historical, theoretical, and methodological overview. Chapter 1, "Social Work Practice and Its Historical Traditions," is a new chapter and traces social work's historical dialectics such as cause or function (social action or clinical treatment), generalist or specialist, and science or art. The current societal context, (economic, political, legislative, and cultural), and its impact on current professional developments, are explored. Chapter 2, "The Ecological Perspective," reviews the theoretical perspective, including new concepts from deep ecology and ecofeminism. Chapter 3, "The Life Model of Social Work Practice: An Overview," presents the defining characteristics and anatomy of life-modeled practice at this point in its development. It briefly delineates modalities, methods, and skills used to help people to cope with or meliorate life stressors. Chapter 4, "Assessment, Practice Monitoring, and Practice Evaluation," is also a new chapter. It examines assessment tasks common to all practice approaches as well as a few underlying beliefs that are distinct to life-modeled practice. The chapter also examines the tasks and skills of practice monitoring as well as the strengths and limitations of different research designs used to evaluate practice outcomes.

Part 2 presents the knowledge, values, methods, and skills of life-modeled practice with individuals, families, formed groups, organizations, and social networks. Chapter 5, "Preparation: Settings, Modalities, Methods, and Skills," another new chapter, examines the professional processes of skillfully entering people's lives. People must feel safe and accepted before they can trust and confide in a professional. The chapter also examines the essential preparatory tasks in forming a group and in selecting the appropriate modality and temporal arrangement. Chapter 6, "Beginnings: Settings, Modalities, Methods, and Skills," examines the initial phase of working together, that is, of getting started with individuals and collectivities. All helping rests on shared definitions about life stressors and explicit agreement on goals, plans, and methods.

Chapters 7 through 11 cover the ongoing phase. Specifically, chapter 7, "Helping Individuals, Families, and Groups with Stressful Life Transitions and Traumatic Events," discusses the distinctive knowledge and skills of helping individuals and collectivities deal with painful life changes. Chapter 8, "Helping Individuals, Families, and Groups with Environmental Stressors," considers the interrelated dimensions of helping individuals and collectivities negotiate their organizational, social network, and spatial and temporal environments. Chapter 9, "Helping with Dysfunctional Family Processes," and chapter 10, "Helping with Dysfunctional Group Processes," explore the issues of helping the family and groups reduce dysfunctional interpersonal processes that prevent the fulfillment of members' individual and shared needs. Chapter 11, "Reducing Interpersonal Stress between Worker and Client," explores interpersonal stress in the worker-client relationship, particularly the processes that interfere with helpfulness. Chapter

12, "Endings: Settings, Modalities, Methods, and Skills," considers the ending phase, or termination, of the work together, and evaluation of practice.

Part 3 examines life-modeled practice at community, organizational, and policy levels. Chapter 13, "Influencing Community and Neighborhood Life," focuses on helping communities and neighborhoods to achieve desired improvements in their quality of life. Chapter 14, "Influencing the Practitioner's Organization," discusses professional issues and methods of influencing organizational operations that do not serve their intended beneficiaries. Chapter 15, "Influencing Legislation, Regulations, and Electoral Politics," embraces the commitment to a just society through the participation of practitioners in political activity. Social work's purpose and its value system require us to help change the oppressive life conditions of many clients. We therefore regard community, organizational, and political advocacy for social justice as the responsibility of all social workers.

The appendixes contain samples of individual, family, and group assessments (appendix A); Records of Service, a practice monitoring instrument (appendix B); and Critical Incidents, a practice monitoring instrument (appendix C).

Alex Gitterman and Carel B. Germain

ACKNOWLEDGMENTS

We are deeply grateful to our baccalaureate, master's, and doctoral students—and to administrators and practitioners whom we met in the course of our teaching and consultation work—for their generosity in permitting us to use their practice excerpts. We especially appreciate the remarkable richness and relevance of their materials to the social issues facing our society and to the struggles of our profession to meet increasingly complex human needs. We are indebted to faculty colleagues throughout Canada and the United States who have influenced our work in many ways. Alex thanks Professor Nancy Humphreys for her generous sharing of macro teaching notes and other materials as well as for providing feedback on a number of chapters prepared for this edition. Alex also thanks faculty colleagues Diane Drachman, Carolyn Knight, Jacqueline Mondros, and Lawrence Shulman for their helpful suggestions on various chapters as well as for their friendship and support over many years.

Alex is also indebted to his late, beloved, faculty colleagues and friends George Brager, Richard Cloward, Mary Funnyé Goldson, Charles Grosser, Irving Miller, William Schwartz, and Hyman J. Weiner for their remarkable contributions to social work theory and practice. Their ideas continue to influence the profession and Alex's own work.

Carel would have thanked and Alex thanks our colleagues Ann Hartman, Steven Holloway, Joan Laird, Judith A. B. Lee, and Renee Solomon for sharing their creativity and practice acumen with us over the years.

We also express our appreciation to Jan Lambert, University of Connecticut School of Social Work librarian, for lending us her professional competence as well as for her graciousness and generosity.

Finally, we are grateful to our families for their love and support. Alex is grateful for the professional contributions of his wife, Naomi, as well as for her abiding love and support and that of their children, Daniel and Sharon; daughter-in-law, Amy; and grandchildren, Max and Claire. In their distinctive ways, Alex's late mother, stepfather, and father, Fay, Pincus, and Aaron; his aunt, Maria; and his late mother-in-law, Ilse, taught him the meaning of courage and the value of life. Carel was always grateful for the love and devotion of her husband, William, and daughters, Adrienne and Denise. She was also extremely proud of her daughters' significant professional accomplishments and, most of all, of their humanity.

THE LIFE MODEL OF
SOCIAL WORK
PRACTICE

OVERVIEW

Part 1 introduces the historical context for the life model. The current conceptual framework of the ecological perspective for social work practice follows the historical perspective. A brief overview of life-modeled practice is also presented: its defining features, modalities, methods, and skills. Part 1 concludes with a discussion of assessment, practice monitoring, and practice evaluation.

Chapter 1 traces themes and trends in the United States' historical development of social work's practice purposes and methods. Particular attention is paid to the historical dialectics such as cause-function (social action–clinical treatment), generalist-specialist, and the science and art of practice. The current societal context (economic, political, legislative, and cultural) and its impact on current professional developments are explored.

Chapter 2 reviews the major ecological concepts that underlie life-modeled practice:

1. Ecological thinking focuses on the reciprocity of person:environment exchanges, in which each shapes and influences the other over time. (The colon is used to repair the conceptually fractured relationship suggested by the hyphen in *person-environment*.)
2. Varied levels of fit between people's needs, goals, and rights, and their environment's qualities and processes, within a historical and cultural context; adaptedness and adaptation, achieved by making changes in the self, the environment, or both in order to improve or sustain the level of fit;

maladaptiveness leading to dysfunctional perceptions, emotions, thinking, and action; and positive and negative feedback processes.

3. Salutary and nonsalutary human habitats and niches.

4. Vulnerability, oppression, abuse or misuse of power, and social and technological pollution.

5. The "life course" conception of nonuniform pathways to human development and functioning, replacing traditional formulations that consider development a journey through fixed, sequential, universal stages. The life course conception incorporates human, environmental, and cultural diversity, and it is applicable to individuals and groups. It also makes use of temporal concepts—historic, social, and individual time—in considering psychosocial functioning.

6. Life stressors that threaten the level of fit and lead to associated emotional or physiological stress, and the coping tasks that require personal skills and environmental resources for managing the life stressors and reducing the associated stress.

7. Resilience reflects moment-to-moment consequences and outcomes of complex person:environment transactions and not simply attributes of a person. Protective factors that help people to negotiate high-risk situations include (1) temperament, (2) family patterns, (3) external supports, and (4) environmental resources.

8. Deep ecology deepens our understanding that all phenomena are interconnected and interdependent as well as dependent on the cyclical processes of nature. The interdependence of networks, the self-correcting feedback loops, and the cyclical nature of ecological processes are three basic principles of deep ecology.

9. Ecological feminism or ecofeminism challenges the culture/nature dichotomy. To ecofeminists, the oppression of women and ecological degradation are intertwined: both evolve from hierarchical, male domination. Hierarchal structures and oppression are always together.

Chapter 3 provides a brief overview of the origins and characteristics of life-modeled practice. Ten features, in unique combination, define life-modeled practice: (1) professional purpose and function, which includes practice with individuals, families, groups, and communities, and organizational and political advocacy; (2) ethical practice; (3) diversity-sensitive and skillful practice; (4) empowering and social justice practice; (5) integrated modalities, methods, and skills; (6) the client:worker relationship regarded as a partnership; (7) agreements, assessments, and life stories; (8) a focus on personal and collective strengths and on client action and decision making; (9) the pervasive significance of social and physical environments and culture; (10) the evaluation of practice and contribution to knowledge building.

The preparatory, initial, ongoing, and ending phases of work structure life-modeled practice, even in one-session and episodic services, where the phases are temporally collapsed. Life-modeled practice focuses on (1) painful life transitions and traumatic life events; (2) poverty, oppression, and unresponsiveness or harshness of social and physical environments; and (3) dysfunctional interpersonal processes in families or groups and sometimes between the practitioner and the people served. These and many other aspects are considered in greater detail and depth in parts 2 and 3.

Chapter 4 examines assessment tasks common to all practice approaches as well as a few underlying beliefs that are distinct to life-modeled practice. Life-modeled practice strongly values and encourages *client participation* in the assessment tasks, and emphasizes assessment of the *level of fit* between human needs and environmental resources. Graphic representations—ecomap, genogram, and social network map—and force-field analysis provide a visual "snapshot" of individuals', families', groups', communities', social networks', and organizations' capacities to deal with stressors and change.

The chapter also examines the tasks and skills of practice monitoring. To truly monitor practice interventions, they must be evaluated by how the client experiences and evaluates their connectedness to the underlying messages being conveyed rather than by what the professional intended to accomplish. Various practice-monitoring instruments are discussed and illustrated. The chapter concludes with an examination of the strengths and limitations of different research designs used to evaluate practice outcomes.

We hope that the examination of historical context and contemporary societal and professional themes, the ecological concepts, and the overview of the totality of life-modeled practice and issues related to assessment, practice monitoring, and practice evaluation in part 1 will help the reader move confidently and eagerly into parts 2 and 3 and their detailed study of a complex professional practice. It is complex because it is designed to prepare students and seasoned practitioners to move knowledgeably and skillfully among varied modalities (individual, family, group, neighborhood and community, organizational, and political) as needed.

SOCIAL WORK PRACTICE AND ITS
HISTORICAL TRADITIONS

The generalist and integrative methods of the life model of practice are both an outcome of historical trends and a response to current issues within the profession. New or emerging forms of practice need to be understood in the light of professional traditions that have spurred their development. They need to be understood also in the light of demands placed upon the profession by external forces in its environment and by internal forces within the profession. Both past and present shape the characteristics of practice. In this chapter, we trace themes and trends in the historical development in the United States of social work's practice purposes and methods. We pay particular attention to the historical dialectics such as cause or function (social action or clinical treatment), generalist or specialist, and science or art. These historical dialectics help to explain the existence and nature of contemporary practice issues and efforts to integrate divergent traditions.

Early Societal and Professional Themes

Occupational Forerunners

The process of divergence began in the United States when two streams of thought appeared in the nineteenth-century arena of social welfare, then called "charities and corrections." One was more interested in theory, and the other in methods of help. Both streams arose out of the social events, requirements, and ideologies of the times. Profound transformation in the social order had taken place in the years after the Civil War. Change was everywhere: in the westward push by wagon and later by rail; in the migration from farms to the towns and cities; in the movement of vast tides of immigrants away from old world oppressions and famines to new world freedoms and opportunities; in the expansions of knowledge, science, and technology; and in the development of graduate education and increasing specialization and professionalization in the occupational structure. Greatest of all, perhaps, were the changes in values and norms as the nation shifted from an agrarian to an industrialized, urbanized society. To most white citizens, these movements, changes, and expansions seemed to offer unlimited opportunities for those who wished to respond to them.

In actuality, the twin forces of industrialization and urbanization, with which these movements and expansions were interdependent, were accompanied by severe social disorganization. Industrialization (as well as the rationalization and bureaucratization of production) led to the concentration of wealth and power and the growing alienation of labor. Persistent poverty was aggravated by cyclical depressions. Wretched housing, inadequate schools, and oppressive work arrangements characterized crowded urban slums and poor rural areas. The government itself favored and was, in fact, in thrall to the nation's business interests. The principle of laissez-faire was for the poor; the principle of free enterprise advanced the interests of the rich and the powerful and the white; and the U.S. Supreme Court upheld property rights at the expense of human rights. Slavery and segregation had a devastating impact on black citizens.

After the Civil War, more and more of society's "dependent classes"—its paupers, insane, and criminal groups—came under the aegis of state administration. Increasingly, their public care and control moved from a single locus of responsibility in the village overseer and the local almshouse to state boards of charities, state insane asylums, and prisons. Child-saving agencies and voluntary associations for relieving the plight of the poor appeared in the private arena. A number of persons who were engaged in such public or private work joined with a group of New England intellectuals, interested in the new social science in England, to organize the American Social Science Association (ASSA) in 1865. Soon after the initial meetings, however, conflicting concerns overshadowed their mutual interests. The interest of the ASSA intellectuals lay in developing knowledge about the operations of the social order so that social conditions could be changed. By contrast, the interest of those directly engaged in the care and control of society's "misfits" lay in developing the best methods for such control, care, and containment. The latter practical group believed their pressing and present concerns were overlooked by the emphasis of the intellectuals on theory development geared to achieving an uncertain gain in an unknown future.

In 1874, the practice people withdrew from the ASSA and established Conference of Charities (CC), which, in 1879, became the National Conference of Charities and Corrections (NCCC), and subsequently became the

National Conference on Social Welfare (NCSW). An interesting question is whether "Corrections" was added in its traditional field of practice meaning or, more likely, as a prelude to notions about changing people as well as distributing charity. Temporarily, at least during the 1880s, the tension between theory of social causation and methodological concerns receded; exchanging experiences in the use of different methods received primary attention. Until journals and other organizations developed, the NCCC was the principal forum for this kind of exchange.

Ideologically, the dialectical development in social work practice was more complex. Several currents of conflicting ideas appeared, and even within each current there was little unanimity of opinion. One stream of ideas was associated with the Poor Law philosophy of the colonial and antebellum periods. It included, for example, the principle of less eligibility and the settlement laws, which themselves had earlier roots in England and Europe. This stream was often accompanied by a concern that charity might lead the needy into pauperism by weakening their moral fiber. The Puritan ethic, which viewed dependency as the consequence of sin, and the Calvinistic emphases on work and on individualism fortified by the frontier spirit were congruent with a repressive stance. It was an ambivalent stance, however, since there were strong threads of piety involved, especially in attitudes toward the poor. One such thread was a humane concern for the suffering of others as in the parable of the Good Samaritan. Another and perhaps stronger thread was the promise of salvation through the giving of alms. In this view, the poor existed so that the rich might give to them, receive grace, and enter the kingdom of heaven.

Another ideological current was a growing interest in science and its promise of unlimited progress through knowledge and technology. Indeed, it was this interest coupled with idealistic reformism that had led to the establishment of the ASSA. If physical laws governed the universe with such magnificent precision as Isaac Newton and others had shown, the argument ran, then laws governing society and the interaction of human beings might also be discovered. It seemed to ASSA intellectuals, and later to some groups within the NCCC, that such laws could then be used to create a better society. They assumed that the social world was governed, like the physical world, by a set of immutable laws and that the purpose of social science was to discover and understand these laws. Many who held this conviction appeared also to believe that environmental causes were more salient than personal waywardness in most forms of human distress. Thus, the conflict between theoretical and practical interests was also related to tensions around the nature of causality, which developed in the 1880s and continued in the decades that followed. In general, the theoreticians believed causality lay in the environment, while the methodologists believed causality was to be found in the wickedness, shiftlessness, and weakness of individuals.

Connected to the interest in science, yet ultimately nonscientific in outlook, was the rise of social Darwinism that applied (actually, misapplied)

Charles Darwin's ideas about evolution to societal processes.[1] Social Darwinism provided a rationalization for the exploitation of the powerless by the powerful. Political thought, interacting with capitalistic developments, became increasingly dominated by conservatism and its emphases on economic freedom and the sanctity of private property. Political, philosophical, religious, and pseudo-scientific ideas thus combined to help create a point of view in society that opposed environmental reform.

Within this matrix of social ideas and events, two more groups joined the newly formed occupational group, exemplified by the NCCC, in the late 1880s. These were the charity organization societies that began in the United States in 1887 (Buffalo, New York), and the neighborhood settlements that began in 1886 (e.g., the Neighborhood Guild in New York City). During the Progressive era (ca. 1890–1920), both movements responded to major economic, social, and political changes. In search for employment opportunities and an improved quality of life, African Americans migrated from the South and white ethnics emigrated from Europe to northern and midwestern urban centers. These migrants and immigrants provided inexpensive labor for industries and factories. By 1914, the workforce increased seven times from the workforce in 1859. Similarly, while in the 1880s only 28.7 percent of the population in the United States (50.1 million) lived in urban areas, as compared to 35.1 percent of 63 million in the early 1900s, by 1920 the overall population had increased to more than 105 million, with 51.2 percent living in urban areas (Iglehart & Becerra, 2000, pp. 17, 19). Many social problems such as slums and crime became associated with this dramatic urban population growth.

In response to these social problems, charity organization societies and settlements appeared almost simultaneously. Each was imbued with ideas and structures that originated in Victorian England. Both spread rapidly around the country, and, although the two movements took somewhat different ideological positions and different practice outlooks, they possessed important similarities. Both appealed to young, upper- and middle-class, well-educated idealists of the day, and most especially to young women. Higher education for women had only just begun on any recognizable scale, and a new group of young women students and graduates were eager to be of service. They were looking for ways to apply their newly acquired insights and understanding to society's growing problems. The young women were also looking for ways to become financially independent. Both they and the young men at the new graduate schools, who also joined both movements, sought to have an impact on the social problems increasingly visible in the 1880s, 1890s, 1900s, 1910s, and 1920s.

Both movements had a strong religious cast, influenced by the ministry of the social gospel. Many charity organization society (COS) secretaries, especially in the early years, and several settlement head-residents were ministers. Most were Protestants, but later there were also Catholic and Jewish settlements, as well as nonsectarian charitable associations. Deeply committed to serving others (within a segregationist context), both the COS and the settlement groups believed they had found the structure that would solve the grave social problems of their era. The leader of the COS movement, Mary Richmond, and the leader of the settlement movement, Jane Addams, were both committed to social reform; however, Mary Richmond distinguished two types of social reform: "wholesale and retail reform." The settlements participated in "wholesale" reform, and the COS in "retail" reform.[2]

Despite their similarities, however, the differences between the two movements were to have a profound effect on the dialectical development of social work practice.

The Settlement Movement

To the founders of the settlements, the sources of most urban misery lay in the environment. To live among the poor, sharing their joys and sorrows, their struggles and toil, was to be a good neighbor. The "settlers," as they called themselves, asserted that their work was not charity but good neighboring, and so they worked to provide such amenities as clubs for boys and girls, classes for adults, and summer experiences in the country for children and adults. For the settlers, conflict between the classes stemmed from a lack of understanding of each other, and thus, they needed to relate to each other. Such interaction between the poor and the settlers would improve the former, and through the "gentle attrition of interaction," people would begin to understand each other and resolve their conflicts.

The settlers' devotion to democratic and liberal social philosophy went hand in hand with an abhorrence of anything that smacked of charity and what the settlers saw as charity workers' stinginess in the face of need. In times of economic depression, neighboring included creating work projects for workmen who had lost their jobs and had no way to provide for their families. The required investigation and verification of need, however, were repugnant functions to the settlers, and they considered them appropriate only in times of great emergency.

The settlers soon concluded that their well-intentioned efforts to improve the quality of life for their working-class neighbors were minimally effective in reducing the hardships imposed by the nature of the physical and social environments. They became intensely aware of tenement conditions, lack of sanitation, poor schools, inadequate play space, long working hours in factories and sweated industries, child labor, and the many obstacles faced by immigrant populations in their attempts to adapt to their new environment. The interests of the settlers broadened to include the painstaking collection of data and careful social research to support their legislative activities on behalf of environmental reforms.[3] Increasingly, settlement residents aligned themselves with the Women's Trade Union League. They supported the strikes of organized labor; they were instrumental in forming the consumer movement that worked to improve working conditions through the use of the boycott; they played a significant role in the early women's movement; and they worked for sanitation, tenement reform, the playground movement, and child labor legislation (Addams, 1910, 1930; Wald, 1915). They were in the vanguard of social reform all during the Progressive era until its end in World War I. Many worked for the unpopular peace movement of the time, and Jane Addams of Hull House, severely criticized during World War I, received the Nobel Peace Prize many years later in 1931 for these very efforts. She was very involved in political activities, including seconding Teddy Roosevelt's nomination as the candidate of the Bull Moose Party in 1912, and serving on the drafting committee of the party's platform.

From the beginning, the settlers were affiliated with colleges and universities, and sometimes were based in them. Graham Taylor of the Chicago Commons, with the help of Jane Addams and others from Hull House, established the Chicago School of Civics and Philanthropy, which, in 1920, became the University of Chicago's School of Social Service Administration.[4] Settlement connections to the social scientists of the day were strong. John Dewey and his friend and colleague, James Tufts, were frequent visitors at Hull House, and Jane Addams often referred to their influence (Dewey, 1916, 1938; Tufts, 1923). It appears to have been a reciprocal influence, since Dewey, upon joining the Columbia University faculty, continued his settlement affiliation at the University Settlement in New York City. Dewey's philosophy of pragmatism, his interest in the experimentalism of science and the instrumentalism of ideas, reintroduced humanistic values into the materialism of the times and profoundly influenced the settlement leaders. Other social scientists lived and worked in the settlements around the country to gain experience and to collect social data concerning community and neighborhood problems. Still others came as guests to conduct classes for the residents and for the neighbors. While the settlement leaders embraced social science, some were ambivalent and others rabidly opposed the idea of becoming professionalized. They believed that professionalization would result in a more conservative practice and dull the passion for social reform.

Through their participation in the NCSW (Jane Addams, in 1910, became the first woman to be president in the organization's thirty-six-year history), the settlers exerted influence on the occupational group that was beginning to think of its calling as social work. Their interest in the environment as a causal factor in human distress, their alliance with social science as the means for understanding environmental relations, and their commitment to social reform were important aspects of the discussions and debates in the forum of NCSW through the 1890s and until World War I. With the end of the Progressive era, the settlement movement lost its momentum. Although some reforms were achieved after the war, the settlers were never again as powerful in the occupational circle; they remained outside the mainstream of practice and theory developments. Their objections and resistance to professionalizing their practice diminished their potential contributions to practice and theory.

The Charity Organization Society Movement

The charity organization societies, whose philosophy was characterized by the watchword "scientific philanthropy," aimed for the rational, efficient distribution of alms, modeled after the division of labor and other methods of the new capitalistic bureaucracies. These aims were implemented by a careful study of each case, the development of central registration procedures, and coordination between charity organizations. This objective was to be achieved by organizing the various charitable organizations within a community in order to eliminate duplication and fraud. Methods were designed to separate the unworthy from the worthy poor, and included investigation and verification of need, registration, classification, conferencing, and written records. The unworthy poor were deemed to be the responsibility of public indoor (institutional) relief, while the worthy poor (victims of circumstance, such as widows with children) were considered deserving of outdoor aid (in their own homes) provided by privately sponsored charitable agencies (Lubove, 1965). Charity had to be provided in a manner that would not foster dependency.

Because there was constant apprehension that alms might destroy the individual's drive toward independence, an important additional component of the COS method was the "friendly visitor." Where possible, help was to be "not alms but a friend," or when alms were needed, such help would be given in conjunction with the services of the friendly visitor. Possessing middle- and upper-class virtues, the visitor would be able to bring to the poor an example toward which they could aspire. Like the settlement residents, the friendly visitors were volunteers, and a paid agent or secretary directed their work. Some university faculty were affiliated with the COS, seeing them as laboratories for the development of sociological knowledge, and some college and university students served as friendly visitors. The emphasis within the COS, however, was on developing the most effective methods of rehabilitating the poor one by one, while relatively little attention was given to uncovering environmental causes of poverty. Nevertheless, some COS leaders were deeply concerned about environmental issues, just as some settlers cooperated with the charitable societies and even served as friendly visitors.

When the need for advanced training was recognized by charity workers as a way to increase the effectiveness of their method and to gain professional status, the New York City COS created the first school of philanthropy in 1898, which later became the New York School of Social Work and, later still, the Columbia University School of Social Work. In contrast to the schools established by settlements, many COS-sponsored schools resisted university affiliation. During the early years, the east coast schools furnished apprentice-type training in agencies, provided by agency personnel and supplemented by class work, rather than a university-based education drawing upon social philosophy and social science, as in the schools founded by settlement leaders. The COS resistance to becoming involved in university education stemmed, in part, from the fear that an emphasis on theory would blunt the visitors' natural warmth and helpfulness. Eventually, however, all schools incorporated the apprenticeship model as the field work component in graduate education. Similarly, all schools eventually became affiliated with universities, since this offered the surest avenue to professional status. Theory and practice then became blended in the graduate school, although greater emphasis tended to remain on method and less on theory and social philosophy.

Settlements, Charity Organization Societies, and People of Color

At the turn of the twentieth century, African Americans were the overwhelmingly predominant racial minority (11 percent of the total 12 percent of the nonwhite U.S. population; American Indians, Chinese, and Japanese comprised the remaining 1 percent. During this period of time, Mexicans were not counted separately from whites (Iglehart & Becerra, 2000, p. 26).

African Americans.   Rural blacks migrated in record numbers from the South to midwestern, eastern, and northern cities. In order to escape poverty and oppression, an estimated 300,000 to 1 million African Americans migrated from the South (Iglehart & Becerra, 2000, p. 28). While the Civil War emancipated slaves, African Americans continued to confront the terrors of lynchings, beatings, chain gangs, and the Ku Klux Klan. For example, between 1882 and 1901, an estimated average of 150 yearly lynchings took place (Martin & Martin, 1995, p. 62). The rural blacks sought employment in industry, greater freedoms, and new lives in urban centers. For the uneducated, poor, and rural peasants, adapting to life in the crowded slums of large cities posed enormously complex challenges. Instead of hope and opportunity, they experienced housing, educational, and employment segregation and discrimination. The segregation they experienced in the South followed them to the North. Before long, high rates of poverty, crime, and disease occurred, "and they were soon being contemptibly dubbed by white city officials as the 'Negro problem,' the primary threat to urban progress and stability" (Martin & Martin, 1995, p. 23).

What did the settlements and charity organization societies do to help African Americans? Very little! While a few settlement houses welcomed the influx of African Americans and a few located themselves in African American communities, most settlements refused to provide services to African Americans, or simply relocated to other areas (Berman-Rossi & Miller, 1994). Iglehart and Becerra (2000) provide the following examples:

> The Board of Eli Bates House in Chicago voted to close the house rather than admit African Americans; Kingsley House in Philadelphia excluded African Americans entirely; one New York settlement substantially increased its membership

fee to discourage African Americans from joining; the board of Christamore settlement in Indianapolis decided to move the settlement rather than integrate it. (p. 119)

Charity organization societies investigated and published reports about the deplorable conditions confronting African Americans. However, their investigations and reports (for example, about housing and employment discrimination) "did not translate into hands-on services to African Americans" (Iglehart & Becerra, 2000, p. 99). Charity organization societies provided African Americans with significantly less alms and services than the white ethnic groups received. Since racism and discrimination led to African American unemployment, the charity organization societies conveniently concluded that their services could not be helpful to African Americans. The "friendly visitor" was not responsible for and could not mitigate discriminatory practices. Their mission was to change individuals and not to change society. Therefore, the charity organization societies concluded that they "had little to offer this impoverished group" (Iglehart & Becerra, 2000, p. 99).

In order to fill the void left by settlements and charity organization societies as well as other white institutions, and building on the African American self-help and mutual aid traditions, African American leaders duplicated and recreated a parallel social service system for their own communities.[5] With dogged determination, they created settlement houses, women's clubs, hospitals, orphanages, schools, and residential centers and established organizations like the National Association of Colored Women (NACW), the National Association for the Advancement of Colored People (NAACP), and the National Urban League (NUL) (Carlton-LaNey, 2001a; Jackson, 1978). The black churches continued to serve as a primary source of social support. In 1920 in North Carolina, for example, African Americans supported 2,591 churches and 179 parsonages (Burwell, 1995, p. 26).

In the face of profound racism and sexism, black female social workers courageously provided the primary leadership to the black communities. They mobilized the traditional informal black helping systems (churches, women's clubs, and fraternal orders). During the Progressive era, Victoria Earle Matthews, for example, founded White Rose Mission, a settlement house. It provided varied services, including a mother's club, adult classes, kindergarten classes, relief assistance, and a library. Ms. Matthews was also a founder of women's clubs (along with Mary Church Terrell and Ida B. Wells) and the Industrial Association in 1897, a home for working black women. At the turn of the twentieth century, she developed travelers' aid services. She devoted her life to improving the lives of black women (Waites, 2001).

Mary Church Terrell, for another example, the daughter of an emancipated slave, was one of the few black women in the nineteenth century to both attend college and earn a master's degree. Deeply affected by the lynching of a close friend (his "crime" was running a successful grocery store) and the death of her infant in a poorly equipped and staffed segregated hospital, she dedicated her life to social activism. She actively participated in the women's club movement. In 1892, she cofounded the Colored Women's League of Washington, D.C., and served as its first president (Cook, 2001). She also served as the first president of the NACW when it formed in 1896, and she played an active role in the formation of the NAACP in 1910 (Peeble-Wilkens & Francis, 1990). Her autobiography, *A Colored Woman in a White World*, was published in 1940 (Terrell, 1940/2005).

Ida B. Wells-Barnett, a crusader for human rights, fought relentlessly for the rights of black women. She championed the anti-lynching movement and "changed the fate of lynch laws in the United States almost single-handedly" (Bent-Goodley, 2001, p. 87). She was a gifted journalist (referred to as the "Princess of the Press"), and wrote many articles advocating for racial justice. She equated lynching to racial terrorism—an inhuman response reflecting whites' fears of blacks' political, economic, and social progress (Bent-Goodley, 2001). In 1893, she organized the Ida B. Wells Club, establishing the first kindergarten for children in Cook County, Illinois. The club provided parental education, recreation programs, employment services, and youth and elderly services (Peeble-Wilkens & Francis, 1990). Ms. Wells-Barnett's courage and foresightedness are evident in her being the only woman in her era known to have hyphenated her maiden and married name.

Birdye Henrietta Haynes, for another example, was the first African American to graduate from the Chicago School of Civics and Philanthropy, graduating in 1914. She made significant contributions to two settlement houses, one in Chicago (Wendell Phillips Settlement) and the other in New York (Lincoln House Settlement) (Carlton-LaNey, 2001b).

With mass migration to midwestern, northern, and eastern cities, the rural communities were left in a state of disorganization. Margaret Murray Washington, our final example of female black social workers who made important contributions during the Progressive era, determinedly organized communities on behalf of poor rural blacks, serving as the first president of the Federation of Colored Women's Clubs. Married to Booker T. Washington, she also became a major independent force at Tuskegee Institute, the Alabama university that he founded. She founded the Tuskegee Women's Club and joined forces with the Russell Plantation Settlement House to establish a local school and church. The women's club members taught in the school, organized clubs and classes, and engaged in social service and reform activities (Dickerson, 2001).

African American male social workers had greater opportunities than their female counterparts. They often were the public face of progressive developments. They identified with the emerging scientific method, advocating for the training of black social work professionals rather than building on the traditional informal black helping systems. They also sought interracial alliances. For example, Dr. George Haynes, the brother of Birdye

Haynes, was trained at the New York School of Philanthropy. As the founder and first executive director of the National Urban League, he was a leading advocate for the recruitment and training of black social workers. In 1911, he played a critical role in establishing the first undergraduate social work program at Fisk University, a black college (Martin & Martin, 1995).

For an additional example, E. Franklin Frazier, a leading social work educator, was also committed to the scientific method. He believed that the traditional black helping systems lacked an essential scientific knowledge base. He established (in 1922), directed (from 1922 to 1927), and achieved accreditation for the first African American graduate school of social work, the Atlanta School of Social Work at Morehouse University (Chandler, 2001). He became even more prominent as a sociologist, becoming the first African American president of the American Sociological Association and the author of two texts (as well as six other books and over 100 articles): *The Negro Family in the United States* (1939) and *The Negro in the United States* (1957).

Finally, Lawrence A. Oxley, between 1925 and 1934, directed an experimental division of the North Carolina State Board of Charities and Public Welfare. His major contributions included (1) directing a state social welfare division in a southern state, (2) employing the first cadre of black social workers, and (3) promoting social work education and the training of African Americans through institutes and the support of the Bishop Tuttle Memorial Training School of Social Work at St. Augustine College in Raleigh. Utilizing the mutual aid tradition, he believed that "African Americans helping each other was the most effective method of ameliorating desperate social conditions in a racially segregated country" (Carlton-LaNey, 1999, p. 312). He also promoted and advanced community organization as a professional method and public welfare among African Americans as a viable field of practice (Burwell, 2001).

Black social workers operating from both the indigenous African helping traditions as well as assimilationist and scientific traditions were fully committed to mobilizing resources for black families and communities and made enormous contributions to improving the quality of life for African Americans (Carlton-LaNey, 2001a; Martin & Martin, 1995). Unfortunately, their courage and heroism have been too often ignored in white, "bleached" historical accounts.

Native Americans. Unlike immigrant groups and African American slaves, Native American were not needed for inexpensive labor; the white settlers wanted their land. Native Americans fiercely fought against the annexation of their land, and domination over their way of life. After many tribes were massacred and their lands overtaken, Native Americans were relocated on barren reservations. Without the ability to hunt, fish, and be self-sufficient, Native American tribes became dependent on governmental support for survival necessities. They were denied the opportunity to develop their own educational and social service systems by a government that allegedly provided for them—"food and materials supplied were insufficient, inadequate and often inappropriate" (Iglehart & Becerra, 2000, p. 39).

During the Progressive era, "reformers" sought to assimilate Native American children. In their view, education was Native Americans' pathway into Christianity and the American mainstream. Reservation day schools were perceived to be inadequate for "raising American Indians to the standards of Christian civilization" (Iglehart & Becerra, 2000, p. 38). Therefore, children as young as six years of age were forcefully removed from their families and tribes and sent to boarding schools to be "civilized" and educated. The boarding schools were expected to resolve the "Indian problem" by teaching the children to "shed the blanket" (i.e., to shed native ways) and become assimilated. These schools emphasized industrial training and Christianity.

By portraying Native Americans as "savages" who needed to be civilized, political leaders justified and rationalized the blatant racism and discrimination in the actions of overtaking their land, relocating them on barren lands, taking their children away, and attempting to eliminate their culture.

> Since the economic development of the United States could not have progressed without the displacement and neutralization of the Native population, the polices of extermination, isolation, and assimilation, that have competed, for ascendancy all required the definition of Natives as savage, inferior, and less than human, and their cultures as inferior and deservedly doomed to extinction. (Kemnitzer, 1978, p. 9, as cited in Iglehart & Becerra, 2000, p. 37)

Mexican Americans.   White settlers were welcomed when they moved into Texas in the early 1800s when it was part of the state of Coahuila in Mexico. These settlers rebelled against the Mexican government. While Mexico was victorious in the first two battles, the Mexican Army was defeated in 1836 at San Jacinto. With this defeat, the Republic of Texas replaced the Mexican Texas. Following the Mexican American War in 1848, thousands of Mexican Americans lived in Texas and the Southwest Territory (later to become the states of California, New Mexico, Utah, and Nevada, and parts of Colorado, Arizona, and Wyoming), and became citizens of the United States.[6] As white Americans migrated to Texas and the Southwest Territory, they began to seize the Mexican Americans' lands and exploited them for cheap labor. The Mexican Americans' economic and social conditions further deteriorated with the influx of Mexican immigrants after 1900. The Mexican population more than tripled. At the turn of the twentieth century, "Mexican immigrants and Mexican Americans made up 80 percent of the agricultural work force, 90 percent of the western railroad workers, and 60 percent of the mine workers"; some migrated to the northern urban centers for work (Iglehart & Becerra, 2000, p. 55).

In "appreciation" of their hard work at low wages, they confronted consistent racism and discrimination. For example, in Texas in 1902, the white settlers instituted a poll tax that prevented Mexican Americans from voting. A master-slave caste system evolved in which Mexican Americans were relegated to serve as a cheap labor force for the white settlers and were racially segregated (Iglehart & Becerra, 2000, p. 53).

Chinese Americans. During the 1880s thousands of Chinese fled China due to political upheavals, peasant uprisings, and deteriorating economic conditions. Between 1885 and 1887 approximately 191,000 Chinese immigrated to the United States They provided an invaluable labor supply for various industries, accepting undesirable positions at very low wages (Iglehart & Becerra, 2000, p. 58). The Chinese laborers' lack of assimilation threatened dominant groups, and they began to vilify them as being clannish and inferior. A wave of anti-Chinese sentiments resulted in the 1882 Chinese Exclusion Act, which prohibited Chinese immigrants from becoming naturalized citizens as well as Chinese laborers from entering the United States. By the time the Progressive era began, Chinese immigrants "moved from being an invaluable labor supply to being the scourge of the earth" (Iglehart & Becerra, 2000, p. 58). They were the victims of racism and suffered oppression similar to that of African Americans, Native Americans, and Mexican Americans.

Japanese Americans. In the late 1880s, a significant number of Japanese laborers emigrated from Japan and Hawaii to work as farm laborers, domestics, and miners in California. From approximately 150 Japanese in the United States, their numbers grew to 127,000 by 1908 (Iglehart & Becerra, 2000, p. 63). The Chinese Exclusion Act eliminated a cheap supply of labor, and a new source was needed. The Japanese laborers filled this void and worked for even cheaper wages. However, they were committed to upward mobility, perceiving these jobs only as a way to enter the economic system. Before long, they organized successful farm labor strikes and, consequently, achieved higher and more comparable wages. Gradually, some Japanese laborers began to purchase their own farms and businesses. They were more successful than other immigrant groups.

> In 1909, 1,380 Japanese-owned businesses were counted; land ownership grew from 2,422 acres in 1904 to 16,449 in 1909. By 1919, Japanese farmers owned over 74,000 acres, leased another 383,287 acres, and shared crops in still another 59,000 acres. In 1920 Japanese farm income reached $67 million. (Iglehart & Becerra, 2000, p. 64)

Viewing the Japanese as economic competitors, the dominant white population became threatened by their successes and activated anti-Japanese rhetoric. By 1900, the anti-Japanese campaign gained momentum. For example, the mayor of San Francisco stated, "The Chinese and Japanese are not bona fide citizens. They are not the stuff of which American citizens can be made . . . they will not assimilate with us" (Daniels, 1962, p. 21, as cited in Iglehart & Becerra, 2000, p. 65). The press whipped up a fear and paranoia of a potential Japanese takeover of California businesses and lands. Japanese businesses were boycotted; white businesses were promoted. Legislation was also passed to curtail Japanese business success. For example, California's 1913 Alien Land Act allowed Japanese to lease agricultural land for up to a three-year period, but disallowed additional land purchases. Moreover, Japanese children were not allowed to inherit land owned by their parents. Similarly, the Immigration Act of 1917 prohibited emigration from southern and eastern Asia (Iglehart & Becerra, 2000, p. 67). Apparently, the Japanese were too successful, too productive, and too effective in business. Consequently, they were vilified, excluded, and restricted.[7]

Professionalization

The Casework Method

By 1895 the principles of scientific philanthropy had become organized into what was called the casework method, and were further codified by Mary Richmond's (1917) *Social Diagnosis*. During the first two decades of the twentieth century, the method spread from the COS (soon to be known as family agencies) to hospital social service departments, child-placing agencies, the school social work field, court clinics, and state mental hospitals. Paid workers, who were eager to achieve professional status, had superseded volunteer friendly visitors. COS staffs were joined in this aspiration by the caseworkers in psychiatric and general hospitals, who were themselves achieving some measure of status by their collaboration with physicians. During World War I, the usefulness of the casework method for work with soldiers' families had demonstrated that it could be applied to a range of problems in family life beyond those associated with poverty. In 1915, the NCCC was shocked to be told by Abraham Flexner, in an invitational address, that social work was not a profession, since its liaison function between its clients and other professions was not a professional function (Flexner, 1915).[8] This observation is particularly ironic in the light of the increasing importance attached to social work's mediating function in the dehumanized and depersonalized organizational world of the late twentieth and early twenty-first centuries.

Flexner also asserted that social work did not have a unique, transmissible method, which would qualify it as a profession. For the next fifty years, the casework segment of the profession devoted energy and thought to develop such a method, and obscured the importance of its unique mediating function. The quest for method was aided by knowledge gained in experience in the mental hygiene and child guidance movements of the 1920s. It was spurred on by Virginia Robinson's (1930) *A Changing Psychology in Social Casework* and was further advanced by the theoretical contributions from Sigmund Freud, who offered both a theory about human behavior as well as a method to help it. During the Great Depression, the former COS now became known (as mentioned above) as family agencies, having undergone a change in function by which relief giving was transferred to the new public programs. The private agencies were thus provided with the opportunity to experiment with the new psychoanalytically oriented procedures. This freedom also supported the search for a method, especially a method focused on individual change.

Beginning in the mid-1930s, a new controversy erupted within the casework segment, one that also supported the preoccupation with method. Faculty at the University of Pennsylvania School of Social Work constructed a view of casework, which was not to be treatment in the disease sense, but was rather to be a service offered in terms of agency function (Taft, 1937). They based many of their ideas on the psychoanalytic concepts of Otto Rank, who himself had broken away from Freud. They added the concept of agency function as the limiting aspect against which clients tested their ability to ask for and use help (Gomberg, 1943). The term "functional" came to be applied to the new school of casework thought to distinguish it from the traditional or "diagnostic" school of casework thought. Throughout the 1940s the conflict raged between the two schools, and it began to subside only in the late 1950s. Despite the uneasy strains that persisted over those two decades, many practitioners today acknowledge the incorporation of important ideas from the functional school into the mainstream of practice. These include ideas about relationships, uses of time, and the influence of the agency setting on social work practice (Dore, 1990). Others have asserted that both schools of thought were guilty of overemphasizing method within a psychological orientation that led caseworkers away from social concerns. The controversy was supplanted by the important theoretical contributions of Helen Perlman (1957) and the pressing social issues of the 1960s and 1970s, including civil rights, the war on poverty, and the Vietnam War, all of which threatened the role of casework in the profession and in society.

A significant feature of the casework method was its having been cast in a medical metaphor (Germain, 1973a). As early as the 1880s charity workers, speaking in the medical idiom, referred to dependency as a "social disease" to be cured by "social physicians" prescribing remedies on the basis of a "diagnosis" of individual need. The gradual institutionalization of the metaphor that occurred in the 1920s, 1930s, and 1940s reinforced a preoccupation with internal processes so that diagnosis and treatment tended to focus on the person while environmental forces—seemingly fixed and intractable—receded further into the background. Even when Hamilton (1940) introduced a more holistic view of the person-in-situation, most caseworkers and casework agencies found it difficult to move beyond a vague conception of environmental manipulation limited to foster care, work with collaterals, and concrete services. As important and essential as social provision was, it did not lead to a critical examination of features in the environment that were associated with the problems caseworkers "treated."

In their long effort to perfect the method, caseworkers succeeded in developing an individualizing service that subscribed to the canons of logical thought and drew upon knowledge and values as a base for the method. They struggled to maintain openness to new ideas in order to develop greater effectiveness. What appeared to be missing from the casework method, however, was a conceptualization of the environment that would take into account its complexity, and from which interventions could be derived. This fact, together with the infusion of psychoanalytic theory, a tendency to model the style and trappings of practice on that of the psychoanalytic-psychotherapist practitioner, and the prestige associated with psychiatric casework, assured the continuation of the medical metaphor of diagnosis and treatment (Germain, 1970).

The transition from an earlier psychoanalytic emphasis on drives and defenses to an emphasis in the 1950s on the adaptive functions of the ego helped to encourage greater interest in environmental interactions. Hollis (1964, 1968, 1972) made a significant contribution by studying case records and developing a typology for interventions. Similarly, additions to the knowledge base from the social sciences in the 1950s and from general systems theory in the 1960s expanded the caseworker's diagnostic understanding to include the dynamic environment (Hearn, 1969). Specialized developments such as in milieu therapy and crisis intervention in the 1960s and 1970s also broadened practice (Parad, 1965). While each of these influences, to differing degrees, broadened the location problems, they did little, however, to change the focus of casework treatment, because diagnosis continued to locate problems mainly within the person.

Bertha Reynolds was an important exception to this obfuscation of the environment. Reynolds had been trained as a psychiatric social caseworker and practiced many years in that capacity. She was also a noted social work educator and gained national eminence for her writings on practice and the teaching of practice and supervision (Reynolds 1934/1982, 1942, 1951). But with the Great Depression and the coming of World War II, she was radicalized and became committed to Marxist thought. She also became committed to union organizing and played a significant leadership role in the union movement. She was one of only a few social work leaders who fully embraced unions while also arguing that social work was a profession. Because of her radical views, she was ostracized by her profession, and retired long before she had intended.[9]

Reynolds (1934/1982) wrote from deeply humanistic convictions about human rights, and human potential for growth and health, as well as out of love and respect for her profession. She declared that social work can serve *both client and community*:

Only if the processes of social change lead to an organization of society in
which the interests of all are safeguarded through the participation of all in political and economic power, a society in which none are exploited economically
and none are deprived of some form of expression of individual will. (p. 126)

Reynolds also believed that exploitation could be countered by the principle of self-determination, which today we might call self-direction or non-
coercive personal power. She shifted responsibility for identifying and
solving a client's plight from the social worker to the client. Thus, the client has the right to decide when help is needed, what help will be useful,
and when it is no longer needed. The social worker cannot grant that right
for it is the client's own. Those being served are the source of authority for
their own affairs. This does not mean that the social worker has no professional input but, rather, that professional input must be situated along the
road to the client's goals. She felt that practitioners should not find their
rewards in changes they make in people—as proof of their own professional achievement—but in human beings able to make their own conditions better. Reynolds also believed that the social worker must be willing to
discuss with clients *their victimization by injustice*—almost foreshadowing
feminist and empowerment theories. These were, indeed, radical ideas at a
time when social casework, the primary social work method, focused on
personal change, and community organization focused on coordination of
agencies' programs and funding.

The Group Work Method

During the 1920s, social group work emerged from the settlement, recreation, and progressive education movements (Gitterman, 1979). From the
settlements, the group work method derived its institutional base. Some
early group work leaders had been settlement residents and were influenced
by the settlers' devotion to the base of democratic groups for the development of responsible citizenship, mutual aid, and collective action (Lee &
Swenson, 2005). They were experienced and skillful in leading groups for
children and for adults.

From the recreational movement, social group work gained its interest in
the value of play and activities. Many early group workers had been associated with youth-serving organizations, the camping movement, and community centers. Group workers were influenced by organized recreation as a
means for building character. They believed that participation in leisure-time
group activities leads to personal development and to the acquisition of desired social attitudes and values.

From the progressive education movement, group work acquired a philo-
sophic base. Dewey (1930) had stressed that democratic citizenship was best
assured through democratically oriented classrooms, in which the group
experience was used to help pupils learn and discover together. To live democracy represented the most effective means for learning democracy.

Creative group life in the schools could lead to responsible citizenship on which the future of democracy depends (Follett, 1924, 1950; Kilpatrick, 1940; Lindeman, 1924, 1926).

The first group work curriculum in a school of social work was introduced at Western Reserve University in 1927, although a group work course had been offered there since 1923. By the 1930s, the recreational and educational components of group work practice had been clearly identified, and practitioners from various fields were invited into the American Association for the Study of Group Work (AASGW), founded in 1936. Over the next two decades, until the mid-1950s, group workers maintained their commitments to the reciprocity between individual satisfaction and the social good, and to the positive impact of group experience upon both the individual and society (Coyle, 1947, 1948). Coming as they did from the settlements, recreation settings, and the progressive education movement, they conceived group work functions as including the development of personality to its greatest capacity, the fostering of creative self-expression, the building of character, and the improvement of interpersonal skills. For them, group work functions also included the development of cultural and ethnic contributions, the teaching of democratic values, the support of active and mature participation in community life, the mobilizing of neighborhoods for social reform, and the preservation of ethical and middle-class values. This conception of group work functions has been termed the "social goals" model of group work (Papell & Rothman, 1966).

The need for clarity of purpose and for the development of systematic knowledge led to the establishment of the American Association of Group Workers (AAGW) in 1946. Although group workers had initially resisted identification with any one discipline, they now began to move closer to the social work profession. In 1956, the AAGW was incorporated into the National Association of Social Workers. In the process, group work gained greater professional acceptance and legitimacy. The practice committee of the group work section of the NASW assumed responsibility in 1959 for developing new working definitions of social group work practice (Hartford, 1964). While unable to agree on a common definition and frame of reference, the discussions renewed interests and identified critical knowledge gaps, but professional group work methods and skills continued to be underdeveloped (Konopka, 1949, 1954; Phillips, 1951; Trecker, 1955, 1956).

The search for a unifying statement of professional function may have been, in part, a response to McCarthyism and the hostile political environment (Andrews & Reisch, 1997). The prevalence of a repressive philosophy and mood undermined group work's assumptions and aspirations. An emerging view of groups as conspiratorial and subversive, rather than as microcosms of democratic society, stripped away the social goals ideology. Because method was still undeveloped, social group workers were now left without a theoretical and philosophical base. They turned inward to self-evaluation and professionalization, and they turned away from the social action and social reform traditions.

Unable to agree on a common, precise definition of social group work's purpose and function, the practice committee invited several group workers to offer their frames of reference. In his remedial model, Robert Vinter (1959, 1966) moved toward the more developed casework paradigm of social study, diagnosis, and treatment. Through similar processes, individual group members having problems in social functioning were to be treated within the group context. The group itself possessed no collective function, and especially not one of social action. As casework agencies and casework departments became increasingly interested in group approaches, the model's conception of group work function found increased support. In its move away from group work's historic commitment to developmental services, democratic processes, and social causes, this model placed the burden of change upon the individual. The environment received little or no attention.

William Schwartz shared Vinter's commitment to the development of a professional methodology. Rather than moving toward casework's medical metaphor, however, he proposed a systemic and generic conception of social work function. While maintaining the vision and, at times, the romanticism of the social goals model, Schwartz (1959, 1961, 1962) developed a "reciprocal" conception (also referred to as the "interactionist" and as the "mutual aid" approach) of group work in which the worker maintains a dual focus on the individual and the social system (the group, the agency). The idea of "reciprocal" captures the mutually dependent relationship that exists between members within a group and between the group and its social environment. "Interactionist" emphasizes the interaction between people and their systems. Schwartz was probably the first to introduce the term "mutual aid" into social work scholarship and was its major proponent (Gitterman, 2004; Shulman, 1986; Steinberg, 1997).

Both the social goals and reciprocal models viewed the group as having the potential for mutual aid. In the reciprocal model's formulation the worker is to have no preconceived goals or "hidden agenda," but is expected to "mediate" between agency services and client needs. The relationship between the individual and society is viewed as symbiotic, even though the mutual need may, at times, be unrecognized or ambivalent. The worker's function is to mediate between the individual and the group, and between the group and the agency. The symbiotic conception, however, tends to becloud the power inequities in social structures, and thus gives insufficient attention to methods of influencing organizations, communities, and legislative processes.

In spite of the limitations noted above, both models made important contributions to the development of the group work method and to the increased use of group workers in various settings. In the late 1960s and 1970s, spin-offs and accretions to both models appeared. Theorists associated with the remedial model incorporated behavioral therapy and task centered into their practice (Garvin, 1974; Sarri, 1974). Gitterman (1971) and Shulman (1979) elaborated on and deepened Schwartz's ideas. Tropp (1971), whose ideas resemble the "interactionist–reciprocal–mutual aid" approach, developed a humanistic, developmental perspective on group work practice. His approach presents a clear alignment with life transitions and their associated tasks. The realities of practice have pushed group work to synthesize and integrate its major models. Distinguishing among them has become increasingly difficult both in practice and in school curricula (Lang, 1972).

The Community Organization Method

While casework as a method originated in the COS, and group work as a method originated in the settlements, community organization as a social work practice method derived some of its characteristics from both the COS and the settlements. Community organization took some of its tasks from the COS interest in pioneering new services to meet needs, coordinating existing services, and establishing central informational and statistical services for all agencies. This inheritance was a primary emphasis in the decades between 1910 and 1930, when community organization sought an institutional base in the developing community chests and councils.

The characteristic settlement emphasis on neighborhood services also persisted in the community organizers' interest in developing, expanding, and coordinating services. The settlement interest in action and social reform, however, was missing in the early development of community organization, perhaps because of the reactionary climate after World War I and the dominant emphasis on rugged individualism within the culture. Instead of challenging institutions, the community organizer coordinated agencies and won the support of business interests in the community. Any effort to encourage citizens to band together in attacking social problems was experienced by the local political structure as threatening, and was quickly defeated (Dinwiddie, 1921).

Although the period of the 1930s through the 1950s was characterized by the chaos of depression, World War II, and postwar recovery, community organization remained largely unchanged. The social action and social protest movements of the 1930s took place outside of community organization, which maintained its involvement in chests and councils and in the newly developing United Funds. The period did see, however, the beginnings of theoretical development. Even here, the emphases were chiefly on the adjustment between social resources and social welfare needs, intergroup processes within the councils themselves, and such generic social work features in community organization as problem-solving and various helping roles utilized in working with committees and council groups (Berry, 1956; Carter, 1958; Lane, 1939; Newstetter, 1947). The lack of a social change perspective and a focus on process instead of on goals meant that issues of power and controversy were not addressed or recognized (Harper & Dunham, 1959; Ross, 1955).

Modern community organization practice emerged in the 1960s and 1970s. The impact of massive poverty existing side by side with affluence, the persistence of social pathologies despite the advances in knowledge, and the civil rights movements influenced community organization beyond anything experienced by casework or group work. Community organization shifted from its role and function of coordinating services to a concern with social problems as the targets of its intervention. The earlier preoccupation with process gave way to an emphasis on goals related to social change (Grosser, 1965, 1973). Like the social goals model of group work, community organization lacked a professional knowledge base and a practice method with which to implement its aspirations for social change. By the early 1970s, however, new social science theories supported the shift from cooperation and coordination to intervention into various societal, bureaucratically organized systems on behalf of the disadvantaged segment of the community. Brager and Specht (1973) published the first formulation of the theory and practice of community organization in its modern form.

The central concepts on which community organization is based are power, social change, and conflict. Emphasis is placed on power within a social system: its location, its sources, and the levels where it appears. The degree of accessibility to power and the potential for organizing countervailing power are assessed in order to plan the strategies and tactics for achieving social change on behalf of the powerless. Social change can create conflict, and conflict can lead to social change. The community organizer is therefore concerned with issues of conflict management in the attempted resolution of social problems. At first there was an occasional tendency to view agencies in an undiscriminating way, and to use adversarial strategies undifferentially, as though the agency were the enemy in every instance. The development of tools for organizational assessment and the formulation of interventive procedures have provided a differentiated view of agencies based on an increasingly sophisticated understanding of their complexities (Brager & Holloway, 1978; Patti & Resnick, 1972; Wax, 1968).

External events and internal professional processes moved community organization to examine broader societal problems, and to develop new curricular emphases upon administration and social policy practice. Rothman (1995) formulated three major approaches to community interventions: locality development, social planning, and social action. Locality development represents a neighborhood-based strategy of engaging significant stakeholders for the purpose of improving community life. Social planning represents the engagement of professionals in a technical problem-solving process for the purpose of designing social service programs and policy frameworks. Social action represents the organization and mobilization of a disadvantaged subcommunity or community for the purpose of gaining increased resources or fairer treatment from those in positions of power and influence.

The Social Administration Method

Business leaders provided the financial resources for the charity organization societies, and aimed to transfer methods of administrative efficiency from the world of business to the societies. Boards of directors (or trustees) oversaw the societies' operations. The board chair often held the position for many years and overlapped the functions of the executive director by being involved in the day-to-day operations of the agency. Board committees were involved in case decisions, with board members' wives frequently serving as "friendly volunteers." The board was also responsible for the coordination of relief efforts among the various charitable organizations. In contrast, the settlements (at least the early ones) were not dominated by board involvement. The head worker with a social reform mission provided the charismatic leadership. However, when the head worker had to be replaced, the board was responsible for finding a new head worker. And through the interviewing and hiring processes, boards became more involved in the organization (Austin, 2000).

Two distinct models of social welfare administration emerged: (1) administration in the private nonprofit sector, and (2) administration in the public social welfare sector. In the private nonprofit sector, professional education and practice experience were considered requisites for administrative positions. Colleges and universities provided a new source for administrative leadership. For example, Amos Warner was one of the first university-educated administrators. Warner (1894) wrote a classic text, *American Charities: A Study in Philanthropy and Economics*, which set forth the principles for poor relief and programs to assist those in need. Mary Richmond succeeded Warner at the Baltimore COS and subsequently (1900–1909) served as the general secretary of the Philadelphia COS. Austin (2000) suggests that since Mary Richmond was dependent on her salary, she was in many ways the first woman to have a career as a social welfare administrator (p. 31).

By the 1920s, men were recruited to serve as administrators from a larger pool of professionals with casework social work education and with experiences in nonprofit organizations. These administrators sought to develop greater functional clarity between the function of the board of directors and the executive function. An important concept of private sector administration evolved: the board's function was to establish policy; the executive's function was to implement the policy. Along with greater functional clarity came certain structures such as "rotating board membership, board nominating committees, limited terms for board officers, and annual election of board officers" (Austin, 2000, p. 32). Mary Parker Follett's (1941) *Dynamic Administration*, published posthumously, conceptualized essential structures and methods for nonprofit administration. She emphasized notions about organizational integration, staff participation in decision making, and the sharing of power. Administration's core function was to support and facilitate the work of the social work practitioners. Administrators served a linkage function "between the board of directors and the professional staff, interpreting the perceptions of each group to the other with the objective of maintaining a harmonious operation" (Austin, 2000, p. 41).

During this time period, public welfare began to expand, with a few states developing worker compensation, old age pensions, blind pensions, mothers' pensions, and child welfare programs. Sophonisba Breckinridge's *Public Welfare Administration in the United States* (1927) dealt with the administration of public welfare programs. The Great Depression fundamentally changed the role of the federal government in caring for its citizens. Through the Social Security Act of 1935, a variety of federal social welfare programs and services were established and administered by federal and state welfare organizations. In order to protect the workers from political interference, they were granted civil service status. Initially, experienced workers from COS were recruited for supervisory and administrative positions. However, over time, the public welfare agencies turned to the field of public administration for the staffing and establishment of administrative procedures, and social work education and practice experience became not perceived as particularly useful for administrative positions (Austin, 2000, p. 36). Administration of public agencies emphasized accountability and the standardization of practice.

Graduate social work programs, mostly located in private colleges and universities, focused on preparing social workers for casework roles in private, nonprofit agencies. Growing out of a concern that social workers were not being prepared to practice in the public sector, Hollis and Taylor (1951) conducted a study and issued a report that recommended that social work curricula be expanded to include content on administration and supervision (as well as teaching and research) (Austin, 2000, p. 44). Following the publication of the report, the Council on Social Work Education, in 1952, circulated a curriculum policy statement that mandated the inclusion of content on organizations and administrative procedures for all students, "but only schools with 'adequate resources' would be able to offer a practice concentration in administration" (Austin, 2000, p. 44). Subsequently, the Council on Social Work Education initiated a national curriculum study under the leadership of Warner Boehm. The Boehm (1959) report recommended that social administration should be available to students as a social work method. However, the council failed to adopt this recommendation. Instead, it conceptualized social administration as an "enabling" method, providing relevant knowledge for direct service workers. Schools with sufficient resources were allowed to offer a social administration method. Gradually, increasing macro content and macro concentrations were added to graduate curricula. Social administration texts began to be published (Schatz, 1970; Trecker, 1961).

Latent Consequences of Historical Trends (1900–1980)

Methodological Divisions

One consequence of social work's historical development has been the tendency to define people's needs or problems on the basis of the method of service. Because of the separate development of practice methods, agencies and workers defined themselves as casework agencies and caseworkers, or as group work agencies and group workers, or more recently as grassroots organizations and community organizers. While an occasional host setting, such as a hospital, might have both caseworkers and group workers and even community organizers on its staff, most practice maintained sharp methodological distinctions. In the 1970s, this tendency diminished as more group workers recognized the need for helping individuals, and more caseworkers experimented with group approaches.

Such methodological divisions in social work education practice prevented an examination of the commonalities across methods, and thus inhibited the development of a distinctive social method of practice directed to the transactions between individuals, groups, and families and their social and physical environments. The divisions led to past and present struggles to establish the generic or core knowledge base for all social workers and to many complex curriculum accommodations, such as courses in basic concepts, first-year generic and second-year specific courses, and the dissension over generalists and specialists. The casework method itself had been concerned in the 1920s about the diversity of casework practice in many different settings, the difficulties in communicating across settings, and the modifications of method imposed by the nature of the setting. The Milford Conference of leading casework practitioners and educators concluded that all caseworkers required a generic core of knowledge, on which specific knowledge according to setting could be built (Lee, 1929a). The method itself, however, was thought to be recognizable across settings. The profession continues to struggle with the generic or core knowledge issue, made more complex by the differential levels of professional education, the place of in-service training after such education, and the question of where generic and specific knowledge can best be located educationally.

Social and physical environments impose an array of adaptive tasks on people whether they are functioning as individuals or in families and groups. It therefore is unreasonable to define needs in terms of a particular practice method and the restrictive self-definitions of worker and agency. For Professor Germain and I, when we worked on the first edition of *The Life Model of Social Work Practice* (Germain & Gitterman, 1980), it was, and continues to be, the nature of the need itself, and the associated life tasks involved in meeting the need or solving the stressors, that determines where to draw the boundaries that "encase" the individual, the family, or the group. Advances in systems and ecological theories provided us (Germain, 1973b, 1976, 1978a,

1978b, 1979; Germain & Gitterman, 1979; Gitterman & Germain, 1976; Gitterman, 1977; Gitterman & Schaeffer, 1972) and other scholars (Bartlett, 1970; Goldstein, 1973; Gordon, 1969; Hartman, 1970; Meyer, 1970, 1976; Middleman & Goldberg, 1974; Pincus & Minehan, 1973) with the conceptual tools to advance integrated methods. Pincus and Minehan (1973) prepared the first generalist text.

Cause and Function

Earlier in the chapter, we described the tension between those who supported environmental reform and social action ("cause"), and those who favored a focus on individual change and the development of a method by which to achieve such change ("function"). In general, the first group included members of ASSA, settlement workers, and, much later, a significant segment of the group work practice. They were interested in social science theory as a basis for environmental reform, and maintained an alliance with the social sciences, at times even seeing themselves as applied social scientists. They were also humanistic in their concern for human rights and equality between themselves and those they served, and in their later emphasis on democratic values and social participation (social goals). They lacked, however, a well-developed methodology for carrying out their sense of mission.

The second group, in general, was comprised of state board members, charity workers of the 1880s and 1890s, and, much later, the casework segment of practice, joined later still by the segment of group workers practicing on the remedial model. This second group began as antitheoretical and practical, and later developed rational, efficient methods in order to generate a scientific philanthropy. As the casework method of study, diagnosis, and treatment developed, it sought to become increasingly scientific through constructing a base of psychological, biological, social, cultural, and practice theory, and through observing the principles of evidence, logical thinking, and evaluation of outcomes for a scientific orientation and a systematic approach to practice. The second group believed itself also to be humanistic in its espousal of self-determination, respect for client difference, and support of client dignity and worth. Yet in the 1960s and 1970s, the second group suffered criticism for a latent antihumanist, social control bias in its problem definitions, service procedures, and role definitions for clients.

The casework segment of practice had assumed the dominant position in the early occupational group largely because it possessed an organized method and was represented by many more practitioners. It was the caseworker's preoccupation with method that led in 1929 to the first explicit formulation of the cause-function issue. Porter Lee (1929b), in his presidential address to the NCSW, traced a changing conception of social work from being a movement concerned with a cause to assuming the character of a function. In Lee's view, both cause and function are valuable and essential for social welfare: a cause won depends upon organization, method, and techniques for its implementation. A tendency to become overly preoccupied with method and process, however, can lead to a blunting of commitment. Goals associated with client need then become displaced by goals associated with organizational maintenance. Lee envisioned a synthesis in which social work would develop its service as a function of well-organized community life, without sacrificing its capacity to inspire enthusiasm for a cause. In the succeeding years, practitioners and social work educators took opposing positions, some supporting cause and others supporting function, thus effectively polarizing the profession. (In contrast, Reynolds [1964] and Schwartz [1969] attempted the bridge the polarity.) This polarity tended to interfere with the development of a practice that takes both positions into account as two complementary features of a profession concerned with human distress and the fostering of human growth in diverse life situations. In the ensuing chapters, we provide practice concepts and principles designed to reduce the polarity between cause and function, and between social action and treatment, and to address the issue of social purpose.

Current Societal Context

The last three decades have witnessed major developments that have dramatically affected people's lives as well as social work practice. The confluence of economic and legislative forces has conspired to oppress poor families, particularly poor families of color. The shift from liberal to conservative views in the United States (and also Canada) throughout the 1980s, 1990s, and early 2000s led to severe cutbacks in services and programs developed during the eras of the New Deal and the Great Society of the 1930s and 1960s, respectively. Deregulation, the spending of most of our resources on overkill armaments, greed, and the abuse of power in public and private life damaged national, state, and local economies, and banking and insurance systems to a frightening extent, the full cost of which to all Americans is still not known at this writing and may never be publicly acknowledged. Inevitably, this will burden all citizens for several generations to come with higher taxes; lower purchasing power; less funding of domestic needs including health care and AIDS research, prevention, and treatment; social welfare; education; affordable housing; restoration of transportation systems that are worn out and overburdened by population concentration; the search for alternatives to oil for energy; and repair of damage to the environment by global warming, toxic wastes, and hazardous materials.

Economic globalization, massive cuts to social programs, increased military expenditures, tax cuts for the wealthy, privatization of social services, profit-making and faith-based services, the spread of managed care in the health and mental health fields of practice, and restrictive welfare and immigration legislation have pushed poor families of color and immigrant families further below the poverty line. A politically conservative era has fundamentally changed the role of government in meeting human needs. Consequently, large sectors of our client population have experienced increased distress and degradation.

The miseries and human suffering encountered by social workers in the late twentieth and early twenty-first centuries are different in degree and kind from those encountered in the 1950s, 1960s, 1970s, and 1980s. Social work interns and professionals confront daily the crushing impact of such problems as unemployment and its devastating consequences; homelessness and the disappearance of affordable housing; HIV infection, AIDS infection, and deaths among drug users, gay and heterosexual men, women, teenagers, and the newborn; unintended teenage pregnancy and childbearing, especially but not exclusively in impoverished communities; alcohol and drug abuse among all social and age groups; brazen white-collar crimes of greed and corruption; violent crimes, including rape, drive-by murders, and assaults; and family violence, including incest and sexual molestation of children, neglect, and physical abuse (Gitterman, 2001b).

Social workers in practice today and tomorrow will deal with profoundly vulnerable populations, overwhelmed by oppressive lives and by circumstances and events they are powerless to control. The problems are often intractable because they are chronic and persistent, or acute and unexpected. When community and family supports are weak or unavailable and when internal resources are impaired, these populations are very vulnerable to physical, cognitive, emotional, and social deterioration. While, historically, the profession of social work has assumed the task of providing social services to disadvantaged and vulnerable populations, this task has become significantly more difficult to fulfill. For the stubborn truth is that problems have been increasing, while resources to mitigate them decrease. Those with less get less!

Poverty

The gap between the poor and the wealthy, and between the unskilled and the skilled, has widened. For example, Bill Gates has greater wealth than half of the people in the United States put together. Larder (1998) reported that "since the 1970's, virtually all our income gains have gone to the highest-earning 20 percent of our households, producing inequality greater than at any time since the 1930s, and greater than in any of the world's other rich nations" (p. C1). In 1991, President George Bush and the U.S. Congress cut taxes on capital, further exacerbating the disparity between the rich and the poor. By 2003, the top 1 percent of households amassed 57.5 percent of corporate wealth, growing by half since 1991, when it was 38.7 percent (Johnson, 2006).

In contrast, 12.6 percent of people live below the poverty line in the United States (U.S. Bureau of the Census, 2005). Moreover, the Census Bureau provides the following demographic risk data about people living in poverty: 17.6 percent of children under 18, 25.9 percent of African Americans and 21.8 percent of Hispanics, and 29 percent of female-headed households. Black men are progressively becoming disconnected from society. In the inner cities, more than half of all black men do not complete high school, with unemployment reaching remarkable proportions. For example, in 2000, 65 percent of black male high school dropouts in their twenties were jobless. By 2004, 72 percent were jobless, compared with 34 percent of white and 19 percent of Hispanic dropouts. When high school graduates are included, half of black men in their twenties are jobless. Concomitantly, incarceration rates of black men continue to rise: by their mid-thirties, six in ten black men who had dropped out of high school have spent some time in prison (Eckholm, 2006, p. A18).

While poverty begins early in life for black men, most people experience poverty during the course of aging in their lives. For example, by the age of twenty, 10.6 percent of people live below the poverty line; by the age of forty, 35.6 percent will have lived in poverty; and by age seventy-five, more than half of our citizens, 58.5 percent, will have lived below the poverty line (Rank, Yoon, & Hirschl, 2003, pp. 19–20). Obviously, as seen by the fact that at some point the majority of the general public will live in poverty, poverty must represent a structural failing of our economic and political system rather than the failings of individuals.

Global Economy

Working and lower-income families have been victimized by broad changes in the global economy. Beginning in the 1970s southern countries attracted outside capital and labor income by establishing free trade zones. These free trade zones permitted transnational corporations to operate with minimal restrictions in relation to minimum wage, working hours, and the use of child labor. By the 1990s and early 2000s, the dismantling of trade barriers and erosion of labor standards have resulted in a "massive movement of jobs" from the factories of the northern countries in the direction of sweatshops located in the southern countries (Polack, 2004, p. 285). Consequently, in the United States low-skilled jobs have significantly declined and blue-collar and lower-income workers' wages have eroded. Gradually and consistently, many manufacturing plants have closed and service jobs have been "outsourced." The result has been significant job losses. Thus, the major factor responsible for poverty is an insufficient number of decent-paying jobs for all people seeking employment (Rank et al., 2003). The elimination of these jobs has created severe economic hardships.

Those fortunate enough to have jobs have had to deal with a decline in their real wages. Among males between the ages of twenty-five and forty-four, only those who completed more than a college degree, a very small percentage, had higher inflation-adjusted earnings in 1993 than in 1973 (Danziger, 1997). Passell (1998) identified the enormity of the decline in blue-collar and lower-income wages:

The median wage of those with only a high school diploma fell by 6 percent, adjusted for inflation from 1980 to 1996, while earnings of college graduates rose by 12 percent. . . . In 1982, people in the top one-tenth of the work force made $24.80 an hour, 3.95 times the $6.28 an hour for workers in the bottom one-tenth. By 1996 the wage gap widened with then high-end workers averaging $25.74 an hour, or 4.72 times the $5.46 an hour of those at the bottom. (p. 1)

Blue-collar and lower-income workers are less marketable and have difficulty competing in an information- and technologically driven economy. Two-wage-earner families have become a necessity. Hence, solo-parent households are more likely to suffer poverty. For example, 16.9 percent of one-parent families live below the poverty line as compared to 9.9 percent of married-couple families. If one raises the poverty line slightly (to about $8,000 for a family of four), 36.6 percent of one-parent families as compared to 23 percent of married-couple families live in poverty (Rank et al., 2003, pp. 11–12).

The environment of poor people is particularly harsh. They are unable to compete for societal resources. For example, as of 2002, 43.6 million people are not covered by health insurance (U.S. Bureau of the Census, 2003). Without health insurance, poor people receive less preventive as well as restorative medical care. Black adults suffer higher death rates than whites from most major health-related causes and live an average of seven fewer years than white persons (Anderson, Kochanek, & Murphy, 1998). The differentials in white and black mortality rates begin at the onset of life and persist throughout the life span. For example, African Americans have the highest incidence of cancer and are more likely to die from cancer than any other ethnic and racial group. Thirty-eight percent more African American men die of cancer than white men; 17 percent more African American females die than white females. Only 29 percent of white males with prostrate cancer die from the disease, as compared to 65 percent of African Americans. Similarly, while 74 percent of white men with lung cancer die from the disease, a shocking 98 percent of African Americans die from it (American Cancer Society, 2007).

With the government reducing its role in providing a safety net, the plight of poor people of color can only worsen.

Immigration

Both the United States and Canada have become pluralistic, multicultural societies. Since 1990 approximately 1 million immigrants a year enter the United States (Drachman & Ryan, 2001, p. 656). In contrast from the late-nineteenth- and early-twentieth-century European immigrants, the present immigrants are emigrating from Asia (China, Philippines, India, Pakistan, Bangladesh, Sri Lanka, Korea, Cambodia, Laos, and Thailand), Mexico and Central America (Guatemala, El Salvador, Nicaragua, Colombia, Chile, Peru, Ecuador, Dominican Republic, and Cuba), and

Eastern Europe (Russia and Poland) (Padilla, 1997). Recent estimates from the U.S. Census Bureau, as reported by Iglehart and Becerra (2000), indicate 40.5 million Latinos and Latinas in a U.S. population of 285.7 million. Immigration and new births are annually adding 1.5 million Latinos and Latinas (Schmid, 2006). The U.S. Census Bureau projects that by the year 2050, ethnic minorities will comprise almost half of the U.S. population, with non-Hispanic whites decreasing from its present 75 percent to 53 percent.

Canada has as many or more newcomers from India and Hong Kong than does the United States, since many hold British passports and entry into Canada is therefore easier. Both Canada and the United States also gave refuge to Jewish and other ethnic and religious groups from the Soviet Union and its satellites. The marvelous cultural diversity of the newcomers enriches both North American societies, while at the same time strains are created because systems of education, health and mental health care, housing, and social services have not been adequately prepared for diverse values, norms, and needs. Indeed, the provision of culturally appropriate services and programs to impoverished American Indian, African American, and Latina/o populations is long overdue, and the struggle to achieve them continues. Only since the mid-1970 have the United States and Canada embarked on self-direction and self-governance for some Indian, Eskimo, and Inuit populations in tribal affairs, including their own social services, education, and health care systems.

Recent immigrants confront numerous stressful and traumatic life events such as separation from family, exposure to life-threatening situations, finding employment and housing, and learning a new language and culture. Some are legal immigrants. They have the support of family and/or employment sponsorship, immigration prerequisites. Others are lawful permanent residents. They have an organizational sponsor who guarantees economic support for a designated period of time. Legal immigrants and lawful permanent residents tend to fare better than other immigrants.

Still others are refugees, also legal immigrants. They are usually forced to leave their home countries out of fear of persecution. They have witnessed and/or directly suffered from violence, genocide, and wars. For example, after World War II and during the cold war, refugees from communist bloc countries and Cuba were admitted to the United States. Subsequently, after the Vietnam War, refugees from South Asia were provided with asylum. In contrast, people fleeing persecution from the Haitian government were treated harshly by being interdicted at sea, deported, and placed in detention. Two explanations have been offered for our government's differential treatment of Haitians: (1) an effort to placate the Haitian government as an anticommunist ally and (2) blatant racism (Drachman & Ryan, 2001).

Yet others are undocumented people, who are unauthorized to be in the United States. They either enter the country illegally or remain after their visas have expired (Drachman & Ryan, 2001). Since 2000, 850,000 illegal immigrants have entered the United States, growing to approximately 12 million. It is estimated that they fill 25 percent of all agricultural jobs, 17 percent of house- and office-cleaning positions, 14 percent of construction jobs, and 12 percent of food preparation potions (Ohlemacher, 2006, p. 3B). Due to the fear of being deported, undocumented people are at high risk of being exploited by ruthless employers and landlords, and are fearful of accessing needed health, educational, and social services. By and large, the poverty levels of recent immigrants are higher than those of native households (Padilla, 1997).

Role of the Federal Government

The federal government decreasingly assumes responsibility for ameliorating economic inequities and associated social consequences. The lack of commitment to the concept of a "safety net" represents a significant structural failure at the political level. Severe cutbacks in Medicaid and public assistance result in poor people not having their basic human needs met. They often find themselves in desperate situations, having to choose food over essential medication. The exaggerated cost of housing and utilities (for those who do not qualify for assistance) trumps all other expenses.

The United States provides much less resources to support the poor than other Western industrialized nations. Rank et al. (2003, p. 15) cited Noble (1997, p. 3) for the trenchant observation: "The U.S. welfare state is striking because it is so limited in scope and ambition." In comparing eight European countries and Canada with the United States on what the level of poverty would be without any government income transfers (welfare grants, unemployment insurance, and Social Security) and what the poverty rate actually is with the income transfers, the comparisons are striking. For example, with income transfers Sweden reduces its nation poverty rate by 92 percent, Finland by 88 percent, Norway by 85 percent, France by 79 percent, the Netherlands by 77 percent, Germany by 76 percent, and Canada and the United Kingdom by 66 percent, as compared to the United States by only 38 percent (Rank et al., 2003, pp. 16–17). The United States provides minimal support to poor families. The federal government's decreasing role in ameliorating economic inequities is evident in recent legislation.

Legislation

In 1996, President Clinton signed into law the welfare "reform" act—the Personal Responsibility and Work Opportunity Reconciliation Act (PRWORA). This act replaced the federal entitlement program of Aid to Families with Dependent Children (AFDC). Since AFDC's passage as part of the Social Security Act of 1935, for sixty years poor families were provided with a safety net of financial assistance. In July 1997, AFDC was replaced with Temporary Assistance for Needy Families (TANF). This federal law imposed work requirements and a sixty-month lifetime time limit, promising to "end welfare as we know it." The law requires involvement in some work-related activities as defined by each state within twenty-four months of receiving assistance (Abramowitz, 2005; Albert, 2000). The new law's manifest purpose was to end public assistance recipients' dependence on the government and create economic independence and self-reliance by limiting benefits to a maximum of five years and by providing job training and employment opportunities. Some believe that the new legislation's latent and real purpose was to punish poor women for having children "they shouldn't have had." Punish them through stigma, economic deprivation, work requirements, and lack of provision of child care.[10]

Supporters of the new legislation conveniently ignored the fact that in 1995, approximately two-thirds of the recipients receiving AFDC were children and only one-third were adults (U.S. House of Representatives, 1996). The legislation does not differentiate between short-term and long-term public assistance recipients. Apparently, a surprise to many legislators (but not to most social workers) is the fact that black and Latina mothers and their children are at much greater risk than white mothers of reaching the time limits. While the number of people receiving public assistance has dramatically declined, white recipients are finding employment and leaving the welfare system at a disproportionately faster rate than black and Latina recipients (DeParle, 1998). The legislation also made legal immigrants (with the exception of refugees) ineligible for most forms of assistance, including cash benefits, Supplemental Security Income (SSI), and food stamps (Kim, 2001).

In the same year, 1996, the Illegal Immigration Reform and Immigrant Responsibility Act (IIRIRA) was enacted into law. This legislation disqualified legal immigrants from public benefits and set up serious obstacles to family reunification. Similarly, undocumented immigrants were ruled ineligible for state and local programs, with their confidentiality unprotected by such programs. Moreover, persons without valid travel documents face immediate deportation (Drachman & Ryan, 2001). With the terrorist attacks of September 11, 2001, on the World Trade Center and the Pentagon, an even more repressive legislation was enacted. The Uniting and Strengthening America by Providing Appropriate Tools Required to Intercept and Obstruct Terrorism Act (USA PATRIOT Act) provides the U.S. Justice Department with broad powers for the surveillance and detention of immigrants. The immigrant has no rights to review evidence or to legal counsel (Drachman & Paulino, 2004).

Religion and Public Services

The Personal Responsibility and Work Opportunity Reconciliation Act of 1996 contained a "charitable choice" clause that encouraged states to involve faith-based and community organizations in providing federally funded welfare service. President George W. Bush extended the policy shift as part of his faith-based policy initiatives. While some view this development as increasing the access of poor people to public services, others view it as swinging open the door for mixing religion and public services and as a significant threat to the separation of church and state (Cnaan & Boddie, 2002, p. 225). Some aspects of faith-based practice reflect a regression to colonial sectarian relief that perceived immorality as the cause of poverty. Still others view this policy direction as reducing funding for public and private nonprofit service providers and, therefore, eroding the quality of our social welfare system. Since faith-based services rely heavily on volunteers rather than professionals, this policy direction is also seen as eroding the professional status of social work. While volunteers can play an important role in the delivery of services, this role should be limited to performing uncomplicated and concrete tasks. Volunteers lack professional competence, discipline, and commitment to a code of ethics, and, therefore, can do harm when placed in the position of performing professional tasks.

Cultural Changes

The final decades of the twentieth century and the beginning of the twenty-first century have seen stunning shifts in values, norms, and behaviors. Some changes originated in the counterculture of the 1960s that influenced drug use, modes of dress, lifestyles, and changes in sexual attitudes and practices—aided by access to safe, effective contraception, which freed women and their families from the burden of too many children. Sexual norms for the young changed markedly, with sexual activity beginning at younger and younger ages. At the college level, both men and women acknowledge lifetime experiences with several sexual partners, a considerable difference from pre-1960 norms.

Other striking changes were generated by the feminist movement of the 1970s and 1980s directed to liberating women from the oppression of a patriarchal social order in family, work, and community life. By 2000, approximately 77 percent of women between the ages of twenty-five and fifty-four were in the workforce, up from about 40 percent in the 1950s. While more recently the employment rate for women has leveled off, the percentage of single mothers in the workforce jumped to 75 percent from 63 percent (Porter, 2006). Child care services lag far behind the need and comprise a major stressor, particularly for single mothers. Sexual harassment at the workplace continues to increase despite the passage of laws that carry severe penalties.

The feminist movement also led to some change in gendered family roles, mostly among middle-class adults and particularly among those men who themselves are liberated from the masculine mystique with its emphasis on work achievement at the expense of family life and participation in child rearing. While committed relationships without marriage increased markedly in the 1980s, 1990s, and early 2000s, marriage is statistically still the preferred option. The U.S. divorce rate soared during the same period but in the last several years has tapered off. Nevertheless, some 50 percent or more of American children are destined to live part of their childhood in solo-parent families, although some will move into blended families.

Gay men and lesbian women have achieved some reduction of negative public attitudes, social stigma, and punitive and discriminatory laws. Gay rights are recognized in some large cities, but the struggle continues elsewhere. More are taking the risk of coming out to family members and friends, and some to their workplace, high school, and/or college. However, homophobic attitudes prevail, as is evident in the public debate about gay and lesbian marriage, adoption, and foster parenting and child custody.

Independent living for those with physical and/or emotional challenges has also taken on the nature of a liberation movement, with an emphasis on the right to physical and social access to all aspects of community life. Despite recent federal statutes, however, liberation has not yet occurred everywhere. Children and adults with emotional and developmental disabilities, AIDS, and chronic diseases, and the poor elderly, have not fared very well, and their struggle continues.

Finally, a significant cultural change is the well-known "graying of society." The population over sixty-five is the fastest growing segment in the United States. Within that population the numbers of the very old, age eighty-five and older, are growing the fastest. The number of older persons is expected to almost double (from 35 million in 2000 to 71.5 million in 2030), and people living to eighty-five years of age will grow from 4.6 million to 9.6 million. While the white population sixty-five years and older will increase by 77 percent, older people of color are expected to increase by 223 percent (Department of Health and Human Services, Administration on Aging, 2003). However, for the next fifteen years, with the nonwhite and the elderly white populations simultaneously growing, a racial generation gap is emerging—an older white electorate and a younger, more diverse population (Roberts, 2007). For example, nearly half the children under the age of five are Hispanic, black, or Asian. Concomitantly, 78 million baby boomers (born from 1946 to 1964), as they turn sixty, "drive the racial generation gap" (Roberts, 2007, p. A21).

Strains are felt as women—the usual caregivers of older family members—are no longer available because most are now in the workforce. Strain is also felt in the health care system, as the elderly have a higher utilization rate, and in institutional care that frequently impoverishes those who need it. Controversy mounts over Social Security, its costs, and its coverage. With growing numbers of the old and very old, social services become increasingly necessary. The aging of the population over the next twenty-five years will create new challenges for the profession.

Technological Revolution

Although it is part of the culture, technology has grown so fast and become so complex that it merits its own discussion. In many ways technology has enriched and extended human life, beginning with the first tools used by early hominoids and extending to current marvels of household aids, entertainment, scientific investigation of the largest and smallest known natural phenomena, medical and public health control of infectious diseases other than AIDS (and the return of tuberculosis), rapid transportation, and instant communication devices that wire all of us around the globe into one giant organism, but without increasing our ability to live together peaceably. The list of perceived benefits is almost endless and is cause for celebration. However, many technologies that seem beneficial—at least over the short run—damage the planet and threaten our survival and other life forms. Natural disasters such as the tsunami of 2004, the Indonesian earthquake of 2006, Hurricane Katrina of 2005, other hurricanes, coastal storms, and flooding alert us to the potential consequences of our ecological abuses.

Technology has also created powerful tools that are deliberately destructive. In the United States, these range from huge continuing stockpiles of nuclear arms to assault weapons and small firearms that even very young children operate with ease. In the search for more and more energy, technology ignores the vast, safe potential in solar energy and instead creates nuclear power plants and accumulates enormous amounts of poisonous wastes from these and other dangerous manufacturing facilities that will take vast sums of money and many decades to clean up.

Medical technology has created means of reducing the impairment of some chronic and genetic diseases. In other instances, however, grave moral issues and ethical dilemmas accompany technological marvels. For example, persons in terminal and vegetative states whose lives a short time ago would have ended in natural death are now kept alive by machines. Similarly, extremely premature infants and gravely ill or injured infants survive on machines who, a short time ago, would have died in utero, at birth, or very soon postnatally. The moral-ethical issues raised by these advances are twofold. One is the quality-of-life issue, made even more complex by legal implications when the courts take over decision making (for which they are in no way prepared) from families and their physicians. The second—one that we avoid talking about—is the use of costly resources for such purposes when so many infants, children, and adults who are poor are deprived of routine health maintenance or treatment of serious but remediable conditions.

Reproductive technology has enabled infertile couples to have children genetically related to one or both of them and fertile parents to control the number of offspring. Surgery and other treatments of a fetus in utero are now possible to prevent certain genetic or accidental conditions. These are the benefits of reproductive technology. But other ones are redefining motherhood, fatherhood, and the birth process with as yet unknown psychological consequences for the child later, especially in the light of adopted children's deep interest in their biological parents.

Current Professional Developments

Four professional developments have been selected because of their profound impact on social work education and practice. They are (1) managed mental health care, (2) practice outcomes and evidence-based practice, (3) professional uses of technology, and (4) the ascent of policy-practice and the decline of group work practice in graduate social work education.

Managed Mental Health Care

Managed care has revolutionized health and mental health services in the United States. During the last twenty years, managed care has become the prevailing philosophy and organization for health services. Spurred by rising health costs, managed health care evolved to contain costs and as an alternative to fee-for-service health care. This philosophy and organization were also applied to mental health care and have had a profound impact on the quality of services people receive as well as funding of social service agencies and departments. Managed care's main objective is to reduce costs: either by placing limits on client services and/or by increasing co-payments and deductibles. Mental health services were transformed "from a purely professional undertaking to a business providing professional services" (Lens, 2002, p. 27, citing Abraham & Weiler, 1994, p. 395). These "business" administrators' primary function is to scrutinize services and look for ways to reduce costs. They determine what services are appropriate and necessary. Having managed care "business" administrators make crucial professional decisions has reshaped professional practice and limited the focus and scope of services to clients. Brief, goal-directed therapy approaches (solution-focused and cognitive-behavioral therapy) that focus on acute symptom relief have been defined as the preferred modes of treatment (Cohen, 2003; Gibelman & Shervish, 1996). The emphasis on short-term symptom reduction too often neglects the underlying life stressors that often create the symptoms or, at the very least, exacerbate them. Since inpatient psychiatric services are costly, its uses have been severely limited, placing people suffering from mental illness in harm's way (Geller, 1996).

In both inpatient and outpatient mental health settings, as well as in private practice, social workers experience profound ethical dilemmas and conflicts (Davidson & Davidson, 1996; Furman & Langer, 2006; Reamer, 1997). What is in the cost-saving self-interest of a managed care company is often not in the best interest of the client. Clients experience pressure to sign consent forms and release information to managed care companies, information that may lead to rejection of services and that may be insufficiently protected. Similarly, mental health agencies and social workers experience tremendous pressure to conform to time limits imposed by managed care. If they do not conform, they risk serious sanctions. Strom-Gottfried and Corcoran (1998, p. 110) identify the pressure to conform: "The threat of adverse 'provider profiles' and 'deselection' from referral networks can subtly or overtly challenge social workers willingness to put the client's best interests before their own." Essentially, the intrusive nature of the managed care oversight function and the limits it places on professional autonomy fundamentally change the worker-client relationship.

Minimizing costs and maximizing profit impose corporate values and ideology on health and mental health agencies. These values and ideology radically differ from social welfare's commitments to human rights and the provision of safety nets and buffers to our capitalist system (Schamess, 1998, p. 24). These values and ideology have a particularly deleterious affect on poor people. A "quick fix" relief of symptoms and a six-session limit do not readily ameliorate intractable and overwhelming life stressors associated with poverty, oppression, and discrimination.

Practice Outcomes and Evidence-Based Practice

With the onset of managed care's emphasis on cost reduction and accountability, the social work profession has experienced intense external pressure to demonstrate the efficacy of interventions and its professional worthiness. Concomitantly, schools of social work in research universities have experienced great pressure to acquire income-producing research grants. As a result of managed care's and universities' fiscal pressures, the profession turned inward toward a narrow focus on evaluating and demonstrating the effectiveness of professional interventions in inducing individual behavioral change—whether it be changing thinking processes, managing one's anger, or learning parenting skills. This turn inward has been at the expense of our commitment to environmental interventions and the social action tradition. Focusing on narrow measurable individual behavioral changes ignores the struggles for survival and complexities of life in oppressed families, groups, and communities. The attempt to present social work as a hard science represents an effort to make it a convincing competitor in the marketplace (Phillips, 2006). The focus on individual behavioral change ignores the basic fact that people are quintessentially social beings, existing with each other in symbiotic as well as parasitic relationships. Schon (1987) poignantly captures the distortion created by removing the people from their social context:

> In the varied topography of professional practice, there is a high ground overlooking a swamp. On the high ground, manageable problems lend themselves to solution through the application of research-based theory and technique. In the swampy lowland, messy confusing problems defy technical solutions. The irony of this situation is that the problem of the high ground tends to be relatively unimportant to individuals or society at large, however great their technical interest may be; while in the swamp lie the problems of greatest human concern. (p. 3)

Our research focus has been on the "high ground" rather than in the "messiness" that oppressed people experience in the "swamp."

The proliferation of behavioral change studies provided the foundation for the evidence-based practice "movement" in social work. Evidence-based practice emerged from the discipline of medicine and promoted basing medical decisions on the best available current external evidence. In medicine, Sackett, Rosenberg, Muir Gray, Haynes, and Richardson (1996) created the term "evidence-based medicine." Sackett, Richardson, Rosenberg, and Haynes (1997, p. 2, as cited in Gambrill, 1999, p. 346), define evidence-based practice as "the conscientious, explicit, and judicious use of the current best evidence in making decisions about the care of individuals." In social work, Gibbs and Gambrill (2002) suggest that practice decisions should emerge from an electronic search and critical review of available research findings. In other words, after meeting with a client and developing a critical assessment, the practitioner should search the major data Web sites to determine the best ways that have been demonstrated to help a person with this particular problem. The best available practices determine the course of "treatment."

Certainly, professional practices "guided" by research findings are in the interest of both our clients as well as our profession. However, when research findings are expected to prescribe rather than to guide practice, we run into serious difficulties. Understandably, the notion that a specific intervention exists to solve a specific type of problem within the context of the "real world" of people with messy and complicated life troubles has a seductive appeal. How can one not find the idea appealing that if you use specific technique "x" with client "y" with problem "z," you will achieve the intended outcome? Duncan (2001) suggests that this idea represents "the psychological equivalent of a pill for emotional distress." This association assumes a linear relationship between research and practice when in actuality the connections between theory, research, and practice are complex and illusive.

Since evidence-based practice "can only be as good as the research on which decisions are to be made" (Margison, 2001, p. 174), a central question becomes how confident can we be in the findings of available outcome studies? Certainly some evidence is available that can provide guidelines for social work practitioners (Austin, Macgowan, & Wagner, 2005; Moore, 2005; Reid, 2002). Overall, however, the designs of many outcomes studies are problematic (Wampold & Bhati, 2004), the evidences are not that strong, and the findings are not sufficiently relevant to the realities of social work practice with oppressed people. Unfortunately, in their zeal, the evidence-based practice proponents may unwittingly exaggerate the extensiveness and validity of outcome evidence. Greater humility and skepticism about how much we actually know are called for.

In a comprehensive review of a decade of social group work research, for example, Tolman and Molidor (1994) carefully examined fifty-four studies. Most of these studies evaluated the effectiveness of cognitive-behavioral interventions. The authors' discovery is astonishing: namely, only four out of the fifty-four studies "reported systematic measurement of any aspect of group process." Moreover, most studies made no mention of group process at all, and only several studies even "acknowledged the importance of group process." Only two studies "attempted statistical analysis to examine the impact of small group differences" (p. 155). How valid and relevant can the findings of these studies be when they exclude mutual aid and peer learning as part of their treatment intervention? These studies ignored the findings from the famous Hawthorn experiments in which the hidden and unexpected informal group culture turned out to be responsible for increased levels of worker productivity rather than the experimental treatment variables. By ignoring group process, "it is impossible to tell what the outcomes were outcomes of" (Smith, 1987, p. 406). In reality, what people take out of counseling might not be what we think we are giving to them (Andrews, 2000). For group practitioners undertaking a computer search, these studies' invalid outcomes may lead them to poor rather than effective practice.

When social work practitioners undertake computer searches, how are they to know whether a study's findings are reliable and valid? Unfortunately, being published is in itself insufficient evidence of validity. Peer reviewers, by and large, only examine researchers' summary presentation of data and rarely examine the raw data itself. Since evidence-based practice began in medicine, we should pay special attention to a post review of articles published in medical journals. Altman (2002, p. 1) found "considerable evidence that many statistical and methodological errors were common in published papers and that authors failed to discuss the limitations of their findings" and that the importance of findings was consistently exaggerated. Moreover, the misinformation would be widely spread because once errors were published, others would unknowingly cite them (p. 12). And even if initial peer review successfully weeded out some scientifically unsound studies, Altman further discovered an astonishing phenomenon, namely, most papers that were initially rejected found acceptance in other medical and scientific journals. Like in medicine, the proliferation of social work journals assures that most submitted articles will be published in one journal or another.

Research designs for evaluating effectiveness outcomes, another concern, are increasingly controlling practice rather than being creatively responsive to the realities of practice. In order to strictly control the independent or predictor variable being tested, a significant number of designs require carefully scripted protocols, curricula, and manuals (Duncan, 2001; Galinsky, Terzian, & Fraser, 2006). Using a medical drug-testing paradigm, a cognitive-restructuring intervention (the experimental drug), for example, is delivered, and the amount and manner of information provided to the client about cognitive distortions or managing anger (the dosage) are standardized and prescribed by a protocol or manual for the purpose of maintaining the integrity of the experimental or treatment variable. In other words, practitioners apply a standardized intervention to clients and evaluate its "effectiveness." An important question is as follows: how do the standardization and control of the treatment variable affect the actual practice itself, as well as the practice outcomes?

Practitioners have become more preoccupied with protocols, curricula, and manuals than with their clients' narratives. In classrooms, workshops, seminars, and consultations conducted by the author, participants present, for example, meeting with semivoluntary adolescent groups whose members are sitting with their arms folded and sending strong signals of frustration, anger, and resistance.[11] The group leaders worried about manuals and meeting "dosage" requirements simply ignore the deafening silent "noise." They present, for another example, their difficulties in dealing with the testing of group members in anger management groups. They focus on the prescribed curriculum and try to ignore the testing. Of course, ignoring testing only leads to its escalation. In the classroom and workshop, when the participants role-play a testing incident, the lack of congruence is startling between how the social workers teach members to deal with anger and how they themselves deal with the anger in front of them. While they are following their manuals and protocols about how to appropriately express anger, they themselves indirectly and inappropriately express their own frustration and anger. Essentially, while they teach the correct way to deal with and express anger, they model how not to manage and express anger. And as we have learned in most incongruent communications, much more is "caught" than "taught"; people pick up what we do much more than what we say should be done.

The author's professional experiences are supported by a study conducted by Castonguay and others (Castonguay, Goldfried, Wiser, Raue, & Hayes, 1996). They studied thirty depressed clients and compared the impact of a specific cognitive-behavioral technique of correcting distorted cognitions with two other, less specific treatment variables. They discovered that the cognitive-behavioral technique of eliminating negative emotions by changing distorted cognitions was negatively associated with successful outcomes. In fact, they found that the greater the emphasis a therapist placed on the distorted cognitions, the lower the treatment outcomes were for clients. What happened in this study is very similar to the author's workshop, seminar, and consultation experiences. When the workers developed interpersonal tensions with their clients (ranging from mild dissatisfaction to overt hostility), they ignored the tensions and their sources. Instead, they increased their adherence to scripted practice. When the interpersonal strains were addressed, they were identified as manifestations of the client's distorted thoughts and dysfunctional beliefs. These researchers discovered that these defensive interventions only increased the clients' resistance toward the model and the treatment.

Strupp (cited in Duncan, 2001) studied the work of therapists before and after they were trained in using manuals. He found that those who followed the manual tended to be more authoritarian and less supportive of their clients. He poignantly cautioned that manualized practitioners might develop better relationships with their treatment manuals than with their clients. The "manualization" of practice bureaucratizes social work and reduces professionals to being technicians rather than disciplined, improvisational, and artistic professionals (Duncan 2001). This type of research design rules out the inevitable interactional improvisations that are essential in the real world of practice. By viewing "social workers and clients as social billiard balls, passively bounding (from one cushion to another) through a world of causal and objective relations," social work practice is decontextualized (Webb, 2001, p. 2000). In relying on manualized experimental designs, we ignore the evidence that interpersonal and interactional variables acting within social, cultural, and organizational contexts often are critical predictors regardless of models and protocols or, at least, have to be considered as important contributors to the outcome. Meyer (1996) insightfully cautioned:

> The practice world is messy—events are out of sequence; clients are multilayered and complex, inconsistent and often defensive; the environment is a powerful force in the life of a case; and the distinctions of class, ethnicity, gender and age are always defining in cases. (p. 104).

The preoccupation with protocols, curricula, and manuals not only distorts social work practice but also weakens the validity of the research findings themselves. In the end, both practice and research suffer.

The profession must be very careful that scientific inquiry does not become equated with scientific practice management. Webb (2001, p. 71) cautions that the evidence-based practice approach "sits too comfortably alongside the new managerialism" by becoming aligned with the "idea that practice should be first and foremost objectively accountable to administrative functions and controls." In other words, what works for managed care may not work for our clients. We have to make sure that evidence-based practice does not unwittingly entrap social work practice within a bureaucratic framework of standardized interventions.

Professional Uses of Technology

Surfing and downloading from the Internet, using electronic mail (e-mail) and attachments, participating in listserv groups or in chat rooms, leaving or retrieving messages from voice mail machines, and logging into organizational networks have become part of our daily personal and professional lives. The technological revolution has brought wide-ranging social, cultural, and economic changes. People are simultaneously living in two worlds, the "real" social and physical world, and the "virtual" world of cyberspace (Gonchar & Adams, 2000). For most people, these two worlds fit well together. However, some do escape from the real world and live too much in the virtual world. The virtual world takes on its own reality, with people using "virtual interactions to substitute for real social interaction—and seeing their real relationships suffer as a result" (Krieger, 2006, p. 9B).

Technology is an extremely useful tool in social work practice (McCoy & Vila, 2002). In our professional lives, we use modern technology to keep

abreast of the latest research findings, newest knowledge about diverse issues, and the latest information; to maintain immediate connections with
our colleagues all over the world; to build and strengthen referral networks
for our clients; to improve coordination of care; to organize at the grassroots
level; to engage legislative processes; and to provide individual, family, and
group services. The telephone, an older telecommunication technology,
and the computer, a more recent communication technology, have been
creatively used in social work counseling (Galinsky, Schopler, & Abell,
1997; McCarty & Clancy, 2002; Rounds & Galinsky, 1991; Smith, Toseland, Rizzo, & Zinoman, 2004; Stein, Rothman, & Nakanishi, 1993). Counseling by e-mail or by interactive e-mail in chat rooms is also emerging.
These technologies attempt to overcome service barriers such as distance
and transportation, physical and emotional disabilities, and time constraints.
They provide the client (member, consumer) greater anonymity, less social
pressure, and more flexible meeting arrangements—which can support or
detract from the helping process. Anonymity, for example, may lead to more
spontaneous and creative or more impulsive and acting-out participation.
Telephones and computers place certain technological demands on participants, such as communicating without visual cues, intense listening, and
cutting and pasting. Schopler, Abell, and Galinsky (1998) offer clear conceptual and practical guidelines for the use of these technologies.

While the newer technologies offer special opportunities for social
worker practice, they also create some ethical challenges, particularly in relation to computerized data and confidentiality. Whenever a person fills out
any information (e.g., an application, warranty, credit card, or subscription),
it ends up in a database. The gathering, storage, transfers, and retrieval of
computerized personal information create opportunities for abuses and
breaches of confidentiality (Davidson & Davidson, 1996). People leave "electronic footprints" that are accessed by third parties and used in unethical
and illegal ways (Rock & Congress, 1999). Gelman, Pollack, and Weiner
(1999, p. 245) offer numerous illustrative examples and warn, "Violations of
confidentiality and invasion of personal privacy increase exponentially, as do
the number of individuals and organization[s] that have potential access to
recorded information." Computers and printers are networked both within
and between hospitals, social welfare organizations, and educational institutions to store and transmit information. These networks are accessed by
hackers and unauthorized personnel. For example, in a 2005 survey of university and college technology administrators, 30.4 percent identified computer security as their most important concern. Half of the sample surveyed
identified that their networks had been attacked in the past year, and 19.6
percent reported major security breaches leaving students vulnerable to
identity theft (Foster, 2006). Similarly, e-mails and attachments, voice mail
messages, and faxes can be intercepted and compromise people's confidentiality and privacy. Social workers must know the extent to which confidentiality is protected in their employing agency and seek to improve the levels of

protection. Clients (members, consumers) should be verbally and in written form informed of the limits of confidentiality.

The Ascent of Policy-Practice and the Decline of Group Work Practice in Graduate Social Work Education

As noted in the prior discussion, social work education and practice developed through the triad of casework, group work and community organization, and, to a lesser extent, social administration. These specializations allowed for the development of depth in a method. However, developments in education and practice created an impetus for change. In the late 1960s and early 1970s, social work baccalaureate programs were developed. These programs needed to differentiate themselves from the graduate social work programs. In 1974, the Council on Social Work Education specified that a generalist perspective was fitting for a baccalaureate education and in 1984 identified the baccalaureate as the first professional degree. The council further specified that the foundation knowledge of baccalaureate education and the first year of graduate education "should consist of the knowledge, values, and skills essential to generalist practice" (Landon, 1995, p. 1102). This common knowledge and skills provided the foundation for second-year specialization in graduate programs. Over time there have been shifts in specialization emphases—methods, fields of practice, and populations. This structural arrangement continues to the present.

Policy-Practice. Policy-practice, a relatively recent professional development, has developed greater scholarly attention and curricula space in social work education. Through the 1970s, social welfare policy was taught as a context for individual, family, group, and community practice as well as social administration, but not as a distinctive method of practice. In the 1980s, an increased focus on clinical social work practice, including the movement into private practice, led policy-oriented educators to search for ways to integrate social policy and social work practice. They were troubled by

> the lack of policy content in social work curricula, the lack of integration of policy content with social work practice curricula, or the tendency of clinical social workers to see policy issues only as context for the interpersonal or intrapersonal dilemmas of clients, thereby defining those policy issues as outside their professional responsibility. (Wyers, 1991, p. 242)

Jansson (1984) merged policy and practice by conceptualizing the method as policy-practice. During the 1980s, other policy scholars (Pierce, 1984; Schorr, 1985) reinforced the policy-practice conceptualization. Jansson (1990) defined policy-practice as "efforts to change policies in legislative, agency, and community settings, whether by establishing new policies, improving existing ones, or defeating the policy initiatives of other people" (p. 10). This inclusive definition insufficiently differentiated policy-practice as a method specialization from policy-practice as an expansion of traditional conceptions of direct practice. The failure to differentiate the specialist and generalist dimensions of policy-practice led Wyers (1991) to ask the following questions:

> Are policy experts performing policy-practice or conducting policy analysis when they analyze policy to predict its effects? Are direct practitioners who try to change policy on behalf of clients conducting policy-practice? Are administrators and planners policy-practitioners by definition because they design or implement policy? How might policy-related activities differ by roles, education or training, and functions of those who conduct them? (p. 243)

In reality, policy-practice is both a method specialization that only certain social workers undertake, as well as a repertoire of methods and skills for all social workers. In order for the profession to fulfill its social justice goals, policy-practice must be carried out by advanced specialists as well as by direct practitioners in their day-to-day activities. In order for social workers to help oppressed and disadvantaged populations, both specialists and generalists must engage in legislative advocacy (Dear & Patti, 1982; Figueira-McDonough, 1993). Similarly, organizing communities and influencing employing and external organizations should be the province of both specialists and generalists. In contrast, policy specialists must carry out the more complex tasks, such as reform through litigation (environmental, welfare, and employment) and social policy analysis and planning. These policy specialists serve as experts; their activities and expertise are integral to their job.

In 1989, the Social Welfare Policy and Policy Practice Group (SWPPPG) was formed to provide a national forum for social welfare policy and policy-practice faculty (Wyers, 1991, p. 247). SWPPPG effectively raised consciousness about the need for policy to receive greater curriculum attention and space. Over time, most graduate schools developed a macro concentration in social policy and planning. For the direct practitioner, most undergraduate and graduate programs introduce students to content dealing with organizational and community influence.

Group Work Practice. In the 1970s, practitioners were increasingly expected to practice across methods. The arrangement of having a caseworker provide individual services in a group work agency and a group worker provide group services in a casework agency became structurally too cumbersome. Increasingly, social workers and social work students were expected to have skills in "multi" or "cross" methods. Eventually, the triad of casework, group work and community organization, and "cross" methods was replaced by an integrated method of practice and generalist curriculum.

The author's experience as a young group work faculty member at a large metropolitan school of social work may illuminate the transition. The first significant change at the school occurred in the mid- and late 1960s. Group work students eschewed placements in the traditional settlement and community center field training sites. Beyond the after-school club programs, these settings provided limited diversity in student assignments. Students preferred and selected National Institute of Mental Health training units in public housing and public welfare, and hospitals and more traditional casework settings of family agencies and health and mental health settings for their field placements. Group work faculty recruited interested and creative casework field instructors, provided special group work seminars for them, and assigned them to field-instruct group work students. In these placements, most students were assigned individual and family as well as group work assignments. Since students were providing multimethod services, the group work courses became more inclusive of the other methods. Group work faculty scholarship followed suit and became broader in scope.

In the early 1970s, an increasing number of students self-designated themselves as double majors in casework and group work. They used their elective credits to double-major. By and large, students found this curriculum design to be burdensome, as they were left with the difficult tasks of integrating the casework and group work content and methods. The group work faculty became uncomfortable with placing the main responsibility of integration on the students, while we ourselves avoided this complex task. Moreover, we also became uncomfortable with a curriculum design that prepared graduates to specialize in only one method. Our students' practice experiences reinforced our conviction that professional specialization should not determine whether a client receives individual, family, or group services, but rather the received service should be based upon client needs and preferences. We developed a strong commitment to this educational direction while, at the same time, we were concerned about its implications for future group work practice.

When the school decided to implement an integrated method curriculum, Professors Germain, Goldson, and I were asked to develop the first two integrated method courses (the forerunner of the foundations curriculum), and in 1974 the new curriculum was institutionalized. While emphasizing the common method of social work practice, distinct individual, family, and group work content was also specified. Group practice case illustrations and video materials were developed to assist casework faculty in teaching the group work content. In our contract with field work agencies, we required a group assignment, and provided advanced field instructional seminars on group work knowledge and methods. During the first ten years, 70–80 percent of the students carried a group assignment. We developed a stable corps of field instructors who were committed to teaching group work content.

For approximately the first ten years (from the mid-1970s to the mid-1980s), the group work content and skills were by and large systematically taught. However, over time, the commitment to teaching the group work content waned in both class and the field. This pattern is evident on a national level. In 1963, 76 percent of graduate schools had a group work concentration. By 2000, less than 5 percent of the graduate schools offered a group work concentration (Birnbaum & Wayne, 2000). In the early 1990s, only 19 percent of graduate schools required a group work course, less than half of the graduate schools offered a group work elective, and only 15 percent of the students registered for a group work elective (Birnbaum & Auerbach, 1994). Survey findings also demonstrated the lack of familiarity with basic group work concepts about group formation, mutual aid, and phases of group development. The dramatic decline in the teaching of group work has had a profoundly negative impact on professional practice.

While group work has been disappearing from social work curricula, practice with groups has dramatically increased in the field. However, in keeping with the conservative times and managed care's emphases, these groups primarily focus on individual behavior change in a group context, with the potential of mutual aid remaining unrealized. These groups are externally controlled with prescribed curricula content, timing, and sequencing. Notions about democratic participation and mutual aid are replaced by leader prescriptions and control. These groups do not have a "suggested" curriculum; they are not curriculum-based groups—"rather they are curriculum-DRIVEN groups" (Kurland & Salmon, 2002). The settlement vision of members learning democratic citizenship in small groups, of the potential of small groups to universalize and legitimize people's life troubles, and of the small group as a potential agent of social change rather than social control is being lost. How sad!

THE ECOLOGICAL PERSPECTIVE

Because ecological theory emphasizes the interdependence of organism and environment, it is especially suitable as a *metaphor* for social work, given our historic commitment to the person-and-environment concept. The ecological metaphor helps the profession enact its social purpose of helping people and promoting responsive environments that support human growth, health, and satisfaction in social functioning.

Bronfenbrenner (1995, as cited by Lerner, 2005, p. xv) identifies four interrelated components of the ecological perspective. The first component is the developmental process that is shaped by and shapes the dynamic relation between the individual and her or his context; the second component is the person's repertoire of biological, cognitive, emotional, and behavioral dispositions and characteristics and its impact on the developmental process; the third component is the context for human development, that is, the nested systems levels; and the fourth component is the multiple dimensions of temporality that influence changes across the life course. The life model draws on several major sets of these ecological concepts, including (1) ecological thinking and reciprocity of person–environment exchanges; (2) person:environment fit, adaptedness, and adaptation; (3) habitat and niche; (4) abuse or misuse of power, oppression, and social and technological pollution; (5) the life course; (6) life stressors, stress, and coping; and (7) resilience and protective factors. The model also draws on newer ecological concepts from deep ecology and ecofeminism. Together, these concepts form the current theoretical foundation of life-modeled practice.

Review of Ecological Concepts

Ecological concepts are derived from the natural science of biology and the study of the relations among components of a biotic community. This community includes flora and fauna, as well as features of the physical environment such as terrain, climate, and natural disturbances. Human beings act within physical, social, and cultural environments. Physical environments include the natural world; structures built by people; the space that supports, contains, or arranges these structures; and the rhythms of environmental and human biology. Social environments include family, friends, and social networks of two or more significant people; larger groups such as organizations, institutions, and the community (which are also physical settings); and society itself, including its political, economic, and social structures and the law. Culture is part of the environment and part of the person, and is expressed through each person's values, norms, beliefs, and language. The cultural environment affects how people "structure their behavior, their worldview, their perspective on the rhythms of life and their concept of the essential nature of the human condition" (Devore & Schlesinger, 1995, p. 903).

From a holistic view, people (and their biological, cognitive, emotional, and social processes) and physical and social environments (and the characteristics of those environments) can be fully understood only in the context of the relationship between and among them, in which individuals, families, groups, and physical-social environments continually influence the operations of the other. These dynamic arrays of linked influences always occur in a cultural context.

Ecology also rests on an evolutionary, adaptive view of the development of human beings. Darwin (1874, 1988) formulated that human beings gradually evolved and were transformed from apes. The premature births of some upright walking apes triggered human evolution. These prematurely born apes may have held on to certain youthful traits longer, and when they mated, their offspring were more likely to be born prematurely and held on to even more youthful traits. An evolutionary trend may have begun that eventually resulted in a hairless species. The helplessness of these prematurely born infants required support from families, which formed tribes and communities and created the foundation for human civilization (Capra, 1996).

Darwin hypothesized that all forms of life evolved from a common ancestry. In the evolutionary process, a natural selection takes place in which some species survive, whereas others become extinct. For example, if an animal species requires thick fur to survive cold weather, those who wind up with thick fur because of random genetic changes will survive and produce more offspring with thick fur. Those who do not wind up with thick fur will be unable to survive (Capra, 1996).

As human cultures evolved, they enabled people to transcend limitations imposed by environmental conditions or the genetic structure of the species developed in the evolutionary past. There were, however, some negative consequences to human development through cultural instead of genetic change. We became disassociated from the rhythms of nature that had shaped our physiology and psychology, and we were exposed to conditions of our own creation that were very different from those in which our earlier organic evolution had proceeded over the millennia.

Ecological Thinking

"settlement" method

Ecological thinking focuses on the reciprocity of person–environment exchanges, in which each shapes and influences the other over time. This mode of thought differs markedly from the simple cause-and-effect linear thinking that now pervades our language, culture, education, systems of ideas, and practice research. According to linear thinking, we assume that an antecedent (experimental or treatment) variable, A, leads to an effect on B at a certain point in time, while A remains unchanged. There is a certain *vs* inescapable determinism in this: Given A, effects on B necessarily follow. Unquestionably, linear thinking explains some simple human phenomena, but ecological thinking explains more complex phenomena, such as those encountered every day in social work practice.

For example, a teenage son is striving for an age-appropriate degree of autonomy from parental control. The parents, not aware or not accepting of the teen's normal desire for greater independence, try to keep their son close and compliant with their wishes. Rather than seeing either the parents or the son as the cause of escalating battles (linear thinking), the life-model social worker, using ecological thinking, is likely to hold the view that the age-appropriate behavior of the son evokes stringent countermeasures from the parents, particularly from the father. These lead to the son's increased rebellion, which eventually may take the form of total rejection of parental values and expectations—a situation that neither son nor parents want. Each stride toward such an undesirable end leads to further restrictions on the son, which then tends to encourage his rebellious behavior. This pattern represents a circle of negative exchanges.

Instead of attributing the escalation of anger and resentment to either party, the social worker focuses with the family on the exchanges and how they lead to the unsatisfactory behaviors of parents and son. At the same time the social worker is sensitive to environmental factors, such as possible help or interference from kin and friends, the nature of school and peer forces, and workplace and health issues, recognizing that the family is not a closed system.

Ecological thinking also recognizes that A and B are in a reciprocal relation rather than a linear or unidirectional one. A may act in a way that leads to change in B, whereupon that change in B leads to change in A, which in turn affects B—a continuous loop of reciprocal influences over time. Each element in the loop directly or indirectly influences every other element. As a consequence, simple linear notions of cause and effect lose their meaning.

Therefore, we should be *less concerned with causes than with consequences*, and concentrate on helping change maladaptive relationships between people and their environments. We should ask, "What is going on?" rather than "Why is it going on?" and ask, "How can the 'what' be changed?" rather than "How can the 'who' be changed?"

In the previous example, the worker may learn that the father has recently lost his job due to cutbacks in his company. Attempts to find other work have been fruitless. He is ashamed and depressed. The new behaviors of his son now seem a personal affront. We now can see that the *what* includes job loss, and the worker's tasks will need to include encouraging the father to join community support groups, helping him with résumés, networking, examining his potential for retraining, and so on as well as addressing the relationship with his son. Similarly, the worker may learn that the son is experiencing difficulty in school, lost a girlfriend, and so on. Moreover, the strain between father and son has had a negative effect on the husband–wife relationship (or possibly the strained marital relationship affected the father–son relationship.) The life-modeled social worker focuses on the strained family relationships with a focus on influencing relationship and communication patterns rather than changing individual family members. Ecological thinking emphasizes the reciprocal relationships among people and their environment, not simply to a lone characteristic of an individual or the environment, but to particular relationships between them. Werner, Altman, Oxley, and Haggard (1987) capture the complexity of these reciprocal relationships:

> Psychological phenomena are best understood as holistic events composed of inseparable and mutually defining psychological processes, physical environments and social environments, and temporal qualities. There are no separate actors in an event; the actions of one person are understood in relation to the actions of other people, and in relation to spatial, situational and temporal circumstances in which the actors are embedded. These different aspects of an event are so intermeshed that understanding one aspect requires simultaneous inclusion of other aspects in the analysis. (p. 244)

Person:Environment Fit

Over the life course, people strive to deal with and improve the *level of fit* with their environments. When a "good" fit evolves between a person and her or his environment, the person perceives the availability of sufficient personal and environment resources and experiences a condition of *adaptedness* (Dubos, 1968). Put another way, *adaptive* person:environment exchanges support and release human potential and growth, health, and satisfaction. When a "poor" fit evolves between a person's perceptions of environmental resources and his or her needs and capacities, he or she experiences stress. How overwhelming and disabling clients experience their daily life stress and how effectively they manage the associated life tasks will largely depend

Table 2.1
Ecological Thinking and Person:Environment Fit Concepts and Their Definitions

• *Exchanges:*	Continuous transactions between people and their environments, in which each shapes the other over time.
• *Person:environment fit:*	Favorable or unfavorable fit between the needs, capacities, behavioral styles, and goals of people, and the characteristics of the environment.
• *Adaptedness:*	A favorable person:environment fit that supports human growth and well-being, and preserves and enriches the environment.
• *Adaptation:*	Actions designed to achieve personal change, environmental change, or both in order to improve the level of person:environment fit.
• *Adaptive:*	Person:environment exchanges that release and support human potential for adaptedness.

upon *the perceived level of fit* between their personal and environmental resources. When the perceived fit between person and environment is unfavorable, or merely adequate, the person—alone or with help—may improve the level of fit by adaptive behaviors.

Adaptive behaviors are active efforts to (1) change oneself (e.g., learn new skills) in order to meet the environment's perceived expectations or demands, and take advantage of its opportunities; (2) change the environment (e.g., emigrate) so that the social and physical environments are more responsive to one's needs and goals; or (3) change the person:environment transactions (e.g., teacher and student) in order to achieve an improved fit. Whatever the adaptation, people must continue to adapt to the changes they or the environment has made. Hence, adaptation is a never-ending process. Social work values support the profession's preference for person:environment exchanges that release people's potential for further growth and promote diverse, supportive environments that release human potential.

Adaptedness and *adaptation* are sometimes confused with passive or conservative adjustments to the status quo. However, in the ecological social work perspective and in life-modeled practice, adaptedness and adaptation are firmly action oriented and change oriented. Neither adaptedness nor adaptation avoids the issues of conflict and power that are as prominent in nature as they are in society. Table 2.1 summarizes the concepts discussed so far.

Habitat and Niche

In the science of ecology, *habitat* refers to the places where the organism can be found, such as nesting places, home ranges, and territory. Human beings' particular physical and social settings within a cultural context represent their habitat. For humans, physical habitat may be rural or urban, and include residential dwellings, transportation systems, workplaces, schools, religious structures, social agencies, hospitals, and amenities such as parks, recreation facilities, entertainment centers, libraries, and museums. Habitats that do not support the growth, health, and social functioning of individuals and families, and do not provide community amenities to an optimum degree, are likely to produce isolation, disorientation, and helplessness. Thus habitats may interfere with basic functions of family and community life (Germain, 1985a).

Niche refers to the position occupied by a species of organisms within a biotic community, that is, their place in a community's web of life. In this book, niche refers to the status occupied in a community's social structure by its groups and individuals. What constitutes a growth-supporting, health-promoting human niche is defined differently in various societies and in different historical eras. In the United States, a set of rights, including the right to equal opportunity, generally shapes a niche. Yet millions of children and adults occupy niches that do not support human needs, rights, and aspirations—often because of some personal or cultural characteristic devalued by society. These niches are shaped and sustained by society's tolerance of the misuse of power in political, social, and economic structures (Germain & Gitterman, 1987, 1995).

Power, Powerlessness, and Pollution

Although power and its abuse may have always been a part of collective life, the 1990s and the beginning of the 2000s saw the exposure of corporate abuses of financial power to an extent never previously seen. The depletion of retirement pensions, the manipulation of stock prices, and insider trading devastate and victimize the unsuspecting public. Private corporations and governmental agencies pollute the air, food, water, and soil. Toxic materials continue to be present in dwellings, schools, and workplaces, especially in blue-collar and poor communities. In politics, lobbyists and their self-interests, rather than legislators representing the public, increasingly enact laws. Even in public bureaucracies, abusive power excludes and oppresses large segments of our population.

The abuse of economic and political power leads to poor schools, chronic unemployment or underemployment of those whom the schools failed to educate, lack of affordable and safe housing, homelessness, inadequate health care, and differential rates of chronic illness and longevity among people of color as compared to whites. This abuse of power creates and maintains such social pollution as poverty; institutional racism and sexism; repressive gender roles in family, work, and community life; homophobia; and physical and social barriers to community participation by those with disabilities. These conditions are major stressors that afflict the entire population, but their burden falls heaviest on the vulnerable, disenfranchised, and excluded. Disempowerment and social as well as environmental pollution threaten health, social well-being, and life itself. They impose enormous adaptive tasks on the oppressed. They are expressions of destructive relationships between person and environment, in which the social order permits some to inflict grave injustice and suffering on others.

Life Course

The concept of the life course is a far-reaching advance in life-modeled practice. The term refers to the unique pathways of development that each human being takes—from conception and birth through old age—in varied environments, and to our infinitely varied life experiences. *Life course* replaces the traditional "life cycle" models of human development in which so-called life stages are assumed to be fixed, sequential, predictable, and universal. Stage models tend to conceal the fact that stages and developmental tasks originate in the social norms of a particular society in a particular historic context. Psychological transformations are viewed as due exclusively to natural processes of psychological growth and ignore the formative influence of society's practices, interpersonal exchanges, socialization processes, and diverse cultures and subcultures.

By contrast, the life course conceptualization rests on an ecological view of nonuniform, indeterminable pathways of biopsychosocial development within diverse environments and cultures. Hence, as adopted for life-modeled practice, the life course conceptualization readily incorporates and emphasizes the following elements:

1. The distinctiveness of human diversity (race, ethnicity, gender, culture, socioeconomic status, religion, sexual orientation, and physical/mental states). The life course conception permits us to individualize personal and collective life experience, instead of forcing all people into predetermined, universal developmental stages.
2. The self-regulating, self-directing nature of human beings and their innate push toward growth and health.
3. Environmental diversity (economic, political, social, and historical) that takes into account the effects of poverty or prejudicial discrimination on human development and functioning.
4. Newly emerging family forms and structures and their unique tasks and developmental issues in addition to those faced by traditional family structures and forms.
5. Rapid shifts in societal and community values and norms in today's world.
6. The critical significance of global as well as local environments.

Perhaps most significant of all, the life course conception can be organized around matters of life stressors, stress, and coping that are generated by difficult life transitions, traumatic life events, poverty, and prejudicial discrimination. Life transitions, for example, are then viewed not as isolated, separable, fixed developmental stages but as ongoing biopsychosocial processes occurring or recurring at any point in the life course. They may be expected or unexpected, and they may be stressful or challenging, depending on the unique interplay of personal, historic, cultural, and environmental factors. The resolution of these processes leads to growth, whereas the lack of resolution can lead to the physical, emotional, or social dysfunction and possible disorganization of family, group, or community (Germain, 1990).

Life course theorists place human development and social functioning in a matrix of historical, individual, and social time (Hareven, 1982). *Historical time* refers to the formative effects of historical and social change on birth cohorts (segments of the population born at the same historical point) that help account for generational and age differences in biopsychosocial development, opportunities, and social expectations. For example, cohorts of North American women born between 1970 and 1980 differ—in psychosocial development, opportunities, and expectations of marriage, parenting, and work—from earlier cohorts. Social workers need to understand the differences across cohorts, in addition to the more telling differences in personality, culture, and life experiences, which are understood in terms of individual and social time.

Individual time refers to the experiences, meanings, and outcomes of personal and environmental factors over the life course, within a given historical and cultural context. Individual time in this sense is reflected in the self-constructed life stories or narratives, about which more will be said in chapter 3. For now, we merely note Neugarten's observation (1969) that predates by a quarter of a century practitioners' current interest in narrative theory:

> The adult, surely by middle age, with his highly refined powers of introspection and reflection, is continually busying himself in making a coherent story out of his life history. He reinterprets the past, selects and shapes his memories, and reassesses the significance of past events in his search for coherence. An event, which, at the time of its occurrence, was "unexpected" or arbitrary or traumatic, becomes rationalized and interwoven into a context of explanation in its retelling 20 years later. (p. 123)

Social time refers to the timing of collective life issues in a family, group, or community, and the transformations that occur as consequences of individual and collective processes. Many families and natural and formed groups develop cherished rituals and myths about their origin and experiences. A community may also develop rituals, such as parades or ethnic celebrations, and myths about early events, such as its founding or its crises.

Until the 1960s, social time consisted of sequential "timetables" that prescribed the timing of certain life transitions: the proper time to enter school, leave home, marry, have a child, and retire. Such timetables are no longer viable, a manifestation of the accelerated rate of social change (historical time). The early childhood education movement created a new age group—preschoolers—who attend day care and nursery schools, Head Start programs, and so on. Elders go back to school for high school certificates or college degrees, grown children remain at home after finishing college, some children bear and rear children, whereas some adults postpone child-bearing until the last possible moment. Many elders do not regard themselves as old until their late seventies or eighties. These and other life transitions are becoming age independent. In parallel fashion, the phenomenon of gender crossover has progressively expanded. Gendered family roles and work roles have dramatically changed in regard to childrearing, household management, and careers.

In adapting to life experiences accumulated over historical, individual, and social time, human beings change themselves and their environments for good or ill. To understand the positive and negative changes, we must understand the interplay of personal, environmental, cultural, and historical factors that produce change. The implications of these and other elements of the life course conception are expanded in subsequent chapters through their application to practice methods and skills. Table 2.2 summarizes the concepts of habitat and niche, power, and life course and their definitions.

Table 2.2
Habitat, Niche, Power, and Life Course Concepts and Their Definitions

• *Habitat:*	Place where an organism is found. Used metaphorically, all the physical and social settings of human individuals or groups.
• *Niche:*	Position occupied by a species in a biotic community. Used metaphorically, the social status occupied in a human community by an individual or a group.
• *Coercive power:*	Withholding of power by dominant groups from other groups on the basis of personal or cultural features.
• *Exploitative power:*	Abuse of power by dominant groups that creates technological pollution around the world, endangering the health and well-being of all people and communities and, most especially, poor people and their communities.
• *Life course:*	Unique, unpredictable pathways of development that humans take within diverse environments and cultures, and their diverse life experiences from conception and birth to old age.
• *Historical time:*	The historical contexts of social change and its differential formative effects on different birth cohorts (segments of the population born in the same decade or period of time).
• *Individual time:*	The life experiences of the individual, the meanings attributed to them, and their outcomes, within a given historical context and a particular culture (exemplified by people's life stories).
• *Social time:*	The expected and unexpected transitions, traumatic events, and other life issues in a family, group, or community, and the consequent positive transformations of the collectivity or grave disorganization that may occur.

Life Stressor, Stress, Coping, and Challenge

People seeking social work services are trying to manage a stressful situation, even though they do not necessarily present their request for service in those terms. The same may be said for those who are referred for services by a third party and those for whom services are mandated by an outside agency or institution. Lazarus's (1980) stressor–stress–coping paradigm fits well with the ecological perspective and the life-modeled practice as it takes into account the characteristics of the person and the operations of the environment, as well as the exchanges between them. Like all ecological concepts, the paradigm helps the social worker to maintain a focus on both person and environment.

Life stressors and internal stress are expressions of negative relationships between person and environment. The *life stressor*, which is usually externally generated, takes the form of a real or perceived harm or loss, or threat of a future harm or loss (e.g., illness, bereavement, job loss, difficult transition, interpersonal conflict, or countless other painful life issues and events). The resulting *stress*, which is internally generated, may have physiological and/or emotional consequences. Frequently, it has both. Physiological and emotional stresses are the consequence of people's intuitive or reasoned *appraisal* that a difficult life transition, traumatic life event, or environmental or interpersonal pressure exceeds their perceived available personal and environmental resources to deal with it. Stressful feelings aroused by the stressor are negative and usually immobilizing, and should not be equated with internal anxiety because anxiety is only one possible internal response to an external life stressor. Feelings may include anxiety, guilt, anger, despair, helplessness, or depression (Lazarus & Folkman, 1984).

The stress caused by difficult life transitions, traumatic life events, and environmental and interpersonal pressures is related to dimensions of the stressor and its meaning to the person. These dimensions include the following:

Whether a stressor is chronic or acute affects its impact.

Whether a person experiences ambivalence about the stressor and its resolution also affects its impact.

Whether a critical event is anticipated or unexpected can affect the amount of time available for a person to prepare for the life change. Unpredictable life events are more difficult to cope with than predictable ones.

Lack of control over a stressor has a profound effect.

Timing, the point on the life course at which the stressor strikes, is a significant factor in the degree of stress experienced. Most of us anticipate that certain events will take place in accord with certain social or biological expectations.

Expected desired events may not take place, as when an engagement is broken, a miscarriage occurs, or a promised job does not materialize.[1]

When a person encounters a life issue, he or she engages in *primary appraisal*, which may be conscious or unconscious, to assess its potential threat. In asking oneself, "What is the meaning of this issue?" and "Am I in trouble, or is this a challenge?" the appraisal results in a judgment that the issue is irrelevant, benign, or a stressor (Lazarus, 1980). If the person decides that the issue is a stressor, further appraisal determines whether it represents a current harm or loss, a future threat of harm or loss, or a challenge. In the case of a harm or loss, efforts to cope are directed to overcoming, reducing, or tolerating the stressor. In the case of a threat, efforts to cope are directed to maintaining the current state of affairs, preventing an anticipated harm or loss, or easing the effects. For example, careful planning of the use of time and financial resources following an announced factory closing or an upcoming but unwanted retirement is an effective coping measure.

We appraise a life issue as a *challenge* when we believe we have the personal and environmental resources to deal with it. Although challenge can be stressful, it is nevertheless accompanied by feelings of zest, relatedness, competence, and self-direction. In contrast, a stressor is accompanied by a sense of being in jeopardy. One person may experience a difficult life situation as a stressor, while another may experience the same situation as a challenge. Some people even under the most adverse conditions experience challenge. These differences appear to arise from the interplay of personality, physical condition, environment, past experiences, personal- and cultural-based meanings of a serious life issue, availability of resources for coping, and absence of too many concurrent stressors. People who experience a difficult life situation as a challenge are probably less likely to seek social work services than are people who experience the same life issue as a severe stressor.

Sometimes our initial appraisal contains an error in perception or thinking. For example, a person may believe that a life issue is a stressor when it is not, or may think the environment is hostile when it is supportive. A person may overestimate her or his resources for dealing with the stressor and thereby fail to cope with it successfully, or underestimate her or his resources and believe that the situation is hopeless. Such a belief is often seen in instances of *internalized oppression*, with consequent self-hatred or lowered self-esteem (Bulham, 1985). Erroneous beliefs, perceptions, and thoughts may intensify the stress. At the same time, it is important to avoid merely considering the truth or falsity of the cognitions. Defenses, for example, falsify situations, yet they can help with coping over the short term.

Once a life issue is appraised as a stressor that exceeds a person's perceived personal and/or environmental resources, the *secondary appraisal* consists of "What can I do about this state of affairs?" The response to this secondary appraisal question initiates *coping measures*. Coping occurs over time. Some stressors may pass quickly, as when a firing is followed by another job. Or stressors may be present for a long time, as in mourning, in raising an autistic child, or in the case of a solo mother living in poverty. Coping efforts may demand frustrating delays (Lee, 1992) or the toleration of a lengthy in-terval between meeting the demands posed by the stressor and the onset of relief. Now and again, demands may momentarily exceed personal resources because of temporary depletion of an individual's usual capability. Progress is often characterized by ups and downs, especially in some chronic ill-nesses. Coping expresses a person's person:environment relationship since both personal and environmental resources are required.

Personal resources for coping include motivation, management of feelings, problem solving, relationship skills, a hopeful outlook, optimal levels of self-esteem and self-direction, the ability to identify and use information from the environment about the stressor and how to deal with it, self-restraint, and an ability to seek environmental resources and to use them effectively. Flexibility is also a personal coping resource. Like hope, it reflects recogni-tion of positives despite the stressor, a trust in the certainty of future satis-faction, and seeking and accepting help when needed.

Environmental resources include formal service networks such as public and private agencies and institutions. Their availability depends on soci-ety's and the community's social provisions, eligibility requirements, hours of service, and transportation facilities. Resources also include informal networks of relatives, friends, neighbors, workmates, and coreligionists. Such informal support networks serve as buffers against stress. Even the perception of their availability can make it easier to cope with a life stressor by altering appraisals. The natural and built physical environment (parks, oceans, transportation, and dwellings) may also contribute to physical and emotional well-being and support coping efforts.

When efforts at coping are ineffective, physiological and emotional stress are likely to be intensified and may lead to physical, social, or emo-tional difficulties. The stress generated in one area may cause other stresses, so that multiple stressors become involved. For example, stressful family relationships may affect a child's school performance and thereby make school an additional stressor. It should be noted that stress alone does not cause dysfunction. Rather, a maladaptive outcome depends on either per-sonal vulnerability and/or ineffective coping. Some coping attempts are doomed to fail, and their outcomes become added stressors. For example, alcohol or drug use may represent an effort to cope with a life stressor and may result in temporary relief. However, chemical substances do not eliminate the stressor or change the person:environment relationship; furthermore, excessive use can intensify the stress and generate additional stressors.

Most people can cope relatively well with difficult life stressors. In some instances, the stressor is ameliorated or its consequences mastered. Many people grow as a result of coping with stressors; their self-esteem and sense of competence, relatedness, and self-direction are strengthened by their tri-umph over adversity. This growth is much the same as that achieved in mastery of challenge, although less pain and personal and familial upset in

Table 2.3
Stressor–Stress–Coping Concepts and Their Definitions

• *Life stressor:*	Life transitions, traumatic events, and environmental and interpersonal pressures that disturb the level of person:environment fit and a prior state of relative adaptedness.
• *Stress:*	Internal (physical or emotional) responses to a life stressor that exceeds one's perceived personal and environmental resources to cope with it.
• *Primary appraisal:*	Conscious or unconscious processes through which a person judges whether an issue is irrelevant, benign, or a stressor. If the latter, whether it poses a harm or loss (damage already suffered), a future threat of harm or loss associated with an anticipated life issue, or a challenge (anticipated mastery). A stressor is associated with negative feelings, while a challenge is associated with positive feelings.
• *Secondary appraisal:*	Consideration of measures and resources to deal with a life stressor.
• *Coping:*	Behavioral and cognitive measures to change some aspect of oneself, the environment, the exchanges between them, or all three in order to manage the negative feelings aroused.
• *Feedback:*	Error-correcting internal and external signals and cues from a person's cognitions and sensory perceptions and from the environment about the effectiveness of the coping efforts.

the process accompany challenge. Table 2.3 summarizes stressor–stress–coping concepts and their definitions.

Resilience and Protective Factors

Resilience is an ecological concept, reflecting complex person:environment transactions rather than simply attributes of a person (Gitterman, 1999, 2001a, 2001b; Gitterman & Shulman, 2005).[2] Webster defines resilience as "the tendency to rebound or recoil, to return to prior state, to spring back." The process of "rebounding" and "returning to prior state" does not suggest that a person, family, group, or community is incapable of being wounded or injured. Rather, in the face of adversity, a person or collectivity can bend, or lose some of his, her, or their power and capability, yet recover and return to a prior level of adaptation. Protective factors are biological, psychological, and/or environmental processes that contribute to preventing a stressor, lessening its impact, or ameliorating it more quickly (Fraser, Richman, & Galinsky, 1999; Turner, 2001). In dealing with poverty, oppression, and/or discrimination, for example, some people do not succeed in spite of personal attributes of resilience. Some even collapse from the pressures and stress.

Yet, most lead normal, happy lives. In fact, some people do not simply survive but also thrive in the face of life's inhumanities and tragedies (McMillen, 1999).

Various theories attempt to explain what differentiates a victim from a survivor. Since many of our theoretical approaches are based on people who do not rebound well from life's adversities, we know much less about those who do and how they do it (Barnard, 1994). Bronfenbrenner (1977, as cited in Lerner, 2005, p. x) criticizes artificial developmental research designs, "the science of the strange behavior of children in strange situations with strange adults for the briefest possible periods of time. . . . [O]nly experiments created as real are real in their consequences." "Real" research into children living in highly stressed, trauma-inducing environments informs us about the protective factors that help them negotiate high-risk situations. The protective factors include (1) temperament, (2) family patterns, (3) external supports, and (4) environmental resources (Basic Behavioral Task Force, 1996; Fraser, 2004; Smith & Carlson, 1997).

Temperament includes such factors as activity level, coping skills, self-esteem, and attributions. In relation to activity level, overactive children often encounter much greater rejection, anger, and abuse than children who are not overactive. Adaptive coping requires the ability to manage one's feelings and to solve problems. Children dealing with parental alcoholism or substance abuse or divorce, for example, must find ways to disengage and to develop psychological distance from daily conflicts and hassles, while pursuing and sustaining external connections. In contrast, a flight into social as well as emotional isolation symbolizes risk factors and processes (Berlin & Davis, 1989). Self-esteem is a dynamic, complex concept as "individuals have not one but several views of themselves encompassing many domains of life, such as scholastic ability, physical appearance and romantic appeal, job competence, and adequacy as provider" (Basic Behavioral Task Force, 1996, p. 26). Feelings of self-worth seem to emerge from two types of experiences: (1) positive intimate relationships, and (2) successful task accomplishment (e.g., academic, sports, music, and employment). Children's attributions also serve as protective as well as risk factors. Generally, a self-condemning attribution style has a strong negative impact (Feinauer & Stuart, 1996).

In *family patterns*, one nourishing parent–child relationship serves as a protective factor in cushioning dysfunctional family processes as well as increasing the child's self-esteem. The presence of a caring adult such as a grandparent leads to similar outcomes (Basic Behavioral Task Force, 1996; Hawley, 2000; Walsh, 2002).

External support from a neighbor, parents of peers, a teacher, clergy, or a social worker serves also as a significant cushioning and protective factor. Cushioning and protecting an individual in harm's way are achieved through the provision of four types of support (Auslander & Levin, 1987): (1) *instrumental* (goods or services), (2) *emotional* (nurturance, empathy, and encouragement), (3) *informational* (advice and feedback), and (4) *appraisal* (information relevant to self-evaluation). These supports provide essential ingredients for effective protection and coping, including a sense of physical and emotional well-being, and also help shape one's worldview.

Finally, the *broader social and physical environment* and the opportunity structure create the conditions that influence all other factors. When social structures and institutions provide essential resources and supports, they are critical buffers, helping people cope with life transitions, environments, and interpersonal stressors.

The direction of a life trajectory is often determined by what happens at critical *turning points* in people's lives rather than long-standing attributes. For example, the decision to remain in school often leads to more positive trajectories than dropping out from school. In contrast, the birth of an unwanted child to a well-functioning teenager who is then rejected by family creates a negative trajectory (Rutter, 1987). Another significant protective factor is the extent of *planning in making turning point decisions*. Exercising foresight and taking active steps to cope with environmental challenges are critical factors.

Although planning and foresight are important protective factors, there is always the simple element of *chance, good fortune and misfortune*, or *"God's will."* Although our efforts to be scientific may distance us from explanations involving chance or spiritual beliefs, they may well enhance our understanding of and feeling for the human experience (Canda, 2002). For example, most survivors of the Holocaust know that they survived because they happened to be at the right place at the right time. For another example, people involved with Alcoholics Anonymous (AA) commit to and align themselves with a spiritual force larger than themselves. They develop a spiritual homeostasis by adopting and abiding behaviorally by "a value or belief system that provides guidelines for living" (Richardson, Neiger, Jensen, & Kumpfer, 1990, p. 35).

Humor, an additional protective factor, has a profound impact on everyday interactions (Gitterman, 2003a). Laughter is essential to life. For oppressed and vulnerable populations, humor and laughter provide a safety valve for coping with painful realities. Religious, ethnic, and racial forms of humor help a stereotyped group to vent anger and to dismissively laugh at the dominant culture's stereotypes. Humor also surfaces the subtle and less visible forms of prejudice and discrimination. By making the less visible more visible, oppression is challenged (Gordon, 1998). To be able to laugh in the face of adversity and suffering releases tension and provides hope. Eli Wiesel poignantly noted (as quoted in Baures, 1994):

> The truth comes into this world with two faces. One is sad with suffering, and the other laughs; but it is the same face, laughing or weeping. When people are already in despair, maybe the laughing face is better for them; and when they feel too good and are sure of being safe, maybe the weeping face is better for them to see. (p. 31)

Table 2.4
Resilience and Protective Factors Concepts and Their Definitions

• *Resilience:*	"The tendency to rebound or recoil, to return to prior state, to spring back."
• *Protective factors:*	Biological, psychological, and/or environmental processes that contribute to preventing a stressor, to lessening its impact, or to ameliorating it more quickly.
• *Temperament:*	Includes such factors as activity level, coping, self-esteem, and attributions.
• *Family patterns:*	One caring adult serves as a protective factor.
• *External supports:*	Social networks provide four types of support: instrumental, emotional, informational, and appraisal.
• *Broader environment:*	Social structures and institutions that provide essential resources and support.
• *Turning points:*	Life trajectory affected by critical turning points.
• *Planning and turning points:*	Exercising foresight and planning in making important decisions.
• *Good fortune (God's will):*	A person being in the right place at the right time.
• *Humor:*	Laughter serves as a safety valve for coping with painful realities.
• *Helping others:*	Through helping others, people help themselves.

A final protective factor is an ability and willingness to *help and give to others*. By helping and giving to others, we heal ourselves. One finds meaning in life, meaning in one's suffering through the process of giving and sharing rather than through the pursuit of self-gratification (Frankl, 1963). Essentially, when people lend their strength to others, they strengthen themselves. Table 2.4 summarizes resilience and protective factors.

Additions to the Ecological Perspective

Two newer sets of ecological concepts emerge from deep ecology and from ecofeminism. These concepts extend and refine our understanding of the complex transactions between people and their environments.

Deep Ecology

Deep ecology enhances our understanding that all phenomena are interconnected and interdependent as well as dependent on the cyclical processes of nature (Naess, 1989; Reed & Rothenberg, 1993). Living systems are viewed as *networks* interacting with other systems of networks—"in intricate pattern of intertwined webs, networks nesting within larger networks" (Capra, 1996, p. 82). These intertwined, interdependent networks—the "web of life"—have certain common properties (Capra, 1996). These intricate patterns are nonlinear—they go in all directions and develop feedback loops, which allow them to self-regulate by learning from and correcting mistakes. Through the processes of self-regulating and self-organizing, new behaviors, patterns, and structures are spontaneously created and the networks' equilibrium constantly evolves. The interdependence of networks and the self-correcting feedback loops allow the living system to adapt to changing conditions and to survive disturbances. Thus, the *interdependence of networks*, the *self-correcting feedback loops*, and the *cyclical nature of ecological processes* are three basic principles of deep ecology.

Deep ecology also captures the creative evolution of network patterns, which unfold in increasing complexity and diversity, replacing the earlier view of evolution as a consequence of random mutations and natural selection. The emerging theory emphasizes "life's inherent tendency to create novelty, in the spontaneous emergence of increasing complexity and order" (Capra, 1996, p. 228). Because the environment changes and fluctuates all the time, living organisms must keep themselves in a flexible state and adapt to changing conditions. Thus, *flexibility* is another ecological principle—"the web of life is a flexible, ever-fluctuating network" (Capra, 1996, p. 302). However, living organisms have certain "tolerance limits" with how much change they can manage. If changing conditions go beyond with what a network can deal, the network faces the danger and threat of collapse and disintegration. *Diversity in the system* will increase its potential resilience as stronger parts can replace the weaker ones. Diversity has the potential to enrich all the relationships and the system as a whole. However, if the system is *fragmented by the differences* among the parts and characterized by prejudice and discrimination, the diversity may decrease the system's resilience and its chances for survival (Capra, 1996).

Unger (2002) adapts deep ecological principles to inform social work practice:

Each individual has intrinsic values apart from the meaning or usefulness of the individual to others in his or her community.

The diversity of culture and social organization offers the potential for unique solutions to emerge to shared human challenges.

Structured alliances between communities and the services that provide for them must act to increase the diversity of resources that are directly available to individuals and families to help them help themselves.

A service delivery system that is managed by community stakeholders, not bureaucracies, is the least likely to contribute to social disintegration.

Human service delivery systems work best when they are kept small, allowing resources to be divested to the communities being served.

Table 2.5
Principles from Deep Ecology

- Networks are intertwined and interdependent.
- Networks evolve feedback loops.
- Networks are self-regulating, learning from and correcting mistakes.
- Networks spontaneously create new adaptive behaviors.
- Networks remain in a flexible state to adapt to the cyclical nature of ecological processes.
- Networks have limits to how much change can be managed.
- Network diversity increases resilience.
- Network fragmentation increases vulnerability.

> Public policy is needed that expands the capacity of communities and their members to function on their own by providing the resources they need to sustain their well-being.
>
> What is good for individuals and their communities is the benchmark of enlightened social and economic development.
>
> Those who believe in the above points have an ethical obligation to achieve these goals by changing the methods of their practice and the structure of the organizations for which they work. (p. 488)

These deep ecology principles will be applied to practice throughout the text. Table 2.5 summarizes these principles.

Ecofeminism

Feminist scholars brought about the new consciousness of gendered roles in family, work, political, and economic life, as well as of historical and contemporary violence against women. Concepts from feminist theory have been entering the practice of many, if not most, social workers over the past twenty-five years. Feminist social work scholars called specific attention to some points of convergence in the feminist perspective and the ecological perspective and life model in social work:

> Social work's integrated thinking with its ecological view of processes between the individual and the environment is consonant with feminist thought. Both ideologies envision the desirable as transactions between people and their environments that support individual well-being, dignity, and self-determination. Both reflect a holistic consciousness not bound or limited by what feminists would argue [are] artificial androcentric polarities. (Collins, 1986, p. 216)

And:

> Feminist analysis mandates viewing reality in a holistic, integrated, and ecological fashion. The ecological perspective pertains to the interrelatedness in-

herent between persons and their environments. (Van Den Bergh & Cooper, 1986, p. 4)

We find an additional convergence between feminist thought and ecological thinking (including the values and principles of life-modeled practice) in their shared concern for the ultimate liberation of all people everywhere (including males) from oppression imposed by dehumanizing social, economic, and political institutions and structures.

Van Den Bergh and Cooper (1986) suggest that the following feminist principles are specifically relevant to social work education and practice:

1. *Eliminating false dichotomies and artificial separations.* Feminist practice shuns such dichotomies as specialist versus generalist practice and any view of direct practice as unconnected to indirect practice of research, policy, and administration.

2. *Reconceptualizing power.* Feminist social work practice seeks to facilitate client empowerment. It emphasizes assisting clients to develop the skills needed to influence their environment, such as assertiveness training, improved communication skills, managing stress and time, conflict resolution, and negotiation and bargaining skills.

3. *Valuing process.* Process is perceived to be equally important as the final product or outcome.

4. *Validating renaming.* This is an interesting and powerful idea. Van Den Bergh and Cooper (1986, p. 21) suggest, "Claiming and renaming one's heritage is an empowering process and is integral within both ethnic-sensitive and feminist practice." For example, Pinderhughes (1982) found that renaming her African American heritage through genealogical research was both liberating and therapeutic. People can choose how they name their own experiences. This concept validates and supports personal experiences and choices. Consciousness-raising groups for women and people of color, for example, lead to recognition of collective experiences and to reclaiming and renaming what it is like to be who they are. Life stories also reflect renaming processes.

5. *Believing that the personal is political* (Evans, 1997). This refers to the relationship between personal troubles and political realities. Van Den Bergh and Cooper (1986, p. 23) poignantly state, "When a client encounters resistance in the way of a desired goal and is able to differentiate whether the restraint is internal or external, then that individual is indicating an evolving political consciousness." External restraints refer to political, economic, and social systems, and internal restraints refer to one's own resistance to changing one's problematic behaviors.

Life-modeled practice reflects and respects these values.

The adage "The personal is political" reflected an effort by feminist scholars to challenge the dualistic arrangement underlying the sexual hierarchy in Western views (Mack-Canty, 2004). Hierarchical structures and oppression are always together. Ecological feminism, or ecofeminism, challenged the culture/nature dichotomy—the "twin oppression of women and nature within the dominance structure of patriarchal social conventions" (Besthorn & McMillen, 2002, p. 223). Western industrial societies assumed the destructive domination of nature as their right. This destruction reinforces the subordination of women, long identified with nature. Ecofeminists identified nonhuman nature and its exploitation for purposes of economic gain as feminist concerns. To ecofeminists, oppression of women and ecological degradation are intertwined (Carlassare, 1999). They both arise from hierarchical, male domination.

In the United States, ecofeminist thought originated from women in the peace movement who identified the interrelationship between materialism, sexism, racism, classism, and environmental destruction (Mack-Canty, 2004; Sturgeon, 1997). Committed to eliminating dualities, dividedness, polarizations, and hierarchical dichotomies, they rejected "dominance, competition, materialism, and technoscientific exploitation" (Besthorn & McMillen, 2002, p. 226). To ecofeminists, social justice cannot be achieved separately from the earth's well-being (Mack-Canty, 2004). They took up the cause against toxic waste, animal abuse, and deforestation, and for nuclear disarmament. In essence, nuclear proliferation is the "the ultimate ecological issue. And so ecology, feminism, and liberation for all of nature, including ourselves, are joined" (King, 1983, p. 127).

Ecofeminism perspectives deepen and enrich ecological theory and life-model practice. We now turn to applying these ideas in practice.

THE LIFE MODEL OF
SOCIAL WORK PRACTICE

An Overview

Origins and Defining Characteristics
of Life-Modeled Practice

The *life model* is rooted in the philosophy and traditions of the settlement house movement. To the founders of the settlements, living among the poor, and sharing their struggles and joys, was to be a good neighbor. If a neighbor "hurt," one rolled up one's sleeves and helped. One joined people in their natural life processes. Social history and the study and verification of need were abhorrent to the settlers.

The actual term *life model* of social work practice was initially inspired by the work of the late Bernard Bandler, a Boston psychiatrist who worked closely with social workers. In advancing ego-supportive practice in social work, Bandler (1963, pp. 42–43) introduced the idea of modeling practice on "life itself, its processes of growth, development, and decline, its methods of problem-solving and need-satisfaction as understood in the trajectory of the life span." Such a life-modeled practice fits the social work profession's purpose of releasing the potential for growth and satisfying social functioning of individuals, families, and groups, while increasing the responsiveness of their environments to people's needs, rights, and aspirations. Bandler challenged social workers to learn from people who cope effectively with the inevitable stressors in life and from those who nurture their children well. Instead of relying on artificial clinical processes, social workers can utilize these real-life processes in interventions that will mobilize forces of health and continued growth and also relieve environmental pressures.

Ten features, in their unique combination, characterize life-modeled practice.

1. Professional function, which includes practice with individuals, families, groups, communities, and organizational and political advocacy
2. Ethical practice
3. Diversity-sensitive and skillful practice
4. Empowering and social justice practice
5. Integrated modalities, methods, and skills
6. Client:worker relationship regarded as a partnership
7. Agreements between client(s) and worker on all aspects of the work, life stories, and assessments
8. Focus on personal and collective strengths and on client action and decision making
9. Pervasive significance of social and physical environments and culture
10. Evaluation of practice and contributions to knowledge

Professional Function

The purpose of life-modeled practice is to *improve the level of fit* between people and their environments, especially between human needs and environmental resources. In providing direct services to individuals, families, and groups, the social work purpose is to (1) eliminate or alleviate life stressors and the associated stress by helping people to mobilize and draw on personal and environmental resources for effective coping and (2) influence social and physical environmental forces to be responsive to people's needs.

Over the life course, most people confront life stressors in one or more aspects of living: difficult life transitions, traumatic life events, environmental pressures (including poverty and oppression), and dysfunctional processes in family, group, or community. *Life transitions* include developmental (biological) and social changes in status and role. *Traumatic life events*, often unexpected, include grave losses such as the death of a child, natural disasters, loss of a home, and sexual assault.

Environmental pressures can arise from the lack of resources and social provisions on the part of some social and physical environments. This might include destructive or nonsupportive social networks, organizations that arbitrarily withhold resources, and societal toleration of poverty, violence, and other major social problems. Physical settings can be serious life stressors because of deteriorated dwellings and neighborhoods that may lack amenities of any kind. *Dysfunctional communication and relationship patterns* in families, formed and natural groups, communities, and human services organizations might also create serious life stressors.

When a life stressor strikes and is not successfully managed, additional stressors can erupt in other areas of life.

The Williams family, of African American heritage, consists of the parents and two daughters, one in high school and the other in kindergarten. Mr. Williams was a valued employee of a moving company until he began to suffer from migraines and fainting spells, accompanied by progressive alcoholism. Eventually, he was suspended from his job. Nevertheless, his employer is eager for his return—but only with medical assurance that the fainting spells and alcoholism are under control. However, Mr. Williams's health care is not coordinated. He receives large doses of different medications, prescribed by several doctors, on which he is becoming increasingly dependent. Debilitating migraines and fainting spells immobilize him. When Mr. Williams lost his job, he also lost the status and self-esteem he had gained as a successful professional mover. This undermined his sense of competence, intensified his depression, and worsened his drinking problem. He also needs help in considering hospital detoxification programs. Mrs. Williams works part-time in a fast-food restaurant and has become the dominant force in the family as her husband's condition deteriorated. Life stressors appear in the following areas:

The family faces eviction because Mr. Williams's troubles resulted in nonpayment of rent and complaints about his noisy behavior.

Mr. Williams now occupies a community niche of "helpless alcoholic." He enacts the role of victim, sleeping late and withdrawing from family life. Reciprocally, Mrs. Williams encourages him to stay away from home, treats him as if he were a naughty child, scolding him and withholding money. Their conflict becomes increasingly severe and is marked by physical violence, emotional explosions, and absence of sexual intimacy.

Mr. Williams is withdrawing from his children, and the children are beginning to withdraw from both parents. The older daughter is beginning to have difficulties in school.

These stressors are interrelated, but each takes on its own life. Together, they can overwhelm the individual, group, family, or community. This family is in need of immediate help to prevent its disorganization. Life-modeled practice would intervene at individual, family, and environmental levels. Family members would be asked to set priorities among the stressors to be worked on immediately, and the social worker would seek out personal, family, and environmental strengths. The professional function is represented in Figure 3.1.

In mediating the exchanges between people and their environments, social workers daily encounter the lack of fit between people's needs and the environment. Thus, the purpose of life-modeled practice also includes

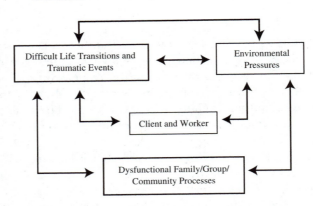

Figure 3.1   Professional Function and Life Stressors

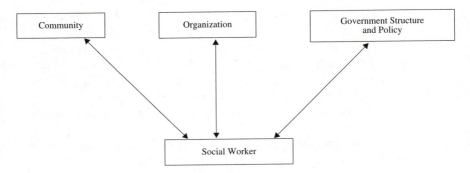

Figure 3.2   The Life Model Social Change Conception of Professional Function

professional responsibility for bearing witness against social inequities and injustice. This is done by *mobilizing community resources* to influence quality of life in the community, by *influencing unresponsive organizations* to develop responsive policies and services, and by *politically influencing local, state, and federal legislation and regulations* to support social justice (Figure 3.2).

Ethical Practice

Social work values are a set of beliefs that define what the profession considers to be desirable and good. Most social workers, for example, hold the basic values of the dignity and worth of each person; respect for diversity; a commitment to social justice, equality, and nondiscrimination; and the importance of human relationships. These broad values, and other more specific ones such as self-determination, confidentiality, and informed consent, constitute the core value base of all social work practice (Reamer, 1995a, 2006).

Ethical practice is firmly rooted in professional values, the National Association of Social Workers (NASW) *Code of Ethics* (1999), and laws and legal rulings. The *Code of Ethics* provides a codified statement of everyday obligations and guidelines for professional behavior. The *Code of Ethics* consists of prescriptive ethical principles (i.e., what a social worker must do) and proscriptive ethical principles (i.e., what a social worker must not do). The *Code of Ethics* also serves as a guide for adjudication when the conduct of social workers is alleged to deviate from the profession's standards (Strom-Gottfried, 2003).[1]

While the *Code of Ethics* is a helpful guide, the contemporary social worker often confronts contradictory and competing professional obligations that create ethical conflicts and dilemmas such as truthfulness in client–worker relationships (e.g., should the worker respond truthfully to a dying patient who seeks a frank answer to the question "Am I going to die?" when the family refuses to have such information shared with the patient?); the worker's obligations to the employing institution versus obligations to the client (e.g., obeying a formal rule or informal policy that seems unjust versus acting in the client's best interests); ethical issues arising from confidentiality and privileged communication, not only in court situations but also in family practice and team practice; informed consent (when ending services against a client's wishes because the client is not cooperating or is not benefiting from the service); and self-determination (imposing services that were mandated by a court or imposed on a person who refuses help while living on the streets without shelter and food and needed medical care) (Bergeron & Gray, 2003; Dean & Rhodes, 1992; Millstein, 2000; Mishna, Antle, & Regehr, 2002; Reamer, 1990; Regehr & Antle, 1997).

Ethical conflicts permeate social work in all fields of practice from child welfare to residential care, schools, and health and mental health settings. For example, much is known about the effects on fetal well-being of such maternal behaviors as smoking, alcoholism, drug abuse, and inattention to treatment of diabetes. Many social workers are engaged in working with pregnant women. When fetal and maternal health conflict, the health of the mother is usually the first priority. But what should be done where maternal behavior is endangering fetal health? Does the fetus, when the mother intends to carry it to term, have the right to be born healthy? In situations where the mother fails to discontinue dangerous behavior, what is to be done? Two courses of action are available: pursuing civil commitment to restrain the mother, or seeking custody of the fetus (and hence of the mother) under child protection laws. What should the social worker's ethical stance be toward conflicting and competing claims, rights, and responsibilities in this situation?

Ethical issues proliferate with managed care and the application of computer technology (Davidson & Davidson, 1996; Gelman, Pollack, & Weiner, 1999; Reamer, 1997; Rock & Congress, 1999). Organizations, professionals, and technology increasingly mandate interventions (Walden, Wolock, & Demone, 1990). Managed care policies and practices undermine self-determination and competence motivation, and ethical principles of autonomy and self-determination. While at times such paternalistic interventions might be necessary for the person's well-being, too often they are used to exercise social control on behalf of the social order or to support an organization and its practices (Abramson, 1985, 1989).

Ethical issues also arise in social welfare policy. For example, should an agency open a group home for offenders or mentally disturbed people in the face of neighborhood protests? Conflicts between the service ethic and the profit motive will confront social workers as a growing number of proprietary organizations enter the human services field. Ethical issues in research can arise in truth telling, methods, analysis, and inferences (Gray, Lyons, & Melton, 1995). Ethical issues in social action and advocacy are connected to truth telling and informed consent, and client vulnerability and risk. Ethical concerns in collegial relations include the extent of a practitioner's responsibility for reporting colleague incompetence or wrongdoing to supervisors or other authorities (i.e., whistle blowing) (Reamer, 2006).

Practice concepts, principles, and methods are not sufficient to resolve ethical issues and value conflicts when they do appear. Social work scholars have created guidelines for ethical decision making (Dolgoff & Skolnik, 1996; Healy, 2003; Linzer, 1999; Loewenberg, Dolgoff, & Harrington, 2000; Mattison, 2003; Reamer, 1990, 2006). Such guidelines can help social workers identify the ethical dimensions of a practice situation and understand particular ethical positions. When confronting an ethical dilemma, Loewenberg, Dolgoff, and Harrington (2000) suggest that the first step is to examine the NASW *Code of Ethics* (1999) to determine if any of its rules apply. However, since most ethical dilemmas confronted by workers are not directly dealt with by the *Code of Ethics*, Loewenberg, Dolgoff, and Harrington developed an "Ethical Principles Screen" (see Table 3.1) to help social workers deal with ethical conflicts.

Their ethical principles are presented in the order of priority. In making ethical decisions, satisfying the higher-order principle takes precedence over satisfying a lower-order principle.

1. *Protection of life*. Protecting a client's life and the lives of others takes precedence over any other professional obligation. A severely diabetic

Table 3.1
Loewenberg and Dolgoff Ethical Principles Screen

- The protection of life
- Equality and inequality
- Autonomy and freedom
- Least harm
- Quality of life
- Privacy and confidentiality
- Truthfulness and full disclosure

adolescent, for example, refuses life-saving insulin injections and diet restrictions because they interfere with her quality of life. Using the ethical principle screen, the worker is justified in compromising the girl's privacy because protecting her life is of primary importance. In such situations, the client must be told what is being done and why.

2. *Equality and inequality.* People have the right to be treated equally, but people with less power and greater vulnerability have the right to be treated differently. In the case of an abused child, the child is not in an equal position relative to the abuser. The worker's obligation to protect the child is of a higher order than the rights to privacy and confidentiality of the child and the abusing adult.

3. *Autonomy and freedom.* The profession has an unyielding commitment to support and foster a client's autonomy and freedom. In order to be autonomous, people must be able to act in accordance with their own decisions. Others (especially the social worker) have to respect and support the person's right to do so. However, this principle is superseded when people plan to harm themselves or others.

4. *Least harm.* The worker is required to choose the option that results in the least immediate or permanent harm, or the most easily reversible harm. For example, before a social worker suggests that a client withhold rent payment to protest dilapidated housing conditions, less risky alternatives should be attempted.

5. *Quality of life.* The social worker should not ignore a client's poor quality of life, but client and practitioner should work together to improve it to a reasonable degree.

6. *Privacy and confidentiality.* Social workers must make ethical decisions that fortify every person's right to privacy. Confidential information has to be kept confidential (to the extent that is possible by law).

7. *Truthfulness and full disclosure.* This demands that social workers speak the truth and fully disclose all significant information to those served.

The authors present a vignette of a twelve-year-old sixth grader who is ten weeks pregnant. The school nurse referred her to the social worker. The youngster said she does not want an abortion and does not want her parents to know that she is pregnant. The worker confronts an ethical dilemma: to respect the child's wishes for confidentiality or to respect the parents' right to protect their daughter from potential health risks. In reviewing the *Code of Ethics* (NASW, 1999; the authors' suggested first step), no discussion is directly applicable to this situation. In the ethical principle screen, principle 6 (above) states that a social worker should not violate a person's right to privacy and confidentiality without permission. Ethical principle 3 emphasizes respect for an individual's right to be self-ruling. These principles support honoring the youngster's decision about pregnancy and her right to confidentiality. However, since pregnancy poses an immediate danger to a twelve-year-old, the worker is justified in violating the principle of confidentiality and notifying her parents. Ethical principle 1 requires the protection of life and survival. The social worker must tell the youngster first that her parents have to be notified, affording her time to tell them herself or in the company of the social worker.

We must consider our own values and ethics in relation to those whom we serve: our clients, the profession, the agency, and society. The literature on professional ethics has focused primarily on decision making, rather than on the values and ethics of the decision maker. Social workers must develop self-awareness about their personal ethical and value standards (Rhodes, 1992). Abramson (1996, p. 199) offers a framework for ethical self-awareness, using the example of an advance directive about personal care at the end of life. In examining potential prejudgments, social workers should ask themselves how their culture, religion, and life experiences affect perspectives on "do-not-resuscitate" orders and artificial nutrition and hydration. Where does one fall on the continuum between planning for the end of one's life and leaving it up to fate and/or God? How intensely does one feel about this issue, and how might one's perspective potentially affect professional practice? With whatever the client is dealing, the social worker must consider her or his personal ethical and value stance, making sure not to impose it on the client.

Joseph (1985) provides this example: a social worker is counseling a sixteen-year-old girl on a regular basis about her interpersonal relationships. The adolescent discloses that she has been shoplifting, and she insists that the information be kept in strict confidence. The initial contract included confidentiality of all content except suicidal or homicidal threats. Another worker in the agency was seeing the adolescents' parents. Must the worker maintain confidentiality, or is she obliged to reveal the information to the parents and to her colleagues? The worker's ethical decision making must not be influenced by personal ethical standards regarding stealing. First, the worker reviews the *Code of Ethics*, which states that sharing information without the client's consent cannot be done except for "compelling professional reasons." Are the reasons in this case compelling? The *Code* also obliges the worker to fully inform those served about the limits of confidentiality. Is the promise implicit in the contract? This dilemma poses one good, the teenager's right to confidentiality, versus another good, the right of the family to this information. After reviewing the data, reflecting on personal values, and analyzing the dilemma and alternative actions, one might argue that "the parents, on the basis of their authority, have a right to the information . . . based on the claim that the well-being of the adolescent takes precedence over her right to confidentiality. On the other hand, one might argue more forcefully in favor of the client's right to confidentiality on the basis of the fiduciary relationship and the contract, a further moral force" (NASW, 1999, p. 214). Since shoplifting does not represent a threat to life, the youngster's confidentiality must be protected. The worker has to monitor her own feelings to make sure that personal ethics and values are not determining factors.

This example demonstrates the potential interaction of personal standards, practice knowledge, and skill with ethical concerns. For instance, failure to be precise in the original contract regarding confidentiality may lead to the dilemma. Also, practice skill might encourage the young woman to discuss the shoplifting with her parents. Joseph (1985) contrasts this to the action of a less skilled worker who might, on the basis of the parents' authority or because of personal values, have given the information to the parents.

Maintaining or violating confidentiality is a common ethical dilemma (Berman-Rossi & Rossi, 1990; Gewirth, 2001; Jonson-Reid, 2000; Kopels & Kagle, 1994; Raines, 2004; Ward, 2002). Abramson (1989) found that it is a major issue for social workers serving people with AIDS or who are HIV-positive. When their clients refuse to inform sexual partners of their infection, workers confront a difficult ethical issue. In these situations, workers have to examine legal statutes as well as ethical guidelines (Reamer, 2005). For example, does the ethical principle screen justify a violation of confidentiality? Or does the ruling in *Tarasoff v. the Regents of the University of California* (1976; cited further in this chapter) require the worker to warn the third party? Or does a state law prohibit the social worker from notifying the third party, and solely entrust that responsibility to the physician?

Boundary violations are an extremely serious form of professional ethical misconduct (Reamer, 2003). Social workers' sexual misconduct with clients is a blatant example of a boundary violation. Sexual misconduct represented the largest number of complaints filed with the NASW over an eleven-year period (Strom-Gottfried, 2003). During the last twenty-three years, 41 percent of the NASW's insurance company payments were the result of claims of sexual misconduct (Reamer, 1995b). The NASW *Code of Ethics* (1999) explicitly prohibits social workers from having sexual contact with clients:

1.09 (a) Social workers should under no circumstances engage in sexual activities or sexual contact with current clients, whether such contact is consensual or forced.

(b) Social workers should not engage in sexual activities or sexual contact with clients' relatives or other individuals with whom clients maintain a close personal relationship when there is a risk of exploitation or potential harm to the client. Sexual activity or sexual contact with clients' relatives or other individuals with whom clients maintain a personal relationship has the potential to be harmful to the client and may make it difficult for the social worker and client to maintain appropriate professional boundaries. Social workers—not their clients, their clients' relatives, or other individuals with whom the client maintains a personal relationship—assume the full burden for setting clear, appropriate, and culturally sensitive boundaries.

(c) Social workers should not engage in sexual activities or sexual contact with former clients because of the potential for harm to the client. If social workers engage in conduct contrary to this prohibition or claim that an exception to this prohibition is warranted because of extraordinary circumstances, it is social workers—not their clients—who assume the full burden of demonstrating that the former client has not been exploited, coerced, or manipulated, intentionally or unintentionally.

(d) Social workers should not provide clinical services to individuals with whom they have had a prior sexual relationship. Providing clinical services to a former sexual partner has the potential to be harmful to the individual and is likely to make it difficult for the social worker and individual to maintain appropriate professional boundaries.

Some states have passed laws imposing criminal penalties for such transgressions.

Generally, practitioners have to be cautious about engaging in dual or multiple relationships with clients, supervisors have to be cautious with workers, and classroom and field instructors must be cautious with students (e.g., business and professional). Yet, many dual-relationship situations remain unidentified. The basic principle is that there should be no potential conflicts of interest or appearance of potential conflicts of interest in dual or multiple relationships. Thus, for example, a person should not serve in the dual roles of agency board member and paid consultant to the agency. These dual roles have the potential to conflict with each other, or at least to have the appearance of impropriety. An instructor, for another example, should not hire a student to babysit or to mow the lawn. This seems like a relatively benign arrangement; however, what if the instructor is not satisfied with the student's performance or the student is unhappy with the course grade? How will the other students experience this arrangement? Similar problems emerge from bartering professional services for client goods and services. For example, to exchange clinical services for house painting or homemade jams complicates the professional relationship.

Some *boundary-crossing* dual relationships may be subtler and less clear (Reamer, 2003). While dual relationships that cross boundaries have the potential to create tensions and should be avoided, in certain agency contexts and situations they may be helpful. For example, the author has attended clients' graduations, exchanged symbolic termination gifts, and attended funerals. In home visits to Latina clients, for another example, the author consistently accepted an offered cup of coffee or a bite to eat—to reject these gracious offers would be perceived as a slight. These crossings were helpful to clients rather than causing them harm. Thus, judicious boundary crossings that are in the clients' interests should not be ruled out. However, any dual relationship that is exploitative, manipulative, or coercive in nature represents a serious ethical breach.

Professional ethics must be considered within a legal framework. Laws sanction organizations and professionals to serve the public. Laws also provide users of services certain protections such as privileged communication. Laws assure minimum professional standards through licensing, and they mandate certain professional behaviors such as reporting suspected child abuse. Kutchins (1991) suggested that the relationship between client and worker is a fiduciary relationship (a relationship of trust) and offers the client legal protection, including informed consent, confidentiality, and privileged communication (with important limitations).

Informed consent protects clients' rights to self-determination and privacy. Reamer (2006) identifies six standards that must be met to fulfill the requirements of valid informed consent:

1. Absence of worker coercion.
2. Capability of client to provide informed consent.
3. Consent is specific.
4. Consent forms are clear and understandable.
5. Clients must feel they have the right to refuse or withdraw consent.
6. Client decisions must be based on sufficient information.

While these standards reflect a consensus on what constitutes informed consent, exceptions exist. State statutes, for example, differ on the legal rights of parents to make decisions for their children, and how much autonomy their children are granted to make decisions for themselves. In some states, an adolescent is allowed to provide her own consent for contraception or an abortion, or to enter substance abuse treatment. In other states, however, parents have to be notified, and only they may give consent. The employing organization and the worker, therefore, must know how to acquire informed consent and the limitations of and exceptions to consent. The process includes furnishing information to clients over time and engaging them in a dialogue about assessment and interventions. Informed consent is much more than simply securing a signature.

While a client's right to confidentiality is an ethical principle rather than a legal one, its violation by a social worker can result in a lawsuit. In *Mac-Donald v. Clinger* (1982), for example, a psychotherapist divulged personal information to a patient's wife. A court ruled this was a breach of confidentiality and allowed the patient to sue for damages (Kutchins, 1991).

Privileged communication is a legal exemption that limits the government's right to force a social worker to break confidentiality. By and large, state law determines whether a social worker is protected from disclosing confidential material. If a client is abusing a child, for example, a worker's actions are legally mandated: all fifty states have mandatory reporting statutes, and many specify the reporting as an exception to client privilege. A social worker might also be expected to breach confidentiality if the client represents a danger to others (Kopels & Kagle, 1993). In one case, a client told his psychologist, who was employed by a university hospital, that he planned to kill his former girlfriend when she returned from her summer vacation. The psychologist informed the campus police, seeking their help in having the client committed to a psychiatric hospital for observation. The police judged the client to be rational and released him after he assured them that he would not harm his former girlfriend. Subsequently, he murdered her. In *Tarasoff v. the Regents of the University of California* (1976), the girl's parents sued the psychologist, the campus police, and the university for their failure to warn their daughter and them (Givelber, Bowers, & Blitch, 1984). On appeal, the California Superior Court ruled that the psychologist had a legal obligation to warn the victim and failed to exercise reasonable care. Since state statutes differ, employing organizations and social workers must be familiar with their respective state laws.

In *Jaffee v. Redmond* (1996), the U.S. Supreme Court had to decide whether the conversations between social workers and their clients were privileged and protected from civil complaint in federal court (Lens, 2000). Jaffee administered the estate of a person who was killed by a policewoman, Redmond. Jaffee filed suit in federal court that Redmond had used excessive force. Jaffee had learned that Redmond went into counseling with a social worker after the event and sought the notes from fifty counseling sessions. Redmond and the social worker assumed the position that the notes were covered by privileged information. A lower court ruled in favor of Jaffee. In accepting the case on appeal, the Supreme Court embarked to determine (1) whether the communication between a psychotherapist and a client should be privileged and (2) if the communication is privileged, should social workers be covered by it? In relation to the first question, the Supreme Court ruled that privileged communication was essential to protecting the mental health of the community and "outweighed the evidentiary needs of the court" (Lens, 2000, p. 274). In relation to the second question, the Supreme Court decided that social workers are in fact covered by the protection of privileged communication. The Supreme Court ruling represents a major victory for the social work profession. In civil proceedings, clients can be assured that confidentiality "stands on the same ground as the confidentiality between a lawyer and her client and a husband and wife" (Lens, 2000, p. 275).

Reamer (2005, pp. 164–165) identifies five areas of law with which social workers must be familiar: constitutional law (e.g., students' privacy and free speech, and women's right to terminate a pregnancy), statutory law enacted by U.S. Congress and individual states (e.g., mandatory reporting), regulatory law promulgated and enforced by government agencies (e.g., eviction from public housing, and protection of information), court-made law and common law (e.g., *Jaffee v Redmond* [1996]), and executive orders (e.g., freezing hiring). In certain circumstances, legal standards may conflict with professional ethics. While social workers are expected to abide by laws and legal precedents, occasionally they may conflict with professional ethical standards and client interests. At these times, the social worker may decide by commission or omission to ignore the law. For example, the social worker learns that the client, after a long period of abstaining from smoking marijuana, celebrated her birthday with a smoke. The client has been making great strides, and the social worker decides not to notify protective services. She determines that the ensuing investigation would create a crisis, undo the gains, and jeopardize the professional relationship. Ignoring or bypassing laws should be done on rare occasions and, when done, the social worker must make sure to be self-protective. In the example above, it would be in neither the client's nor the social worker's interest to record the birthday "celebration."

Diversity-Sensitive and Skillful Practice

Social workers must consistently accept and respect each client's (1) race, ethnicity, religion, and spirituality; (2) gender; (3) sexual orientation; (4) age; and (5) particular mental and physical challenges. Such sensitivity requires specialized knowledge about a particular population or person being served by the practitioner and a high level of self-awareness. The combination of specialized knowledge and self-awareness helps to assure a practice that is sensitive to diversity (objective) and difference (subjective) as well as sameness, and is responsive to the needs and aspirations of vulnerable and oppressed populations and to the consequences of discrimination. Sensitivity to diversity also requires respect and understanding of people whose characteristics and values may differ from those of the group around them or of the worker. At times, working with people whose backgrounds are similar to ours creates its own special challenges.

Sensitivity to Race, Ethnicity, Religion, and Spirituality. Social workers must familiarize themselves with the characteristics of the diverse racial, cultural, and religious groups whom they serve or are likely to serve (Abbott, Berry, & Meredith, 1990; Bullis, 1996; Congress, 1994; Congress & Lyons, 1992; Denby & Alford, 1996; Dore & Dumois, 1990; Drachman, Kwon-Ahn, & Paulino, 1996; Hodge, 2004, 2005; Hurd, Moore, & Rogers, 1995; Lum, 2004; Malgady & Zayas, 2001; Roer-Strier & Rosenthal, 2001; Rosenbloom, 1995; Schiele, 1996; Swigonski, 1996; Wade, 1994). Formal social work education provides general information about people of color, and perhaps more specific information within the region served by an educational program. Nevertheless, all social workers must continually update their knowledge about the history and culture of the racial, ethnic, and religious groups whom they serve. In relation to recent immigrants, for example, the practitioner needs knowledge about

- civil war, revolution, traumatic expulsions, mass murders, and atrocities;
- regional and class differences within the group;
- characteristics of family structure, gendered role expectations, the status of women, and generational relationships;

- values, attitudes, and beliefs, and the significance of religion;
- health and illness patterns, the meaning attributed to physical and mental symptoms, and natural helping traditions;
- worldview and the social construction of reality;
- the group's acculturation experience in North America; and
- the ways in which a particular individual or family differs from cultural patterns usually found in the group.

In addition to continual updating of knowledge about the history and culture of the racial, ethnic, and religious groups whom we serve, social workers must also continually develop greater racial, ethnic, and religious self-awareness. The process begins with a curiosity about one's own world-view (i.e., philosophy of life) and about differing worldviews. In the United States, the Western European– or American-centered worldview dominates. Sue and associates (1998) characterize this worldview as follows:

> Rugged individualism, competition, mastery and control over nature, a unitary and static conception of time, a religion based on Christianity, separation of science and religion, and competition are [a] few of the values and beliefs indicative of this orientation. (p. 19)

The Industrial Revolution replaced commitment to a primary group and its traditions, rituals, and values by requiring and rewarding individualism, independence, and autonomy. Sue and associates (1998) cogently capture other attributes of this worldview:

> Competition (winning is everything, win/lose dichotomy); Action orientation (must master and control nature; pragmatic/utilitarian view of life); Communication (written tradition, direct eye contact, limited physical contact, control emotions); Time (adherence to rigid time, time is viewed as a commodity); Future orientation (plan for future, delayed gratification); Emphasis on scientific method (objective, rational, linear thinking, cause and effect relationships); Status and power (measured by economic possessions, credential[s], titles and positions, owning goods, space, property). (p. 20)

These basic life beliefs and values have a profound impact on the delivery of social services as well as on the actual processes of supervising, helping, and influencing. When we assume that everyone subscribes to dominant traditions, beliefs, and values, difficulties arise in practice as well as in supervision.

In contrast, an Afrocentric (or Africentric) worldview emerges from three crucial African traditions, beliefs, and values: collective identity, spirituality, and affective knowledge and expression. In this worldview, individual identity is rooted in the traditions, rituals, and values of the primary group and community, and its collective survival efforts. Schiele

(1996, p. 286) captures the essence of this belief through an African adage used by Mbiti (1970, p. 141): "I am because we are, and because we are, therefore, I am." The individual can only be understood within the context of her or his social group and cannot be separated from the collective. Spirituality, the second important belief and value, receives equal prominence to Western emphases on body and mind. According to Schiele (1996, p. 287), "soul, mind, and body are considered interdependent and interrelated phenomena." Finally, an Afrocentric worldview values affective knowledge and expression. The expression of emotions is essential to all aspects of life: to the development of scientific inquiry, knowledge, communication, community, and oneself. Thinking and reasoning are deeply influenced by the experiencing of emotions. Similarly, thought processes affect emotions. Neither thoughts nor feelings act alone—they are interdependent. In all, the Afrocentric perspective, in contrast to the Western European– or American-centered worldview, encourages a holistic view of individual and collective identity, soul and body and mind and rationality and emotionality (Swigonski, 1996). The perspective makes sense of the world by joining rather than separating into dualities and opposites.

The Latin and Asian cultures' worldviews, similar to the Afrocentric perspective, emphasize primary family and community identity over individual identity. Maintaining group identification and cooperation is valued more than individual achievements and competition. Life circumstances are perceived to be a matter of faith, chance, and luck and, by and large, out of a person's control. The status quo is accepted and respected. In contrast, the Western European– or American-centered worldview "places high value on personal output of energy for solving all problems; pragmatic ingenuity, individualism that is self-reliant and status achieved through one's own efforts; power or ability to influence and control others, things and forces of nature" (Ryan & Hendricks, 1989, p. 31). Moreover, in contrast to the Western European– or American-centered egalitarian worldview, Latin and Asian cultures tend to have a hierarchical orientation. People in authority are granted expert status and are accorded respect. The hierarchical orientation also ties people to their elders and ancestors. In Asian cultures, death is more likely to be honored than birth. In contrast to the Asian ties to the past, the Western European– or American-centered worldview values preparing for the future (e.g., "saving for a rainy day"), and the Afrocentric view emphasizes living in the present (e.g., "One has to live for today because tomorrow is not promised"). While Latin cultures share Asians' strong ties to the past, the value of "personalism" encourages warmth and spontaneity in the present (Becket & Dungee-Anderson, 1996, pp. 33–34).

In developing racial, ethnic, and religious self-awareness, all social workers should examine where they fall on the continuum between monocultural and multicultural worldviews. Models are available to help the social worker assess her or his racial and cultural development in relation to "one's feelings, thoughts and behaviors concerning oneself, others within one's racial group and others not belonging to one's racial group" (Chang, Hays, & Shoffner, 2003, p. 124.) In the first phase, "contact," one is only aware of the dominant culture. The second phase, "disintegration," emerges from contact with other nondominant cultures as one begins to be exposed to different cultural values, beliefs, and cognitive and communication styles. Initial reactions may denigrate and reject the different worldviews and idealize the dominant culture (the "reintegration" stage). From further exposure to nondominant cultures, one may develop increased awareness of differences while continuing acceptance and preference of the dominant culture (the "pseudo-independence" phase). Over a period of time, through continued exposure to nondominant cultures and through self-appraisal, one develops a nonjudgmental and nonaggressive cultural identity (the "immersion/emersion" phase). In the final phase, "autonomy," one learns to value and appreciate diversity rather than be threatened by it, and develops a multicultural perspective (Stone, 1997, p. 276).

In dealing with oppression and racism in their personal and professional lives, social workers of color must sort out how they feel about themselves, others in their cultural group, other minority cultural groups, and the dominant white society. A Minority Development Model proposes five phases of cultural identity development (Atkinson, Morton, & Sue, 1998). In the first phase of cultural identity, "conformity," the person of color has internalized and shows preference for the dominant white, western European– or American-centered worldview and undervalues or devalues her or his own culture. The second phase, "dissonance," is often characterized by feelings of confusion and ambivalence. The person "experiences a breakdown of his or her previously held denial system" and develops a beginning identification with her or his own cultural group (Sue et al., 1998, p. 75). During this period, the person often has to manage feelings of guilt, shame, and embarrassment.

In the next phase, "resistance and immersion," the person begins to idealize and endorse her or his own cultural group and to actively reject the Western European– or American-centered worldview (Stone, 1997, p. 275). In the fourth phase, "internalization," the person continues to develop a cultural identity and a strong commitment to her or his cultural group. In the fifth and final phase, "synergetic articulation and awareness," the person develops an integrated awareness of oneself, one's cultural group, and other minority groups as well as of the dominant culture. In this phase, one feels at peace with oneself and confident in one's ability to work and live with members of one's cultural group and other cultural groups.

In many urban agency settings, a white social worker and clients of color is the most pervasive service pattern. The structural positions represent a microcosm of the power relationships in the larger society. White social workers must be sensitive to the power and privilege associated with their organizational and professional statuses. These daily privileges include:

not being questioned or viewed suspiciously every day because of one's race; not seeing one's values and history validated and reinforced in the media and popular culture; not having to be the representative of the entire White race in groups and discussions about racial issues; and not having to worry about being targeted by police, employers, or some else due to race. (Fong & Lease, 1997, p. 391)

White social workers must be vigilant to detect racist stereotypes and attitudes. Stereotypes about poor clients of color may lead to assessments that emphasize pathology and vulnerability rather than strengths and resilience. White social workers also must listen for cues from clients of color that their "whiteness" represents a tension or obstacle in the work. Feigning "color blindness" is an unhelpful response when clients suggest subtly or not so subtly that color is in fact an issue. Racial, ethnic, and religious sensitive practice requires a skillful invitation to openly discuss how difference in background is affecting the work (Gitterman & Nadelman, 1999; Gitterman & Schaeffer, 1972). The white social worker must also be cautious about attributing all strains in the helping process to racial, ethnic, and religious differences.

Social workers of color working with white clients also represent a complex structural arrangement, a reversal of the power relationships in the larger society. The "newness" of the experience for some white clients should be legitimized and discussed. When a white client's facial expression registers a surprised look upon meeting a worker of color for the first time, a benign response, "Not whom you expected," with a follow-up reach, "I gather you are surprised that you have been assigned to a black (Latina, Asian) social worker," may create the tone for a conversation about the dynamics of race and ethnicity in the helping encounter.[2] While being sensitive and supportive, the social worker of color has to be cautious to remain in the professional role and not respond defensively or aggressively.

The dynamic may also be quite complex when social workers of color attempt to help clients of color. Based on common experiences of racism and oppression, the social worker of color may feel caught between the policies and practices of the employing organization and the needs of the clients. In contrast, based on internalized racism, the social worker of color may unwittingly be hypercritical of a self-destructive client. All social workers have to be careful about not treating a client "as a member of a race rather than as an individual who has a race" (Coleman, 1991, p. 149).

Similar principles apply to ethnic and religious differences and similarities. Reactions to race, ethnicity, and religion are omnipresent in social work micro and macro practice. These reactions are likely to provide some static in the helping and influencing encounters, and, if not addressed, they have the potential to fester into significant practice obstacles.

Social class cuts across race, ethnicity, religion, gender, and sexual orientation. Sameness in race or ethnicity coupled with differences in social class may strongly affect the helping process. The social worker of color will have to examine his or her potential reactions to the behaviors of a low-income client of color, particularly if the behaviors reinforce dominant cultural and racial stereotypes about dress, language, and sexuality. Similarly, the middle-class, Jewish social worker will have to examine her or his potential reactions to the homeless, alcoholic Jewish client. Social workers have to self-assess their social class biases and stereotypes.

Sensitivity to Gender.   The perspective on racially, culturally, religiously, and spiritually knowledgeable, sensitive, and skillful practice is applicable to gender-sensitive practice. The feminist movement has explored the pervasiveness of institutional sexism in education, work, health care, and family and community life (Lancaster & Lumb, 1999; Orme, 2002; Sands, 1996: Saulnier, 2000; Taylor, 1998; Van Den Bergh & Cooper, 1986). Gender-sensitive practice requires enlightened avoidance of compliance with male and female socialization of male dominance. Social workers must examine their own gender identity, and take stock of potential biases. Self-reflection is an essential prerequisite to helping clients as well as influencing communities and organizations with gender issues. Social workers must reflect on their formal and informal conversations with support staff, colleagues, supervisors, interdisciplinary team members, clients, and community residents; participation in agency and community meetings; and professional correspondence and recording. Based on these reflections, social workers examine their "conventional assumptions about gender related issues" (Ford & Jones, 1987, p. 11).

Gender self-reflection is an essential prerequisite to the development of sensitivity to the oppression of female clients by a male-dominated society and how their lives have been affected by discrimination and exploitation within their families, their communities, and the larger society. All social workers must examine their gender-based beliefs and behaviors. Self-recognition will lead to greater sensitivity and understanding of female clients and group members whose internalized oppression results in behaviors such as self-mutilation, depression, substance abuse, and high-risk sexual activity, or who have externalized oppression and turned anger and violence against family and community members.

In modeling gender-sensitive and skillful practice, the male social work practitioner helping a female client or the male social work supervisor supervising a female social worker must be sensitive to the symbolic societal representation of a man asserting his dominance over a woman. The male social work practitioner or supervisor must be attuned to potential style differences in communication, problem solving, conflict resolution, and orientations to authority and intimacy. Gilligan (1982, in Granello, 1996), for example, identified that females use conversations to build social networks, while men use conversations to build hierarchies. A meta-analysis of research studies suggests a marked difference in male and female leadership styles. Men tend to be more comfortable with a direct, autocratic, and dominant style, whereas women tend to adopt a more democratic and participative style (Granello, 1996).

The female social work practitioner helping a male client or the female social work supervisor supervising a male social worker also must be attuned to possible differences in communication, problem solving, conflict resolution, and orientations to authority and intimacy. Since the overwhelming majority of current social work graduates are female, one can deduce that females will supervise most male workers. The female social work supervisor supervising a male student or helping a male client must be sensitive to the reversal of the gender power dynamics and how both parties react to it. The female social worker will have to pay special heed to how she handles the authority invested in her role, being careful not to yield that authority to an assertive or aggressive male worker or client or to overcompensate by becoming autocratic.

Similarly, in the female–female and male–male combinations, the social work practitioner and supervisor must be cautious about being overly or insufficiently demanding or overly or insufficiently supportive because of the gender sameness. "Sameness" creates its own dynamics and potential complications.

Sensitivity to Sexual Orientation. The perspective on racial-, cultural-, religious-, spiritual-, and gender-knowledgeable, sensitive, and skillful practice is also applicable within the context of the sexual orientation of organizational representatives, social workers, and clients. Sensitivity to sexual orientation requires the understanding that with race, ethnicity, religion, and gender, families often provide a supportive context for identity formation and for teaching how to deal with prejudice and discrimination. In contrast, heterosexual parents and relatives who expect their children to be heterosexual and who may daily convey negative judgments about alternative sexual orientations often raise gay and lesbian children. While the process of coming out often creates a family crisis, parents, siblings, and other relatives remain important to gay and lesbian people. While some families may not accept homosexuality, a family truce often evolves (Laird, 1998).

By and large, homosexual, bisexual, transgender, and heterosexual men and women live in somewhat overlapping and separate subcultures. In the United States, the nonconformity of lesbians and gay men to traditional societal roles is often used to stigmatize, pathologize, and ostracize them (Caron & Ulin, 1997; Green, 1996). For example, the U.S. government military policy of "Don't ask, don't tell" allows homosexual soldiers to enlist or be drafted as long as they hide their sexual orientation. In social work schools and in field agencies, we must be aware of a subtler version of this military policy: "Don't ask, don't tell, don't teach about it, don't write about it" (Green, 1996, p. 389). Ignoring sexual orientation in organizational and clinical practice introduces "a covert system of understanding about what can and can not be discussed" (Russell & Greenhouse, 1997, p. 29).

Current practice requires knowledge of the effects of oppression and multi-oppression on gays, lesbians, bisexuals, and transgender individuals; the strengths and resources within gay, lesbian, bisexual, and transgender communities; the process of coming out and its personal costs and joys; gay and lesbian family life; alternative lifestyles; and gay and lesbian rights (Berger, 2001; D'Augelli, Grossman, Hershberger, & O'Connell, 2001; D'Augelli, Hershberger, & Pilkington, 1998; Fukuyama & Ferguson, 2000; Hartman & Laird, 1998; Horowitz, 2000; Laird, 1996; Morrow, 1993; Patterson, 2000; Ryan, 2000 ; Schloemer, 2000; Smith, 1997; Strommen, 1993; Tully, 2000; Van Voorhis & McClain, 1997).

To develop self-awareness, the social worker begins by exploring his or her potential homophobia and heterosexual bias (Berkman & Zinberg, 1997; Newman, Dannenfelser, & Benishek, 2002). In their formative years, most social workers have been exposed to a strong heterosexual bias and have incorporated some homophobic reactions (discomfort, fear, and/or hatred of homosexual people). Without self-awareness and knowledge about homosexuality, they will experience difficulty in providing sensitive and skillful services to gay and lesbian clients. Even of greater concern, the social worker may unknowingly reject the lesbian or gay client and communicate that issues related to sexual identity are not to be discussed. Social workers with religious beliefs that homosexuality is a sin must find ways to separate their personal belief system from their professional values, ethics, function, and roles. The professional value and ethical principles must take precedence over personal views.

Sadly, too many agencies and social workers are insensitive to gay and lesbian colleagues and clients (Jones & Gabriel, 1999). Gay and lesbian staff members are routinely exposed to homophobic and heterosexual-biased comments and practices. The following is an entry in an employed social work student's journal:

> I am extremely lucky that I have been able to be open about my sexual preference in my agency with no apparent negative backlash. It's not only a matter of luck but also my willingness to take some risks. I think that one of the strongest factors in reaching that decision was the knowledge that if another social worker were to verbalize or react negatively to some aspect of homosexuality, I would be ready to point out that the profession is ethically mandated to be open-minded, tolerant of all differences, and prepared to help all who are in need regardless of personal values, beliefs, and cultural traditions. To process the values of difference without practicing them and making them part of our core beliefs is not a position of strength. I am never really sure if my openness is accepted or simply tolerated. But I have made a beginning by giving my fellow workers the opportunity to re-evaluate the concept of homosexuality and the stereotypes and attitudes that they grew up with. In the near future, I hope to organize a workshop on homosexuality within my agency. It is long overdue.

Social workers must confront their own prejudices and stereotypes about gay and lesbian clients. A colleague was invited to consult at an agency providing services to gay and lesbian clients. In the elevator, he felt the stares and smirks of a few workmen. He had the urge to inform the workmen that he was not gay. He was unsettled by these thoughts and feelings, and, confronting his own homophobia, he began the consultation with agency staff by sharing his experience with them. They, in turn, appreciated his candor, and their work together began in a real and moving way.[3]

Sensitivity to Age.   Social workers must develop age-knowledgeable, age-sensitive, and age-skillful practice. Social workers need to be careful about not talking down to children and treating them in a patronizing manner. Children should be thought of as short people worthy of respectful and direct communication (Lucco, 1991). In work with adolescents, honesty and directness and not personalizing their testing are essential (Halleck, 1963; Malekoff, 2004). With young adults, tasks of intimacy and employment are most often the foci of helping efforts. Midlife represents a transition between earlier and later life. Helping clients to embrace life and to look forward rather than reliving the past is a core task.

When working with younger people, most social workers can draw on personal life experiences. However, when working with elderly clients most social workers do not have direct experiences with the physical, cognitive, emotional, and social dimensions of the aging processes (Lazarus & Lazarus, 2006). Consequently, social workers must develop aging-relevant knowledge, self-awareness, sensitivity, and skill. Knowledge about aging demographics, age-related changes, developmental tasks, and different cohorts is essential for contemporary practice (Berman-Rossi, 2001; Toseland & Rizzo, 2004). Self-awareness about one's own biases and stereotypes is also essential to sensitive and skillful practice. Age and developmental issues will be discussed throughout the text.

Sensitivity to Particular Mental and Physical Challenges.   All social workers—and not only those in the fields of health and mental health care—must be knowledgeable about major physical and mental challenges and the impact of discrimination. Social workers, regardless of their field of practice, are likely at times to be professionally engaged with individuals, families, groups, and communities struggling with severe, chronic mental and physical disorders. Practitioners must familiarize themselves with the nature, course, and prognosis of the condition, and the stressors faced by those who directly or indirectly suffer from it (Callahan & Turnbull, 2001; Christ, Sormanti, & Francoeur, 2001; Getzel & Willroth, 2001; Gitterman, 2001b; Lukens, 2001).

Mental illness carries a powerful societal stigma. Labels such as schizophrenic and borderline are too often used pejoratively. When the author's students refer to a client as schizophrenic or borderline, they are asked to consider the social construction of the label. For example, some people's difficulties are difficult to diagnose as they fall on the "border" of affective disorder, neurological impairment, and schizophrenia. With the simple words "Oh, she is a borderline," we have projected our professional diagnostic and intervention difficulties and made them negative attributes of the person. Similarly, the "schizophrenic" is in fact not a schizophrenic, but a person suffering from and dealing with a mental illness. Knowledge about mental and physical challenges and self-awareness about one's own biases and stereotypes are critical to sensitive and skillful practice.

Empowering and Social Justice Practice

Knowledge and self-understanding must be supplemented by reflection on racism, sexism, homophobia, ageism, and mental and physical illness, that is, by reflection on the abuse and misuse of power, the effects of powerlessness, and the need for a practice based on *empowerment* (Freeman, 2001; Gutierrez & Lewis, 1999; Lee, 2001; Mondros & Wilson, 1994; Simon, 1994; Tully, 2000; Wise, 2005). Various social work traditions deal with the issues of power and powerlessness. On a micro level, the concept of empowerment is limited to the development of *personal power*. On a macro level, empowerment is limited to the development of collective action and *political power*. Life-modeled practice is committed to helping people gain both personal and political power as well as *interpersonal power* in families and small groups. People need help with feeling in control over their lives as well as being able to influence the behaviors of significant people in their social networks and organizations (Gutierrez, 1990). Empowerment practice in the life model is conceived as the help given by social work practitioners and administrators to clients and colleagues to increase their personal, interpersonal, and/or political power for greater control over their lives.

Life-modeled practice has been greatly influenced by Bertha Reynolds (1934/1982), who believed that the client has the right to decide when help is needed, what help will be useful, and when it is no longer needed. She suggested that social workers find their professional goals on the client's own road. She did not deny that the worker had the power of knowledge, skill, and resources, but she reminded us that those served also have knowledge and skills. Their knowledge of their environment and culture, for example, exceeds that of the worker. Working together, the client and the worker are better able to achieve agreed upon goals and tasks than either would be alone. Reynolds also believed that the practitioner must be willing and ready to discuss a client's victimization by social injustice.

Solomon's work on disempowerment, powerlessness, and empowerment in social work practice in oppressed African American communities advanced the conceptualization of an empowering practice (Solomon, 1976, 1982). Later, other social work theorists (Breton, 1994, 1998; Gutierrez, 1990; Gutierrez & Lewis, 1999; Lee, 1994, 2001, 2005; Pinderhughes, 1983,

1989; Simon, 1994; Wise, 2005) made important contributions to empowerment practice. Gutierrez (1990; see also Gutierrez & Lewis, 1999), for example, described an empowering relationship between client and worker as one of shared power. Workers need to perceive themselves as enablers, organizers, consultants, or compatriots. Empowering skills include accepting people's definitions of their life issues; identifying and building on existing strengths; engaging in a power analysis of their situation; mobilizing resources and advocating with them and on their behalf; and teaching specific skills such as problem solving, community and organizational change, parenting, job seeking, assertiveness, competence, and self-advocacy.

Social justice is the cornerstone of a democratic society.[4] In a just social system, equity and fairness determine the distribution of resources, rewards, and punishments. In contrast, in an unjust social system people with more power (economic, political, physical, and emotional) dominate and exploit those with less power. Poverty and all its negative consequences (including hunger, homelessness, crime, and incarceration) reveal coercively maintained and established injustices (Gill, 1998). The concept of social justice and injustice is further specified in distributive, procedural, and retributive justice and injustice (Tyler, Boeckman, Smith, & Huo, 1997).

Distributive justice emphasizes social reform and policy making to alleviate economic deprivation and injustices. Part 3 of the book examines the macro methods of influencing organizations, communities, and legislative and political processes to achieve distributive justice. Social workers also attempt to help families and small groups achieve equity in distribution of affections, recognition, status, as well as instrumental resources. Fairness in distribution of instrumental and affective resources becomes a significant focus of social work interventions (Wakefield, 1988).

Procedural justice emphasizes being treated fairly in the resolution of differences, conflicts, and grievances. People of color, gay and lesbians, women, physically and mentally challenged people, young children, and the frail elderly are particularly vulnerable to procedural injustices. Social work as a profession often lends its professional status to influence social systems to be procedurally just and to help people suffering from procedural injustices to achieve fair treatment.

Retributive justice refers to the extent of fairness or unfairness with the consequences for breaking family, small-group, community, organizational, and societal rules. Small systems tend to use informal norms and sanctions to achieve conformity, while large systems use rules, policies, and laws to achieve compliance. Retributive justice requires that the punishment fit the crime and that the punishment be distributed "blindly." In reality, the primary function of the punishment is not to rehabilitate the rule breaker, but "for the victims and observers of the infraction to feel that the retributive justice has taken place" (Gitterman, 2003b). Social workers work with both victims as well as rule breakers and, therefore, advocate for both sets of rights. Both require fairness and justice.

Sensitivity to difference and empowerment and social justice practice are inseparably and intimately connected to ethical practice. Each supports the other two.

Integrated Modalities, Methods, and Skills

Life-modeled social work practice consists of eight modalities: work with individuals, families, groups, social networks, communities, physical environments, organizations, and politics. Contemporary practitioners must be equipped to work effectively within all eight modalities, moving readily and skillfully from one to another, as situations require and with client (individual, family, group, or community) agreement. Some methods and skills are common to all modalities, while others are specific to one. Commonly held methods and skills are used for developing explicit agreements and exploring client concerns. Specific methods and skills are those used to form groups; develop mutual aid; deal with internal group obstacles; help families change dysfunctional relationship processes; help communities or neighborhoods acquire needed resources, networks, and self-help groups; create needed programs and services; and influence organizational and legislative activity.

Practitioner style and creativity are indispensable in life-modeled practice. Clients respond best to social workers who are willing to reveal their humanness, vulnerability, and spontaneity (Shulman, 1991). Clients do not expect social workers to be models of perfection and virtue. A practitioner's empathy, commitment, and desire to be helpful speak louder than any possible awkwardness or mistake. Successful practitioners are "dependably real" rather than "rigidly consistent" (Rogers, 1961, p. 50).

Professional education and socialization sometimes stiffen practice and discourage purposeful and spontaneous humor. Yet, used appropriately, humor might relieve a client's (and the worker's) tensions, anxiety, and embarrassment. For instance, after heart surgery, a blue-collar hospital patient was very anxious about possibly being impotent. He had been unable to discuss the concern with his physicians. The social worker dealt with the awkward silences between them by asking with a smile, "Are you worried about whether the lead has run out of your pencil?" He responded with laughter, and a frank discussion followed (Gitterman, 2003a).

Relationship between Client and Worker

In life-modeled practice, the professional relationship is conceived as a humanistic partnership, with power differences between the partners reduced to the greatest degree possible. Thus, the relationship between client and worker shifts from subordinate recipient and superior expert to a relationship characterized by mutuality and reciprocity. Social workers bring professional knowledge and skill to the therapeutic encounter. Those served bring experiential knowledge of their life issues and their life stories. They are responsible for work on their goals and tasks; social workers are responsible for creating conditions that will facilitate clients' work.

To be effective, the relationship also must be strongly rooted in empathy. Absence of empathy inevitably leads to therapeutic errors and failures, and to client dropout.

> In order to empathize, one must have a well-differentiated sense of self in addition to an appreciation of and sensitivity to the differences as well as sameness of the other. Empathy always involves surrender to feelings and active cognitive structuring; in order for empathy to occur, self-boundaries must be flexible [to allow] perception of the other's affective cues (both verbal and non-verbal) followed by surrender to affective arousal in oneself. . . . For empathy to be effective, there must be a balance of affective and cognitive, subjective and objective, active and passive. (Jordon, 1991, p. 69)

The capacity for empathy is relative rather than absolute. For example, some people may be empathically attuned to certain feelings but not to others, to sadness but not to anger, to pride but not to shame. With practice experience, however, social workers' ability to empathize with most clients is expected to increase. But if one cannot empathize with certain people or their feelings, this limitation must be recognized.

Inexperience, together with lack of empathy, may occasionally lead to underestimating people's strengths and their potentials for growth. This is especially true in settings that serve profoundly disturbed people. A beginning social work student reports on how her low expectations were turned around:

> My client in a day treatment program for those suffering from chronic schizophrenia was riding with me in the program's van. The driver stopped the van and asked my client to go across the street to buy a pack of cigarettes. I began to argue that Matthew does not speak, cannot make change, and doesn't know how to cross the street. The driver said, "Gee, I didn't know that. If I had, I wouldn't have asked him, but he's been getting my cigarettes for me for weeks now."
>
> I think I had been seeing my clients as bundles of symptoms rather than as living, growing human beings. Our driver didn't know about the "hopelessness" of the symptoms, and therefore he set his expectations higher and more accurately than mine. This was an important lesson for me.

Agreements, Life Stories, and Assessments

Mutual agreements and assessments are characteristic of many practice approaches. In life-modeled practice, social worker and client are partners as they work together throughout their time together. When the worker–client partner relationship is defined and manifested, as it is in life-modeled practice, resistance, testing, withdrawal, or unplanned termination in the initial phase is minimized.

Agreements. All helping in life-modeled practice rests on shared definitions of life stressors and explicit agreements on foci, priorities, selection of modality, goals, plans, next steps, and other arrangements of the work. In themselves, an applicant's statement of need, an agency's offer of service, or a mandated service does not represent agreement until the applicant and worker reach a shared, specific, and clear understanding about their foci and methods. Reaching agreement is a critical aspect of the initial phase of social work practice and continues in the ongoing and ending phases.

Agreement between worker and client protects the client's individuality, enhances self-direction, and strengthens coping skills. Most importantly, arriving at an agreement structures and focuses the work, decreases anxiety associated with the fear of the unknown and the ambiguity inherent in beginnings, and mobilizes energy for work. It also reduces some of the power discrepancy between client and worker at a time when the client is vulnerable to manipulation or misuse at the hands of the agency or professional authority.

Life Stories. The life stories that we tell to others and ourselves over our life course are natural, real-life processes—our human way of finding meaning and continuity in life events. "One's identity, then, is built on the sense one can make of one's own life story" (Laird, 1989, pp. 430–431). The value of life stories lies in the connections these stories create among life events, lending coherence to individual and family life (Docherty & McColl, 2003; Gilbert & Beidler, 2001; Jones, 2004; Kelley, 2002; Knei-Paz & Ribner, 2000; May, 2005; Norman, 2000; Pietsch, 2002; Wood & Frey, 2003). With the empathic, active listening of the social worker, a life story gains increased intelligibility, consistency, and continuity. The teller of the story reinterprets and reconstructs a narrative, which ultimately will contain new conceptions of oneself and of relationships with others. Because they are offered voluntarily after trust is established, life stories become part of the work. The extensive "life histories" taken by the practitioner in intake interviews are obtained from probing questions before a trusting relationship is in place; as a result, they yield less significant content. To the extent that is possible, given our professional role, the social worker invites clients to tell their stories in their own words and helps them make meaning of their struggles and lives.

Assessment. Client participation in continuous assessment ensures shared focus and direction. Life-modeled practice emphasizes assessment of the *level of fit* between human needs and environmental resources. Professional assessment takes place at every moment in the helping encounter, and after each session. Collecting, organizing, and interpreting data are the social worker's major assessment tasks. Conceptualizing life issues and stressors as difficult life transitions and traumatic life events, environmental pressures, and dysfunctional family and group processes provides a schema for collecting, organizing, and interpreting data.

Practice Focus on Personal and Collective Strengths and on Client Action and Decision Making

In life-modeled practice, the focus is on individual and collective strengths rather than on deficits (Saleebey, 2006). All people have strengths and resilience, although for some, those strengths have been dampened by circumstances. Practitioners must identify, mobilize, and build on people's strengths and resilience. When social workers are preoccupied with deficits, psychopathology, and diagnostic labels, individuals, families, and groups are merely broken objects to be "fixed" (treated) by powerful experts. This obscures the humanity of both clients and practitioners. Life-modeled practice, as closely as possible, mirrors natural life processes, builds on people's strengths, and seeks to remove or reduce environmental obstacles.

All people need opportunities to make decisions about their own situations and take action on their own behalf. When people are able to have an impact on their environment, take responsibility for an aspect of their situation, or make decisions in significant areas of life, their self-esteem and sense of competence are strengthened, and their skills for continued mastery are developed. Individuals, families, groups, and/or communities' motivation has to be mobilized and followed through with specific actions. Tasks, activities, and actions are carefully considered to ensure that they are achievable and appropriate to the client's (member's) lifestyle, interests, and capacities. Risks of failure must be minimized.

The Pervasive Significance of the Environment

Society's varied social and physical structures are often closed to some populations by virtue of race, ethnicity, social class, gender, sexual orientation, age, or physical and mental challenges, generating many painful life stressors. Organizations designed to meet fundamental needs (welfare, schools, and health care systems) frequently create stress because of their harsh or unresponsive policies and procedures. A social network of relatives, friends, or neighbors might be emotionally and materially supportive, or it might be unresponsive, or the network is characterized by interpersonal conflict. A network might not even exist, leaving the person or family socially isolated.

Physical habitats must support human needs for stimulation, comfort, challenge, and family and community life, and provide access to the natural world. They become life stressors when they create overcrowding, fail to provide sufficient protection from the hazards of crime and pollution, or lack affordable housing that supports family life.

Life-modeled practice emphasizes the importance of social workers helping clients to negotiate their environments and directly intervening in them on their behalf.

Evaluation of Practice and Contribution to Knowledge

Different methods are available to evaluate social work practice and to contribute to knowledge. Through detailed documentation of practice, the *case study method*, the social worker tests out intervention hypotheses. By examining the processes and details of a case, the subtle nuances of practice are captured. Increasing concerns about validity and reliability led investigators to study comparison groups of clients or programs. By creating experimental and control groups of people with similar background and problem characteristics, the *group comparison method*, interventions are provided to one group (the experimental group) while interventions are withheld from the other (the control group). By measuring the differences between the groups on some outcome measure, the effectiveness of an intervention is evaluated. The *single-case design method* provides an alternative to the group comparison method. A baseline measure of a person's behavior, mood, attitude, or perception is developed and then remeasured on completion of the intervention.

Naturalistic qualitative methods are ecologically sensitive and compatible with social work's client-centered traditions. The social worker skilled in inviting and exploring clients' stories is a natural investigator into people's transactions with their social and physical environment. The social worker explores, observes, and follows cues throughout the phases of helping, capturing subtle nuances of meaning and behavior. In the ending phase, the social worker engages clients in a joint evaluation of the service, including satisfactory and unsatisfactory elements. The evaluations may help workers further develop positive aspects and correct negative ones.

Over time, accumulated evaluations may suggest interesting questions to the worker: what seems to work best with certain life issues but not with others? What seems to work best with certain individuals, groups, or cultures but not with others? Questions that arise from practice experience can lead the practitioner to undertake a quantitative study that may yield contributions to social work theory.

Goal attainment scaling methods bridge the separation of process and outcomes by monitoring clients' progress over time. Client involvement in specifying desired outcomes has therapeutic as well as practice evaluation value. By using jointly developed scales, clients and workers mutually track progress in their work.

Four Phases of Life-Modeled Practice

The phases of helping further characterize the life model. Four phases—preparatory, initial, ongoing, and ending—constitute the processes and operations of practice. These processes ebb and flow in response to the interplay of personal and environmental forces. While the phases are separated in order to organize our presentation, they are not always distinct in actual practice.

Preparatory Phase

Empathy.   Even before the first session, social workers need to prepare themselves to enter applicants' or clients' lives by reflecting on available information concerning the probable objective situation, its possible cultural meaning, and its potential impact on the first session. Practitioners need also to reflect on an applicant or client's subjective reality by empathizing with their likely perceptions and feelings. Drawing on such anticipatory processes readies the social worker to "hear" both the more obvious as well as the more disguised content. A high level of professional empathy is correlated with a high level of client sharing (Truax & Carkhoff, 1967). Social workers must demonstrate empathy by showing interest and concern through nonverbal and verbal means and by paying close attention to the client. While demonstrating empathy is always important, it is essential with mandated and/or ambivalent or confused and anxious clients.

Developing anticipatory empathy and demonstrating empathy are essential to practice with all modalities. Additionally, each modality requires distinctive preparatory skills. For example, in forming groups, workers have to formulate proposed group purposes, select appropriate group types, effectively compose the groups, and determine the number, frequency, and duration of meetings and group size.

Initial Phase: Getting Started

Stressor Definition.   The client and worker must first identify and define the life stressor(s), since how the life stressor is defined largely governs what will be done about the issue. For some people, multiple stressors lead to disorganization, as with the Williams family described earlier in this chapter. Sometimes, effective work on one life stressor supports coping with others. At other times, worker and client may agree to rank-order the stressors and work on them one by one. Occasionally, however, the shared work is simultaneously directed to two or more stressors, as in the following example, in which the client himself defines the stressors.

Mr. Hall, a childless widower age eighty-seven, came to the United States from Russia with his mother when he was seven. He is a high school graduate who, at age sixty-five, retired as a bridge toll collector. He entered the institution after two strokes left him paralyzed on one side. He has chronic heart failure, limited vision due to glaucoma, and a hearing impairment. Before her sudden death three years ago, his wife visited daily. They had divorced four years ago so that Mr. Hall could receive Medicaid without her becoming penniless. He rarely socializes with other residents and infrequently leaves his room. The social work intern records:

When I read his chart, the nurse told me, "He turns off anyone who tries to help." My field instructor also warned me that Mr. Hall is angry, manipulative, self-destructive, and rude. As I prepared to meet him, I reminded myself that people are often unfairly labeled. When I introduced myself to Mr. Hall, I met a friendly, receptive, elderly man. I explained who I was, my role, and how long I would be at the institution. He said he was desperate to have someone to speak with. In our early sessions, Mr. Hall expressed some feelings and concerns and gave me small, select glimpses into his past. During those times he frequently tested my loyalty and the boundaries of our relationship. I understood his occasional gruffness and was undaunted by it. Mr. Hall wished to work on three painful life issues:

1. His wife's death (a difficult life transition). She died in the winter—Mr. Hall is confined to a wheelchair, and he has never visited her grave. Hence he has not been able to work through his grief and to experience a sense of closure with her death.
2. A change of room (environment). Mr. Hall feels he is "shriveling up" on the third floor, where the most limited reside. He wants to move to a more independent floor.
3. Institutionalization and loss of personal control (a painful life transition and environmental stressor). Mr. Hall's ultimate life stressor is his sense of lost control over his mind and body due to his disabilities and being institutionalized.

Degree of Choice.   The initial phase is strongly influenced by the degree of choice about the service. People usually seek professional help, taking on the applicant or client role, when stressors become unmanageable (Alcabes & Jones, 1985). They are propelled into social work services either out of their own quest for help or out of the concern of other people or organizations, who then initiate referral. When services are *sought*, finding common ground between the client's and practitioner's definitions of the life stressor(s) and goals, and the agency services, is usually easier to achieve than when client choice is more constricted.

When services are *offered* to preselected groups or populations, as in outreach programs, the social worker must maintain an ethical balance between active presentation of anticipated benefits and people's right to refuse service. By identifying and relating to people's perceptions and definitions of their needs, practitioners are more likely to engage them in the offer of service.

When a court order or other authoritarian institutions and their representatives *mandate* services, the practitioner must acknowledge the mandate and directly deal with its implications. Both the nature of the mandate and

Table 3.2
Social Worker Skills in the Initial Phase

• *In general:*	Prepare to enter the applicant's or client's life by reflecting on available information concerning probable objective and subjective realities, their possible cultural meanings, and potential impact on the first session.
	Create an accepting and supportive environment by demonstrating empathy by showing interest, curiosity, and concern through nonverbal and verbal means and paying close attention to what client is saying and doing.
	Define people's life issues and stressors as expressions of relationships between people and environment, and emphasize increased adaptive capacity and increased environmental responsiveness.
• *In sought services:*	Create welcoming atmosphere when client *seeks* services, encourage applicants or clients to share their concerns, reach for details, and explore possible doubts and hesitations about the agency and the worker.
• *In services offered:*	Identify the applicant or client's potential perceptions and definitions of life issues and stressors when offering services; maintain an ethical balance between active presentation of anticipated benefits and people's right to refuse *offered* service.
• *In mandated services:*	Acknowledge the *mandate* when offering services; deal directly with the implications of both the nature of the mandate and the extent of possible sanctions for violations, and locate and respond to client discomfort.
• *In all:*	Describe and explain agency services and social work procedures, and invite client questions and discussion. Develop a tentative shared assessment of person:environment exchange.
	Develop explicit initial agreement on next steps, tentative goals, priorities, reciprocal tasks and responsibilities, and other arrangements affecting the proposed work together.

the extent of possible sanctions on violations must be specified. Efforts to locate and respond to people's discomfort with mandated services are also important. Table 3.2 summarizes worker skills used in the initial phase.

In a first session, practitioners need to describe and explain agency services and social work procedures, and invite client questions and discussion about them. Exploring and defining the life stressor(s) then begins. A tentative shared assessment of person:environment exchanges, including coping skills and environmental resources, may be reached in the first session and in other early sessions of the initial phase (or in the only session in one-session and episodic services). Explicit initial agreement on next steps, tentative goals, priorities, reciprocal tasks and responsibilities, and other arrangements affecting the proposed work together must also be covered in the initial phase. Clients' active participation in these processes is empowering because it enhances the sense of competence, relatedness, self-esteem, and self-direction.

These professional skills are differentially applied according to applicants' and clients' backgrounds, their life experiences and level of functioning, the particular practice modality in use at a given point, and temporal arrangements.

Ongoing Phase: Working toward Goals

Methods.   Strengthening and supporting person:environment relationships (such as level of fit and personal coping skills and environmental resources required for managing life stressors) are central in the ongoing phase. Modalities were briefly described earlier in this chapter and are more fully examined in the next chapter. Methods and skills associated with the various modalities are more fully examined and illustrated throughout part 2 of this book.

Supporting and strengthening people's adaptive capacities and problem-solving abilities can be achieved through the methods of enabling, exploring and clarifying, mobilizing, guiding, and facilitating. *Enabling* mobilizes or strengthens clients' motivation to deal with difficult life stressors and the associated stress they arouse. Enabling clients to elaborate their concerns requires skills that include using minimal responses to encourage; waiting out silence; reaching for facts; verbalizing feelings; legitimizing and universalizing thoughts, reactions, and feelings; emphasizing and highlighting specific cues; rephrasing concerns; using metaphors; using appropriate humor; and sharing one's thoughts and feelings as appropriate. Other skills such as identifying strengths, conveying hope, and offering realistic reassurance help clients to marshall and sustain their motivation and personal strengths.

Exploring and *clarifying* provide focus and direction to the work. Conveying "Can you help me understand your situation?" the social worker draws on skills such as developing focus, specifying concerns, reaching for underlying meaning, clarifying ambivalence, identifying discrepant messages, patterning concerns, offering interpretations, providing and inviting feedback, and inviting self-reflection. Exploring and clarifying deepen the "therapeutic conversation" between the partners.

Mobilizing is used to strengthen people's motivation to deal with difficult life stressors and manage the associated disabling feelings. In dealing with painful life issues and events, people need help with mobilizing their personal strengths and motivation based on skills such as identifying strengths, offering realistic reassurance, and conveying hope.

Guiding helps clients learn the steps in the problem-solving aspects of coping. Social workers must attend to the different ways in which people learn. Some learn primarily by doing, whereas others learn primarily by summarizing—visualizing and organizing perceptions into patterns and images. Still others learn primarily by abstracting and conceptualizing (Bruner, 1966). Effective guidance depends on providing opportunities for activity, modeling, role-play, and discussion and exchange of ideas. The following skills guide problem solving: providing needed information regarding the stressor and coping tasks; clarifying misinformation; offering advice when requested; supporting clients' accurate interpretations; discussing, visualizing, and acting; specifying action tasks; and planning for task completion (Gitterman, 1988, 2001b).

Facilitating encourages clients to remain committed to the work. Some will be reluctant to examine and work on difficult issues. Avoidance is indicated by passive behaviors such as withdrawal, overcompliance, and extreme diffidence; by nonpassive behaviors such as provocation, intellectualization, interruption, verbosity, and seductiveness; or by flight behaviors such as changing the subject, withholding information, and minimizing concerns. If avoidance persists, the worker needs to challenge and demand purposive work by commenting on the avoidance pattern, challenging illusions of mutual agreement, and remarking on discrepant messages. These interventions can stimulate and mobilize energy for the work. However, if used indiscriminately, they may increase defensiveness or lead to clients dropping out.

All life stressors require work with the environment. Social work methods for this work include coordinating, mediating, advocating, innovating and organizing, and influencing organizational and legislative policies and regulations.

In *coordinating*, the social worker links clients to available resources. After bringing about agreement on shared tasks, the worker draws on skills, including preparing the way for informed consent and involvement, defining a division of labor, evoking and drawing on clients' energy and personal resources, and lending the worker's professional status to the client.

When the environmental pressure arises from distorted exchanges, the worker *mediates* between the client and the organization or social network so they effectively connect to each other. Skills of the external mediating method include developing and using informal and formal contacts; demonstrating understanding of the perspectives held by other organizational staff; knowing and using formal policies, procedures, and precedents; and persevering.

If mediation fails, worker and client consider potentially adversarial actions through the use of *advocacy*. Because both client and worker are often vulnerable to retaliation, probity and caution are necessary. Before taking an adversarial position, the social worker needs to evaluate available organizational, professional, and personal resources for dealing with potential consequences. In using external advocacy, the social worker assumes a polite, respectful stance, rather than one of outraged righteousness. Ethical practice requires an adversarial position and external advocacy when essential entitlements are denied or client rights are violated regardless of risks. The method includes such skills as hinting at plans of further action; organizing protests; refusing compliance; and reporting to the media, civil rights groups, and the NASW.

Through *innovation*, the social worker seeks to fill gaps in services and resources and to help establish preventive and growth-promoting programs. When clients lack a social network or when communities lack informal networks, the practitioner can organize social support and self-help groups centered on members' common life stressors, interests, or tasks. Social support groups help members assume an active role in reducing the stress generated by social and emotional isolation and loneliness. Self-help groups focus on a shared painful stressor such as job loss, bereavement, a physical or mental disorder, or family violence. Innovation skills include assessing need, developing a programmatic response, acquiring organizational consent and support, identifying community leaders, and recruiting the population in need.

Social workers and clients seek to influence organizational practices and legislation on social policies and regulations at local, state, and national levels in the cause of social justice. The *influencing* method includes such skills as coalition building, positioning, lobbying, and testifying.

In responding to difficult life transitions and harsh environments, families, groups, and communities can encounter interpersonal obstacles such as maladaptive behaviors, conflicted relationships, and blocked communication. Withdrawal, factions, alliances, and scapegoating are examples of dysfunctional patterns in groups. Dysfunctional patterns in families include misuse of power and authority, violence, neglect, and sexual abuse. Dysfunctional patterns in communities include unfair allotment of scarce resources, intergroup hostilities, and power structures that exclude vulnerable residents. Helping groups, families, and communities to change these and other dysfunctional patterns is a critical arena for preventive and restorative interventions. The social worker helps members to recognize obstacles, learn to communicate more openly and directly, and attain greater mutuality, trust, and concern for collective well-being. *Internal mediating* and *advocating* skills include identifying and commenting on dysfunctional patterns, challenging collective resistance, inviting and exploring conflicting ideas, establishing protective ground rules, lending support, and crediting work. Social work methods and skills associated with the ongoing phase are summarized in Table 3.3.

Natural Life Processes.   Clients are not responsible for "confirming and conforming to our interests; our professional responsibility is to join their natural life processes, to follow their leads and to be responsive to their cues"

Table 3.3
Professional Methods and Skills Associated with the Ongoing Phase

Life Stressors	Professional Methods	Skills
Difficult Transitions and Traumatic Events	Enabling	Use minimal responses to encourage; wait out silence; reach for facts; verbalize feelings.
	Exploring	Develop focus; specify concerns; reach for underlying meaning; clarify ambivalence.
	Mobilizing	Offer realistic reassurance and hope.
	Guiding	Provide information regarding stressor and coping tasks; clarify misinformation.
	Facilitating	Comment on avoidance patterns; challenge illusion of mutual agreement; generate anxiety to promote movement.
Environmental Issues (organization, social networks, natural world, built world)	Coordinating	Prepare the way for informed consent and involvement; define a division of labor; elicit and draw on client energy.
	External Mediating	Develop and use system contacts; demonstrate understanding of others' perspectives.
	External Advocacy	Imply further action; organize protests; refuse compliance; report to other organizations and the media.
	Innovating	Assess need; develop program in response; acquire organizational and community support.
	Influencing	Build coalitions, position, lobby, testify.
Maladaptive Interpersonal Processes (family, group, worker:client)	Internal Mediating	Identify and comment on dysfunctional patterns; challenge collective resistance.
	Internal Advocating	Invite and sustain conflict; establish protective ground rules; lend support.

(Gitterman & Shulman, 2005, p. 34). The following provides an example of joining natural life processes in life-modeled practice with a family (a solo mother and her twelve-year-old daughter). It also illustrates how bypassing serious pathology facilitates this joining and releases the potential for growth and social functioning. The social work intern records:

When I arrived at Mrs. Richards's home for the first visit, she seemed to be under considerable stress, complaining of sleepless nights and an increasing inability to concentrate on anything besides her "noise problem," caused by "vicious upstairs, downstairs, and next-door neighbors." The neighbors all persist in "ganging up" on her by "purposely annoying" her, beginning at 5:00 A.M. and continuing until 1:00 A.M. the following day. They speak loudly, play TV and radios on high volume, repeatedly drop shoes, and "go out of their way" to walk very heavily. Mrs. Richards also refuses to pick up mail, fearing a bomb may have been mailed to her. Further proof of the "conspiracy" against her is the notice she just received from the landlord that her lease is being terminated because neighbors have complained of noise coming from her apartment. Mrs. Richards has also received a summons from a neighbor charging her with harassment. Mrs. Richards admits she rings her neighbors' bells frequently to ask them to be quiet. She views the termination of the lease as an act by "malicious people who are jealous" of her because she is so quiet.

After my visit, Mrs. Richards had another agency call the department to verify I had no secret intent to harm her. In the second visit, Mrs. Richards told me she always did well in school, but all her life she has felt out of place and inferior to those around her. She states her social life consists of Debbie (her daughter) and one friend, whom she rarely sees. Debbie also has only one friend and prides herself on being a "bookworm." Mrs. Richards also said that for ten years she has lived in various buildings with "noisy, inconsiderate neighbors," whom she has often unsuccessfully taken to court, but the present noise level is the most bothersome of all because she can't rest or even think of anything else.

In Mrs. Richards's transactions with her environment, disturbances and disruptions occur frequently. She perceives a powerful imbalance between external demands placed on her by the environment and her self-defined ability to meet these demands with her own external and internal resources. This imbalance creates intense stress and anxiety. These transactional imbalances create daily transitional, environmental, and interpersonal stressors (Gitterman, 1996; Gitterman & Germain, 1976). The social work intern viewed Mrs. Richards's paranoia as poor perceptions of the inside and outside worlds preventing adaptive interchanges between Mrs. Richards and her environment and impairing her ability to cope with the tasks of adult-hood. Mrs. Richards saw the problem as "vicious people out to get me." The consulting psychiatrist, noting that Mrs. Richards had been a patient in a state hospital twenty years before, defined the problem as a long-standing psychosis exacerbated by threat of eviction. Life-modeled practice puts an emphasis on the troubles Mrs. Richards is experiencing. Whatever her diag-nosis, she nonetheless has to manage serious life issues. The life-modeled emphasis helps the social work intern to find common ground so Mrs. Rich-ards could have what she calls "a friend" to talk with her about her "noise problem," since she is alone all the time and has no one with whom to dis-cuss the problem. They agree on the goal of a solution to Mrs. Richards's discomfort with her environment. Accepting Mrs. Richards's environmental concerns is the "ticket" into the work. It provides the social work intern with time to assess Mrs. Richards's level of functioning and her capacity to ex-plore such life issues and transitions as thwarted tasks of adulthood, or to accept the status of a person with an illness who might need medication to improve her daily functioning, or interpersonal issues of establishing appro-priate boundaries between her daughter and herself.

10/24—I asked Mrs. Richards if she has thoughts about the possibility that she has to move. She says she has, and she has begun to look in the papers to see if anything is available in the neighborhood. She stated she had seen what sounded like a beautiful apartment advertised in the pa-per, and when she called up it was already taken. Mrs. Richards feels sure the vacancy never existed at all, and that they played a trick on her so that she'd call and inquire about a more expensive apartment. I agreed that might be possible, but wondered if the apartment had sounded so attractive to her that someone else might have thought so, too, and tele-phoned before her. Mrs. Richards said that she doubted that—she's pretty sure it was all a "gimmick" to trick her. On further discussion, she remembered she had, in fact, bought the newspaper late in the day, and said, yes, maybe I was right.

During the next month, at Mrs. Richards's request, the social work intern accompanied her to court several times. Each time, they went to a coffee shop afterward. Whenever Mrs. Richards's anxiety mounted, the social work intern offered support.

11/11—Mrs. Richards stated that she was not at all sure why she had asked me to coome, since there was nothing that I could do to help her with her case. I said I knew sitting alone in a courtroom is not the most pleasing thing, and I would not like to wait alone. Mrs. Richards then turned and thanked me for coming with her today.

When the case was postponed a week, Mrs. Richards expressed fear that her attorney might not come back.

She seemed very anxious about this, saying she wouldn't know whom else to call. I then told Mrs. Richards that if he couldn't make it for the 19th, the date of her next appearance in court, I would try to help her find another lawyer. She said that she would appreciate that. She stated again that her noisy neighbors are "picking on" her. I told Mrs. Richards that while she may be bothered by the noise, it is something that we must all put up with while living in the city. Mrs. Richards did not deny this, but expressed fear that she would have to go through moving again. She anxiously stated that she's afraid that she "won't live through" the court case. I reassured her that she will, and that if she has to move I will be there to help her clear things through the Department of Welfare. Mrs. Richards then seemed much calmer and said it was nice to talk to me, adding that Mrs. Peterson at the other agency really hadn't understood her, and she would like to have coffee with me again.

At the next court hearing, after a long wait:

11/19—Mrs. Richards seemed to be getting more and more nervous and suddenly, sounding as if she were going to cry, stood up and said, "What will happen to me if I get thrown out? I have no family, no one to go to, I'm all alone." I immediately reassured her that whatever happens, she won't be out on the street. If she is evicted, I will make sure that everything is cleared at the welfare center. Mrs. Richards then worried that she won't get permission to move because she has not been living in her present apartment for the required two years. I assured her that under the circumstances, the time element will not count, and that I will try to have everything arranged for her quickly. Mrs. Richards looked at me, smiled, and thanked me for being there with her today.

The case was postponed indefinitely, and afterward, at the coffee shop, Mrs. Richards asked if the social work intern would go looking for an apartment with her.

I pointed out that she may not even have to look for another place to live—she may not be evicted at all. Mrs. Richards then asked if she would be able to move even if she weren't evicted. I said that I had been under the impression that she wanted to stay in her apartment. She said she does, but she can't stand her "vicious neighbors." I reminded her that wherever she would move in the city she'd be faced with neighbors and noise. Mrs. Richards said I was right, even the lawyer had said the same thing, and she'd been bothered by neighbors for ten years. I reinforced this, and wondered if she would feel less aggravated by trying to get out of the house a little more. Mrs. Richards nodded and said that maybe that's what she should be doing, and she'll try it. Mrs. Richards then said she did not want to discuss it today, but asked if on Thursday we might discuss the possibility of her getting a part-time job because she wants to be more independent. As we walked together to the corner, Mrs. Richards thanked me again many times, and before my leaving, she turned to me and said, "I like you." I said I liked her too.

Guiding

A month later, Mrs. Richards reported some changes in her situation.

She said she sometimes still hears her neighbors, but they "seemed to be bothering her" less. She is trying not to pay so much attention to them; she "has her own life." Mrs. Richards said that all day yesterday she had not been home, having gone to the Y for swimming, and then to the library. I said that was good, and she might find the more she continues to pay attention to other things, the less bothered she may be by her neighbors. Mrs. Richards nodded in agreement. She said she knows she is "smart" because she has an IQ of 132, but she always felt inferior to others. She could never mingle or feel at home with others. She remembers reading that people who are smart are good in everything, and should be able to get along well with others. She said that she has been thinking about it lately, and there's no reason for her to think she's not as good as everyone else. I nodded in support, and she said she's thinking of being more independent and getting some part-time work. She asked if I could find out if this would be possible under the WIN (Women and Infants Nutrition) program.

Mobilizing

Not only did the social work intern focus on Mrs. Richards's strengths, but also she successfully bypassed the pathology. While it may not always be possible (or advisable) to bypass pathology, we believe that the social work focus should always be on the daily hassles and serious life stressors rather than on "treating" the pathology. Instead of treating a paranoid schizophrenic person, the social work intern viewed Mrs. Richards's difficulties as arising from exchanges between her and the environment. The social work intern sought to interrupt transactional processes that had created and sustained the present life stressors, and did this successfully by a focus on strengths. She purposefully increased Mrs. Richards's badly damaged self-esteem while engaging her perceptual-sensory capacity by distinguishing between inner and outer experiences at every opportunity. Together these two areas of work created a beginning trust in interpersonal relationships.

As Mrs. Richards's anxiety diminished, progressive forces in her personality were released. She began to feel better about herself; her thinking, perceptions, and behavior began to change. The behavioral changes elicited different responses from her environment (neighbors, landlord), thus supporting the restitution process. Within two months, Mrs. Richards began to transact differently with her environment. Instead of spending her days frantically listening for traces of noise, she readied herself for taking action that could lead to learning and competence. Several months later, with the social work intern's help, she successfully planned for Debbie to attend summer camp, made arrangements for her own vocational counseling at the division of vocational rehabilitation, and was expressing an interest in meeting men.

Mrs. Richards was able to relinquish her preoccupation with inner phenomena and to reestablish connections with the outer world through the social work intern's support and clarifications provided. The social worker intern's caring, respect, and positive expectations nurtured Mrs. Richards's sense of self as a worthwhile person. Successful experiences led to growth, and growth increased the likelihood of further successes. The previous cycle of frustration and failure in transactions with the environment was interrupted. Mrs. Richards was beginning to build a sense of trust and was more ready to take action for developing competence in the tasks of adulthood.

To identify and pursue an appropriate focus, the social work intern first identifies the client's perceptions of her *most pressing and stressful life issues*. By paying close attention to the client's own sense of her greatest vulnerabilities, the social work intern is provided with critical points of entry into her life situation. Mrs. Richards's possible eviction and the risk of becoming homeless represented the most serious threat to her and her daughter's survival. Therefore, joining and supporting her in coping with the eviction hearing comprised the crucial point of entry into her life situation.

Second, the social work intern *avoids mobilizing defenses*. With reluctant or ambivalent clients, for example, the practitioner focuses on safer and more comfortable definitions of life issues, thereby fostering credibility and trust. Accepting Mrs. Richards's initial definition of "noisy neighbors" avoided mobilizing her defenses and her paranoia.

Third, the social work intern and client *select tasks that provide opportunities for success*. Success is a powerful motivator for involvement in the partnership, the development of hope, and commitment to the work. When Mrs. Richards confronted an overwhelming environmental stressor, the social work intern divided it into manageable tasks. The partners could begin with the simpler ones and experience some success before tackling the more complex tasks.

The Ending Phase: Bringing the Shared Work and the Relationship to a Close

Clients and workers often experience phases of termination, including avoidance, negative feelings, sadness, and release. In preparation for ending with clients, the social worker considers the potential impact of the agency or department, the frequency and number of meetings, and individual, family, or group modality. Each phase requires distinctive skills used in a timely fashion.

Avoidance is a conscious effort to ward off pain or loss; denial is an unconscious defense against pain or loss. With the worker's help, clients can begin to relax the avoidance effort and allow feelings of anger and sadness to surface. Social workers must remain empathic and sufficiently detached for this to happen. They need to maintain sufficient empathy to understand the aroused feelings. At the same time, they must move far enough away from the experience to invite the expression of negative thoughts and emotions. As the reality of ending is directly confronted, both client and social worker are freed to experience their positive feelings and their shared sadness at ending. Not all clients will feel sad; some will feel relieved, neutral, or cheated. Workers must be careful to avoid forcing an expression of feelings that may not exist.

Having faced and shared the termination, the social worker next helps the client evaluate gains and consider whether some work is still to be done; develop plans for the future, such as transfer or referral; and say goodbyes and disengage.

FOUR

ASSESSMENT, PRACTICE MONITORING, AND PRACTICE EVALUATION

Assessment

Assessment Tasks

Assessment is an essential attribute of all practice approaches. Social workers must make informed choices as the helping process begins, including where and how to enter an individual's, family's, or group's situation; what modality and temporal arrangements to suggest; which client messages to explore; and when to work on factual content or feelings, or on verbal or nonverbal material, or on goal setting and next steps. Assessment relies on reasoned thought when making judgments at any moment during the session, and when constructing a formal assessment of person:environment exchanges following several sessions. To be valid and useful, clinical decisions and the assessment itself must be rooted in logical reasoning, and inferences based on available evidence (Gambrill, 1992, 2006; Meyer, 1993).

To develop reliable and clinical judgments, social workers must construct assessments in partnership with those served. Their shared tasks include collecting, organizing, and analyzing and synthesizing the data:

1. *Collecting* salient data on the nature of the life stressors and their degree of severity, the person's perception of and responses to the stressors, and personal and environmental resources available for coping. Data are also collected that clarify the operation of cultural and historical contexts, and biological, emotional, perceptual, cognitive, and environmental factors in the current situation. Strengths and limitations must be identified.

2. *Organizing* data in ways that reveal significant patterns. Clients' overwhelming life stressors may overwhelm social workers. Therefore, a system is needed that can organize data in a way that clarifies their meaning and reveals significant patterns.

3. *Analyzing* and *synthesizing* the data in order to draw inferences about client strengths and limitations, environmental resources and deficits, and level of fit between person and environment.

Accurate assessment rests on the collection of relevant information, its systematic organization, and the analysis and synthesis of the data. Without information on the nature of the life issue and the social and *cultural* contexts in which it exists, the practitioner is unable to determine an appropriate purpose and direction. With immigrant applicants and clients, the social worker has to collect culturally relevant data. Congress (1994, p. 533) identifies the following areas: reasons for immigration; immigration status; length of time in the country and community; age at time of immigration; impact of crisis events; language spoken at home; contact with cultural institutions; health beliefs; holidays celebrated; and values about family, education, and work. Culturally sensitive assessment also deepens the understanding of a client's spiritual perspective. Hodge (2001, 2005) encourages social workers to be curious about client's *spiritual* histories as a method of identifying potential strengths (as well as weaknesses). A series of questions can be used to explore spiritual and religious themes in people's lives, for example, "I was wondering if spirituality or religion has played an important role in your life," and "In what ways does your spirituality help you cope with the difficulties you encounter?" (Hodge, 2004). If the client's response suggests that spirituality or religion play an important role, Hodge (2004, p. 38) recommends follow up with such questions as "Are there certain spiritual beliefs and practices that you find particularly helpful in dealing with your problems?" and "I was wondering if you attend a church (synagogue, mosque) or some other type of spiritual community?"

Sources of data include the client's *verbal* accounts, the worker's observations of *nonverbal* communication, verbal and nonverbal presentations by others (obtained only with the client's informed consent), and *written reports* (obtained only with the client's permission, except for the agency's own earlier records). Large amounts of data are overwhelming; therefore, a schema is needed to grasp and organize the data.

Inductive and *deductive reasoning* draw inferences from the collected objective and subjective facts. Inductive reasoning uses collected and organized data to generalize: if the social worker asks a client how she feels about her job, her responses can be used to infer the degree of job satisfaction. The validity of an inference may be questionable. If the social worker observes a client's hand trembling and infers that the client is anxious, it may not be a valid inference. If the client does not respond to the worker's invitation to explore the anxiety, the client's "denial" may be perceived as strengthening the original assumption of anxiety. Yet the explanation could be cerebral palsy, recent physical exertion, or fever. Social workers need sufficient facts to support tentative inferences.

Deductive reasoning applies practice knowledge and research findings to a client's life situation. For example, depression is manifested by a combination of certain symptoms such as difficulty in sleeping, loss of appetite, internalized anger, low self-esteem, agitation, and feelings of helplessness and despair. If all or several symptoms are present, practitioners can reasonably infer depression. Consultation with other social workers or other mental health professionals can strengthen or eliminate the assumption in less clear situations.

In interpreting data, social workers must be careful about distortion and misinterpretation. For example, in helping immigrant clients, social workers must be particularly sensitive to the impact of culture and language. Marcos (1994, cited in Malgady & Zayas, 2001, pp. 45–46) identifies four areas susceptible to misunderstanding. First, the applicant or client's response to the social worker and to the interview might be incorrectly assessed. When people are uncertain about their ability to communicate in their second language, they might act in a guarded, self-effacing manner. The social worker should not infer from this behavior that the applicant or client is uncooperative, is withholding, and lacks self-esteem. Second, the applicant or client's motor activity may reflect a language problem rather than an underlying mental health symptom. Problems in cognitive sequencing and logic should not be confused with difficulties caused by communicating in a second language. Third, the social worker has to be careful about misinterpreting the meaning of an applicant or client's affective and emotional communications. Malgady and Zayas (2001, pp. 46) attribute to Marcos (1994) the insight that "flattened affect is common among bilingual individuals, leading clinicians to infer emotional withdrawal or inappropriate emotional reaction." Finally, the social worker has to be cautious about inferences about self-identity and self-esteem. The applicant or client may convey a completely different sense of self in his or her native language than in the secondary language.

Life-Modeled Assessment

These assessment tasks (collecting, organizing, and analyzing and synthesizing data) are common to all practice approaches. However, a few underlying beliefs are distinct to life-modeled practice. First, life-modeled practice strongly values and encourages *client participation* in the assessment tasks. Involvement ensures shared focus and direction, and supports a difference-sensitive, empowering, and ethical practice.

Second, as mentioned above, large amounts of data can overwhelm the worker; therefore, a schema is needed to grasp and organize the data. The life stressors formulation of difficult transitions and traumatic events, environmental pressures, and dysfunctional family or group relationship and communication patterns provides both a schema to organize data as well as guidelines for potential professional interventions.

Third, life-modeled practice emphasizes assessment of the *level of fit* between human needs and environmental resources. For example, Mrs. Stein, a sixty-year-old widow, has suffered a stroke. How much stress and difficulty she will experience when discharged from the hospital and confined to a wheelchair will depend on her physical condition (extent of physical loss and of stamina), inner resources (her motivation, outlook on life, and coping skills, and the meaning of the illness to her), access to organizational resources (competent medical staff, homemaker, nursing care, physical rehabilitation, and speech therapy), availability of social support networks (family, relatives, friends, and neighbors), supportive physical environment (wheelchair accessibility of building and apartment), and financial resources.

Figure 4.1 suggests the combined impact of a client's internal resources and limitations and environmental resources and limitations (Gitterman, 1991). If Mrs. Stein has strong internal and external coping resources (D), the social worker's activity might be limited to uncomplicated referrals, suggestions, and emotional support. In contrast, if Mrs. Stein has limited personal resources (cognitive impairment, chronic depression, and lack of physical strength), and limited environmental and financial resources (no children and few friends) (A), she is at serious risk for disorientation, deterioration, and disorganization. In this case, the immediate attention of an active and directive social worker with sufficient time to become a critical resource for an extended period would be called for. If Mrs. Stein has limited personal resources and strong external resources (B), it is essential to find organizational and network resources to compensate for her biopsychosocial deficits. Finally, if Mrs. Stein has strong personal but limited environmental resources (C), the social worker might help her to seek alternative resources or construct new ones. By jointly assessing the person:environment level of fit, social workers and clients can make informed decisions about focus and direction.

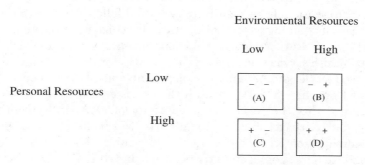

Figure 4.1 Person:Environment Fit

The amount of physiological and emotional stress suffered by Mrs. Stein will depend on her (1) inner resources (her motivation and outlook on life, coping skills, and meaning attributed to the illness), (2) family and social network (emotional and instrumental supports, geographic proximity, and motivation), (3) access to organizational resources (competent medical staff, nurses, homemakers, and physical, occupational, and speech therapists), and (4) entitlements and financial resources for achieving flexibility in the physical environment (outside ramp; wide entrance, interior doors, and corridors to accommodate the wheelchair; movable furniture; and suitable bathroom and kitchen equipment).

Finally, life-modeled practice emphasizes assessment as a *moment-to-moment* process. In the helping encounter, the worker faces an array of simultaneous issues and varied cues. At any moment, the practitioner must determine which ones to respond to, which to ignore, and which to put aside. There is little time to think about a "correct" intervention. Conceptualizing life issues and stressors as difficult life transitions and traumatic life events, environmental pressures, and dysfunctional family and group processes provides a schema for moment-to-moment assessment. To illustrate, at an early moment in the fourth session with Mrs. Stein, she complains about her loneliness and isolation. The social worker has to obtain additional data (e.g., "Can you tell me a little more?") in order to determine with Mrs. Stein whether at this particular moment she is asking for help in

exploring her grief and requesting help with mourning her loss of physical mobility and independence (seeking help with a life transition).

exploring her feeling of social isolation from her friends and family, and asking for help with reaching out to natural support systems or help in constructing new support systems (seeking help with the environment).

complaining obliquely about the worker's inattentiveness and subtly pressing for attention to their own transactions and to obstacles to communication between them (seeking help with the interpersonal).

From one moment to another, the focus may change, demanding the worker's ability to sensitively and skillfully assess and follow Mrs. Stein's cues.

A caveat: the dominance of the American Psychiatric Association's (1994) *Diagnostic and Statistical Manual of Mental Disorders*, 4th edition (DSM-IV) in mental health services poses special challenges for the life-modeled social worker. For services to be reimbursable, clients must be assigned a clinical diagnosis from the DSM-IV, which is then registered with the state. Many have claimed that the reliability and validity of DSM-IV categories are questionable (Kirk & Kutchins, 1994; Kirk, Wakefield, Hsieh, & Pottick, 1999; Kutchins & Kirk, 1987, 1988; Mattaini & Kirk, 1993; Pottick, Wakefield, & Kirk, 2003), and others have believed that a diagnostic label tends to reinforce behaviors that are associated with it (Gingerich, Kleczewski, & Kirk, 1982; Lind, 1982). During the late 1980s and 1990s, a National

Association of Social Work (NASW) chapter in California developed a Person-In-Environment (P.I.E.) Manual for describing clients' difficulties in social functioning, using the concepts and terminology of social work (Karls, Lowery, Mattaini, & Wandrei, 1997; Karls & Wandrei, 1992, 1994, 1995). The hope was that social workers could substitute this manual for the DSM-IV. However, this hope has not been actualized.

Individual Assessment

In developing an individual assessment, four areas need to be understood: (1) the *nature* of the particular life issues, (2) the *client's expectations* of the agency and worker, (3) the *client's pertinent strengths and limitations* (De Jong & Miller, 1995; Early & GlenMaye, 2000; Hurd, Moore, & Rogers, 1995; Perkins & Tice, 1995), and (4) *pertinent environmental supports and gaps.* Together, these reveal the current adaptive balance or imbalance: (5) *level of person:environment fit.* Discrepancies might arise between the client's and worker's expectations of how active or inactive, directive or nondirective, personal or impersonal, and/or spontaneous or detached each should be (Specht & Specht, 1986). Based on the examination of the data, the worker and client assess the level of fit between the stressor's demands and the personal and environmental resources for meeting them. The assessment must be difference sensitive (Congress, 1994; Hess & Howard, 1981; Rodwell & Blankebaker, 1992) and conclude with a sense of future case focus and direction. (See Appendix A for an individual case assessment—Mrs. Ross.)

Family Assessment

Helping individual family members to have their needs met by other family members and the needs of the family unit met by the external environment are the core social work functions in family work. Thus, a family assessment needs to capture the family's *distinctive patterns of communication and relationship, identifying adaptive and dysfunctional mechanisms and processes* as well as the family's *patterned transactions with its social and physical environments.* A family assessment, the Carters, is illustrated in Appendix A.

Group Assessment

In developing a group assessment, the following areas require attention: (1) *temporal arrangement, group size,* and *space* (e.g., single-session, short-term, time-limited, or open-ended); (2) *compositional balance* (homogeneity and heterogeneity, and their effect on group functioning); (3) the level of *mutuality* about focus and role expectations; (4) *interaction, friendship,* and *role patterns* (who speaks to [sits with] whom, when, and how; division of tasks; initiators and followers; instrumental and expressive roles; motivators and depressors; polarizers and compromisers; and scapegoaters and scapegoats); (5) *normative and sanctioning patterns* (a collective value system regarding rights and responsibilities; right and wrong; preferred, permitted, proscribed, and prohibited behaviors; members' explicit or implicit threats of punishment ranging from mild rebukes and teasing to more severe responses; and a system of rewards ranging from mild praise and recognition to increase in privilege and position used to enforce conformity); (6) *phases of group development* (authority and intimacy); (7) a group's *transactions with its environment* (agency, other organizations, family, and friends); and (8) *next helping steps*. (See Appendix A for an assessment of a bereavement group.)

Visual Representations

Graphic representations help our understanding by providing a visual "snapshot" of individuals', families', groups', communities', social networks', and organizations' capacities to deal with stressors and change. An *ecomap* helps us visually grasp the complexity of clients' environments and the transactions involved (Hartman, 1978; Hartman & Laird, 1983). One begins by drawing a circle to represent the client. If the client is a family, the circle is further divided into the subsystems (e.g., parent–child, marital, sibling units, or individual members). The next step is to identify the environmental elements that involve the client, and they should be pictured as circles outside the central circle. Some of these might be further broken down to show their complexities: for example, the various subsystems in the health care circle (doctor, nurse, dietitian, occupational therapist, physical therapist, and outpatient departments) or the school system (teacher, guidance counselor, principal, bus driver, and school guard). Other systems may include the extended family, the church, the welfare system, the workplace, the public utilities, and neighbors. Lines are drawn connecting the client circle to each of the other circles, and between those that communicate with one another with respect to the client's situation. Arrows at the end of each line show the directional flow of the transactions—sometimes they are reciprocal, sometimes unidirectional, and sometimes blocked (blocked transactions are depicted by broken lines). Destructive transactions are shown by cross-hatching the lines. These lines highlight the need for action to improve reciprocity and achieve positive transactions. The employing agency is portrayed with whatever specificity its own complexity requires. The completed map is enclosed in a circle that represents the client's life space (as completely as we can depict it at this time). It also represents the practitioner's unit of attention, the "case," whether neighborhood, community, family, group, or individual. Mattaini (1993a, 1993b) has attempted to quantify these exchanges and also has developed computerized approaches to simplify the visual presentation.

The ecomap shown in Figure 4.2 depicts the situation of Mr. and Mrs. Brown and their three young children. Mr. Brown is disabled. The hospital social worker is from the Department of Physical Medicine and Rehabilitation. Mr. Brown effectively transacts with various subsystems of the hospital. Mrs. Brown is seeking work but is having trouble placing her children in day care. The family is being threatened with eviction by the housing authority for nonpayment of rent. Relatives are helping to the extent possible.

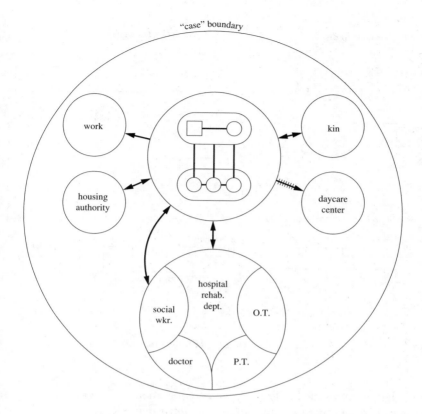

Figure 4.2 Ecomap

The *genogram* is an intervention tool developed for social work practice by Hartman (1978, 1979; Hartman & Laird, 1983). The genogram is a family tree that incorporates major family events, occupations, losses, migrations and dispersals, identifications, role assignments, alignments, and communication patterns across two or more generations (Swenson, 1979). It also brings to the foreground how family aspirations, myths, secrets, expectations, and perceptions are transmitted from one generation to another. In the illustrated example, it clarifies the impact of migration, abandonment, and the addition of new members over time and across space.

Richard and his mother have been referred to the protective services division of the Department of Children and Family Services by the school, which reported that Richard regularly comes to school with bruises on his face and limbs and is unhappy and withdrawn. Initial interviews with the mother reveal that she and Richard's father came to New York from Puerto Rico. Richard, then age three, and his brother, then age four, remained with the maternal grandparents, several youthful aunts, and an uncle. Five years

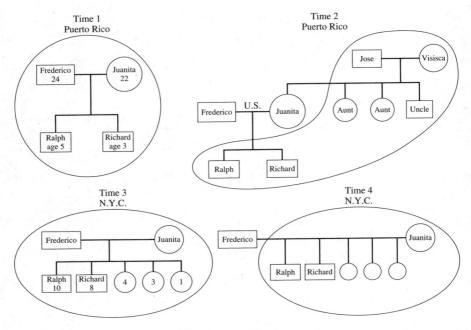

Figure 4.3 Genogram

later, the parents sent for Richard and his brother. This was the first time the boys had seen their parents since they left Puerto Rico.

They also met their three sisters for the first time. From the beginning, Richard and his father did not get along. The marital tie was weakening, and the constant strife between Richard and his father was perceived by the mother as Richard's fault and as the reason for the father's abandonment of the family. She was forced on welfare and continued to berate Richard for causing all of this. As Richard became unhappier and more difficult to control, his mother beat him more often. She told the worker she hated the boy and wanted him removed from the home. Figure 4.3 depicts the genogram.

The *social network map* examines social relationships in more detail. Mrs. Roberts and her son, John, age nine, have been living with her widowed mother, Mrs. Green, since Mrs. Roberts divorced her husband. Mr. Roberts continues to see John. Mrs. Green agreed to take care of John after school when Mrs. Roberts took a job. Conflict developed when Mrs. Roberts started returning home later than agreed because she developed new friendships at work. Mrs. Green was angry because she now has less opportunity to be with her own friends. John's schoolwork started to decline after the divorce, and recently he withdrew from his friends in school. His teacher suggested to Mrs. Roberts she take him to the local child guidance clinic. He is being seen by a social worker, and another worker sees Mrs. Roberts, but unfortunately no one is seeing the family as a whole. See Figure 4.4.

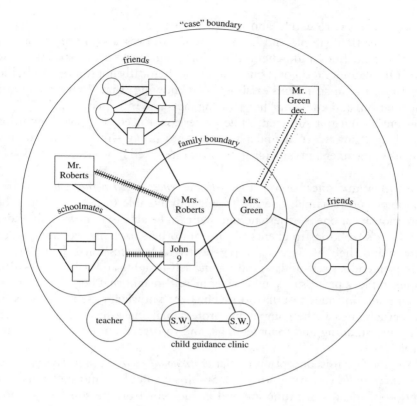

Figure 4.4   Network Map

These visual and graphic representations have various derivatives. For example, Congress (1994, p. 522) discussed the uses of "cultugrams" to assess culturally diverse families, and Hodge (2005) presented the assessment methods of "spiritual life maps," "spiritual genograms," "spiritual ecomaps," and "spiritual ecograms." The "force-field analysis" assesses organizational forces that promote and restrain a specific change effort. Instructions for constructing an organizational force-field assessment and illustrative force-field charts are provided in the text (see chapter 14).

Practice Monitoring

Monitoring Interventions

Our profession has experienced difficulty in teaching practitioners to conceptualize and monitor helping interventions. We have held on to mistaken beliefs that interfere with the acquisition of professional competence.[1] A primary misconception is that *knowledge is self-actualizing.* The connections between theory, research, and practice are complex and mutually dependent rather than simple and linear. Theory and research findings provide practice guidelines and general directions, but rarely prescriptions for action. One cannot do theory; one cannot mechanically apply a research finding. Important distinctions exist between knowing "that" (having facts and information) and knowing "how" (using facts and information). Knowledge is essential, but not sufficient. The professional needs to learn how to use knowledge, how to turn understanding into doing—into skillful actions. Clients (consumers, members) are mostly interested in what we can "do" for them.

Another misconception is that *self-awareness is self-actualizing.* To be a competent professional, one has to not only be able to use knowledge but also know what one is experiencing; that is to be able to monitor and understand one's reactions to clients (significant others, organizational representatives) and their life issues and perspectives. A professional, however, can have tremendous self-understanding and self-insights and still be unskillful. For example, a professional may have the self-insight that he or she talks too much and continues to talk too much. Like knowledge, self-insight is not self-actualizing. To be competent, professionals have to learn to use their self-understanding and their feelings, and to turn them into skillful interventions.

Yet another misconception is that *professional method can be prescribed into mechanical skills.* Learning professional skills cannot be removed from a conception of social work function and purpose or from personal styles. Prescribed and memorized skills become mechanical and dehumanize practice. For example, in learning the skill of "mirroring," the client says, "I am angry," and the worker has been taught to lean over 45 degrees and provide a mirror response, "You are angry." The client may think that she is in an echo chamber. The danger of prescriptive and mechanical skills is that the practitioner may become more interested in the technique than the client. Professionals' distinctive and creative styles must be integrated with methods and skills.

A final misconception is that *effectiveness of interventions can be evaluated solely by client outcomes.* As the profession is increasingly accountable for externally determined outcomes, clients' progress or lack of progress is attributed to the workers' skills or lack of skills (Gitterman & Miller, 1992). This represents serious means–ends confusion and negates the power of an oppressive environment, of a worker trying to be helpful and a client consciously or unconsciously deciding not to use the help from this particular worker at this particular time. In reality, a worker's behaviors may be skillful, and yet the client may not progress or may even regress. Similarly, the worker's behaviors may be unskillful, and yet the client may progress. That is why lawyers who lose a case may be justly praised for their fine work. In medicine, a surgeon may receive praise from her or his colleagues for a masterful heart surgery even though the patient died. In these instances the question is, "Was the right thing done under the circumstances given the state of the art and available options?" The outcome was beyond her or his control. Our profession tends to vacillate between a stance of impotence and one of omnipotence. The professional needs to learn to separate the behavior of helping from the behavior of using help. Certainly outcomes can be evaluated in aggregate terms. However, to credit or blame a worker for a client's (family's, group's) progress or lack of progress dismisses the critical influences of environmental supports and gaps as well as client strengths and limitations and the timing of the interventions in relation to a person's and environment's readiness to change.

The professional task is to turn knowledge and self-reflection into creative, personalized interventions. To truly monitor these interventions, they must be evaluated by how the client experiences and evaluates their connectedness to the underlying messages being conveyed rather than by what the professional intended to accomplish. In other words, the emphasis is on the client's reception of an intervention rather than the worker's intentions. For example, a worker confronts a client's denial that he is an alcoholic and defines the intervention as skillful because that was precisely his intent. This type of practice monitoring is self-justifying and leaves little room for practice improvement. However, if the worker is curious about the client's underlying message—let us say that the message is "I am not an alcoholic, but drinking is creating troubles for me"—then the worker will recognize a missed opportunity and be able to reverse the practice focus. The author has found two practice instruments, the record of service and the critical incident, extremely helpful in the monitoring of professional practice.[2]

Record of Service

The record of service traces in depth a worker's effort to help an individual, family, or group with a specific life stressor. In the record of service, a life stressor is conceptualized, the client's view of the stressor is identified, the degree of fit between client and environmental strengths and limitations for dealing with the life stressor is assessed, the specific helping interventions over time (whatever the temporal arrangement) are conceptualized and evaluated, the progress or lack of progress in the work is analyzed, and specific next steps are defined. The student or worker draws on the theoretical and research literature with respect to the particular stressor, and applies relevant concept and research findings. (A summarized sample record of service is presented in Appendix B.)

The Critical Incident

This instrument is designed to help practitioners examine in depth one incident in the course of the helping process and the transactions between client (individual, family, or group) and worker in the incident. A critical incident consists of eight to twelve consecutive transactions, beginning with client (member) response(s). Each intervention, including purposeful nonverbal gestures and silence, is italicized and numbered. A critical incident represents a microcosm of the themes in the worker's practice and, therefore, can be generalized beyond the particular incident and the particular case. The emphasis is on the practitioner's abilities to maintain a continuing process of assessment, and on relating one's interventions to the understanding of the client's manifest and latent responses. The critical incident analysis requires application of pertinent theory, knowledge, research, and practice concepts and principles, and consideration of values and ethical issues. Two sample critical incidents follow, each with slightly different emphases. The first examines analysis of individual transactions; the second presents an analysis of the total incident. Both illustrate the potential uses of a critical incident to monitor practice. (See Appendix C for summarized samples of critical incidents.)

Practice Evaluation

Practice and Research

Social work practice research and contributions to knowledge emerged from diverse traditions. In the *case study method*, the investigator tests out intervention hypotheses through detailed documentation of practice (some of the life model's intervention hypotheses have been inducted from the case study method). This research method is grounded in the processes and details of a case and captures the subtle nuances of practice. However, problems of validity and the reliability of the investigator's observations represent a critical limitation of the case study method. The case writer may not be a neutral observer, and may overclaim practice "successes." Similarly, the findings from a particular case or program, in a particular setting and culture, may be overgeneralized and inappropriately applied to other clients or programs, settings, and cultures.

Concerns about validity and reliability led investigators to study comparison groups of clients or programs. In the *group comparison method*, two groups composed of people with similar backgrounds and characteristics are established. Interventions (the independent variable) are provided to one group (the experimental group) but are withheld from the other (the control group). By measuring the differences between the groups on some outcome measure (the dependent variable), the investigator evaluates the effectiveness of the intervention on the clients in the experimental group. In one famous study, for example, the group comparison method was used to examine the treatment of depression by pharmacotherapy, interpersonal psychotherapy, and cognitive-behavioral therapy. These three experimental groups were compared to a control group that was given a placebo and some general emotional support (Elkin, Parloff, Hadley, & Autry, 1985). Validity and reliability are more effectively established in the group comparison approach than in the case study approach.

Group comparisons, however, also have significant disadvantages. In aggregated data, the interventions' effect on an individual is averaged into a group score. Thus, the individual response is lost in the aggregated data. Similarly, the impact of the environment is extremely difficult to control. A new job or a sudden loss of a relationship may have a more profound positive or negative effect than the professional intervention itself. Another disadvantage is that interventions are often defined ambiguously and not precisely specified. Moreover, when interventions are specified, they are evaluated on their own terms as if they were separate from a worker's style and persona. The art of social work practice is removed from the science of social work practice. Individual practitioner skills and the reciprocal transactions between social worker and client are often ignored. Finally, the problem of withholding treatment from those in the control group and the technical sampling problems of composing two or more similar groups raise ethical issues.

An alternative to the group comparison is the *single-case design method*. It represents a more rigorous elaboration of the case study approach and a return of focus from the group to the individual. The proponents of the single-case method have two primary objectives for practice-researchers: (1) to demonstrate empirical evidence of the effectiveness of interventions (Fisher, 1993; Ivanoff, Blythe, & Briar, 1987) and (2) to apply empirically tested interventions (Klein & Bloom, 1994). For a period of time, the single-case method became the predominant method of evaluating the effectiveness of a planned intervention. The design had much to offer the practitioner in its requirements for clarity about intervention methods and specification of client outcomes. This rigor alone often increases practice focus, discipline, and accountability. Moreover, when clients are actively involved in defining their life stressors, identifying hoped-for outcomes, and participating in the interventions, they become engaged in evaluating their own progress.

The sequence of the single-case method design consists of phase *A*, establishing a baseline measure of a person's behavior, perception, attitude, or feeling; followed by phase *B*, introducing an intervention and remeasuring the behavior, perception, attitude, or feeling (Blythe & Tripodi, 1989). The first step in evaluating a practice outcome (the dependent variable) is the collection of baseline data at various points in time prior to the introduction of the treatment intervention (the independent variable). If one collects baseline data at only one point in time, the standard may be idiosyncratic and not representative of the individual's behavioral patterns. To have confidence that the baseline is truly representative of the individual's behavioral pattern, data have to be collected at various points prior to the introduction of the helping intervention. Establishing baseline criteria is fundamental to the single-case outcome evaluation of changes in behavior (perception, attitude, feeling). At times, this complex process of remeasurement creates ethical dilemmas related to the postponement of needed services and the logistical problems of repeating baseline measurement (Barlow & Hersen, 1973). For some clients, postponing services results in an unmanageable increase in stress, or in impatience and dropping out.

Nelsen (1985, 1988) identifies four dimensions to be considered in defining the intervention: form, content, dosage, and context. Form refers to the type of communication used. Partializing (breaking up large concerns into smaller, more manageable ones), for example, reflects a type of intervention. Content refers to the message provided by the intervention. Reaching for a client's anger, for example, may communicate that the emotion of anger is acceptable and legitimate to express. How extensively and intensively interventions are repeated reflects dosage. Context refers to such factors as the client's prior experiences with professional and social agencies, the worker's reactions to the client, the degree of trust and conditions of safety established in the helping relationship, and messages communicated in voice tone and nonverbal behaviors. These four dimensions are considered in the process of developing conceptual and operational definitions of the experimental intervention. However, a natural overlap between these dimensions makes the task of developing these definitions a most difficult and challenging step for the practice-researcher.

After establishing the baseline measure and conceptualizing the intervention, one introduces the intervention and then compares the client's starting point behavior to behavior at later points in time. For example, a worker requests that a woman suffering with the symptoms of depression (e.g., difficulty sleeping and eating, internalizing anger, and expressing self-doubts) complete a self-anchored depression scale and a problem inventory at three different times. After establishing a baseline measure of her depression through the self-anchored scale and identifying the major stressor as her boyfriend through the problem inventory (phase A), the worker helps by teaching her assertiveness skills. After ten sessions, the woman completes the depression scale once again (phase B). A decrease in the depression score is suggestive of an effective and successful intervention.

The helping process, however, is rarely so linear and simple. Factors other than the treatment intervention may confound or account for the actual outcome rather than the treatment intervention (Jayarante & Levy, 1979; Nelsen, 1981). A major confounding factor, which affects internal validity, is a change in the person's environment. In reality, the practitioner-researcher has limited control over the person's social and physical environment. For example, the depressed woman's boyfriend may have been promoted in his job and, feeling better about himself, changed his behavior toward his girlfriend. This environmental change may be more responsible for her improvement than the helping intervention. Another factor is the individual's own internal development. The depressed person becomes "tired of being tired" and sets out to make changes in her life. Moreover, the treatment environment may have its own built-in confounding factors. For example, the worker's unconditional support and nurturing of the depressed person may have had more to do with the improvement in her depressive state than the assertiveness intervention. Possibly, six months later, without the therapeutic relationship, the woman might have become as or even more depressed than the initial baseline measure of her depression. Finally, while single-subject practice-researchers may effectively conceptualize and operationalize an intervention, there is a tendency not to verify its actual use (Nelson, 1985). The worker in this example may have modeled reasoning skills rather than assertiveness skills. Without the safeguard of external verification by independent observation, the specified intervention may be delivered in a manner other than intended.

To develop greater experimental controls, various adaptations of the *AB* design shown above have been developed. One such adaptation is the *ABC* design, also referred to as the "successive intervention design" (Nelson, 1988, p. 371). In the case of the depressed woman, after establishing the baseline data (phase *A*), the assertiveness intervention is evaluated after ten weeks (phase *B*). If the person makes no or limited progress, a new intervention (e.g., cognitive restructuring) is applied, and progress evaluated after ten additional weeks (phase *C*). The design can be further expanded. After establishing a new baseline, the worker introduces a new intervention (cognitive restructuring and unconditional support), and after ten additional weeks evaluates the intervention (phase *D*). While in this design external factors are not controlled, however, some impressionistic comparison of interventions might be made.

Another such adaptation is the *ABAB* design, which can be either a reversal design or a multiple baseline design. Like the *AB* and *ABC* designs, the reversal *ABAB* design begins with the establishment of baseline behavior (phase *A*) followed by the introduction of the experimental intervention and evaluation of the outcome (phase *B*). The outcome serves as the new baseline (second-phase *A*), but this time the intervention is withdrawn and, after the same period of time, the outcome of the withdrawn intervention is evaluated (second-phase *B*). If the person had improved after the original intervention was applied and regressed after it had been withdrawn, the effectiveness of the intervention is demonstrated. If the intervention can be reintroduced and the individual once again improves, there is greater confidence in the outcome. This final application actually expands the design to *ABABAB*. To illustrate, after establishing the baseline behavior of a disruptive child in a group (phase *A*), the worker for a period of five sessions uses nonverbal methods to demonstrate acceptance of the child and evaluates the child's disruptions at the end of the time period (phase *B*). After establishing the new baseline (second-phase *A*), the worker ignores the child's disruptive behavior for the next five sessions and evaluates the child's behavior at the end of this time period (second-phase *B*). Finally, after establishing the new baseline (third-phase *A*), the worker reintroduces the accepting nonverbal interventions for the next five weeks and then evaluates behavioral changes (third-phase *B*). A decrease in the youngster's disruptive group behavior followed by a regression and in-crease in disruption, and then followed by a subsequent decrease in disrup-tions, establishes the positive impact of the worker's accepting, nonverbal interventions.

While this design has greater empirical controls, the withdrawal of a po-tentially effective intervention raises serious ethical and service issues for the social worker. To remove an effective intervention from the depressed woman in our example may do her irreparable harm. Even though the re-sults might be more definitive, the human costs may be too great.

Pressure to demonstrate effectiveness of interventions may result in the selection of more motivated clients with less severe problems because they fit the design better than those less motivated for behavioral change and those economically disadvantaged. Thus the most significant problems may not be selected for outcome evaluation. In short, a finding might be statisti-cally but not clinically significant. Reagh (1994, p. 81) makes a poignant ob-servation: "Social work has gone too far in its quest to validate its existence when it forgets that clients can lose a great deal while they are 'studied' in relation to the treatment outcome."

Ecologically Sensitive Scientific Traditions

The quest for a scientific base of social work is as old as the profession itself, and continues unabated today. Epstein (1996) made a profound distinction between *research-based practice* and *practice-based research*. In search for causal relationships, research-based practice is prospective, primarily utilizing ex-perimental, random-control group designs. To rigorously test hypotheses, practice interventions must be standardized. Research requirements of stan-dardization outweigh professional considerations. In practice-based research, designs and information-gathering techniques are responsive to the realities of practice. The purpose of the research is "to answer questions that emerge from practice in ways that inform practice" (Epstein, 2001, p.17). Practice requirements outweigh research considerations.

Practice-based research approaches provide alternative methods for studying, learning, and contributing to the profession's knowledge base. Life-modeled social work practice itself is based on the *systematic examina-tion of the detailed and rich descriptions* of seasoned and student social workers' interventions over more than forty years. By reviewing audiotapes and vid-eotapes, direct observation, records of service, critical incidents, and process and summary recordings, the complexities of the transactions between per-son and environment, and between client and worker, are studied. By exam-ining this mass of information, transactional patterns and practice principles are inducted. The primary advantage of inductive case patterning is that clinical generalizations develop from "inside" and represent an "insider's" view of the helping process.

Naturalistic qualitative methods widely used in anthropology and biology are compatible with social work's client-centered traditions. In naturalistic explorations, the investigator is the major instrument of study. The social worker skilled in inviting and exploring clients' stories is a natural investigator into people's transactions with their social and physical environment (Blacher, 2005; Riessman & Quinney, 2005). By exploring, observing, and following cues, the practitioner is able to capture subtle nuances of meaning and behavior.

> The human instrument is the only instrument that can process a complex, holistic picture all at one time and be able to generate and test hypotheses immediately in the very situation in which they are created. The human instrument also has the unique capability of summarizing data on the spot and feeding them back to the respondent for clarification and explanation of any atypical or idiosyncratic responses that might have occurred. (Reagh, 1994, p. 92)

By immersing ourselves in clients' stories and environments, social workers are in a natural position to describe adaptive and dysfunctional patterns, as well as processes of change. Through detailed and rich descriptions, including direct quotes from clients and significant environmental figures, we capture the whole person within a life course and ecological perspective. The biologist Albert Szent-Gyorgyi (1967, p. 11) referred to the ecological field as the most complex and difficult to research. To study this field, "we must be in direct personal contact with it and we must use all our senses, including two outdated instruments: eyes and brains."

Constructivist researchers study *personal meanings people attribute to events in their lives.* They believe that human experience cannot be studied by standing on the outside and can only be understood as a subjective reality (Morris, 2006, p. 194). Therefore, subjective data must be gathered via people's narratives. People's narratives represent their social construction, that is, their intra- and interpersonal engagement in the world, and how they create personal meaning in their lives. Narratives are the stories people tell themselves about themselves, as well as the stories they tell others about themselves. Narratives explain how the episodes and events in peoples' lives are meaningfully linked (Arvay, 2002, pp. 207–208).

Constructivists pay special attention to ways in which their own roles in the research process affect the gathering of data. They eschew the view that "the relationship between observer and observed is a value-free interaction in which the observer gains insight from measurements of an objectified data source" and in which the "powerful researcher is unquestionably the owner of the data produced in this process" (Schlutsmeyer & Pike, 2002, p. 188). The constructivists reconstruct the three-way relationship between researcher, participant, and data as a collaborative one. The researcher is viewed as an appropriator, using the participant's artistic work to create a new artistic work (Schlutsmeyer & Pike, 2002, p. 194). In this new artistic work, the constructions of the participants must be differentiated from the construction of the researcher.

Arvay (2002) provides an illuminating illustration of investigating secondary traumatic stress experienced by female trauma therapists. The study consisted of six stages. In the first, *setting the stage*, the researcher met with all participants and discussed the research question, design, process, and respective roles and responsibilities. The objective was to develop commonality of focus and clarity of purpose, and to establish a collaborative relationship.

In the second stage, *performance*, the researcher invited participants to share their narratives about their experiences in helping people suffering with trauma. The researcher paid attention to both the individual's experiences (verbal and nonverbal expressions) and their cultural context. The researcher was "engaged at both an experiential level and a reflective level—in other words, holding dual consciousness." In this process, the researcher shared her experiences with helping trauma survivors, mutually exploring the meanings of their common experiences. The participants were "envisioned as co-investigators and co-actors in this research performance, not as respondents answering upon request, nor as informants merely imparting information." The participants and the researcher "laughed together, cried together, and struggled to understand what it all meant" (Arvay, 2002, pp. 212, 214).

In *the transcription process*, the third stage, a first rough verbatim draft was transcribed from the audiotapes, including pauses, silences, laughter and crying, and nonverbal observations from notes. A second draft separated themes within the total narrative. Subsequently, in the fourth stage, participants were asked to undertake four readings of the final transcription. They were asked to *interpret* the transcript, evaluating each of the four readings from different standpoints (the content, the self, the research question, and the relations of power and culture.) The researcher reviewed the transcription from similar perspectives. The interpretive conversation with participants was also audiotaped. "We retrospectively, collaboratively, and reflexively discussed the interpretation from the four readings, then listened and responded to each other's renderings" (Arvay, 2002, p. 217).

In the fifth stage, the researcher *wrote* in the first person the participants' *narrative* into coherent text, placing the "heart back into research" (Arvay, 2002, p. 219). *Sharing the narrative with the participants* represented the sixth and final stage. In all six stages, constructivist researchers invite and search out input from the participants. They perceive themselves to be appropriators rather than data owners.[3]

Clinical mining of available data provides yet another method for studying, learning, and contributing to the profession's knowledge base. Social workers in all fields of practice record a great deal of information about clients and their social and physical environments, the workers' professional interventions, and the clients' and environmental representatives' responses to these interventions (Cordero, 2004; Cordero & Epstein, 2005; Epstein, 2001). By and large, this valuable information is ignored in social work research. Yet, by aggregating and statistically analyzing available agency data, we can study important individual, family, group, organizational, social network, and policy practice issues. While these data are originally collected for accountability purposes, they can be "mined" for valuable retrospective studies (Auslander, Dobrof, & Epstein, 2001; Ciro & Nembhard, 2005; Mirabito, 2001; Peake, Surko, Epstein, & Medeiros, 2005; Zilberfein, Hutson, Snyder, & Epstein, 2001).

Goal attainment scaling attempts to bridge the separation of process and outcomes by monitoring clients' progress (Kiresuk, Smith, & Cardillo, 1994; Smith, 1981). Clients are involved in specifying desired outcomes and, with the worker's assistance, in developing scales to measure progress. Several studies have found that the process of involving clients in goal setting improves the treatment outcomes (Kiresuk et al., 1994, p. 3). By using self-anchored scales, clients and workers track progress in their work. The clients and worker begin by setting three to five goals, including process outcomes (e.g., participation in counseling) as well as behavioral outcomes. The goals need to be clear, specific, and stated in observable and measurable terms. They should be realistic and achievable. The goals must be formulated as an accomplishment rather than a reduction of negatives. Achievable time frames must also be specified. After the goals are established, workers and clients establish five levels of goal attainment outcome descriptors that identify progress or lack of progress toward the identified goals. The middle point (0) represents the expected outcome, while the endpoints represent the least favorable outcome (−2) and the most favorable outcome (+2).[4]

The use of goal attainment scaling is illustrated in the James family. Mr. James and Mrs. James have serious difficulties in providing sufficient structure and limits for their four children, Jack (age thirteen), Jillian (ten), Edna (eight), and Debra (four). The Jameses provide contradictory and inconsistent directions, and are unrealistic about what children at different ages are capable of doing. Discipline vacillated from parental withdrawal to corporal punishment. Chaos and conflict have become a daily family occurrence, and the children were increasingly acting out in the home, school, and community. The school personnel became increasingly concerned and contacted the Department of Children's and Families Services. Mr. James was indicated for child abuse, and the family was referred for mandatory counseling to a community mental health center. After meeting with the James family for three weeks, a set of goals, with eight-, twelve-, and eighteen-week time frames and outcome measures, was jointly developed. Table 4.1 depicts the James Family Goal Attainment Scaling.

Mr. and Mrs. James were also referred to a parents' support group. To further illustrate goal attainment scaling, Mr. James's group attainment goals are specified in Table 4.2.

By monitoring their own progress in counseling, clients are empowered to own the focus and direction of their work. The responsibility for change is in their hands, and they are self-accountable. Doable potential outcomes make life's difficulties seem more manageable and give clients hope that

Table 4.1
The James Family Goal Attainment Scale

Outcome Goals	1. All family members will participate in and complete counseling (12 sessions, one time per week).	2. Parents will learn and apply alternative methods of discipline.	3. Parents will develop more realistic expectations of children.	4. Parents will learn to act together as a team in the parenting role.	5. Children will become more responsible regarding household chores.
Levels of Goal Attainment					
−2 Least Favorable Outcome	Family drops out of counseling after a few sessions.	Parents are reported again for child abuse.	Parents continue to make age-inappropriate demands on children.	Parents continue to give opposing orders. Father continues to undermine mother's authority.	Children continue to fight with parents when asked to do assigned tasks—refuse to carry out jobs.
−1	Family misses 50% of appointments and fails to call to cancel.	Parents recognize need but are unable to apply alternative techniques.	Parents are open to learning about child development but are unable to apply concepts.	Parents recognize and discuss problems. They plan new behavior but are unable to follow through.	Children carry out tasks with consistent reminding and some back talk.

0 Expected Outcome	Family keeps over two-thirds of planned appointments and calls ahead to cancel.	Parents learn and apply two new behavior management techniques, such as time out and limit setting, with some consistency.	Parents read one book on child development and discuss its relevance to their own expectations.	Parents actively work on problem. Father checks with mother fairly consistently before giving directives. Mother is sometimes able to assert herself.	Children carry out assigned tasks with one reminder and no grumbling.
+1	Family misses less than one-third of scheduled appointments and always calls to reschedule.	Parents learn and apply several new behavior management techniques in a variety of situations.	Parents actively try to apply new learning regarding child development in daily interaction with their children.	Parents discuss how to handle children most of the time.	Children carry out assigned tasks with no reminding and no grumbling.
+2 Most Favorable Outcome	All family members attend all scheduled appointments.	Parents are consistent in applying new behavior management techniques in all situations.	Parents' expectations of children are entirely consistent with their developmental capacities.	Parents are consistent in their approach to childrearing and they work as a team.	Children do extra tasks in addition to assigned tasks without being asked.

Table 4.2
Mr. James's Group Goal Attainment Scale

Outcome Goals	1. Client will recognize and act on need for change in parenting behavior knowledge.	2. Client will learn and apply more effective and non-abusive methods of child discipline.	3. Client will develop developmentally appropriate expectations of children.	4. Client will develop a more effective and nurturing communication style with children.	5. Client will use group members as a support network.
Levels of Goal Attainment					
−2 Least Favorable Outcome	Does not accept need for change. Refuses to attend group meetings.	Uses inappropriate and/or abusive methods of discipline. Refuses to consider alternatives.	Continues to make age-inappropriate demands. Refuses to alter expectations.	Makes blaming or insulting comments to children—unable to consider children's view.	Negative or no response to problems expressed by other group members.
−1	Verbalizes need for change but attends group inconsistently and does not participate when present.	Listens to but usually rejects suggestions of alternatives: "Yes, but . . .".	Verbalizes openness to learning about child development but unable to apply new concepts to own situation.	Verbalizes recognition of need for better communication but does not alter behavior.	Gives verbal support to others in group.

0 Expected Outcome	Attends group and participates most of the time; avoids confronting an issue and/or unable to respond to others appropriately.	Listens and responds positively to suggestions of alternative methods, but unable to carry through in action.	Able to discuss relevance of child development concepts to own situation.	Demonstrates recognition of need for better communication by trying new methods, although inconsistent and unskilled.	Makes self available by telephone to other parents in crisis.
+1	Attends group consistently and participates actively. Beginning self-awareness; occasionally able to give and/or receive help.	Listens and responds positively to alternatives. Able to try new methods and report results.	Actively tries to apply child development concepts in interaction with own children.	Demonstrates knowledge by reporting incidents of active listening and appropriate responses to children.	Calls another parent to help when experiencing a crisis.
+2 Most Favorable Outcome	Participates in group regularly and actively; able to give and accept help; demonstrates self-awareness and insight.	Accepts and gives suggestions on alternative methods of discipline. Consistently applies new methods at home.	Expectations and behavior are consistent with the developmental capacities of participant's children.	Express feelings about children's misbehavior in a nonblaming manner—consistently uses active listening and responds appropriately.	Shares outings with other parents and children.

situations can change. Experiencing progress motivates and mobilizes energy for further work. For the worker, goal attainment scaling provides similar advantages. The clients' troubles seem less overwhelming, there is greater mutuality of case focus and direction, and they are building on successes rather than being demoralized by case failures.

To further develop the process method of empirical inquiry, some social work practice scholars attempt to *relate helping processes to differential client outcomes.* Shulman (1978) initially investigated the association between twenty-two skills with the development of a positive relationship and client perception of worker helpfulness. Later, Shulman (1981) developed a category observation system for systematizing observations of interactions between workers and clients. In this early research, he examined the clients' perceptions of the helping process in an entire agency at one point in time. In a subsequent study, a number of "hard" outcomes (such as maintaining children at home rather than in foster care, or court status) were added to client and worker subjective impressions about the helping process (Shulman, 1991). Shulman found that the professional skills of helping clients to manage their feelings showed a direct and strong path to caring. In turn, caring suggested a causal path to court status and the number of days a child spends in foster care.

Naturalistic inquiry is life oriented and is directed to context as well as people.

PART TWO

THE HELPING PROCESS IN LIFE-MODELED PRACTICE

Like life itself, life-modeled practice is phasic. Four phases, preparatory, initial, ongoing, and ending, constitute the processes and operations of the practice. These processes ebb and flow in response to the interplay of personal and environmental forces. While the phases are separated in order to organize our presentation, they are not always distinct in actual practice.

Chapter 5 examines the professional processes of skillfully entering people's lives. Beginning a professional relationship requires careful preparation in order to create a supportive environment. People must feel safe and accepted before they can trust and confide in a professional. Chapter 6 focuses on the actual beginnings in practice. All helping efforts rest upon shared definitions about concerns, needs, and explicit agreement about goals, tasks, and reciprocal roles.

The ongoing phase is ushered in by the joint recognition that client and worker have reached a shared, possibly tentative, understanding of the nature of the stressor(s) and its amelioration. In the ongoing phase, the professional purpose is to help people effectively cope with the biological, social, emotional, cognitive, and behavioral demands posed by life transitions and traumatic events and to influence the social and physical environments. Effective help requires attention to (1) painful life transitions and traumatic life events, (2) associated environmental stressors, and (3) dysfunctional interpersonal processes. An interpersonal focus applies when the social worker is involved with a family or group system or with issues between the worker and client. If a social worker, for example, is working with an abused woman, but not with the partner, the focus is on life transitional concerns (e.g., separation or grief) or environmental concerns (e.g., linkage with community resources, negotiating with her partner, or securing a court order of protection). By contrast, a focus on dysfunctional interpersonal communication and relationship patterns requires conjoint work with both partners and/or the children.

The reader will see in the bereavement group presented in chapter 7 that the worker and members had to work simultaneously on the traumatic life event and the interpersonal tensions that erupted in the group, while at the same time constructing a safe social environment that could support the painful grief work. For purposes of discussion, however, we believe that considering the three arenas of practice in separate chapters yields greater clarity. We ask the reader to remember that actual practice is not as separated as our presentation might seem to imply.

Ending a professional relationship also requires careful preparation to deal with the feelings aroused by the ending; a review of what has been accomplished and what has yet to be achieved; planning for the future, including, where indicated, transfer to another worker or referral to another agency; and evaluation of the service that was provided. Like the initial and ongoing phases of helping, the ending phase requires sensitivity, knowledge, careful planning, and a range of skills on the part of the social worker.

PREPARATION

Settings, Modalities, Methods, and Skills

Initiating a professional relationship with another person requires careful preparation, ready compassion, and professional skills burnished by creativity.

Creating an Accepting and Supportive Service Environment

Anticipatory Empathy

The worker creates an accepting and supportive service environment by demonstrating empathy—the capacity to get "inside" another person's life and to experience how the person is feeling and thinking. To convey empathy, the practitioner begins by examining available data.

For example, a hospital social worker receives a referral from a nurse of a sixty-year-old, unmarried, African American patient who had spent her working life as a domestic. She had been admitted to the hospital a month earlier for a severe circulatory disorder related to chronic diabetes. Her gangrenous foot was amputated; shortly thereafter, a further amputation of the leg to the knee was performed. The patient refuses to talk or to follow medical orders, and is regarded as a management problem. The worker reflects on this information. She considers the assault of losing a limb, piece by piece. She thinks about the impact of age and age-specific tasks related to the loss of work and financial independence looming ahead. She wonders how the surgery was explained to her, what social supports she can call on, and what discharge options are available to her. She reflects on the fact that the patient is African American while the physicians, nurses, and social workers are white. And she considers the culture of the particular ward, including the staff's tolerance of difficult behavior.

Essential to this preparation was her viewing the world from the patient's probable perception of reality and the meaning she might attribute to her current situation. A social worker's struggle to achieve empathic feeling and thinking within another's frame of reference is an ongoing one (Raines, 1990). The process of anticipatory empathy aids achieving this level of empathic understanding. The four steps in anticipatory empathy are (1) *identification*, through which the social worker experiences what the client is feeling and thinking; (2) *incorporation*, through which the worker feels the experiences as if they were personal; (3) *reverberation*, through which the worker tries to call up personal life experiences that may facilitate understanding those of the client; and (4) *detachment*, through which the worker engages in logical, objective analysis (Lide, 1966).

Some social workers might find it difficult to identify with life circumstances such as poverty, grave injury, racism, homophobia, or job loss if they have not themselves experienced such conditions. They can evoke parallel memories of their own—for example, the worker's childhood memory of a parental divorce can parallel to some degree the client's mourning the death of a loved one. However, this can also lead social workers to project their own emotions and thoughts onto the client. Social workers must move "inside" another's experience *as if* it were their own, but "without losing the 'as if' quality" (Rogers, 1961, p. 284). They must also anticipate their own characteristic patterns of handling certain situations and life issues. Detachment permits a pulling back and reestablishment of a more objective view of the client's situation. Detachment takes into account the tentative assessment of available information, knowledge, and empathy.

A student assigned to a former client returning to the agency for help with several life issues began by reviewing the case folder:

After reading the folder, I had misgivings about working with Mrs. Stein. Early entries portrayed her as a physical and emotional invalid: cerebral palsy, chronic paranoid schizophrenia, legal blindness, mental retardation, and placement as a foster child. As I read, I became emotionally removed, hiding my fears in diagnostic speculations. Then I allowed myself to become curious about the person rather than the labels. This time her life story as a human being unfolded. I found myself feeling her feelings of being overwhelmed, alone, and scared. I sensed her inner strength and her capacity to endure despite numerous traumas. I pictured her sitting next to me, and I wondered what she would be like and how she would react to me. If I were she, I would be curious about why I was getting a new worker. She might feel that the change of workers was her fault, a reflection of her unworthiness. She might be angry and upset about beginning anew with another social worker. At the same time she might be curious about me and hopeful that I could help. As I anticipated her possible reactions, several opening statements occurred to me: explaining why I was assigned to her, eliciting her understanding of why the other worker left, listening for her feelings about starting with someone new, sharing what I know about her situation, and inviting her to bring me on board her current situation.

The student's sensitive preparation increased the possibility of engagement and decreased the possibility of provocative, prolonged testing of the worker; nonverbal expressions of anxiety; unresponsiveness; or the client's failure to return.

Another student described how she prepared to meet with Mr. Sachs, whose wife was terminally ill with cancer.

In preparing for the first session, I considered how to introduce likely issues that might be of concern to Mr. Sachs. I also tried to anticipate his reactions. The interview itself confirmed my anticipation. However, I stopped short of dealing with his wife's approaching death, and failed to invite discussion in this area. At the time, I was aware of what I was doing; yet I continued to avoid the painful topic, thus undermining my intention to help. In preparing for my interview and Mr. Sachs's possible reactions to his wife's death, I had not included my own reactions. I "forgot" to consider how the loss of a loved one would make me feel.

Practitioners' preparation for understanding clients' life issues and feelings needs to be flexible, individualized, and multidimensional. At the same time, workers must be careful that the anticipatory preparation does not become a rigid script. Effective empathy always remains open to additional data and impressions, and avoids stereotypes and preconceptions.

Cohort history can also play a part in anticipatory empathy. For example, a school social worker plans to reach out to seriously troubled, thirteen-year-old Laura, who is repeating the sixth grade because of extensive truancy. Laura, her eleven-year-old brother, and their alcoholic, diabetic mother are on welfare. They share a bedroom in a small, dilapidated, dirty, three-bedroom house in a dangerous and impoverished neighborhood. Also living in the household are a cousin, her boyfriend, and her two children, ages twelve and thirteen. Interfamily conflict is continuous. Laura and her sixteen-year-old boyfriend spend much time together, but she denies sexual involvement. Laura's parents were divorced when she was five years old. Her father remarried and now has two young children. Laura occasionally visits her father and his family.

As the social worker prepares to meet with Laura, she considers cohort history. Laura and her cohort grew up in the 1990s, a decade in which the poor became poorer. These children arrived at puberty and adolescence in the 1990s, when drugs and guns were devastating the United States. Divorced parents, blended families, and solo-parent families are also a reality for these young people. We need to be sensitive to (1) what it meant to Laura to grow up poor in a decade when greed and wealth were glorified; (2) the reality of illicit drugs and alcohol as part of Laura's life, peer pressures involved in their use and in early promiscuity, and pervasive fears in living in a dangerous neighborhood; and (3) the possible influences of the several differing family forms in her home. By locating Laura in the context of a historical cohort, the worker gains greater empathy for her life issues.

The authors realize that with the large caseloads, enormous paperwork, and intense time pressures associated with contemporary practice, social workers have hardly any time to catch their breath and rarely enough time to go through the steps of anticipatory empathy. We ask you to do the best you can—that even a few seconds of preparation is better than none. Moreover, these steps can also be used at any and every moment in the interview itself. With practice, like in driving a car, the steps become automatic and integrated with personal style.

Demonstrating Empathy

Cognitive understanding and anticipatory empathy are important in the creation of a supportive, accepting service environment. However, the most significant task remains to demonstrate understanding and empathy in the sessions with the applicant or client. The social worker must communicate attitudes of caring and being emotionally "with" the person. Social workers convey interest, curiosity, concern, and caring through numerous nonverbal and verbal behaviors. Nonverbal skills are presented in this section; verbal skills are presented in later sections and chapters.

Nondefensiveness and self-exploration manifested by clients are directly related to high levels of practitioner empathy (Duehn & Proctor, 1977; Håkansson, 2006; Håkansson & Montgomery, 2002, 2003; Truax & Carkhoff, 1967). The more vulnerable and anxious applicants or clients feel in the early sessions, the more necessary is the worker's immediate demonstration of interest, concern, and caring.

Practitioners must always take account of physical, developmental, and cultural influences—and their own biases—in order to avoid misinterpreting nonverbal behaviors (Arkin, 1999; Dyche & Zayas, 2001). Most people are initially reluctant to express thoughts and feelings directly to a stranger, even a professional. Empathic practitioners note significant shifts and changes in nonverbal behaviors that might reflect intense discomfort (eye contact, posture, gestures, facial expressions, physical reactions, and changes in vocal qualities). For example, when a social work intern probed the recent murder of a client's husband, she observed the client's sudden rigid body posture, uncontrolled perspiration, frequent body shifts, and increase in voice volume and pitch. All these behaviors indicated intense discomfort.

The worker uses *posture, gestures, and facial expressions* to show attentiveness, and *maintains eye contact* during discussion of tabooed or painful material. In such moments, the social worker can comment on the painfulness of the material and ask clients if they prefer exploring the difficult area later. This is done without directing attention to a particular behavior, which might intensify the client's self-consciousness.

The worker observes and listens for *discrepancies between nonverbal and verbal behavior*, and between the *manner of speaking and the verbal content*. Observing an applicant or client smiling while her body is rigid, or asserting she is not upset or angry in an agitated tone of voice, suggests that she has not grasped or fully processed her emotional reactions. In a first session, the worker might demonstrate empathy by supportive verbal and nonverbal means rather than by directly confronting the discrepancies. However, commenting on discrepancies is usually necessary and helpful in later sessions. Generally, social workers tend to make more mistakes of omission than of commission. In beginnings, we encourage practitioners to make the active mistakes on the empathic side and be more cautious on the confrontational side. Timing is an essential practice element.

An important professional nonverbal behavior is *touching*. Shaking hands, guiding the client to the office by the elbow, patting a child, and touching a hand during a crisis or an emotional upset are nonverbal demonstrations of empathy (Edgette, 1999). Touching also has different meanings in different cultures. The worker must be cautious that an applicant or client does not confuse warmth with sexual interest, or perceive it as a threat.

Empathy is also demonstrated by the social worker's *manner of speaking*. A soft and gentle tone can show caring and sadness for client pain; a louder and animated tone can suggest pleasure in client accomplishment. A bland tone conveys indifference. Language that is forced, unnatural, or pitched above or below the client's level increases distance between client and worker. The social worker must speak directly, clearly, and without jargon.

And finally, empathic practitioners create a *welcoming atmosphere* in their offices by adding plants and pictures and providing alternative seating arrangements. They are also careful to assure *uninterrupted time* for sessions by minimizing telephone calls and other interruptions. Table 5.1 summarizes anticipatory empathy skills and nonverbal skills used to demonstrate empathy.

Forming a Group

Developing anticipatory empathy and demonstrating empathy are essential to practice with all modalities. The tasks and skills of forming a group are distinctive to the group modality.

Table 5.1
Skills of Anticipatory Empathy and Demonstrating Empathy Nonverbally

- Examine available data.
- Understand the person's perception of reality through identification, incorporation, reverberation, and detachment.
- Respond to nonverbal cues and manner of speech.
- Observe discrepancies between nonverbal and verbal behavior, and between manner of speech and content.
- Demonstrate interest and concern through responsive body postures, facial expressions, and hand gestures.
- Welcome the applicant or client by attractively and comfortably setting up one's office.
- Provide uninterrupted meeting time.
- Use a responsive tone of voice.
- Speak directly, clearly, and without jargon.

Group Purpose

In preparing to form a group, the worker has to develop certain specialized skills such as *clarity about the group's purpose*.[1] A group has to evolve from a common need, concern, and/or interest around which prospective members are brought together. The commonality is essential to the development of mutual aid. Mutual aid is more likely to evolve in a group where members need each other to deal with common needs, concerns, and/or interests. In preparing, the social worker rehearses a statement about potential group purpose, translating commonality into specific operational tasks (Gitterman, 2005; Kurland & Salmon, 1998; Wright, 1999). The life model's three interrelated stressors (life transitions and traumatic events, environmental pressures, and interpersonal processes) can be used to formulate group purpose.

Groups with a *life transitional* focus are formed to help people with developmental issues over the life cycle, such as adolescents dealing with issues of sexuality, ethnic identity, and independence versus dependence (Irizarry & Appel, 2005; Jagendorf & Malekoff, 2000; Levinsky & McAleer, 2005; Malekoff, 1994, 2004). Physiological, cognitive, and emotional impairments complicate the accomplishment of developmental tasks (Bloch, Weinstein, & Seitz, 2005; Garvin, 1992; Lynn & Nisivoccia, 1995). A group experience for learning, emotionally, developmentally, and/or physically disabled adolescents and adults can be formed to help members to deal with their common and distinctive life struggles.

Groups can be formed to help people with stressful life changes such as school transitions, marriage and parenthood, divorce, retirement, immigration, and bereavement (Knight, 2005b). Some transitions may come too early in life, such as adolescent pregnancy. Others may come too late in life, such as elderly people carrying primary responsibility for childrearing. Helping people with organizational transitions such as agency admissions and discharge provides yet another potential focus for groups (Hanson, 1998).

Groups can also be formed to help people who are burdened by stigmatized life statuses such as a prostitute, drug addict, alcoholic, mentally ill person, homeless person, sexually abused child, or person with AIDS (Efron & Moir, 1996; Getzel, 2005; Getzel & Mahony, 1993; Hardman, 1997; Lee, 2005). Moreover, some people carry the burden of dually stigmatized social statuses such as homosexuality and HIV/AIDS, and drug abuse and mental illness (Shulman, 2005). These people are at double jeopardy, and groups can be formed to help deal with life's pressures (Kelly, 2005).

Traumatic events represent complex life transitions. People may confront various traumas: before or after surgery (e.g., cardiac surgery or a mastectomy), physical assaults (amputation, sexual abuse, rape, or homicide), or the sudden and unexpected loss of a loved one (a child, spouse, or parent). When a sudden, unexpected, overwhelming loss occurs (or is about to occur), the victim or survivor and relatives urgently need emotional and instrumental support from significant others. Group services can provide those "significant others" to help cope with the overwhelming stress (Hack, Osachuk, & De Luca, 1994; Knight, 2005a; Reid, Mathews, & Liss, 1995; Schiller & Zimmer, 2005; Stokes & Gillis, 1995).

Social and physical environments are a major source of stress, and groups can be formed with an environmental focus. A group formed to help with life transitional issues may also need to deal with external organizational concerns. Parents of developmentally disabled children, for example, can help each other with childrearing concerns. However, they may also need to work on the lack of community resources and deal with the unresponsiveness of organizational representatives. Similarly, a group formed for life transitional issues may also need to deal with intraorganizational obstacles including the agency's structure (for example, lack of evening hours) or the quality of services (such as institutional food) (Berman-Rossi, 2005).

Group services may be also formed explicitly to deal with internal and/or external organizational issues. Thus, groups may be formed to involve consumers more fully within the agency's planning and decision-making structures. A planning committee, an advisory group, or a leadership council fulfills important functions for both members and agencies (Ephross & Vassil, 2005). Social workers also can organize groups with a social action focus to help consumers negotiate organizational structures and services (such as welfare rights and tenants' associations). These services enable people to gain greater control and mastery over their environments (Cohen & Mullender, 1999; Lee, 2005). Unfortunately, many agencies underestimate the therapeutic value of attention to environmental concerns and do not offer such group services. However, for people to act upon their environment and to develop social and emotional connections is, in fact, most therapeutic.

Natural units such as families, patients on wards, students in classrooms, roommates in hospitals or dormitories, and residential cottages may experience relational and communication problems (Miller & Donner, 2000). These units may develop interpersonal stress from dysfunctional communication and relationship patterns that promote scapegoating, factions, or mutual withdrawal. In a residential cottage, for example, children may experience difficulties in living, working, and communicating together (Nadelman, 2005). A social worker can intervene within the natural unit (e.g., the cottage, the classroom, or the hospital ward) and identify and challenge the dysfunctional patterns and facilitate communication. Beyond intervening in natural units, workers form groups with an explicit interpersonal focus. Couples and multifamily groups, for example, provide a natural modality to examine and work on relational and communication patterns.

Life transitional, environmental, and interpersonal stressors emphasize natural life processes around which people at risk, in need, or with common interests may be clustered. Clarity of commonality increases the likelihood of engaging members' motivation and strengths in the mutual aid and problem-solving processes.

Group Types

After formulating the group's purpose that will be presented to potential group members, the social worker considers the type of group from which members will most likely benefit. Five different types of groups allow for mutual aid (Gitterman, 2005; Toseland & Rivas, 2005; Wayne & Cohen, 2001). Groups can be formed with an (1) educational, (2) common stressor–solving, (3) specific behavioral change, (4) task, and (5) social development focus. In a group with an *educational* focus, participants acquire relevant knowledge and information, such as coping with a schizophrenic child, dealing with diabetes, practicing safer sex, and preparing for surgery (Kuechler, 1997). In these groups, the worker must find a balance between presentation and discussion in which members have an opportunity to process and help each other use the information. In the current emphases on prescribed curricula and protocols, the potential for mutual aid too often remains unrealized.

In a group with a *common stressor–solving* focus, members help each other with common life transitional, environmental, or interpersonal concerns, such as raising a developmentally challenged child, coping with divorce, dealing with the death of a parent, or confronting spousal abuse (Irizarry & Appel, 2005; Knight, 2005b; Lee, 2005; Nadelman, 2005; Orr, 2005; Schiller & Zimmer, 2005; Trimble, 2005). In these groups, the social worker must pay equal attention to helping the group develop a mutual aid system as well as, at the same time, to the needs of each individual member. To focus only on one or the other limits the capacity of members to help each other and to receive help for themselves.

In a group with a focus on *specific behavioral change*, the group serves as a context for individual change, such as eating disorders, substance abuse, phobias, and anger management (Patrick & Rich, 2004; Smith, Smith, &

Beckner, 1994; Straussner, 1998). In this type of group, the worker faces the challenge of helping with individual problems without turning the experience into doing casework in a group (Kurland & Salmon, 1992). Adolescents often resist these types of groups because the problem is lodged within them.

In a group with a *task* focus, members help one another to complete pre-scribed objectives, such as planning and advisory committees, social action groups, and ad hoc task forces (Gummer, 1995; Speer & Zippay, 2005). In these groups, the worker must pay equal attention to the identified tasks as well as, at the same time, to the interpersonal group processes. To focus on task accomplishment over process or process over task limits the full potential of the group experience.

Finally, in a group with a *social development focus*, members learn the interactive skills of making friends and building emotional and social connections, such as in a regressed schizophrenics' coffee club, a widows' or widowers' group, a men's cardiac club, isolated elderly adults, or an elderly music reminiscence group (Cusicanqui & Salmon, 2004; Hartford & Lawton, 1997; Lynn & Nisivoccia, 1995; Schopler, Galinsky, & Abell, 1997). The worker's task is to integrate having fun, doing activities, and helping with developmental life tasks and issues.

The social worker selects the type of group that most fits the prospective members' expectations and comfort. For example, a worker the author supervised formed a group for parents of developmentally challenged children to develop community resources for their children. Although members enthusiastically agreed to the offer of service, they did not invest energy into the work or follow through on agreed upon tasks. After a few weeks, the worker reached for the obstacle and learned that the members wanted to share their concerns about having a developmentally challenged child; they wanted an opportunity to ventilate their frustration about the child and lack of social supports, and to help each other with childrearing. While the worker had proposed a task group, members desired a group that focused on common life issues and stressors. The reverse just as easily could have happened. The suggested principle is that whatever type of group is selected, the social worker has to be *flexible and responsive to renegotiation*.

The process of renegotiation includes acquiring agency sanction and support for the proposed changes in the group's focus. The social worker pays attention to both group member needs as well as agency expectations. The worker's consistent focus is on finding and nurturing the common ground between the agency and group members.

Group Composition

Group composition is yet another specialized group formation task. Generally, groups composed of members with common backgrounds (age, sex, ethnicity, and social class) and common personality capacities and behaviors (in ego functioning, role skills, and authority and intimacy orientation) tend to be stable and supportive, and quickly develop a group identity and esprit de corps. Similar backgrounds provide members with a sense of commonality. These commonalities create a sense of immediate comfort. However, when members are too alike, their "likeness" may reinforce dysfunctional patterns. Thus, a gang may support antisocial and delinquent behavior, a depressed patients' group may exacerbate hopelessness and despair, or a court-mandated group of substance abusers or batterers might reinforce minimization and denial. Excessively homogeneous groups limit the diversity and vitality essential to challenge the status quo, to create the necessary tension for change, and to provide models for alternative attitudes and behaviors.

Groups composed of members with diverse backgrounds (age, sex, ethnicity, and social class) and diverse personality capacities and behaviors (that is, in ego functioning, role skills, and authority and intimacy orientation) tend to be less stable and less predictable. Members may experience difficulty in developing a sense of group identity and cohesion. Differing backgrounds may create internal obstacles to achieving a common agenda and open communication. Members may be too different, and their differences may become the central issue rather than the group purpose and tasks. The author, for example, formed a racially balanced group of youngsters with school difficulties. The youngsters focused on the racial differences with factionalism and scapegoating rather than on their school difficulties. These internal barriers inhibited the group from working on its purpose. However, if a social worker can help members to overcome their differences, they have the potential to have a dramatic impact on each other. The inner diversity provides vital and rich resources for members to draw upon.

Ideally, groups require both stability (homogeneity) and diversity (heterogeneity). At the very least, prospective members need to have common concerns and interests—a commonality of purpose. Once the common purpose has been identified, the social worker considers the desired range of commonness or difference on important background and personality factors. In developing a group service for pregnant adolescents, for example, the social worker considers the relative advantages of commonality or difference for such other factors as first pregnancy, stage of pregnancy, plans for baby, religion, ethnicity, parental and boyfriend relationships, health, and geographic location.

Generally, members tolerate and use greater diversity when common interests and concerns are experienced intensively. Thus, for example, the author organized a group of women with limited life expectancy due to advanced breast cancer. Group members were quite diverse in their backgrounds. While their differences in age, class, and stage of the life course introduced very important differences for each of them (e.g., dying with young children was different than dying with grown children), their profound commonality of breast cancer made the differences in age, class, and ethnicity seem inconsequential. In contrast, in the racially balanced school group, members experienced the need for the group service much less intensely. Thus, the less the members perceive common concerns and interests, the more homogeneously composed groups have a better prognosis.

The social worker should be particularly careful not to isolate a member on important background or personality factors such as a "butterfly chaser" would be in a group of athletic youngsters. This youngster is likely to be either scapegoated or isolated. Because group composition plays such a significant role in a group's life, the worker must assume responsibility for group composition. Relinquishing this responsibility to someone else, for example, a teacher in a secondary setting, may result in a group of only acting-out children, or, if to a nurse, a group composed of diabetics with severely mixed symptomatology (i.e., early diagnosis and late amputation stages). Such combinations do not encourage mutual support and end in conflict, despair, or both. To avoid potential isolation and alienation, each member should have at least one other member in regard to factors assessed to be important. Yalom and Leszcz (2005) refer to this compositional guideline as the "Noah's Ark Principle."

Temporal Arrangement, Group Size, and Physical Setting

The final tasks in forming a group are to consider the temporal arrangement, the group's size, and the physical setting for the group. Group purpose, type of group, and organizational context influence the group's temporal arrangement. Most groups are planned for the short term. The time boundary helps members focus quickly and maintain purpose, direction, and a sense of urgency. For certain populations, a time limit is imperative. The previously mentioned group of cancer patients with a limited life expectancy would have been devastated by a gradual loss of membership, even if new members had been substituted. Thus, a one-session orientation group (Kosoff, 2003), a two-session postsurgical group, a four-session adoptive parents group, an eight-session couples group, or a twelve-session group of foster care adolescents provides the essential time boundary. In some situations, as the group nears completion and evaluates its progress, members and worker may decide to recontract another cycle or for a specific number of additional sessions.

All the principles of planned short-term services are utilized in time-limited (six- to twelve-month) group services. The worker, for example, clearly identifies the ending date in the first session. Certain settings such as schools have a natural time calendar in the academic year to take stock. For example, Christmas/Hanukkah, Easter/Passover, winter/spring breaks, and the end of school are either natural time breaks to end the group service or benchmarks to evaluate progress and determine if additional time is needed.

Long-term and open-ended group services in which departing members are replaced by new members best serve members with chronic, intractable personal and environmental stressors. For example, chronically mentally and developmentally challenged members benefit from the continuous instrumental and emotional support provided by long-term groups. These group members need much more help than short-term services can provide. The open-ended groups, however, do have two chronic problems: (1) the ongoing, long-term nature may lead worker and members to lose their original sense of purpose and vitality; and (2) the shifts in membership result in the group's inability to move beyond an early stage of group development (Galinsky & Schopler, 1985, 1989; Schopler & Galinsky, 1984). To minimize disruptive membership shifts, the worker, to the extent possible, attempts to control group entrances and exits. If only one new member joins a group, the group is able to incorporate the new member into its current phase of development. In contrast, the arrival and departure of a few members require the group to slow its processes and return to beginning group issues.

The worker needs to process with departing, new, and ongoing group members the departure of old and addition of new members. Group members need to be involved in the change process rather than experience it as arbitrary and out of their control.

Other time considerations are the frequency and duration of sessions. Frequency and duration of sessions should be structured and arranged in ways that are responsive to the special needs of the population being served. For example, in providing group services to young children in schools, the author discovered that weekly sessions for an hour were insufficient. During the interval between sessions, the youngsters confronted various school and family crises, and the group was unavailable for assistance. Consequently, the worker restructured meetings for greater frequency (twice or three times weekly) and for shorter duration (thirty minutes). This time change made a dramatic impact upon both the substance and intensity of our work. Generally, children and mentally impaired adults are responsive to more frequent and shorter sessions, while well-functioning adolescents and adults are responsive to weekly and longer sessions (one and a half to two hours). In medical settings, physical discomfort and pain make sessions of shorter duration necessary. Essentially, the worker must creatively structure time by taking into account group members' developmental stages and special population attributes and their effect on attention span and capacity for session-to-session carryover.

The worker also has to consider the potential consequences of the scheduled time for the meetings (Steinberg, 1999). Some members may only be able to attend meetings in the daytime because their children are in school or because of safety concerns. Others, due to employment and other reasons, may be only able to attend during evening hours. To the extent possible, involving potential group members in identifying the most and least preferable times for scheduling group meetings increases the likelihood of their participation.

Appropriate group size is related to group purpose. Generally, large groups (more than fifteen members) by necessity become formalized through establishing rules and procedures and possibly electing officers. Communication tends to be channeled through the formal or indigenous leader, with limited opportunity for individual attention, accessibility to the worker, and intimate, spontaneous participation. For some mental patients or the frail elderly, the size of community meetings may be overstimulating and confusing, leading to inappropriate behavior or withdrawal. To shy, anxious, or less adequate members, however, the large group may provide a sense of identification and belonging without a loss of autonomy and the desired degree of interpersonal anonymity.

In contrast, small groups (three to six members) offer greater opportunity for individualization, providing each member with sufficient time and accessibility to peers and the worker. Members in crises, for example, often need the attention afforded by small groups. Similarly, emotionally deprived children need the continued and special attention more likely in a small group. Small groups, however, do make greater demands for participation, involvement, and intimacy. For shy, anxious, or less adequate members, the pressures may be too great. The level of demand may exceed their level of tolerance. A moderate-sized group (approximately seven to ten) can provide regressed schizophrenics, for example, the necessary interpersonal space that may be unavailable in a smaller group. Moreover, a small group may have insufficient resources for diversity and vitality, or for linking up with a "buddy." Finally, absences leave a small group extremely vulnerable to disintegration.

Finally, the physical setting also has a significant impact on a group's activities and interactions. Light, ventilation, room size, and furniture arrangement facilitate or inhibit the development of a mutual aid system. In arranging space, the worker assesses members' comfort and communication style. A circular sitting arrangement facilitates member-to-member communication and is usually the preferred sitting arrangement. However, in certain situations the circular arrangement may create self-consciousness and unease. When the author met with a group of adolescent girls, for example, he discovered they were initially uncomfortable with chairs arranged in a small, intimate circle. They were self-conscious about what to do with their miniskirts, hands, feet, and so on (parenthetically, the author was unsure what to do with his eyes). The small circle also can be threatening to members who do not seek or are not ready for the degree of physical and emotional intimacy such a structure demands. In these situations, tables provide the necessary spatial boundary and distance members require. If, however, members need physical movement, the tables are restrictive. Since predicting members' spatial needs is difficult, the worker should involve members in assessing and planning for their own spatial needs, including changes during a session and over time.

Staffing the Group

Solo leadership is usually the most effective model for the staffing of groups. When roles are clearly delineated as in some interdisciplinary settings, co-leadership may be an effective arrangement. A nurse or doctor for medical expertise and a social worker for interpersonal and environmental expertise can jointly provide an integrated service that is more responsive to patients' total needs than what either one can do alone. For the arrangement to be effective, the co-leaders must reach an explicit agreement on their respective roles and tasks, particularly in beginning, ending, and focusing sessions. Contracting respective co-leadership roles with group members is also helpful (Nosko & Wallace, 1997). Co-leadership may be also used to gain sanctions for group services by providing two disciplines and mutual accountability, and by acquiring interdisciplinary involvement and support. Toseland and Rivas (2005) identified the salient benefits of co-leadership: an additional source of support, opportunity for feedback and professional development, greater objectivity achieved with two sets of eyes and ears, a situation in which inexperienced leaders gain skills and comfort, leaders who role model open communication and dealing with differences, and support in setting limits and structuring activities.

While these benefits do exist, the authors caution that co-leadership should only be used purposively and discriminately. While numerous rationales are offered, co-leadership too often reflects workers' discomfort and anxiety about working with groups: "There are so many of them and only one of me." Besides being an uneconomical arrangement, co-leadership adds a complex dynamic to the group process, namely, the workers' struggles to synchronize their interventions and to cope with role ambiguities, competitiveness, and discrepant interventions (Toseland & Rivas, 2005). Unwittingly, this arrangement may inhibit the group's mutual aid processes by encouraging withdrawal, testing, or identification with one worker at the expense of the other.

Creating a Responsive Organizational Climate

Organizational sanctions are essential to the development of group services. Without vertical, administrative approval, the worker "walks on eggshells." In response to any perceived problem, such as "uncooperative patients" in a hospital or "noisy children" in a school or social agency, the medical or psychiatric chief, the school principal, or the agency director may precipitously terminate the group (Dane & Simon, 1991; Gitterman & Miller, 1989). Similarly, without horizontal, interdisciplinary, and peer staff involvement, the service is easily undermined or sabotaged—coworkers do not refer appropriate clients, nurses suddenly have to take the patients' temperatures, or teachers decide to punish children for class behavior by disallowing group participation.

Structural supports are also essential to the development of group services. Without them, group services are doomed to fail. A worker's office or an auditorium may inhibit children's activities or encourage destructive behavior, and therefore more suitable space is required. Working parents require the agency to provide group services in the evening or on weekends. Single mothers require child care assistance. Special populations may need transportation. The worker may need petty cash to purchase light refresh-

Table 5.2
The Professional Tasks in Forming a
Group

- Formulate group purpose clearly.
- Select type of group.
- Compose group.
- Select temporal arrangement.
- Decide on group size.
- Arrange room.
- Staff group.
- Create a responsive organizational climate.

ments. If workers are to maintain investment and time for preparation and follow-up, the agency must provide statistical credit for the service. When these supports are not negotiated beforehand, the result is administrative, worker, and client frustration. Chapter 14 discusses the method and skills for acquiring institutional sanctions and supports. Table 5.2 summarizes the professional tasks in forming a group.

Selecting Practice Modality and Temporal Arrangement

Practice Modality

Selecting the appropriate practice modality requires consideration of the advantages and disadvantages of individual, family, group, community, social network, or organizational and legislative modalities. This is a difficult area: organizational constraints and fears—rationalized by "Our job is not to organize," "We're not set up to supervise work with groups or families," or "Our mandate is short-term solution-focused therapy"—inhibit a flexible response and the exercise of professional judgment. Theory and research-based criteria for selection of modalities are limited. Few explicit criteria exist for the informed selection of modalities beyond custom, tradition, and the medical model. Client choice and comfort should be the most significant factors.

Certain clients are most effectively helped through use of the individual modality.

Mrs. Melvin, fifty-five years old, is depressed and anxious, and reports sleep and appetite disturbances. She has experienced severe losses in the past six months. Five years ago Mrs. Melvin was awarded physical custody of her two cerebral palsied granddaughters after an investigation of their mother by child protective services. Last year she was granted permanent custody of the children. This year the children's mother, who had since borne three more children by her second husband, went to court to regain custody. Despite overwhelming evidence in favor of Mrs. Melvin, the court recommended that the mother be given temporary custody with weekend visitation rights for Mrs. Melvin. With little counseling or preparation, the children were removed from Mrs. Melvin's home. Six months later Mrs. Melvin's father died. Last week her sister died of breast cancer. The youngest of seven children, Mrs. Melvin was the caregiver for her aging parents and siblings. She continues to care for her mother, who lives in a nursing home a few blocks away from Mrs. Melvin.

Mrs. Melvin is motivated and resourceful, and displays good judgment. She and the social worker agree on the following goals: (1) resolution of grief, (2) new relationships with the grandchildren and their mother, (3) new sources of meaning in addition to caregiving, (4) possible employment that makes use of her strengths, and (5) a new support system to replace the community and agency supports that were related to the care of children with disabilities. Mrs. Melvin and the social worker plan to meet weekly and to reevaluate the situation in three months.

A client experiencing severe stressors may require frequent and immediate contacts. Some people are relatively private, and sharing and confiding in groups could be disconcerting and uncomfortable. Similarly, extremely anxious and shy clients usually require a period of support before they feel comfortable in a group. Clients in need of a long-term, trusting relationship in which past traumas and their effects on current functioning are explored benefit from individual work. Finally, certain situations may make the family modality unsafe for an individual. For example, if an abusive partner is violent and unmotivated to change, conjoint or family service places the abused partner at risk. If an abusing husband is mandated to enter family therapy or agrees to attend only to appease his wife, she risks retaliation. Unless the abusive husband identifies his abuse as the foremost marital issue to be discussed and changed, marital counseling can be contraindicated (Bogard, 1984).

The definition of the life stressor can determine the choice of modality. If worker and client locate the stressor in family relationships, communication, and structure, the living unit related by blood, marriage, or association is the natural modality of choice. Within the living unit itself, the sibling, marital, or parent–child subsystems may represent an appropriate focus. A combination of family, subsystems, and individual contacts are sometimes used, depending on the nature of the issue, the rhythm and tempo of family life, and the developmental tasks of individual members.

In many agencies, individual services are assumed at the outset. It would be useful to explore the relative advantages of group and family modalities with clients. The group modality provides multiple opportunities for relatedness, mutual aid, and learning coping skills. A group is particularly responsive to people who share a common set of life events such as violence,

Table 5.3
Selection of Appropriate Practice Modality

Select practice modality responsive to client choice and comfort.

Select practice modality responsive to the type and definition of life stressor.

Select *individual modality* for people
- under intensive stress, requiring frequent and immediate contacts.
- in need of specific, concrete, entitlement resources.
- in need of privacy.
- in states of extreme anxiety and shyness.
- in need of a long-term, trusting relationship.
- in situations in which the family modality is inappropriate.

Select *family modality* for
- life stressors located in family relationship and/or communication patterns.
- life stressors located in family developmental transitions, traumatic life events, and other critical life issues.

Select *group modality* for people who
- share a common set of threatening life events.
- share a common set of life tasks and issues.
- suffer from isolation or stigmatized status.
- need to act and gain greater control and mastery over their environments.

Select *community modality* for people who
- need to work to improve community or neighborhood conditions.

bereavement, serious illness, or common life tasks and issues. By its very nature, the group can universalize individual and family troubles, reduce isolation, and mitigate stigma. As group members share and reach out to each other, they experience a "multiplicity of helping relationships" and experience their life issues as neither unique nor deviant. Group members may receive support for definitions and perceptions of their concerns, or they may be challenged to examine them further. Since they have had similar life experiences, they are apt to be more receptive to fellow members' definitions and suggestions than to those offered by professionals. The group modality also provides a force with which people can act and gain greater control and mastery over their environments. Collective action is likely to gain organizational or community attention. It reduces the risk of reprisals and also is apt to be more successful than individual action. Table 5.3 summarizes principles for selection of the appropriate modality.

Temporal Arrangement

With managed care, most clients now receive short-term services. Some are seen episodically; others are seen during periods of severe stress; still others receive planned short-term services. A small percentage of clients receives time-limited services, and an even smaller percentage receives long-term, open-ended services. Each temporal arrangement requires distinctive contracting skills.

In episodic services, the contact is brief and temporary, and the worker immediately involves clients in a rapid assessment of life issues; their nature, longevity, and severity; the availability of supports in the environment; and the level of fit between their personal and environmental resources for effectively coping with the issues. Based on the assessment of issues and the resources, workers and clients develop a plan for focus and direction in service at irregular intervals as needed.

In emergency services, clients require focused and immediate services, with sessions occurring as frequently as needed. The primary goal is to restore the client's prior level of functioning. The worker takes a directive and structured approach and immediately focuses on the severe stressor, assessing precipitating factors and whether other people are involved. The social worker assesses the client's level of functioning, particularly his or her cognitive grasp of the situation ("What happened?"), level of anxiety and immobilization ("How are you managing?"), and potential sources of personal and environmental support ("Have you been able to discuss this with anyone else?"). By eliciting details associated with the severe stressor, the practitioner explores objective and subjective perceptions. Through empathic support, the worker conveys an understanding of the stressor and related pain. The worker specifies the issues and focuses the client on making essential immediate decisions and specifying goals. Specification, clarification, and focus help people to master stressors. The worker provides a sense of hope and confidence in the client's ability to master the stressor. The worker also actively engages and mobilizes personal, family, community, and institutional resources to help the client in coping with the critical life event. Throughout, the focus is on personal and environmental strengths.

In planned short-term services, because of the time limit, the worker assumes a more active role in the initial interview, adhering to essential professional tasks: (1) specifying one or two stressors, (2) demonstrating empathic understanding, (3) creating a sense of hope, (4) developing an agreement to work on a specific stressor, and (5) setting a clear time limit (Wells, 1982). The first task should be identified in clear operational terms. Limited time leads individual, family, and group members to focus quickly on their concerns and to maintain purpose and direction. The time limit creates a sense of immediacy and urgency for both clients and workers; it must be clearly established in the first session. A one-session caregivers' group, two sessions of postsurgical counseling, a four-session adoptive parents' group, or eight sessions for a couple considering divorce sets the time limits within which work is to be accomplished. As an individual, family, or group service nears completion, however, clients and worker may (as mentioned above) decide to begin another cycle of services or a specific number of additional sessions (Gitterman, 2005).

Time-limited services utilize all the principles of planned short-term services. The termination date is clearly established in the first session and can be anywhere from six months to a year. Certain settings such as schools have, as previously discussed, a natural time calendar in the academic year. Therefore, social work services can be timed with this natural limit. We recommend the use of preestablished time periods to evaluate progress on a mutually agreed focus. If client and worker agree that objectives have been met, the work comes to a natural end. If, however, client and worker agree that more time is needed, the work continues until the next natural calendar benchmark.

Long-term, open-ended services can best serve clients with chronic, intractable personal and environmental stressors who need more help than episodic or planned short-term services can provide. Clients who experienced childhood traumas such as physical and sexual abuse are unable to immediately identify and focus on these issues. Others are prone to continuous crises such as those associated with homelessness. Chronically mentally ill and developmentally challenged clients require continuous support, and they benefit from long-term, open-ended services. The long-term professional relationship becomes a lifeline for everyday functioning. However, clients may learn to become too dependent on the relationship. The dependency could lead to lingering self-doubts about their competence. In open-ended group services, frequent shifts in membership often result in a group's inability to move beyond an early stage of group development. Table 5.4 summarizes professional tasks and skills related to length of professional contact.

People experience time in different ways according to culture, age, and physical and psychological states (Germain, 1976). Cultural orientations to time, for example, affect people's regard for punctuality, their interpretations of long waits, their attempts to prolong or to shorten interviews, and the value placed on the past, present, or future. Such variations need to be considered in developing a mutual agreement, and throughout the contact, in planning the respective responsibilities of client and worker. Stressful life events do not accommodate themselves to agencies' and institutions' temporal structures, so meeting more frequently or less frequently, for longer than an hour or less than an hour, could be helpful. Temporal arrangements agreed to by worker and client should, to the degree possible, fit the nature of the stressor, agreed-on goals, and the client's own temporal resources and orientations rather than the organization alone.

Depending on members' physical and emotional states, most adult groups, even those for the elderly, can sustain work on group tasks in sessions of one and one half to two hours in duration. Open-ended groups with changing membership gain more from frequent meetings than do time-limited groups. Crisis groups such as those for hospitalized cardiac or postsurgery patients benefit from several sessions a week, at least until the crisis is past. The frequency and duration of sessions with children must be geared to their

Table 5.4
Skills Related to Temporal Arrangement: Length of Contact

• *Episodic services require:*	Developing rapid assessment of life issues.
	Developing immediate plan for focus and direction.
• *Emergency services require:*	Providing rapid, focused, and immediate services with frequent sessions as needed until the crisis is past.
	Assuming a directive and structured approach.
	Assessing precipitating factors and identifying significant people involved.
	Assessing cognitive grasp of the situation, level of anxiety and immobilization, and potential sources of personal and environmental support.
	Inviting the details associated with the crisis event.
	Providing empathic support.
	Specifying issues and focusing on essential, immediate decisions and specification of goals.
	Providing a sense of hope and confidence.
	Engaging and mobilizing personal, family, community, and institutional resources.
	Identifying and working on personal and environmental strengths.
• *Planned short-term services require:*	Assuming a very active role in the initial interview.
	Specifying one or two stressors.
	Demonstrating empathic understanding.
	Creating a sense of hope.
	Developing agreement to work on a specific life stressor.
	Setting clear short-term time limit.
• *Time-limited services require:*	Establishing termination date in the first session.
	Developing agreed-on focus.
	Developing preestablished time periods to evaluate progress.
• *Long-term, open-ended, services require:*	Providing an ongoing, supportive long-term professional relationship.
	Sustaining original sense of purpose and vitality.
	Exploring potential impact of dependency on the relationship.
	Introducing concept of time-limited services.

Table 5.5
Skills Related to Temporal Arrangement: Personal Factors

- Assess person's experience of time according to culture, age, and physical and psychological states.
- Select temporal arrangements that fit the nature of the stressor, the agreed-on goals, and the client's own temporal resources and orientations.
- Provide a quick response to a physically ill client.
- Communicate a sense of commitment and urgency in contracting with the elderly, avoiding delays or postponements.
- Provide individuals, families, and groups in crisis several sessions a week, at least until the crisis is past.
- Provide young children with frequent, shorter sessions.

orientation to present time and their limited awareness of future time. In providing group services for children having difficulty with school, as previously stated, we discovered that weekly sessions for an hour were insufficient. Between group meetings, the youngsters confronted various difficulties, but the group was unavailable for assistance. In these situations, we recommend sessions that meet twice or three times weekly and for shorter duration (thirty or forty minutes). Young children, very active children or adolescents, and mentally challenged adults usually are responsive to more frequent and shorter sessions. In contrast, well-functioning adolescents and adults are responsive to longer, weekly sessions. Table 5.5 summarizes the selection of temporal arrangements that are responsive to needs.

BEGINNINGS

Settings, Modalities, Methods, and Skills

All helping rests on shared definitions about life stressors and explicit agreement on goals, plans, and methods.

Developing Mutual Focus

Degree of Choice

People seeking services are applicants until they accept the agency's service and the agency agrees to provide it (Alcabes & Jones, 1985). People who are offered the service by an agency become clients only when they agree to a need for the service and to the specified conditions. Even when service is mandated, the person's participation and acceptance of the service are equally necessary. Even continuing clients, when transferred to new workers, must agree to reinvolve themselves. Engaging clients in a social work service and in developing a mutual agreement with them depends on the choice people have in accepting or rejecting the service.

Services Sought. Applicants usually seek social work services at the point when life stressors have become unmanageable. If the agency does not respond to a service request in a timely manner, the length of delay between service request and initial appointment significantly predicts nonattendance (Benway, Hamrin, & McMahon, 2003; Reitzel, Stellrecht, & Gordon, 2006; Wierzbicki & Pekarik, 1993). Service delayed represents a service denied. The act of seeking help can itself be another stressor. In a society that values self-reliance, a need for help might be interpreted as personal inadequacy and loss of control over one's affairs. A sense of shame or fear of how one will be received by the social worker mingles with hope that one's needs will be met, the stressor resolved, and stress eased. Hence, many applicants face the first session with ambivalence.

After introductions, the applicant is invited to tell his or her story and specific concerns and needs. The approach is nonthreatening and encourages specific responses. The worker may ask, "What brings you here?" The question focuses attention, yet gives the applicant latitude in replying. When the person readily shares concerns, the worker uses minimal encouragers to invite elaboration with sounds such as "Uh-huh," "Ah," and "Mmm," and words such as "I see," "Go on," and "I understand." Such minimal encouragers are "like the pats you give to a swing in motion to keep it in motion" (Kadushin, 1983, p. 160). Where needed to help applicants continue, the worker makes supportive statements: "You were badly hurt," "That was rough," "Most parents would worry about that." Inability to follow clients' presentations in these ways is significantly related to dropout from services (Duehn & Proctor, 1977; French, Reardon, & Smith, 2003).

When an applicant falls silent, the worker waits out the silence. Silence is uncomfortable for most people, but effective social workers are cautious about rushing to fill it. Judiciously waiting it out might release the applicant's expression of underlying painful life issues. The wait, however, has to be brief (although it may not feel short) because prolonged silence intensifies the person's anxiety. Social workers should not engage in power struggles over who will talk first. Timing is critical: not to respond too quickly and thus cut off thinking, nor too slowly and thus increase anxiety.

When uncertain about the meaning of a silence, reach directly for its meaning. For example, "I wonder what you are thinking at this moment" invites further exploration. Unfortunately, our own discomfort leads us away from silence and from the applicant's concern that it expresses. Shulman (1978, 1991, 2006) found that the skill of reaching for silence is one of the least used of all the skills that he studied. He also found that in the face of silence, workers tended to change the subject instead of exploring it.

Mrs. Carlini, an Italian American woman, age thirty-two, sought help from a community mental health center. She left her husband a year ago when he told her he was seeing another woman. She described herself as feeling depressed, and began to tell her story:

As good as the weekend had been, she still had to go home alone and face the reality of her husband's leaving her for another woman. What made it worse was her feeling that she had failed miserably as a wife, lover, companion, and source of support, and failed as a mother since her children would no longer have their father at home. She felt alone and pessimistic. She would have a hard time "getting it together with another man" and added that she can't get it out of her mind that she was to blame. "I'm even a failure at getting better." (During this time I responded nonverbally, occasionally nodding or making short comments to show that I understood what she was saying. She related her story without emotion in her voice, but I did not comment on this.) After a brief silence, I asked Mrs. Carlini what she was thinking at this moment. She said she was thinking about her expectations of what a woman was supposed to do—get married, run a household, raise kids, give support to her husband. She must have failed him in some way for him to leave her for another woman. I said that the last few months must have been very painful for her, especially with thoughts of failure on her mind. She said she worked hard in her marriage to make things work, but they didn't, and all of a sudden he told her he was seeing someone else. She was surprised and is still shocked because she thought he was a "man of integrity." I responded, "He hurt you very badly." She had hoped that he would be willing to discuss and work on whatever problems existed in their marriage. She realized that he might think about leaving but never expected him to go so far. For that to happen, she really must have botched things up. I said, "Mrs. Carlini, you are taking a tremendous amount of responsibility onto yourself." She nodded and said others tell her the same thing, but she can't seem to get rid of that idea.

As Mrs. Carlini speaks, the worker picks up nonverbal messages that might indicate anxiety, depression, guilt, or relief. He notes what is emphasized, what is left out, and any discrepancies between verbal and nonverbal communication, and also considers the client's affect. When people actively seek service, minimal, supportive interventions usually suffice. In these situations, "less is more."

When people begin to describe their troubles, workers must sort the ensuing data into three areas: (1) the life stressor, its nature, and its duration; (2) what was done or not done to manage or resolve the stressor; and (3) how the client is reacting to the situation. In thinking about these three areas, social work interns and new social workers have to be careful not to cut themselves off from their feelings. We have to think at the same time we are feeling. By requesting facts, objective and subjective (feelings are also facts), the worker invites further details for greater range and depth of the applicant's presentation of concerns. Open-ended questions—what, how, when, and where—encourage further exploration. For example, "What happened then?" "How did you respond?" "When did he say that?" and "Where were you when you saw him?"

Questions that ask "why" should be avoided; they are usually experienced as challenges or accusations, and they encourage self-justification and rationalization. Asking why someone is depressed may imply there is something inappropriate in that feeling, or that the person is expected to produce an insightful answer. The question "Why?" is usually unanswerable, and blocks applicants' spontaneity in discussing their situation.

Closed-ended questions such as "Did you tell your husband how you felt?" result in a restrictive "yes" or "no" response. The author's content analysis of case recordings by student and experienced workers suggests that interviews characterized by closed-ended questions take on an investigative flavor. The worker maintains substantial control of the interview, and the applicant follows the worker's direction and structure rather than the reverse. Occasionally, however, closed-ended questions do help applicants get started and can also slow down premature "spilling" and overconfiding.

In the early presentation of their stories, people might include subtle, indirect, or qualified messages, such as "I thought he was a man of integrity," "He beats me but I am generally satisfied with him," or "I'm kind of pleased with what she has done." By repeating a key phrase, such as "A man of integrity?" "Generally satisfied?" or "Kind of pleased?" the worker highlights the hidden message. Rephrasing and paraphrasing in the form of a question (e.g., "Are you saying that for once she . . . ?" "Does what I am hearing mean that he is doing . . . ?") communicate the worker's interest in understanding the hidden message. They also encourage further elaboration. A caveat: when rephrasing, paraphrasing, and other skills are used in a rote and mechanical manner rather than as reflections of the worker's genuine concerns and feelings, applicants and clients will immediately experience the worker's lack of authenticity. All professional skills have to be integrated with the social worker's natural and distinctive style.

As people explain the factual aspects of their concerns, the associated feelings are usually also expressed. Thus, for example, when a worker asks a youngster about being thrown out of his class, his anger mounts as he tells his story and he may shout or raise his voice while reliving the experience. An empathic response, such as "He embarrassed you in front of your classmates" or "You have felt all along that he picks on you," may help the youngster to continue his story. Both interventions are a step ahead of the client's feelings and help him to share his narrative. A caution: our profession has a tendency to verbally overspecify people's feelings. The youngster's anger does not have to be labeled. Telling the youngster, "You must have been angry," when he is shouting is superfluous. Minimal encouragement, supportive statements, waiting out silence, reaching for the meaning of silence, and securing more data are often more likely to elicit the associated feelings.

When people have difficulty expressing feelings, putting the feeling into words is helpful (e.g., "You felt very hurt"). Verbalizing and acknowledging the person's feeling encourage continued development of the narrative. For example, reaching for a specific feeling (e.g., "How did your husband's behavior with the children make you feel?") highlights a feeling and invites further discussion as the focus shifts from the situation to reactions.

In telling their life stories, some people feel shame about events and situations in their lives such as incest, violence, or drug use. Legitimizing and universalizing the client's thoughts, emotions, and reactions facilitates continued elaboration. Comments such as "Most people in such an experience would feel abandoned" or "Many people wrongfully blame themselves when such things happen" convey acceptance and invite further discussion.

Metaphors and figures of speech demonstrate understanding and invite further discussion. When clients are stuck in their perceptions, thinking, and verbalizations, the social worker can use a parallel situation, an analogy, to achieve release. For example, a father unable to understand a child's embarrassment at being yelled at in class by her teacher might learn from the worker's analogy of being yelled at by his boss in front of others at the workplace. Parents who are defensive and vulnerable in an intake interview for the hospitalization of their adolescent schizophrenic son might respond to a worker's analogy to diabetes (i.e., both having a biochemical and genetic nature, and both conditions being activated by stress).

Telling one's troubles to a stranger is uncomfortable and painful for many people. If the worker is detached and impersonal, pain and anxiety mount. The ability of workers to share their thoughts and feelings was ranked by clients as the most important skill in Shulman's 1978 study. Social workers' self-disclosures often invite further and deeper disclosures by clients (Goldstein, 1997; Katz, 2003; Raines, 1996; Schloemer, 2000; Wall, 2001). Appropriate sharing of the worker's personal feelings that are neither too powerful nor too superficial bridges the distance between worker and client. Statements such as "I also get upset when . . ." or "I understand your pain, for I also lost my father . . ." must always be responsive to the person's need and not to the worker's efforts to be liked.

At the right moment, gentle humor can relieve anxiety or embarrassment and ease suffering (Gitterman, 2003a; Siporin, 1984). Humor helps to equalize power and to normalize the helping process. Feeling more at ease and not judged, clients are more likely to share their thoughts, feelings, and experiences. However, humor is risky unless it comes naturally to the worker, and it should never be couched in sarcastic or hostile terms.

After the applicant or client has shared considerable material, the worker briefly summarizes concerns and life issues, bringing salient themes to the foreground, consolidating lengthy messages, and providing continuity beginnings within the first session and from session to session. A statement such as "Let me pull together what we have talked about to make sure I understand . . ." provides an opportunity for clients to amplify messages not heard by the worker, take stock, and continue the exploration.

As the social worker helps applicants and clients describe the stressful life issues they are facing, they are actually working together on the beginnings of a mutual assessment of the life issues (stressors), how they are manifested, and the personal and environmental resources available for coping with them. Together, applicant and worker consider a stressor's onset, duration, and intensity; what has been done about it so far; and the results. By maintaining balance between a focus on the life stressor(s) and responsiveness to

Table 6.1
Skills Related to Degree of Client Choice: Service Sought

- Invite person to identify concerns.
- Use minimal encouragers to invite elaboration.
- Provide supportive statements.
- Wait out silence.
- Reach directly for the meaning of silence.
- Invite facts.
- Ask open-ended questions.
- Repeat key phrases.
- Rephrase and paraphrase questions.
- Acknowledge and verbalize feelings.
- Reach for specific feelings.
- Legitimize and universalize feelings.
- Use figures of speech and analogies.
- Share own thoughts.
- Use self-disclosure when appropriate.
- Use timely humor when appropriate.
- Summarize discussion.
- Explain agency function and services.
- Describe and explain social work service and professional purpose.

verbal and nonverbal cues, the worker encourages applicants and clients to tell their story in their own way. This gives a beginning sense of the interplay of forces in the life situation. The practitioner might then be able to tentatively confirm the applicant's definition of the life stressor(s), suggest an alternative definition to consider, or agree to postpone further exploration to a later time. Then they together examine what each believes might be helpful, including objectives, priorities, respective tasks, and next steps.

Only when applicant, practitioner, and agency agree to work together does an applicant become a client. At this point, given the tentative assessment, practitioners may again describe the agency's function, the social work purpose, and how the work together will proceed. The description must be concise, explicit, and clear. Table 6.1 summarizes the skills applicable to services sought.

Services Offered. In offering a service, social workers begin with a clear, concrete description of the agency, of social work services, and of professional purpose without falling into jargon and with due attention to the potential clients' values and lifestyles. For example, a woman became very depressed over a recent transfer to a new job. Contrast the following two statements: "The focus is to restore your sense of self-esteem" and "The focus is on helping you to deal with your new job pressures and the increasing strains at home with your husband and children." Identifying specific, concrete life issues that occur in daily human interactions helps both client and worker to be less overwhelmed and more hopeful and focused in their work. The worker suggests how the offered service connects to the person's life situation. Next, the worker invites the potential client(s) to respond in terms of that connection. People who are well informed about what is offered are less apt to fear a hidden agenda, such as a practitioner describing one service while intending another.

For example, in a psychiatric hospital serving adolescents and their families, social workers were expected to interview parents for the stated purpose of securing a developmental history of their teenager. The latent purpose, however, was to engage the parents in treatment:

> In our first session, I explained to Mr. and Mrs. Dalton that the hospital provides regular interviews with a social worker in order to secure developmental and family history and information about recent events in the patient's life. Families are informed about patient progress, and their questions answered, and their help with discharge plans is sought. Mr. and Mrs. Dalton accepted my invitation and agreed to provide the necessary information. In subsequent interviews, however, they resisted my efforts to "treat" them. I had never acknowledged the covert aim of our meetings. I was too uncomfortable to state directly that they may be partially responsible for their son's disturbance.

Most parents worry about their possible roles in their child's illness. A practitioner's covert agenda mobilizes their anxiety and defenses and closes off any possibility of engagement. Contrast the Daltons' experience with that of Mr. and Mrs. Parker, an African American couple whose daughter, age sixteen, was hospitalized for schizophrenia after attempting to strangle her four-year-old foster sister:

> I discussed the purpose of our getting together and mentioned that parents often have worries about how their children became ill and also what happens to them in the hospital. They also wonder what to expect when their child goes home for the weekend. I said I would like to help them with any worries and questions they may have, and at the same time, I need their help with our efforts to understand Linda's illness. Mrs. Parker responded that Linda as a baby had no troubles, tantrums, or feeding problems. "We always thought she was a happy child, and it's hard for us to understand what went wrong. I want to know what went wrong. What caused this to happen? Can you tell us, or don't you know? Or do you know and won't tell us?" I replied, "We don't really understand how this came about, but I will always share with you anything I know. Right now, we want you to know that in this disorder

there is usually no single factor, no single experience that one can point to as the cause. There are biochemical and genetic factors, which are still not fully understood. There may be emotional experiences that only Linda perceived to be significant, yet they could have triggered this reaction. She might have felt pressure that built up anxiety, and you and I need to understand that too." Mr. Parker noticeably relaxed and shared some recollections of when he began to suspect that Linda was having trouble.

The direct statement that all parents have natural worries was both reassuring and welcoming. It relieved the parents' fears of negative judgments and blame.

Social workers' discomfort with intruding in people's privacy is readily conveyed to clients. A worker might focus on forming a positive relationship with the intent of easing gradually into the "serious" business later. This erroneously assumes that a relationship is the goal of the work. Overlooked is the fact that the relationship can only arise out of the quality of the work together. Preoccupation with forming a "good relationship" deflects the client's concerns and hinders the worker's ability to help. Inviting potential clients to accept an agency service requires anticipatory empathy to understand potential clients' perception of their life situations. Introducing the service by correspondence, telephone calls, or personal contact requires conveying genuine concern and responsiveness to those perceptions. When an agency decides to offer a service, someone has already decided that a need exists, or a source of funding has become available. However, perception of needs will vary. For example, a teacher refers a child for being a "troublemaker." While the teacher calls the child troublesome, the worker calls him troubled, and the child says he is being picked on. While developmentally challenged young adults are likely to be upset by a social worker identifying them as "mentally retarded," they will be much more likely to engage in a discussion of how the status affects their lives—for example, being teased for being slow, being treated like a child, or being labeled as "retarded." Similarly, while an adult is likely to resist being labeled an alcoholic, he or she is more likely to accept that alcohol has created troubles in his or her life. By verbalizing the potential clients' perceptions of their life issues, the worker demonstrates empathic understanding and, thereby, increases the likelihood that the potential client will accept the agency's services.

People offered a service may already be experiencing stress and are vulnerable in the face of any manipulation or misuse of authority by agency or practitioner. Hence, in offered (outreach) social work services, establishing mutuality is essential to the acceptance and engagement of potential clients, many of whom already feel powerless and perhaps resentful of the offer. A worker's offer of service is not formalized until potential clients and the worker reach explicit agreements about goals, means, and mutual

Table 6.2
Skills Related to Degree of Choice: Service Offered

- Define and describe agency function and services.
- Describe professional function.
- Describe the service being offered.
- Identify person's potential perceptions of his or her life issues or needs.
- Reach for doubts, hesitations, and ambivalence.
- The elaboration skills listed in table 6.1.
- Establish priorities.
- Specify respective tasks and responsibilities.
- Specify temporal arrangements.

responsibilities. Setting priorities among life stressors and translating them into coping tasks offer worker and potential clients a focus for their work.

Table 6.2 summarizes social work skills in offered services.

The first priority is given to the most critical life issue. If potential clients face eviction, a medical emergency, or lack of food, such issues must be immediately addressed. Beginning with the person's definition of the life issue minimizes resistance. If parents declare their child to be the stressor but the worker immediately redefines it as a marital issue, the couple's defenses will be mobilized. Trust and credibility must be in place before a fixed system can become more flexible. Then the worker considers which tasks might successfully resolve or reduce the stressor; success is a powerful motivator.

A social work faculty member volunteered at a women's homeless shelter. She offered residents a group service (Lee, 2005, pp. 384–385):

Present for the meeting were Jean, age thirty-one; Carla, twenty-five; Anna, twenty-four; Iris, twenty-four; Sheryl, thirty-two; and Dora, thirty-five. All are African American except Anna, who is Hispanic. Jean and Sheryl were waiting for me in the appointed place. Jean called out the window and the others arrived. We put chairs in a circle and began.

I asked their names and ages and told them I was a social worker who worked here voluntarily on a part-time basis because I wanted to help. There were so many people here, and not enough help to go around. "You can say that again" and "There's no help" were the replies. I told them that the rest of the time I was a teacher at a school of social work, but I felt concerned that women were in such trouble and living under these conditions—maybe I could help them to help each other. This group, if they wanted to become a group, would talk about making this place better and about getting out and back on your feet again. I didn't need to ask what they thought because they were telling me as I spoke by saying, "Yeah" and "Right on." Now Iris angrily and very loudly said she didn't want to meet with me as a go-between—I should send them the director or the big boss above all the shelters. I said I couldn't do that today, and I couldn't promise any fast results, but I would act as mediator or go-between until I could arrange that if they wanted to do it later. Iris reluctantly agreed. They all expressed fear that there would be reprisals for coming to this meeting. Staff would "get them" for it. I said I didn't know if that were so or not, but they should tell me if anything happened. I asked for their concerns and they began. In a steady stream, Iris, Jean, and Carla shared what the problems were. Anna and Dora agreed with all that was said by nodding. Sheryl seemed uncomfortable with the tone and barrage. At various points I turned to her to get her in. A few times she clarified where the others were not aware that the service they wanted did exist in some form. They went on with a list of fifteen grievances. All this was said with much feeling of anger, depression, and desperation, and I related to these feelings with empathy as the process unfolded, naming the feelings when they were particularly strong.

The social worker offers a group service in a clear and respectful manner and explains her professional role. She invites their specific concerns as well as discrepant feedback.

Later in the meeting, Carla said there is frequent cursing at clients, and hitting of residents has also been observed. "We're all treated like we're crazy or in prison. It's hard enough to be down and out, but to be treated like dirt gets us desperate." Then Jean said, "This place is tense, it's going to explode." Everyone agreed. Iris said she felt really close to hurting somebody and going to jail. I said I understood how angry they were. I asked if Iris really wanted to go to jail; she said no. I asked the group what she could do then. Jean suggested, "Just what we're doing, talk about it here. I'm so glad you came. I don't explode, but I'm so depressed." I said I heard her pain and asked how the others felt. Everyone agreed to being very depressed. Carla said, "You need hope, you need to know your options, and how you can get out of here or you don't know what you'd do in time." Sheryl said people who felt they were so angry they could hurt someone should get some help. Many would not hurt anyone, and didn't want to be hurt. I said that I heard her and understood she didn't feel that way, and it was scary when other people did. But everyone here is hurting in her own way. This brought for more outpouring. . . .

Jean said she'd sum it up for us: "There's a lack of compassion here. Everything is hard and tough and soon you become hard and tough. You get treated like dirt, so you feel like dirt. To be treated like a criminal is the worst part of the pain. You already hate yourself for messing up and landing here. Where's the compassion?" It was a moving moment. I said I agreed, and everyone nodded solemnly. I said I saw today that they cared about each other and that's why I brought them together as a group. Jean said, "God bless you for coming here. This is the first time I talked my heart out and felt caring from anyone since I got here." Everyone agreed. I thanked them for giving me a chance to hear them and work with them and share their pain and frustration. I suggested they could become a group here with me and we could worry about taking care of each other. I honestly didn't know how much I could do about the shelter system. I would be pleased to try. But I did know they could care for each other and I could help with that. Jean said, "It's happening right here, right now. I'm so glad I spoke up this morning." Iris starting joking and singing about everyone needing a little love.

The social worker helps the group members to share their experiences and empathize with their pain. She reinforces the group members' potential to help each other and help them experience the beauty of mutual aid.

In developing a common purpose with groups, the social worker directs and redirects member transactions to one another and helps them to express their common and different perceptions. Members are invited to build on one another's contributions, enhancing mutual involvement. Practitioners identify and focus on salient collective themes that provide the "glue" that binds members together and helps them with their shared concerns. They encourage respect for individual opinions, creating a culture that permits expression of difference. Family, group, or community members may not agree about definitions of needs, goals, and tasks. The social worker helps members develop understanding of one another's views by eliciting and accepting discrepant perceptions and opinions. Collective support is as strong as its capacity to tolerate differences. At times, certain members may be reluctant to participate. In a caring and supportive manner, the worker invites participation of the "outside" members. Finally, the worker establishes ground rules that facilitate open communication and allow for expression of difference without fear of recrimination. Explicit rules that bar physical violence, verbal abuse, or threats have to be established (Gitterman, 1989b).

A hospital social worker had invited eleven cardiac patients to form a group. Her interventions illustrate several distinctive skills of the group modality.

After the refreshments and introductions, I said, "As I had explained to each one of you individually, you were invited to participate in a four-session group for patients with recent heart attacks. The staff believed you could be helpful to one another in dealing with your concerns about hospitalization, the heart attack, and what the future has in store for you."

Bill indicated that work worries him the most. Mario, Hector, and John agreed. In an agitated way, Bill continued, "If the doctor won't let me go back to work, what can I do? It's been twenty-seven years of my life, and I always put in an honest day. Now the doctor says give it up. What kind of bullshit is that? Doesn't he realize that I have family and financial obligations?" Lenny agreed, stating angrily that the doctors don't care that a medical recommendation could destroy a man's life.

I asked if they were mostly annoyed about what their doctors said, or how they said it, or both. Hector explained that he thought it was a doctor's responsibility to make work recommendations in order to protect health, no matter the economic consequences. He has ended up on welfare, and that's been hard to swallow. Bill responded with intensity that no doctor was ever going to do that to him, and he released a barrage of angry words. Mario suggested that Bill was doing what he himself has stopped doing—taking out the anger at the doctor's recommendation on his own heart. Hector understood Bill's being fighting mad because he, too, is having a hell of a time living with his "bum ticker." He is just beginning to calm down and to realize that it will never be the same. Bill shook his head in disbelief and asked, "How can I be calm? I have a family to take care of." Lenny explained that he also has a family, but getting excited and upset will only lead to another heart attack. Andy supported Bill.

Peter exclaimed, "But, shit, common sense will tell a man that health is the only important thing and everything else has to become second." Most members agreed that if they let themselves get excited or experience too much pressure, they will only hurt themselves. Bill became angry again, telling group members that they had to be as dumb as the doctors to be forgetting their problems. Bill's eyes became tearful as he shouted, "If the doctor says give up truck driving where I feel like a real man, what am I going to turn to? Who is going to hire me? What good am I?" Lenny suggested that Bill calm down. Mario suggested that Bill talk to his boss and ask about a light job. Bill was insulted by the suggestions and shouted that he has pride and isn't going to degrade himself and tell the boss to pity him, to give him crumbs. What kind of man did Mario think he is, anyway? Mario answered, "I think you are a good man, and I respect you. I know a wounded animal has to fight for his brood, but Bill, you have brains, you have to listen to your body and accept its limits. It takes a man to talk to his boss about lighter work."

I said that it seemed some of them have made peace with their hearts, while others are still fighting. Either way, I realize how much pain they are experiencing. Peter implored Bill to take it easy, to accept his heart condition. Bill insisted that his boss wouldn't give him light work because it would raise insurance rates. He feels he is no longer a man. At this point, Bill began to sob. Several members tried to change the subject, but I encouraged others to share their struggles. Walter referred to the mortgage and his family food needs. Hector talked of his pension and how it helps. In a disgusted tone, Bill wanted to know how he was going to get by with workers' compensation.

Mario spoke quietly but firmly: "Bill, I can see you are a big man, strong, and you can beat anybody here in a fight, but I'm gonna tell you something, you gotta stop crying and be a real man; that means accept what is, do what has to be done, face the facts. You want to help your family, you ain't gonna help them by killing yourself. You have to cut down on your expectations, do what the doctors say, and start to build a new life."

Everyone waited for Bill's reaction. He stared at Mario as if trying to decide what to do. After a while, he said, "I guess I could sell my home and buy a smaller one. My oldest son can go to work." Peter put his hand on Bill's back, saying that it was much better to be a live father than a dead one. Hector agreed, suggesting that they are all afraid of the same thing but handle it differently. Each man then spoke of how they changed or plan to change lifestyles and habits, and of their fears and common objective: "Life!" Bill said the guys had been helpful. He continued, "I'm a man, and I'll do what has to be done."

At the end, I asked what they thought of the first meeting, and many said it was helpful to see that others struggle with the same kind of problems. Mario's comment caught the essence: "It's like we are in the same boat trying to keep from drowning. Talking can help us stay afloat." We agreed on the place and time of our next meeting.

The social worker's straightforward statement of the group's purpose, her reference to their common concerns, and her interest in their feedback are all the group needed to begin developing its own processes of mutual aid. The intensity of feelings and concerns associated with heart attacks propelled the group into their common tasks of dealing with life-and-death fears and concern about their families' well-being, their ability to work, and their self-images as "whole" men.

An oncology hospital social worker provided services to patients and their loved ones. She decided to offer a one-session group to caregivers. Three members were present on this particular week: Linda (whose husband's cancer had metastasized to his liver and spine), Karen (Linda's sister), and Lenny (whose wife's cancer had metastasized to her brain).

The social worker started, "Each one of you is dealing with a loved one's chronic and terminal illness. Your husband, wife, and brother-in-law are back in the hospital and you have had to face the pain of their decline. Your loved one's long illnesses have placed great pressures on you. The hospital social work department felt that this group would give you an opportunity to help each other with the emotional pain and also get some ideas of how you best take care of yourselves in the caregiver roles."

Linda immediately responded, "I know that I need some time away from him for myself, but he always wants me to be with him. Then, I think about that and get angry at him for making unfair demands on me. Then, I feel guilty for getting angry with him because he is, after all, very sick and it is hard to be in pain and know that you are dying. Then, I feel angry for feeling guilty because it is normal to want some time to myself and I need the time to recuperate so that I can come back and be present to take care of him. And now the only person who has been helping me, my sister, is moving and I do not know how I will manage without her. She has been extremely helpful to my husband and me, and I can't imagine doing this alone." I replied that this is very important for us to discuss, but if it would be OK with her I thought it would be helpful for the members to introduce themselves and briefly talk about their loved one's diagnosis and what is happening with their loved one and them. All three of them nodded in agreement.

Linda introduced herself and gave a summary of her husband's diagnosis. He was admitted with severe pain, and a long hospital stay is anticipated: "I don't know how I am going to do it. He wants me at his bedside all the time, and I just can't do it. I need some sleep. My sister has been coming to stay with him in the mornings, but now she will be leaving." I replied, "Linda, you are dealing with a great deal," and asked Karen to share her experiences. Karen nodded and said that she had been staying with her sister for five weeks, but that she has to get back home. She said that Bill (the patient) does not like to be alone and that she helped as much as she can, but she really had to get back to her life. I thanked Karen for filling us in and asked Lenny to introduce himself and share his wife's situation.

He said, "OK, well, my name is Lenny and my wife has breast cancer and it went to her brain. She has been treated with a mastectomy first, then chemo, then radiation, then chemo again, and now we are back to radiation. We have been going through this for eight years now." Linda responded, "How terrible." "Don't get me wrong," Lenny continued. "We had some good years in between some of those treatments. But she is really sick now. In fact, the social worker just recommended a hospice placement for her. I have had a hard time caring for her—it has been very hard for me, especially the last few months."

I replied, "Now that we have a sense of who you are, and what's happening, I suggest that we use our hour together to help each other with the stress you are experiencing and strategies to alleviate some of the stress in your lives—does that sound OK?"

The social worker's clarity of purpose, specification of commonality, and identification of the one-hour time limit focus group discussion and provide the structure for mutual aid. Table 6.3 summarizes distinctive skills of helping a group develop common focus.

Table 6.3
Skills for Helping a Group Develop Common Focus

- Direct and redirect member transactions to one another.
- Invite members to build on one another's contributions.
- Identify and focus on salient collective themes.
- Invite expression of differences.
- Reach for contradictory perceptions and opinions.
- Invite participation of all members.
- Establish protective ground rules.

Services Imposed or Mandated.   Increasingly, social workers serve involuntary clients (Rooney, 1992). Imposed service presents ethical dilemmas that arise from the dual social work functions of care and social control. Hutchison (1987) suggests that care for individuals and control of the general social welfare are complementary rather than antithetical and that ethical practice requires that "social workers, especially in mandated settings, remain sensitive to the inherent dangers of becoming repressive forces in support of the dominant special interests" (p. 590).

Mandated social work services range from completely involuntary to somewhat involuntary. Court-mandated services carry prescribed consequences for clients if they fail to comply with court orders (i.e., coercion; Regehr & Antle, 1997). To some extent, the court's legal authority is transferred to the agency and the social worker. Compliance becomes the minimal condition for escaping a status of parolee, probationer, or juvenile offender or for achieving a desired goal such as return of one's child from foster care or discharge of a child from institutional care. While legally mandated services are the most coercive, institutions or agencies can also impose a social work service as a condition for methadone maintenance, homemaker service, or adopting or fostering a child.

While institutional sanctions may be less restrictive than legal mandates, they can nonetheless be formidable threats to prospective clients. The authoritarian nature of a particular agency can create ambiguity about the extent of client choice. For example, a welfare recipient might feel compelled to accept a group service for fear of jeopardizing the assistance grant. Public housing tenants may accept service lest they be evicted. Hospitalized mental patients and residents of geriatric facilities may fear negative sanctions if they refuse a service. Agency and worker may assert freedom of choice, but potential clients may experience it as coercion.

When services are imposed, people are not likely to welcome an organization and practitioner who would have extensive power over their lives. Social workers in mandated services need to remember that they represent a serious threat, even an obstacle, to potential clients' own aims. Some people acknowledge their need for help, finding the service to be congruent with their own definitions of life issues and aspirations. Others resent having problems attributed to them and being coerced by external authority. Some people hide their resentment by superficially cooperating in order to obtain a desired goal. Others reject the agency definition of their goal or life issue and actively resist the social worker.

Cingolani (1984, p. 442) views the encounter of mandated client and social worker as a political process, "one that involves the socially sanctioned use of power or influence in a context of conflicting interests between the client and some part of his or her social environment." Within this context, social workers have to anticipate struggle and conflict against their power and authority (Gitterman, 1983, 1989a). Many social workers in mandated settings commit one of two common practice errors. Because they are intimidated or angered by these clients, they avoid dealing with the question of legal, organizational, and professional authority, or they set out to build a relationship before risking the client's anger, failing to recognize that the relationship can only emerge from effective work together. In either case, the difficulty in engaging a distrustful and angry client is increased. If the social worker also becomes angry, unnecessary confrontations may follow. Misuse of authority and power increases client distrust and resistance. The practice task is to turn formal authority into professional influence.

Effective social workers are direct and honest about the source of the mandate, their own authority and responsibility, limits on confidentiality, potential consequences of noncompliance, and definitions of noncompliance. The guiding principle is to provide the least intrusive service. Ethical practice requires social workers to use their authority to provide resources to mandated clients as they would for nonmandated clients and not impose personal standards that are not part of the mandate. And, even in mandated settings, social workers must influence employing organizations to "further a progressively constructive relationship between the individual and society" (Hutchison, 1987, p. 587). Professional directness and honesty reduce mistrust, thwarted expectations, and resistance.

The social worker also shares available information and invites the mandated client's perceptions and reactions. The worker must demonstrate warmth and caring if the person is to hear the worker's description of the service (De Jong & Berg, 2001; Rooney & Bibus, 1996; Thomas & Caplan, 1999). Professional "straight talk" has to be mediated by compassion for the client's predicament and life stressors over which any semblance of control is being lost. Also, the description of service should fit the client's perception of reality (for example, "You feel the parole officer is hassling you"). The aim is to actively engage the client in an area in which a commonality of interest is greater than a conflict in interests (Cingolani, 1984). At the same time, nonnegotiable legal requirements and agency policies have to be separated from negotiable rights, choices, and options (Rooney, 1992). In many instances, common goals can best be described as "helping you to get the agency and me off your back." This includes helping neglectful or abusive

Table 6.4
Skills Related to Degree of Choice: Service Mandated

- Prepare to be perceived as a potential threat to the client.
- Anticipate struggle and resistance.
- Be direct and honest about the source of the mandate, potential consequences for noncompliance, and limits of professional authority.
- Specify conditions for termination of mandate.
- Identify limits to confidentiality.
- Share available information.
- Demonstrate compassion for person's life stressors.
- Identify areas in which the commonality of interests is greater than the conflict in interests.
- Use the elaboration skills listed in table 6.1.

parents to improve their child care so they will be free of surveillance, or helping probationers or parolees to meet the conditions for changing their status. Sequencing objectives in accordance with client priorities is frequently involved. The pressing, concrete needs of neglectful or abusive parents often have to be met before they can even think about and respond to the needs of their children. Table 6.4 summarizes the social work skills in imposed and mandated services.

When people are voluntarily or involuntarily referred for services, the social work response needs to be timely. Benway, Hamrin, and McMahon's (2003) review of five family clinic studies found that potential client nonattendance was significantly predicted by the length of time between referral and initial appointment.

Degree of Owning One's Difficulties

Based on their research in the field of substance abuse, Prochaska and DiClemente (1982, 2005) and DiClemente and Prochaska (1998) help us better understand the process of how people change. They and their associates (Connors, Donovan, & DiClemente, 2001; Prochaska, DiClemente, & Norcross, 1992) differentiate between *intentions* to change and taking specific *actions* to change. They conceptualize five stages of change, each characterized by different levels of motivation and awareness. In the first stage, "precontemplation," the person is unaware of the core problem, and has no intention or takes no action to change her or his behavior. The person's life difficulties are divorced from the problematic behaviors. In the second stage, "contemplation," the person is highly ambivalent. While she or he may have some awareness of the core problem, she or he has not made a commitment to deal with it. The person has intentions to change without taking any specific actions toward that goal. The person is "not quite ready yet." This stage is often characterized by "Yes, but . . ." declarations. In "preparation," the third stage, the person is more serious about changing problematic behaviors;

however, the actual effort is not sustained. In the "action" stage, people commit themselves to modifying their behaviors and/or changing their environments in order to deal with their core problem. Their actions are deliberate and sustained in commitment, time, and energy. Finally, in the fifth stage, "maintenance," the person has implemented new behavior, sustained gains for a significant period of time, and also worked on preventing the problem from coming back or relapsing.[1]

Although the schema was developed for the addictions field, it has immense applicability for all types of life stressors and situations. In beginnings, the worker can use the schema to quickly assess the applicant or client's readiness to deal with his or her salient life issues. If in an initial interview the social worker meets with an applicant or client who, being in the *precontemplative* phase, does not link her depression, or her abusive relationship, or her sexual trauma, or her parental abandonment to current life difficulties, the worker should not force the connection.[2] Forcing the connection will lead to a power struggle, argumentation, and/or premature service withdrawal. To avoid these outcomes, Miller (1983) discourages premature interpretations and labeling: "labeling is not essential . . . what matters is this: what problems is the person having in relation to alcohol, and what needs to be done about them?" (pp. 154–155). In other words, the person need not accept a label of "alcoholic" (or "depression") in order to work on the troubles alcohol (or depression) is creating in his or her life.

When individuals or family or group members are ambivalent about working on their difficulties, they may be in the *contemplative* phase of change. While they may be thinking about their difficulties, they have mixed feelings about taking any remedial action. For example, a couple may consider that their problematic marital relationship might influence their child's acting out in school; they vacillate between accepting and rejecting this possibility. At this point in time, they make no commitment to working on their marriage. They need their child to serve in the role of "identified patient" to deflect the spotlight from their relationship. If the social worker insists that the child is acting out their marital difficulties, the couple will likely argue against the interpretation. The more strenuously the worker promotes her interpretation, "the more vigorously clients defend themselves to minimize stress and to maintain some sense of balance" (Hanson & El-Bassel, 2004, p. 44).

Some applicants or clients right at the outset seem committed to dealing with salient life issues. While their intentions are strong, the actual follow-through is uneven and inconsistent. They are *preparing* themselves to explore new ways of thinking and acting. In this phase, as in the prior ones, social workers create a safe and accepting service environment. The focus is on cultivating the clients' motivation to engage in the helping process and in alleviating their life stressors. In the *action* phase, social workers reinforce the clients' motivation and commitment to remain engaged in the helping process and the work at hand (Hanson & El-Bassel, 2004).

Diversity Sensitive Beginnings

In response to racism, sexism, homophobia, attendant poverty, and power-lessness, some oppressed people react with rage. Others internalize society's rejections and turn the rage against themselves, their own families, and their communities. Many, in spite of the heavy toll of oppressive social and economic conditions, maintain a positive outlook and high levels of self-valuation.

The initial contact of a person of color with a social worker takes place in a racist environment in which persons of color are labeled and stereotyped, their families and lifestyles disparaged, and their survival strengths and adaptability ignored. To applicants or clients of color, a white social worker is likely to represent institutional power and a threat to desired goals. Clients may directly or indirectly express their resentment by hostility or exaggerated compliance. For example, an African American adolescent mandated by the court to a residential treatment center might respond to a white social worker with direct hostility, staring at the floor, or monosyllabic, noncommittal responses. African American teenagers have reason to resent the poverty and racism that rob them of their adolescence and rapidly propel them into adulthood. Why should they trust white social workers (Gitterman & Nadelman, 1999; Gitterman & Schaeffer, 1972)? African American social workers might create powerful ambivalent feelings and so be distrusted. Both white and African American practitioners might experience guilt, defensiveness, and resentment because their efforts are not appreciated.

The worker must anticipate some degree of distrust, and not personalize it. Trust has to be earned. A client's initial testing behaviors and resistance have to be understood and accepted as adaptive efforts. Social workers must explore their own attitudes before they can demonstrate that they genuinely care and are committed to trying to understand the clients' pain and oppression even when it is turned against themselves, their families, or their communities. Social workers must understand their clients' dual worlds: the local community of people of color, and the institutions and mass media of white society (Lum, 2004; Sue, 2006). Social workers need to identify and be sensitive to potential racial differences. They must avoid blaming clients for the "messes" in their lives, and connect on a human level.

George R., age fifteen and black, lives in a western city with his mother and two younger brothers in a recently integrated neighborhood that they had just moved into. His mother is a registered nurse. She divorced her husband ten years ago, and George sees his father about once a year when he drifts into the city. George was referred to the mental health clinic by a probation officer. Since his arrival he had been repeatedly involved in fistfights. When he was suspended from school, he threatened to kill school personnel. Following the next fight, an "unprovoked attack" on a smaller boy, police were called and George was to be taken to juvenile hall. However, when handcuffs were used, he became so out of control and threatening that he was taken instead to the psychiatric ward of the county hospital, where he remained for ten days until his court hearing. He was diagnosed as schizophrenic, with a paranoid reaction, and commitment was recommended. However, disposition was delayed because his mother agreed to seek outpatient treatment for George and to take a leave of absence from work to care for him at home. He was ordered by the court to stay away from school until a second hearing in two months.

The social worker, a mature, white female, is employed by a community mental health agency. The first two interviews illustrate the worker's efforts to engage George.

First Interview. In my office, George was almost ostentatiously menacing as he stood over me and glowered, fists clenched, shoulders held in such a way as to make him appear even more broad shouldered than he is. At first, he seemed to struggle against speaking, then he exploded, "I'm not coming here, I don't care what they do to me, I don't care, I'm not crazy. I'm going to sue the judge, he can't get away with this, let them send me to a state hospital, I don't care." I cut in, "OK, so sit down and let's talk about it. I don't know whether you belong here, either—all I know right now is that you are very upset." (He sat down.) I continued, "Now, tell me, what's happened to you?" His story was incoherent and interspersed with threats to kill the principal, the judge, and particularly the school counselor. He insisted that he did not start the school fights, but that everyone was against him. He told, in a particularly frightened fashion, of the arrival of the police, the handcuffs, and the days on the psychiatric ward. He repeated many times, "I don't care." I said, "Handcuffs and the psychiatric ward is no place for a fifteen-year-old boy. It's terribly frightening. You weren't prepared to go there, and you didn't know what would happen next." He said, "They were going to send me to state hospital. I don't want to go anywhere. I'm not crazy, I'm not coming here, I don't care what the judge's or psychiatrist's report says about me." He stood up to leave. I said, "George, I don't know what the report says about you because I don't have it, but I will in three days. Let's set up another time so I can tell you what's in the report, OK?" He reluctantly agreed.

Second Interview. George's first words were "I'm only going to stay five minutes." He turned my clock to face him and stared at it. He did not look at me. I said, "I hope you will stay longer, but let's make the most of the time we have." George asked me if I received "those" reports. I said, "Yes, the report says that you have had a lot of hurts. When you were a little kid, first and second grade, the kids picked on you, and they would not stop no matter what you did. You wanted to but didn't know how to make them your friends. You must have been very lonely. . . . That's rough on a little kid, and you were very small and thin, in a neighborhood full of bullies." He remained silent, looked at me, and then said, "Five minutes is up," but he did not get up from his chair. I added, "The report also describes the hurts from your father." He stopped me and said that he wanted to talk about grade school. He described how the bigger boys would waylay him to tease him for wearing a cap and would knock it off his head. He jumped to the present, describing his loneliness. He had been kicked out of the YMCA; he was out of school; a month ago, he'd been told to leave the roller rink and never come back. He added sadly, "I still got no friends, see? Nobody wants me around, but I don't care." At the end of the hour, George agreed to return next week.

The social worker realized that George is in the precontemplative phase, and her high degree of empathy and acceptance helped alleviate some of his fears and anxieties. The worker was not intimidated by George's menacing stance, but instead recognized and responded to George's feelings at the moment and throughout the case. The social worker's approach is racially sensitive. She realizes the racist context of George's experiences: the school's lack of sensitivity to its newly transferred student, the police's harsh response, and the mandated referral to the psychiatric ward of a county hospital. These experiences are more likely to be confronted by black than white adolescents.

In working with diverse populations, social work practice has to be racially and ethnically sensitive. For example, Puerto Rican Americans, Cuban Americans, Dominican Americans, Mexican Americans, and Central Americans share a common language while having distinguishing customs and folkways. Latin cultures do not generally support the use of social agencies. Institutional help is sought only if all other informal options have failed (i.e., family, friends, neighbors, shopkeepers, clergymen, and spiritists). Spiritism is an important belief system in many Hispanic cultures (Paulino, 1995). Spiritism is the belief that spirits have a powerful influence on human behavior. Since problems are primarily defined as caused by spirits, spiritists resist hospitalization and drug treatment. They believe these "external" treatments undermine people's ability to gain control over invasive spirits. For example, in Puerto Rican culture, *ataques*—hysterical reactions or seizures—are accepted as normal means of coping with pent-up stress. The medium communicates with spirits to eliminate the evil ones and replace them with protective spirits (Delgado, 1988). Since the dominant culture defines these attacks as pathology, Hispanic clients are reluctant to share their spiritual lives with physicians, psychiatrists, and social workers. In addition to the spiritist, other folk healers include the *santero*, who uses rituals of song, music, and animal sacrifice; the herbalist, who treats "hot" and "cold" illnesses with combinations of foods, teas, and herbs; the *santiguador*, whose cure requires the will of God and various treatments such as massage, herbs, and prayer; and the *curandero*, who strengthens ties with the Roman Catholic church (Delgado & Humm-Delgado, 1982). A caution: diversity exists within diversity. While different Latin cultures (e.g., Puerto Rican American, Dominican American, Mexican American, Cuban American, and Central American) share some common customs and folkways, they also have distinguishing customs and folkways.

Mrs. Morales, a Puerto Rican solo parent of two young children, casually informed a Latina settlement house worker that she is in danger of being evicted from her apartment. The worker invited her into an office.

MRS. MORALES:	I got until September to move out. Next month, I have to go to court again.
WORKER:	What happened so far?
MRS. MORALES:	Last time I went to court, the landlord tricked me. They say the receipts I have of payments are no good.
WORKER:	Did you have a lawyer with you?
MRS. MORALES:	No.
WORKER:	Do you want me to help you get a lawyer from Legal Aid?
MRS. MORALES:	No, it's OK.
WORKER:	I am afraid you will lose your apartment.
MRS. MORALES:	They will have to put me into a hotel.
WORKER:	A hotel may be rough for you and the kids.
MRS. MORALES:	It is OK. I lived in a hotel before, and you could cook there with a hot plate. It's OK.
WORKER:	I sense you are not pleased with your apartment.
MRS. MORALES:	There are things going on in that apartment.
WORKER:	What do you mean?
MRS. MORALES:	Last night Hector woke up and started to talk but he was really still asleep, but with his eyes open. I did not call him by his name because if you do that the child could die. Then I am half asleep and I feel this hand that grabbed me by my neck. I really had to struggle to get rid of it. The woman who was in the apartment before me also had a lot of trouble with her husband, and had to move out. You see, a man died in the bedroom. I don't feel right with it—his spirit is still in the apartment. I am afraid of it. I am glad you are also Puerto Rican. White people do not believe in spirits.
WORKER:	How have you managed so far?
MRS. MORALES:	I try to stay in the street as late as possible. Sometimes, I bring the mattress into the living room. I don't get much sleep. A friend slept over one night and felt the spirit also. I bet you wouldn't sleep there one night by yourself (she began to laugh). The other night I felt this man and he was trying to

touch my parts. I woke up in the morning with pains all over my body. I am a strong woman, and in the morning I have no energy to get up. I feel like someone has beaten me up.

WORKER: This is very scary for you.

MRS. MORALES: I went to a *santero* a couple months ago. He told me to go check my parts and to be careful in the kitchen. Everything he said was true—a doctor found a cyst, and the frying pan moves in the kitchen. I am afraid to cook there.

WORKER: I hear how difficult it is for you to stay in the apartment. Let's put our heads together and figure out what we can do. OK?

Latin cultures emphasize an informal, expressive style of relating, requiring *personalismo*, or trust in a person. The worker needs to establish an informal atmosphere (e.g., sit in the kitchen, have a cup of coffee together, and exchange observations about the children) for the prospective client to feel comfortable. The worker also has to demonstrate a willingness to be incorporated into the client's informal social system rather than remain solely a representative of a formal bureaucracy. This Latina worker's knowledge of and comfort with the cultural concept of spirits helped Mrs. Morales to reveal her fears. By shifting from advocating for Mrs. Morales's legal rights to inviting her fear of evil spirits, the worker engages her. The culturally sensitive intervention led to an ingenious solution: inviting the spiritist to the apartment to expel the evil spirits and replace them with protective ones. The culturally sensitive intervention enabled Mrs. Morales to maintain her apartment, instead of risking homelessness.

Encouraging the client to reach out to supportive kin and kin networks to reach out to the client can be helpful. These networks can have a profound impact on people's use of institutional resources. Whether people apply for social work services and whether they remain connected to the agency and the worker may depend on what their networks think of applying for formal help, social workers, or the agency itself (Lum, 2004; Schiele, 1996; Sue, 2006; Swigonski, 1996).

People's *sexual orientation* ranges along a continuum from an exclusively homoerotic sexual orientation to an exclusively heteroerotic one. People with a homoerotic sexual orientation confront the choice of keeping their orientation secret and remaining in the "closet," and thus suffering from the split between their public and private lives, or being public about their orientation and risking suffering discrimination and scorn (Caron & Ulin, 1997; Green, 1996).

Two graduate students, Helen and Kaye, interned in an urban agency that provides programs for elderly homosexual people. From reviewing agency records, they learned that many elderly gays and lesbians have remained in the closet in order to survive in a homophobic culture. Some married, and others continually worried about possible exposure. Now that many are retired or have lost their spouses, older gays and lesbians are contacting this agency. Yet the students observed that many older women applied for service yet failed to continue. Some welcomed telephone calls, but did not wish anyone to come to their homes. Several reported that they disliked the drop-in center because gay men dominated it. The students concluded that a group might best serve the psychosocial needs of isolated older lesbian women. If a mutual aid system were to develop, such a group would have the potential to universalize individual life issues, reduce isolation, and relieve feelings of stigma (Gitterman, 2005). Ten women were selected from the students' case-loads, and handwritten invitations were mailed to each one followed by a phone call a week before the meeting date. Refreshments were mentioned as well as transportation for those needing it. All appeared interested, and all said their attendance would depend on the weather and their health. On a rainy night, four women came to the first meeting. Carolyn, sixty-nine, and Virginia, sixty, both African American, have been a couple for thirty-five years. Virginia is employed as a professional, and Carolyn is a retired professional. Mary, also African American, sixty-eight, is a friend of Virginia and Carolyn. Betty is white, sixty-six, and has never married. Her lover of many years is a bisexual woman. The students are white. Kaye, forty, is a lesbian and has lived with her lover for five years. Helen, twenty-four, is heterosexual. Helen records a summary of the first meeting:

After welcoming the members to the group meeting and a period of introductions, I stated, "You have a great deal in common—as I mentioned on the phone, you are all older women who share a lesbian sexual orientation. That's being in triple jeopardy in a sexist, ageist, and homophobic world. Those of you who are black also share the experiences of living in a racist society. [Since the agency had served only seven people of color in a total of 615 service units during the prior month, we were especially happy with their group attendance.] We invited you to the group because we thought you would help each other in dealing with common experiences that you have to confront because of your sexual orientation—such issues as whether to tell friends and family you are lesbian, how to deal with discrimination and prejudice." The members immediately connect with each other and begin to share life experiences. They agree to work on life issues such as their social isolation and the struggles and joys in their lives as older lesbians. They also express interest in helping recruit more members. Halfway into the meeting, the subject of work and "coming out" is brought up. Carolyn (addressing the students) inquires, "What do you think of coming out?" I responded, "I think coming out is a very personal decision that a woman makes every day. Are you thinking of a particular situation?" (My response was brief and impersonal because I felt uneasy offering an opinion on a choice that I have never had to make. I also realize that the current generation of older lesbians have had to "pass" as straight as a way of coping with their homosexual identity.)

Technically, the student moves from the general to the specific. She recognizes that Carolyn could have been asking several questions: do you think people should be out? Are you out? What do you think of gay people? She realizes that group members' coping styles have been developed and maintained for several decades, and respects them by not responding with a simplistic opinion that would frame the discussion. At the same time, if she could have used her discomfort and said, "I feel a little uneasy offering a decision about choice because I am not gay. What do you think about Carolyn's question?" she would have clarified her role and modeled directness. Instead, her discomfort increased when her co-leader identified her own homosexual orientation. Before the initial contact, a worker must explore her own self-comfort with her sexual orientation and potential homophobic feelings.

Virginia picked up on Carolyn's question and asked, "Well, for example, what do you think about coming out on the job?" Kaye responded, "It depends on the job. Many people who volunteer at this agency are in the closet at their regular jobs. I am out of the closet all the time. I just am. I know I want to work where I can be out. Of course, that limits my options for jobs." I was feeling terribly "on the spot." I felt all the group members were staring at me, expecting my testimony as well. Because of my unease, I redirected the attention to Virginia, asking, "How about you, Virginia, are you closeted or not?"

The student's dilemma is understandable: she is white, young, and heterosexual. She decides to keep her heterosexuality in the closet. As part of her education, the student will learn to trust group members' capacity to handle difference; after all, they have been handling difference for most of their lives. Encouraging discussion of differences in sexual orientation, race, and age—even in the first session—can advance the group process, build trust, and help develop mutual aid.

In reviewing this first session, Helen analyzed her reluctance: "I made the choice at this time not to tell the group members that I am not gay. I feared their rejection. I thought if I revealed myself, the group might not trust me and would be more guarded in their discussions." Fortunately, there was another opportunity at the next meeting for Helen to be more candid and to come out of her own heterosexual closet. The ensuing discussion not only helped resolve the ambiguity but also advanced the group's development as they struggled with the inevitable issue of difference. In a later session, the group reminisced.

VICTORIA:	Do you think it is easier to be gay now than then? [Meaning Stonewall and the gay rights movement.]
ANN:	Oh no, it was easier for me years ago. I used to be quite popular. I was accepted in several different cliques. A bunch of us would meet at the Eastgate, it was a very popular bar then, and we'd have a great time. We'd all stay over someone's apartment and go to the park the next day and back to the Eastgate Saturday night. A whole group of us would spend the weekend together. It was so much fun.
MARLENE:	Oh yes, we used to have a wild time up at that bar.
ANN:	I used to be there, too.
MARLENE:	Yes, that was a great place. We'd have barbecues and go to the beach and meet in people's homes.
HELEN:	It sounds like there were a lot of bars for lesbian women to go.
LORI:	There were many more than today.
HELEN:	I've heard there used to be more places for women to go out. It must be quite a loss for all of you now.
JANET:	Oh yes. [Marlene and Lori nodded, and Ann agreed.]
HELEN:	Are you all feeling isolated?
LORI:	Yes, we need a center like this in Queens where people can just sit together and talk.
JANET:	A place where we could meet other gay women to be friends with.
MARLENE:	Yes, we need a center for gays in Queens. I go to a senior center, but most of the women there are complaining about their children. The other day a woman asked me if I had a husband because she and her husband are looking for a couple to socialize with. I just said no.
ANN:	I'm "in the closet." The people in my building would never tolerate a gay person. It's a building for senior citizens. I'm friendly with the super's wife. She has me down for dinner and stuff like that. If she knew—oh boy.
HELEN:	You've been forced to give up a very important and special part of your life; that's sad.
ANN:	Yes, it is very depressing.
MARLENE:	I have always been in the closet. That is my personal life. I have my public life and my personal life.
HELEN:	How does that make you feel? Do you wish you could let people know?
MARLENE:	No, that's just the way it is. I have my group of gay friends whom I socialize with, but as for everyone else, I keep it quiet.

The group members communicate feelings of loss, loneliness, and isolation. The lesbian world they belonged to and enjoyed no longer exists for them. However, the review of common life experiences connects group members and encourages mutual support. Passing through life as someone other than who you are, feeling that you have to hide your sexual orientation, and fearing that you might be caught and uncovered take a heavy daily toll. The group provides a safe environment for acceptance and unconditional regard.

People with *physical, intellectual, and emotional challenges* also experience oppression. In chapter 3, we presented the situation of Mrs. Richards to illustrate the life stressors experienced by a person with paranoia. The more overwhelmed and disabled a person is, the more directive and active a worker needs to be in helping the client to identify life stressors, goals, and coping skills. Mrs. Richards's social worker assumed an active, orchestrating stance in their work together.

In beginning with a chronically depressed client, the person's intense despair may well threaten the worker's own private demons. Hence, beginning practitioners must guard against a wish to simply "shake" a client out of a depression, or to detach themselves and flee from the threat of being engulfed by it. Most chronically depressed people manifest a lack of energy and bland affect; others may be agitated and even psychotic. A few will readily share the content and feelings of their depression. Practitioners must monitor their reactions to the client's depression and its manifestations in order to avoid judgments, impatience, and premature interpretations. The depressed client needs to feel the worker's acceptance, caring, and interest through helping the client confide his or her life story, express associated feelings, hew to reality, and comply with prescribed medication (Callahan & Turnbull, 2001).

People *addicted to alcohol or drugs* pervade social work caseloads. Whatever physical, emotional, and social stressors people have, alcohol abuse exacerbates their suffering and worsens their life circumstances. Alcohol and drug abuse makes the depressed more depressed, the hyperactive more hyperactive, the spouse abuser more abusive, the homeless more likely to remain homeless, and the employed more likely to become unemployed. A person who abuses alcohol and drugs presents special challenges to the social worker (Freeman, 2001; Hanson, 2001). Our profession in general has accepted the notion that alcohol and drug abusers must be immediately confronted with their addiction. However, when confronted in the precontemplative and contemplative phases, before they are ready to accept the labels of alcoholism and alcoholic or drug addiction and drug addict, many deny the problem and refuse to stop drinking. The belief is "I am not an alcoholic . . . I don't have to abstain from alcohol for the rest of my life." While denial is considered the core defense of the alcoholic, the denial might be a response to the practitioner's early confrontation. The more forcefully the social worker confronts, the more intensely the applicant or client counters with denials (Miller, 1983; Miller & Rollnick, 2002). We suggest that workers initially avoid confrontation. At the outset, people are more likely to accept only that they have some problem with drinking. Focusing on problem drinking or life issues created by the drinking is less likely to produce defensiveness. A group's first session is illustrative:

I began by stating, "It must have been hard to come in such terrible weather. I appreciate your coming. Before I ask you to introduce your-selves, let me restate what I see as the purpose of the group. I have spo-ken to each of you about the difficulties in your life and how your drinking was making them worse. Your drinking creates difficulties for you with your wives, girlfriends, children, relatives, and bosses. Since you have had similar experiences and current difficulties, I thought you could offer each other a great deal of support and help with the stress in your lives. What are your reactions?" Nick suggested we begin by in-troducing ourselves. I asked the other group members, and they agreed.

Nick began, "My name is Nick, and I want to make it clear that I am not an alcoholic, but I do drink a lot. I used to drink a lot of V.O. and ginger ale, and then I switched to wine. I used to buy two bottles of wine a day. It was costing me a lot of money. Now, I'm trying to drink less because I have big dental bills. I drink only in the apartment. I don't go to bars. I drink a bottle of wine every night before I go to sleep. I know I am not an alcoholic because I cut down with no problem. My main problem is that I don't work, I am on 100 percent disability, I don't know what to do with all my free time. I get very bored and down in the dumps."

Ralph spoke next. "I'm Ralph. I don't consider myself an alcoholic because I don't really crave it. I do have problems when I drink too much. Whenever I start to drink, I drink too much, and something hap-pens to me. I get into fights, or am attacked, or my wife gets crazy. I would like to stop drinking, but it's hard, man."

"My name is Jack, and I work at the post office. My supervisor tells me I am an alcoholic and insists I attend the postal alcoholic recovery group. My job depends on my participation in the group. Man, I know I got a problem drinking, but I ain't no alcoholic. But I don't want to lose my job. I don't know what to do."

The last member introduced himself. "Hi, my name is Gary, and I am an alcoholic. I drink on the spur of the moment, and I can't control it. I don't kid myself anymore. I drive a cab at night. I have a good night, and I say, well, before I go home I'll stop for one drink. I know that if I have that one drink, I am going to continue drinking, but I still have that one drink. I have lost some great jobs, and now my wife has moved out with the kids. I gotta find some ways to get control over my life."

The worker focuses on the stress in their lives created by drinking and avoids a struggle over their accepting the label "alcoholic." Several members assert "for the record" that they do not accept the label, immediately describe their problem drinking, and energetically begin to share their life patterns. By focusing on life stressors created by drinking rather than on the label, we tap into the positive side of the ambivalence. This supports potential for engagement. Miller and Rollnick (2002) emphasized that people with alcohol-related problems need to be treated as responsible adults capable of making decisions, rather than as weak, inferior, and diseased. Only they can decide whether to drink or not to drink. If they relapse, they can make a new decision to abstain. The social worker can only help the addicted person to struggle with life stressors and decisions, but cannot take responsibility for the drinking itself. The social worker has to convey empathy and respect for the client's struggles.

Trauma-Sensitive Beginnings

Applicants and clients dealing with traumatic events require specialized knowledge, sensitivity, and skills. The exploitation of a child for an adult's sexual pleasure, for example, is a devastating betrayal and abuse of power. The closer the child is to the offender, the greater the hurt (Alaggia & Kirshenbaum, 2005; Guelzow, Cornett, & Dougherty, 2002; Lovett, 2004; Sperry & Gilbert, 2005). A further betrayal transpires if the child discloses the abuse and is not believed, or is insensitively treated by family or an institution. Sexual abuse distorts the child's self-concept and undermines the child's sense of control over the environment. The linkage of sexuality with manipulation, force, fear, or secrecy traumatizes the child. The sexual trauma then shapes the child's behavior in inappropriate ways, including erotic relating to others, compulsive sexual play, obsessive masturbation, and withdrawal from peers. As teenagers and adults, sexually abused children will be at risk of self-destructive behaviors such as promiscuity, prostitution, anorexia, bulimia, suicide, addictions, hypervigilance or impaired judgment about others' trustworthiness, or reenactment of their own abuse (Finkelhor & Browne, 1985; Finkelhor, Hotaling, Lewis, & Smith, 1990; Vera, Alegria, Pattatucci-Aragon, & Pena, 2005). In beginning with a sexually abused child, the worker must follow the child's sense of timing and pacing in discussing the trauma.

Barbara is a bright, engaging, nine-year-old white youngster. Her mother's boyfriend sexually abused her for three years from the age of four to seven. When she turned seven she told her mother, "Bill hurt me downstairs with his finger." Protective Services investigated the accusation, but the matter was dropped when Bill passed a lie detector test. Barbara was not even taken for a medical examination. Six months later, Barbara's mother resumed her relationship with Bill. Two years later the mother lost her job, and she and Barbara left the area and moved in with Barbara's grandmother, thereby ending the relationship with Bill.

Barbara came to the attention of the community mental health center when she was found engaging in oral sex with a neighborhood friend. She was also having difficulty in adjusting to a new school and complained of nightmares and anxiety. In the first session, Barbara and the social worker agreed to work on difficulties she and her mother were having in getting along and on her own confusing memories about Bill.

The social worker hypothesized that the relationship to her mother had been affected by Barbara's likely feelings of having been left unprotected by the person she most expected to protect her. She trusted her mother and risked disclosure. Yet Bill remained an active member of the household. In fact, Barbara's mother was reluctant to believe that her Bill could be capable of such abhorrent behavior. Barbara may have blamed herself since "something unexplainable, out of the child's realm of understanding, is being done furtively or coercively, or both, so it must mean that the child is bad" (Friedrich, 1990, p. 149). Barbara turned confusion and despair against herself. She overdosed on her asthma medication and exhibited hypersexualized behaviors such as inappropriate sex play, provocative dress, and seductiveness. She also suffered anxiety and nightmares in which Bill was watching her and sneaking into her room through a window.

Barbara and the worker agreed that every week the worker would ask Barbara if she felt ready to talk about the "hard stuff" concerning Bill. This gave the child some sense of control over what and when to disclose. The social worker knows that Barbara has to begin to learn to trust. In an early session, while playing a game with Barbara, the worker asked if Barbara felt ready for the hard stuff:

BARBARA:	But I just got here!
WORKER:	I know time goes by very quickly when we are playing together and having a good time.
BARBARA:	(After a short silence) Well, I did have a nightmare the other night.
WORKER:	What happened in the nightmare?
BARBARA:	(With heightened anxiety) Well, I was in my bed and I thought Bill was climbing in my window. I thought he was coming to get me.
WORKER:	Oh, how scary!
BARBARA:	Yeah, it was, and I had to get out of bed and tie my closet door and my bedroom door with a hair ribbon because that covers the window.
WORKER:	It was so scary—you had to figure out some way to keep him out?
BARBARA:	Yeah, because my window doesn't have a shade, and my room is so small.
WORKER:	What an awful nightmare. Bill could come through your window and then you would be trapped with him in your

little room and he would hurt you. (Barbara, looking worried, nods her head in agreement.)

WORKER: What did you do—how did you get to feel safe?

BARBARA: I ran into Mommy's room—I slept in her bed.

WORKER: And Mommy helped you to feel better? (Barbara nods yes.)

WORKER: I am glad because that was a very scary dream. Do you have these dreams often?

BARBARA: Yeah, last night I had another dream—it was more like a nightmare!

WORKER: (Nodding her head to encourage her to continue) Tell me about it.

BARBARA: Well, my uncle took me swimming and we were having a lot of fun in the pool, but then I turned around and couldn't find him.

WORKER: (Looking concerned) What happened next?

BARBARA: I went to look for him at the bar, but he wasn't there. But when I turned around, I saw Bill and then I screamed really loud.

WORKER: You must have been really shocked and scared to see him.

BARBARA: Yeah, but I don't think I could have screamed in real life. I think I would call him a bastard or something.

WORKER: Because you're so angry with him for what he did to you?

BARBARA: Yeah, and then I thought, well . . . maybe I should write this part down.

WORKER: (Handing Barbara pen and paper) Okay?

BARBARA: (After writing down what she wanted, she handed the piece of paper back.)

WORKER: Is it OK if I read it aloud?

BARBARA: (Nods)

WORKER: (Reads) "And I was thinking he might have touched me there. I know I said it happened in his bedroom, but I think it happened more than once."

WORKER: It's terribly confusing for you.

The worker legitimizes Barbara's fear and creates a climate in which she feels safe in a supported environment to begin to discuss her fears. The worker follows Barbara's cues about how and when to proceed, pursuing suppressed traumatic material at the child's pace. She stays focused, and the ongoing phase begins.

We now turn to helping people with stressful life transitions and traumatic events.

SEVEN

HELPING INDIVIDUALS, FAMILIES, AND GROUPS WITH STRESSFUL LIFE TRANSITIONS AND TRAUMATIC EVENTS

Helping people manage stressful life transitions and traumatic events requires distinctive knowledge and skills.

Transitional Processes as Life Stressors

Stressful Life Transitions

Across the life course, human beings must cope with numerous social transitions. They must cope with stress associated with a developmental phase. Puberty, for example, is biological, but adolescence is a social status. They are not the same. Adolescence has been recognized as a social category in our own society and culture only since the late nineteenth century and has slowly been extended well beyond the duration of puberty. Adolescence is not recognized in all societies: in some cultures, puberty alone marks the entry into the rights and responsibilities of adulthood, with no intervening state. In Western societies, adolescence is often associated with rebellious behavior. Social workers mostly meet troubled teenagers in their practice (Armstrong, 2001).

The value placed on particular biological changes varies across cultures. In traditional Asian societies old age is venerated, as it is among Native Americans. In many segments of American society, however, becoming old is frequently regarded with dread. The aging process begins at birth and continues until death. But the upper end of the life course presents universal, biologically based life transitions with cultural and psychological components and social consequences. For some elderly, life stressors associated with the biological transition and the change in social status may include poor health, diminished financial resources, social isolation, and losses. If such stressors exceed coping resources, aging is experienced as a difficult life stressor (McNeil, 1995).

Human beings also cope with stress associated with new experiences and relationships, or leaving familiar ones. Beginnings require a change in status and new role demands. Whether entering a new school, a new relationship or marriage, or a new job, or having a child, status entries create some degree of stress. Exits from desired social statuses imposed by divorce, loss of employment, placement of a child, or widowhood are usually more potent stressors than entry into new statuses.

Thwarted life transitions can also be extremely stressful. The diagnosis of infertility for a couple can be as painful as coping with the loss of a valued relationship. A child or a parent suffers terribly when his or her desires to be reunited are thwarted. A high school student who is unable to attend college also suffers from thwarted aspirations. Blockages to desired life transitions create frustrations and stress in people's lives.

Certain life transitions carry powerful societal as well as internalized stigma. Transitioning from a physically or mentally healthy person to a person with a diagnosis of HIV/AIDS or mental illness, from a heterosexual to a homosexual person, from a person with some difficulty with alcohol to an alcoholic, or from an ambulatory person to a wheelchair-bound person carries significant adaptive burdens and challenges. The external judgments and personalized meanings attributed to these transitions substantially add to the level of stress experienced.

The timing of a status transition and life event affects cognition and perception. When entering into a new experience comes too early or too late in the life course, the potential for stress is increased. For example, a young adolescent who becomes a parent, a young child who is not ready for day care, and a grandmother who must take on parenting tasks may all experience intense stress because of the problematic timing.

Some people have the additional burden of dealing simultaneously with developmental changes, social life transitions, and traumatic events. For example, Louise, a Jamaican thirteen-year-old, was admitted to the hospital for correction of a slipped epiphysis (part of a bone that ossifies separately and then becomes attached to the main part of the bone). Since the surgery she has been in a spike cast, which keeps her flat on her back. After the cast is removed she will be in traction, and following discharge she will require weeks of recuperation at home. The head nurse, because of crying fits, tantrums, and uncooperative behavior, referred Louise to social service. The worker learned the following from Louise and her family.

When Louise was five months old, her parents left Jamaica for England and better economic conditions, leaving the baby with her grandmother. Many years passed, and they had seven more children. Louise knew of her parents and siblings in England, but had no contact with them. The only mother Louise knew was her grandmother, and her first nine years were apparently happy and stable ones. Three years ago her grandmother became ill and could no longer care for her. Louise was sent to the United States to live in a large city with her aunts, who were married with children of their own. The aunts accepted full responsibility for and financial support of Louise.

The aunts said that Louise adapted well to living in the city. She made friends. She is cooperative and helpful around the house and babysits for her young cousins. Although bright, she is lazy about studying and had to repeat the fifth grade. She is now in the sixth grade. Recently her grandmother died, and the aunts said Louise took the loss very hard. Louise's medical problem was only recently recognized. She started walking awkwardly a year ago, and the aunts urged her to lose weight (the worker noted her obesity). But her walking became worse, and they brought her to the hospital.

Her aunts told Louise's mother about the surgery, and she flew to the United States. The visit was extremely painful for Louise. In front of the aunts and Louise, her mother complained that Louise was being "spoiled." She talked of taking Louise back to England but stopped short of any action. She visited Louise three times, one of which went badly. Crying, she told Louise how homesick she was and how she wanted to go back to England. Louise told her mother that if she wanted to go, she could. When her mother left, Louise began to have crying fits and temper tantrums.

This "normal" early adolescent youngster has endured many grave losses. She faced pressing tasks of adapting to a new environment; a new family; a new school; a different climate, culture, and lifestyle; the loss of her beloved grandmother; rejection by her own mother; the medical trauma of hospitalization, pain, and surgery; and the prospect of a long convalescence.

All transitions have to be understood within an ethnic or racial context. In the above illustration, knowledge of Jamaican culture suggests that West Indian families are closely knit, and extended members are significant resources. While white social workers may assume Jamaican culture is the same as African American culture, their historic and contemporary experiences have been very different. Jamaica's history of slavery began and ended much earlier than that of the United States. West Indian blacks have a strong sense of ethnic identity and identification with their particular island's culture, shaped by their African roots and island life.

Traumatic Life Events

Traumatic life events represent losses of the severest kind—the death of a child, rape, the birth of a genetically defective child, a natural disaster, or a terrorist attack. Such events are experienced as disastrous and overwhelming and, therefore, tend to immobilize us. While a traumatic event can provide opportunity for growth and mastery, inherent is the hazard of regressed functioning if the tasks in resolving the trauma are not successfully completed (Bussey & Wise, 2007).

The chronic pain and obsessional thoughts often associated with the traumatic life event may last a long time. The crisis caused by the unexpected death of a spouse may be limited, but the stressful process of mourning may continue. The stressful transition from husband to widower will continue long after the crisis of bereavement has subsided. A condition such as AIDS leads to progressive phases of functional impairment. Each phase of deteriorating health may precipitate its own trauma and associated stress (Getzel & Willroth, 2001). Traumatic life events can remain a significant issue throughout the life course. A ninety-five-year-old resident of a nursing home shared with her social worker for the first time that she had been sexually abused by her father. To cope with the trauma, she had repressed the experience for a lifetime, not feeling safe enough to share her secret. Although the defense of repression helped manage the pain of betrayal, it blocked her from dealing with the assault and from learning to trust and to be intimate. At ninety-five, she took the first steps and risked asking her younger sisters whether their father had also sexually abused them.

Social Work Function, Modalities, Methods, and Skills

The Worker and Stressful Life Transitions and Traumatic Events

With people who are experiencing life stressors that arise from difficult developmental and social transitions and traumatic life events, the social worker helps them effectively cope with the biological, cognitive, emotional, behavioral, and social demands posed by the life issue within a particular environment and cultural context. The social worker helps people move through stressful life transitions and deal with traumatic life events in such a way that their adaptive capacities are supported and strengthened, and the environment's responsiveness increased.

Professional Methods and Skills

Helping individuals, families, and groups cope with life stressors of painful transitions and traumatic events requires a repertoire of professional modalities, methods, and skills. By enabling, exploring and clarifying, mobilizing, guiding, and facilitating, the social worker supports and strengthens people's adaptive capacities and problem-solving abilities.

Enabling is encouraged by a professional stance of "I'm with you, and want to help you with your concerns." Enabling clients to present their concerns requires skills that include encouraging with minimal responses; wait-

Table 7.1
Enabling Skills

- Use minimal responses to encourage.
- Wait out a silence.
- Reach for a silence.
- Reach for facts.
- Verbalize feelings.
- Legitimize and universalize thoughts, reactions, and feelings.
- Reach for specific feelings.
- Highlight specific cues.
- Rephrase concerns.
- Use metaphors, analogies, and euphemisms.
- Use humor.
- Summarize concerns.
- Share thoughts and feelings.

ing out silence; reaching for facts; verbalizing feelings; legitimizing and universalizing thoughts, reactions, and feelings; emphasizing and highlighting specific cues; rephrasing concerns; using figures of speech and, occasionally, humor; and sharing one's thoughts and feelings as appropriate. These skills were discussed in the previous chapter and are summarized in Table 7.1.

Through *exploring and clarifying*, focus and direction are provided to the work. Some clients confide and explore their life stressors with relative ease, others ramble without focus or direction, and still others remain painfully silent. In helping clients to confide and explore their concerns and feelings, the social worker's tasks are to help the person explore the objective and subjective facts about the life transition. The following skills are used to address these tasks:

- *Developing focus and direction.* The social worker explores and clarifies with a professional stance that conveys, "I'm with you and I need your help in understanding better." By developing a clear and mutual focus in the work, client and social worker minimize the emergence of competing or overlapping concerns. Focus and attention are associated with the achievement of agreed-on goals.

- *Specifying concerns.* People express their concerns in vague phrases such as "My husband is unfair" or "And I thought he had integrity." A general term may cover an important life story and also have different meanings to clients and social workers. Abstractions such as "integrity" and "unfair" require clarification: "In what way is he unfair?" or "Can you give me an example of his being unfair?" Specifying what clients mean improves clarity in communication.

- *Reaching for the meaning of experiences.* People attribute different meanings to life experiences. The worker explores such hidden or understated meanings by direct questioning: "What does the idea of divorce mean to you?" or "Telling the truth is very important to you?" By reaching for the meaning of experiences, the social worker explores belief and value systems that influence behavior (Levine & Lightburn, 1989).
- *Exploring ambivalence.* In exploring ambivalence, the practitioner examines the duality of conscious feelings: "Let's identify the main reasons and feelings you have for wanting and not wanting to leave your lover." People are sometimes aware of one side of their ambivalence, but not the other. Thus gentle questions or comments are needed to bring the other side to awareness: "You say you have decided to leave your lover. Sometimes people have doubts about big decisions. What about you?" Often the ambivalence is unconscious and therefore exerts a powerful influence on behavior, without the person's awareness.
- *Identifying discrepant messages.* Mixed thoughts and feelings are communicated through contradictory messages. To explore the extent and depth of life transitional concerns, discrepancies between verbal and nonverbal behavior are identified and clarified: "You say it doesn't bother you, but I notice you are clenching your fist," or "I am confused by your saying how angry you are at your lover's coming home at 2:00 A.M., but then having sex with him."
- *Recreating experiences.* Some people intellectualize concerns; efforts to focus and specify fall short because associated emotions have been removed from the content. At these times, the worker helps the client reexperience the situation by dramatizing events and episodes: "So you remember your brother sneaking into your room late at night. What were you thinking and feeling when you first saw him coming toward you?" By recreating the experience, the client's affect is more likely to be engaged in exploration.
- *Sharing being puzzled.* Communications are complex and difficult to follow. Practitioners should not pretend to understand when, in fact, they don't understand people's communications: "I am unclear about what you just said; could you tell me again?" Asking for help in understanding can clear up contradictions in behavior and ideas for the client as well as for the worker.
- *Patterning concerns.* In presenting stressors, people may focus on repetitive details or behaviors. Helping them to see patterns and themes encourages greater depth in exploring and clarifying (e.g., "I noticed your major battles with Billy seem to have started over his coming home and putting on the TV. Let's examine this"). By observing a pattern, the person, family, or group is able to examine various isolated incidents in a new way.
- *Offering a hypothesis.* A hypothesis provides a new frame of reference for people to consider; for instance, "Do you think it is possible that a lot of your hurt and anger with your father is being transferred to your son?" or "I wonder if your husband gains control over you through his silence." Suffi-

client data and timing are essential before sharing one's inference or hypothesis. Premature interpretation could prove to be incorrect, or the client might not be ready to accept it. Skilled, tentative questions can evoke a client's own recognition and acceptance.

- *Inviting feedback.* Inviting the client's reactions should follow directive interventions: "What's your reaction to what I suggested?" The client may directly respond whether the hypothesis is helpful or unhelpful. Other responses may be more indirect: "I guess you're right," or "Yes, but . . . !" The worker reaches for hesitation, lack of clarity, or negative reactions. Even if the advice or interpretation is perceived as unresponsive and unhelpful, the client's feedback stimulates further work. Without client feedback, the worker may sound "smart" or be insightful, but the work is not deepened.

- *Providing feedback.* People may be unaware of how others perceive them. By sharing one's own reactions to a client, the social worker provides valuable feedback. When offered out of caring and concern and not because of frustration or anger, such feedback is more likely to be accepted. After trust has been developed, the worker may share reactions directly: "When you answer only 'yes' or 'no' to my questions, I feel frustrated in understanding and I really want to understand." The worker's reaction is presented in concrete, behavioral terms and expressed calmly in a caring manner.

- *Inviting self-reflection.* Self-reflection and self-discovery have more profound and lasting outcomes than giving advice and interpretation. When a client grasps the relation between current and earlier experiences, the realization is more likely to be "owned" and transferred to other situations and experiences. Encouraging clients to reflect on and to consider self-defeating patterns is initiated by tentative questions such as "Do you sense any similarities among the last three men you have dated?" or "What happens to you when you feel out of control?" Such questions enable clients to see patterns in their life experiences. By encouraging a client to self-reflect, dependence on the worker for advice and interpretations decreases, and self-direction and self-regulation increase.

These exploring and clarifying skills are used in various combinations. The worker assumes the initiative in stepping out in front of the client in order to deepen their professional interchange. These interactions must be responsive to people's signals that they are ready to explore and clarify, rather than reflecting the worker's impatience or need to be in control. Helping requires the worker to follow the client's cues and signals rather than the reverse. Table 7.2 summarizes exploring and clarifying skills.

In *mobilizing*, the social worker strengthens people's motivation to deal with painful life stressors and manage disabling feelings and stress. For some, the support, caring, and interest they experience in elaborating their life story and the help provided in exploring their concerns are sufficient to

Table 7.2
Exploring and Clarifying Skills

- Develop focus and direction.
- Specify concerns.
- Reach for the meaning of experiences.
- Explore ambivalence.
- Identify discrepant messages.
- Recreate experiences.
- Share being unclear.
- Pattern concerns.
- Offer a hypothesis.
- Invite feedback.
- Provide feedback.
- Invite self-reflection.

release energy and provide a sense of well-being. Others, however, require more help with mobilizing their personal strengths and motivation.

- *Identifying strengths.* People who seek out (or accept the offer of) professional help may feel inadequate and insecure. Self-doubt and preoccupation with life issues and limitations can be immobilizing. The worker breaks through this by identifying the person's or group's strengths: "Raising three children as a single parent and working full-time takes so much energy, determination, and skill; let's look at all the things you do to manage so effectively." Helping people to review their competencies creates a foundation for coping (Saleebey, 2006).
- *Offering reassurance.* At times, realistic reassurance provides important support: "The doctor told me you are undergoing a simple surgery, and she is confident there is absolutely nothing to worry about." However, if the reassurance is unrealistic the worker's credibility is seriously damaged.
- *Offering hope.* Without hope that things can improve, people despair. The social worker offers needed hope by conveying confidence that something beneficial will emerge from their work together. Specifying tasks ranging from simple to more complex provides potential for success: "I know you can be firm with Jennifer the next time she stays out all night; you can stick to your guns in the way we rehearsed."

Some people are unable to manage their feelings and resolve a life issue because they lack necessary information or are hampered by misinformation. Others have difficulty because they do not recognize their dysfunctional, possibly self-destructive patterns. They are overwhelmed by life events despite their potential abilities to manage feelings and to solve problems. Perhaps they are immobilized by a particular life event (e.g., surgery or divorce). In these situations, the worker calls on the method of *guiding* to encourage inherent coping abilities.

- *Providing relevant information.* Information about their concerns principally flows from clients to social workers. However, clients also need and expect relevant information from their workers. For example, information about the common phases of bereavement and community resources is an essential tool for effective coping with loss. If the need for information is unfulfilled, people feel frustrated.
- *Correcting misinformation.* Misinformation about physical, emotional, and social functioning is an additional stressor. For instance, adolescents who believe that crack is not addictive until used a few times, or that the rhythm method or withdrawal will prevent pregnancy, must be given accurate information.
- *Offering advice.* In seeking or accepting an offer of social work services, people expect advice about what to do and are dissatisfied when little advice is forthcoming. Advice is offered to encourage people to try a new approach: "I suggest you present Jessica with an 11:00 P.M. weekday curfew and enforce it by . . ." or, to discourage the use of a maladaptive behavior, "When Jessica misses dinner, I think it's best if you did not reheat the food for her." The practitioner determines how direct the advice should be depending on the severity of the issue and the person's level of anxiety or impairment. The advice can range from suggesting, to urging, to warning, to insisting. In offering advice, social workers must avoid imposing their own values and coping styles. The advice should be responsive to what a client is requesting and is prepared to hear, rather than to the worker's need to demonstrate concrete help. For clients who cannot manage emotions and solve problems, the worker may become an important teacher of life skills, calling on the method of guiding to develop problem-solving strategies as needed. The worker pays attention to the differing ways in which people learn. Some learn primarily by taking action ("enactive" learners); others learn primarily by summarizing, visualizing, and organizing perceptions into patterns and images ("iconic" learners); still others, "symbolic" learners, learn primarily by abstracting and conceptualizing (Bruner, 1966). The worker uses a diverse repertoire of guiding skills, depending upon individual and social factors.
- *Discussing.* Discussion helps people learn coping behaviors. By focusing discussion on the meaning of the life transition, the social worker explores faulty perceptions, reasoning, and beliefs, and helps clients learn ways of restructuring maladaptive thought processes. As discussion leader, the worker (1) poses questions to stimulate clients' reflective thinking aloud; (2) supports and encourages client examination and evaluation of alternative coping responses; and (3) maintains a flexible focus to provide clients sufficient "space" to examine, explore, and try new behaviors.
- *Presenting.* Informal and brief exposition of issues and ideas by the worker can increase people's problem-solving abilities. Practitioners share what they know simply and without jargon. Introducing such simple ideas as ignoring a child's tantrum, praising a child for appropriate behavior, and

developing their own observing and listening skills helps parents. New knowledge has a profound effect. Helping people master the steps in problem solving is important: delaying immediate action, defining issues, developing means to deal with the life issue, evaluating means, and selecting and carrying out specific action.

- *Visualizing.* Graphic presentations can illuminate heretofore unidentified patterns of relationships and behavior. Genograms portray family trees over several generations, including illnesses, occupations, nicknames, and migrations. Similarly, ecomaps delineate the complexity of people's transactions with the environment. For people who are primarily visual learners, graphic representations especially enhance understanding.

- *Participating.* In work with children and severely impaired adults, games and activities facilitate comfort in interaction. For some, it is much easier to talk while doing something. Activities are also used to help people learn to manage their feelings and problems (Leahy, 2004; McFerran-Skewes, 2004; Middleman, 1980; Tillyn & Caye, 2004). Managing feelings is also learned by relaxation exercises as well as by systematic desensitization and cognitive behavioral interventions. Role-play can prepare a survivor of incest for a conversation with her mother. Role reversal permits a person to examine her own as well as her mother's experience and reactions. By mirroring the incest survivor in a role-play, the social worker demonstrates how her mother will perceive her. By role recreation and dramatization, the woman examines the actual conversation with her mother, analyzing its effectiveness. By role modeling and coaching, the social worker demonstrates effective communication skills (Regan, 1992; Rose, Duby, Olenick, & Weston, 1996). Family sculpture dramatizes interpersonal patterns in families. By sculpting, family members consider and reflect on their interpersonal roles (Hartman & Laird, 1983).

- *Specifying action tasks.* People might require assistance in planning next steps. For example, with a couple planning to separate or divorce and worried about their children's reactions, the social worker might say at an appropriate time, "Let's decide when and where you want to tell the children, how you want to tell them, and what you want to tell them." The more active and specific the task, the more likely it will be put into action. Similarly, the more actively people are involved in specifying and selecting their tasks, the more likely progress will result (Reid, 1992).

- *Preparing and planning for task completion.* In addition to specifying actions to be taken, clients prepare and plan for such actions. Assignments such as "During the week, how about you write down what you want to tell your father about his abuse . . ." or role-play such as "I'll be your father—let's rehearse what you will say to him" are helpful in preparing clients to carry out agreed-upon tasks. Such preparation helps them to anticipate and handle possible responses, as when others remain silent, refuse to listen, or deny

Table 7.3
Guiding Skills

- Provide relevant information.
- Correct misinformation.
- Offer advice.
- Discuss.
- Present.
- Visualize.
- Participate.
- Specify action tasks.
- Prepare and plan for task completion.

responsibility for their actions. When preparatory planning is completed, it is useful to review and summarize the agreed-upon approach.

Table 7.3 summarizes guiding skills.

Clients can be reluctant to work on painful life transitions and traumatic life events. Discomfort arises when one must reveal, share, confide, and explore one's troubles. Even the most skillful practitioner cannot easily overcome the client's tendency to avoid the vexing and painful. Avoidance is expressed by active provocation, intellectualization, interruption, verbosity, and seductiveness, or by passive withdrawal, compliance, procrastination, and extreme diffidence. Flight behaviors such as changing the subject, withholding data, and minimizing concerns are often encountered. If avoidance persists, *facilitating* encourages clients to remain committed to the work. The worker challenges and demands purposive work, but does so in a supportive manner.

- *Identifying avoidance patterns.* Identifying the avoidance pattern is the first step. The social worker makes an explicit, direct statement about the pattern and its self-defeating consequences: "I notice you have many excuses for not seeing a doctor about your diabetes when you know it's very important for you to do so," or "Every time we begin to talk about your son and his homosexuality, you change the subject; we have to find a way to talk about it because it is upsetting you very much."
- *Challenging the illusion of engagement.* When a social worker and client become too comfortable with each other, an illusion of work may develop (they may in fact collude to avoid pain). Engagement in the helping process requires focus, direction, and investment of energy and motivation. The illusion of work has to be challenged by the worker: "I sense a lack of urgency and energy in our work." Schwartz (1971, p. 11) identified a core professional task as "continually challenging the client to address himself resolutely and with energy to what he came to do."

- *Generating anxiety.* To break through avoidance, people need to experience some discomfort: "You have to make discharge plans because the hospital will kick you out." Out of concern and caring, the social worker challenges a person's defenses and generates a degree of anxiety needed to advance the work. By demanding focus on core issues, the worker creates sufficient tension to mobilize coping efforts.
- *Responding with directness to discrepant messages.* At times, pointing out discrepancies between verbal and nonverbal messages helps to move the work ahead. Sometimes, a more direct approach is required ("How come you tell me you stopped drinking when I can smell the alcohol on your breath?" or "Look at all these things you have done that are self-defeating, yet you tell me you're not hurt by his leaving you"). The worker makes the contradictions explicit and prods the client to deal with them.

These interventions challenge avoidance and seek to stimulate and mobilize energy for work. They work only if trust and confidence in the worker's caring have been established. Thus, these skills are used selectively and with caution. If they are used inappropriately, defenses are intensified and dropout from service is likely.

How practitioners use these diverse methods and skills depends on their individuality, creativity, and experience. In this section, we present practice materials to illustrate how social workers have helped individuals, families, and groups deal with difficult life transitions and traumatic events.

Practice Illustrations

Stressful Life Transitions

In chapter 6, we described the initial phase of the work with George R., a fifteen-year-old African American. Here we pick up on the ongoing phase, starting with the third interview.

Before George's third interview, a relative commented on George's coming to the clinic. This reinforced George's fear that everyone considered him crazy. He refused to return to the clinic. (Adolescents attach stigma to mental health services, and many black and other minority communities also view such services with suspicion.) George's probation officer and the worker decided that George should be told that the court ordered him to continue until his next court hearing. The probation officer was a young African American who liked George and felt strongly that the precipitating factor in George's emotional upheaval was the move to a new school where he was poorly handled from the beginning. However, the probation officer exerted benign but firm authority by spelling out rules of conduct, repeating them weekly, and gradually allowing George more freedom as he seemed able to tolerate it. Mrs. R. trusted the probation officer and supported his decisions. The social worker recorded:

Third and fourth interviews. George did not bring up his earlier decision to drop out of service, and when I mentioned it, he grinned and acknowledged that it was all right as long as no one thought he came because he wanted to. In these two interviews, we dealt with George's feelings about the recent traumatic events. There were some wild threats to "get" the school counselor and to sue everybody, and one or two lapses into fantasy. As George gave a detailed account of his experiences with the police, it was obvious that he could not tolerate the feelings of helplessness associated with handcuffs. His fears on the psychiatric ward were similar. He told me about patients who were strapped down, and he was particularly concerned about a patient who suffered delirium tremens. George had been put in restraints when he first arrived. As he told of this, he groaned and was perspiring. I answered his questions and tried to underline the fact that, given a very difficult and frightening situation, he had handled some things very well. I did this to cut through some of the grandiosity and also the abject feelings of inferiority and inability to cope effectively.

He told of a second time he had been threatened with restraints. This had occurred after he had been told he could not go home prior to the court hearing, and he understood that he was considered crazy and dangerous. He then began threatening to kill ward personnel, and he behaved in a psychotic manner. As we talked, he agreed he would label as crazy someone who behaved as he had. I suggested that whenever he felt someone in authority was criticizing him, "You seem to knock yourself out proving they are right." He was amused by my choice of words and agreed. I tried to carry this further by bringing up the way he had behaved in school in an instance he brought up, but he would not accept this, as he was still too angry with these people. George brought the subject back to the psychiatric ward, and said it wasn't just that he had to prove he was as bad as they thought—he was also scared. I agreed. By the end of this fourth hour, he was speaking coherently, calmly, and with surprising self-understanding.

The worker identifies George's strengths in dealing with a very frightening situation, and through clarification offers an interpretation of a dysfunctional behavioral pattern. When George agrees with the interpretation, the worker prematurely offers a second interpretation. George disagrees and returns to his primary message of concern about being scared when placed at the psychiatric ward. Timing is an essential factor in a client's ability to "hear" an interpretative comment.

Fifth interview. George's improvement was striking. He began by telling me of a new boy, his age, who had moved next door. They had swapped music tapes. (Later, his mother telephoned to tell me this was the first time George had a friend in a long time. She was extremely pleased.) After a short silence, George said he was thinking about school. He wondered if they'd let him re-enroll after the court hearing. The semester is "mostly gone, and what will I do? I don't know, but I'll get A's. They can't stop me if I try hard enough." I said, "Why do you have to get A's? Superman again?" He tried to deny that getting A's was impossible. I said, "It will be a triumph if you can pass any of your courses." He finally admitted this. I said, "So how come you set such goals? You know, I think when you do this, you are very mean to yourself." He said it was the school personnel who were mean to him. I said, "You are the one who says you have to be Superman. It's you who won't give yourself credit for doing the best you can." After a long pause, he said, "You have to get A's to be a doctor. I'm going to be a doctor, not just any doctor; I'm going to be the head doctor. My mother says they try to keep blacks from being doctors, so a black has to be better than any white doctor. I'll run the whole hospital; I'll be the one who tells the white doctors what to do." He stopped, then said firmly, "And don't go talking about Superman. On TV, Superman is not a doctor." We both smiled, then I said that regardless of our smiles, I felt this subject meant a great deal to him.

He said, "Ever since I was born, I guess I was going to be a doctor." He told of his mother buying him a set of encyclopedias "when I couldn't even read much at all. And I read them too. I read all the way to the M's." He sounded very depressed. I said, "Then what happened?" He said, "I just stopped, that's all. I got too tired, maybe, I don't know. It is like being tired." I asked when that was, and he said, "in junior high." As he talked, he told how hard he had tried to get good grades, but he never got better than a C in junior high. I said, "And that is why you stopped reading the encyclopedia?" He said, "It wasn't any use. My brother could read all the way through them, if he tried. He doesn't even have to read them; he always gets A's. I guess he will be the doctor." Long pause, then, "I don't know what will happen to me." He sat silent for a time, and then said, "It is strange here. We talk and talk and then everything is said, and there is nothing more. Only silence." I said, "Yes, that is how it can feel, when you have finally been able to tell so much about yourself."

When George informs the worker of his expectations to receive all A's, she challenges the illusion and invites him to view the unrealistic expectations in a new way. Using the metaphor of Superman helps George to connect his grandiose statements with his feelings of inferiority. The worker uses various exploration skills to invite elaboration of his feelings of inferiority to his brother.

Four days later, the worker received a frantic call from George's mother. The police had picked up George for attempted shoplifting, took him home, and notified the probation officer.

Sixth interview. George said he was falsely accused of stealing. He went into the store to buy a bicycle pump, had the money in his pocket, and was holding the article "in plain sight" when he decided to go out on the sidewalk to tell his brother something. He carried the pump with him. He was planning to prove in court that he had stood in the doorway rather than on the sidewalk and therefore was not guilty. He would then sue the store for false arrest. He said, "They could send me to the youth authority for nothing!"

I shared my concern that at times it seems he gets himself into precisely this kind of trouble, in which he feels both abused and innocent. I pointed out that it seemed this had happened before and referred to his telling me in an earlier hour about being falsely accused of vandalism. He finally acknowledged that maybe he had behaved in a suspicious manner.

I said that two things might have upset him this time. One was the notice of the court hearing, which came the day of the attempted theft. The other was what we had talked about last time. He said, "And I wouldn't want to do something suspicious before court, that doesn't make sense. I want to go back to school." I said, "Last time we talked about grades." "Oh yes, how could I forget that?" Then he said, "One other time I was out of school, and I didn't flunk. It was when I had my operation." He said that in the third grade, he was operated on "because my navel stuck out like a pickle."

We talked of the operation in terms of how a "little kid" would have felt about it. He said, "It's when you wake up that it's bad. I saw this scar. It's long enough they could have done anything inside me. I didn't know what they could have done. They could reach just about anywhere from so big a scar." I said, "What did you worry they had done?" With great hesitation and embarrassment, he revealed his fantasy: "Is there a tube, I mean a connection, from your navel to your . . . sex parts?" He felt they had shortened or somehow badly damaged his penis, and this was why he hadn't grown. "When a little kid is the smallest in the whole school, even smaller than his brother, and he sees a midget, you know what he thinks? He thinks he's a midget too." He then asked me to tell him what had happened during the operation. I described a hernia repair as well as I could, and he said with great relief, "Only muscles? Well, then, I'm all right. My stomach muscles are all right, you use them to lift weights." (Later I learned from his mother that he had not only a hernia repair but also a circumcision and tonsillectomy during the same operation at age six.)

I asked if he had current fears about his penis. He said, "No, I think it's OK. But you can be scared of things just the same." I then brought him back to the fears surrounding the operation and said maybe the operation had something to do with some of his current fears. I wondered, for instance, if he wasn't afraid of being helpless, tied down, and handcuffed, in much the same way a boy is afraid of submitting to an operation. He thought about that very seriously, and said, "I'm always afraid of being at the mercy of someone. Like someone is going to do something terrible. That part's like an operation." I said, "So you have to pretend to yourself you are Superman, because you are afraid of being helpless. You're really not as helpless anymore. In fact, I imagine you'll be able to get through court this time without being so scared and without pretending you're Superman either." He said, "I'm sort of worried about that." We decided we'd talk more about it next session, several days before the hearing.

The worker offers an interpretation about George's setting himself up to be an abused victim in relation to the forthcoming court appearance. The worker moves ahead of George's readiness to assess her interpretation. Thus, this interpretation seems premature, lacking sufficient client exploration and involvement, and possibly reflecting the worker's own frustration with his self-defeating pattern. When George shares the trauma of his surgery at the age of six, the worker skillfully invites his major worry ("What did you worry they had done?"). This moves them into the taboo area of concerns about possible damage to his penis. The worker provides relevant information about a hernia operation, clearing up misconceptions and greatly relieving George. However, after reaching for George's current concerns about his penis, the worker does not explore his tentative response, "I think it's OK. But you can be scared of things just the same." The worker changed focus, and lost an opportunity to reach for his fears and insecurities. The lengthy interpretation of George's current behavior and its relation to this childhood experience illustrates a worker regaining control over an uncomfortable situation rather than making a helpful intervention.

Seventh interview. George said he was worried about court and what the judge might do to him. The judge would never believe he hadn't tried to steal the bicycle pump. He said the probation officer was going to get a report from me to give the judge. I asked if he was wondering if I would say he hadn't tried to steal it. He asked what I would say. I said I believed him when he said he hadn't, but I also believed he had tried to make it look as if he were stealing, even though he wasn't aware of it at the time. We then discussed my perception, primarily in terms of his doing these things when he is upset and feeling not good and unable to defend himself. I related this to his feelings about court and about not being able to do as well in school as his younger brother.

For the first time, he admitted that he started that final school fight by hitting a boy who called him "brainless." He said, "But I don't want to admit this in court. The judge will think I'm no good." I said, "Again, I think you are meaner to yourself than any judge could possibly be. You look at one thing you consider a failure, and you damn yourself. I think the judge will consider other things, too, like the fact that you have been able to go to the park and play baseball these past two weekends, have had no fights, and even with the bicycle pump business, you didn't lose control of yourself. I don't think he will find you a worthless person because you can't get the world's best grade, an A." He gave a short laugh, as if in relief. Then he asked what I was going to tell the judge. I said I was going to tell him that "you are much less upset than when I first saw you, and you seem to be doing well. In fact, I will tell him that I think you are going to be a good man." He was very touched by this, and looked as if he might weep. Instead, he stood up, said, "I have to leave early today, is that OK?" and hurried out.

The social worker's reassurance about the judge's benign behavior is risky. No one can ever safely predict how an organizational representative will behave. The worker could and should only have described her own behavior in his behalf. Telling George that she would tell the judge that he will "be a good man" is powerful, and George is obviously moved by her sensitivity and confidence in him.

In discussing the hearing with the probation officer, the worker interpreted the "stealing" episode as primarily a fearful reaction to the court appearance. George needed an incident that would allow him to feel injured, perhaps punished, and utterly innocent. The worker asked the probation officer's assistance in not allowing the episode to thwart George's progress. The probation officer said he would discuss this with the judge before court so the judge could give George an opportunity to tell of his success in meeting the terms set by the court at the first hearing. The judge was so impressed with the change in George that he allowed him to return to school. The social worker was worried that neither George nor the school was ready for this development.

Eighth interview. George described the hearing and said, "This time I had a nice judge. He was the nicest white man I ever met." I told him it was the same judge at both hearings. He was dumbfounded, and we were able to discuss how one's own upset can color one's views of other people—the hateful judge and the likable judge were the same person. In addition, we discussed his apprehension about returning to school and his hopes that he could stay out of trouble.

The worker continued seeing George for six more interviews devoted to his real and imagined difficulties at school, his feelings that his father had never "even cared enough about me to know how old I am," and a reworking of issues from earlier sessions, including fears of sexual damage and inadequacy stemming from the operation.

At the end of the school term, he recited Robert Frost's "A Road Not Taken" to me. "Had to memorize it for English," he muttered. He saw the two roads as representing good and bad, or perhaps emotional sickness and health. He said, "The trouble is, they do look alike. They don't have the right markers so you can know. Or maybe you only see one road, you never know the other is there. That's when you need someone to show you there are two roads after all."

The work was terminated over the summer vacation. In the fall, the worker telephoned George's school and learned that he was still considered a pest and a poor student, and bragged too much, but had been in no fights. He made friends and is no longer thought to be dangerous. Probation was also ended as George had been in no further trouble.

Institutional racism, social and economic inequities and injustices, and their impact on an adolescent's development must be thoroughly understood by the practitioner for ethnic-sensitive practice. While George's social worker does not refer to these factors, the work shows some implicit recognition that disruptive behaviors are defined as psychopathology more often with black than with white youth. George had been inappropriately diagnosed as schizophrenic and paranoid on the psychiatric ward of the county hospital. The worker ignored the label and elected to work with George's potential for growth and his existing strengths. Indeed, disruptive behaviors at school can mask difficulties that stem from inequities experienced in an oppressive and racist school environment.

However, there were two missed opportunities for the social worker to acknowledge and explore the impact of institutional racism on George's life. Doing so would have raised his consciousness. The first occurred in the fifth interview, when George talked of becoming a doctor: "My mother says they try to keep blacks from being doctors." The second occurred in the eighth interview, when George said, "This time I had a nice judge. He was the nicest white man I ever met." The worker did well in helping George to see that how we feel can affect how we view people, but overlooked considering together some effects of racism in George's life, which would have been empowering.

Two observations about other environmental factors: first, we know less than we need to know about George's mother and their relationship. More effort was needed to engage her in a supportive partnership directed to releasing George's potentials. She is involved, she does care, but we really know too little about the nature and quality of the mother–son relationship.

Second, we need to know more about George's school. It would have been helpful had the worker, with George's permission, visited the school to talk with the guidance counselor, principal, and teachers. They could have discussed George's needs and his strengths in order to increase the school's understanding of him as a unique individual, block their continuing perception of him as a pest and braggart, and ensure their supportive contact with him. From the beginning, the social worker was candid, direct, and at ease with George. The worker conveyed hope and confidence in George's ability to change his behavior and to recognize his own actual feelings. The social worker helped George gradually to construct his own inner controls, reduce his impulsiveness, analyze possible consequences of planned or actual actions, and acquire some self-understanding.

Yet an apparently unrecognized ethical issue related to self-direction arose when George refused to return to the clinic after his relative's comment. The worker and the probation officer agreed, "George should be told that the court ordered him to continue until his next court hearing." The wording suggests that the court did not actually issue this order. If it did not, then both the worker and the probation officer acted unethically and paternalistically.

Particularly striking was the excellent work on George's fantasies about his surgical experience at age six, an important source of his insecurity about his masculinity and a possible basis of his aggressiveness. Also striking was the work done by George and the practitioner on his crippling grandiosity. The worker used the effective metaphor of Superman to connect the grandiose statements to George's deeply felt inferiority. The worker's acceptance and empathy permitted George gradually to relinquish the defense and begin to accept the reality of both his abilities and his limitations. This freed him to cope more effectively with the life stressors.

The methods used by the worker included enabling, exploring and clarifying, mobilizing, guiding, facilitating, and collaborating with the probation officer. The worker used various skills (e.g., minimal responses and nonverbal gestures, and verbalizing feelings) to enable George to elaborate his concerns. In exploring and clarifying, the skillful use of focus and direction, specification, interpretation, and direct feedback enhanced George's self-awareness. Hewing to the reality of George's actual capacities reduced defensive grandiosity. The worker consistently responded to George's signals of distress by affirming strengths and self-worth, accepting negative feelings, legitimizing his concerns, and supporting self-awareness by the use of symbolic descriptions of what George had suffered and felt as a "little kid." In mobilizing, the worker identified George's strengths, and offered reassurance and realistic hope.

In guiding, the worker helped George to identify possible actions and their likely consequences. She gave advice as needed, and modeled relatedness and competent problem solving. She enhanced the growth of self-direction by providing information in an appropriate cognitive mode (e.g., the metaphor of Superman and the work on the surgery) at the appropriate time and in the appropriate amount. In facilitating, when George appeared to be ready, the worker confronted the grandiosity and reframed the coping demands (e.g., "You're meaner to yourself than any judge would be"), managed episodes of regression (e.g., the shoplifting incident), and provided adequate time and metaphorical space (in accord with George's own temporal rhythms and readiness) for him to develop new ways to cope with loneliness and anxiety.

Together, the social worker and probation officer constructed a strong collaborative relationship that facilitated George's trust in them and in their caring. No doubt his trust was enhanced by the fact that the probation officer was a black male like himself and a strong role model for caring and competence. The social worker drew on the collaborating method, using skills of conferring, cooperating, and consulting with a person who represented official authority vis-à-vis George.

Mrs. Kenyon is a forty-five-year-old widow who works full-time as a secretary (her husband, Tom, died of cancer four months ago). She is extremely thin and looks ten years older than she is. She has four children: two daughters, Bernice, age twenty-three, and Alice, age twenty-two, who attend separate colleges and do not live at home; and two sons, David, age nineteen, and Bob, age sixteen. David is single and employed, and lives in an apartment in the same town. Bob lives at home with Mrs. Kenyon and attends a technical high school. Home is a house in a lower-middle-class community.

She told her family doctor that she was nervous and upset and that everyone was talking about her. At times she heard voices. Mrs. Kenyon had a history of severe emotional illness. Her doctor referred her to a psychiatrist. Dr. A saw her once. His view was that she was not coping effectively with the life stressors she was facing. He believed she had not yet mourned her husband's death. He referred her to a family agency social worker.

When Mrs. Kenyon called the worker to set an appointment, she spoke for half an hour describing how nervous she was and how she needed to talk with someone about it. She goes to church every lunch hour since her husband's death and repeatedly asked if this were normal. An appointment was made for three days later. However, Mrs. Kenyon called the worker the next day very upset. She had spent the day at work believing that her name had come up for promotion and that people had discussed her all day; she was not promoted and was very hurt. She added she was not even qualified for the position and did not want the job. She felt she had made a fool of herself by calling a fellow worker when she got home from work. The woman denied that Mrs. Kenyon's name was mentioned, much less considered. "The woman had a big mouth, and now the whole office will know I called."

Mrs. Kenyon's repeated themes in the first interview were that no one cares about her feelings, no one understands what she is going through, and, with her husband gone, she has no one she can trust and to whom she can talk. The worker's major concern was to help Mrs. Kenyon begin to mourn and reach a beginning resolution. Clearly, she was feeling acute and painful stress and was unable to manage the tasks of bereavement or the associated negative feelings. The worker suggested a connection between her grief and her current feelings at being alone. Mrs. Kenyon saw the connection, and agreed to work on both.

In an early session, Mrs. Kenyon was upset because of her need to change things. She had changed her hair color and changed the way she dressed. The worker supported the difficulty of all the changes she has had to confront. Mrs. Kenyon also found that giving clothing and jewelry away frightened her because when she became emotionally ill "the last time," she also had begun to give things away. Because Mrs. Kenyon kept referring to that time, the worker felt it was important to discuss it with her.

Mrs. Kenyon said she had been very ill, had tried to commit suicide, and has the marks on her arm. She rolled up her sleeves and showed me the scars. She said she took a bottle of pills and turned on the gas, all in one morning. "I became like a hermit, I was afraid to go anywhere. My husband worked shifts. I just felt everyone would be better off without me, because I was so sick, and I heard these voices and was haunted. It was terrible, like there was only one way out of my misery." I asked, "Are you afraid you are going back to being this ill?" Mrs. Kenyon said, "I think I have this fear again, now. For a long time I had Tom to talk to, and now he's gone." I replied, "That makes a difference, it is real. Tom is not around to talk with, and it is scary to lose the person you talked to the most. It must have been difficult all the three years he was sick, and particularly the last six months when you knew his death was imminent." Mrs. K replied that it was, and she had no one to talk to. I asked if her husband knew he was dying, and she said he did but they never discussed it. I commented, "It had to be very painful for you to have to deal with his dying all by yourself." Mrs. Kenyon replied, "I used to leave work at five and cry all the way home. His room, really Bob's, was turned into a hospital room. David moved back home when I told him his father's situation, and Alice came home from college. She was stronger than I. She would get up at night with Tom and never wake me." I asked, "Did the family ever talk about his illness?" Mrs. Kenyon: "Not really. In the beginning, everyone was screaming at one another. I had a talk with each one, and I said there's a great deal of pressure, and you usually take it out on the one nearest you, and that's what we're all doing. I told them I would understand if they were cranky or abrupt, but they would have to understand me too. One time I was crying, and Bernice said I just wanted someone to feel sorry for me. I really wanted her to understand me. . . . If you don't have someone to talk to, you begin talking to yourself."

I believe Mrs. Kenyon has real reason to fear regression to psychiatric illness. However, if we can keep her in touch with reality, and reassure her that what she is going through is normal and applies equally to those who have not had a breakdown, she may be able to stay intact. I will try to help her (1) develop greater cognitive clarity about her situation, (2) manage her feelings through ventilation with my emotional support, and (3) seek and use social support through family and through new friends and activities. I think it is imperative that she accept and integrate the stressors generated during her husband's illness and death, and her own stress reactions. I will try to help her to allow herself to feel the grief in recognizing that she will never see him again.

The worker's empathic and supportive stance enables Mrs. Kenyon to begin to deal with her loss and the status transition. Elaboration and explorations skills helped Mrs. Kenyon to begin to unload the pain of her husband's death. The worker also developed a responsive plan of action. We note that Mrs. Kenyon is Catholic, and she could be hoping for or expecting reunion in eternal life. Indeed, it might have been supportive to ask Mrs. Kenyon if she and the children had talked with her priest or visited the grave together.

Over the next couple of weeks, Mrs. Kenyon went to church daily, and talked to her husband's picture every night. In her grief, she seemed to want to recover him, at least in fantasy. In the early phase of mourning, a person often yearns and searches for the lost figure. The social worker took every opportunity over the next five sessions to refer to Mr. Kenyon in the past tense and to the fact that he is dead. She did this in a sympathetic and matter-of-fact way to help Mrs. Kenyon through the first phase of the mourning process.

Fifth session. I asked if she and her husband ever talked about what she should do after he died. Mrs. Kenyon responded, "No, we had three years. I wished sometimes that he would talk about it. He would lie in bed and just stare at me. Sometimes I would take his hand and wish I could make him well. I just miss him so (much crying). I lost my father two years ago and my mother twenty years ago. My only relative is my brother, and he's in a state mental hospital. I always feel for him, but I think I have to straighten myself out first. He's forty-seven and has been there since he was nineteen. I had a rotten life, too. Our father and mother drank. We never had Christmas. Sometimes they would start cooking a turkey and then they would get so drunk it would be the end of the turkey." I held her hand as she continued to grieve for the childhood she never had, the love and support she never received, the lost relationship with her brother, and most of all the emptiness of life without her husband.

From this session on, Mrs. Kenyon began to marshal her strengths as preparation for reorganizing her life and environment. In the next session, she talked of wanting to make new friends as she and her husband had few friends. He wanted her to take up a hobby, but she had felt her job and taking care of the home were enough. Maybe she took the wrong attitude. When the worker asked what she meant, Mrs. Kenyon responded, "I do get very depressed. I'd like to have more people around me." The worker encouraged this quest. Mrs. Kenyon soon joined a group in a neighborhood crafts store where she can either work on a project there or take it home. She reported pleasure in this.

During this period, Mrs. Kenyon also described ways in which it had been difficult to live with her husband. Sometimes he was moody and wouldn't communicate, and that left her with no one to talk to. Earlier, she talked of how supportive he was, but now she referred to his coldness, how much he was away, and how much of the childrearing was left to her as the children were growing up. In the seventh interview, she reported going out to dinner with a married man from her office and then going to Confession. Her priest absolved her of sin, and told her she was a very lonely woman. Grief work includes resolving anger and guilt one might feel toward the deceased, but the worker notes that, for the time being, she is touching lightly on this aspect because of Mrs. Kenyon's fragility.

The worker notes that Christmas is coming, and it is a source of much fear and insecurity for Mrs. Kenyon and the whole family. It points to the need for setting up new ways of dealing with each other and new ways of viewing themselves within the family structure. Mrs. Kenyon and the worker prepare for this together by anticipating situations or processes that could produce anxiety and depression. Their hope is that the holiday, always extremely difficult after bereavement, will bring the family members closer together if they can now at last express and share their grief, and incorporate their painful loss and mourning into their own life stories.

Prentice is a sixteen-year-old African American male who resides in Brooklyn with his paternal grandparents and his older sister, Brenda, age eighteen. Prentice's grandmother referred him to Family and Children's Service, an outpatient mental health clinic. She was very concerned about his increased angry outbursts and oppositional behaviors at home, and academic and behavioral difficulties at school.

As a young child, Prentice experienced parental conflict, substance abuse, and abandonment. When Prentice was two years old, his father abandoned the family and has had no subsequent contact with him. When Prentice was eight years old, the Administration for Children's Services (ACS) became involved because of substantiated maternal emotional and physical neglect. Subsequently, Prentice and Brenda were removed from the home and were placed with their paternal grandparents, who assumed legal guardianship of the two children. Their mother maintained weekend visitation for a few years, and then her contact with the children became sporadic and inconsistent. Prentice has not seen or heard from his mother for the last four months.

In the first session, Prentice was open and easily engaged. He acknowledged his difficulties at home and at school and described his grandmother as being "caring but too strict." He complained about "too many house rules" that lead to frequent arguments. He identified "feeling angry lately" and wanted to reduce conflicts between him and his grandmother. After three sessions, Prentice began to talk about the feelings of loss and anger about his mother's lack of involvement in his life. He had hoped that his mother would petition the court and resume full custody of him. However, over time, he began to realize that his mother was either unwilling or unable to care for him. He insightfully stated, "She always breaks her promises, and I know that she never will be a real mom."

During the fifth session, Prentice began to grieve the loss of his mother. He was able to express his anger, but not his sadness. In the sixth session, the social work intern invited Prentice to share his life experiences with her. He shared his remembrances as a young child of his mother being frequently drunk.

INTERN:	So you remember Mom drinking?
PRENTICE:	Yeah, she would stumble around the apartment and yell at us and then somehow Grandma would always have to come over and get us.
INTERN:	What was it like for you before Grandma came over—what was it like for you watching mom stumble around the apartment and yelling at you?
PRENTICE:	I don't know. . . . I sometimes wondered if it was something that my sister and I did?
INTERN:	What do you mean?
PRENTICE:	Well, I just wonder if me and my sister had been better, then Mom wouldn't have drunk so much, maybe we wouldn't have had to leave her and then we would still be living with her now. Things could have been different.
INTERN:	You think if you and your sister would have been better, your mom would not have drunk, and you would still be living together?
PRENTICE:	I don't know. . . . (Looks down toward floor, shakes leg)
INTERN:	I don't think two small children could do too much to help a mother not to drink.
PRENTICE:	I guess, but I think that had she gotten clean in the beginning things would be different. Then again, maybe not, because she's been clean now and she still doesn't want us. I just wanted to help her, but she is so damn immature. She doesn't take responsibility for anything. I wish I could have lived with her so I could have talked to her about it, you know, helped her with stuff.
INTERN:	What could you have helped her with?

PRENTICE:	I could have been there for her. Tell her she needs to get a job, save money for a car so she could give my grandma money to support us and she could drive over here to pick us up instead of Grandma driving over to her place all the time to drop us off. Well, actually to drop me off because mom couldn't deal with both my sister and me at the same time because we were too much for her to handle at once.
INTERN:	Wow! You take a lot of responsibility on your shoulders.
PRENTICE:	I do. I love her and I hate her. Well, I don't hate her really. I just wish she could be different. I wish everything could have been different.
INTERN:	I understand—you have mixed feelings about your mother and miss her.
PRENTICE:	I feel bad. . . . I keep thinking that if I never yelled at her on the phone, everything would be fine.
INTERN:	I feel terrible that you blame yourself so much—your mother was supposed to take care of you, not the other way around.
PRENTICE:	(Silence.)
INTERN:	What are you thinking, Prentice?
PRENTICE:	I guess I do take too much responsibility—she is supposed to be the mother (tears start to well up in his eyes).
INTERN:	Yes, she was supposed to be the mother, and you the child.
PRENTICE:	Yeah (pause)—but how do I stop thinking about her, and wondering if she is ever going to call me again? (Tears start to roll down his cheek.)

Prentice conveys his intense guilt, self-blame, helplessness, and longing for his mother's love. The social work intern helps Prentice to grieve the loss of his mother by using elaboration, clarification, and exploration skills. She helps Prentice to recreate his experiences of living with his mother during childhood to help him be able to express his profound loss. She acknowledges his painful feelings and creates a safe place for their expression.

The next two illustrations demonstrate the helpfulness of group mutual aid in bereavement. In the first illustration, the group is one of many provided by a social service agency for family members of cancer patients at all stages of the illness. The groups provide a supportive environment in which members can share their feelings and experiences, engage in the tasks of mourning, reduce their feelings of isolation and loneliness, and learn from one another how to cope with their many life stressors.

Prior to the first session, the worker met with each person individually to describe the group's purpose and tasks and assess the person's readiness for the group and the appropriateness of this particular group. Thirteen people from the waiting list were screened for membership, allowing for expected dropouts. Nine were women (six white, two Hispanic, and one

African American), and four were white men. Their ages ranged from thirty-eight to seventy-three. Although the group was quite diverse, the common need to relieve pain was powerful enough for members to develop a collective identity and mutual aid system (Gitterman, 2005). No one dropped out, so the work was a little more difficult because of group size. As group size increases, possibilities for potential relationships increase, yet fewer opportunities and less time are available for everyone to communicate as fully as each might wish (Toseland & Rivas, 2005). The group met one evening a week for ten consecutive weeks. Following the second session, the group was closed to new members. Although members were at different points in the mourning process, the group instilled hope in those at earlier points and permitted those at later points to recognize their growth. During the seventh session, members recontracted to meet for two additional sessions.

All members expressed the difficulty of sharing their pain and sorrow with family and friends. Hence, a collective need emerged: to talk in the group about their experiences from the past, to understand their current feelings, and to figure out how to go on living. Members also agreed to share their experiences of taking care of their spouses and to express their feelings about the loss.

By the fourth meeting, members began to help each other with specific life issues. For example, Elyse described her difficulties talking with her twelve-year-old daughter about death. The group helped her to explore her concerns, and members suggested alternative ways to initiate discussion with her daughter. Members developed problem-solving skills and began to balance the sessions with work on both general themes and specific concerns. At first, members were polite in entering into the discussion. By the fifth session, they were interrupting others and asserting themselves. Less assertive members were consciously included in the discussions. Gradually a norm developed that permitted expression of a wide range of emotions. Use of the pronoun "we" grew as group cohesion, loyalty, and commitment increased.

In the sixth session, the discussion focused on their spouses' final days: the feelings they had as they realized their spouse was going to die, and the words that were spoken during those last precious days. Lorraine said her husband never acknowledged he was going to die, while Carol told of the intimate conversation she had with her husband about death. Diana cried for the first time since her husband's death. Tara opened up for the first time and told of feeling relief when her husband died because his suffering was over. More members shared their pain and underlying feelings in this session than in any other. The incident occurred when Lorraine said, "I want to tell the group something."

She looked at me. I nodded my head and encouraged her to share her thoughts.

LORRAINE:	I think this discussion is very disturbing. I don't see the point of going back over the terrible details of the hospital, the doctors, and the illness. I don't think it's productive for us to dwell on this. I don't want to remember the bad times; I try to think about the happy times when my husband was well. (Elyse was in tears.)
CAROL:	Stop! Lorraine, you are going on too long.
WORKER:	Carol, can you tell the group what was going on for you as Lorraine was talking? (My intent was to help Carol to clarify and express in the group what she was feeling at this moment, to encourage the group to talk about what had just happened, and to explore the interpersonal tension.)
CAROL:	OK, this might help Lorraine. I'm not a psychologist or anything, but I am aware that there are two major breakthroughs tonight.
WORKER:	(Looking around the room, saying softly) Yes, there were.
CAROL:	I thought tonight's discussion was very important.
JESSIE:	I think it has been a significant meeting. This is what the group is all about.
ELYSE:	It was very helpful to me to talk about the last few days with my husband. You see, I have such pain inside me, and I don't have anyone I can talk to about this.
DIANA:	It was hard for me to talk about my husband's death, but tonight the group helped me. It's the first time I've cried, and Lorraine thinks it was a waste of time. I'm hurt.
WORKER:	The group is a place where you can talk about the experiences that are painful for you. You all have so many memories and feelings about your experiences in the hospital, watching your husband or wife endure treatment, and watching them die. These experiences bring up painful feelings, and yet, they are important to talk about in the group.

To realize her intent of exploring the interpersonal tensions, the social worker would have to reach for Lorraine's reactions and experiences. In the record, the worker is struggling with her reactions.

I was uncomfortable as Lorraine expressed her thoughts. I was aware that bereaved people have a strong desire to avoid experiencing the pain and emptiness of a profound loss. I was torn between wanting to acknowledge and validate her feelings and concerns and wanting to point out the meaning this session had for the others. A part of me was angry that she was negating the value of our work.

The worker struggles to control and hide her anger by becoming somewhat wordy and "sticking up" for the group. Lorraine is really saying she must forget the sad times and remember the happy ones. At seventy-three, Lorraine is much older than the other members. Most people in their seventies value the time left. Their happier memories are boosters as they get on with the tasks of life's closure and the satisfactions that may remain despite the loneliness imposed by loss. If the worker could reach beneath her anger, she would experience the empathy she feels for group members' pain, and Lorraine's individual expression of that pain. Pain is an essential part of mourning, and is a means to feeling better. The worker is fearful that Lorraine's comments undermine an essential area of work. But, in reality, Lorraine's comments actually increase the demand for work on this painful life transition.

LORRAINE:	It brings back the feelings I had while I was at the hospital with my husband. I felt nauseous, and I had a headache. I could almost imagine the smell of the hospital and see all the tubes. This is how I was feeling here tonight.
WORKER:	So, as other people were talking about their experiences, it was almost like reliving the awful experience you went through with your husband.
LORRAINE:	Yes, and I try not to dwell on that. Now I feel terrible.
WORKER:	You know, sometimes it's very hard to be in the group, and it can be uncomfortable to sit through a discussion that brings up painful feelings. You have all endured so much over the last several months. It hurts to relive all the pain of those experiences, and yet, it's part of healing. (I felt very connected to the pain of the group. My own natural instinct is to want to make everything better, but I realize that the pain is an essential part of their healing. I can identify with Lorraine's desire to move away from the pain. The group's pain brings forth my own pain about losing my husband to cancer.)

It would have been helpful to the group if the worker had shared her own loss and personal feelings with the members. Some practitioners consider self-disclosure inappropriate or unprofessional. We believe referring to the commonality of a status or experience for the client's benefit, and not for the practitioner's, deepens the work.

CAROL:	I'm sorry Lorraine for cutting you off, but I thought the discussion was helpful to many people. You know, I didn't want to come tonight because it can be so painful, but I also knew it would be helpful.
WORKER:	It takes a lot of courage and strength to come to the group each week.

The work becomes too intense for the worker, and she focuses on Carol's courage rather than on her natural ambivalence about the group. In her analysis, the worker recognized that her intervention closed off further discussion. A more helpful response would have been, "It's been an intense session. It can be painful to come each week. We are almost out of time, but I think it's important that we begin to talk about how we can help each other when it gets too painful." This affords support and is a facilitating demand for work at the same time.

For the following week, the group agreed to share photographs of their spouses. Most had pictures of their spouses when they were healthy and happy. Lorraine brought in the "happy" pictures she displays around the house. But she also brought in some photos of her husband just before he died. She pointed to his physical deterioration and told the group how painful it was to watch this happen. She said this was the first time she had shown these pictures or shared this pain with anyone.

In the ninth session, Jessie brought a problem to the group for help. She appeared extremely agitated, and reported she was dealing with a stressful legal and financial situation that involves her husband's business. Jessie is legally responsible for running the business and feels miserable in her role. She dreamt of pursuing her ambition to be an opera singer. She recently discovered stipulations in Robert's will that tied her to the business and left her in a financial bind. (They were married only six months before his death several months ago. He had cancer and a heart condition, and died after a heart attack.)

The group began to offer suggestions and advice, but Jessie was too upset to accept their help. She said, "I'm so mad at Robert. How could he do this to me? You just don't tell someone something and then do something different." I said, "Jessie, you feel let down by Robert. You trusted him, and now you're not so sure what he did or why." Jessie responded, "You're damn right." Barbara said, "He probably didn't have time to make the changes in the will that he intended to make. Look, he didn't know he was going to die. People just don't plan ahead." Jessie looked ready to explode. She said, "Look, he told me to my face that he was going to put something in the will, and he didn't. I really don't know if he loved me." Diana said, "Oh Jessie, I'm sure he loved you." By Jessie's nonverbal response, it was clear that the well-meaning reassurance was not helpful. Jessie was probably thinking, "How can she know whether Robert really loved me?"

We social workers sometimes also provide reassurance out of our own anxiety, cutting off further exploration and expression of feeling.

JESSIE: I've given up my whole life for this business. I haven't had time to sing, and now I'm left with nothing. How could he do this to me? He's probably getting back at me.

WORKER:	Jessie, how would he want to get back at you?
JESSIE:	I wasn't there for him before he died. I was so busy taking care of the business that I didn't have time to go with him to chemotherapy. I shouldn't have let him walk up that flight of stairs. I should have known he couldn't take it.
BARBARA:	Jessie, how could you have known? I kept pushing my husband to walk three days before he died. Jessie, you took care of his business because that's what he wanted you to do.
CAROL:	Jessie, you didn't know he was going to die so suddenly.
JESSIE:	You know, he died of a heart attack after trying to walk up that damn flight of stairs. Autopsy showed the cancer was in remission. That's just like Robert—oh, he was determined. He did such a great job getting rid of the cancer that it killed him. (She began to cry again, and I put my hand on her shoulder.)
AL:	Jessie, we all probably think about things we could have done or should have done differently. My wife went to the same gynecologist for years, and she really trusted him. She complained for four years about irregular bleeding, but he insisted it was nothing to worry about. I went along with her, without questioning any further. She had cancer of the cervix. If it's detected early, it's curable. If only I had done some reading, or insisted on a second opinion, but it didn't occur to me or I would have done it.
WORKER:	And yet, Al, you did the best you knew at the time. You trusted your wife's faith, and that was important too.
GLADYS:	Look, I still feel guilty about allowing the brain biopsy to be done on my husband. I didn't know what to do. Everyone encouraged me to sign for it. But when he was left in a semicomatose condition, his family blamed me. (She began to cry, and Elyse passed her the box of tissues.)
JESSIE:	Gladys, it had to be done; you had no choice.
WORKER:	Each of you was faced with difficult decisions based on so much uncertainty. It's hard to look back with the knowledge you have now.
LORRAINE:	We did the best we possibly could.
AL:	We all wanted our husbands and wives to live, but we couldn't do much to change that.

Jessie's anger seemed to be directed not so much at the misunderstanding in the will but at Robert for dying and leaving her alone with many dreams unfulfilled. As the group was helping Jessie, they began to express their own feelings of guilt and anger. Having heard some speak the "unspeakable," they openly express the same emotions. Bereaved people commonly go over the events leading up to the loss and find someone to blame, even themselves. For many, this is less disturbing than accepting that life is uncertain and one is helpless.

The social worker's intent was to help all members explore and express those negative feelings. She wanted them to know it was OK to have such feelings and to share them. As the group became more involved in problem solving, the worker gave them room to provide mutual aid to one another. She felt that the emotional support of peers was a more powerful healing force than the support of the worker. This was a powerful episode for both the members and the social worker. The empathy, knowledge, exploring, mobilizing, guiding, and facilitating of this practitioner enabled all members of the group to integrate their bereavement experiences and feelings into a new and more growth-oriented life story.

In the second bereavement illustration, a social work intern formed the group for people who had experienced the death of a spouse or parent. The group's purpose was to bring together bereaved individuals who were struggling with or felt alone in their grief and to provide them a safe and supportive place where they could help each other deal with their losses. The group was offered by a hospital and met once a week for six weeks, from 6:00 to 7:30 on Tuesday nights in a well-lit, clean, and attractively decorated room. The group was composed of six African American members and eight white members. Twelve members were females and two were males, with ages ranging from the twenties to the seventies (most members were in their fifties). The group was quite heterogeneous in terms of age, ethnicity, religious affiliation, and socioeconomic background. However, every member had experienced the death of someone whom they loved, and that profound commonality made their differences in background inconsequential (Gitterman, 2005).

The issues and feelings surrounding the death of a loved one are strong and complex. For the members who lost a spouse, they felt terribly alone and incomplete. For the members who lost a parent, they felt the loss of their longest consistent and often most precious relationship. Friends and relatives unable to tolerate the sadness urged group members to bury their grief and to move on with their lives. This pressure added to the members' adaptive burdens. The mutual aid group provided grieving members with a safe place to share their painful losses, their loneliness, their memories, as well as their struggles to cope and survive. A vignette from the third session follows:

JENNIFER: I hear what my family and friends are saying. But I don't understand, how do I simply forget my mother and go on with my life?

INTERN: Your friends tell you to forget your mother in order for you to move on?

JENNIFER:	That's how they make me feel (begins to cry). . . . I don't want to forget her. We loved each other.
INTERN:	Do others feel the pressure to forget and get over your grief (looking around the room)?
EVA:	No matter how hard I try, I can't forget and I won't.
OTHERS:	(Verbalize agreement)
JOAN:	I feel like I have to forget my mother, place her behind me, or I'm never going to be OK again, but I think about her all the time.
INTERN:	Maybe you can stay connected on some level while still trying to go on with your life.
GINA:	Yeah, I never want to lose that connection. I mean, I know my husband is dead, but he was a huge and important part of my life. How could I ever forget him—why would I ever want to forget him?
BETTY:	(Nodding) If I forgot my husband, it would be like he never existed—like my life never existed. Why do people want us to forget?
GEORGE:	Maybe they think that by telling us to forget, our pain will go away. They do not realize that they increase our pain.
INTERN:	(I noticed that Debbie looked like she wanted to speak. Tears were streaming down her cheeks.) Debbie, you are feeling a lot right now.
DEBBIE:	Everyone is talking about forgetting, but I can't forget my husband. Maybe I am crazy, but I feel him with me all of the time. At night I wait for the door to unlock at 6:30. Sometimes I even hear his voice. I must have something wrong with me, right?
GINA:	If there is something wrong with you, then there is something wrong with me too. I'm sure I'm going nuts (laughs). My husband loved his car—he had it washed every week. Well, I was out driving it the other day and I realized that the car had not been washed in several weeks. I heard his voice asking why I hadn't washed it lately. So if anyone is crazy, it's me. (Group members laugh.)
INTERN:	It is very common to feel a sense of presence or to hear the person saying things that they said before. It's how we all handle loss. I know I did when I lost my father.
GINA:	(Laughing) Whew . . . so you mean I'm not going nuts.
INTERN:	Certainly not, but worrying about going nuts must be scary (looking around the room).
LINDA:	I don't feel my husband's presence or his voice, but I want to. I want to remember him and feel his presence more than anything, but I can't. I only remember his sickness and his

pain. His illness lasted so long that I couldn't remember him any other way. It's funny because I find myself talking to him, asking him to let me know that he is out of pain now. I also ask him everyday questions. I just wish he could answer me.

OTHERS: (Group members were silent.)

INTERN: (I remained silent to let us all process what just had been discussed.)

Group members movingly express the depth of their pain and confusion. They yearn for their loved ones and can't express their feelings and thoughts to family members and friends. The mutual aid process universalizes and legitimizes their distress, mitigates their fears of losing sanity, and reduces their social and emotional isolation.

In the fourth meeting, group members decided to bring in photos or mementos of their spouse or parent to share with the group. Most of the session was devoted to the exchanges of experiences and memories. In the next session, Debbie begins the meeting with the photos she "forgot" to bring the previous week.

DEBBIE: I remembered my pictures this week (she pulls them out and proudly shares them).

OTHERS: (Group members silently look at them, then start talking among themselves.)

INTERN: How was it for all of you to share your pictures and mementos? We didn't get a chance to talk about it last week.

EVA: It was good, but I'm glad it's over.

BETTY: I agree.

LINDA: It is still hard for me to look at his pictures.

MARTA: I agree; he looked so healthy and alive—it's hard to imagine.

JOAN: Yeah. It was hard to look at the pictures because it was the first time I looked at them since my mother died. I am glad you all suggested it because I ended up feeling good. I decided to leave them out to look at every now and again.

INTERN: You had mixed reactions. . . .

JENNIFER: (Interrupting) I left my pictures out also. I thought it would make me sad, but it didn't. I was surprised that it brought me great joy. I could see the sparkle in my mother's eyes. I loved that sparkle.

GEORGE: I need to ask you a question (looks at me). When does the presence of somebody leave your memory?

INTERN: I am not sure what you mean, George—could you explain what you mean?

GEORGE: What I mean is how strong should a deceased person's presence remain with you and for how long?

INTERN: George, I am not sure; for each of us it's different. How strong is your wife's presence for you?

GEORGE: I was going through some things in the basement and I ran across some of my wife's things—the pictures (his voice cracked) and some invoices from her business. Anyway, it was like she was standing right next to me—I could feel her presence so strongly—it was like I could touch her (a tear ran down his cheek), but I couldn't—I kept trying to, but I couldn't.

GINA: I feel my husband's presence all the time. It is comforting to me. I don't want to lose it, but I am scared that it will decrease over time. It probably has already.

LINDA: (Looking at George) Everyone experiences things differently—no one can tell you how long it will last. Maybe you need her presence now but not later.

GEORGE: I really do need her right now—I miss her terribly.

INTERN: Sonia, you seem to want to say something.

SONIA: I feel my father's presence often. I find it comforting, and I use his comfort. When I need to, I recall my memories.

Members discussed the need to keep an active connection rather than forget their loved ones as others had urged them to do. They learned from and reassured each other that their grief responses were normal. The social work intern gently encouraged exploration or wisely stayed out of the way of the free-flowing mutual aid processes.

Helping people face dying and death is a painful experience. Ms. Simpson, a thirty-eight-year-old African American, has been diagnosed with AIDS. She has been treated on and off for the last ten years and has resisted taking medications. Due to failing health, she began to attend the clinic about six months ago. The clinic physician informed her she was close to dying. At first, she did not accept the terminal diagnosis. However, in time she accepted the reality and agreed for the social worker to help her through the process of dying. Ms. Simpson worked through the phases of denial, anger, sadness, acceptance, and release. In the process, she has changed from a highly defensive person who lacked insight to a woman trying to make the most out of her life in the remaining time. She was determined to improve her relationship with her daughter, who was born with the HIV infection. Initially, Ms. Simpson's deteriorating physical condition overwhelmed the social work intern—"I felt I was staring death in the face." The intern also struggled with annoyance that Ms. Simpson had been noncompliant with her medications over the years. In order to be helpful, the social work intern had to move past her own reactions to Ms. Simpson's physical appearance and the feelings of blaming her. The following practice vignette occurred after a few sessions with Ms. Simpson. At the time, while she was in denial about the seriousness of her illness, she was beginning to let in the reality for brief periods.

MS. SIMPSON:	I don't believe the doctor about being really close to death. I've been sick for so long. That doesn't mean I'm going to die.
INTERN:	Do you have any idea how come the doctor is saying that you are close to dying?
MS. SIMPSON:	I don't know. I guess because of my numbers being so bad and because I keep getting pneumonia. But I can get better.
INTERN:	I am glad that you are feeling better, but you also did tell me that you can feel your system shutting down.
MS. SIMPSON:	When I feel really lousy, then I do believe that I'm dying. But when I don't feel too bad, then I can't think about death.
INTERN:	What is it about death that you don't want to think about?
MS. SIMPSON:	I don't know. It just doesn't seem real. I see pictures in my head of what people with AIDS look like when they are dying. I'll never look like that.
INTERN:	Is it scary to think about looking like that?
MS. SIMPSON:	I can't let myself think about it. It is too scary. I guess I know that I am going to go through the same process—I just don't want to think about it—I am not ready.
INTERN:	Dying is a really scary process. I can understand your not wanting to think about it.
MS. SIMPSON:	When I think about dying from AIDS, I really get mad at myself.
INTERN:	Mad?
MS. SIMPSON:	Because it's my fault. I have it either because of unprotected sex or because of IV drug use. If I hadn't been so stupid, I wouldn't have it. Do you know what it's like to know that you are dying because of something that you did?
INTERN:	Just terrible, terrible.
MS. SIMPSON:	Just imagine the worst thing you did, but thousands of times worse. I'm so ashamed of myself. I want to hide.
INTERN:	I am so sorry. How come you want to hide?
MS. SIMPSON:	You know what people think when they hear someone has AIDS. They want to get away from them as soon as they can. They think that they'll catch it. They think that you're an awful person.
INTERN:	Do you feel awful about yourself?

Ms. Simpson struggles with dying, with self-blame, and with the stigma of AIDS. The social work intern empathically invites Ms. Simpson to talk about dying, reaching for the feelings of powerlessness and stigma often associated with the AIDS diagnosis (Getzel & Willroth, 2001). The intern's acceptance and support provide Ms. Simpson with essential psychic healing.

The following practice vignette occurs two months hence.

MS. SIMPSON: I just wish that I could die right now. I don't want to go through what I've seen other people with AIDS go through when they are dying.

INTERN: What don't you want to go through?

MS. SIMPSON: I don't want to waste away and not be able to do anything for myself. I don't want to have to go to the bathroom in bed because I can't get up (starts to cry). I don't want to be hooked up to tubes. It scares me to say that because I don't want to be in pain. I'm already experiencing the beginning stages of dementia—I know it'll get worse. I don't want it to happen.

INTERN: These are all scary things. Are there other things that you are afraid of?

MS. SIMPSON: I'm afraid of not seeing my daughter anymore. She is HIV-positive also. I'm worried that she won't take care of herself. I don't want her to go through the pain that I'm going through.

INTERN: That is a terrible burden for you, knowing that your daughter has HIV.

MS. SIMPSON: It's awful! But we have become closer as I've gotten sicker. I wish it hadn't taken this to bring us closer. I want to spend as much time with her as I possibly can. It's hard to think that soon I won't be seeing her anymore. It's hard not knowing when my last day will be. Like today, I'm doing really well. But last week I was in the hospital and it was questionable whether or not I would make it out alive. I feel like I need to say goodbye to her every time I see her just in case it's the last time.

INTERN: Is there anything else that you want to say to your daughter?

MS. SIMPSON: I've tried to tell her everything that I want to say the past few times I've seen her. It's just hard. I tell her that I love her. It doesn't feel like that's enough. I can't make up for all of the past years. I can't tell her how terrible I feel that I was HIV-positive when I was pregnant and I passed it on to her.

INTERN: I know it's hard to say these things. If you could, what would you say to her?

MS. SIMPSON: I'm sorry I passed the disease on to you. I love you to death, and I feel so guilty that I am causing you pain.

INTERN: What would make it hard to say that to her?

MS. SIMPSON: I don't know. I guess that I've never been the type of person to express my love directly. I feel like I just freeze up when I try to talk about AIDS and what I did to her.

INTERN: Would you like me to help you say that to her or to give or leave her a letter with your feelings?

MS. SIMPSON: I would be more comfortable with leaving her a letter. Would you help me pull it together?

Ms. Simpson is invited to share her intense feelings of grief and guilt over her daughter's HIV. The social work intern verbally and nonverbally ("I was leaning forward and I was nodding my head") communicates her genuine caring and interest. She is trying to help Ms. Simpson to place her "emotional world in order." During these interviews, the intern struggles with her own feelings about Ms. Simpson's imminent death. She wrote, "I wanted to let her know how special she is to me, and that I will miss her when she dies. I held back because I was finding it difficult not to cry and I did not want to burden her with my tears." Her class instructor, the author, encouraged the intern to give Ms. Simpson the gift of her tears and to model for her direct expressions of emotions. Interestingly, when the intern did express her feelings to Ms. Simpson, she was, in turn, able to do so with her daughter.

An educational group for "at-risk" 17–24-year-old gay males was led by a social work intern.[1] The group members were sexually active, and were at high risk of HIV infection. They practiced unsafe sex with their friends as well as anonymous partners. In response to these "at-risk" behaviors, the agency formulated an educational group through which information about safe sex and harm-reduction behaviors would be emphasized. A curriculum was prescribed that would teach members to reduce their self-defeating behaviors.

In this particular ten-session group, three group members were white, two Latino, one African American, and one Asian American. While their parents partially or fully financially supported members, most lived independently. Members were open about their high-risk behavior as passive partners of anal intercourse without condoms or active partners of oral sex without condoms. While they all agreed to try the group, they were not invested in changing these behaviors.

After actively describing their self-destructive behaviors in the first session, by the third session, they began to lose interest in the intern's didactic presentations and began to withdraw from the group. The prescribed curriculum structure interfered with group members' desire to discuss their concerns and to reach out to each other. When the intern presented his difficulty with this group in the author's class, he was encouraged to pay greater attention to the group members' underlying pain and the group's potential for mutual aid. As the intern naturally integrated the curriculum content with members' own expressions and concerns, and shifted away from the prescribed curriculum and didactic presentation, the group's mutual aid processes instantly became a powerful healing force.

Jack stated, "I had a really rough day yesterday. I told my parents that I was not going back to school next semester and that I am going to take the semester off and they became really upset. They think I am lost or something. My mother was crying and she never cries. It really upset them. I didn't expect it. They've been worried about me. They think my life is going nowhere. They told me that I am not the son they wanted me to be and that I had disappointed them." I emphatically shook my head from side to side. Jack went on, "I know they think I am not going to finish school because I am gay. Ever since I came out to them three years ago, they think my life has gone downhill. They think I have all of these negative influences in my life and that the negative influence made me decide not to return to school. I'm so pissed off at them, but it's hard because they have done so much for me." The room was silent. John, Mike, and Steve exchanged glances indicating that they understood. I said, "I see you guys nodding your heads. You know exactly what Jack is talking about?"

Steve nodded yes and said, "I feel the same way." He looked at Jack and said, "I identify with you totally. I am so angry with my parents, but it is hard for me to be mad at them because they are doing so much for me, you know what I mean. I can't help it, though. Whenever I am at home there is all this tension and I know I am the cause of it. You know what I mean?" I asked, "What do you think the tension is about, Steve?" He answered, "I don't know. I mean, I guess I am tense because they don't really accept me. Like sometimes when we are all at home and watching some TV, a show comes on and there is the token gay character. You know what I mean?" We all laughed knowingly. Steve continued, "Well I always try to bring it up and talk about it. But they won't discuss it. I really try to talk about it, but they just won't. It's crazy. It's as if a wall comes down (Steve placed his hands out as if he was making a wall). Sometimes, I push a little, but then they get really tense; so I stop. It makes me mad. I mean as far as the gay thing. Like, OK, so I am gay, but it's not like it's the end of the world. You know what I mean?" "Yes, it really hurts not to have your parents accept who you are," I replied. Steve continued, "After I graduate, I am going to move into the city and be on my own and I won't have to deal with them."

Mike replied, "My parents are great, they really are, but I am mad at them too. I treat them like shit. They have always been there for me, even when my lover died, and everything. I don't know why, but I am just a total bitch to them." I asked Mike, "Any hunches what makes you so mad at them?" "I don't know," he said. "I really don't. I can't help it. Do you know?" With that question all the members looked at me. I said, "I am not sure, but on the one hand you are appreciative of the help your parents give you, but, on the other hand, you all feel different levels of acceptance about who you are, ranging from mild disappointment to total rejection." John agreed, "My parents pay for my apartment, my tuition, my living expenses, but I am not allowed to talk about being gay. It's a nonsecret secret!" "Yeah," Jack added. "In order to afford school, I had to live with my parents and they are financially generous with me, but not in their acceptance of who I am—I always see the disappointment and hurt in their eyes." After a silence, I added, "You know most guys your age go through a rough time separating from their parents, but being gay makes it much tougher, much more confusing. We grow up having our parents love us and then they find out we are gay and we become someone else. We are no longer the child they used to play with, protect, embrace. Their son is gay and for some, at least initially, they experience it as a terrible loss—a loss of their hopes and dreams. And we discover that some of their love is conditional. And then we too feel a powerful loss. What is like for you when your parents make you feel that you are not the son they had hoped for?"

Mike said, "It's awful—the pain shoots throughout my body." He looked down at the floor. John said, with tears welling in his eyes, "Terrible doesn't describe it—especially with my Mom. We used to be so close before I told her, and now she treats me as if I don't exist." A painful silence followed. Steve and Jack began to cry. Steve looked at me and said, "It really hurts, you know what I mean?" I said, "I do know, Steve. I know what you mean and I know how it feels." John said, "I miss my mom so much. She used to play with me and love me. It's really strange. She always had gay friends, but when it came to me, she couldn't accept it. Things have never been the same." John continued to wipe away his tears and asked me, "Does it ever get better?" I said, "Yes, it does get better—we all find ways to heal. But what I worry most about is that you guys are acting out your pain in very self-destructive ways—like punishing yourself through unsafe sex—like, my parents don't care about me, so why should I care about myself?"

Steve responded, "You know, right now I feel better than I have in a long time, I really do." John and Jack replied, "Me too! I am not alone with this pain." Mike agreed, "I feel much clearer—I didn't hear any of your lectures on safe sex. Today I heard you that you cared about me—about us."

This courageous social work intern gives up the security and structure offered by a prescribed curriculum. He demonstrates faith in himself, in the group, as well as in the group process. He makes the decision not only to work with the members but also, more so, to fully involve himself in their lives. As a gay man, he identifies with their struggles, recognizes their loneliness and isolation, and identifies with their pain from parental disappointment and disapproval. He experienced their tormenting dilemma, namely, to remain in or out of the closet in relation to their family members. He experienced the painful struggle of being true to oneself and one's gay identity and, consequently, inflicting pain on one's parents. In the members sharing their gayness, he understood that their parents' reactions probably ranged from identifying their son's behavior as immoral and sinful, to declaring that their son had a disease that needed to be treated, to a milder view of a slight sexual imperfection and abnormality. He is with their pain.

The social work intern served as an important adult gay role model who skillfully helped members to help each other. Previous sex education had not reached them. As they explored their common painful experiences and their internalized self-punishment, they began to make connections between unsafe sex, their search for love and acceptance, and their fear of rejection. As one member explained his participation in unprotected sex, "I was afraid he wouldn't like me, and that he would ask me to leave."

The social work intern uses enabling, exploring, clarifying, mobilizing, guiding, and facilitating skills and integrates them with genuine caring and personal style. He harnesses the constructive and healing power of mutual aid, helping members to help each other to examine their risk-taking behavior and to consider changing these behaviors.

Transitioning from the aspirations associated with being a mentally healthy person to a person with a mental illness is quite stressful. After being hospitalized for five days in a psychiatric hospital, Jerry, a forty-year-old white man, was discharged to a psychiatric day hospital. At the age of eighteen, Jerry had his first psychotic episode with delusions of persecution and auditory hallucinations, and was hospitalized for the first time. He responded well to medication and enlisted in the navy. During his tour of duty, he suffered his second psychotic episode, and during the next twenty years he lived at home and suffered five additional psychotic episodes. While medications stabilized his condition, he would stop taking them. His most recent hospitalization was also precipitated by his not taking his medications. He explained his noncompliance by stating, "I just want to feel normal, like everyone else, no pills." The practice incident takes place in the second week of the day hospital program.

Jerry slumped down in the chair across from me. He began to tell me about his difficulties getting started in the morning. He spoke rapidly, "I'm tired of my mother telling me every day to get up, get up. Sometimes I feel like I hate her. What does she want? She gets my check (disability). I pay her rent, and she gives me one, maybe two dollars to buy lottery tickets. She always has to control me." I replied, "That has to be frustrating for you." He nodded and continued, speaking more slowly, measuring his words, "And that's the way it has always been, well since I was twenty or so. Everyone wants to know why I like my fantasy world. Well, that's why. Nobody can control my thoughts. It'll never be any different. It's OK, it's fine. I go out to the coffee shop and meet the guys. I go to see my nephew. It's OK." Noting the difference between his words and his affect, I inquired, "Do you want it to be different?' He paused and opened his eyes wide. He sat up straighter, and folded his hands in his lap. "I'm forty years old, and I've never had a woman in my life. I did have one woman that I bought. I don't have a wife or children." I commented, "Something is missing for you. You want a family of your own." He looked at me for a moment, hung his head, nodded, and stated, "I want to be normal." He appeared relieved. I asked him to help me understand what "normal" means to him. He thought for a moment and replied, "I take the meds because everyone tells me, 'Jerry, you have to take your medications.' But I don't want to. Not all the time.

"Sometimes I like to go to my fantasy world. That has been so since I was a young kid. Everyone tells me that those fantasies are not true. I know that, but sometimes I like to be there. But, I'll go along. I'll take those pills. That's what you all say I have to do." He continued, "I feel like a guinea pig, by agreeing over the years to different medication regimes. But I don't want to be a guinea pig—I want to be normal." I commented, "You feel stuck—trapped between wanting to be without meds, but everyone around you feels that you need them." He nodded vigorously.

He remarked that in the earlier meeting today, the psychiatrist suggested that he consider a regimen on the antipsychotic drug clozapine. Jerry expressed his doubts. I asked, "How would that be for you if clozapine changed you and you no longer had your fantasy world?" He replied, "But I still would not have a woman. I mean, how would my life be any different? I don't think I could ever be like other people. I would be the same person, but without fantasies." I heard the sadness in his voice and commented, "You don't think clozapine can change your life—you are saying that we are offering you medication, but that's not enough, you want more help than that." He looked at me, shrugged his shoulders, and commented, "All the doctors do is give you pills, but I still have to go back to my mother's house every night and live the same life." He slumped further into the chair. His body showed despair. Then he said, "You people are the experts. If you think I should take it (clozapine), then maybe I should. I mean, what do I know? I don't know what I don't know."

Sensing a shift in him, I said, "It seems that everyone wants to change you, wants you to be different than you are, and that really hurts." He sat up in his chair, sighed, and responded, "So, now you see where I am. You all tell me this is my decision, to take this drug. And I say it really doesn't matter. All the shrinks and my mother care about is that I don't act crazy. Not whether I am happy, but that I don't act crazy." The poignancy of his pain had an impact on me and I replied, "You feel that the people who are supposed to help you are letting you down." He looked up, his eyes widened, and he nodded vigorously. He hastily said, "It is not you. I don't blame you." Hearing that he needed to know if he could be honest with me, I nodded, smiled, and reflected, "I don't feel blamed. I appreciate your honesty and candor. I want to help you through this." His face relaxed, and he smiled.

Jerry's aspirations to be a normal adult and mastery of the associated developmental tasks are thwarted by his mental illness. He movingly conveys the depth of his pain, sorrow, hopelessness, and, concomitantly, fear of being symptom free. He experiences difficulty transitioning from living without a mental illness to living in recovery. For many people suffering from schizophrenia, while life is difficult, change is frightening (Grotstein, 1995). Living in recovery requires "the development of new meaning and purpose in one's life as one grows beyond the catastrophic effects of mental illness" (Munetz & Freese, 2001, p. 2). The social worker taps into Jerry's grieving for all the things that are missing in his life. She also grasps the poignancy of his message—that the key difference between belief and delusion is who holds the power to assign such a label.

Traumatic Life Events

Mary is a twenty-five-year-old single white woman. She is well educated and works as a stockbroker in a large investment firm. She has worked very hard to reach the goals she set for herself, and she spends a great deal of time at work. Until a year ago, Mary always had a roommate; she is now living alone and moved into a new apartment about a month ago.

Mary called rape victim services seeking counseling. A coworker with whom she became friends a few months ago raped her. She had "tried to put this behind me, and go on with my life." However, she described how things seemed to continue to get worse. Friends suggested that she speak to a counselor. She also realized that she was not coping well with what had happened and felt isolated, confused, and frustrated.

One of the first issues Mary and the worker discussed were feelings of guilt, self-blame, and distrust of her own instincts. "There must have been something that I did to invite the rape." She held herself responsible for not preventing the rape. She verbalized that the rape has defined who she is: she no longer is the person she used to be. "I should be able to get over it, stop thinking about it, and forget it." She attempts to cope by working even longer hours, keeping herself busy, and fighting against flashbacks. However, after "trying to get over it" on her own, she realized that she is unable to move on and that she is still feeling many of the feelings she felt right after the rape. In fact, the feelings have intensified.

The worker realized that she had to explore with Mary the meaning of the rape before she could help her to assimilate and desensitize the traumatic event. In the first two sessions, Mary talked "around" the rape itself, discussing relationships and trust in general terms. The worker respected Mary's sense of space and timing. In the third session, Mary indicated that sufficient groundwork had been established for the more intense and painful work to come. She began by stating that she has no control over the things that have been happening in her life.

MARY: I feel like so many things that have been happening to me have happened to me in the past and are all building up to one horrible ending.

WORKER: What are some of these things that you have been focusing on?

MARY: I remember about seven or eight years ago when I lived in Washington, D.C., and I passed by a construction site and one of the construction workers said to me as I passed, "You are going to die." I thought nothing of it at that time, and well, it doesn't seem like much now, but I keep thinking of that, and there are other incidents.

WORKER: What kind of other incidents?

MARY: Well, I remember coming back to this city after living in Washington and I got off the train and this homeless woman picked me out of everyone, got right in my face, and yelled, "You're going to be murdered." I couldn't believe it, and I thought very little of it at the time. And there have been other things that have happened. When I am with a bunch of people for some reason an incident always happens to me, whether it is getting yelled at, a nasty comment, or being spit on, which happened to me once on a subway. Someone has it in for me, it always happens to me, and the incidents just seem to get worse, and I always find myself thinking about what could be worse, what will happen if I continue along this path?

WORKER: What have some of your thoughts been about what might happen?

MARY: I really feel that all these things are leading up to a violent death, and it could happen any time. Or, this could happen to me again, and the thought of it being a stranger next time really scares me. I feel there is a greater chance of it being a stranger, although this time it was someone I knew or thought I knew.

WORKER: You feel that all these incidents are leading up to the possibility of your being raped by a stranger, is this what's most frightening to you?

MARY: What I am worried about is that I have no control over what happens. This really frightens me, but I feel that anything is possible because of all the things that have already happened.

WORKER: A lot of people feel that because they were raped once, something like this could more easily happen again.

MARY: What I am worried about is I have no control over what
             happens. I limit myself so much already—it is not fair.

WORKER: It is not fair, and it's frightening to think of these incidents
             and what you think could happen.

MARY: I never felt this way before and I just want to feel the way I
             used to feel. I used to do things to prove to myself that I could
             take care of myself, that no one could hurt me. I used to take
             walks at midnight and not think anything of it. Now I come
             home from work, I have a hard time walking on my street
             because I pass all of the reminders of that night. I lock myself
             in my apartment, and even if it is 7:30 and I would like ice
             cream, I decide it is not that important because I do not want
             to leave my apartment. I do not have any control over what I
             do. I feel there is so much I do or not do that one incident has
             defined whom I am and what I can do.

WORKER: The rape has defined who you are?

MARY: There are so many things I did before that I no longer do, just
             in my everyday routine of walking down the street or meeting
             people. I did not have much trust in people before this
             happened, and now I have even less, practically no one. I feel I
             have taken steps backwards; I just want to feel like myself
             again.

WORKER: The rape has made you feel a terrible loss of control over your
             life?

MARY: Yes, I feel that before, I did what I wanted and when I wanted
             to do it. And now I feel that I can't do anything except what I
             have to do, like go to work. It is an effort for me to go out
             with friends because I have to be so careful about when I go
             out, with whom, when I will be coming home, at what time.

WORKER: To feel so little control is very frustrating and scary.

   In this practice excerpt, Mary conveys the intensity of her helplessness.
She is a trauma victim. Mary is also asking the social worker to make her
feel whole again, to help her find her former identity and regain control over
her life. The worker sensitively reaches for Mary's fears ("What have some
of your thoughts been about what might happen?" and "You feel that all
these incidents are leading up to the possibility of your being raped by a
stranger, is this what's most frightening to you?") and empathizes with her
fears ("it's frightening to think of these incidents and what you think could
happen"). At one point, the worker moves too quickly to universalize and
teach about reactions to rape ("A lot of people feel that because they were
raped once, something like this could more easily happen again"). Mary is
not ready to examine universal reactions: she wants to discuss her own distinct reactions. The worker skillfully refocuses and continues to explore
Mary's fears, "simply" listening and empathizing.

There are no easy formulas to help someone regain feelings of control. The first step is for Mary to tell her story and to examine the experience itself (Herman, 1992). In order for the rape victim to become a rape survivor, she has to regain control over the experience (Clemans, 2004; Wasco, 2003). In the next session, the worker helps Mary to discuss the trauma of the actual rape.

MARY: I do not feel like I can trust my own instincts. I trusted them with a person I thought I knew and could trust, and look where it got me. Why should I trust my own instincts, my own judgments? There were things that happened, that he said or did that I should have been clued into, but I thought he was being flirtatious. He had always been so nice, and I liked him so I didn't want to make him feel bad or for him not to like me.

WORKER: Sometimes it is very hard not to trust someone that you know as being nice, especially if you like them and they like you. What are some of the things you believe you should have clued into?

MARY: Well, first I really feel as though this all would have been avoided if I hadn't called him, I feel partly responsible for making the date. Maybe he thought I was being forward so I wouldn't mind what happened.

WORKER: There is no reason, no excuse, why he should have believed that because you called him for a date you wanted more than just a date with him, or that you agreed to sex.

MARY: Yeah, I guess I know that, but it makes me wonder. What makes me feel a little better is that I think he has done this to other women, so maybe it is not what I did.

WORKER: No, it is not what you did, it is not your fault no matter what you said, did, or didn't do. It does not give him any right to do what he did to you. You are probably right that he did rape other women, but what makes you think so?

MARY: Well, it is the things he said, like after we had sex I realized I was bleeding and I told him. He responded, "Oh don't worry, that happens all the time." Well, I thought, it never happened to me before. And he didn't even make an effort to help me or to offer to bring me to a doctor. Although I do not know why I even wanted him to stay around. He left and I couldn't believe that he left me like that, as if nothing had gone wrong. It didn't hit me that anything was really wrong until after he left and I sat and thought about it. I just tried to put it out of my mind at the time. But the more I think about it now, the more I feel that he has done this before to other women, and although it makes me feel awful, maybe it wasn't my fault.

WORKER: He probably has raped other women. It is not your fault. There was no way for you to know that he would rape you, and that he should not be trusted.

MARY: There are other things that should have clued me in to what he was capable of doing—what he did when we were at the bar. I can't believe I didn't do something at the time. We were talking and drinking; he had been drinking a lot. He flirtatiously said to me, "Tonight either you are going to rape me, or I am going to rape you," and then laughed. I kind of just laughed with him, not knowing how to respond. I thought it was a little strange, but I didn't take it seriously. Now thinking back on it, I guess I should have ended the date and I definitely should not have gone to my apartment with him. There were so many signs I should have recognized, and then I could have stopped it from happening. Maybe he did this, but maybe there was enough that I knew in order to have stopped this rape from happening, before it went so far. (When she started to blame herself, my eyes lifted and my eyebrows raised. I paused at first because I could feel the expression on my face. Before this point, I could feel my eyes were squinting and my eyebrows furrowed and I was biting my lip.)

WORKER: What happened was not your fault. He violated your trust and your person. He took that control against your will. It sounds like it really frightens you to think back to what happened not only because of the rape but because of what you believe to be your role in it all.

MARY: I just don't understand it, why did this happen? It is not fair that this has affected my life so much, and I feel the rape has defined my life and who I am now. I just want to be back to normal.

WORKER: It is very understandable that you are having these feelings. It takes some time to get over the trauma of being raped.

MARY: I feel this takes up so much of my life—this is all I focus on. But talking about it with you does help. It not only helps me to hear myself say what I am feeling, but also to think about the incident and what happened because much of it I have to put in the back of my mind. It helps to talk to you and get feedback and to hear someone say that my feelings are not ridiculous, nor am I going crazy.

WORKER: Is it comforting for you to know that your feelings are normal and that it is OK to talk about those feelings and about the rape?

MARY: It is great to know that it is OK to talk about my feelings here, and I know that you do not blame me. You are more objective

	than most people I talk to about what happened because you did not know me when I came here, but you believed my story and me. But my real concern is, how will I know how to trust others? I do not trust my own instincts.
WORKER:	This is something that will take time, something that you can rebuild, and something we can work on together.

Mary describes her own behavior on the date, testing to see if the worker will support her self-blame. As the worker passes each respective test, she releases additional information. The worker repeatedly corrects misinformation regarding Mary's contribution to the rape. Mary begins to develop a new cognition in the change in her reference from sex to rape. However, Mary continues to struggle with assuming responsibility and self-blame in the next session. After discussing a number of concrete issues, the worker identifies and reaches for Mary's apparent reluctance to continue working on the rape.

MARY:	I am ashamed to talk about it. I really do think at least to some degree that I brought this on myself, that I did not stand my ground with him. I acted differently than I thought I would act and have acted in the past. I don't know why.
WORKER:	Differently, in what way?
MARY:	Well, with other men, when I have told them no, I did not feel that I needed to give them an explanation. With Jim, I told him no, but I then gave him some lame excuse. It was so bad, and I don't know why I felt I had to give him any excuse; "no" always had been good enough for the others (her voice trailed off, and I nodded my head all the time she was saying this, sitting silent for no more than two or three seconds before she continued). I told Jim that I did not have any new condoms; all the ones I had were old and it would not be safe to use them. He agreed, and said he understood and that I was being good. We would talk about something else for a few minutes, but then he would start pressuring me again. We must have gone through this four or five times and I thought he really understood; he said that he did. But I do not understand why I felt that I had to give him an excuse. I never did before.
WORKER:	Did you feel so much pressure from him that you felt "no" was not enough for him to understand?
MARY:	Yes, I think that is part of it, but it is still confusing. I am not sure what I was thinking at the time before he raped me. But I liked him and maybe he realized this, and so he did not think that my "no" really meant no.
WORKER:	Whether or not your "no" meant *no*, it is not something for him to decide. He should take that *no* meant *no*.

MARY: That is true, and I know that I said NO.

WORKER: That should have been enough, which is all you had to say to him. You tried to make it even more clear to him and that did not help either. He chose to rape.

MARY: There are other things that I have started to think about that should have clued me in.

WORKER: Can you give me an example?

MARY: Before we went out we spoke on the phone. I don't know if I told you he has his master's in poetry. Well, anyway, we were talking and he told me that he was going to tie me up and read to me. That sounded weird to me, but I thought he was just trying to be funny. However, I was really thinking about it so I asked a few people what they thought. And I got a range of reactions from "That's good, Mary, he's flirting with you" to "Oh, that is kind of scary, I hope that is the worst thing he'll do to you." And there were other conversations that now that I think about it, I should have paid more attention to what he said.

WORKER: It's natural to look at a comment like "I am going to tie you up and read to you" as something a little odd but funny, especially if you like someone and you want them to like you. He sounds like he is good at charming people, getting people to become interested in him. When you look back, suddenly things he said provide clues. But at the time, he is simply charming. So you are being real rough on yourself when you blame yourself for not knowing his intentions. It is human nature to trust, especially when you want to become romantically involved.

MARY: That is true, and I did like Jim. I even broke up with another boyfriend partly because I wanted to have the chance to start dating him.

WORKER: Is this adding to feelings of self-blame because you did like him and because up to that point he had been nice?

MARY: Yes, very much so. I feel ashamed that I could have ever liked him, and that somehow he must have known this. So I begin to think that maybe it was partly my fault for not giving him a clear message.

WORKER: The message you gave him was "no," and that was enough not only for him to get the message, but for him to understand it as well. This is not your fault. You are not at fault because you liked him, or because there were things said that you think should have given you a clue. The bottom line is that you said "no," he violated your trust and your body, and he committed a violent crime. (Mary began to sob, thanking me for my support.)

The worker's support invites Mary to provide further details to explore her feelings of self-blame. She refers to the rapist by name for the first time. The worker creates a safe space for Mary, repeatedly emphasizing the rapist's responsibility for his actions. When Mary is able to direct her rage at Jim, she will become less depressed and can begin moving from victim to survivor.

In the next session, Mary relived the experience of the rape itself. She sobbed uncontrollably as she described the invasion of her body and self-identity. Mary referred to this session as "taking a hundred pounds off my back" and the "lifting of a huge black cloud." The worker also helped Mary to explore her fear of AIDS from the rape and mobilized her to get a blood test. Finally, she helped Mary to reconnect to family and friends, and to join a rape survivors' mutual aid group. Mary is also considering pressing charges against Jim. This became the current focus of counseling.

The human capacity to create and narrate a life story and to make a healing process of it is a compelling life force available to client and practitioner in their joint work. Most practice vignettes in this chapter illustrate life stories of loneliness, despair, illness, or loss, and the search for meaning and coherence in these and other critical life stressors. With social work help, the narrators were better able to integrate difficult and traumatic events into a more positive, helpful life story.

With the empathic, active listening of the social worker in each of these case examples, each person reinterpreted and reconstructed a life story that ultimately contained new conceptions of the self and of relationships with others. As the storyteller was reconstructing it, each life story gained increased intelligibility, consistency, and continuity (Docherty & McColl, 2003; Jones, 2004; Kelley, 2002; May, 2005; Wood & Frey, 2003). The telling of the story, together with the listening, is a healing process. It is our human way of finding meaning in life events, of explaining our life experience to others and ourselves so that we can move on. The point of origin of the person's troubling life issue may be located at any point in actual time over the life course and not necessarily at some theoretical point in very early life. It may not be necessary to uncover memories of very early life to find a trauma that can explain the present life issue. It is enough to seek out its narrative point of origin in the remembered past, that is, the time and the circumstances under which it entered the life story. That narrative point is viewed as the first edition of the life issue, not a re-edition of earlier life events.

EIGHT

HELPING INDIVIDUALS, FAMILIES, AND GROUPS WITH ENVIRONMENTAL STRESSORS

In this chapter, environmental stressors are limited to organizations, social networks, and built and natural settings. Organizations, social networks, and physical space can be important supports or significant life stressors.

Environmental Processes as Life Stressors

The Social Environment

Contemporary urban society is characterized by the prevalence of complex organizations in most areas of life, including health, education, and social service organizations. Such structures are themselves embedded in social and physical environments. They affect and are affected by political, economic, and cultural forces. Growing numbers of people served by social workers face such grave life issues as family and community violence and neglect; unemployment; and social and physical disability and chronic illness, including AIDS, homelessness, and substance abuse (Gitterman, 2001b). Limited attention is given to economic stressors that arise from institutionalized blockage of access to stable and sufficient resources.

Social Welfare Organizations.   Initially, health, education, and social service organizations are established with financial support from private or public funds. Once established, however, social service organizations must maintain a balance among pressures exerted by legislative bodies, regulatory agencies, funding sources, the community, changing definitions of social need, and new knowledge and technologies (Reitan, 1998; Schmid, 2004). These forces continually threaten organizational obsolescence. Once established, how an organization defines its function and boundaries has an impact on the experiences of applicants and service users (Gitterman & Miller, 1989). A social work agency may define its function in terms of helping people change, with little account taken of the complex transactions between people and social variables. In some schools, for example, pupils are referred to social work services as disruptive or disturbed because teachers find them unmanageable. The social worker is expected to help such children passively adjust to the school environment. By acquiescing in this definition of professional purpose, the social worker overlooks the need to intervene at the classroom, family, educational policy, or community level. Yet one or all levels may be creating or sustaining the life stressors. An unintended consequence of this definition of social work's purpose is to stigmatize service. Preventive help to all children and their families in their exchanges with the educational system lies outside the boundary of social work in such a school system.

All organizations gradually develop a structure of statuses and roles for division of labor. If roles constrict professional function and negatively impact services, they increase stress for service users and providers. The function of inpatient medical or surgical social workers, for example, is severely limited by the current emphasis on rapid hospital discharge. This deprives patients and their families of social work help with the psychological and social consequences of illness and disability. The pressure of large caseloads, limited time for discharge planning, and shrinking resources create pronounced ethical dilemmas and increased stress for social workers (Moody, 2004; Sulman, Savage, & Way, 2001).

Stress may also be created by organizational boundaries. Some agencies locate services away from those they seek to serve, thus inhibiting client use because of transportation costs, babysitting costs, or social intimidation in an unfamiliar geographic area. Agency gatekeepers such as telephone operators, receptionists, and intake personnel may be unwelcoming and gruff. Physical aspects may be unattractive and uncomfortable; long waits may be involved (Germain, 1983; Seabury, 1971).

Boundaries of other social service organizations may be too easily penetrated. For example, children may be taken into substitute care without sufficient effort to keep them in their own homes, or with other kin, or at least in their own neighborhoods and schools so that all social ties will not be broken.

Intraorganizational boundaries might be too loose, particularly in those interdisciplinary settings where useful role distinctions are blurred. The distinctive contribution of the social worker may be lost in the general welter of "everyone can do everything." Clients could then be confused by ambiguity in professional function and the competitiveness among varied professionals (Reese & Sontag, 2001).

Where interorganizational boundaries are drawn unrealistically or where there is a lack of linkages to ensure effective referral and service pickup, some clients become "lost" and do not receive needed service. An aged person in need of medical care may be deemed ineligible by a clinic because he is financially unable to purchase insurance to supplement Medicare. A mental patient discharged from a state hospital but lacking an aftercare program may be denied service by a family agency because of poor prognosis, weak motivation, or other personal "deficits."

An organization develops structures, policies, and procedures to manage external and internal pressures. An authority structure allocates responsibility and coordinates tasks. It provides a chain of command through which decisions are made. Some authority structures are rigid; they reward conformity, discourage innovation, and block horizontal and vertical communication. The layers of authority may become so numerous, or the communication channels so clogged, that the time span in decision making discourages both practitioner and client from pursuing individualized needs or even common entitlements. In other cases, authority structures may be too flexible, allowing inappropriate discretionary power to practitioners having minimal accountability. Clients are then vulnerable to individual whim, prejudice, or narrow interpretation of service provisions (Reitan, 1998).

The organization develops a set of policies and procedures to assure fair and neutral treatment for all service users regardless of personality traits, ethnicity or race, sex, age, physical or mental disabilities, sexual orientation, or social status. In some organizations, policies and procedures proliferate as circumstances change or exceptional situations arise. They assume a life of their own and take precedence over client need and the organization's avowed goals. Some organizations demand strict adherence to policies and procedures: the agency manual supersedes the applicant's or client's needs and interests. In effect, individual needs are held hostage to bureaucratic needs. Some organizations use procedures and policies to ration or deny services. A welfare agency, for example, may rely on long waits and complicated forms to discourage applicants, delay service, and block referrals. Other organizations may not formalize or codify practices, and clients are subjected to nonuniform practices and to workers' idiosyncratic judgments. When procedures or policies are either underformalized or overformalized, they are potential stressors for clients (Fischer & Siriani, 1994; Gibson, Ivancevich, & Donnelly, 2000).

Informal structures also develop within organizations. These may support the organization's responsiveness to client need or subvert it. Just as formal structures socialize each organizational member to the agency's culture, the informal system socializes members to its culture (Gitterman & Miller, 1989; Jaskyte & Dressler, 2005). Formal and informal sanctions influence members to accept formal and informal structures and processes as natural and immutable.

Even the informal system sometimes exerts pressure toward conformity with the organization's own norms and practice and discourages creativity or innovation. When staff dissatisfaction with personnel practices and working conditions exists, the informal system may support scornful, punitive, or uncaring attitudes toward clients as displacements of feelings aroused by the authority structure of the agency itself.

People's transactions with the organizational environment represent a critical arena for social workers. In helping clients to secure services from an organization other than their own, workers' tasks may be difficult, but not hazardous. The task is more delicate when one seeks to influence one's own organization in order to secure services or resources required by clients and withheld by the agency. Particular skills are required so that neither client nor worker is placed in jeopardy. Issues of job security, agency loyalties, and professional reputation may be involved. Above all, the social worker's responsibility and accountability to clients, with recognition of the vulnerability inherent in the status of client, must be constant and unflinching.

Social Networks. Social support systems consisting of kin, friends, neighbors, workmates, and acquaintances are recognized as important elements of the social environment (Saleebey, 2004). Social networks are embedded within a cultural context and comprised of various circles that move outward from the innermost (which includes people with whom one lives and has the most intense investment), to the next circle of people (which includes those whom one highly values and interacts with frequently), to the next circle (with whom one interacts frequently but who are less important, or important people with whom one interacts less frequently), to the next circle (which includes people who are known but considered of less importance), to the final circle (which includes people who are known about or linked through significant others) (Lewis, 2005; Specht, 1986; Tracy, 1993; Weisner, 2005). As the child grows, the circle of friends grows and becomes in youth and adulthood a network of affiliations that may consist of friends and relatives as well as neighbors, workmates, religious affiliates, and so on. People's networks have a history, change over time, and are the central means through which integration is achieved during each phase of the life course (Bidart & Degenne, 2005; Takahashi, 2005).

Social networks can become very important support systems that buffer the impact of life stressors or serve as coping resources for both problem solving and managing negative emotions in the face of life stressors (Li, Edwards, & Morrow-Howell, 2004). They are important sources of our self-concept and also help shape our worldview (Miller & Turnbull, 1986). Social networks may meet the need for human relatedness, recognition, and affirmation (Lin, Ye, & Ensel, 1999). Some members may consciously serve as effective informal helpers, eliminating the need to seek institutionalized services (Patterson, Germain, Brennan, & Memmott, 1988; Patterson, Memmott, Germain, & Brennan, 1992). For these and other reasons, social networks are critical buffers against life stressors or the stress they generate (Berkman, 2000; Cleak & Howe, 2003; Dominguez & Watkins, 2003; Hurdle, 2001; Luckey, 1994). Social networks can cushion an individual through four types of support (Auslander & Levin, 1987): instrumental (goods or services), emotional (nurturance, empathy, and encouragement), informational (advice and feedback), and appraisal (information relevant to self-evaluation). Knowing that networks are available for support results in people being less anxious and more confident in dealing with new stressors.

Modern information and communication technologies have had a profound influence on the forming, sustaining, reconstituting, and redrawing of social networks and their boundaries (Licoppe & Smoreda, 2005; Wellman & Haythornthwaite, 2002). People use the communication technologies to maintain easy contact with social networks regardless of geographic distance and time zones. People also develop distinct networks in two worlds, the "real" world, as well as the "virtual" world of cyberspace (Gonchar & Adams, 2000).

While informal support systems may exist, some people are unable to make use of them (Johnson, Whitbeck, & Hoyt, 2005). People who perceive themselves as vulnerable tend to occupy closed networks of weak connections (Kalish & Robins, 2006). Mentally ill people, for example, often suffer from impoverished networks. Background and personality affect people's perceptions and help-seeking behavior. For example, women are more likely than men to identify life issues, acknowledge the need for help, and seek help (McMullin & Gross, 1983). Seeking help may threaten a person's self-esteem. For some, seeking help from social networks evokes a negative social comparison. Seeking help generates and reinforces relative feelings of inferiority and failure. Self-esteem might also be threatened when help seeking is unidirectional rather than reciprocal. Receiving without reciprocating may have negative consequences. Finally, people who attribute their life issues to internal rather than external causes are more likely to feel threatened and to avoid seeking help from significant others.

For some, the needed degree of privacy and anonymity affects their ability to seek help. Public admission of need evokes shame and humiliation. Prior experiences in obtaining assistance from the network could have left a residue of negative feelings, inhibiting future use. A life stressor that conflicts with the network's value or moral system is yet another deterrent. In certain issues pertaining to sexuality, for example, individuals may be reluctant to turn to their network because of the network's restrictive or repressive norms. Harsh judgments or rejection anticipated by a gay person may deter him from reaching out to the network for help with such a devastating life stressor as AIDS (Hough, Magnan, & Templin, 2005; Shippy & Karpiak, 2005). Cultural emphases on independence and self-reliance may inhibit some people from asking their network for help.

Loosely knit networks may be unaware of a member's stress. Lacking meaningful contacts, members' stress remains invisible. In addition, some networks do not offer their resources to members even when stressors are actually visible. When network resources are stretched out, some members may fear incurring additional pressures and burdens, while others may fear encouraging dependency.

While it is generally assumed that social network resources are always useful and helpful, they could at times have a negative impact on members facing life stressors (Schilling, 1987). Some networks are subject to internal exploitative and competitive processes that could undermine one's sense of identity and autonomy. A network with rigid boundaries could isolate the client from growth experiences outside the close-knit network. Some networks have ill-defined boundaries, and are so loosely knit that the network is actually unavailable for material or psychological support.

Other networks can be a negative influence, as in violent teenage gangs or adult groups of drinking companions. They reinforce deviance, holding to values that contravene healthy or normative strivings of the client (Duncan-Ricks, 1992). A member of a drug-oriented network or a delinquent network may want to end his affiliation in order to modify his values and aspirations. Yet the network may exert a strong counterforce, leading to severe stress and even danger. Some families have difficulty combating the influence of peer networks on younger members or combating unwanted interference by kin networks on the day-to-day functioning of the family. Other networks may be emotionally destructive because of hostile attitudes toward a person, family, or group.

Life transitions such as school changes, marriage, migration, job promotion, and retirement are sometimes difficult. Critical life events such as job loss, sickness, and death interrupt or dissolve linkages to others. The sense of self is dependent in part on involvement with others. Some of the most painful and stressful experiences of humankind are loneliness, isolation, and unwanted distance from others (Weiss, 1973, 1982). In old age, friends and kin die, one's activities are curtailed, and the acquisition of new networks is limited. Women appear to make greater efforts than men to establish and maintain friendships and kinship networks. For elderly men, the death of a spouse frequently means more than a lost attachment. The widower has also lost social ties, which were maintained by his wife. This stressor might be intensified by concurrent retirement and the loss of the network created at work.

The Physical Environment. The human services tend to neglect the physical settings of human behavior. The physical environment was long viewed as a static backdrop for biopsychosocial forces that were believed to be the only influence on human behavior and development. Our clients require a more balanced view. The physical environment is an important factor in the development and maintenance of relatedness, competence motivation, and self-concept (Kahn & Scher, 2002). Trust, for example, is based on the security of stable physical arrangements, as well as on stable companionship. Children refer to *my toys, my clothes, my room, my house,* and *my neighborhood* as part of themselves (Bronfenbrenner, 2005; Cohen & Horm-Wingerd, 1993; Lindholm, 1995; Mota, Almeida, & Santos, 2005; Nicotera, 2005). Some adults identify the outdoors as the most significant place in their childhood. Children experience the natural world in a "deep and direct manner, not [as] a background for events, but rather as factor and stimulator" (Sebba, 1990, p. 395). Stressors are generated from the loss of familiar and cherished places and structures that comfort and protect, and are part of one's individual and group identity. The life stressor of uprootedness is attributable, in part, to the sense of being torn from an identity base.

In order to analyze complex exchanges between people and physical settings, we distinguish between the built world and the natural world. The built world includes personal space, semi-fixed space, and fixed space. *Personal space* refers to an invisible spatial boundary that people maintain as a buffer against unwanted physical and social contact and to protect one's privacy (Altman, 1975). Some people react to intrusion into their personal space with gestures, withdrawal, or aggressive responses.

Semi-fixed space refers to movable objects and their arrangement in space. Furniture, curtains, plants, pictures, colors, and lighting provide spatial meanings and cues. People rely on environmental props (locks, labels, fences, etc.) to regulate interactions with the social environment. Too much interaction is experienced as crowding. Too little interaction is experienced as social isolation. Both can be life stressors. Families and groups experience differing levels of fit between their interactive patterns and the physical design of their living space (Minami & Tanaka, 1995). The degree of interpersonal coordination required in a limited space is often a stressor. High density limits physical movement, demands behavioral coordination, and increases the number of people with whom coordination is necessary. The close proximity, social overload, and spatial constraints lead to irritation and conflict. Laying claim to an area and defending it are difficult (Cutler, Kane, & Degenholtz, 2006; Pruchno, Dempsey, Carder, & Koropeckyj-Cox, 1993). Such behaviors are influenced by culture. For example, Asian cultures are strongly oriented to collective, communal use of space, whereas Western cultures emphasize private use of space.

Seabury (1971) examined the uses of semi-fixed space in six different types of social service settings. He found a significant association between arrangement of space and the social class of an agency's clients. The public welfare center and hospital social service departments were the most unattractive and uncomfortable, while the private offices and private agencies were the most attractive and comfortable. Iris, Rafaeli, and Yaacov (2005) investigated the uses of office space on three separate dimensions: instrumentality, aesthetics, and symbolism. McCoy (2005) linked the physical designs of organizational environments with the creative achievement of teams.

Reception areas make important symbolic statements to applicants and clients. A social work intern describes an agency serving poor elderly clients:

The Senior Service Center (SSC) is located in the basement of a two-story project building entered directly from the street. The building is not conspicuous. It has two doors, one for administrative offices and the other for clients. Wire fences hidden by overgrown plants and weeds surround the two doors. A small sign is posted on the door bearing the initials SSC. A passerby could easily miss the agency.

On entering, one climbs down a few steps to reach the reception/waiting room. The room is small, dimly lit, and unpretentious. The secretary's desk is located in the middle of the room. Covering one wall is a bookcase containing magazines; various pictures and diplomas hang on the other two walls. Chairs are lined up side by side, forming a line along two walls.

Most interviews are held in an office in the administration building. The office is shared by ten social workers. It contains a table and desk; two chairs are located next to the desk, and two others face the desk from across the room. No lamps or pictures adorn this room. When this room is unavailable, I must use a staff office that I share with four other social workers. It contains five desks, and is sparsely decorated. The agency's drab features probably reinforce feelings of helplessness and despair in those served.

In institutional settings, the need for supervision and surveillance often leads to concentrated use of a limited portion of available space. Unchanging spatial arrangements limit residents' opportunities for privacy and spatial identity. Arrangement of open and closed spaces in institutions, treatment cottages, and schools either invites or discourages certain behaviors in children; arrangement of furniture and other objects in mental hospitals and geriatric facilities promotes or discourages social interaction among the residents (Devlin, 1992; Fein, Plotnikoff, & Wild, 2005). Ward "geography" in any inpatient setting either supports or inhibits patients' shifting needs for privacy or for socialization. A social worker intern reports:

When I enter a resident's room, I feel immediate discomfort as a result of the limited space shared by two people, the intrusive proximity of the beds, and the lack of adequate provision for personal objects. The organization's policy is to have nothing on the walls except the bulletin board provided each resident. The policy is aimed at keeping walls clean and without holes, and at avoiding frequent repainting. Each board provides a few square feet of space for displaying cards and pictures. The only other space the residents have access to is a small bedside table and a small space by the sink. This feels very un-homelike.

The dayroom is located far from the nurses' station, the elevators, and the bathroom. The chairs and sofas are neatly arranged shoulder-to-shoulder around the perimeter of the room. A television is at one end, and a small table piled with books and games is at the other. There are no tables for games. Residents rarely use the room. Conversations are rare except when visitors are present. They usually arrange the furniture to make small groupings. I thought to myself, "Why can't this be arranged more like a living room?"

I observed several residents in wheelchairs lined up in the hallway, and I realized that it was close to lunchtime. They were waiting for someone to escort them onto the elevator and into the dining room. The wheelchairs were lined up one behind the other. Needless to say, no conversations could take place.

The answer to the student's question, "Why can't this be arranged more like a living room?" is that patients and staff who are confined to an environment for a long period of time eventually view semi-fixed, movable space as fixed and immovable. Habit and tradition become institutionalized and achieve "institutional sanctity." The absence of color, sound, and adequate light in bleak unchanging environments is stressful, and coping with it is difficult.

The character of the physical setting, including climate, and its cultural styles and meanings, influences the design of dwellings (*fixed space*). The structure and design of high-rise, low-income public housing violate cultural and psychological aspects of the self-image. Such housing is a warehouse symbol of lost identity, rather than a personal symbol of the unique self. High-rise, low-income housing provides tenants with no defensible territory within, and no safe territory on the ground. Vandalism and lack of care by tenants may represent their angry responses to stressful assaults on their identity and dignity, and lead to further social, psychological, and physiological stress. Other physical settings such as mental hospitals, prisons, schools, and residential facilities for the aged or the very young reflect similar social and cultural processes, which dehumanize and devalue society's "outsiders."

The *natural world*, too, influences human functioning more than most of us realize (Wilson, 2001). People experience relatedness not only with others, but also with the natural world. People directly, indirectly, symbolically, or vicariously experience the natural environment (Kahn & Kellert, 2002). Studies of accidents, suicides, crimes, psychiatric hospital admissions, and even rates of social interaction have revealed suggestive associations with features of the natural environment such as hours of sunlight, climate, and phases of the moon (Barlett, 2005; Besthorn, 2002; Clayton & Opotow, 2003; Dufrechou, 2004; Gale, 2003; Mayer & Frantz, 2004; Miller, 2005; Proshansky, Ittelson, & Revlin, 1976). Barometric pressure, wind, excessive temperatures and humidity, and seasonal variations in climate influence the moods and behavior of people, and contribute to stress. The influence of the natural world may be intensified in rural areas, where climate, lack of public transportation, and greater distances from neighbors, friends, and relatives are more important than in urban areas.

Landscape features such as islands, mountains, seashores, coasts, deserts, lakefronts, and marshlands have different effects on lifestyles and identities. Human beings must learn not only to respect the natural world, our life-sustaining environment, but also to remain in touch with its restorative, healing, and spiritual forces. These forces explain the powerful therapeutic influence of wilderness programs, organized camping, and nature excursions. They also explain the stressful adaptation required of people moving from open spaces to urban living. Puerto Rican migrants to a northern mainland city, for example, must contend with differences they meet when leaving a self-contained tropical island and entering a seemingly limitless continent and a city located in a temperate zone with marked seasonal changes in climate. If the migrant comes from a rural area of Puerto Rico, the impact of urban life is all the more stressful. In the United States, Native Americans or Chicanos who move to the urban centers of the North may encounter similar stressors. In Canada, migrants from India and Southeast Asia, and Canadian Indians who move to cities, are subjected to similar stressors.

The natural environment has a temporal texture in its alterations of day and night, seasons, and annual rhythms as the earth journeys around the sun. Such rhythmic variations have been entrained in all forms of life through adaptive processes over evolutionary time. Biological rhythms in human beings such as rapid eye movement (REM) sleep, hunger cycles, pulse, and respiratory rhythms reflect these terrestrial cycles. For example, the spring shift to Daylight Savings Time and the consequent loss of sleep produce an increase in accidental death (Coren, 1996). Temporal rhythms imposed by schools, hospitals, social agencies, and even work arrangements may conflict with fundamental biological rhythms and cause physiological and psychological stress.

Toxic pollution and contamination threaten the health and life of people and their natural environments. While pollution is relatively visible, contamination represents an invisible layer of the environment. Children's exposure to lead has been found to reduce IQ, create reading deficits, lower class ranking, and lead to more high school dropouts (Needleman, Schell, Bellinger, Leviton, & Allred, 1990; Wigle, 2003). Similar adverse effects have been found for children who were exposed to polychlorinated biphenyls, or PCBs (Jacobson & Jacobson, 2000). When families discover that their communities have been exposed to hazardous wastes, they suffer significant distress. Their symptoms included "fear and panic, sleep disturbance, feelings of loss of control and helplessness, fatalism, and elevated family conflict" (Evans, 2006, p. 423). Toxic pollution and contamination deteriorate the relationship between people and their ecological surround (Edelstein, 2002).

Plants and animals may be defined by cultural values and human needs as useful, supportive, unimportant, endearing, or symbolic. Gardening activities have been used with community minority elders and people suffering from stroke, brain and spinal cord injury, dementia, aphasia, developmental disabilities, and mental illness to stimulate and engage people with life in the moment (Catlin, 1998; Goff, 2004; Haas, Simson, & Stevenson, 1998; Larner, 2005; Sarno & Chambers, 1997; Shapiro & Kaplan, 1998; Strauss & Gabaldo, 1998; Wichrowski, Chambers, & Ciccantelli, 1998). The therapeutic values inherent in gardening activities are becoming recognized by hospitals, hospices, clinics, and residential care institutions (Kavanagh, 1998).

As valued companions, pets are part of an individual's or family's social network (Greenebaum, 2004; Prato-Previde, Fallani, & Valsecchi, 2006). Dogs provide numerous functions and meet diverse needs. Some people use dogs to mediate family conflicts and strengthen their identity as a family (Tannen, 2004). Other people desire the security and protection of a watchdog. For still others, a dog (or a cat or a bird) serves as a companion. For socially isolated and shy people, dogs serve as icebreakers, acting as a social lubricant (Brickel, 1986). People even pick a pet that, at some level, resembles them (Roy & Christenfeld, 2004). Guide dogs serve the legally blind, and the hearing impaired are aided by other animals (Naderi, Miklósi, & Dóka, 2001; Redfer & Goodman, 1989; Sanders, 2000; Valentine, Kiddoo, & Lafleur, 1993). Dogs also serve an important function in disaster preparedness and response (Hall, Ng, & Ursano, 2004). At times, newly adopted dogs do not fit in well, and the decision and process of returning them can be quite stressful (Shore, 2005). Other pets, such as cats, counter loneliness for people suffering with AIDS (Castelli, Hart, & Zasloff, 2001).

Social Work Function, Modalities, Methods, and Skills

The Social Worker and the Environment

With limited power and limited awareness of their rights, some service users become resigned to the unresponsiveness of organizations. For poor people, particularly poor people of color, the environment is particularly harsh. Because of their economic position, they are unable to command needed goods and services or to exercise their rights. They are closed out of opportunities for good education, preventive health care, jobs and promotion, safe housing, and neighborhood amenities. Their mobility is extremely limited. Morbidity rates are higher, infant mortality rates are high, and life expectancy is low in comparison with those of higher income families (Gitterman, 2001b). The social worker's attention and actions must be directed to helping clients make use of available resources and on influencing organizations to provide responsive services.

Agencies are a source of some power; our profession is a source of some status. Both can be used to improve people's environments and provide them with leverage for meeting their needs. While we may believe our influence is slight, our actual impact might make the difference between disintegration and survival for individuals, families, and groups who obtain needed food, shelter, medical care, and other entitlements through our advocacy on their behalf. Similarly, social workers' attention and action must be directed to the exchanges between an individual, group, or family and their social network. Mobilizing or strengthening "real-life" ties, finding new linkages and reestablishing old ones, enlisting the aid of natural helpers, and helping clients disengage from maladaptive affiliations help improve transactions between clients and social networks.

Practitioners must also be prepared to act upon those aspects of the physical environment that, alone or in concert with social and cultural processes, create life stressors for an individual, family, or group. For example, social work staff in a nursing home can successfully personalize resident space. Residents can be encouraged to exhibit meaningful possessions (pictures, books, and knickknacks) and to care for plants. In one home for the aged, the communal dining room now has small circular tables for interaction, television and card lounges are available on each floor, and a bar has been added. Such changes in the physical environment enrich the social environment with sites for social interaction.

Professional Methods and Skills

When clients' knowledge, experience, and physical state permit, their taking action on the environment is an important means to achieving psychological empowerment and actual power. If social worker and client agree that client action is not feasible, thought must be given to whether the worker and client should act together or if the worker should act alone, continually apprising the client of any progress.

Coordinating, mediating, advocating, innovating, and influencing methods are used to help with and influence environmental processes. We again remind the reader that work with environmental issues is usually concurrent with work on difficult life transitions and dysfunctional family and group patterns, so these professional methods are used in tandem with those of enabling, exploring, mobilizing, guiding, and facilitating, as well as other methods described in later chapters. All ebb and flow throughout the service contact, as circumstances and client needs and interests require.

Assessment, exploration, and agreement on focus and action usually continue in the ongoing phase. They often disclose sources of stressors between client and organization, between client and network, or between client and physical environment. The worker might use guiding, for example, if a client has insufficient knowledge of the availability of resources and services, or if a client requires help in using them; or facilitating if psychologically or culturally based resistance to using service or seeking the resources is present, or if fear of the unknown or unrealistic concern for independence interferes with using available organizational or network resources. For example, an elderly client refused to apply for much needed food stamps. The worker encouraged him to "tell his story." His narrated experiences, behaviors, thoughts, and feelings explained his reluctance to seek the entitlement. To help this elderly man hold on to his dignity, manage his feelings, and solve his life issues, the worker used the skills discussed in chapters 5–7 and in this chapter. A routine referral would have failed.

In most instances, however, the problem is not the client's inability to use the social environment, but distorted communication between client and the organization or the social network. In *coordinating* services, the worker links the client to available resources. In *mediating*, the social worker helps client and social system connect in more realistic and reciprocal ways through intercession, persuasion, and negotiation (Berman-Rossi, 2005; Schwartz, 1976). Increasingly, the problem lies within the organization. If collaborating and mediating do not accomplish the desired end, the social worker seeks to influence the organization to be more responsive by *advocacy* and its skills of pressure, coercion, or appeals to third-party intervention (Freddolino, Moxley, & Hyduk, 2004; Lens, 2004, 2005; Mickelson, 1995). The social worker might also use the media; mobilize a group, neighborhood, or community; or involve legislative, fiscal, or regulatory agencies in the organization's environment.

There may be unresponsive or punitive individuals within the social network whom the worker must engage on the client's behalf. Authority figures outside the network are sometimes unresponsive or punitive toward a client. A landlord, policeman, creditor, physician, or others may need to be approached in an attempt to increase their understanding of the client's needs and responses, or to secure concessions, delays, access to rights, or entitlements. When the client lacks a network, or wants to disengage from a network, the social worker might arrange an introduction to other networks of neighbors, fellow tenants, or institutionalized sources such as parent–teacher associations or church-sponsored groups (Bell & Bell, 1999; Morrison, 1991). Or worker and client may decide on referral to a self-help group such as Parents Without Partners or Alcoholics Anonymous as a network substitute or to improve coping (Ben-Ari, 2002; Wituk, Shepherd, Slavich, Warren, & Meissen, 2000; Wituk, Tiemeyer, Commer, Warren, & Meissen, 2003). Computer-generated and telephone self-help groups are yet another potential resource (Finn, 1995, 1996; Galinsky, Schopler, & Abel, 1997; McCarty & Clancy, 2002; Smith, Toseland, Rizzo, & Zinoman, 2004). If the client lacks networks or network substitutes, the worker, alone or with clients and colleagues, and usually with agency support, might develop an informal network or a more structured self-help group. A social worker might help the client and others with similar interests or needs form a network for elderly neighbors or physically challenged people, a babysitting exchange among young mothers, or a support network in a homeless shelter (Lee, 2005; Orr, 2005).

Enabling, exploring and clarifying, mobilizing, guiding, and facilitating are appropriate when a client lacks information, is fearful, or is unable to

Table 8.1
**Relation Between Sources of Environmental Stressors
and Responsive Professional Methods**

People's Environmental Stressors	Professional Methods
1. People are unwilling or unable to use available social or physical resources.	Enabling Exploring Mobilizing Guiding Facilitating
2. Client needs and social or physical environment resources lack sufficient fit; communications and transactions are distorted.	Coordinating/connecting Mediating
3. Social environment is unwilling to provide available resources.	Advocating
4. Formal and/or informal social environment resources are unavailable.	Organizing Innovating

use or respond to the natural and built worlds (Resnick & Jaffee, 1982). Mediating and advocating are appropriate when service systems or powerful individuals in the social environment must be influenced before the physical environment can be improved. *Innovating* is appropriate when mobilization of group or community efforts is necessary for modifying the physical environment. Table 8.1 summarizes environmental stressors and responsive professional methods.

In *coordinating* and *connecting* clients with available organizational resources, the first task is reaching an agreement on a division of labor in dealing with environmental difficulties:

- *Obtaining informed consent and involvement.* While doing "with" a client is preferable, doing "for" is better than ignoring the problem out of misguided insistence on client participation in all situations. Differences in power relations often call for social workers to intervene on behalf of clients, with client consent and involvement. To proceed without informed consent and involvement is unethical and conveys a lack of faith in the client's abilities.
- *Defining a division of labor.* Hopeless and vulnerable clients often expect social workers to do for them; some practitioners, however, are concerned about encouraging dependence and are reluctant to intercede directly. A clear division of labor encourages client involvement and meliorates discrepant expectations: "I will make the call for you, but we need to prepare for the landlord's possible reactions and for how you want to respond." Even when doing "for" a client, the social worker engages the client in the process. Otherwise, feelings of powerlessness and helplessness are reinforced.
- *Mobilizing client's energy and personal resources.* People need to experience some control over their lives. If that need is frustrated, motivation and

self-direction suffer (Gold, 1990; Miller & Rollnick, 2002). People can slip into victim roles, apathy, and learned helplessness (Hooker, 1976; Seligman, 1980). The worker must challenge this response. To mobilize an elderly client's energies and personal resources, the worker makes a direct appeal: "To stop your neighbor's verbal abuse, we have to find small things you can do to change his behavior . . . the problem will not go away, unless we take small steps." This approach to coping helps to make the stressor more manageable.

- *Lending the social worker's professional status to the client.* Although practitioners may feel relatively powerless in relation to their own and other organizations, for clients to have a professional "on their side" provides support and hope. Sitting with a client in a waiting room, telephoning on a client's behalf, and making appointments for a client make a difference. Our presence conveys to the other person that the client is not alone. The presence of an observer or witness reduces the possibility of peremptory treatment. How we define our roles and how we engage formal and informal structures and networks can either reduce or intensify a client's vulnerability and powerlessness. Client-oriented motives must be pursued in an organizational context of other imperatives and people, if we are not to become isolated and ineffective.

- *Demonstrating professional competence.* Organizational effectiveness usually depends on achieving informal influence through demonstrated professional competence. Competence must be visible.

- *Developing and using informal contacts within the employing organization.* The worker who is an insider, attentive to colleagues' interests and concerns, acquires an interpersonal network. Having lunch or coffee, sharing greetings and support with colleagues, and exchanging personal and professional favors activate a "norm of reciprocity" and provide the basis for a favor from a colleague on behalf of a client in a "special" circumstance.

- *Building and using interorganizational resource networks.* For effective contacts with other organizations, social workers need to develop and maintain an interorganizational resource file in which they log helpful (or unhelpful) personnel. Similarly, if the practitioner has been helpful to a staff member from another organization, the "norm of reciprocity" can be activated. By developing a resource file, staff is able to pool their contacts and elevate the level of fit between client need and organizational resources. Continuous updating and searching are needed. Resource files developed by the agency or published centrally within the community are useful adjuncts, but formal files are no substitute for the professional exchange of favors or for building a professional reputation as a competent practitioner.

- *Developing and using formal system contacts.* Active, skillful involvement on committees, teams, consultations, conferences, staff meetings, task forces, and community meetings provides opportunities for contacts. A staff person from another organization is more likely to respond to a social worker who has exhibited clarity, discipline, and good humor in interdisciplinary contacts.

- *Demonstrating awareness of the perspective of other staff.* Before meeting with a staff member, the social worker prepares for the encounter by anticipatory empathy with probable reactions to still another request for service. By identifying with feelings of pressure and of being harassed ("I know how terribly busy you are") and yet appealing to self-interest ("I think Mrs. Smith will become less demanding and complaining if . . ."), the social worker presents requests in a nonthreatening manner. The aim is to achieve positive rather than defensive or resentful responses.
- *Knowing and using organizational policies, procedures, and precedents.* In dealing with others in organizations, knowledge of relevant policies, rules and regulations, research findings, practices, technical procedures, and professional language is critical. In a medical setting, social workers must be familiar with medical terminology. In psychiatric and mental health settings, practitioners must be knowledgeable about categories in the American Psychiatric Association's *Diagnostic and Statistical Manual of Mental Disorders*, 4th edition (DSM-IV). In a public assistance setting, social workers must know the policy manual. Being able to cite a specific policy or procedure useful to a client is most effective in securing entitlements.
- *Demonstrating perseverance.* Being a "charming" pain in the neck is an art worth developing and is a useful collaborative intervention: "It's Louise again, I'm sure you have been waiting all day for my call." Red tape and unresponsive functionaries can certainly evoke anger, despair, and behavioral extremes. We must move past these responses and demonstrate dogged endurance: "Let's call one more time," "Let's write one more letter," and "Let's try just showing up."

To be helpful to clients with environmental stressors, the social worker must have *collaborating* and *mediating* skills. These skills are summarized in Table 8.2.

Collaborating and mediating are not likely to result in negative repercussions. If they fail, more *directive*, *assertive*, and *persuasive* interventions might become necessary:

- *Creating organizational tension.* Elaborate defenses develop in organizations, through which a client's life issues are minimized, avoided, or denied. Before the organization will bend an agency policy, make an exception, or stretch service boundaries, the social worker might have to generate general discomfort with the status quo and its consequences for the client. "I know our policy discourages financial assistance, but I spoke to John's aunt in Virginia. She's willing to have him stay with her, but needs our help with buying him a bus ticket. If we don't do that, he will be homeless and vulnerable to all kinds of violence."
- *Climbing the organizational hierarchy.* If a worker receives a negative response from another agency, a polite request for the name and phone number of the supervisor is advisable. In one's own organization, suggesting that a colleague or supervisor check with the respective supervisor should precede skipping a level.

Table 8.2
Coordinating/Connecting and Collaborative/Mediating Skills

• *Coordinating/connecting skills:*	Reach for informed consent.
	Establish a division of labor.
	Mobilize client's energy and personal resources.
	Lend the worker's professional status to the client.
• *Collaborative/mediating skills:*	Demonstrate professional competence.
	Develop and use informal system contacts within the employing organization.
	Build and use interorganizational resource networks.
	Develop and use formal system contacts.
	Demonstrate awareness of the perspective of other organizational staff.
	Know about and use organizational policies, procedures, and precedents.
	Demonstrate perseverance.

- *Asserting client entitlement or need.* Disciplined assertiveness is a major means of improving the fit between client need and environmental resource. Assertive behavior requires abilities to (1) objectively describe the concern, (2) express associated feelings, (3) specify the desired change or outcome, and (4) explicate consequences; for example, "I know how it is—Mrs. Jones starts to yell and it's hard to resist yelling back at her [1], but when you yell at her, she feels totally helpless, begins to cry, and becomes unmanageable [2]. Maybe if you explain to her that if she only rings her buzzer once, you'll try to come within five minutes and won't yell at her [3]. In that way, she will be a more cooperative patient [4]."
- *Arguing on behalf of the client.* Making a case includes clearly defining the issue, specifying its boundaries, and proposing possible solutions. Next, the social worker tries to anticipate potential opposition to the proposal and the expected and unexpected consequences of adopting it. Throughout the process, one respects others' opinions, but presses one's own position out of expressed concern for the client, the organization's good name, and its mission.

If mediating, asserting, and arguing fail, worker and client might consider *adversarial* actions. Professional ethics actually require such action if essential entitlements are denied or client rights are curtailed (NASW, 1999).

Before taking such action, the social worker evaluates potential consequences. In taking an adversarial position, the worker assumes a polite, respectful stance, not one of outraged righteousness. Expressing outraged righteousness might make the outraged feel better, but it could cost the desired end. Also, client and worker could be vulnerable to retaliation so that probity and caution are always needed.

- *Implying further action.* An even-tempered assertion—"We are running out of patience. My client and agency are prepared if necessary to seek a fair hearing, or to move to a class action, or both"—can, by shifting the balance of power, release a client's entitlement. Sometimes the action has to be initiated before willingness to negotiate or to concede is brought about.
- *Refusing compliance.* Social workers might sometimes be expected to take actions that conflict with established professional standards and ethics. Polite firmness can be highly effective: "I am sorry, but the client has to be informed about her legal rights and options—professional ethics requires it. I am also concerned about the negative impact upon our department's reputation if this practice became known." Unwillingness to carry out a wrongful departmental policy is a part of organizational loyalty.
- *Organizing protests.* Clients gain strength and security from joining with others in similar circumstances. Group action usually diminishes client isolation and risk of reprisal, and it increases chances of success. Group action gets institutional attention. In some severe instances, the social worker helps groups to express grievances through sit-ins, vigils, marches, rent strikes, picketing, the use of mass media, and engaging the interest of political figures. These actions increase client visibility and bargaining power.

Table 8.3 summarizes adversarial and persuasive skills.

Skills with organizational issues are also applicable to network issues. Some require simple modification. "Knowing and using organizational policies, procedures, and precedents" becomes "Knowing and using network structures and processes"; "Climbing the organizational hierarchy" becomes "Traversing network boundaries" (Adams & Blieszner, 1993; Biegel, Tracy, & Corvo, 1994; Lee, 2005).

Table 8.3
Persuasive and Adversarial Skills

- Create organizational tension.
- Climb the organizational hierarchy.
- Assert client entitlement.
- Argue on behalf of the client.
- Imply further action.
- Refuse compliance.
- Organize protests.

The physical environment offers the social worker an additional dimension in helping people. Improving the degree of fit between people and their physical environments requires distinct professional skills.

- *Responding to the client's spatial needs.* People with schizophrenia have been found to have a large personal distance and often react with flight if too closely approached, even by eye contact. In responding to their spatial needs, the social worker might sit beside them rather than across from them, minimizing eye contact and thereby providing greater distance. An aging client, because of declining sensory perception, or a physically challenged client might hunger for physical nearness, and the worker could respond by moving closer, touching, and so on. By responding differently to clients' differing spatial needs, help is more effective.
- *Arranging professional space.* Spatial arrangement of a worker's office provides significant clues to clients and affects their comfort and interaction. Appropriate posters and plants convey welcome and receptiveness. Personal mementos such as pictures of one's children or pet convey a willingness to be personal and involved. In working with a female adolescent group, the author assumed that chairs arranged in a circle would create an intimate atmosphere and facilitate interaction. The adolescents, however, experienced self-consciousness about their hands and their miniskirts. The small circle demanded too much physical and emotional intimacy with an unknown professional.
- *Arranging agency space.* In a family agency waiting room, a social work student noticed the lack of toys or reading matter for children and organized an effort to add inexpensive ones. In a public welfare setting, another student asked staff to contribute magazines, children's toys and books, and plants to make the waiting room more attractive and welcoming. Sensitivity to arrangements of physical space reflects staff interest and caring.
- *Coordinating spatial access and use.* In families where many members share a limited amount of space, stress can result from the interpersonal coordination required to manage restricted space. Sharing a bathroom, room, closet, dresser, or television places a strain on civility. Helping a family develop a schedule for morning use of a bathroom, for evening use of a television, or for planning meals may significantly mitigate interpersonal tensions and facilitate mutual support and assistance. Sometimes a worker-initiated discussion about privacy and clearer spatial agreements is sufficient. In other cases, the worker may suggest a simple environmental prop such as a lock on a bedroom, a room divider, or a screen. Living space is an important area for professional attention and intervention.
- *Encouraging and teaching clients to use the built and natural environment.* The physical environment can be overwhelming and threatening. Deinstitutionalized mental patients and developmentally challenged clients frequently lack the basic skills needed for moving through and using the built environment. Some residents of inner cities are fearful of leaving their neighbor-

Table 8.4
Skills of Influencing the Physical Environment

- Respect the client's spatial needs.
- Arrange professional space.
- Arrange agency (department) space.
- Coordinate spatial access and usage.
- Encourage and teach clients to use the natural and built environment.
- Use animals to provide companionship, assistance, and nonthreatening relationships.

hood. The worker can provide trips to the zoo, parks, seashore, and countryside; camping experiences; and hikes. These refresh the spirit and renew energies, as do visits to libraries, museums, and concerts. They bring relief from urban and rural isolation as well as the stress of overcrowded living. For these reasons, wilderness therapy has been found to be helpful for troubled adolescents (Cooley, 1998; McGowan, 1997).

- *Using animals to provide companionship and unthreatening relationships.* Pets meet people's unmet needs for companionship. Animals are also used for specific therapeutic purposes (e.g., rebuilding trust in abused children; Mallon, 1994). Pets provide people certain control over their environment. A pet provides its human companion an opportunity to be nurturing and responsible.

Table 8.4 summarizes the skills of influencing the physical environment.

Practice Illustrations

Organizational Environment. In work on dysfunctional exchanges between client and service system, social workers rely on the *mediating* method and its *collaborative skills* of interceding, bargaining, and persuading. The effectiveness of these skills depends, in part, on familiarity with the client's situation, careful assessment of the organizational components in the problem, and knowledge of organizational properties and operations.

In the following illustration, a nursing home group is meeting with the social worker, and the members are discussing their concerns about the food:

Mrs. Schwartz said she thought we should spend time talking about all the things that go wrong during meals. Mr. Ball agreed, saying that the food is lousy and the service is lousy. If he didn't have to eat to survive, he wouldn't even bother going to meals. Several other members nodded. I asked the residents to say specifically what was bad about the food and service.

Mrs. Schwartz said the napkins either arrive wet on the trays or they're given out at the very end of the meal, which defeats the purpose. I said I could understand how annoying this is. Mr. Silverman added that silverware is often missing from the trays. By the time the missing pieces are brought, the food is cold. He sighed, "For all they care, we can eat with our hands." Mrs. Schwartz commented that it would be logical for the kitchen to send up extra silver, so the aides could replace the missing pieces right away. Mr. Phelps added they often get different food from what they ordered. Mrs. Schwartz confirmed this, saying she doesn't know why they put things on the menu if they have no intention of giving them to the residents: "They pretend to give you a choice, but in the end, they give you whatever they damn please." I acknowledged their frustration and asked when these substitutions occur. Mrs. Schwartz said it usually happens with things like dessert—you order ice cream and get Jell-O. . . .

I said, "So, you have three specific complaints: napkins that are either wet or not given out until the meal is almost over; missing silverware; and the substitution of items that you've selected from the menu. I wonder if you have ideas about what we might do about these problems?" Mrs. Liebner asked, "Who could we speak to?" Mrs. Schwartz responded, "We could meet with Miss Jackson [the kitchen supervisor]." I asked the others what they thought. Mr. Goldstein said, "Talking to the supervisor won't help." Mr. Lazar agreed, "No one will listen to us anyway, so why bother?" I sensed their hopelessness, but suggested that it was worth a try and I would like to help them improve the situation. This led to a discussion of the advantages and disadvantages of my doing it or of a member's inviting the supervisor to a meeting. We decided that a positive response was more likely if I extended the invitation. We reviewed what I would say to her.

I then asked them how we should present their concerns to the supervisor when she comes. Mr. Silverman suggested we make a list and read off the items. This was agreed on, and I asked who would begin the meeting and read the list. Mr. Goldstein said that as the group leader, I should. I responded that I could, but I felt it was important for the supervisor to hear directly from them about their experiences. Mrs. Schwartz volunteered to start the meeting off. We role-played what she would say. Mr. Silverman volunteered to offer specific examples of his own experiences. Others volunteered to share theirs. We then considered possible responses and how to handle them.

Before she approaches the supervisor with the group's request for a meeting, the social worker prepared herself for the encounter. She put herself into Miss Jackson's shoes, and imagined the likely impact of still another pressure on a busy, harassed staff member, and her possible responses. She considered how best to present the request without stimulating resentment against the residents and with a view of engaging Miss Jackson in collaborative problem solving.

I said, "The group members have been discussing their dietary problems, and they feel it will be very helpful to have your input, so they have asked me to invite you to our next meeting." She said she didn't know if she could make it. I responded that I knew she was very busy. She explained she is responsible for several floors, and it's hard to find time for everything. I acknowledged it was, but added that the group members really feel she can be helpful to them, especially since their concerns are quite specific. She asked me what their complaints are, and I mentioned several. She smiled and shook her head. I said, "I imagine you're really tired of hearing complaints, especially when you're working so hard." She responded, "You're not kidding." There was a pause, and she asked me what time the meeting would be. I told her, and she said she would come. I expressed my appreciation.

In mediating, the worker conveyed her understanding of the supervisor's perspective and commiserated with her difficulties. At the same time, she persisted in stating the clients' need for Miss Jackson's assistance and clarified their concerns. In such efforts, the worker must be willing to risk tension and even conflict while persevering. In this instance, perseverance succeeded, and Miss Jackson agreed to come.

Miss Jackson entered the meeting. As we agreed, I began by stating the general purpose of the meeting, and suggested Mrs. Schwartz describe the first concern. Mrs. Schwartz began by asking who was responsible for setting the tables. Miss Jackson said she usually oversees the preparation of the dining room. Mrs. Schwartz explained the problem with the napkins. Miss Jackson explained that staff is sometimes rushed and water spills on the napkins. She assured the group she will try to correct the problem. Group members said they would appreciate it. There was a pause, and I asked if anyone else wanted to say something about this particular problem. This was a prearranged cue for Mr. Silverman to ask about the pieces of silverware missing from the trays. Miss Jackson replied that she knew this was a problem and that she would have two extra sets of silverware sent up. I asked the members if they felt this was a good solution. They all agreed. Mr. Phelps said he would like to know why he gets Jell-O every day when he hates it and orders other desserts. Ms. Jackson asked him if he had dental problems. He said no. She explained that when a dessert on the menu has to be changed at the last minute, they substitute applesauce or Jell-O. Mr. Phelps said he prefers applesauce. Ms. Jackson made a note of his request. I asked why substitutions have to be made. She explained that when menus are made up, the department assumes a certain item will be on hand. When it isn't, or they run out of a popular dish, substitutions are made. Mrs. Schwartz said she could see how these become problems. After discussing how residents could be given some choice, the meeting ended with Miss Jackson's agreement to return in a month for a review of the results.

The changes were immediately implemented and institutionalized. Members felt a sense of accomplishment, and they were now more willing to work on other environmental tasks.

In this instance, the transactions between the service system and its residents had unintentionally become distorted. The residents, fearful of asserting themselves to the appropriate authorities, had continuously but ineffectively complained to the dietary aides. This only increased their sense of powerlessness. Meanwhile, the kitchen supervisor was vaguely aware of inefficiencies, but since she already felt overburdened and no one approached her directly, she did not address these problems. After mobilizing the group's interest in taking action, the worker interceded by persistently requesting the supervisor's meeting with the residents. Had the supervisor been less willing to come, or had she or the group been antagonistic, other skills would have been brought into play. Here, the worker used the least amount of pressure needed to bring about the desired outcome. From the outset, she correctly assumed goal consensus that required direct, effective exchanges.

In mediating, a critical area to assess is how much clients can do for themselves to increase their sense of competence and self-direction. For example, Sal, a sixteen-year-old, and his eleven-year-old brother Paul were placed in a residential treatment center before being placed with foster parents six months ago. Sal had lived until age ten with his natural mother and her husband, both heroin addicts. Five years ago, because of severe neglect, the child welfare agency placed him in a foster home, where he and the other children were subjected to extensive physical and sexual abuse by both foster parents. Sal was removed to a residential treatment center, and six months ago, he was placed with other foster parents.

The supervising foster care agency decided that Sal and his brother should visit with their mother in her social worker's office. The mother has no permanent home, but stays on and off with a current lover, Jerry, who had once beaten Sal for refusing to call him "Dad." Jerry also frequently attends the sessions with the mother's social worker, Mr. Briggs. At their last visit to Mr. Briggs's office, while they waited for their mother's late arrival, the boys were bored and acted up. Mr. Briggs threatened to send them "back to the residential treatment center." According to the foster parents, when the boys returned home that evening, they were pale and shaken, and Sal vomited. When I spoke to Sal, he exclaimed, "I am never going to see either my mother or Mr. Briggs again, because I don't need people like this. I finally live in a normal home, and I intend to keep things that way." Sal asked the worker to intervene for him. However, she thought that he was capable of fulfilling this task by himself with her assistance.

SAL:	Did you call Mr. Briggs?
WORKER:	Remember, Sal, what we talked about before? You have the ability to call Mr. Briggs yourself. I want to help you make this call, so let's figure out what you want to say to him.
SAL:	I will not go to see my mother tomorrow! My brother wants to go, but I can't go with him anymore. He has to go alone, and that's too bad. But I am not going!
WORKER:	Tell me in more detail what you would like to say to Mr. Briggs about why you don't want to go.
SAL:	I hate him. I wish he were dead. I can't believe a grown-up can behave like that—a man with schooling and a social worker, besides. He's a jerk. Because I didn't behave in his office, he actually threatened to put me in placement! Can you believe that?
WORKER:	I understand your anger and hurt, Sal. Let's think about what you want to say to him so he can hear your complaints.
SAL:	I'm going to say I hate him and I'm not going to see him or my mother ever again.
WORKER:	Besides wanting to tell him how angry you are because he threatened you with placement, are there other things about the meetings you don't like?
SAL:	I can't stand it that Jerry is there. I want to be alone with my mother. He doesn't belong to our family. And I don't want to see Mr. Briggs there either. And I also can't stand my mother being always high and always telling me, "your friends in the Bronx are always asking for you." Especially since they haven't seen me for years and years.
WORKER:	I think it is very important that you tell Mr. Briggs all the things bothering you—not that you hate him, but the specific things that you hate. He needs to know exactly how you are feeling and reacting. You must tell him how deeply his threat affected you.
SAL:	Mr. Briggs should really call and say he is sorry. That would be the right thing to do.
WORKER:	You already know that grown-ups don't always do the right thing and are not always aware when they do things wrong. You're right—it should be different.
SAL:	I hate his guts! That's what I want to tell him.
WORKER:	I understand that, Sal, but do you remember how, not very long ago, you stood up against your former foster father in court? You told him in front of everybody how you felt about him and all that he had done to you. Do you remember how

	the judge came up to you afterwards and told you that she had never before seen so young a man do so well in court?
SAL:	(After a long pause) Y-e-a-h, I did tell him what I thought of him in front of the whole courtroom full of people.
WORKER:	You did. And you were very brave to tell the whole story, the total truth. I would like you to be brave again and continue being brave.
SAL:	You're right. I can call Mr. Briggs. I'll tell him what my reactions are to everything that's been going on.

Sal called Mr. Briggs from the worker's office and told him everything he felt about his visits to the office. He added that because he was so upset, he would discontinue future visits. Mr. Briggs apologized for his threat and informed the worker, "I can hear that Sal is improving. And he does have the right to decide for himself. I will tell his mother that he will only consider seeing her if she is by herself and is not high."

The worker encouraged Sal to stand up for himself and to be self-directing. She knew Mr. Briggs and was confident that he would be responsive to Sal. If she had not had the confidence in Mr. Briggs, she would have had to prepare him for the phone call and gain his support. Supported by her presence and in her office, Sal ably confronted his mother's social worker. With his worker's support and demand, Sal demonstrated competence and self-direction. The worker's demand was a statement of confidence in his competence.

When a disparity in power exists between client and service system, the social worker must assume an active and directive role. In helping young children and clients with impaired cognitive, emotional, and social functioning, the worker's active presence in the mediation process is crucial.

For example, Latisha is a sixteen-year-old girl of Jamaican descent from East Plainview, Connecticut. She is currently in foster care and resides with her foster mother, her foster brother, and her biological five-year-old sister. Latisha is in a ninth-grade special education class at the local high school. She has been in and out of foster care since she was six months old. At age four, Latisha was placed with her maternal grandmother, who physically abused her by slamming her head against a wall, causing cognitive disorder and partial paralysis on her right side. As a result of this abuse, Latisha is paralyzed on her right side, her right arm is bent at the elbow with her hand fisted, and she wears braces on both legs. She is unaware that her grandmother caused these disabilities. Instead, she believes that she was in an accident. Latisha's father recently died, and her mother, Mrs. Yates, fell apart and began to use drugs. Latisha was returned to foster care and has a loving relationship with her foster mother, Mrs. Simms.

The social work student is interning at an agency, which provides evaluation, planning, and clinical services to foster children with developmental, behavioral, and mental health needs and their foster and biological families. The intern is assigned to Latisha; Mrs. Yates receives services from the Department of Family Services (DFS). The social work intern has been meeting with Latisha once a week for the past eight months. She was initially referred to the agency because of difficulties in dealing with the recent death of her father. In the beginning sessions, the focus was on the loss of her father and her return, once again, to foster care. In addition, they worked on her mother's substance abuse and her brother's incarceration. Latisha has been verbal and receptive to the intern's help.

As the end of the internship was approaching, the student spoke with the caseworker at DFS, who informed her that the agency planned to return the children to Mrs. Yates this summer. This news shocked the intern because Latisha verbalized fear of her mother's rage and because Mrs. Yates is not currently attending any parenting training at the agency, which usually precedes children being discharged to their home. In addition, no one could confirm that Mrs. Yates had been clean or attending any drug program. The intern felt that the DFS caseworker had become allied with the mother and lost sight of the children's needs. For example, when the intern inquired why the visitations had been unsupervised in view of the history in this case, the caseworker abruptly answered, "Why shouldn't they be alone together—she is their mother!" When the intern reminded the caseworker about the long history of family problems and the past concerns about unsupervised visits, the caseworker responded, "I have no concerns."

During subsequent sessions with Latisha, the intern reached for her feelings about returning home to her biological mother. Latisha vacillated between not wanting to hurt her mother's feelings and not wanting to go home with her mother.

I opened a session by saying, "Last week, you shared with me your mixed feelings about not wanting to hurt your mother's feelings and not wanting to live with her. Have you had time to think more about this?" Latisha said, "I love my mother and I love my foster mother." I responded, "It is very confusing to love both your mother and your foster mother." Latisha agreed. I encouraged her to describe her life with both "mothers." Latisha replied, "It is peaceful with my foster mom. We all get along." "And how about living with your mother?" Latisha replied, "I am scared when my mother gets angry and starts screaming and throwing things. She blames me for anything that goes wrong." I asked, "Can you give me an example?" Latisha explained, "My mother asks me to wake her in the mornings. I can't, and then she begins to scream at me to leave her alone, and then later she screams at me again for not waking her up." I commented, "You can't win—whatever you do, you get yelled at." "Yes. I have to take care of both Desmond and Alicia (younger siblings). I have to cook, clean, and do the laundry. And no matter how much I do, I get yelled at." I asked, "Do you have to do these tasks also for Mrs. Simms?" "At Mrs. Simms's home, I also have chores and responsibilities, but I am allowed to play and participate in many school activities. Also, Mrs. Simms talks to me quietly—she hardly ever yells at me." I commented, "Latisha you love your mother, but you seem to be more comfortable living with Mrs. Simms." She replied, "Yes, I am." I explained, "We will need to tell others about your preference at the forthcoming Service Plan Review, where you, your mother, the DFS caseworker, and I will participate. Based on this meeting, DFS will make the decision on where you will live. We will need to convince them that right now you prefer living with Mrs. Simms. What would it be like for you for your mother to know your preference?" She replied, "I will be scared—will you be with me—will you help me?" I assured her, "I want you to know that I agree with your decision. Mrs. Simms is sincerely concerned and committed to you. I will be with you—we will prepare how and when to tell your mother and her caseworker."

Exploring Latisha's fears and her mother's potential reactions, and developing strategies, became the focus of the next two sessions. The intern offered Latisha a great deal of support and credited her decision to take care of herself instead of taking care of everyone else.

In assessing the environmental stressor and developing intervention strategies, the social work intern identified the following factors that promoted a successful problem resolution: (1) Latisha's ability to express her wishes and concerns about returning home; (2) the field instructor's assistance and support; (3) a court-appointed special advocate (CASA), Ms. Trumbel; (4) another social worker from the agency, who sees Latisha's younger sister and who recognizes the biological mother's need for intensive help with parenting; and (5) the foster mother's caring for Latisha and her concerns about the biological mother's ability to handle all three children. The factors that restrained the problem resolution were (1) the DFS caseworker, who was identified with the mother and negated concerns about her mothering abilities; and (2) the fact that DFS had the authority to make the final decision.

In preparing for the Service Plan Review meeting, the intern suggested to Latisha that Ms. Trumbel, who had been working with her for four years, join them for a session and that she explain to her advocate how she felt. Latisha agreed and during this meeting, she was able to tell Ms. Trumbel that she did not want to return home to her mother. She even gave examples of her mother's irrational behavior and explained how scared she would become when her mother acted in this manner.

"Latisha, do you remember Ms. Trumbel?" I asked. "Yes," Latisha answered with a grin. Ms. Trumbel said, "Hello Latisha, I was happy to hear that you agreed to have me attend a session." "I remember you," Latisha answered. "Of course you do. We've known each other for quite a while. I used to visit you when you lived in Bridgegate with your mom." Latisha nodded and smiled. I said, "Latisha, as you know we asked Ms. Trumbel to join us so that you can tell her where you want to live and why you want to live there. I know it's difficult for you, but can you try and tell Ms. Trumbel how you feel?" Latisha had difficulty beginning. I asked, "Do you want me to start?" "Please," answered Latisha. "As you know, Ms. Trumbel, Latisha and I have been discussing her returning home with her mother or remaining with her foster mother." Latisha blurted out, "I don't want to go home. I love my mom, but I don't want to live with her. She gets very angry." Ms. Trumbel asked, "What does she get angry about?" Latisha replied, "My mom gets angry about everything."

A Service Plan Review was scheduled for the following week at the DFS office in Plainview. The DFS caseworker wanted the meeting participation limited to her supervisor, the mother, Latisha, and the intern. The intern insisted that Ms. Trumbel, the other agency worker, and the foster mother also be invited. She stressed that all the people involved with Latisha should be invited—that their "voices" had to be heard to determine what was in Latisha's best interest. The intern requested that the caseworker call the supervisor for a decision. The DFS supervisor agreed to honor the intern's request. The intern wrote in her process recording, "I wanted the supervisor involved because I remembered from the class discussion that the higher you go in a public agency's organizational structure, the more likely you will reach a professional social worker. I was prepared to go as high as possible."

On the day of the Service Plan Review, the intern made arrangements to meet Mrs. Simms in advance, helped her to think through what she wanted to present, and briefly rehearsed how she would present. On the way to the meeting, Latisha became increasingly frightened and requested that the intern speak first. Latisha specifically wanted the intern to state that she loves her mother, but is scared by her angry outbursts. She has been in the foster home for many years and feels very comfortable and happy there. The intern agreed to this request, feeling that Latisha was very brave to have these sentiments expressed, even though she feared her mother's reactions.

Upon speaking at the Service Plan Review, the intern wanted to make sure that she was clear and concise. She felt a great deal of pressure to influence the DFS supervisor and achieve a favorable disposition for Latisha. She introduced herself and explained that she provided individual services to Latisha on a weekly basis since September. She faced the biological mother and stated,

---

"Latisha was so nervous about today's meeting that she told me she did not sleep last night. She asked me to speak on her behalf. She first wanted me to let you know, Mrs. Yates, that she loves you very much." Mrs. Yates smiled and nodded her head. I continued, "Latisha has given a great deal of thought and decided that for now she wants to continue to live with Mrs. Simms. She feels very safe and comfortable there. This was a very hard decision for her, because she is so worried about hurting your feelings. However, she is also scared of your angry outbursts, and wants you to get rid of them before she comes home. She also explains that when she lived with you, she had too many responsibilities in taking care of her younger brother and sister and with housework and cooking—she could not just be a kid." The DFS caseworker interrupted me and praised Mrs. Yates—that she had been drug free for a year, and that the children would be going home in the summer. Mrs. Yates's drug counselor spoke and confirmed that the mother has been clean for almost a year. I congratulated Mrs. Yates for being free of drugs for an entire year and encouraged her to work as diligently on dealing with her anger and gaining parenting skills. I looked at the DFS supervisor and commented, "I hope that the decision has not been already made and that you will listen to what the other people in the room have to say." The DFS supervisor replied, "I assure you that I have made no decision yet and am interested in what you all have to say." The caseworker scowled.

The social worker who sees Latisha's younger sister stated her concerns about the children returning home to their mother without any improved parenting or anger management skills. Then the CASA worker spoke. "I joined a session with Latisha and the social worker and can confirm your daughter wishes not to return home. As the court-appointed advocate, I believe that Latisha's request has to be honored and that DFS acts in Latisha's best interests. I fully support the recommendations of the two social workers—that before Latisha returns home, Mrs. Yates has to demonstrate the ability to manage her anger and allow Latisha to be a child." Ms. Trumbel stated her views so forcefully that a period of silence followed. I invited Mrs. Simms to speak next, who quite timidly expressed her concern about Mrs. Yates being able to manage the children. (I immediately recognized my mistake. I had prepared Mrs. Simms for the meeting, but not for speaking in front of Mrs. Yates. Mrs. Yates had the reputation of erupting in violent outbursts. Mrs. Simms was clearly intimidated.)

The DFS supervisor thanked all of us for our feedback. "We all have a common goal for Latisha and Mrs. Yates to be able to live happy lives together. At this time, I think we have a better chance to achieve the goal if Latisha stays a little longer with Mrs. Simms. Let's use the next six months to get you some more help and support, Mrs. Yates, so that when Latisha comes home it will be a permanent reunion."

Over time, the intern developed a trusting relationship with Latisha. This trust enabled her to express her wishes and have the intern represent her interests. Having Latisha speak with Ms. Trumbel proved to be a critical intervention, as it lent Latisha the credibility and power of two agencies and two professionals' statuses. Mrs. Simms's attendance was also important, although the intern needed to have spent more time in preparing her for the pressures she faced at the meeting. Finally, the intern skillfully represented Latisha, speaking forcefully in her behalf at a meeting attended by many professionals with differing points of view and by the biological parent. She "gave voice" to a child who could not represent herself (Dalrynmple, 2003; VanBergeikj & McGowan, 2001).

For another example of a social worker assuming an active and directive role: Mrs. Simpson, a "tired" teacher in an elementary school, acted out her frustration by scapegoating nine-year-old Jill. She often singled out Jill in front of the class or wrote her name on the blackboard for misbehavior or unfinished work. Jill worked hard to fulfill Mrs. Simpson's expectations of her, but with fussiness, interruption, and other inappropriate behaviors. The school social worker's helping efforts were sabotaged by Mrs. Simpson's negative reinforcement of Jill's behavior. One afternoon, Mrs. Simpson drew the worker into her inner office to begin yet another tirade against Jill.

"That kid is driving me crazy . . . she draws attention to herself in the most inappropriate ways, constantly bothers people, and doesn't do her work. The nice kids in the class will not give her the time of day." (Since little progress was being made, I decided to focus Mrs. Simpson on a search for positive attributes—to try to dramatically change their ways of interacting.) After listening and empathizing with Mrs. Simpson's frustrations, I suggested the only way we can change Jill's behavior is to identify and focus on some of her strengths. "Well, she is bright," Mrs. Simpson responded, "does good atlas work and does a good job explaining things in Friday class discussions." I supported Mrs. Simpson's assessment, noting I had seen similar qualities, and also commented on Jill's creative imagination. I asked, "Can you think of any ways that we can use and channel Jill's abilities in imagination and theatrics (the same attributes that repeatedly get her into trouble)?" She was willing to try, but wanted to know, "Meanwhile, what are we going to do about her behavior?" I replied, "How about if the three of us get together and talk about your frustrations with her in light of her special abilities and the things Jill has to offer?" Mrs. Simpson agreed, and I prepared both her and Jill for our three-way meeting.

Mrs. Simpson began the meeting by berating Jill for her behavior and waving a note from a volunteer art appreciation teacher about Jill's rudeness. She also emphasized her lack of cooperation on a class outing. Jill was quiet, sad, and despondent. (I began to feel that still another of my efforts was being sabotaged. But I was determined to focus on Jill's many assets.) I tried again. "You know, Jill, the other day Mrs. Simpson was telling me about some of the things she thinks are very special about you. Mrs. Simpson, I would appreciate your telling Jill what you told me." As Mrs. Simpson began, she opened herself up more, telling Jill she was a talented girl and highlighting her special qualities. She also told Jill about her frustration when Jill doesn't follow rules, how it disrupts the class and upsets her. Jill listened, and said she would try to behave better, but she doesn't like Mrs. Simpson's singling her out and yelling at her. After discussion, I suggested they might try a private signal between them when Mrs. Simpson thinks Jill is going too far—it would be their secret signal. They agreed. I also asked Mrs. Simpson if she could credit Jill more in front of teachers and students. She agreed to try. We also decided to meet in a week to evaluate the results.

During the week, Jill represented her class in the all-school assembly. She talked about Martin Luther King Jr., and was outstanding. Mrs. Simpson praised Jill on her articulate, informative presentation. Jill also received praise from classmates and the principal. Positive reinforcement increased Jill's motivation to cooperate. The following week, Mrs. Simpson enthusiastically informed me of Jill's cooperation on a class project. For the project, Jill called various companies and obtained information for the class. Jill proudly showed me the mass of information she had received in the mail. She read and explained the information to the class. Jill asked Mrs. Simpson if she would send her mother a "happy note," like she sends to other kids when they have a good week. Mrs. Simpson was obviously embarrassed since she had not done this for Jill, and she readily agreed to send her mom two notes—for the last two weeks. When I saw Mrs. Simpson later, I thanked her for her efforts and praised her ingenuity. She beamed and said it was all worth it to have a week like this!

The social worker's determination to improve the fit between student and teacher was contingent on her ability to build on the strengths of both. Each needed to feel better about herself in order to feel better about the other. Jill was particularly vulnerable to scapegoating, so change had to be initiated by the more powerful teacher. While each party contributed to and had a stake in the issue, the teacher had the power to reward and punish. The worker's mediating changed the degree of reciprocity to a more favorable balance for Jill.

The worker often has to intervene on behalf of clients, guided by their involvement if possible and by the ethical principle of informed consent.

Karen, age thirty-two, had been given alcohol by her alcoholic mother. Her mother's boyfriend also sexually abused Karen when she was eleven years old. She stopped drinking approximately six years ago, attends AA meetings regularly, and has seen a family agency social worker for a year, trying to "get her life together." Recently, Karen had been having severe digestive distress and menstrual problems. She consistently resisted the worker's suggested medical referral: "They're all alike, those gentleman doctors." The worker referred her to a women's health service. Ulcer medication and vitamins to reduce heavy menstrual flow were prescribed. The physician also strongly recommended dilation and curettage (D and C). Karen refused to consider D and C, emphasizing that she wasn't "going to lie down in front of a doctor and a bunch of medical students and open my legs."

The social worker called the physician, who confirmed that medical students would observe the surgery. The worker empathized with Karen's aversion to the lack of privacy, given her history of sexual abuse, and offered to intervene with the hospital. Karen welcomed the worker's offer:

I called the hospital's Obstetrics/Gynecology Department, introduced myself as a social worker from Family Services calling on behalf of a client, and asked to speak to the medical director of the department. He was unavailable, and I left my phone number. A week later, I called again, spoke to the same receptionist, and left the same message. After three days, I called again and asked to speak with a female gynecologist. That afternoon, Dr. Park returned my call. After introducing myself, I explained Karen's background and situation, and her aversion to undergoing surgery with medical students observing. I also mentioned that Karen would only respond to a female gynecologist. Dr. Park suggested I send a letter to the medical director. I expressed my concern that the letter would receive a response similar to my phone calls, and inquired whether I could send the letter to her. She agreed to follow up on my request. I wrote the letter with a return permission form for Karen to have a private operation with a female gynecologist and no students present. Approximately a week later, the signed permission was returned to me with instructions for next steps.

Powerless and vulnerable clients often need workers to do "with" and "for" them to obtain essential services. *Doing for* the client is opportune when conflict exists between client and organization, particularly when the client's presence may exacerbate or increase the potential for negative outcomes. Under these conditions, it is more productive for the worker to mediate on the client's behalf.

Mrs. James, a homeless client living with her two-year-old daughter in a suburban welfare motel, had no food. She asked the social worker in a child abuse prevention program to drive her to the district office for a required referral card from her caseworker. The social worker called for Mrs. James and her daughter, stopped for the referral card, and drove to the pantry. On the way, Mrs. James explained the procedure: the client turns in the referral card and is assigned a number; on a first visit, the client must see the pantry minister for a brief intake and counseling session; when the number is called, the client must show an identity card; the amount of food needed is determined; the client returns to the waiting room until her number is again called; and the client signs for food and waits in the hall until the bags are brought out.

Mrs. James and I waited two hours until her number was called. I was sitting nearby and could see her engaged in heated discussion with Mrs. Folk, the coordinator. Mrs. James came out and said she was refused food, and went out into the hall. I went out after her. She said the coordinator was a nasty woman who had previously banned her from the pantry. I asked how come and she said, "I was with a man who got mean and swore at Mrs. Folk." Mrs. James felt that Mrs. Folk is taking it out on her even though she was not directly involved in the incident.

I suggested we figure out how to obtain some food, for it would be a shame to leave after such a long wait. She said usually a priest is around. We finally found him. Mrs. James immediately explained that Mrs. Folk had banned her, even though she "did nothing wrong." The priest explained to us that Mrs. Folk was in charge and that he couldn't intervene. He volunteered to speak to her and suggested we return next week. I explained that Mrs. James didn't have any food and inquired whether something could be done today. He suggested we talk to Mrs. Folk again, and walked away. I asked if she wanted to talk to Mrs. Folk again. She felt it would be no use and she wouldn't change her mind: "I tried to apologize, but she didn't care!" I wondered if it would help if I tried to talk to her. Mrs. James didn't think it would make any difference, but agreed to my making the effort. I asked if we should go in together, and she responded, "No way—I'm not going back in there with that bitch."

I returned to the waiting room. Mrs. Folk was seated behind a desk. I introduced myself and hunkered down in front of the desk so we would be at eye level (there were no chairs). I said, "I know you are very busy, but would you have a few minutes to discuss Mrs. James's problem?" She exclaimed, "She's banned. I told her she's banned. I banned her three months ago." I explained that I really didn't know what happened. She reported that Mrs. James came in three months ago with Mr. Brown. They had cards for a Mr. Smith, which they had stolen from somewhere. When she informed them that Mr. Smith had just picked up his food and that he was right here, they started cursing her. I inquired whether both of them behaved this way. She replied that Mrs. James was as much involved as he was: "Believe me, she was really nasty to me. And I take a lot. Believe me, it's only happened two or three times that I've had to ban someone. They were really violent." I said it sounds like they gave her a rough time and she has a big job. She replied, "Yes. It really is. For no appreciation." I asked if there was some way she might make an exception, because Mrs. James and her daughter had nothing whatsoever to eat. She repeated, "But she really was nasty. And structure is important here. If I let her get away with it, there will be chaos." I responded, "I agree with you about how important structure and rules are. And I understand your concern about losing authority if you change your mind. But is there some sort of possible compromise we can come to . . . some way that will keep your authority intact and allow Mrs. James some food?" Mrs. Folk asked if Mrs. James is my client. "Yes. This is the first time she has asked for my help. And even though it is a very small step, I think if we work this out, she'll start using me more for things going on in her life." Mrs. Folk exclaimed, "Do you know why she asked you? She knew she was banned. I told her caseworker that, too. She's just using you!" I replied, "You may be right. But if you can think of a way out of this problem, I'd really appreciate it." She said, taking out Mrs. James's card, "Look at what I have written here. You see. I'll tell you, this has happened only two or three times." I tried once again, "I can see you feel strongly about this. But I would really appreciate if you could find a way to give her some food—nobody should have to go hungry, particularly a two-year-old child." Mrs. Folk threw up her hands and replied, "I'm not going to do this for her. I don't care about her. I'm doing this for you because I see how much you care. She can get food here, but only if you come with her. Alone, she is still banned." I thanked her and said that I thought her decision was a fair one. Her last words were "Remember—only if she's with you!"

Mrs. Folk and Mrs. James saw themselves as adversaries. They both felt humiliated and angry. The worker could do little to remedy the situation. She realized that Mrs. Folk needed some appreciation for her work on behalf of homeless people. She accepted Mrs. Folk's perceptions of reality (i.e., the need for authority and structure) and Mrs. James's need for food. The worker remained calm, used various arguments, and persisted. Since her relationship with Mrs. James was tenuous, she did not press her to examine her part in the problem or to participate in the negotiation. The worker sought to get her foot in the door. And with skill and determination, she succeeded.

Case management is a system of community-based care for defined populations who suffer profound, long-term, or permanent disabilities. The chronically mentally ill are the largest population served, followed by the physically and developmentally challenged. A growing population of older persons who are unable to provide adequately for their health, social, and economic needs without in-home services are also maintained in the community through public and private case management agencies. Similarly, physically challenged persons in the community who require multiple social and health services in order to maintain independent living are served by case managers attached to rehabilitation agencies or provided by case management and community-based agencies, including those who also serve the elderly (Germain, 1994).

Those suffering profound long-term or permanent mental or physical disorders often encounter difficulties in finding their way through the complex of formal services and programs. They may be unable to deal with difficult eligibility requirements and restrictive policies. Coordinating services and linking vulnerable people to entitlements and needed services such as Social Security, Supplemental Security Income (SSI), public assistance, and health care are essential. Monitoring entails regular contacts with service providers and clients to ensure that appropriate and effective services are provided in a timely way (Anthony, Cohen, Farkas, & Cohen, 2000; Bigby, Ozanne, & Gordon, 2002; Ferry & Abramson, 2005; Moxley, 2002; Parrish, Burry, & Pabst, 2003; Wodarski & Williams-Hayes, 2002). In exchanges with organizational personnel, the worker's knowledge of relevant laws, policies, research findings, technical procedures, and professional jargon within the field of practice is a critical source of influence (Gitterman & Miller, 1989).

Mark, forty-two years old, had been diagnosed with multiple sclerosis (MS) ten years ago. A family agency with a case management service assigned a worker to assess his need for homemaker services.

On the first home visit, Mark narrates that before the MS he was happily married to his high school sweetheart, adored his two children, and had a responsible and financially rewarding job. Suddenly, his life was shattered. He lost his job; and last year, his wife and children. Currently, he is wheelchair bound and homebound, and lives with his elderly mother who does the cooking. Since last year, he has become incontinent. He freely describes the progression of his disease and the consequent losses. He talks movingly about his loneliness and sadness.

At Mark's invitation his sister, Jackie, entered the increasingly desperate situation. She and her teenage children are major resources in

Mark's care. She told of her unsuccessful efforts to obtain a Medicaid card so that she could obtain three shifts of homemaker services for Mark. "I have a family. We all help out, but my children are in school and my husband and I both work. My mother can't do too much anymore." When I returned to the agency, I persuaded the supervisor to provide Mark with at least one shift of homecare prior to his receiving Medicaid. The agency agreed to wait to be reimbursed.

As I helped Mark follow Medicaid eligibility procedures and submit the paperwork, he told of the intense pain of being abandoned by his wife. While we awaited a response from Medicaid (his Medicaid worker left on vacation, then his papers were transferred to a new department and worker), we agree to work on his loneliness and isolation. His main objective is to get out of the apartment to be with people. Because of his reluctance to make telephone calls, I called Paratransit to help Mark gain transportation, and the MS Society to learn about available programs. I discovered a local YMCA with a program for the disabled that will meet Mark's interest in swimming. I connected him to a monthly conference-call book club and a biweekly conference-call game group sponsored by a community agency. From these phone contacts, Mark found new friends who share his loneliness and courage.

After several months, my agency began to pressure me about Medicaid reimbursement, threatening to discontinue homecare. I won an additional month. Jackie, Mark, and I developed a strategy to expedite Medicaid. Jackie wrote a letter to her congressman, describing the many delays and consequences for her brother. The Paratransit card arrived, and I connected Mark to a loosely organized social group for the physically disabled that meets three times a week. He loves his new friends and the activities.

Meanwhile, Mark received his Medicaid card. A Medicaid worker and public health nurse visited him to determine how many shifts of aides he requires. In a few weeks, he was granted three shifts.

With the worker's assistance, Mark has gone from being completely dependent and isolated to having homecare assistance; participating in a social group, conference-call groups, and swimming; and having a level of privacy appropriate for his age.

Occasionally the social worker needs to consider advocacy and the use of pressure, coercion, and appeals to third-party intervention. The advocacy method calls for data gathering, assessment, and planning to minimize the risk of failure.

The following example illustrates a transition from mediating to advocacy. It also illustrates missteps along the way caused by the worker's neglecting to secure necessary information.

Mrs. Thomas, a twenty-five-year-old African American with two children, came to a community service agency requesting help in obtaining SSI benefits for her daughter, who suffers from cerebral palsy. She explained that her daughter's claim was approved, but no checks arrived. When she went back to the local Social Security office, she received an emergency grant of $200. Still no checks came. When she went back again, she was told she was not eligible. Since then, she has moved to another district but continued her efforts through the local Social Security office in the new neighborhood, again to no avail.

Mrs. Thomas and I agreed to work together: she will bring in all her documents, and I will call the Social Security office. When she returned with the documents, we went over them. Then I telephoned the local office, identified myself, and described the problem. The staff person responded that Social Security doesn't handle that kind of problem and we should try welfare. I suspected he was wrong, and I challenged his assertion. He said, "Listen, we can't help you." I asked to speak to a supervisor. She took the phone, and again I described the problem. I fared even worse with the supervisor, who said that cerebral palsy does not qualify Mrs. Thomas's daughter for benefits. I said, "Are you sure?" The supervisor responded with a firm yes. I thanked her and hung up.

The worker made a serious error by contacting the organization before learning Social Security policies and structures. Fortunately, the social worker and Mrs. Thomas were undaunted, and they set about learning the rules regarding disability claims. The worker obtained the SSI manual, and together they studied its contents. Several sections seemed to establish Mrs. Thomas's eligibility, so they decided to retrace Mrs. Thomas's earlier attempts. The worker called the first Social Security office.

I related the problem. The staff person listened without much interest and referred me to the current office. Playing a hunch, I said I understood records of initial claims were held in the original office. He then referred me to the records representative, Mr. Ross, who turned out to be responsive. He asked for documentation, and I said that Mrs. Thomas had received an emergency grant from that office, so her claim must have been accepted. Mr. Ross agreed to look into the matter. He called back and said the application had been initially accepted and processed. He believes a large retroactive sum is due, and outlined the steps to be taken. I thanked him for his help.

I was elated and called Mrs. Thomas to tell her the good news. We talked about remaining steps, and she felt she could take them alone. I encouraged her to do so.

One month later, however, Mrs. Thomas advised the worker that she still had not received a check, and she asked the worker's help. They discussed the steps she had gone through and agreed that the worker would again telephone the first Social Security office.

Mr. Ross was not in, and I spoke to another person. I informed him of the situation and asked him to find out what had happened. After a few minutes he returned, saying Mrs. Thomas's grant had not been processed because she first had to go to the welfare department and notify them of the large retroactive benefits she would receive, which she would be obliged to turn over to welfare (Mrs. Thomas had been receiving welfare for her daughter in the interim). I asked if this was agency policy, because the SSI manual did not mention formal collaboration between the two organizations. The staff person insisted it was policy, and Mrs. Thomas could not receive checks until she fulfilled the requirement. I asked him to mail me a copy of the policy, and he refused to do so. I then asked to speak to his supervisor, who confirmed the policy and who also refused to forward or even to read the policy to me over the phone.

Up to this point, the worker had depended on the mediating skills of requesting, pleading, and persisting with staff members. He also used negotiating skills to the extent that the situation allowed. Still the organization withheld the daughter's entitlements. The Social Security office denied Mrs. Thomas' rights by not informing her of the basis on which benefits were denied. After conferring with Mrs. Thomas, the worker decided that he must go beyond mediating to advocacy, utilizing adversarial skills of pressure and coercion. He began with pressure, that is, with threats and challenges.

After searching, I found a lawyer whose expertise was in welfare and Social Security legislation. He explained to me that the agency has no right to withhold payments from clients because of informal agreements with the Department of Welfare. The practice is clearly illegal. He offered to intervene, and I said I would first discuss the matter with Mrs. Thomas and get back to him, if necessary. I expressed our appreciation. Mrs. Thomas decided that she and the worker should make one more effort before turning the matter over to a lawyer. She preferred to avoid legal escalation, fearing reprisals. So they prepared for another telephone contact, selecting and rehearsing the worker's approach.

I asked to speak with the supervisor [at the second office] and brought him up to date on our previous contacts with the office. I said Mrs. Thomas and my agency had retained a lawyer who informed us that the daughter is the legal recipient of the disability allowance and welfare has no claim to the retroactive payment. I informed him that we are presently prepared to seek a fair hearing, and the lawyer may wish to move to class action. I continued that this was our final effort to handle the matter ourselves, before seeking legal redress. The supervisor asked for half an hour to look into the matter. When he called back, he apologized for the misunderstanding and announced that the claim had been processed. I asked for specific commitment, and he said that Mrs. Thomas would receive her first check and all retroactive benefits within three weeks. She did, indeed.

As frequently happens, the bureaucratic organization's formal policy is more responsive to client need than are its actual practices. What seemed to be the real lever of change in Mrs. Thomas's situation was the threat of legal challenge. It is often the case that individual members of organizations are responsive to the threat of crisis, making it unnecessary to go further. The worker's decision to move beyond collaborative strategies of interceding, persuading, and placating to the adversarial strategies of pressure, challenge, and threat was effective in securing his client's entitlement. His entrance into the situation, especially as he gained knowledge and competence in the two roles, lent weight to the cause of a vulnerable client. The unfavorable balance of power was corrected in some measure. In receiving her entitlement, Mrs. Thomas experienced satisfaction in taking effective action on her own behalf.

When persuasion and negotiation are ineffective, the social worker needs to involve the client in considering adversarial strategies of pressure, challenge, and threat. In turning to the adversarial method, worker and client must understand that risks increase and consider their respective vulnerabilities.

In dealing with organizational obstacles, the problems are frequently overwhelming, the tasks complex, and the process frustrating. The client may experience despair and a sense of futility. Social workers must provide realistic support and encouragement, and invite clients to express doubts, hesitations, fears, or resentments. In pursuing environmental objectives, social workers must not forget the person in the process. Whatever the method, workers must continuously take possible consequences for clients into account.

The Social Network.   Social network intervention has characterized social work practice since its beginning. The settlement movement's founders conceived good neighboring as the essence of its practice philosophy. College students and youthful professionals who became settlement house residents sought to be good neighbors to the poor among whom they lived. They wanted to help their neighbors organize themselves to improve the quality of neighborhood life through mutual help. They appreciated the ecological validity and value of intervening in networks within their community and cultural contexts. Now, more than a century later, recognition of the importance of natural helpers in people's lives is growing, and many such helpers coalesce into social networks.

To help people who need instrumental and emotional support or who suffer from loneliness and emotional isolation, practitioners work toward mobilizing or strengthening real-life ties between clients and significant others, reestablishing old linkages, or helping the client find and develop new connections. The worker considers various potential network units for professional interventions. For example, the worker may help a client to reach out to one significant person inside the current social network, or help a significant other to reach out to the client.

Maria, an eighteen-year-old single Hispanic Catholic foster child, was voluntarily admitted to a psychiatric hospital by her psychiatrist after one of a series of suicide attempts over two years left her with razor cuts on her arms and abdomen. Maria's mother abandoned her at birth; for several years, she and her sister lived with the maternal grandmother until both were placed in foster care. As a teenager, Maria ran away from several foster homes. At sixteen, she was sent to a residential treatment center, where she made her first suicide attempt.

In two meetings with Maria, the social work intern ascertained that she yearned for family and roots, having lost contact with her older sister, who had enrolled in the state university. She felt isolated, unwanted, and without a sense of place. She found it increasingly difficult to interact with people. The first aim was to help Maria reestablish contact with her sister. One day, Maria approached the social work intern in the hospital corridor, on the verge of crying. Sensing her need, the social worker suggested they sit on the couch and talk.

INTERN:	You look so sad right now. What's bothering you?
MARIA:	(Looking down) I miss my sister (tears falling down her cheeks).
INTERN:	Uh-huh.
MARIA:	I miss her for so long. I haven't seen her since she went to college.
INTERN:	And it's far away.
MARIA:	Yes. We both have no money. I get $60 from the agency each month, but that's not much. So I only see her on Christmas and holidays. I wish it were the holidays.
INTERN:	I sense you feel a special need for her right now.
MARIA:	Yes (cries). We're close. I can talk to her, though she doesn't know what I've done or where I am. I don't even have money to call her.
INTERN:	It's very lonely not to be in contact with someone you need.

MARIA:	Yes. But there's no way to change it, no way (voice shaking). I'll just have to wait until Christmas.
INTERN:	Well, I think there is a way to talk to her. We could go into the staff office and call her right now, if you want.
MARIA:	(Brightens) Could we do that?
INTERN:	Sure. And perhaps you could invite your sister to visit you here. Maybe the hospital might help with the travel expenses.
MARIA:	I doubt she can come. I'm sure she's busy with schoolwork and friends.
INTERN:	Let's try, OK?
MARIA:	I'd love to talk to her now, but how would I explain being here? I'm not sure she'll want to visit me here.

Maria discussed her worries with the social work intern, and together they developed a plan for Maria to explain her hospitalization to her sister.

The intern successfully connected the client to the most valued member of her limited social network. Her sister is the only positive source of continuity in her life, and the reunion generated significant breakthroughs in her treatment. She engaged in counseling, followed prescribed protocols, and invested herself in developing new relationships on the ward.

Extended kin networks can also maintain effective ties, even across geographical distances. For example, Mrs. Bates is an eighty-year-old white Protestant widow living alone in an apartment in a suburb. Her two daughters live across the continent. The older daughter, Margaret, and her husband, Paul, hold jobs that require travel, so they visit Mrs. Bates every two months. The younger daughter can afford to visit her mother only once a year. Mrs. Bates's lawyer called the community family agency at her daughters' request to inquire about services for the elderly. The daughters were very concerned about their mother's mental health.

The assigned worker made several calls to the lawyer and to Margaret, making an appointment with her during her next trip. Margaret said that Mrs. Bates's mental condition sharply deteriorated following a hospital stay a year before, and the doctor explained that she suffers from arteriosclerosis. The daughters were extremely concerned about their mother living alone and so far away. Margaret then asked the worker to visit her mother, assess the situation, and provide whatever services were required. Cost was not an issue.

Initially, Mrs. Bates was uncertain about meeting with the social worker. However, after several home visits, she became more comfortable and admitted to depression and distress about confusion and memory loss. Transactional issues between Mrs. Bates and her kin and others were apparent. To compensate for living far away, her daughters and son-in law frequently called, trying to manage Mrs. Bates's life from a distance and to do "for" her rather than "with" her. Their suggestions and actions clashed and increased her distress, disorientation, and confusion.

The social worker focused on helping Mrs. Bates's family become more responsive to her need to retain control over her life, while at the same time supporting and encouraging their involvement. She wanted them to understand how important it was to Mrs. Bates to feel actively involved in plans for her own care:

The first intervention was to introduce myself to the family members in order to gather data and gain acceptance of my involvement in the plan of care. After two interviews with Mrs. Bates, I called members of her support network with her informed consent. With her lawyer, we discussed how she could involve Mrs. Bates in some legal decisions without causing her too much confusion. Her physician informed me of the etiology of her dementia. He said her condition was apt to progress in stages, and told of his long-standing relationship with Mrs. Bates and how much he likes her. Her cook and the accountant impressed me with their genuine concern and apparent honesty. Mrs. Bates's niece and her niece's best friend both care very much for her and want to be kept abreast of developments. They were openly critical of the daughters for "allowing" their mother to live alone (despite the fact that Mrs. Bates refuses to consider an alternative). The hospital volunteer coordinator told me that every effort is made to support Mrs. Bates and help her to feel needed. The practitioner and network members agreed to stay in touch and to exchange information.

When Margaret and Paul came to visit their mother, she had a panic attack. Pressured by their need to solve everything and tie Mrs. Bates into a neat package before their return home, they overwhelmed her with proposed changes (forming a trust fund to take control of her finances, replacing her cook and accountant with people they would hire, and changing her physician to a specialist in geriatrics and dementia). I met with them, acknowledged their concern and love, but suggested that less can be more. I spoke of Mrs. Bates's comfort with and confidence in the cook, accountant, and physician. It is true that her financial situation is messy—she writes several checks for the same bills and ignores overdue notices on others. But in terms of establishing priority issues, wasn't it much more serious that she still drives her own car? The cook had told me that Mrs. Bates is losing her sense of direction, is easily distracted, and once used the accelerator instead of the brake. I suggested we needed to prioritize changes and begin with her driving. They agreed, and we decided that the most appropriate person to discuss driving with her was her physician. They spoke to him, and he did talk to Mrs. Bates and she agreed to use taxis instead.

A month later, the volunteer coordinator at the hospital called to say that Mrs. Bates was in the emergency room, having fallen outside her apartment. Her wrist was broken, and her ankle sprained. The coordinator also called her niece, who then called Margaret to say she should come at once (she had been scheduled to leave for a business trip to Europe the next day). I immediately visited the hospital, and subsequently called Margaret, the niece, and the friend to reassure them that I was in touch and that Mrs. Bates is being well cared for in a familiar environment, and she will be discharged in a few days. I made reassuring calls over the next few days.

Mrs. Bates was shaken by the fall but was comfortable in the hospital. My concern, and that of network members, was to make a plan of care for her upon discharge. I believed she must be actively involved in this planning. I began by asking her what help she will need when she returns home. She agreed to live-in help, at least for a while. She wanted her cook to be that person. With Mrs. Bates's permission, I talked with the cook. She isn't available, but her young cousin is. I spoke with the cousin to satisfy myself that she had some experience in caring for people with intellectual impairment. Then I encouraged the cook and the cousin to visit Mrs. Bates in the hospital. I wanted to keep the feeling of control in Mrs. Bates's hands. She liked the cousin and informed her daughter, niece, and friend of what SHE had arranged. While live-in help resulted in some loss of privacy, everyone was relieved when she accepted this arrangement as permanent. It had a dramatic positive impact upon Mrs. Bates's daily functioning.

The worker used the coordinating method and its skills of orchestrating and brokering. Mrs. Bates's accident was also an opportunity to make rapid use of environmental resources. The social worker thus counteracted the network's tendency to overload the telephone lines with instructions to one another and to Mrs. Bates about what ought to be done "for" her. The worker demonstrated how to manage Mrs. Bates's care without taking control of her life. Hence, when Mrs. Bates expressed dissatisfaction with her young companion, Margaret and Paul took Mrs. Bates with them to interview an older woman, and let her handle the hiring as well as the firing.

Peer and friendship networks also serve as critical units for professional intervention. While they may lack the permanence of kinship networks, they do provide diverse and relatively durable support. Friends from work, religious, social, or recreational activities can offer potential ties for effective support. The social worker might help the client to assess friendship resources and potential obstacles such as embarrassment, fear of imposing, or reluctance to risk rejection.

Neighbors, since they are usually in frequent direct contact, can help with immediate and short-term tasks (Patterson et al., 1988, 1992). Because neighbor networks have a shifting membership in our mobile society, many are helpful in immediate emergencies ranging from the trivial to the catastrophic. They might lend or provide resources (a ride to the store, use of the telephone, watching the baby, and providing information about neighborhood customs and resources). Natural networks of neighbors are often found in multiple-unit dwellings. In homeless shelters and single-room hotels, natural helpers are not uncommon. They look after the frail, manage their checks, care for them, and see that they take medications, keep clinic appointments, and report to the welfare center as required (Getzel, 2005; Lee, 2005). Although sometimes functioning marginally themselves, these natural helpers enable their neighbors to cope and survive. The social worker must be careful not to undermine the influence or role of natural helpers, which could disrupt the delicate structure of informal aid.

Being emotionally attached to at least one other person promotes and protects physical and mental health (Uchino, 2004). The significant other may be part of the current social field, or, if unavailable, a new tie may need to be forged. For certain situations and problems, the new tie may be linked to an organization such as Big Brothers and Big Sisters, Extend-a-Family, AA, or a volunteer "friendly visitor" to homebound elderly. Mrs. Trask, an eighty-three-year-old widow, reported to a doctor at a community health clinic that she felt nervous, agitated, and unable to sleep. After examination, the doctor found no health problems as the basis for her nervousness. He suggested she might like to talk to the staff social work intern. Mrs. Trask replied that she did not know how that would help but agreed to talk with him. The social work intern made a home visit to her clean, well-furnished apartment. Mrs. Trask could not identify any recent precipitating events that might account for her nervousness. She said she had no one to confide in and had little to do, which left her with too much time to worry about small things that ordinarily she would not worry about, such as her declining health.

Mrs. Trask said she was the last surviving member of her family, the last of her six sisters having died two years ago. Her second husband died seven years ago, and she moved here from Florida, losing touch with her friends. She has only one friend in the apartment complex, a woman thirty years younger. While they occasionally do things together, Mrs. Trask feels she can't confide in her, and she is annoyed because her friend takes financial advantage of her. Her only relatives are a nephew who lives twenty miles away but doesn't call or visit, and a niece. She said she is angry that her nephew is uncaring and added that she terminated her relationship with her niece about six years ago after an argument. Hence, her social "network" is limited to one unsatisfactory person. Her declining health and physical capacities are a source of consternation, and Mrs. Trask finds it difficult to accept her physical limitations. Her own doctor retired two years ago, and she is unable to trust her new one completely—she wonders aloud if a thirty-year-old female physician is capable of providing quality medical care (not an unusual assumption for members of Mrs. Trask's generation).

After several visits and Mrs. Trask's positive response to empathic support, the social work intern concluded that Mrs. Trask was motivated both to act for herself and to be reconnected to people. She wants to end her absorption in her fears and become active. His assessment was that she is energetic, is well organized, and has a sharp mind. Her cognitive style, however, is obsessive, and she usually assumes the worst about any situation. When she is busy, Mrs. Trask is less obsessive and less agitated. Similarly, her level of self-esteem rises and falls with the availability of environmental activity and contacts. When she is inactive and isolated, she feels unimportant and useless.

Together, Mrs. Trask and the worker agreed to look for a productive activity that would also provide opportunities for socialization. They decided on the Retired Seniors Volunteer Program (RSVP). She was interested yet hesitant for fear that she would be unable to manage a new experience and would be a burden to the program.

I continued to point out potential benefits of activity with others and to identify her real strengths. I also encouraged her to talk of her fears about what might go wrong, and empathized with what I described as the universal fear of change. I suggested there wouldn't be dire consequences if things didn't turn out well. After several weeks, she did make an appointment with RSVP and was given a list of openings. We discussed the pros and cons of each. While the decision making was distressing, it did enhance her sense of competence. She decided she would like to work as a data enterer in the local library.

Mrs. Trask was met her first day by the library administrator, who had not been told by RSVP that she was coming and was annoyed. Mrs. Trask felt rebuffed and returned home, vowing never to return. The worker felt this was probably the outcome of an exchange between an overly sensitive, anxious elder and an undersensitive, busy, anxious person. It was not Mrs. Trask's failure as a volunteer.

I wanted to help Mrs. Trask interpret the incident as a misunderstanding (rather than her obsessing about a perceived rejection). I accepted her expressions of embarrassment and anger, and also gently challenged her tendency to perceive events from a self-centered position. She was then able to consider other possible explanations for what had happened. Agreeing that it might have been a misunderstanding, she called RSVP, explained what happened, and cleared up the misunderstanding. With Mrs. Trask's permission, I intervened in the environment: I called the library administrator and explained how frightened Mrs. Trask had been of trying something so new. She again expressed her annoyance, but volunteered to reassure Mrs. Trask and to clarify for her what happened.

Mrs. Trask continued her work at the library, but during weekly interviews with the worker she fretted about not being liked because she wasn't working up to the library's expectations.

Knowing she is a perfectionist who continually underestimates her abilities, I encouraged her to ask for feedback on her performance from her coworkers. She agreed, and asked that I also call to find out how the librarian feels about her work so that we could compare notes. As anticipated, the librarian reported that Mrs. Trask was doing exceptionally well and seemed to prefer working by herself. I mentioned my perception that she does not feel confident in her work and could use a few "strokes" now and then, as well as some rest periods just to chat with fellow workers. This two-pronged approach resulted in a better fit, and Mrs. Trask began reporting pleasurable success in her work and enjoyment in her new friends.

The social work intern and Mrs. Trask then worked on improving her relationship with the younger friend in the apartment complex by heightening Mrs. Trask's awareness of what she wanted from this friend. She stopped relating to her friend as a mother nurturing a nonreciprocating child. This triggered a change in the friend's behavior, and apparently resulted in a more satisfying relationship for both. On her own, Mrs. Trask then decided to write her nephew and to tell him of her library work. In response, he telephoned to let her know he was pleased for her.

Throughout, the intern tried to help Mrs. Trask recognize her personal and environmental resources for coping with the multiple life stressors facing her. These interventions and others through the ongoing phase helped Mrs. Trask build new relationships, reestablish former ones with relatives, find new activities, and accept her increasing physical limitations with less despair. The intern writes, "We agreed that she feels more competent and powerful because she found she is once more able to act for herself."

Built World. Sensitive practitioners have often attempted to improve aspects of the physical environment. Little such work is found in agency records or textbooks, perhaps because its importance went unrecognized. It was viewed as common sense rather than professional knowledge or skill. With the advent of concepts relating the physical environment to the social environment and to the culture, the significance of the physical environment in growth and adaptation became clear, and hastened the development of practice principles.

Shelter is a basic human need. Yet deinstitutionalization, loss of employment, eviction, displacement, intolerable conditions, natural disasters, and the lack of affordable housing leave an increasing population homeless (Cohen, 2001; Lee, 2005). The fastest growing sector of homeless people is families with small children—a national disgrace that leaves people vulnerable to brutality and exploitation and with the basic human need for shelter unmet.

When people lose their dwellings, they do not grieve for their lost home alone, but also for the lost sense of community. People become embedded in their local environment. They know the shortcuts, sidewalk cracks, creaky steps, and elevator's idiosyncrasies. Familiarity with physical aspects of their environment is further reinforced by people's social connections— neighbors, community helpers, store clerks and owners, familiar teachers, and school officials provide a sense of belonging and personal identity. Physical and social connections develop from living in the same place over time and a landscape of memories that are integrated into life stories. For homeless individuals and families who live in a welfare motel, in a public shelter, or on the street, such physical, social, and autobiographical connections are ripped away.

A community agency assigned social workers to reach out to mentally impaired homeless people, who require a great deal of assistance in obtaining needed resources. Their life stressors must be worked on in small coping tasks. Appointments must be made for them; they must be prepared for, and escorted to, appointments. They must learn how to fill out forms, manage money, and take care of themselves. The social worker has to be active, persistent, and directive. Agencies have to be pursued and persuaded to extend additional time and effort, to anticipate problems and regressions, and, most of all, to "hang on." The following illustrates a social worker's struggle to help a homeless man with a mental impairment find housing.

Carmine is fifty-nine years old. His parents were Italian immigrants. As early as he can remember, his parents beat him on the head with a wooden knife handle. He frequently ran away from home, only to have the police bring him back in spite of his many bruises. At age seven, his parents took him to a municipal hospital, where he was diagnosed as mentally retarded. He was institutionalized and released in his late thirties. He met a woman, and married. He inherited his parents' home when they died and moved into it with his wife. Within five years, his wife left him and their two children. Since then, "Everything went down the sewer." It's unclear how he lost his house and children, but he has been homeless for ten years, living in abandoned cars, automobile repair shops, and parks.

Carmine initially responded to the worker's outreach because of failing health. He was losing weight, not eating, just drinking coffee and smoking cigarettes. He denied abusing alcohol (and this was later confirmed). Within several days, he arrived at the agency spitting up blood. The worker accompanied him to the hospital and stayed while he was X-rayed. When she had to leave for another appointment, Carmine bolted. Henceforth, subsequent work included escorting Carmine to his various appointments and participating in the entire process.

The mutually agreed-on goal was placement in an adult group residence. This required Carmine to complete medical and psychiatric assessments. He completed the psychiatric assessment with the worker staying throughout. The psychiatrist felt that Carmine was misdiagnosed as a child. The current psychiatric diagnosis is "borderline personality with borderline intellectual functioning." Even with the worker, he is impulsive, unpredictable, self-damaging, and often inappropriately angry. He frequently yells at the social worker and then storms out of the office. He consistently reaches out to her but then pulls away. He says, "No!" to everything and then shows up for appointments. His judgment is poor in most areas. He offends almost everyone, so he is socially and emotionally isolated. From his own perspective, Carmine is dealing with a hostile environment and he responds with equal hostility. He said he had attempted suicide at least seven times. Yet, in his own way, Carmine adapted to a physical and social environment with which only a few could cope. He has remarkable tenacity and survival skills.

The social worker helped Carmine with health issues and medical care first. As they developed a relationship from this work together, the social worker next helped him with entitlements. In the past, Carmine had applied for SSI, but certain forms were never filled out. A Social Security employee with whom the practitioner had worked agreed to meet with Carmine in the social worker's office (Carmine had had an upsetting experience in the Social Security office a few years ago and refused to return there).

Carmine assumed his usual position in the far corner of my office, wedged between a table and file cabinets. He could see everything that went on while remaining fairly invisible. I introduced him to Bill (I had asked and received Mr. Jackson's permission to introduce him by his first name, as I observed that Carmine is more comfortable and predictable in informal, relaxed encounters). To my surprise (Carmine was full of them), Carmine began speaking Italian. Whether he assumed Bill was Italian or felt more in control speaking Italian, I wasn't sure. However, I complimented Carmine on his ability to speak Italian, and explained that Bill didn't speak Italian. Carmine feigned shock (he seemed very pleased with himself). I reminded him that Bill was here to help him with SSI and it would help if he spoke English. The rest of the meeting went smoothly. Bill asked Carmine some questions, filled out some forms for him, and so on. Carmine agreed to have the first check mailed to the agency and subsequent ones to a bank after we opened an account for him.

The worker structured the situation, created norms of informality, talked to Carmine respectfully, and mediated the exchanges. She also made a supportive demand that Carmine not waste Bill's time but get "down to business."

Before Carmine would accept more testing, he asked to visit a group residence. The worker arranged for Jackie, a social worker she knew at Century House, to show them around and to answer Carmine's questions.

On the way, Carmine was quiet and tense. I reassured him that this was only a first meeting: he doesn't have to make a decision. He is not being interviewed, and if he doesn't like the place we will visit others. He was silent but, as always, listened to every word. On arrival, Carmine announced that he isn't going in—he will sit in the car. I sensed his growing panic and resentment. Fortunately, that signal usually tips me off to MELLOW OUT! I told Carmine that I would really appreciate his just having a look at the place. He didn't have to talk, but if he chose not to come in, I would go inside and then describe to him what I saw. Carmine followed me in.

Jackie gave us a tour, and Carmine was introduced to a benign older Italian resident. They enjoyed speaking Italian, especially since we couldn't understand what they were saying. After the tour, we sat down to talk. Carmine announced that it would take him a year to make up his mind and he would get back to me with his decision. I thought this was meant to be humorous since he had no place to live, but realized it was his pattern of rejecting before being rejected. The resident and Jackie encouraged him to think about it. Carmine and I thanked them and left. He then informed me he wants to live there. He said he was quiet and cautious because he doesn't know "those" people and he didn't feel comfortable trusting them right away. I supported his stance and credited his behavior.

The practitioner avoided a potential power struggle by leaving to Carmine the decision about entering the residence. She fought against understandable personal reactions: "after all I've done for you, how can you do this to me?" She worked at involving him, supported his decision making, and respected his style and manner of coping, thereby increasing his self-esteem and self-direction. At their next meeting, they discussed Century House.

CARMINE:	I've got to think about what I wanna do.
WORKER:	Well, Century House is one possibility and if that's where you want to live, there are certain things we need to work on in order for you to get in. I want to make it clear to you that you don't have to go there. If it's not what you want, then we'll work on other possibilities.
CARMINE:	It's better than living in the garage or on the street. I'll tell you right now, I am getting ready to run away.
WORKER:	I understand your feeling impatient and frustrated, but I don't think running away is the answer.
CARMINE:	I gotta have people to talk to. I can't keep living lonely like this. It's impossible.
WORKER:	And so are you thinking if maybe you go to Century House, since it is a place with lots of others, you'd be able to make some friends?
CARMINE:	Well, I'd be able to live a happy life—I have no life right now.
WORKER:	You know you'll have to have some tests (last time I mentioned this, he exploded—I braced myself).
CARMINE:	Well, I'll tell you, forget it!
WORKER:	But it's the only way we can get you into Century House.
CARMINE:	Forget it!
WORKER:	I have to get you to understand that it's really important for you to have these tests done. Would you be willing to pick a male or female doctor and let him or her examine you?
CARMINE:	Maybe. But no needles! I am afraid of needles.
WORKER:	Are you afraid that they are going to use needles on you?
CARMINE:	Yeah, I don't like getting pricked.
WORKER:	How did you get through it before?
CARMINE:	Crabby. I was real crabby.
WORKER:	I don't blame you, and I don't like it either. But they often need to test our blood and it's the only way. How about if I stay with you and we can be crabby together?
CARMINE:	If you stay with me, then I'll stay, but if you walk away, then I'm going to leave too.
WORKER:	Let's shake—we just made a deal.

Throughout this exchange, the worker balanced support and demand: support to provide the foundation for the next step, and demand to move the work and take the next step. The next step was a medical examination.

The meeting with the physician was a bit tricky. I was outside speaking to Dr. Gwynn about Carmine's fear of needles when a technician entered through another door to take blood samples from Carmine. I heard him scream that he was going to slit my throat and the technician's throat before he would have a blood test. He said a few more choice words as I ran into the room. Dr. Gwynn asked the technician to come back later, and I apologized to Carmine for the mix-up and emphasized that I will be with him throughout the examination. He was cooperative and remained calm, just looking over to see if I were still there.

On the return trip I credited him for his cooperation. Since he was in good spirits, I decided to introduce the next hurdle, the psychiatric examination. He initially responded that he wasn't going to go to "no head shrinker." I reminded him that in order to have all the paperwork done for Century House, he needed to speak to someone about his life (as I said this, it sounded quite ridiculous). I added if he wants me to go with him, I will, and I kidded him that at least there would be no needles. After some bantering, he agreed to see a "shrink" if I accompanied him.

The worker slowly helped Carmine to plug into the various systems to obtain housing. He lacked the skills and trust to negotiate environmental systems. With the worker's presence, persistence, support, and demands, he gained strength and confidence in his own abilities. Each success motivated further willingness to risk and trust, and to feel competent and related. The agency had had positive experiences with a young, female psychiatrist, so the worker set up an appointment for her to meet with Carmine.

When we arrived, Dr. Raimes asked to speak to me alone for a few minutes. I asked Carmine if this was OK. He threatened to leave, and then said he would wait. I told him and Dr. Raimes that if he were going to leave, I would wait till the end of their meeting to talk to Dr. Raimes. Carmine replied it was OK, and we should go ahead.

Dr. Raimes wanted some background information about Carmine and what type of an assessment Century House required. She then met with Carmine, sensitively asking for his life story. He answered all questions. When the interview was completed, Dr. Raimes informed us she would write a supportive report and wished Carmine good luck with his application. As we left the office, Carmine informed me that he felt ready to open a bank account. We set up a time to complete this next coping task.

When the worker received Carmine's first social security check, they opened his savings account and figured out a weekly budget. In the worker's company, he began literacy classes at the library and sustained the task without the worker's direct assistance. He also began to participate in the agency's support group, trips, and educational seminars. Five months later, he moved into Century House and the worker spent his first day there with him.

* * *

Transportation systems are features of the built world that can be over-whelming and unsafe. Private and public transportation systems are often inaccessible to people with physical, intellectual, or emotional impairments. Discharged mental patients, especially after lengthy hospitalization, frequently lack the basic skills of moving through the physical environment.

A social work intern in a program serving developmentally challenged adults was assigned to work with Andrew, a nineteen-year-old African American. Andrew is mildly retarded. He felt socially isolated, especially after completing a school program one year ago. Andrew does not know how to travel; he cannot navigate the bus and subway systems. He wishes he could visit former classmates who live in other parts of the city. He feels he is a burden to his mother and wishes he could shop in the downtown mall or seek a job in a store stockroom.

The student felt that helping Andrew use public transportation would broaden his horizons, make him employable, and enhance his sense of mastery and competence. Andrew was elated: "If I can learn to travel, I'll be independent. I won't have to bother my mother anymore."

The student asked Andrew where he would like to travel to first. He immediately named the shopping mall, twenty minutes away by subway. At their next appointment the student suggested they map out a plan prior to taking the trip together. She had already thought through the multiple steps involved in using the subway system. They traced a map from Andrew's apartment to the subway and discussed how to pay the fare. They thought about how to look for signs and count the stops until his destination. The student described her own first trip and worries in taking the subway.

After they reviewed the steps several times, they agreed to meet at his home and try the trip together the next day. The student met Andrew, pointed out directional signs, tried to let him take the lead, and coached him when he looked to her for advice. The ride went smoothly, and Andrew was very happy when they arrived at the mall.

They reviewed the directions home before embarking on the return trip. Andrew moved cautiously through each step and grew more confident as he mastered each step. When they got back to his home, Andrew dashed up to his mother and proudly announced his accomplishment. They showed his mother their maps so she could remind him of the steps prior to his next trip to the mall.

Such work in the physical environment requires a considerable investment of time and effort on the part of the social worker. Traditional policy and agency caseloads rarely permit such investment. Hence, social workers need to alert administrators and policy makers to the importance of the social work function in such necessary but often overlooked areas, and its implications for preventive work.

Natural World.   Caring for a pet can sustain relationship capacities and a sense of purpose and achievement. Angel, age eight, was placed in residential care for emotionally challenged children. Angel had been severely abused by his father, and saw the continuous abuse of his mother and siblings. His father used sadistic means to enforce total subservience. He demanded quiet in the apartment. Angel had a sock placed in his mouth and duct tape over his lips. He was tied up for long periods of time. After Angel was forced to hold a knife to his mother while his father raped her, he "snapped" at school, breaking furniture and windows.

Angel entered court-ordered placement with minimal language, social, and learning skills. He was withdrawn and fearful of others, and always looked sad. He suffered frequent nightmares about his father escaping and killing his mother and him. His mother visited every weekend and called him several times a week. She is a stable force in his life.

The worker noticed that Angel was gentle with a child care worker's dog. When she had puppies, the social worker persuaded administration and the child care worker that if Angel were willing to assume responsibility for a puppy, the center should keep one. After receiving permission, she discussed the idea with Angel. He responded with rare enthusiasm, and immediately assumed a nurturing role. He named the puppy Beauty and took wonderful care of her. If she had an "accident" in the office, Angel cleaned it up and gently picked her up, saying, "Oh, Beauty, you are too little, you just don't know." The worker drew parallels between Beauty and Angel's experiences.

ANGEL:	Oh, Beauty don't do that. I have to watch you every minute. You need me to take care of you and protect you. You are so little, you don't know. You just don't know.
WORKER:	She doesn't know?
ANGEL:	No. She's just a little puppy. Little puppies don't know.
WORKER:	So, I shouldn't be upset with her because she is chewing on my calendar.
ANGEL:	No, no. She is little. She doesn't know. She doesn't understand. Ahhhh, Beauty. No! See, she does things, but doesn't know she's not supposed to because she's so little.
WORKER:	Uh-oh. She just began to chew on a report I was preparing.
ANGEL:	Important?
WORKER:	Yes, but I should have put it away because I am the big person and Beauty is the little puppy; she doesn't understand.
ANGEL:	Yes, Beauty. I'm the big person who will protect you. No one is going to hurt you. I'm here.
WORKER:	Beauty has a big person to protect and care for her. Did Angel have big people to protect and take care of him?
ANGEL:	My mom, yes. My dad, no. I told you my dad is bad. Not my father. Never.
WORKER:	I remember the things you told me.
ANGEL:	Yes, like when he raped my mother and had me hold a knife on her.

WORKER:	Yes. Remember how I am always trying to help you understand that it wasn't your fault?
ANGEL:	But, I did it.
WORKER:	Yes, but you were little and you didn't know. You were like Beauty. Beauty is little and doesn't know what she is doing, so we don't blame her or get mad at her. And Angel, you were too little and scared, and had to do what your father demanded. He would have hurt you if you didn't obey.
ANGEL:	He would have killed me if I didn't.
WORKER:	Angel, your father was very big. He did know what he was doing was wrong.
ANGEL:	Yes, he should have kept me safe.
WORKER:	Exactly! Like you are keeping Beauty safe.
ANGEL:	Oh, Beauty, I won't let anyone hurt you. Come here. I won't hurt you, never. You're just a little baby puppy who doesn't know.

With Beauty's help and the social worker's skilled use of metaphor and simile, Angel began to understand that as a small child he was unable to protect his mother from his father's violence. He began to understand that he, like his mother, was also a victim of his father in the rape incident. As he felt more protected and less guilty, Angel told terrifying stories of his father's sadistic abuse. He relived being locked in a basement for two days while his father went out to "party." Many elements of his life story were told with Beauty in his lap. They were painful to hear. They were told with increasing anger and decreasing self-blame. Beauty provided a nonthreatening, secure relationship to which Angel made a deep emotional commitment. Beauty was his bridge to gradual human connections with peers, teachers, and child care staff. Taking care of Beauty made Angel feel responsible and valued. He received recognition for his excellent care of her. Without minimizing the contribution of the social worker and others, we recognize that Beauty helped Angel to transform himself from victim to survivor.

We now turn our attention to helping families in distress.

HELPING WITH DYSFUNCTIONAL
FAMILY PROCESSES

Most families experience difficult life transitions, painful life events, and environmental pressures, and they manage the inner and outer demands of such life issues, often by developing new forms of coping with the associated stress. They do not need professional help. For others, the demands may generate additional stress if the family does not recognize the need for change. In many such instances, family members may need only modest help in revising their usual patterns. In other instances, dysfunctional relationships and communications in the family are or become themselves the primary stressors.

Internal Family Functions, Structures, and Processes as Life Stressors

Families may be bound together not only by ties of kinship or by legal rights and responsibilities, but also by self-definition. In addition to traditional nuclear families and extended families, there are growing numbers of families that are childless by choice, two-provider commuter families (where the adult partners live and work far from each other), gay and lesbian families, solo-parent families, blended families, communal families, and augmented families (composed of two or more people who may not have a sexual relationship and may be of the same or different sex and age). These families confront most of the same challenges and stressors faced by the traditional nuclear family plus additional challenges and stressors that may be unique to a particular form.

Family Functions and Forms

The traditional functions that have been ascribed to families across diverse forms, cultures, and historical eras are (1) the procreation and socialization of children; (2) providing shelter, food, and protection for survival (instrumental functions); (3) meeting members' needs for nurturing, acceptance, security, and realization of potentials (expressive functions); and (4) connecting members to the outer social and physical worlds.

In modern life, former family functions such as education, socialization, production, and health care have gradually been taken over in whole or in part by other social institutions. Thus, families must also develop structural channels for connecting their members to schools, workplaces, health care services, day care and respite services, voluntary associations, and, for the affiliated, religious institutions.

Nuclear families face pressures and adaptive demands that may or may not exceed adaptive limits, as when both parents must work or choose to do so. Geographic mobility, previously considered a strength, has become a significant strain in many middle-class families. Constant uprooting in response to corporate demands or the personal quest for achievement places stress on the adult partner and on the children. Likewise, suburban families may suffer from the long daily absence of the employed parent(s), social isolation, heavy indebtedness, and other pressures such as job loss or the fear of it in a global economy. While it was responsive to the demands of industrialization and urbanization, the nuclear family is exceedingly vulnerable to the loss of one parent, since the entire system rests on the marital pair.

Over the last three decades we are witnessing a dramatic change in family structure and living arrangements. Women living alone doubled from 7.3 million to 14.6 million, while the number of men living alone tripled from 3.5 million to 10.3 million (U.S. Bureau of the Census, 1996). The 1997 U.S. Census reported that since 1980, the number of single mothers has increased by more than 50 percent (from 6.2 million to 9.9 million) (U.S. Bureau of the Census, 1997). The Bureau of the Census further reported that married-couple households decreased from 55.2 percent in 1990 to 51.7 percent in 2000, while female-headed family households and male-headed family households increased from 11.6 and 3.4 percent in 1990 to 12.2 and 4.2 percent in 2000. Similarly, one-person, nonfamily households increased from 24.6 percent in 1990 to 25.8 percent in 2000 (Simmons & O'Neill, 2001).

Families headed by women are characterized by poverty. Of the children under six living in single-parent female families, 58.8 percent were poor compared to only 11.5 percent of children in that age group living in married-couple families. In 1995, the median income of married-couple households is triple that of female households and more than double that of male households (Federal Interagency Forum on Child and Family Statistics, 1997, p. 67; Lamison-White, 1998). The disadvantages for the millions of children living in female-headed families, including those of never-married mothers, derive more from the multiple adverse conditions associated with poverty than from the family form per se (Cain & Combs-Orme, 2005).

The situation of solo fathers is qualitatively different from that of solo mothers. Solo fathers confront role ambiguity and the lack of norms for role performance. Solo-father families are frequently presumed to have resulted from the mother's pathology. And the solo father is apt to be perceived as poorly prepared by his very nature for the performance of the expressive functions in childrearing. Social workers have begun to provide support groups and educational programs for solo fathers.

The solo parent must double for the other parent, or may need to cast an older sibling in that role. Stressors may arise in association with household management, child care, personal respite, and personal fulfillment. Society has not yet developed institutional solutions, particularly with viable child care resources, to meet these adaptive needs.

Same-sex families are also markedly different from the nuclear form. In addition to the tasks and environmental opportunities and limitations that characterize nuclear families, these families must also manage additional tasks and environmental strains due to homophobia and discrimination and, in rural areas, to the lack of a gay community. While the majority of people in the United States seem to view same-sex marriage as either conflicting with their religious values or undermining the traditional family, they seem to be more accepting of civil unions and some legal recognition of same-sex couples (Brewer & Wilcox, 2005; Coulmont, 2005; Merin, 2002; Saucier & Cawman, 2004). Lesbian couples seem to be more accepted, enjoy more positive attitudes about relationships, and experience more satisfaction with relationships than do gay couples (Kurdek, 2003). With modern reproductive technologies, lesbian couples are giving birth, and others are adopting. These pioneering and courageous same-sex couples are creating new family definitions and role relationships. The choosing of surnames and explaining two "mommies" or "daddies" are two examples of definitions and role relationships that that have to be negotiated (Almack, 2005). As more lesbian and gay couples have "traditional" families and their children become integrated in school and community life, same-sex families should achieve greater acceptance and experience less prejudice (at least in some parts of the country).

Extended families who live together in the same household are prevalent around the world, but in the United States and Canada they are mainly limited to certain ethnic groups. Nevertheless, most other American and Canadian families remain close to extended kin through visiting and reciprocal care and support or, if at a distance, by electronic technology (and some "even" by letters). Independent living on the part of young unmarried adults became the norm in the white urban middle class beginning in the 1960s. Ethnic families and families of color who still placed value on adult unmarried children (and sometimes married children, their spouses, and their offspring) remaining in the parental home were unthinkingly defined as overly dependent. However, as children out of economic necessity return to live at home, perceptions and definitions have changed. Now living at home represents an effort to save money rather than being overly dependent.

Blended (reconstituted or step-) families have grown in number as the divorce rate and the acceptance of divorce and remarriage increased. Sometimes both partners bring children to the new marriage (or cohabitation), or only one may have children and either the other partner may be childless or the children may be in the custody of the other parent. Those children may visit the remarried family either occasionally or not at all, depending on custodial agreements, proximity, and so on. Children living in the new family not only have a new stepparent but also may have stepgrandparents, stepsiblings, and other adult kin who may or may not accept the new parent and children as relatives. To complicate the structure and relationships even more, the new parents may have a child or children together, who are then half-siblings to all the other children. While possibilities for individual and family identity confusion, jealousy, conflict, and divided loyalties are rife, the potential exists for extended-kin support, loving relationships, stability for the children, a cohesive family life, and the emotional growth of all members (Edwards, 2002; Rodgers & Rose, 2002).

Each family form has certain strengths and challenges (Davis & Friel, 2001). Each needs to adapt to the demands of its external and internal environments. In families with children, the challenge is to meet their needs for stability, security, support, and attachment (Antognoli-Toland, 2001).

Family Structure

From the ecological point of view, attention is also paid to family subunits, usually recognized as the marital (or unmarried) adult partners', parent–child, and sibling subunits. Social work intervention may be with one, two, or all three subunits. However, sometimes practitioners deal with the parent–child subunit as though it were unrelated to the marital subunit, thus leaving the father out of the work. At the other extreme, some workers focus mainly on the adult pair on the assumption that it strongly influences the parent–child subunits. Sibling relationships are frequently overlooked altogether as a possible focus of attention.

Such practice deficiencies are being corrected as more social workers engage in family-centered practice (Hartman & Laird, 1983; Wise, 2005). For example, sibling relationships are significant elements in family life, and may be an important focus for practice. Sibling relationships remain influential throughout the life course. In particular, sisters who were not close in childhood or adulthood often draw closer together as they grow old or outlive their husbands. Increasingly, grandparents living with or apart from the focal family are viewed as important elements in family life and may be included in social work sessions as appropriate. In augmented families, other kin or nonkin (lodgers or friends) live in the household and may provide valued instrumental functions such as child care for the working solo parent. However, some people living with or outside the family may participate in dysfunctional alliances with one or more family members.

Increasing numbers of grandmothers are raising their grandchildren, some of whom have been orphaned by AIDS. These grandmothers can experience intense economic, social, and emotional strains.

In the following example, the grandmother plays quite a different role. Mr. and Mrs. Conroy are concerned about the troublesome behavior of their only child, ten-year-old Annie. She tells lies excessively at home and at school, has no friends due to her "bossiness," and pits her parents against each other. When the parents complain about or describe Annie's behavior, they grin. Smiling, Mrs. Conroy says Annie's behavior reminds her of herself as a child, stubborn and with a fiery temper. Even now when angry, she screams and throws things. She and Annie endlessly struggle about who is going to be in control. Mrs. Conroy is proud that it is she who "rules the roost," and Mr. Conroy seems quite comfortable with that. Both parents work in factories, Mr. Conroy on the night shift and Mrs. Conroy on the day shift. Mrs. Conroy says that her mother, Mrs. Kirk, who lives close by, belittles her in front of Annie by telling Mrs. Conroy that she isn't properly handling a situation. Mrs. Kirk dotes on Annie and constantly undermines the parents' authority. When Annie is angry or loses the battle with her mother, she turns to her grandmother, who either chastises the mother or gives Annie a gift to compensate for the mother's error. Boundaries between the Conroys and Mrs. Kirk appear to be nonexistent, reinforcing the turmoil and conflict. Physical boundaries are breached also as the Conroys have no hot water, so Annie and her mother wash their hair and clothes at Mrs. Kirk's home. And Mrs. Kirk collects the Conroys' dirty dishes twice weekly and washes them. Mrs. Conroy feels helpless in coping with her mother on issues involving Annie and says they never have had a good relationship.

Over time, families develop a structure for dealing with role and task allocation and issues of authority and decision making. Structure helps shape relationship and communication patterns and, in turn, is influenced by the nature and quality of those patterns. In each subunit, characteristic patterns also develop that may or may not be in conflict with those of the family as a whole or with those of other subunits. In some families there may be subunits, which are long lasting, and others that are temporary and shifting, such as coalitions and alliances that cross over age and sex boundaries of the other subunits, usually in dysfunctional ways. A common example is the triangulation represented by an alliance of a child and one parent that closes out the other parent (Nichols, 2004).

Social workers must be aware of the culture—racial, ethnic, or religious—of the families with whom they work, and its influence on family structure, worldview, and functioning (Maseko, 2003; Smith & Montilla, 2004). In the multicultural societies of Canada and the United States, it is unlikely that all social workers can be familiar with all cultural differences within their own society. But all are professionally responsible for learning about the culture of the particular individuals, families, and groups with whom they work.

Family Processes

Social workers must familiarize themselves with family processes that can become dysfunctional, such as secrets, myths, and rituals. A dysfunctional collective process sometimes seen in troubled families is a secret or a ta-booed area of experience that members are skillfully coerced into keeping from spreading to outsiders or particular family members (Dalzell, 2000). In the following example, a family's secret is kept from outsiders, adversely affecting the emotional and social development of the thirteen-year-old son, Tom.

Tom is the youngest of six children and the only one still at home. His teachers are concerned because he is failing most subjects, has no peer relationships, and appears to be continually angry with everyone. Initially, the school social worker thought that Tom was experiencing identity issues, having just entered middle school and its teen culture two months ago; or was mourning the loss of close siblings as they left the family, and the loss of friends at his former school (where Tom had friends and performed well academically).

As his trust in the social worker grew, Tom revealed to her the family secret that seemed to be the dominant source of his troubles. His mother is alcoholic. He was very angry with his mother for drinking and for treating him like a baby when she is drunk. He said he was afraid to make new friends because he might be tempted to divulge the secret of his mother's alcoholism. His mother's drinking problem was not a new family issue, but Tom's entrance into early adolescence might mean he is now meeting an old problem with diminished coping skills. All his energy is invested in maintaining the secrecy, with little left for schoolwork or new relationships.

> Toxic events and themes in intergenerational family systems are often shrouded in secrecy, distorted by misinformation, and made even more powerful and threatening because they are cut off from the family discourse. . . . Sometimes the oppressive presence of these avoided issues interrupts the potential for clear and open communication of any kind in the family. It is almost as if communication must be tightly controlled so the secret will not emerge. (Hartman & Laird, 1983, p. 248)

Included in a family's implicit beliefs are the myths and rituals it develops to explain its experiences through time and across space. Family rituals are usually adaptive. They help maintain channels of communication or open closed channels, maintain relationships or restore fractured ones, and help construct or reconstruct salutary arrangements of the family's interior life.

They provide family members a shared sense of belonging. However, they are dysfunctional if they continue destructive myths, promote illusions, maintain women's lack of power in the family, reinforce maladaptive rules, or exclude members because of their sexual orientation (Oswald, 2000). Rituals embody the "should" and "ought" of the family's implicit rules. Especially important in family life are rites of passage, those rituals surrounding individual and family transitions. They include observances of biological transitions such as birth, male sexual maturation (in some cultures), and death, and of social transitions such as graduation, first job or new job, promotion, engagement, marriage, anniversaries, adoption, return from war, and retirement (Oswald, 2002). Some rituals help families cope with change or discontinuity, while others support stability in family life and bind the members to one another in shared, memorable experiences (Hartman & Laird, 1983). When rituals cover up distasteful facts, however, they may take on a hypocritical quality. Mother's Day, a societal ritual, is such an example if it merely represents one day off a year from domestic chores that a family considers to be the mother's exclusive responsibility.

Family processes are affected by differences among birth cohorts. As the life course of a cohort proceeds, its collective lives set off social changes. For example, the cohorts of young women in the late 1960s and early 1970s—responding to feminist thought—developed new norms, values, definitions of self, and patterns of living. As a collective force, they pressed for change in social roles and social values. Cohorts of young women and some young men brought the new ideas into the open, institutionalized them, and began to seek changes in gendered roles, sexist attitudes, and power differentials in the family and the workplace. These changes led to changes in the life patterns of many of today's cohorts of young men and women, as well as the developmental experience of their children. Cohorts' patterns of living are influenced by unique sequences of social changes in the family, the school, the workplace, and the community; in ideas, values, beliefs, science, technology, and the arts; and in patterns of migration, fertility, and mortality. More powerful influences on individual and family development within the cohort are differences in personality, culture, and life experiences. Nevertheless, cohort influences add important historical contexts and social dimensions to the understanding of individuals and families. Failure to take account of cohort influences in historical time can lead to the erroneous assumption that each cohort follows the same developmental pathway of our personal cohort (Riley, 1985).

Also within the dimension of historical time, the traditional timetables of many life transitions are disappearing: with increased longevity, many of today's elders do not regard themselves as old until their late seventies or early eighties. We also see sixty-five-year-old caretakers of their eighty-five-year-old parents, as well as a particularly tragic age crossover of child-mothers rearing their infants, while some adults postpone childbearing to the last biologically possible age. Therefore, times for learning, selecting sexual partners, marrying or remarrying, first-time parenting, changing one's career direction, retiring, and many other life changes no longer have fixed age connections and have become relatively independent of age.

Family Development, Paradigm, and Transformation

Family members develop simultaneously, with parents and offspring as active agents in their own and one another's development (Germain & Bloom, 1999). That is, parents and children develop in tandem. Individual adaptive and maladaptive processes merge into collective processes, and collective processes lead to family development and change. Over time the family constructs a unique "family paradigm" or worldview (Reiss, 1981), defined as the members' shared, implicit beliefs about themselves and their social world. The paradigm shapes the family's basic patterns in living and its experiences in the environment. A painful life event or other life stressor that causes serious discontinuity in family life requires the family to change its ways of functioning as embedded in its paradigm and structure.

The distinction between first- and second-order life issues clarifies how collective processes involved in family development and transformations are formed out of individual processes (Lazarus, 1980; Lazarus & Folkman, 1984; Terkelsen, 1980). First-order life issues represent individual life transitions that occur frequently and can be expected in average experience, fitting into the continuous flow of family life. They include the developmental transitions of individual members, such as puberty, pregnancy, and aging processes; and social transitions such as school entry, work, marriage, and retirement. Life transitions from birth to old age present both individual and family with new requirements and new opportunities for mastery and growth.

Most families perceive first-order life issues as challenges rather than stressors, and manage them more or less smoothly, without serious disruption. First-order issues can lead to increased mastery and competence that yield pride and satisfaction to family members despite any frustrations involved. The family paradigm does not need to be changed. It is enough that several new behavioral sequences emerge as the family learns to manage the issue effectively. As the new behavioral sequences appear, outmoded sequences drop away.

Second-order life issues, however, are much more frequently encountered in social work with families than first-order ones. Second-order stressors consist of serious, unpredictable life events and other life issues ranging from natural catastrophes to family violence, addictions, unplanned and unwanted pregnancy, sudden and serious mental disorders, onset of disability or chronic illness, job loss, separation and divorce, and premature loss of a loved one. When such unexpected events occur, they represent severe discontinuities in the routine flow of family life. All such life stressors put the family in harm's way. They also may include any first-order issue perceived by a particular family as a harm or threat of harm, either because of the meaning the issue has for the members or because of the absence of internal or external resources needed for moving through it. Second-order issues also include such grievous harms as poverty and oppression, which themselves generate multiple second-order life issues.

Second-order life issues require the family to go beyond the process of simply adding new behaviors and dropping outmoded ones. Often, because of the severe discontinuity and the greatly changed conditions imposed by second-order life issues, many families require formal or informal help to change the fundamental characteristics embodied in the family paradigm. These changes include the reorganization of its structure of roles, tasks, and routines, and the redefinition of the family's values, norms, and meanings. In some instances, a family may have to modify its goals, plans for the future, and interpretation of its past. While these and other alterations are going on, family members also must regulate the accompanying anxiety, guilt, depression, resentment, shame, anger, or despair they feel so that these feelings do not interfere with efforts to change. For example:

Mrs. Abrams, a fifty-two-year-old, white, Jewish woman, is the mother of three daughters, ages twenty-seven, twenty-five, and twenty-three. The youngest, Rebecca, was admitted to a private inpatient psychiatric facility after her attempted suicide by Valium overdose. Rebecca had moved back home five weeks earlier. She is now diagnosed as suffering major depression with psychotic features, including delusions and bizarre behaviors. Three years ago Mr. Abrams had surgery for colon cancer. Currently, he receives chemotherapy and is also being treated for a heart condition. Total home care is provided by Mrs. Abrams. The oldest daughter has two small children and works full-time. The second daughter also works, is very upset about Rebecca, and depends on Mrs. Abrams for comfort and emotional support. Mrs. Abrams says, "Both lean on me too; it's easier to keep them out of it."

The couple has few friends and no kin other than their daughters. Their finances are limited. The cancer center reports that Mrs. Abrams keeps her husband home at times when others would have sought hospitalization. Mrs. Abrams says she has come to terms with her husband's illnesses, but Rebecca's disorder "came out of the blue and is a shock to my system. I don't know how to cope with it and I don't understand it." She worries that somehow she is at fault for Rebecca's condition, and her sense of competence and her self-esteem as a mother are seriously undermined. She also feels angry and cheated as a woman engaged in multiple caregiving who hasn't yet lived for herself. Rebecca is to be discharged to her mother's care in one week, and will be on medication as an outpatient.

If the difficult life issues facing the Abramses are to be managed successfully and the new reality of Rebecca's psychiatric disorder incorporated into the family paradigm, a transformation of its structure of roles, tasks, coping modes, goals and expectations, and views of the environment will be required. But with the lack of resources for Mrs. Abrams, the outlook appears bleak.

Successful first- and second-order changes lead to family development. First-order developments occur frequently, so that the family experiences itself as living in a state of flux. In contrast, second-order developments occur infrequently, so that the family experiences itself as living in a state of constancy. Flux and constancy proceed together. Through successful first-order changes, the family is continually evolving and the members are continually developing. Through successful second-order changes, the structure and the paradigm governing family life are transformed in order to be congruent with changed realities, and the family and its members develop as a consequence.

However, should a family persist in dysfunctional patterns that block needed change, it may become a troubled family. Its implicit paradigm and structure governing life together are characterized by conflicted relationships, destructive negative feelings, contradictory communications, and rigid systems of control. Failure to change can lead to other second-order stressors such as breakup of the marriage, destructive behaviors in either partner or in the children, or physical or social dysfunction.

Social Work Function, Modality, Methods, and Skills

The Social Worker and Dysfunctional Family Structures and Processes

Families that face painful life transitions, traumatic life events, or environmental pressures may find that coping with such stressors is made more difficult by dysfunctional patterns of relationships and communications. Other families may not be facing external life stressors, but their interpersonal processes are a serious life stressor. In either instance, the social worker's function is to help such families identify sources and consequences of dysfunctional interpersonal processes, communicate more openly and directly, and develop greater reciprocity and caring in family relationships. However, if coping efforts continue to be ineffective, the worker will need to help members discard some behaviors and adopt new ones. If that is not enough, the family will need to develop a new paradigm that restructures family roles, tasks, and goals and incorporates the new reality posed by the critical life issue. With the social worker's help, the family transforms itself into a more functional unit that can cope with the stressor and can better support the needs and growth of all members.

Professional Methods and Skills

Given these aims of the family modality, the social worker enables, guides, and facilitates in the ways previously discussed. In addition, in family practice the worker joins a family system, mediates its internal structures and processes, and advocates for the rights and needs of weaker members. This is *internal* mediation and advocacy, as contrasted to the external mediation described in the previous chapter. Unfortunately, analyzing each method isolates the method from all others. In reality, various methods and their skills are called on as needed so that many sessions may present a blend. The method of *joining* is characteristic of the first interview, but it is also remains important throughout the contact with the family. The skill of joining includes the following:

- *Affirming.* Seek out and affirm positives. Affirmation builds on the strengths of family members and may also help to modify some members' negative perceptions of another member.
- *Tracking.* Encourage narratives and life stories of the family and of individual members. Practitioners must track all the members and not only the most verbal. They must be aware of their own tracking processes. Worker reactions such as talking mostly to the mother or failing to ask how come the father did not come to the session may on reflection yield insight into the family structure.
- *Creating therapeutic contexts.* Establish a climate in the sessions that enables members to feel competent or to experience hope of change. Identify family strengths; facilitate the enactment of familiar, positive patterns; or introduce novelty by encouraging members to engage with one another in unusual exchanges (Hoffman, 2002).
- *Monitoring the family's worldview.* Social workers must learn the elements of families' paradigms in order to support the family's reality or to help members construct a new or expanded worldview. The new paradigm must incorporate a new reality, new attitudes and beliefs, and other changes. The worker must learn how family roles, tasks, routines, and goals are organized in order to help the family manage the stressor and change what needs to be changed.

Table 9.1 summarizes joining skills.

To help family members change dysfunctional interpersonal processes, the social worker relies on specialized skills to encourage clear *communication*, positive relationships, and needed *behavioral change*. These skills include reframing, homework, work on rituals and myths as needed, and reflective comments:

- *Reframing.* The worker makes statements to family members designed to change their views of an event or a situation, to modify their conceptions of causality, or to convert what they see as linear communication into exchanges

Table 9.1
Joining Skills

• *Affirming:*	Seek out and validate strengths.
• *Tracking:*	Encourage and value narrations of life stories of family and individual members.
• *Creating a therapeutic context:*	Establish an emotional climate in sessions that enables members to feel competent and/or hopeful of change.
• *Monitoring the family's paradigm (worldview and structure):*	Learn the elements of the family's worldview such as values, norms, beliefs, and assumptions about themselves and their world.
	Learn the elements of the family's structure (organization) of roles, tasks, routines, and goals.

between members (Hartman & Laird, 1983, p. 307). Reframing also includes applying a positive connotation to destructive behavior by naming it as an effort to preserve the family system, defining a problem as a solution to another problem, and using metaphors and analogies to integrate information or to intensify its meaning.

• *Assigning homework.* Homework brings the clinical work into the daily life of the family through assigned tasks to be carried out at home (Hartman & Laird, 1983). Techniques used to ensure the effectiveness of an assignment include relating it to what is going on in that session's work, presenting it as serious and important, and, if possible, imbuing it with a bit of drama.

• *Working on rituals and myths.* Rituals help unite families by infusing events with meaning and value and preserving family paradigms. However, a family may adhere to maladaptive rituals. For example, holiday rituals can be pleasurable and contribute to a shared identity of the members. But in some families they are dreaded for their rigidity, hypocrisy, and emptiness. The social worker may be able to help the family design new holiday rituals that are more congruent with the lifestyles of the children (now adults). Other families may be underritualized. They need help in constructing beneficial rituals such as marking a divorce as a fresh start, celebrating a lesbian or gay partnership, celebrating a new achievement of a seriously disabled family member, or reuniting with estranged family members. Myths help families integrate their history and values, but some myths are dysfunctional. For example, a family explains the suicides of a father, uncle, and grandfather as deaths due to heart attacks. This myth about death is designed to protect a vulnerable child from a terrifying family secret, but it can lead to destructive consequences. The social worker may accept and support some family myths, while avoiding, intentionally ignoring, or

Table 9.2
Skills of Inducing Communication and Behavioral Change

• *Reframing:*	Make statements that can change the family's views of an event or situation.
	Place a positive connotation on destructive behavior as an individual member's effort to preserve the family.
	Define a problem as a solution to another problem.
	Use metaphors and analogies to integrate information or intensify its meaning.
• *Assigning homework:*	Bring the clinical work into the family's daily life by assigning tasks to be carried out at home.
	Relate the assignment to what is going on in that session's content.
	Present the assignment at the end of the session and as serious and important.
• *Working on secrets, rituals, and myths:*	Help members to dissolve a family secret defined as blocking growth.
	Support adaptive family rituals and myths.
	Help members to create celebratory or other rituals when the family is underritualized.
	Avoid, ignore, or raise necessary questions about maladaptive family myths.
• *Reflective commenting:*	Comment on family interpersonal processes to help the family learn about itself.
	Describe behavior as it is happening and as everyone experiences it in the session.
	Make use of enacting, such as family sculpture by the members.
	Observe and comment on family-of-origin issues as family and worker analyze genograms, ecomaps, or enactments such as family sculpture.

Table 9.3
Mediating and Advocating Skills

- Explore divergent views.
- Legitimize differences in perceptions and behaviors.
- Invite feedback on each other's comments.
- Search for common ground.
- Lend support to each partner as needed, most often the weaker member.
- Explore family-of-origin issues.
- Encourage self-awareness and other-awareness in both partners.
- Use initial agreements to maintain focus.
- Make therapeutic demands.

raising a question about others, or helping the family to relinquish a dysfunctional myth and to accept the truth as part of the family's life story.

• *Offering reflective comments.* Comments by the social worker on the family's interpersonal processes help the family learn about itself and even begin to identify maladaptive communication and relationship patterns, implicit rules, and other paradigmatic elements. Comments that describe a behavioral sequence as it is happening and experienced by everyone in the session call the attention of the family to how it is functioning. Families may unwittingly exhibit their patterns or difficulties in the session through their seating arrangements, who always speaks first, and the like. The worker's comment on the displayed behavior brings the maladaptive pattern to members' consciousness and stimulates change. When a member talks to another member through the worker, the worker instructs the communicator to redirect the communication to the other member. Their growing awareness empowers the family to make the changes they desire.

Table 9.2 summarizes skills of inducing communication and behavioral change.

Internal mediation and advocacy are particularly useful in helping couples to reduce chronic marital or family conflict. The skills of internal mediation and advocacy include exploring divergent views; searching for common ground; legitimizing differences in perceptions and behaviors; inviting feedback on each other's comments; lending support to each partner as needed, most often to the weaker member; exploring family-of-origin issues; encouraging self-awareness and other-awareness in both partners; using agreements reached at the outset to maintain focus; and making therapeutic demands. These skills are elaborated and illustrated in this chapter (Table 9.3) and in chapter 10.

Practice Illustrations

Family Structure

Mr. and Mrs. Weiss, a young, white, married couple with no children, sought help from an outpatient mental health clinic. Mrs. Weiss, twenty-four years old, is Italian and Roman Catholic. Her family history includes harsh physical punishment by her mother; repeated rapes by her father from the age of twelve, which continued for an unspecified period of time; and responsibility for caring for an infant sibling during her adolescent years while her mother worked. She graduated from high school and entered a college premed program two years ago at the urging of her husband. She received good grades, but dropped out after a year because she felt too much pressure. Since then, she has been too depressed to seek employment or further study.

Mr. Weiss, age thirty, is Jewish. He is employed as an accountant and is completing an undergraduate degree in accounting. He has attended ten colleges and has frequently shifted jobs, usually after a year. He met his wife at work. She was a clerk, and he was a bookkeeper. After several years of dating, they were married. He is the younger of two children, and says he was "spoiled," always getting what he wanted. His facial expression is bland, with consistently flat affect. In contrast, Mrs. Weiss is distraught, verbal, and expressive.

The primary life stressor was Mrs. Weiss's depressed feelings concerning an abortion two months earlier. The pregnancy was not planned, but Mrs. Weiss stated that she wanted the baby. She decided to abort because her husband did not want a child at this time. Mrs. Weiss complained that he always gets what he wants when they disagree. She felt that her husband was insensitive to her need to have a child and did not care about her: "Bill and I are two different people—we even have trouble talking to each other." She had a severe reaction after the abortion. Everything slowed down, and she perceived people and objects in lights of different colors flashing ahead of her, felt a tingling sensation in her body, and had trouble sleeping and a fear of going outside. The symptoms coincided with her resumption of smoking marijuana. After the first session, Mrs. Weiss experienced a dramatic reduction and subsequent absence of symptoms.

While Mr. Weiss recognized the existence of marital issues, his initial motivation for coming to the agency was not to deal with these, but rather to "get help for my wife, who has a lot of problems." After he described his wife's problems, the worker asked for Mrs. Weiss's perceptions. She is concerned that they are incompatible and probably should never have married. He probably married her only because he felt sorry for her because of her difficult family life. She complained that Mr. Weiss neither expresses emotion nor talks to her. This, coupled with his opposition to their having a child, confirmed his lack of commitment to her and their relationship. Mr. Weiss explained that there were too many problems in the marital relationship to have a child, and he is not ready. He had not even wanted to get married, preferring simply to live together, stating that "marriage meant responsibility, commitment and roots." She resents his attitude, leaving her no choice but to have an abortion. The worker records the following:

I asked Mr. Weiss if he did not want to have the baby. He said he told her he didn't want a baby, but it did not have to be his way. I asked Mrs. Weiss to comment on that, and she responded that he always says, "It does not have to be that way," but he always gets his way. I asked, "How come?" She replied, "I knew Bill never wanted a child; I knew he would never let me have a baby. So when I found I was pregnant, I called a doctor to set up an appointment for the abortion and then I told Bill." I said, "You told Bill after you called the doctor?" She replied angrily that she knew what he would say: "He always gets his way and doesn't care what I think. I said to myself, I might as well get it over with, and I called the doctor." I replied, "It had to be a very painful call to make and to follow through on." She lowered her head, and tears streamed down her cheek. I offered her a tissue, and asked him for his reactions to what his wife said. In an unemotional tone, he said, "I state my opinion, and Mary can state hers. She doesn't have to go along with what I say. I just didn't want her to get pregnant."

I asked if they had agreed on a birth control method. Mrs. Weiss replied that they had not planned the pregnancy, nor had they used birth control. I suggested that this seemed to be a contradiction. She replied that they could not agree on what birth control method to use. I asked what happened after she had the abortion. Mrs. Weiss scowled at her husband. He expressed guilt about leaving his wife right after the abortion (he went on a business trip for a few days), and realized that he should not have left her (expressed without emotion). I said he seemed to be genuinely sorry, but had difficulty expressing his feelings, and added, "Bill, I think you would like to, but find it difficult to do." He responded, "I have always had difficulty expressing my feelings—I don't know why." I asked what it had been like for him in his own family. He began to describe a similar pattern in his own family, with his mother complaining that his father never talked.

After describing his experiences with an overbearing mother and detached father, he made the connection to his needing the freedom to pick up and get away. He doesn't even like any furniture in the apartment—it confines him. He married only to please his wife. Mrs. Weiss said she wanted the "benefits" of marriage if they were going to live together. He abruptly switched focus, stating, "Everything is meaningless. We all just exist." I said what he was saying is important, but I don't understand. He responded calmly that he is just being negative, and needs some space from the conversation. I commented that he seemed to put up a wall when he is under pressure and feels the need for space and privacy. I asked Mrs. Weiss what it is like for her to try to break through the wall. "It's totally frustrating. I try everything possible to get a response from him. The more I scream, the quieter he gets." I asked Mr. Weiss what it is like for him to see his wife become increasingly frustrated and upset. He feels good because it shows that she cared, but at the same time it invaded his privacy. I asked what he meant by "privacy." "To be able to breathe," he said.

Mrs. Weiss has experienced a deep sense of loss and is angry with her husband for his detachment and lack of empathy. The abortion has profound meaning to her. She sees her husband's problems with intimacy and his emotional defensiveness as a lack of commitment and affection. The worker empathically explores the divergent perceptions and invites feedback on each other's comments. She asks clarifying questions and points out contradictions, creating the context for fostering self-awareness, mutual understanding, and open lines of communication. She effectively joins the family system.

A rigidly defended person such as Mr. Weiss requires empathic understanding from the social worker, which the practitioner tried to give by at least controlling any negative reactions she might have felt. It is easy to empathize with Mrs. Weiss's pain at her husband's lack of caring, loving, and concern for her and her very human neediness. It is far harder to recognize underneath Mr. Weiss's defensive armor a desperately hungry but frightened child who himself seldom experienced caring, love, or parental concern for a child's neediness. Slowly, the social worker will need to tune into Mr. Weiss's feelings under the armor and help him to experience and express them to whatever degree might be possible. Once he can love himself a little, he might be better able to experience and convey loving feelings to his wife.

In family systems, the conflicts and tensions between adult partners affect children. They are innocent victims caught between adult partners' crossfire. At times, children take on the symptoms of adult partners, and become the "identified patient" in mental health services.

George and Martha Simpson, white, Protestant, in their mid-thirties, and the parents of three sons, aged ten, seven, and three, sought help from a family agency. They had been seen before, about their "unmanageable" oldest son. After six sessions, they withdrew because Mrs. Simpson felt that the worker sided with her husband. Their current concern is marital conflict, which has escalated to the point where both are considering divorce. A first interview was scheduled for the couple, but Mrs. Simpson was unable to come to the interview or the next two because of illness. Mr. Simpson was seen alone in the three sessions. He told of recently being cheated out of his business by his partners and then suffering a back injury, which left him unable to work. They are rapidly going into debt, but his wife refuses to get a job or to curb her spending. According to Mr. Simpson, she is more involved with her relatives and friends than with him or the children.

The couple came to the fourth session and all subsequent sessions together. Mrs. Simpson had been crying and was still visibly upset. Mr. Simpson was angry and sullen, refusing to direct anything but verbal abuse toward his wife. She said that all their disagreements ended in her "giving in after being tortured by silence or yelling, and threats of desertion." She does not want a divorce, but seriously doubts they can continue together much longer. He admitted the situation is now intolerable for the entire family. Both blamed the interaction on each other.

MR. SIMPSON: We can't even go anywhere anymore because we don't have the money. We're stuck together all day long and getting on each other's nerves.

WORKER: (To Mrs. Simpson) Is that how it is for you too?

MRS. SIMPSON: When George was working, he was gone from early morning until late at night. I'd get the kids off to school and do whatever I had to do in the apartment. Then maybe a friend would come over, and we'd have lunch and watch a soap opera. Or I'd visit a friend. I've also been a volunteer at church and the school. The kids came home in the late afternoon and kept me busy with dinner and all.

MR. SIMPSON: You also like to stay on the phone all day.

MRS. SIMPSON: (Smiling) I like to talk on the phone.

WORKER: What about you, Mr. Simpson?

MR. SIMPSON: I worked ten hours a day, seven days a week. My schedule didn't allow me much time, but I used to play poker with the guys on Monday nights. Now I'm not able to play basketball and I don't have the money to gamble.

WORKER: What about your time together?

MR. SIMPSON: What time together? (Both laugh.)

MRS. SIMPSON: George was always so busy at the store that I guess I got used to living alone and handling things myself. Now I have no privacy. I'm embarrassed to have friends over because he joins us and monopolizes the conversation. He even stands around while I'm on the phone and comments on my conversations. I feel like a fourth child.

MR. SIMPSON: What am I supposed to do, lie in bed all day?

MRS. SIMPSON: Of course not! But you could find something to do besides watching me all day.

WORKER: Mr. Simpson's being out of work has caused some major changes in both your lives. While he was working you were apart all the time, and now you're together all the time. That's a difficult adjustment for both of you.

MR. SIMPSON: I get real bored, but I keep thinking, why start a project or anything when I might be going back to work soon?

MRS. SIMPSON: And I keep putting my friends off until George goes back to work.

WORKER: It sounds as if you've both put your lives on hold and are waiting for things to get back to normal.

MRS. SIMPSON: (Thoughtfully) Yeah. That's exactly right. (Mr. Simpson nodded in agreement.)

The life stressors of injury and unemployment and the stress they generate heighten existing vulnerabilities, trigger emotional reactivity and maladaptive responses, and sharply lower the level of person:environment fit. The worker joins the couple and avoids taking sides. She creates a therapeutic context by validating their difficulties and lowering emotional arousal. The couple's perspective is limited; they blame each other for the state of their marriage. But by focusing on the two critical life events that beset them, rather than on the maladaptive patterns, the worker broadens their perspective and reduces their anxiety and anger. By the end of the session, and motivated by their mutual love for their children, the couple agree to work on their relationship and communication patterns in order to improve their marriage.

The Simpsons were extremely angry at each other when they arrived for the next session. Mr. Simpson began by declaring that he was taking the children to visit his dying father in another state. He had set aside a portion of his insurance settlement for this trip, as he wanted his father to meet the children before he died. He was doing it for the children so they would have a sense of family. He was not doing it for his father—they never got along. He was angry that his wife is against the trip and said he plans to go without her. Although Mrs. Simpson agreed to go, she did so grudgingly. She objected to taking the children out of school, to the cost, and to the fact that her husband had not arranged accommodations. They then bitterly argued about arrangements. Mr. Simpson accused his wife of picking a fight with his sister-in-law and making it impossible for them to stay with his brother.

MRS. SIMPSON: You know she didn't want us there.

MR. SIMPSON: Not now she doesn't. (Suddenly furious with his wife and shouting at her) You could give a shit. You hate my family. Bitch! You destroyed my relationship to my brother and fixed it so we can't stay with them.

MRS. SIMPSON: (More hurt than angry) You know damn well neither he nor she wants us there, and that's not my fault.

WORKER: (Holding hands up in a "stop" gesture) Please hold it a minute.

MR. SIMPSON: (To the worker) She pisses me off.

WORKER: I can see that, but I'm not sure I understand what pissed you off.

MR. SIMPSON: All she ever does is criticize me.

MRS. SIMPSON: It's the other way around. I can never say or do anything right. I'm too fat. I'm a lousy wife, a lousy mother. I ruined his family. (Shrugs.) I don't know. I'm so used to it. He doesn't like anything I do. It's like this all the time—Martha, the punching bag.

WORKER: Each of you feels criticized. What is so sad is that you both are in the same boat and can't seem to help each other. You're both feeling unappreciated, unloved, alone, stuck with things as they are. The longer you wait for the other to change, the more hopeless it all seems.

MR. SIMPSON: (Half-hearted attempt at humor) I didn't think we had anything in common.

MRS. SIMPSON:	(Smiles.)
WORKER:	Let's try to solve the problem without name-calling and blaming. Two people in the same boat, and the boat will sink unless you can learn to work together to resolve issues. So, let's talk about your trip.
MRS. SIMPSON:	Well, we know we can't stay with your brother. The way things stand right now, it looks like we're going to spend five days in the car.
WORKER:	Are there other options?
MRS. SIMPSON:	If we had to, we could stay in a cheap hotel.
MR. SIMPSON:	I really don't want to spend the money. We could sleep on the floor at my father's place, but my stepmother is very sick.
MRS. SIMPSON:	Three kids would be too much for her.
MR. SIMPSON:	Why don't you ask your friend if we can stay there? (To the worker) It seems like the least she can do.
MRS. SIMPSON:	(To the worker) She said it was all right, but I feel she wasn't pleased. She's one of those perfect people who never has a thing out of place. I'd never be able to relax with the kids and all. I mean, our kids aren't bad. I'd just spend the time worrying that they'd spill something or put their hands on the wall. You can't watch children all the time. I don't know—I feel it's such an imposition.
MR. SIMPSON:	The woman said it was OK. SHE HAS TWO KIDS, SO SHE KNOWS WHAT IT'S LIKE. I DON'T KNOW WHAT THE BIG DEAL IS.
MRS. SIMPSON:	That's easy for you to say. You just tune out and leave me to do the chasing around. This isn't going to be a vacation for me.
MR. SIMPSON:	And it is for me?
MRS. SIMPSON:	I wouldn't mind if we were flying down and staying at one of those nice hotels.
MR. SIMPSON:	(To the worker) She knows we don't have the money for that. Why does she always have to rub it in?
WORKER:	Please tell her directly rather than through me.
MR. SIMPSON:	Martha, don't you think I wish this were a nice vacation instead of a trip to see my father dying in the hospital?
MRS. SIMPSON:	(No response)
WORKER:	(To both) This isn't easy for either of you. There are a few problems, but you both agree it is something you have to do. (To Mr. Simpson) You feel this is the last chance for your children to meet your father and for you to say goodbye to him. That's a difficult thing to do alone, and you would like Mrs. Simpson to support you by accompanying you and making things as easy and as pleasant as possible.
MR. SIMPSON:	Right!

WORKER:	(To Mrs. Simpson) And you understand how important this is to your husband and do support the decision. But you can't communicate that to him because you feel alone in having to make all the arrangements. You would like this to be more pleasant for you too.
MRS. SIMPSON:	Yes.
WORKER:	What can be done to make the trip more pleasant for everyone?
MR. SIMPSON:	(Hesitating while regarding his wife's expression) We do have a few days free. . . . (More of a question to his wife than a statement) As long as we're in Pine City, I suppose we could see some sights. We could be out all day and just use your friend's place to sleep.
MRS. SIMPSON:	I would feel better about this trip if we had something to look forward to.

In this excerpt, the worker focuses on the dysfunctional communications. By empathizing with each partner, clarifying latent concerns, and searching for common ground, she promotes cooperative problem solving. In limiting their exchanges to perceived differences, the Simpsons lost sight of their common interests. This impairs their ability to recognize and appreciate their need for each other. The rapid shift in emotional climate was remarkable. The worker stopped the flow of anger by taking control of the interaction and restoring emotional stability to the session. The Simpsons are locked into a win–lose pattern, and the worker suggests a win–win option in which both benefit from resolution of the conflict. After defusing the tension, the worker reframes the blaming in a way they both could accept (Sperry, 2004).

The Simpsons returned from Pine City and were in good spirits. Both were in a light mood, laughing and sharing funny moments from their trip. Mrs. Simpson enjoyed the visit with her friend and the sightseeing, and Mr. Simpson felt satisfied that his children now refer to "Grandpa" and not to "Dad's father." He repeated, "The trip was for the kids—not for me or my father."

WORKER:	It must have been very difficult for you to see your father for what might be the last time.
MR. SIMPSON:	Well, I accomplished my purpose, if that's what you mean. Now that's done, I really don't give a shit what happens to him. I'm serious. He never did anything for me.
WORKER:	That's really sad. (Short pause, then he shrugs off her comment) Can you give me an example of how he disappointed you?
MR. SIMPSON:	(Thinking) Our kids . . . (pause) there were a lot of things, but the kids come to mind.
MRS. SIMPSON:	(Glances at her husband and hesitates before speaking) George was very hurt that his father never acknowledged the

children. He never sent a card or gift when they were born. There just didn't seem to be any interest. I didn't care for myself, but I felt bad for George because he was hurt.

The Simpsons then began to explore both families of origin and dysfunctional family patterns. For example, Mr. Simpson learned to mask his feelings. He dealt with parental rejection by withdrawal and feigned indifference. Later in the interview, the worker pointed out that while he declared indifference toward his father, his nonverbal expressions pointed to great pain and anger. Mrs. Simpson's empathy for her husband made it possible for the worker to help him give verbal expression to those feelings.

In subsequent sessions, the Simpsons continued to move away from blaming each other. They were increasingly able to listen to each other, act collaboratively, and accept responsibility for changing their own behaviors. Their awareness of destructive patterns increased, and they now feel more optimistic about their future as a family. Mr. Simpson's back pain is subsiding, and a possible job has appeared on the horizon. The couple gained (or regained) strengths by learning to cope with serious life issues, including their own destructive relationship, without any apparent change in structure or paradigm. Growth occurred as the worker mediated their relationship and advocated for both.

Homework assignments are often used to guide problem-solving skills. For example, Mr. and Mrs. Tucker, a young couple married two years and recently separated, wanted help on the question of divorce. In the first session it became clear that they did not know how to resolve marital conflict, and they were unable to decide whether to resume living together. The social work intern sensed that they both did want to be together, but each was afraid to make the first move and each feared rejection. The intern was impressed by their ability to talk reasonably without a lot of blaming and name-calling. Hence, the intern proposed a homework assignment:

I suggested that over the next three weeks they meet for at least an hour each time to discuss the sole question of moving back together. They were to discuss both the pros and cons. If the discussion degenerated into argument, they were to discontinue and try again another day. They carried out the task, resisted the impulse to do battle, and moved back together in the fourth week. From then on I assigned weekly tasks aimed at the more difficult demands of coping with day-to-day grievances. Although it was not easy for them, they were increasingly able to complete the tasks and toward the end of our contact were telling me about their new abilities to solve problems (none of which had been assigned by me as tasks). Clearly, both had become more like their real selves. He, taciturn and reclusive at the start, began raising his voice and becoming mildly histrionic. Her withholding behavior diminished, and she became more confident about her emotionality. At the end of nine months the Tuckers had experimented with managing conflict and were successful enough times to feel they were a competent couple. The hardest tasks for them—negotiating finances and dealing with her jealousy of his former girlfriend—became manageable and were dealt with during the last month of our work.

Homework should be assigned toward the end of the session. With some families, especially those that are easily overwhelmed, the task should not be overly demanding. But with families like the Tuckers, assignments should be difficult in order to be challenging (Hartman & Laird, 1983).

Parent–child conflict is a serious and frequent life stressor. While it also occurs between parents and school-age and younger children, it is seen most often in families with adolescents. In this solo-parent family, serious conflict exists between Mrs. Calhoun and her adolescent daughters.

Mrs. Calhoun, a thirty-five-year-old African American, was married at age seventeen. She left her husband two years ago because of his alcohol and drug abuse and his involvement with other women. She placed their five children in foster care until she could send for them, and left the South to seek work in a northern city. In accordance with the requirements of the Department of Children's and Family Services (DCFS) with whom she had been working on reunification for almost a year, Mrs. Calhoun had prepared for the children's arrival by obtaining a four-bedroom apartment in a public housing project, which she furnished inexpensively but attractively. She has been working at two jobs as a nurses' aide. A year after working with DCFS, she applied to the local family agency, as the children's arrival was imminent.

Mrs. Calhoun said she wanted to work on her relationships with the children and on how to manage the multiple demands placed on a working single mother. The oldest child, sixteen-year-old Margie, arrived during the summer. Betty, age fifteen, and the boys (ages seven, twelve, and thirteen) arrived in time for Christmas, three weeks before the session described below. Mrs. Calhoun said she had a strict upbringing, and like her parents she believes in the right of parents to train their children, no babies before marriage, owning nice furniture and a car, and supporting one's family by work, not welfare. Her verbal and nonverbal communications suggested that as a mother she is more authoritative than nurturing. Mrs. Calhoun had said in our earlier interview that she feels competent as a strong woman and breadwinner and puts her efforts into work and making money. She said that is less risky and less difficult than trying to build relationships with Margie and Betty.

Unexpectedly, she brought the girls to this January session. They both looked older than their age. They were stylishly dressed, and

Margie seemed quite fashion-conscious. Neither looked pleased to be here and, like their mother, they looked tense. I began by asking how things were going. Mrs. Calhoun gave an uncharacteristic short answer: "adjustments are being made." When I asked both girls, each merely shrugged. Trying to reduce tension, I asked if Mrs. Calhoun had been able to register the children at school. She said the boys were registered and attending school; they like it and are making friends. Betty can't register for high school until necessary papers are received from her former school. The situation is different for Margie, who was expelled a year ago and is now considered a dropout. At this point, Mrs. Calhoun added, "There's something you should know about Margie. She's carrying a baby." I said, "Oh," then recovered and asked Margie how she feels about being pregnant. She said she is four months along and feels tired but OK otherwise. I asked if she has decided to raise the baby herself, or if the father was in the picture. She said she doesn't know exactly what she is going to do, but the father is out of her life. I asked if she has considered adoption, and she said, "No, I'm keeping the baby." I said she could talk to a teen pregnancy counselor at our agency or she could talk to me about it, and we could set up some separate time if she wants. Mrs. Calhoun jumped in and said, "That would be nice." Margie seemed to resent her mother's comment and said, "I don't exactly know what I want to do." I said, "Well, it's something you can think about."

Several practice mistakes occurred at the start of this first family interview. First, the worker should have made an empathic comment on observing the girls' apparent discomfort, to elicit their expectations and feelings about the session. Second, the purpose of the agency and of social work practice should have been stated in order to engage the sisters, elicit any erroneous perceptions, and facilitate a beginning trust in the worker. Instead of making such comments, or picking up on Mrs. Calhoun's "adjustments are being made," the worker focused on school. This had been the mother's concern in the prior session. The worker did note that she hadn't given Margie and Betty a chance "because I assumed the girls weren't ready to talk."

On hearing the surprising news of Margie's pregnancy, instead of focusing on what this means to Margie, the worker took refuge in factual, nonempathic questions regarding the baby's father and adoption. She then suggested a referral to the agency's teen pregnancy counselor, which could push Margie further away from engagement with the worker herself. Despite these errors, the worker recouped later in the session:

After a silence, Mrs. Calhoun brought up an issue that was obviously upsetting her. Her voice was raised, and her speech was fast and detailed. Margie and Betty, who don't have driver licenses, had taken

Mrs. Calhoun's car and damaged a wheel driving over a curb. She said, "Here I was, out working hard to support the family, and this is what my children do to me. This is what I have to put up with." Margie said she wanted to say something, but Betty warned her not to get into it. I suggested that Margie say what she wanted, but Mrs. Calhoun broke in with "I can't have children in my house who won't respect rules." I said it must be real difficult for her to go to work with the fear that her children, at home without supervision, would break her rules. She recalled other rules they had broken and then switched the subject back to Margie's pregnancy. She asked Margie to tell me why a crisis counselor at the community hospital had told them to get a restraining order against the baby's father. Before Margie could begin, Mrs. Calhoun proceeded to narrate the story herself. (Here the worker might have asked Mrs. Calhoun to let Margie tell the story herself.) John, the baby's father, had come to the house with a knife, threatening to kill Margie and himself if she wouldn't talk to him.

So far, Margie had said nothing, but now she asked me, "Do you know what it's like to have someone threaten to kill himself and you, and really mean it?" I said I had never been in that situation, but I could imagine that she must have been really scared. She said, "He didn't use to be like this—he was nice to me at first." She added that over the summer she spent most of the time on the streets or at friends' houses. She didn't think her mother cared about her, but cared only about work and her own boyfriend. "Now I see she was working so hard to get things together for my brothers and Betty to come live with us. I know I was wrong and did a lot of dumb things over the summer, but my mother was never home." I asked how she feels about it now, and she said that with her siblings here, she sees her mother more. Margie turned to Betty and said, "You didn't see how hard she was working to buy things for you, you didn't see how tired she was, working two jobs. That's why Momma got sick, and I know it's our fault." Betty seemed to want to say something, and I invited her to speak. She said she used to get mad when she was still down South: "I would ask for things, but she'd only send them maybe two or three times a year." She was angry because her mom didn't write to her or call her. Mrs. Calhoun broke in to say that she was always working and tired, and didn't have time to write because she was getting things ready for all of them to be together again. I told Betty that when I first met her mother, all she could talk about was how excited she was that her kids were coming home and how much she enjoyed talking with Betty on the phone. She was sorry she didn't write more.

At this point all three were crying, but the worker does not record whether she responded to their crying.

Betty said she called her worker down South last week and told her that all they do is fight. "I don't know what's wrong, but things aren't working right. I can't talk with my mother anymore." I asked Betty to talk to her now. She said, "Momma, I used to be able to talk with you, but I can't anymore. That's our problem: all we do is fight, and you're always mad." She then brought up an incident when Mrs. Calhoun slapped her for not getting up to bring her a scarf. Mrs. Calhoun said she was angry because the girls were talking back to her and being disrespectful. Betty said, "But you don't listen when we try to say things, Momma." Mrs. Calhoun responded that they had said she wasn't a fit mother. Betty said, "I said that, Momma, but I was mad; I didn't mean it."

The worker commented that the girls were taking some responsibility now for things they had done, and saying that they sometimes say things they don't mean when they are angry.

Mrs. Calhoun said, "This family has been falling apart since the girls were eleven or twelve. I've been through so much." Betty said, "We're going through it too, Momma. It hurts us too." I said, "There is a lot of pressure on all of you, and maybe if you can talk some of it out, things won't hurt so much." (The worker also needed to point out that there was love, too, and a desire to make things work.) Betty said, "Yeah, we don't talk until we're so mad that all we do is fight. This family doesn't talk." Mrs. Calhoun said she still feels like the villain and doesn't think the girls love and appreciate her. They disagreed, and I helped them express this to their mom. Then I moved closer to Mrs. Calhoun, took her hand, and said, "You have a lot of pressure on those capable shoulders of yours. You're working hard to keep the family together. With all this pressure, it's hard for you to take time out to really talk to one another. Your daughters don't seem to see you as a villain. They are expressing problems they see, but they love you." By now all were exhausted. I asked if they felt it helped to talk. All said yes as they wiped away their tears. I said, "This is difficult work, but you really opened up here. Talking and trying to understand each other is the first step to solving the problems. I feel we need to set up weekly meetings with the whole family or at least with you three." I added that I saw our work together as learning how to get along as a family and to feel good about being together. "You've only been together three weeks, and a lot of changes are going on." I walked them to the door. Mrs. Calhoun called the next day to say they had talked some more. She still isn't sure if the girls want to follow house rules. I said we could talk about ways to help them understand the need for some rules and some ways to make things clear to them. She said, "All right, I'll see you Tuesday."

The severely dysfunctional relationships and communication in the Calhoun family need to be understood from several vantage points. One is the typical adolescent struggle for independence from parents and conformity to peer behaviors and norms. The sisters' uprooting intensifies this struggle. They moved from a small southern town where they had lived all their lives to a depressed and dangerous area of a large northern city. We should also consider the long separation of mother and daughters during the crucial years of the girls' puberty and early teens. This reunited family faces intense demands on a working solo mother, and a lack of social supports to make coping with all the new demands easier. And, finally, there is the apparent conflict between Mrs. Calhoun's relatively rigid values and the more relaxed norms of urban working-class families now encountered by the girls.

The social worker's joining skills create a therapeutic context for the sharing of family members' pain. She redirects mother and daughters to talk to each other and reframes their maladaptive communication patterns. "With all this pressure, it's hard for you to take time out to really talk to one another." This situation cries out for a therapeutic ritual celebration of the family's reunion, designed by the whole family (with the help of the social worker, if needed). A celebratory ritual could help with the difficult reunion tasks. It could also be a first step in relieving serious, dysfunctional interpersonal processes that emerged during this family session and to help prevent further family breakdown.

Ahead lies the practice task of helping the Calhouns construct a new paradigm as a reunited family in a new environment. This requires adaptive exchanges, new attitudes and beliefs about themselves and the family, and even new values and norms. They will also need help in developing a new structure of family roles and tasks, and new relationship and communication patterns.

A challenged child, intellectually, emotionally, and/or physically, often presents distinctive adapting and coping issues for parents and siblings. Chronic disability is a persistent life stressor. The Jacob family consists of the wife, Susan, a twenty-five-year-old son, Elliot, and a twenty-two-year-old son, Sam, the identified patient. Mr. Jacob died five years ago. The Jacobs are white, Jewish, and of Polish descent. They live in an upper-middle-income suburb. Sam was referred to a psychiatric hospital after a short-term hospitalization for detoxification of Xanax and alcohol. (Sam self-medicated above and beyond the dosage regimen his physician prescribed.) Psychiatrists diagnosed Sam as suffering from hypochondria, generalized anxiety disorder, and obsessive-compulsive disorder (Axis I, *Diagnostic and Statistical Manual of Mental Disorders*, 4th edition), and from histrionic, narcissistic, and dependent personality disorders (Axis II). His alcohol and Xanax abuse is in remission. Mrs. Jacob admitted Sam to the psychiatric hospital because of his behavior. After admission, the social worker agreed to meet with Sam twice a week, and with Sam and his mother once a week. Mrs. Jacob also participated in a parents' psychoeducation group, which Sam joined after a number of sessions. Initially, Elliot was ambivalent about attending family sessions. In his own counseling, he had been working on setting limits to protect himself from becoming overinvolved in family difficulties. Therefore, the worker and Elliot agreed to weekly telephone contacts. He was also willing to participate in monthly family sessions.

Sam was an average to above-average student until high school. Behaviorally, he did not present any problems to teachers with the exception of socializing during class and excessively interrupting to ask questions. He experienced his greatest social success during junior high school athletics, band, and a leadership position held in student government. He brought friends home. When Sam was in the eighth grade, his mother underwent several surgeries for thyroid cancer. When Sam was in the ninth grade, she had a mastectomy and chemotherapy. At this time Sam began to experience severe anxiety and panic attacks. As Sam progressed through high school, mounting anxiety interfered with his ability to perform. Twelfth grade was especially difficult, and he saw the school counselor several times a week. He entered a small liberal arts college but was homesick, calling his father every day and going home every weekend. He dropped out after the fall semester because of his father's death and mother's hysterectomy. The next year, Sam enrolled in another college and again dropped out after the first semester. Subsequently, he enrolled in three other colleges as a nonmatriculated student and held a series of jobs, unable to sustain study or work. With each move, he established an unsuccessful relationship with a therapist. He was unable to live independently and became increasingly unable to manage his own affairs.

Mourning has been difficult for the family. Mrs. Jacob was not sure she could go on as a homemaker or provider, and became very depressed. Elliot was a supportive listener for both his mother and brother; however, he quickly became overwhelmed and fled by returning to school for an additional semester. He is currently experiencing a delayed grief reaction. Sam is highly defended against his father's death, showing little affect. He buried deep feelings of guilt, believing that he had contributed to or possibly caused his father's death. Mrs. Jacob had no time to mourn. She had to cope with her own illness as well as assume responsibility for her husband's business and the caretaking of three grandparents.

Mrs. Jacob states that her husband fostered intense dependency in both herself and the children. He dominated decisions and communications. His judgment was not to be questioned. In the tradition of second-generation parents, he wanted to give his children all the material things he did not have as a youth. He strongly advocated for his children (e.g., when Sam did not make the town's baseball team, Mr. Jacob intervened and had the decision reversed). He was unable to accept that his children had any problems, offered pep talks, and "fixed" things. As Elliot and Sam grew older, Mrs. Jacob became concerned by the children's lack of ability to follow through with commitments and assume responsibility. Mr. Jacob subverted her efforts to teach discipline and responsibility. He continued to insist that the "kids are just fine, stop worrying." However, in the area of academics, Mr. Jacob expressed his frustrations and disappointments. He expected and demanded excellence. In this area, Mrs. Jacob became the children's protector. And when Sam began to have serious problems, she took over his thinking and feeling. She did it for him.

A grandparent and uncle suffered schizoid and schizophrenic conditions—indicating a possible genetic predisposition. Life experience, and the family paradigm, has made it extremely difficult for Sam to separate from his family. Developing separateness was the focus of the worker's helping efforts. The following excerpt is taken from the third session. Mrs. Jacob, Elliot, and Sam are present. The family had been talking about separation for forty-five minutes, and the session was coming to an end.

MRS. JACOB:	Did you talk to Carol (the worker) about getting a pass this weekend?
SAM:	(Looking at the worker) No, I don't want to go on a pass this weekend.
WORKER:	(Smilingly) Sam, I didn't ask the question—share your reason.
SAM:	(Looking at his mother) I don't want to go on a pass with you this weekend. I want to do something with my friends instead.
MRS. JACOB:	Well, that's fine. It is your decision. I just thought I'd ask.
SAM:	I think I will enjoy myself more with my friends.
MRS. JACOB:	What do you mean by that? Aren't we supposed to do things together to work out our differences? Isn't that bad for his treatment?
SAM:	No, I'm supposed to do things with my friends instead of running to you all the time.
WORKER:	I think it is very important for you to spend time together, but I also remember that you all agreed to work on helping Sam to separate from home. It is very important to develop supports outside the family, and one way to do that is by spending time with friends.
ELLIOT:	That's true. I remember making some good friends at college and realizing for the first time that I didn't have to be exactly like my parents—always together.
SAM:	Yeah, I remember when Elliot decided to go away to college. I could not believe he did that, but I was proud of him.
WORKER:	What do you mean?
SAM:	Because I could never do that. I went to the college close to home my parents picked out for me. (To Mrs. Jacob) What did you and Dad think about Elliot's decision?

MRS. JACOB:	We, we were disappointed—sure we were. We were very upset.
ELLIOT:	I felt guilty about that.
WORKER:	It seems that though Elliot felt bad about making some of his own decisions, he was still able to follow through—that took a great deal of strength.
MRS. JACOB:	I am beginning to see what you are saying. Elliot went with what was comfortable for him, and maybe that was best because he learned to function on his own.
SAM:	It's always been like that. I have never been able to say no to my parents.
MRS. JACOB:	Oh Sam, that's not true.
SAM:	See, she's doing it again—telling me what I think and how I feel. It seems like she knows me better than I know myself. That's the problem. I never know whether she is right or I am right.
WORKER:	Sam, I suggest you ask her.
SAM:	Do you think it happens a lot?
MRS. JACOB:	Well yeah, I do that a lot, not only with you but also with Elliot.
WORKER:	As a family, you are all working very hard at recognizing your patterns, at becoming experts in how you behave with each other. You are a very close family—you even speak for each other as if you knew the thoughts and feelings of each other.
ELLIOT:	That's true. We all need to grow on our own. I take my phone off the hook at night, because after a number of phone calls I am no longer able to talk with Sam or Mom.
WORKER:	You are learning to take care of yourself. Everybody has to learn to take of him and herself.
SAM:	I think we may be on to something here.
MRS. JACOB:	Me too. You know, I never looked at it this way before. I mean—I know that we did too much for our kids instead of teaching them how to do things for themselves.
SAM:	So, how do we get better at it?
WORKER:	Sam, you are making an important start by choosing to be with your friends; Mrs. Jacob, you by your willingness to look at the patterns; and you, Elliot, by placing some limits.
SAM:	This is scary, but it does feel like a good start.
WORKER:	Yes, a start, and we will go slowly—it can't happen overnight. With the love you have for each other, you can do it.

With the social worker's support, Sam is able to tell his mother that he prefers to spend the weekend with his friends rather than coming home. Because the worker had prepared Mrs. Jacob for this objective, she did not respond with panic or guilt-inducing responses. However, when Sam devalued her importance in his life, she became defensive. The worker supports Mrs. Jacob's investment in spending time with her children, but also reminds all that they had agreed to help Sam develop additional supports. She joins with each family member as well as with the family unit, using the agreements to keep the work focused. The fact that Mrs. Jacob acknowledges her pattern of taking over freed Sam to state the crux of the difficulty with his mother. Mrs. Jacob became defensive again; however, when she became invalidating, Sam held his own and turned to his brother and the worker for support. This was the first time that Sam could intervene in his own behalf. He is working very hard to stick with the theme of struggling to express his own thoughts and feelings to his mother. The worker reframes their dysfunctional communication and relationship patterns by crediting their "becoming experts in how you behave with each other. You are a very close family—you even speak for each other as if you knew the thoughts and feelings of each other." Elliot makes the family fusion issue more explicit by stating how he deals with their intrusiveness by taking the telephone off the hook. The worker credits his ability to take care of himself, and encourages the other members to use Elliot as a role model. The session ends with the worker providing hope that their pain could be alleviated.

Family Processes

Differences in values, role expectations, self-definitions, and patterns of daily living can undermine a family's ability to cope with painful life transitions, traumatic life events, environmental stressors, and the attendant stress. Differing generational and cultural factors account for much of the family stress evident in the Benetti family, although neither factor is a focus of the work.

Mr. Benetti, age sixty-five, emigrated from Italy with his parents at age four. For thirty years he owned the shoe store where he first worked as a young man. Mrs. Benetti, age fifty-three, emigrated from Italy as a teenager. She does not work outside the home. The oldest child, Sal, age twenty-two, lives nearby with the maternal grandmother. The other children, Mike, age twenty, and Dena, age nineteen, live with their parents. The grandmother, born in Italy and now eighty years old, lived with the Benettis until Dena was age three. She continues to be an active presence in the family, doing most of their cooking and cleaning because of Mrs. Benetti's crippling anxieties. Mrs. Benetti was hospitalized for depression after Dena's birth and is treated as an incompetent child by the family. When Dena was in her senior year of high school, Mrs. Benetti developed agoraphobia (fear of leaving the house), and her husband sold his store. He is semiretired.

The children did well until adolescence. At seventeen, Sal, rebelling against his father's rules, was ordered by his father to leave the home. He moved in with his grandmother, and is now praised as the only child to hold a job. Mr. Benetti complains about his two "weak" children: Mike is withdrawn, and while Dena did well in school, she dropped out in her senior year and was recently discharged from a psychiatric hospital.

Neither parents nor children have friends. Several family members perceive the outside world as unsafe and suspect. Boundaries between individuals and between subunits are blurred. Mr. Benetti regularly interrupts members during sessions and tells them what they should do. He talks at everyone but does not listen. Grandmother constantly interferes in the family and tends to infantilize Mrs. Benetti. The parents rarely interact, except for his telling her what to do or complaining about the children. Both resist freeing their children to live their own lives, partly because of a cultural norm of two-, and even three-, generation families living together, and partly because of realistic fears and unrealistic anxieties in the parents and the children.

The social worker met Dena at a halfway house after Dena's discharge from the psychiatric hospital. She had been in the hospital for six months' treatment of severe depression and anorexia. The worker continues to follow Dena's progress and is now working with the entire family. The following excerpts reflect serious life stressors that block the family from coping with painful life transitions that involve the adult children's struggle for independence. In the first excerpt (from the initial session), those present are the parents, the grandmother, and Dena. Unexpectedly, the focus shifted from the "identified patient," Dena, to the "unidentified patient," Mrs. Benetti.

MRS. BENETTI:	It's hard to describe. I feel panicky when I'm home alone, and I can't go out of the house alone either. I don't know why I feel like this, but it's getting worse.
MR. BENETTI:	(Interrupting) She's impossible. She's like a child. (To his wife) You're afraid because we were robbed once, but the neighborhood is safe.
GRANDMOTHER:	No, she's not afraid of being mugged. I wish it were that simple.
MRS. BENETTI:	I don't know what I'm afraid of.

Mrs. Benetti is signaling for help. Her husband views his wife's phobias as unnecessary fears, and he is clearly frustrated. He is not yet ready to deal with the implications of his wife's symptoms. The grandmother knows that her daughter needs help, contradicts Mr. Benetti, and invites discussion of the family secret. The worker, having joined the family, now gives support to Mrs. Benetti as the weaker member. The worker tracks life stories in order to gain understanding of family development and structure.

GRANDMOTHER:	I grew up in a small village. I was one of ten children, and all my relatives lived nearby. When we came to this country, my daughter lived with my husband and me. When he died, we lived together until her marriage. We then went to live in her

husband's apartment. I was happy when she married him. He
was older, and I thought he would take care of her. After Dena
was toilet trained, I remarried and moved to an apartment
close by. We were happy for fifteen years together, but when
he died I was so lonely that Sal came to live with me.

MR. BENETTI: I kicked Sal out of the house because he couldn't obey my
rules.

MRS. BENETTI: It was good for everybody because my mother shouldn't live
alone.

WORKER: (Looking at the grandmother) Burying two husbands has
caused you much loneliness and pain.

The worker responds to the grandmother with empathy for her losses, and
wonders if the fact that the grandmother and Mrs. Benetti have never lived
alone as adults has something to do with the difficulties the Benetti children
are having in living on their own. Grandmother wanted the worker to understand the cultural values and norms to which the family adheres. The
worker pointed to how the cultural expectations of two and even three generations of family members living together could interfere with the children
moving ahead in their lives. This interpretation, however, ignores the deep
feelings involved in culturally based expectations. The significant issue of
the "normal" difference in cultural norms between the two immigrant generations and the third generation (in this family) is not brought up again.
Exploration and emphasis appeared to be more on emotional components.
As important as those are, they are not the total explanation. An opportunity to explore and clarify a common cultural impasse between generations
in an immigrant family was missed.

In the next excerpt (second session), the worker explores the parents'
marital relationship:

MR. BENETTI: It makes me angry when we're walking across the street
and a car comes too fast, and she refuses to run.

MRS. BENETTI: I can run if I have to—you're too anxious.

MR. BENETTI: No you can't. You never run. You're going to be killed
because you won't run. You should practice running.

DENA: There you go—telling Mom what she should do instead
of listening to her.

MRS. BENETTI: I think he runs too much. He's going to fall and hurt
himself.

WORKER: I hear that you are both worried about each other and
that you care for each other.

MR. AND MRS. BENETTI: Yes.

WORKER: You're in the same situation, yet you are two different
people and react to it in different ways. I sense your
frustration with each other, and the difficulty you have
in accepting very different styles and rhythms. But I

	want you to know that neither of you has to be right or wrong. Your difference makes you very interesting people.
MRS. BENETTI:	(Beaming with pleasure) I never thought about being different; I just thought that something was wrong with me.

The worker searches for common ground and their mutual caring, and legitimizes their differences in style and pace of life. She reframes their criticism of each other by stating, "Your difference makes you very interesting people," offering a new perspective on their relationship difficulties. Mrs. Benetti is responsive to the comment, but her husband, perhaps feeling threatened, continues to berate her. The worker asks for her reaction:

MRS. BENETTI:	I don't like it when he yells at me. He makes me feel very bad.
MR. BENETTI:	Well, you do nothing all day long, and I have so many problems with work and money. But you can't understand that, can you?
MRS. BENETTI:	Yes, but . . .
MR. BENETTI:	(Interrupting) But what do you do about it? Do you get a job to help the finances?
MRS. BENETTI:	But how can I if I'm afraid to go out of the house alone? (Pause) You always criticize me, and it makes me feel so bad.
WORKER:	(To Mrs. Benetti) You feel yelled at like a child, and (to Mr. Benetti) you feel great pressure and frustration. Mr. Benetti, could you try to tell your wife about your pressures and frustrations without yelling at her?
MR. BENETTI:	Well, I get so mad.
WORKER:	I know it's tough when somebody is very angry to control the anger. What else could you do with it?
MR. BENETTI:	Ummm, maybe leave the room, or take a walk.
WORKER:	That would be a good start. Mrs. Benetti, if your husband forgets and starts to yell, could you remind him to go for a walk?
MRS. BENETTI:	Yes, I could do that, if he won't yell at me.
WORKER:	Mr. Benetti?
MR. BENETTI:	I will leave the room. I won't yell, but she has to try also.
WORKER:	What would you like her to do?
MR. BENETTI:	Last week, you mentioned something about a phobia clinic at the hospital. I want her to go.
WORKER:	Mrs. Benetti, if I help you make the arrangements, and your husband takes you, would you be willing to try the clinic?
MRS. BENETTI:	I'll do anything as long as Mario doesn't yell at me.

Mrs. Benetti conveys how devastated she is by her husband's constant verbal abuse. His rage immobilizes her. Mr. Benetti expresses frustration at not having an adult partner to share his life. Neither feels understood or supported by the other. The situation is maintained by his aggressiveness and her passivity. The worker wants them to empower themselves so they can change their own behaviors. Her hope is to unfreeze the rigid system of exchanges so they may themselves find new ways of relating to each other.

During the third session, Mrs. Benetti complained that her husband never talks to her. Mr. Benetti said he was so tired at night that all he wants to do is watch television. The worker then developed a homework assignment: the Benettis agreed to participate together in a planned leisure-time activity each day (without anyone else present). They practiced how they would do this by discussing a television show they had both seen. The worker notes, "This was the first time I saw this couple have a relaxed conversation; talk without complaining, arguing, or yelling; and actually laugh together."

In the next excerpt, Dena and her parents are meeting with the worker.

MRS. BENETTI:	I've been to the clinic twice now, and I think it's helping me. (Brightening) Look, I have this rubber band on my wrist, and now when I feel anxious, I just do this (showing how she snaps it).
DENA:	I don't know if it's good that you go the clinic, Mom. I'm afraid you may get worse and be hospitalized and then Dad would be alone.
WORKER:	What makes you think she might get worse instead of better?
DENA:	Maybe their relationship will change; they may get divorced.
WORKER:	You're concerned that your mother's getting help may mean that the family may change, and that worries you because you want your parents to stay together. Mr. and Mrs. Benetti, what do you think about Dena's worry that you may get divorced and the family would fall apart?

The parents' declaration that they never would divorce seemed to reassure Dena. Suddenly, the parents shift the discussion to their own concern that the children are leaving home.

MRS. BENETTI:	Mike is thinking of joining the army.
MR. BENETTI:	Sal is leaving for Italy next month to work on a farm. He's crazy. I don't know why he wants to go there to work on a farm. He'll be back soon, I'm sure.
MRS. BENETTI:	Well, I don't know why Mike is thinking about joining the army. He should be at home.
MR. BENETTI:	Yeah, he could get a good job.
WORKER:	It's hard to have your kids leave home. What worries you the most?
MRS. BENETTI:	I just like my kids at home with me.
MR. BENETTI:	Sal needs to be near home to help me with projects.
WORKER:	I sense you're feeling abandoned?

The worker encourages them to express their shared sadness at the prospect of "losing" their children. However, she doesn't pick up on the cultural norm that the generations live together, nor does she grasp the parents' desperation. They pressured Dena to leave the halfway house and return home. Dena soon became very depressed, refused to eat, and was rehospitalized. In the next excerpt, the worker confronts Mr. and Mrs. Benetti:

MRS. BENETTI:	We are so upset that Dena is in the hospital again.
MR. BENETTI:	She shouldn't be in the hospital. She's better than she ever was. I think I should bring her home.
WORKER:	(After a pause) She was doing much better until she stopped eating again.
MRS. BENETTI:	I think she needs to meet with you more often. You've helped her.
WORKER:	Dena feels very guilty about not being home to help you. She hears from her mother and grandmother that they are lonely and from her father that he needs her help with his paperwork. She feels helpless to meet your needs while she is trying so hard to get better. She needs your support and encouragement to stay where she is instead of your pressuring her to come home. She feels you say one thing to me in the office and the opposite at home. This has to stop; otherwise she will not get better.

The worker makes an appropriate therapeutic demand on the Benettis to stop sabotaging their daughter's treatment. They and the worker then agree to work on new ways of relating to their children (but still not in the cultural context). With the parents' knowledge, the worker met several times with the siblings. She helped them to improve their relationship and to support one another's efforts to be more independent. Their trust in the worker and her prior support enabled the parents to support Dena in her decision to remain at the halfway house. Mrs. Benetti continued at the phobia clinic and is proud of her progress. With the worker's encouragement and positive reinforcement, she assumed increasing responsibility for household management and relies less on her mother. Mr. Benetti joined the YMCA for exercise and to meet other people. He still has an occasional outburst of anger toward his wife but quickly leaves for a walk. Both are talking more to each other and, for the first time in years, are going to the movies. Dena, too, is making progress. She often chooses not to go home on weekends but remains responsive to her parents in their daily phone calls.

The family's caring for one another, and the parents' hopes for themselves and their children, facilitated their adaptation to the family transition that required new relationships to the children and to each other. They coped with several serious stressors and learned to manage negative feelings, improve interpersonal processes, and resolve stressful demands by cooperative problem solving. Effective coping raised the level of related-ness, competence, self-esteem, and self-direction in both partners, empow-ering them for continued growth. Mr. and Mrs. Benetti may be on their way to forging a new family paradigm as a couple that incorporates the new real-ity of their American-born children's transition toward independence. They are reorganizing the family structure of roles, tasks, routines, goals, and expectations. The tasks of children, parents, and grandparents might have been easier if the members had been helped to understand the generational and cultural aspects in their struggles.

Family Development, Paradigm, and Transformation

Over time and the life course, family members develop shared, implicit be-liefs about themselves, their environment, and their worldview (the family paradigm). A traumatic life stressor (such as death, severe injury, or illness) may require the family to change its ways of functioning and integrate the new reality into its worldview, transforming itself and creating a new para-digm. Such change is difficult and takes time and energy. Family violence or substance abuse, for example, is difficult to change.

Susan Mulligan, age thirty-one, Catholic and Irish American, lives in a ru-ral, working-class, factory town. She sought counseling at a women's center in connection with three major stressors. She has filed for divorce, and her husband, Richard, is not contesting. But he is asking the court for sole cus-tody of the three children (Seamus, age seven; Maura, age five; and Kevin, age three), which terrifies Susan. She lacked financial resources to obtain effective legal counsel, while Richard had no such problem.

Richard had abused Susan throughout the eight-year marriage. He abused her emotionally and physically, even raping her once when she was extremely ill and on heavy medication. During the past year, he beat her severely on three occasions. He was arrested for the most recent beating a month ago. That precipitated her divorce action.

Susan is an alcoholic who has remained sober for seven months. Susan states that Richard is an alcoholic, and she asked her attorney to request a court order for an alcoholic assessment and treatment of Richard. The attorney did not do so until after four months of pressure by the social worker.

Susan and Richard were ordered by the court to remain in their jointly owned home with their children, creating a dangerous situation for Susan and the children. Susan is very upset about this, as she is afraid of Richard, who continues to harass her. He owns a plumbing business, yet he has not paid the mortgage, car repair, or car insurance, nor has he helped with the daily care of the children, all of which he was ordered to do by the court. Susan works as a bookkeeper and pays for all food, heating oil, and child care expenses.

Susan suffers from a chronic, painful gynecological condition, which be-gan after Kevin's birth. A year ago the symptoms worsened. She finally went to a gynecologist, who prescribed medication. Symptoms continued, and six months later Susan underwent surgery. She still must take medication, and since it does not work well when combined with alcohol she stopped drinking when the medication was prescribed.

Susan's parents and eight siblings live in a nearby town. She has no contact with her siblings, but has a warm yet distant relationship with her father. She resents her mother's continuous criticism about how she raises her children and her mother's doubts that Susan is "really" an alcoholic. Mother contends that Susan has too many meetings. Susan says that her father spends most evenings in the local pub, three of her brothers and two of her sisters also drink heavily, but "my mother, who doesn't drink at all, doesn't like to think of this." Despite her criticism, her mother does help with evening child care as needed (both parents are employed days).

The Mulligans are awaiting the completion of a family study by the family relations officer of the county's superior court. Due to budget cuts and the backlog of cases, the study may not be completed for another eighteen months. In the meantime, Susan is clearly at risk of further violence. Her patterns of communicating with her parents, her lawyer, her alcohol counselor, and the social worker alternate between cooperativeness and blaming everyone else for her problems. Although she is consistent in maintaining sobriety and being responsible with her children, she is defensive and wary. This makes a poor impression on her attorney, the judge, and her alcohol counselor.

The social worker records their work together:

Our immediate agreed-upon aims were to improve Susan's relationships with uncaring personnel in the justice system, and with her mother and her children; strengthen her cognitive and perceptual capacities in order to correct misperceptions and faulty interpretations; and improve problem solving.

Susan attends Alcoholics Anonymous (AA) every day and our center's weekly group for substance-using and battered women. She sees her alcohol counselor and me every week. Her compliance with the various treatments may be fueled by fear of losing her children, but she also says that AA and the group are "my only sources of sanity these days." She was suspicious and wary with me until recently. By now, the judge and three sets of attorneys (representing Susan, Richard, and the children) view both parents as difficult. Her attorney failed to push for Richard's alcohol assessment and treatment, and the judge handled the domestic violence with arrogance and insensitivity. Susan compounds these terrible realities by rude and abrasive attitudes and responses that evoke still harsher judgments and attitudes on the part of the attorneys and judge.

Susan doesn't yet follow through on my efforts to show her that if she deals with her attorney more productively, she may avoid an undesirable custody arrangement. Instead, she blames him for representing her poorly and feels victimized by him. On the other hand, the children's teachers, day care providers, and pediatrician stated to me that Susan is a responsible parent, while Richard has not been to see any of them. The pediatrician reported that the children do not manifest fetal alcohol syndrome. They are physically healthy and of normal intelligence or better.

The children's attorney, whom Susan was forced to engage and pay for because Richard refused to, plans to recommend joint custody. She views both parents as equally dysfunctional and adds that Susan is rude to her and wastes her time with irrelevant information. She rejects my attempts to advocate for Susan and the children, as dispassionate and tactful as I try to be, and "ordered" me to have no further meetings with the children.

Considering all this, Susan is coping well with an extremely stressful and potentially dangerous situation. She continues to hold down her job, care for her children as best she can (at least from outward signs), drive her kids and herself to all the places they need to be, and maintain the difficult relationship with her mother. She takes care of her own health by remaining sober, taking her medication, and seeing her gynecologist regularly. Relations with the children have improved, and her limit setting is calmer and more consistent. She has also complied with every task the judge put to her and takes pride in being able to perform under such pressure.

Susan has also striven mightily to meet the terms of what we both view as a very unfair and potentially dangerous court order (continuing to live with Richard). Together, we worked out a safety plan should Richard become violent, and we taught the children how to dial 911 in an emergency. I talked with Susan's attorney and the children's attorney about the primary need for safety, described research findings about men who batter, and pressed for an alcohol assessment of Richard. After months of my continuous pressure, Susan's attorney filed a motion that she and the children be allowed to live separately from Richard and that he be ordered to undergo alcohol assessment and treatment.

Coping with the attorneys and judge is still ineffective as Susan fails to see how her anger and behavior lead to their rejecting, pejorative attitudes. I am now using rehearsal, role-play, and positive reinforcement to help Susan manage her negative feelings in a more constructive way, bolstered by my emotional support. We're working on correcting her false assumptions and distortions about these people through reciprocal role-play. Improved cognitive and perceptual capacities are likely to empower Susan and give her more control of her own life. These tasks, however, are extraordinarily difficult for Susan in light of the abuse and neglect by her husband and the court, the attorneys (including her own), and the family relations officer.

Susan and the worker may need to undertake further work, for example, "walking" Susan through the judicial process in preparation for the court appearances that lie ahead. This could increase her tolerance of delays and decrease her open, self-destructive anger. Similarly, the worker might help her to revise "self-conversations" that she, like all of us, holds with herself, especially those in which she evaluates and interprets her unpleasant experiences. For example, instead of telling herself that the people in authority hate her, Susan could practice repeating to herself before scheduled encounters, "No matter how unpleasant they are, I am going to be respectful and calm when I explain my difficulties to these people, because everything will be better if they like me." Assertiveness training might also help her deal more effectively with the lawyers and judge, and even with her mother.

Depending on the court's decision regarding divorce and custody, Susan and her children face several difficult life transitions that will require a new organization of family roles, tasks, rules, routines, and goals. Ultimately, a new family paradigm will need to incorporate new values and norms (e.g., sobriety, the centrality of childrearing, and the importance of pleasurable time together) and changed beliefs and attitudes regarding interpersonal relationships both inside and outside the family. In these ways, Susan and her children could transform their abusive, addictive nuclear family to an abuse-free, alcohol-free, healthy solo-parent family. Such an achievement will merit a celebratory ritual.

In the next example, a couple seeks social work help because of escalating verbal and physical abuse. Denise Carter, age thirty-five, and Melvin Carter, age forty-seven, are an African American couple living in a suburb with Denise's two adolescent daughters (see Appendix A for a family assessment). They are nonpracticing Protestants. Mr. Carter is a recovering alcoholic, sober six years; Mrs. Carter is a daily beer drinker. The couple married eighteen months ago after living together for two years. Both have been married before. Mr. Carter has three grown children from his first marriage, all living out of state. After their marriage, their arguing about Mrs. Carter's and her family members' drinking turned to screaming matches. Last May, after Mr. Carter lost his job (he charged the employer with racial discrimination), the constant verbal arguments escalated. Mr. Carter became violent, and Mrs. Carter called the police. In September, Mrs. Carter became violent, and he left home for three weeks. Mrs. Carter initiated counseling two weeks ago, alarmed that the relative calm following Mr. Carter's return is now replaced by days and nights of constant verbal fighting. The couple and the social work intern contracted to meet for eight sessions to deal with their dysfunctional communication and relationship patterns. At the end of the period, they are to consider whether they want to continue to work on their relationship or whether they want help in separating.

Both Mrs. and Mr. Carter come from large families. Mrs. Carter has six siblings, all living in her neighborhood. There is a history of alcoholism in her maternal grandmother's family, and two of her brothers abuse drugs and alcohol. Mr. Carter's siblings live out of state. His father, who died twenty years ago, had been a recovering alcoholic for the last fifteen years of his life. Mr. Carter and one of his brothers are also recovering alcoholics. Six years ago Mr. Carter entered a one-month alcohol rehabilitation program; subsequently, he lived for six months in a drug and alcohol rehabilitation halfway house. He has remained sober since then. His determination to stay sober results in a militant anti-alcohol stance. When Mr. Carter met Mrs. Carter, she was not working and, by both accounts, was living a partying lifestyle. Both Carters attribute Mrs. Carter's change in habits—cutting down on beer drinking, maintaining more regular sleep patterns, and finding and holding a clerical job—to Mr. Carter's encouragement and support.

Mrs. Carter grew up in a family with fluid boundaries. Today, family members and friends sleep and eat at each other's apartments with no prior arrangement and, according to Mr. Carter, little respect for individual or marital privacy. Individuals seldom own problems; the group works on them together. This lack of unit boundaries is a crucial issue in the Carters' marriage. Mr. Carter resents Mrs. Carter's siblings walking into their bedroom at 11 P.M.; he also resents the time she spends at her mother's and sister's homes. He describes his family of origin as fairly formal. Visitors to his extended family were by invitation, and friends never blended easily into family situations. He rarely interacts with his own family; his interactions with Mrs. Carter's family are mostly limited to breaking up their drinking parties in his apartment and telling them to leave.

Communication between Mrs. Carter and Mr. Carter is vituperative, driven at present by Mr. Carter's increasingly toxic reaction to Mrs. Carter's drinking. They are so intensely reactive to each other that they have difficulty sustaining any nonvolatile exchange. They alternate between heated fighting and withdrawal—Mr. Carter into silence and TV, and Mrs. Carter into her family, her friends, and beer. Although both appear to understand the role that environmental factors (unemployment, job, and financial pressures) play in their verbal and physical violence, their animosity is so great that their focus is on blaming each other. The Carters are currently experiencing the effects of breadwinner role reversal, a reversal painful to Mr. Carter and somewhat confusing to Mrs. Carter. Just at the time Mr. Carter was fired, Mrs. Carter received a promotion. Mr. Carter spends his days driving Mrs. Carter to and from her job and looking for work.

The isolation of Mr. Carter's days is not alleviated by contact with peers. Mr. Carter and Mrs. Carter developed friendship patterns as alike as their family relationship patterns are different. They cultivated drinking buddies, people who drifted in and out of their lives and were brought together by their mutual interest in partying. Mrs. Carter still has these buddies. Mr. Carter, encouraged by his association with AA, avoids his onetime buddies and is estranged from people he and Mrs. Carter had in common.

In the first session, the Carters were fully engaged in a discussion of their perspectives on the marital issues. They agreed to devote eight sessions to work on improving their life together. When the intern went to the waiting room to greet them for the second time, they were seated at opposite ends of the room, slumped in their chairs, and glowering. Once in the office, Mr. Carter sat in the farthest corner and Mrs. Carter sat close to the intern.

INTERN: You seem upset; are you having a rough time?

MR. CARTER: Yeah.

MRS. CARTER: We had a big argument over the TV on Saturday and Sunday because I said channel 2 was 3.

MR. CARTER: Yeah. Not only that. She's beginning to irritate me.

MRS. CARTER: Yeah. He's beginning to irritate me. See I said 2 was 3 on TV, and he said that I knew it all.

MR. CARTER: No. You see, first of all you irritated me from before. You know what you did. You irritated me from Friday. You called me up and you were all fired up, and I don't like that. ("Fired up" is Mr. Carter's term for being drunk.) I'm getting aggravated. I'm getting sick of it.

INTERN: (To Mr. Carter) Last time you were here, you said that you didn't like Mrs. Carter's drinking. Is this what you are saying now?

MR. CARTER: Yeah. Because she gets nasty, and I don't like it. She called me to get her at her sister's on Friday; and I came when she said to. I waited fifteen minutes, and she came out and says she is not ready to go. She done that on purpose. I know she did.

MRS. CARTER: But I was gonna send my niece out, but thought (taps her head), "No, I should go myself. He won't like it if I send her." So I went out. But I don't like to always be thinking like that, walking on eggshells. That's not me.

INTERN: Help me get a better picture of when these things happened. It was Friday when you went to pick Mrs. Carter up, and Saturday you had the argument over the TV—and Sunday too?

MR. CARTER: Yeah. She was trying to make me look stupid in front of the kids. I was showing her the paper, just trying to explain. But you don't read. You don't even know what's going on half the time. Channel 2 is not Channel 3!

MRS. CARTER: No! No! Channel 2 is the same as Channel 3—on the cable station—they're the same. I know that. I was right.

INTERN: But Channel 2 and 3 are not what you are really arguing about—your argument started on Friday night.

MR. CARTER: No. I was irritated before.

MRS. CARTER: Melvin can do whatever he wants, but I have to do what he wants. I'm getting frustrated! I'm getting tired! Like I told

you about not sending my niece out there—I don't like to be
thinking all the time.

INTERN: One of the things—if you're going to live more peacefully
with each other—is that even if you don't like to, and you may
not like to, you both have to stop and think. Especially
during the time when you're trying to see if you can make
things good enough to discover if there's something still good
between you. If you don't do that, nothing is ever going to
change because (I snap my fingers) you trigger each other.

MRS. CARTER: Sometimes I don't feel comfortable about things.

MR. CARTER: (Ignoring this) Everything starts out like this. You were
wrong. Channel 2 and 3 are not the same. If you weren't all
fired up all the time, you'd know that.

MRS. CARTER: You're draining me. I can't go to work, and I can't function
because you are draining me.

MR. CARTER: That's always your story. That's your famous story. You better
get another story. I tell you I'm sick of it! (Yelling and lunging
out of the chair)

INTERN: OK! (I cut the air with my hand to separate them.) We can't
get anywhere if we try to deal with five things at once. We're
dealing with the drinking; we're dealing with the way you
argue, the way that you talk to each other; we're dealing with
TV channels. You are arguing about Channels 2 and 3, but it
could be about anything. Mrs. Carter, you could say, "That's
a crow." And Mr. Carter, you say, "No, it's a pigeon." So one
of the things that's very important is to stop and say, "Hey,
we're not arguing about 2 and 3." What are we really arguing
about? Is it the tension about drinking? Let's get to the
bottom line.

MR. CARTER: Yeah. She already knew. It's that drinking that's getting
to me.

INTERN: OK. Let's talk about that.

MR. CARTER: That's the real problem. The drinking. It's making me sick.
The smell of it is making me sick. Most of the things start
with the drinking.

INTERN: Do you see it that way, Mrs. Carter?

MRS. CARTER: Yeah. Most of the time.

MR. CARTER: You always irritate me with that drinking.

MRS. CARTER: Yeah. You ain't so fine, always yelling at my brothers, at my
sisters. You call me stupid. You're the one that's stupid.

MR. CARTER: Bitch! You can't even get up in the morning. (Rising out of his
chair) Bitch!

INTERN: Mr. Carter! Get back into your chair. There will be no
threats! We need to take turns talking. For a while, I just
want you to talk to me. (I reposition my body.) Please, each of

you take turns talking to me—and directly talk to me about the drinking. Please do not interrupt when the other is talking. Mrs. Carter, let's begin with you. Tell me about the drinking. Friday night, for example, describe the evening, what it was like, what happened, how much you drank, and so on.

The Carters are angry and want to continue their fights. They are highly reactive to each other. The worker's initial efforts to develop a structure for the interview and to slow down the pace failed partly because of the Carters' rage, but also because of the student practitioner's discomfort with the intensity of their feelings. When she invites them to "help me get a better picture of when these things happened," she unwittingly invites them to refuel their television channel argument. She exhorts them, "You do have to stop and think," and misses their tremendous mutual pain and confusion. In the student's analysis of this particular intervention, she wrote,

---

I am aware that my nonverbal presentation is that of a preacher. I am sitting erect on the edge of my chair and speaking in a loud projecting voice, scolding. I was thinking that I had to give them an answer to their problems, and I was feeling somewhat desperate. I moved away from their frightening anger.

In the final intervention, the worker prescribed a structure to the session. This was a breakthrough, as the Carters accepted the structure and took turns in directly talking to the worker. Having the communication go through her broke the destructive feedback loop, and they begin to listen to each other. In violent families, the partners need nurturing and expression of concern for their needs before they can use cognitive inputs.

In the next chapter, we examine dysfunctional group processes.

TEN

HELPING WITH DYSFUNCTIONAL
GROUP PROCESSES

Mutual aid is the primary rationale for the development of group services. Dysfunctional processes emerge at different points in a group's life course, and the group becomes blocked from serving as a system of support.

Internal Group Functions, Structures, and Processes as Life Stressors

By their very nature, group mutual aid systems universalize individual issues, reduce isolation, and mitigate stigma through their powerful yet subtle interpersonal processes. A formed or natural group led by a social worker is comprised of individuals who come together under agency auspices to work on a common life issue. Schwartz (1971, p. 7) defines a social work group as a "collection of people who need each other in order to work on certain common tasks in an agency that is hospitable to those tasks." A group's primary functions are to establish and maintain a favorable interchange with its environment and develop a mutual aid system. The same two functions present challenges to the group's survival: to manage environmentally induced stressors and interpersonally induced stressors. When successful in carrying out the twin functions and meeting the two challenges, the group is in adaptive balance.

As members develop a sense of purpose and commonality, they begin to share experiences and concerns. Safe or less threatening issues are raised first to test the worker's and other members' genuineness and competence. Through the testing, members begin to develop and reinforce mutual bonds and alliances as they figure out where each member and the worker belong in the interpersonal system. When collective support and individual comfort are in place, members are willing to risk more sensitive and sometimes even taboo concerns. When they learn to share and to relate to one another, they experience a "multiplicity of helping relationships," with all members investing and participating in the helping process rather than only the social worker (Schwartz, 1961, p. 18). Since they have experienced similar life stressors, they are more receptive to others' views and suggestions. Moreover, as a microcosm of members' interpersonal self-presentations, the group is a rich arena in which members can examine their own adaptive and maladaptive perceptions and behaviors. Through their exchanges, members develop and practice new interpersonal processes and environmental activities and receive feedback from the group on their efforts.[1]

Finally, groups have the potential to be a force through which members act and gain control and mastery over their environments. A passive retreat from one's environment inevitably leads to feelings of incompetence and impotence. In contrast, being active in a group, and influencing one's environment, helps develop competence and a sense of personal, interpersonal, and political empowerment (Berman-Rossi, 2005; Lee, 2005).

Behavioral Expressions of Internal Group Difficulties

Dysfunctional interpersonal patterns in formed groups are often expressed in factionalism, monopolism, scapegoating, withdrawal, and ambiguous communications. While these processes are usually dysfunctional for most members, they can also serve an unrecognized and unintended function of maintaining the group's equilibrium. Thus, they are best understood by focusing on the functions they serve for the individual and for the group.

When *factionalism* becomes a fixed pattern of relations, a clique or alliance provides its members with greater satisfaction and a greater sense of identification than are experienced by the total group. This is desirable for the clique, but it isolates and rejects the other group members. This is dysfunctional for them and threatens the constancy of the group. Autocratic leadership promotes factions as a way to obtain security and protection from punitive interaction with the leader. The members then compete for the leader's attention and for improved status for themselves at the cost of unaffiliated members, undermining their status and security.

In *monopolism*, one member produces overwhelming detail in describing ideas, feelings, and experiences. At the manifest level, this gives the monopolist control over her anxiety and the group process and its content with positive consequences for her (Bogdanoff & Elbaum, 1978; Yalom & Leszcs, 2005). The other group members tolerate and even encourage such communication because monopolist behavior protects them from self-disclosure and personal involvement. At the latent level, however, the behavior has negative consequences for all group members, including the monopolist, by preventing the group from fulfilling its purpose and successfully completing tasks. Most monopolists monopolize within the boundaries of the group's purpose rather than the more difficult to deal with tangential monopolist.

In a day treatment program, a new worker was assigned to an adult group (ages twenty-seven to forty-five) composed of members with a psychiatric diagnosis. The group had been meeting for over a year. The current main theme is dealing with parents and agency staff members. The members justifiably feel that they are not treated as adults in spite of their chronological age. From the first meeting, Mr. Marcotti monopolized group interaction. Whereas in the day treatment center and in individual sessions he was quiet and withdrawn, in the group he has always been the "talker." One could depend on him to keep the session going. Through the group, he learned to assert himself, and experienced how good it feels to talk and to have attention and power. The worker began to view the monopolization as a hindrance to the group's growth and tried to reduce his participation. He experienced the worker's efforts as discrediting his role and fought to hold on to it. The worker recorded:

Mr. Marcotti was talking for a period of time about his sister's death. I stated that it must be very painful to lose a family member, and inquired if anyone else experienced it.

MS. RAINES:	I had a cousin who died last year, and I felt sad.
MR. MARCOTTI:	(Interrupting) I didn't even know my sister was sick.
SOCIAL WORKER:	What do you mean?
MR. MARCOTTI:	Well, my mom told me one day that my sister was in the hospital, and then the next day she died.
SOCIAL WORKER:	This seems like a very painful experience for you, but could you hold it until Ms. Raines finished?
MR. MARCOTTI:	Yeah, I guess so.
SOCIAL WORKER:	(I encouraged Ms. Raines to continue.)
MS. RAINES:	Well, Mr. Marcotti can keep talking—I can wait.
SOCIAL WORKER:	I think it would be a good idea if you each had a chance to talk and if we waited for one person to finish before another starts. What does each of you think about this? (While they nodded in agreement, the group sat in silence.)
MS. SATZMAN:	One time I told my mother I didn't want to have my hair cut and I would tell her when I did, but she didn't even listen to me.
SOCIAL WORKER:	It sounds like you were very frustrated and possibly annoyed because your opinion wasn't respected.
MS. SATZMAN:	That's right. I don't see why my mother doesn't ever listen to me. I'm not dumb, you know.
MR. MARCOTTI:	Yeah, my mom didn't even tell me when my sister was sick and put into the hospital.

SOCIAL WORKER:	Uh-huh, I see. So, Ms. Satzman, you are saying that you would be like to be treated like everyone else.
MS. SATZMAN:	Yeah, I'm not a little kid anymore.
MR. MARCOTTI:	I don't know why my mom didn't tell me that my sister was sick. I have a right to know what's going on, too.
SOCIAL WORKER:	It seems you both are upset about not being treated like adults. Has anyone else had similar experiences?
MR. MARCOTTI:	I have another experience of when I wasn't listened to. One time . . . (After a couple of minutes, I interrupted him.)
SOCIAL WORKER:	Mr. Marcotti, I appreciate your contributions, but maybe we could hear from other members and then we'll get back to you, OK? (This pattern continued, and I found myself increasingly annoyed.)

As we shall discuss later, the worker's feelings and reactions become part of the group system's pattern of dysfunctional communications and relationships.

Scapegoating in formed groups is similar to the process in families. The scapegoat status serves important latent functions for both the individual member and the group. At the group level, deviance helps clarify behavioral norms, sharpens group boundaries, and promotes solidarity. For the individual members, the contrast between the self and the scapegoated member is reassuring and offers protection against the fear of similar behavior or attributes in the self. For the scapegoated member, the status provides satisfaction as well as pain. The scapegoat is often at the center of attention and may also partake of secondary gains in the sense of martyrdom, helplessness, and enslavement of the self in the service of others (Antsey, 1982; Cohen & Schermer, 2002; Shulman, 1967).

Usually the scapegoat is the most vulnerable member of the group. In a school group of African American youngsters, the lone Latina member was scapegoated. Her responses to the members' provocations lead to the institutionalization of the scapegoating role. An adolescent male group was threatened by the behavior of an effeminate member; their communications were replete with ridicule and hostility. Reciprocally, his responses influenced the scope and intensity of members' reactions and his exclusion through scapegoating. In a geriatric facility, the least lucid member evoked hostility from the others. She represented a safe target for the displacement of members' feelings of despair, impotence, confusion, and anger. The disoriented member's inability to fight back only frightened the other members and triggered their further acting out.

While scapegoating controls and suppresses serious group issues at the manifest level, it has negative consequences at the latent level that entrap the group and the scapegoated member. To the extent that a group permits its members to exploit one member in order to maintain their own functioning, all members become vulnerable to stress from personal, group, or environmental processes. The scapegoated individual suffers grave harm, internalizing the negative perceptions of others as self-contempt. The group members develop dysfunctional interpersonal processes that reflect their evasion, negation, guilt, and projections.

Frank is a mildly developmentally challenged member of a "truancy group." He exhibits poor self-control and occasional bizarre clowning. In an early meeting, Stanley was describing how the teacher makes school impossible for him. The work is too hard, and the teacher calls on him when he doesn't know the answers. As all the boys began to laugh, Angel asked Frank, "What're you laughing about?" I asked if anyone else had a similar experience. Frank replied, "Yeah, in dancing class, all the kids laugh at me." He demonstrated his dancing, and explained that the teacher made him stand in the corner because he made mistakes. Billy said, "Frank, you are so damn stupid anyway." Angel added, "You don't even know how to read, write, or the multiplication table." All the boys laughed and joined the attack.

Frank performs a critical function for the group, permitting members to evade necessary work on painful life stressors and to displace frustration and anger. The youngsters' hostilities are managed by focusing attention on one member, the clown, who mediates conflict by providing the group with comic relief. For Frank, the positive consequence is the momentary glow of attention. The fact that both the "deviant" and the group benefit from the scapegoating underscores the transactional nature of scapegoating. But in the long run, the process has negative consequences for the individual and for the group. It further isolates the scapegoated member, and the members do not grow and develop their full potential. Thus, the social worker must understand not only what group and environment processes make scapegoating necessary, but also what processes in the scapegoat lead to his inviting and accepting the dysfunctional communications and relationships.

Sources of Internal Stressors in Groups

Even after much effort some groups never begin, others begin and then disintegrate, and still others reinforce deviant and dysfunctional behaviors. Even groups that achieve an adaptive balance may experience upset in the balance at certain points in the group's development. These upsets are natural and even essential to the group's construction of a mutual aid system. When internal or external stressors upset the balance, the group attempts to regain balance by various coping efforts. However, while some efforts may temporarily relieve stress, in the process members might develop dysfunctional communication and relationship patterns that create further stress. Such dysfunctional interpersonal processes can emerge from formational and structural elements.

Formational Elements.   Lack of clarity about group purpose is a frequent formational problem (Kurland & Salmon, 1998; Sloane, 2003). If members' needs diverge, or the agency's agenda does not fit group interests, or the social worker's conception of group purpose is ambiguous, then members may withdraw, test incessantly, or act out. For example, for five years, a group of mildly developmentally challenged young adults had been meeting as a social club in a community center. A social work student wanted to explain her proposed short-term service to group members. As the director felt that members would have difficulty sharing personal concerns in a formal group setting, he invited the student to their Saturday evening social gathering.

Arriving in a casual business suit, sweater, and scarf, the student immediately felt out of place, as the members were clad in jeans. The club president, Hank, introduced her, stating that she had some services she wanted to offer the group. The student recorded that before she could present her well-rehearsed offer, she was bombarded with questions: "Are you selling something?" "Are you a doctor?" "My name is Gary—what is yours?"

SOCIAL WORK INTERN:	As Hank told you, my name is Joyce, and I am a social work intern.
VARIOUS MEMBERS:	Are you a therapist? I have one already. I'm already in a group in my program; I don't need another group.
SOCIAL WORK INTERN:	I'm here to tell you about a group I thought some of you might be interested in, but before I explain it, maybe everyone can introduce him and herself, so I will know who you are. (All introduce themselves.) I thought the group could discuss the jobs you have, the difficulties you may have had on the job, how it feels to be different, not only on the job, but also . . .
GARY:	Oh, you mean because sometimes we're discriminated against in the job market?
SOCIAL WORK INTERN:	(Continuing) Yes, maybe some of you have experienced discrimination in other ways too, and the group could be a place to talk openly about experiences and to share what has been helpful for you at such times.
DANIEL:	Why do you want to focus on problems? This is Saturday night, time for rest and relaxation . . . why are you so formal, you can talk to us like you talk to anyone else, we're all human, you know.
GARY:	Give the girl a break; she's just trying to help us.
SOCIAL WORK INTERN:	I guess I'm a little nervous, I don't know you that well and . . .
GARY:	Sit down, get to know us, we don't bite. (He laughed, and other members joined in.)
SOCIAL WORK INTERN:	I am really interested in talking with you about some of your feelings about being labeled "retarded" in this society.
NANCY:	I am not going to be in this group.
BARRY:	I don't like that word at all; I have heard that word all my life, and it is like a prison sentence for me.

JACKIE:	(Slamming the table) Let me tell you, I don't let anyone push me around; one time a guy started laughing at me, I let him have it. I don't let anyone push me around!
NANCY:	(Walking around, obviously very angry) So that's what the group is about, that word, that disgusting word? (Gary and Cynthia tried to help me, and an argument broke out among the members.)
SOCIAL WORK INTERN:	Let me try to explain better what I meant. (But it became clear that I had lost the members, created an internal group conflict, and put a damper on their Saturday night activity.)

At the next meeting, the student changed the focus to helping members to share information about health-related, leisure time, and housing resources available to them in the community. They appreciatively accepted the revised conception of group purpose. This focus met their desire and need to focus on the "positives" in their lives.

Group composition dramatically influences interpersonal processes (Gitterman, 2005). Overly homogeneous groups are apt to lack vitality. A group whose members are all depressed, for example, could find communication stifled. Also, a homogeneous group is sometimes unable to absorb a member who deviates from group norms. For instance, a group of light-skinned Puerto Rican girls with one African American member or a parent's group with one father may not be able to assimilate the member who is different (Brown & Mistry, 1994).

A member describes a poignant experience of being "different" in a group:

> My previous social worker referred me to a group at a mental health clinic. She told me it would give me something to do and people other than my children to talk to. Then I found out it was a group for recently released mental patients, many of whom were still psychotic. They talked to themselves and sometimes lost sight of reality for moments. They frightened me. Look, I know I am nuts, but I'm not that nuts. Maybe someday I will be, but let me get there in my own time. When I have a nervous breakdown, I want it to be my very own and not taught to me by members of my therapy group. (Gitterman & Nadelman, 1999, pp. 78–79; Gitterman & Schaeffer, 1972, p. 290)

On the other hand, groups that are too heterogeneous lack stability because members with limited interests or concerns in common find it difficult to relate to one another (Fluhr, 2004; Saino, 2003). In school-age groups, for example, differing personalities skew interpersonal trends as some members act out and others withdraw.

A coed group of eleven children was composed of subgroups (of fifth graders and sixth graders) of students who knew each other from their classrooms. Gender issues also came into play because there were relatively few boys. This created another natural subgroup within the larger group:

Jean began to speak, and Ann, Barbara, and Tracy began to fool around with one another. Richard said something quietly to them about being quiet. Tracy immediately told him to "shut up" and called him a "tub of lard." Barbara and Ann began to laugh. Jean became quiet. I looked over at Tracy, Barbara, and Ann, and told them that Jean was talking and they should not interrupt. Richard looked at the group of girls and said, "See, I told you, you shouldn't be talking." All three girls told him to shut up and continued to call him names, laughing. I told the girls that there was to be no name-calling in this group, and asked them if they remembered the group rules. Tracy looked at me and said loudly that Richard had started it, and called him still another name. I asked Richard if that were true.

Before he could answer, the three girls broke in to say that it was true. I told them to please be quiet and give Richard a chance to speak. Laughing, they all looked at Richard and waited for him to speak. He hesitated and then, with a little smile, said that it was not true. Simultaneously and angrily, the girls called him a liar. I told everyone to be quiet and listen to Jean. I invited Jean to continue. She hesitated for a moment, shyly smiling. The other three began to giggle. I looked at them angrily and said, "I am tired of your being rude to other members." They tried to suppress their smiles, and Tracy pulled her chair in close with exaggerated interest in what Jean was saying. I looked sternly at her, and she moved her chair back with a smile to the other two. Barbara and Ann laughed.

Jean went on to describe an interesting experience. I nodded and asked whether anyone else had experienced something similar. Frank had been drawing something with his body sideways to the group, and Richard was looking over his shoulder. Billy was also drawing, but he kept his face to the group. Frank looked up from his drawing and shared his own experience. I attempted to comment on this, but was interrupted by Tracy, Ann, and Barbara, who were giggling about Frank's drawing, and asking him to show his drawing. I looked at them and asked them to be quiet. Ann said loudly that Frank was drawing and he wouldn't show it to the group. I asked Frank if he would show his drawing. He shook his head with a smile and continued to draw. The girls insisted that he show the drawing to them. I told everyone to please be quiet, and asked Frank and Billy to stop drawing and turn around to be with the group. I waited until they reluctantly did so. The girls taunted them and giggled. Frank told them to shut up, and Billy joined him. I stopped and told Tracy, Barbara, and Ann that I wanted them to sit between the boys and directed them where to sit, starting with Tracy. They resisted loudly, saying that they did not want to sit by those "idiots." Nevertheless I insisted.

The girls became very angry, and Tracy turned her chair around and the other two followed her. I asked them to please turn their chairs around and waited. They did not. I said, "All right, then, everybody leave, the meeting is over. Until you guys can start acting mature in this group and participate, I don't want you to come back." The group froze and everyone became quiet. The three girls immediately turned their chairs back around and said that they would be good now. I told them quietly to leave and that we would discuss this next week.

While the worker's behaviors certainly contributed, heterogeneous composition undermined members' ability to achieve common focus and mutuality.

Group size can also skew interpersonal processes (Bond, 2005; Ohtsubo & Masuchi, 2004; Price, Smith, & Lench, 2006). Groups that are too large cannot provide sufficient opportunities for individual participation. Groups that are too small make excessive demands for intimacy.

Open-ended groups with fluctuating membership tend to develop two chronic problems: members lose their original sense of purpose and vitality, and the group remains stuck in an early phase of development (Galinsky & Schopler, 1985, 1989). The shifting membership impedes the development of mutual aid.

The type of group formed (educational, stressor-solving, behavioral change, task, and social development) can also create interpersonal group obstacles. For example, as previously discussed in chapter 5, the author supervised the worker who formed a group for parents of developmentally disabled children to develop community resources for their children. The members enthusiastically agreed to the offer of service. However, they did not invest energy into the work or follow through on agreed upon tasks. After a few weeks, the worker reached for the obstacle and learned that the members wanted to share their concerns about having a developmentally disabled child; they wanted an opportunity to ventilate their frustration about the child and lack of social supports, and to help each other with childrearing.

Currently, to meet the demands of research protocols, workers are increasingly assigned to lead educational groups. They are provided with prescribed curricula in order to test the efficacy of an intervention. These curriculum-driven groups require the leader to direct the presentation of content, too often at the expense of mutual aid (Kurland & Salmon, 2002). For example, a social work intern placed in a special early childhood center was asked to form an educational group for parents with autistic children. A curriculum was designed to help parents with very specific and challenging needs. The curriculum focused on providing parents with information that would help them to prepare their children (and themselves) for the necessary struggles that lay ahead of them as well as to improve the parent–child interactions. Topics focused on coping with the life challenges of supporting, educating, and caring for a child with pervasive developmental challenges (Moreno, 2001). These parents had to learn to parent a chronologically four-year-old child who was functioning at the level of a one-year-old. The group developed a strong dependency upon the curriculum, the distributed materials, and the leader. This pattern induced a passivity that limited their involvement with and ability to help each other. In the fourth meeting, a member who had a painful encounter with a teacher stated that she wanted to talk about her disappointment with the school rather than continue with the scheduled presentation. This became a turning point in the group (Gitterman & Wayne, 2003), and the intern's practice will be illustrated later in the chapter.

Structural and Normative Factors.   Social structure and culture evolve in the group and mediate between environmental demands and group needs, and between group demands and individual needs. Social structure represents networks of roles through which responsibilities are allocated, decisions are reached, and relationship and communication patterns are established. Roles may shift and change as work continues and as the group passes through phases of its development (Spira & Reed, 2003; Toseland & Rivas, 2005). Some structures are too loose and others are too tight for adaptive interchanges to take place within the group, and between the group and its environment. In a group that is too loosely structured, individual autonomy may be valued, but the members do not experience a sense of identity and support that comes from group solidarity. Members are not sufficiently integrated into a structure, so that patterns of relationship and communication may not permit involvement in developmental or environmental issues. In a group that is tightly structured, over-involvement of group members with one another leads to patterns of relationship and communication that limit adaptive interchange with the social environment. The price for belonging is a reduction in individual autonomy.

As in families, subunits also evolve in groups. Subgroups are usually composed of members with similar interests and interpersonal orientations to authority and intimacy. Members who are similar on these dimensions tend to find or "drift" toward each other, seeking security together. When subgroups are fluid and responsive to the phases of group development, they provide important support to group members. When they are "frozen," inflexible, and exclusionary, however, they are frequent sources of dysfunctional interpersonal patterns (Berman-Rossi, 1992; Kelly & Berman-Rossi, 1999). For example, in a three-parent group at a local Head Start program, Mrs. Davis and Mrs. Patterson had developed a very strong friendship, which included lunch and play dates on a fairly regular basis. Mrs. Smith, however, was new to this area and was rarely included in their social activities.

In the group meetings, she found herself left out of their conversations and, consequently, withdrew from conversations. The preexisting friendship created an "us" and "her" internal group strain.

The social structure and its patterns of relationship lead to the emergence of a *group culture* (Armelius & Armelius, 2000; Toseland & Rivas, 2005). Members set group norms regarding rights and responsibilities, modes of work, bodily and verbal expressions of feelings, and styles of relating and communicating. These unite group members and integrate their behaviors. Norms that are rigidly defined or punitively enforced, however, pose problems for members seeking to develop and maintain individuality and a degree of autonomy. The violation of norms that prohibit certain behavior poses a serious threat to group survival and generates powerful sanctions resulting in expulsion, ostracism, or scapegoating of a member. For example, in a young adult parents' group, one member arrived to the group meeting smelling of alcohol. Other group members confronted her. She had violated a prescribed group norm of sobriety and the notion that members must be working on being good parents.

When group norms are ambiguous, members become anxious and may engage in continuous testing of the leader and the group in order to establish guidelines. Whether ambiguous or clear, norms may be unevenly enforced, reflecting preferential treatment and double messages and creating rivalries. Members may subscribe to discrepant personal norms of morality, logic, and attractiveness. Such discrepancies could also create dysfunctional patterns.

Both the structure and culture of the group are influenced by environmental factors including societal, community, and agency values and norms, as well as opportunities and limitations. Group members may respond to environmental limitations with apathy, which then inhibits their use of whatever resources are available within the group and environment. Others may turn inward and project their anger and frustration onto the group members. In groups composed of minority schoolchildren, the author observed the children's consistent tendency to internalize and to project teachers' negative judgments of their intellectual abilities and potentials onto one another.

The group service may not be adequately supported by the host agency's structures and procedures. Without administrative approval and commitment to the group service, the worker "walks on eggshells." In response to any perceived issue, such as noncooperation by a hospital patient or "noisy" children in a school or social agency, the medical or psychiatric chief, school principal, or agency director may disrupt or even terminate the group. Similarly, without interdisciplinary staff involvement, a group service is easily interrupted, undermined, or sabotaged. It may be time for the group to begin, yet nurses suddenly have to take the patients' temperatures, or teachers decide to punish children for class behavior by disallowing group participation.

Along with agency sanctions, structural supports are also essential. Children cannot participate freely if the worker's office inhibits activity or if an auditorium encourages destructive behavior. If young single mothers are to participate, child care assistance is essential to support attendance. Finally, the worker, as the organizational representative, can overidentify or underidentify with the organization and create internal group problems.

A hospital group was organized to help surgical patients with their common concerns about the critical life event and discharge. The worker expected members to focus on this group purpose. Instead, they raised questions about the setting itself, which the worker felt were inappropriate:

JILL:	I'd like to know why this floor is so dirty.
SOCIAL WORKER:	Have you spoken to the head nurse about it?
JILL:	No, it should just be improved.
SOCIAL WORKER:	I can see you are angry with this.
JILL:	Angry . . . I'm not angry. I'm just stating the facts.
SOCIAL WORKER:	Well, the conditions around here seem to be a real concern for you, but . . .
JILL:	Listen, the showers are not clean, and they are clean on the other side of the hall. Why do you think that is? I shouldn't be expected to walk over there.
SOCIAL WORKER:	No, you shouldn't be expected to walk over there. These are legitimate complaints, but . . .
JILL:	I am not complaining; I'm just telling you I'm aware of what is going on.
SOCIAL WORKER:	OK, the things you are bringing up about the conditions of this floor should be brought up with the head nurse after this group is over. The purpose of this group is to discuss similar concerns about being here and being sick. Now, I'd like the rest of the group to share their concerns.
MARY:	The showers are dirty, though.
JILL:	See, I'm not the only one.
SOCIAL WORKER:	I realize you all may be concerned about the conditions here. What I am saying is that these things can be discussed with the head nurse.
ELLEN:	I don't care what we talk about.

Long periods of silence and withdrawal followed. By attempting to steer group members away from their expressed concerns, the worker mobilized their resistance.

In these varied ways, societal, community, and organizational conditions affect group life and can create dysfunctional communication and relationship processes. Interpersonal processes are also affected by phases of group development. Tension and dysfunctional communication arise from discontinuities in members' personal development or in group developmental tasks. In a group of pubescent girls, one member might already be dealing with biological and social transitions of early adolescence that pose communication and relationship issues for her and for the group as they take one another's measure. In another group, most members may be ready for the group's developmental phase of interpersonal intimacy, but their relationships and communications are already inhibited by one member's continuing preoccupation with testing the worker's authority (Garland, Jones, & Kolodny, 1976; Schiller, 1995, 1997). Thus, group developmental factors are potential interpersonal stressors and sources of dysfunctional behaviors.

Social Work Functions, Modalities, Methods, and Skills

The Social Worker and Dysfunctional Group Processes

With groups whose dysfunctional interpersonal processes interfere with members' efforts to deal with stressful life transitions, traumatic life events, and environmental stressors, the social work function is to help members to communicate openly and directly as they work on common life issues and to develop greater mutuality and reciprocity in their relationships. The worker relies on the enabling, exploring, mobilizing, guiding, and facilitating methods described earlier and also mediates to improve a group's interpersonal processes and the internal forces that generate them. Internal mediation is different from the external mediation directed to the environment.

Professional Methods and Skills

Mutual aid groups are organized around common concerns, interests, or tasks. These groups can universalize individual life issues, reduce isolation, and ameliorate stigma. Skillful group formation mitigates internal stressors.

1. *Beginning a group service.* Support groups emerge from a common life issue or interest. Life transition groups focus on (1) stressful developmental struggles and status changes, (2) painful life issues, (3) difficult status changes, and (4) traumatic life events. Environmental groups relate to a lack of community resources, to problems within an organization, and to consumer involvement within an agency. Interpersonal groups focus on natural units (e.g., patients on wards, students in classrooms, or residential cottages) and forming groups to deal with maladaptive patterns (e.g., couple groups or family groups).

2. *Obtaining organizational consent and support.* A clear presentation increases the likelihood of achieving organizational approval and support, which are important to the development and institutionalization of group services.

3. *Composing the social support group.* Group composition influences development and direction. Groups require both the stability of homogeneity and the diversity of heterogeneity. For example, in developing support groups for pregnant adolescents, the social worker identifies their common concerns about birthing; relationships with parents, boyfriends, peers, and school representatives; and future plans for babies. The social worker then

considers the relative advantages and disadvantages of commonalities and differences in age, first pregnancy, religion, race or ethnicity, and stage of pregnancy. Members usually tolerate and even come to enjoy diversity when common interests and concerns are intensely felt. The practitioner assumes professional responsibility for group composition.

4. *Structuring the support group.* Some groups are long-term and open-ended, with departing members replaced by newcomers. If a membership core remains intact, these groups provide long-lasting emotional support, social contact, and instrumental assistance. But if membership fluctuates, these groups develop two chronic problems: members and worker lose the original vitality and sense of purpose, and the group remains stuck in an early phase of group development. In contrast, planned short-term and time-limited mutual aid groups help members focus quickly, maintaining purpose and a sense of urgency. Group size should be determined by group objectives and member needs. The larger the group, the more formalized it becomes, thus limiting the opportunity for individual attention, intimacy, and spontaneity. Yet the large group provides greater community and organizational visibility, influence, and opportunities for individual anonymity. Smaller groups become informal and intimate but also vulnerable to disintegration if insufficient membership limits the strengths of diverse perspectives.

5. *Recruiting group members.* Random invitation is one form of group recruitment. This includes using a card file with common criteria for sending invitations, putting up signs, and inserting notices in a union newsletter or community newspaper. Random methods invite voluntary participation and avert pressure for involvement. However, the social worker maintains limited control over group composition. Referral is a second common recruitment method. Referrals will not be forthcoming unless the social worker has organizational or community standing and a reservoir of "favors receivable" to draw on. Appropriate referrals are more likely when group purpose and membership criteria have been clearly stated. Lastly, natural group clusters can be recruited such as isolated elderly in a building, patients on a hospital ward, and vulnerable youngsters in a residential cottage. Natural clusters often develop into effective social networks.

Table 10.1 summarizes the skills of organizing mutual aid groups.

Table 10.1
Skills of Organizing Mutual Aid Groups

- Establish a group service.
- Obtain organizational consent and support.
- Compose the mutual aid group.
- Structure the support group.
- Recruit group members.

Support is central to the group modality (Gitterman, 1989b, 2006). Support can be metaphorically viewed as the engine propelling the group process just as electric energy runs machinery. Without exchange of support, groups lose drive and momentum. For members to feel supported and to be experienced by others as supportive, they must demonstrate certain behaviors to one another (Macgowan, 2003; Macgowan & Newman, 2005). These behaviors include acceptance and the experience of being accepted. Offering hope also demonstrates support. When members sense that situations can improve and become less stressful, they more readily invest themselves in the group.[2]

The social worker helps build a mutual support system by *integrating* members through various skills.

- *Scanning.* The social worker scans the group by focusing on all the members rather than only on the member who is talking.
- *Directing members' transactions toward one another.* In the early phases of group development, members often communicate through the worker. The practitioner asks members to talk to each other.
- *Inviting members to build on one another's contributions.* The practitioner encourages members to interact by linking their comments to those of others ("Bill's idea is very close to George's. What do the rest of you think about their idea?").
- *Encouraging and reinforcing cooperation, norms of mutual support, rights, and responsibilities.* Group members develop collective norms about rights and responsibilities, modes of work, and styles of relating and communicating. Dysfunctional group patterns such as competition, withdrawal, and exploitation impede the development of mutual aid. To influence these dysfunctional patterns, the social worker supports and guides members to work together supportively and collaboratively ("I hope you feel great about how you solved this problem—no one yelled or threatened—you really helped one another").
- *Examining members' expressions of approval and disapproval.* Group members verbally and nonverbally approve or disapprove of certain behaviors. Approval is expressed through mild praise to more intense acclaim, and disapproval through mild rebukes and teasing to more severe scapegoating and ostracism. The social worker helps members become aware of both their dysfunctional and adaptive patterns.
- *Encouraging members' participation in activities and collective action.* Activities require planning and decision making, interacting and communicating, specifying roles and tasks, and negotiating the social and physical environments. When members accomplish these, the group becomes a source of mutual support and satisfaction.
- *Identifying and focusing on common themes in members' discussions.* At times, a group theme is readily evident. Other times, a group theme is more elusive and expressed in disparate behaviors. For example, some members may cope with termination by withdrawing, others by acting out, and others by

Table 10.2
Skills of Building Group Mutual Aid

- Scan.
- Direct members' transactions toward one another.
- Invite members to build on one another's contributions.
- Encourage and reinforce cooperative mutual support norms.
- Examine members' expressions of approval and disapproval.
- Encourage members to participate in activities.
- Identify and focus on common themes.

questioning the worker's caring. The social worker actively searches, identifies, and focuses on common themes: "Everybody is reacting to the group's ending—John, you're running in and out of the room; Bill, you have stopped talking to me; Jack, you have put your head down and closed your eyes; and I'm acting like the group is not ending in two weeks." The common themes are the "glue" that binds members together and develops their mutual concerns and skills (Caplan & Thomas, 2004).

Table 10.2 summarizes the skills of building group mutual aid.

Common themes and activities strengthen collective functioning and foster mutual support. The worker should also help group members to negotiate their needs for being *different* and *separate* by developing a satisfactory balance between the demands for integration and individuality.

- *Inviting individual members to disagree and supporting differing opinions and perceptions.* To help group members to tolerate differences, the social worker discourages premature consensus and the stifling of divergent perceptions and opinions. The worker invites individual members to disagree and supports differing opinions and perceptions ("Jane, you don't seem to agree. I'm very interested in your ideas"), encouraging the expression of individual differences.

- *Inviting the participation of reluctant or marginal group members.* In any group, some members may have difficulty in participating, and they may withdraw or engage in parallel activities. With caring and support, the worker invites the participation of the "outside" members. More than one invitation might be necessary.

- *Creating emotional and physical space for individual group members.* Members have different needs for intimacy and distance. Some members are not as ready to trust and expose as are others. Hence, the practitioner helps members to respect one another's needs ("I think Phyllis is saying she needs more time before she can talk about the rape. Am I right, Phyllis?").

The social worker helps members to balance individual needs with group needs. Table 10.3 summarizes the skills of helping with their needs for being different and separate.

Table 10.3
Skills of Mediating Individual Members' Needs

- Invite individual members to disagree on and support differing opinions and perceptions.
- Invite participation of reluctant or marginal group members.
- Create emotional and physical space for individual group members.

Groups develop dysfunctional group processes for many reasons. To help members deal with dysfunctional patterns, the social worker calls on the internal *mediating* method and its various skills.

- *Developing a transactional definition of the interpersonal stressor.* A worker is curious about a dysfunctional pattern and asks herself, "What is keeping this group structure frozen so that it can't move away from this way of communicating and relating?" "What are the primary sources of this pattern?" "What positive and negative consequences, both manifest and latent, does the pattern have for the collective as well as for the individual members?" and "Am I caught up in it and unwittingly contributing to the pattern?" Social workers must consider the effects of their own interventions and take into account the members' disparate views of the dysfunctional pattern. The worker regards the problematic pattern in transactional terms, namely, as lodged in the collective or subunit structures rather than in an individual.
- *Identifying dysfunctional patterns for the group.* Members are often unaware of transactional obstacles. Identifying the dysfunctional pattern is often the first step to consciousness raising: "I have noticed every time someone brings up a painful subject like graduating or cheating boyfriends, someone picks on Yolanda and changes our focus."
- *Reidentifying dysfunctional patterns for the group.* Since dysfunctional processes are often repetitive, the social worker reminds the group of prior incidents. ("OK, here we go again, it's happening right now. Carmen, you started in on Yolanda when we began talking about fathers. . . . Let's take a look at what's happening right now.")
- *Holding members to their agreed on focus and challenging their resistance.* Giving up an entrenched pattern is not easy. Member resistance should be anticipated. The worker holds members to the work: "Everybody's fuming but not talking—what's going on?" Firmness and persistence convey strength and caring, which in turn can help members face dysfunctional processes.
- *Inviting and sustaining the expression of strong feelings.* Suppressed feelings such as anger or frustration block communication. The social worker invites the expression of these feelings and the attendant content: "I would like each one to put your silence into words" or "You are furious at each other. What happened?" By inviting the expression of strong feelings, the practi-

tioner conveys faith in the members' ability to deal with interpersonal stressors and in their capacity for mutual aid.

• *Establishing protective ground rules.* Members require an atmosphere in which differing opinions and feelings can be expressed without threat or fear of recrimination. Protective ground rules barring physical violence or verbal abuse facilitate open and direct communication. ("This is going to be a difficult conversation. Remember, there can be no bullying, threats, or hitting.")

• *Identifying common definitions and perceptions.* As members explore interpersonal stressors, the social worker listens carefully for potential commonalities. For example, in a group for parents and their foster adolescents, the social worker clarifies youngsters' struggles for gaining greater freedom and autonomy and parents' desires for maintaining some control and direction. In helping the arguments unfold, the worker searches for possible common ground: the parents' stake in their children making positive transitions into young adulthood, and the adolescents' stake in their parents providing security and some structure. The social worker might suggest, "You are all struggling to find the right balance between age-appropriate freedom and limits."

• *Crediting members' work.* Members struggle and deal with painful issues. By crediting their efforts, the social worker encourages continued open and direct communication: "The important thing is that as mad as you were with one another, you talked about it. It was hard to do, but you've done it real well."

• *Using activities and programs to facilitate work.* When members are unable to discuss their difficulties, the practitioner uses action, such as working on a craft project or playing a sit-down game, to facilitate communication (Cusicanqui & Salmon, 2004; Glassman & Kates, 1993; Halperin, 2001; Lynn & Nisivoccia, 1995; McFerran-Skewes, 2004).

Table 10.4 summarizes the skills of mediating internal group stressors.

Table 10.4
Skills of Mediating Internal Group Stressors

• Develop a transactional definition of the interpersonal stressor.
• Identify dysfunctional patterns.
• Reidentify dysfunctional patterns.
• Hold members to their agreed on focus, and challenge their resistance.
• Invite and sustain the expression of strong feelings.
• Establish protective ground rules.
• Identify common definitions and perceptions.
• Credit members' work.
• Use activities and programs to facilitate work.

Practice Illustrations

Dysfunctional Group Processes

A social work student named Jackie was assigned to an ongoing open-ended group on the adolescent unit of a psychiatric hospital. The group consisted of Dick (white), Ralph (Latino), and Bill (white). Each had been in trouble with the law, with significant histories of fighting, suicidal thoughts, or gestures. In the last few sessions, the boys had worked on issues related to lying, betrayal, trust, loss of hospital friends, and the departure of a favorite psychiatric resident. Bill, the newest member, was quickly assigned the role of scapegoat, which he readily accepted.

In the next meeting, the pattern continued. Bill was complaining about a youngster who had been discharged from the unit when the other members vented their anger on him:

BILL:	He was just a big bunch of hot air! God! He would make stuff up! Do you know what he said? Man, he said . . .
DICK:	Well what about you? You do the same thing. Can't tell you anything.
BILL:	(Sighs.) I don't mean to.
DICK:	(Glares at Bill, then says something under his breath to him.)
BILL:	(Softly) I already apologized for that. I told you I was sorry. (He looks close to tears.)
RALPH:	(Squirms in his seat, glancing sideways from Dick and Bill to me.)
SOCIAL WORK INTERN:	Ralph, do you know what they are talking about?
RALPH:	(Smiles, looks away.) Yeah.
SOCIAL WORK INTERN:	Dick, what's up?
DICK:	Bill is a liar. He invents stories and no one can believe him. He doesn't know how to stop it. Who wants to hang around someone like that? He's immature.
BILL:	Augh! Jeeze! I do not. I told you about my dad for real. He ran out on us. (Said with head hung low) OK? And I'll tell you something else, but I don't want this to get outside of the room. I mean it. I have an older brother, honest, and he had to go back to Germany because he was in trouble with the law—drugs—he's in the army now. . . . (Tells more of this tale, which I hadn't heard either from his mother or from him.)
SOCIAL WORK INTERN:	(I remained silent: not a purposeful silence, but a confused one.)

RALPH AND DICK:	Liar . . . liar . . . liar . . . liar . . . (Ralph and Dick begin to whisper to each other.)
SOCIAL WORK INTERN:	Yo! (All three look at me.) Let's get back to the whole group. This isn't the place for private conversations. Remember, last time we talked about stretching the truth . . . that everyone stretches the truth sometimes and there are a whole bunch of reasons why people do so. What are some of the reasons why people stretch the truth?
DICK:	See, even Joan thinks you don't tell the truth.
RALPH:	Some of the reasons people don't tell the truth are . . .
SOCIAL WORK INTERN:	(After a brief silence) What can we do as a group to help keep each other from stretching the truth? (More silence.)
BILL:	(Fights back tears.)

The meeting ended with long periods of silence and discomfort. Three sessions later, Dick and Ralph "try to help" Bill. They give him advice on how to act more mature and stop "stretching the truth."

SOCIAL WORK INTERN:	I notice everyone is sinking lower and lower into their chairs and turning away from Bill. I get the feeling that you guys are pissed off at him. Am I right?
DICK:	He's not listening to us. Why bother?
RALPH:	How long have we talked about this, and he keeps doing the same thing.
BILL:	(Sulks, looking away from under heavy lids and hugging his chest protectively.)
SOCIAL WORK INTERN:	Bill, you have been pretty quiet so far today. It's hard to tell if you've been listening. I'm wondering if you've heard what Dick and Ralph have been saying.
BILL:	I have been, too!
SOCIAL WORK INTERN:	(Nudges Bill in a friendly way.) Tell us what they have been talking about.
BILL:	(Repeats verbatim, beginning to straighten up and look around the circle, less rigid, and wearing a half-smile.)
GROUP:	(Laughter from everyone.)
DICK:	So why didn't you say so, you little twerp?
SOCIAL WORK INTERN:	I'm kind of confused here, Dick. You come down on Bill and say all this negative stuff, like you don't like him, but earlier you said you wanted to help him.
RALPH:	We like him. But it's hard sometimes . . . 'cuz he don't tell the truth. Man, we talk to him and stuff during the day. I am just tired of it. He doesn't listen.
DICK:	He is like a little brother to me. He just needs to learn to act . . . be mature. I talk to him a lot and give him advice.

SOCIAL WORK INTERN:	I'd like to know what Bill thinks about this. What do you think, do you agree?
BILL:	(Silence)
DICK:	Answer, Bill. Don't just sit there.
BILL:	(Silence)
SOCIAL WORK INTERN:	Dick, you've been giving a lot of advice about how Bill should change.
DICK:	I feel I can help him. I know a lot about psychological testing and stuff and can coach him to act more mature.
SOCIAL WORK INTERN:	Yeah, you've been a friend here on the unit, but your advice seems to have a lot of negatives. You've pointed out a lot of Bill's problems. Can you tell him some of his positive qualities?
DICK:	He hasn't fought . . .
SOCIAL WORK INTERN:	(Pointing) Tell Bill.
DICK:	You haven't fought here, but you've tried to pick on others. You're funny, but sometimes you don't know when to shut up.

After this meeting, the student attempted to assess the group's scapegoating pattern. She remembered that after another group member, John, had been discharged, Bill joined the group and assumed the scapegoat role. Bill was even accused of the same faults as John. Bill and the other members seemed to perpetuate the scapegoating role over the next few sessions. Dick and Ralph maintained that they did not have problems anymore, that they are merely waiting for placement, whereas Bill needed to mature and learn how to stop lying. They took great interest in "helping" Bill with his problems. What the worker had not realized was that the processes of both helping and scapegoating Bill served a similar function, namely, to divert focus from their own concerns and issues. Dick had great trouble with intimacy and self-image and is defended with a high intellect. His coping efforts blocked the development of mutual aid in the group.

Bill fit into the scapegoating role, having set himself up as victim on the unit and in the therapeutic community. His lying represents a dysfunctional effort to gain attention and avoid painful or unresolved issues. Ralph wavers, unsure of his loyalty and preoccupied with his own discharge plans. Transactionally, scapegoating gives Bill the attention he craves, Dick feels empowered and more competent than the others, and Ralph is reassured of not being the "dummy" and of having some control over his environment.

Beginning social workers quite understandably find it hard to manage conflict (Secemsky, Ahlman, & Robbins, 1999). When Bill informed the group about his brother, the worker was skeptical, but she was at a loss about how to intervene:

Bill blurted out the story about his brother (which I suspected was fantasy) so quickly that I was unsure how to respond. I felt bombarded. I knew his story would invite a round of scapegoating. I wanted to protect him; at the same time, I realize that I was very annoyed with him. So I vacillated between a retreat into silence and a retreat from the specifics of the exchange. I changed the subject to "reasons for stretching the truth," moving to a topic that I thought would be safer and easier to control. And it was. However, by keeping the discussion on a broad, general level, I didn't help them struggle with important common concerns. Moreover, "stretching the truth" was still closely connected to Bill (it was HIS problem), and therefore I unwittingly reinforced his negative status. I struggled to not take sides, but now I see a pattern in which I choose sides and put members on the spot. I am beginning to get in touch with my own vulnerability and anger at being put on the spot. I realize this is what we all had in common—a feeling of being on the spot and vulnerable.

Members are often unaware of their transactional patterns. Identifying a dysfunctional pattern ("I've noticed every time someone introduces painful or scary concern like leaving the hospital, someone picks on Bill and our focus changes") is often the first step to raising consciousness. A social worker's identification of, and invitation to examine, an internal stressor is at times all that a group requires to modify a dysfunctional pattern.

For example, a group was comprised of youngsters in an adolescent partial hospitalization program. Group members experienced difficulty in becoming involved with each other and in sharing their life struggles. Group members avoided interpersonal and personal involvement by simply not listening to each other and engaging in side conversations.

Bob and Mike were engaging in side talk. Susan was talking about how hard her week was in the program. I said, "I appreciate you being able to share this experience with us, Susan, and I want us to talk some more about it in a moment, but there are two conversations going on at the same time and I'm having a difficult time focusing. What does the group think we should do about this?" "Do about what?" replied Donald. "Do about people talking at the same time someone is sharing her or his concerns, just like Bob and Mike were doing while Susan was sharing her troubles." Donald responded, "It really doesn't bother me." "But it bothers me," stated Steve. "Susan is obviously having a hard time, and the least we could do is listen." Susan added, "Yeah, man, it's not cool, I mean I'm doing OK, but would like some help and I think it's really rude of you guys to do that." Bob replies, "I'm sorry, I just get bored sometimes, but I didn't mean to make you feel bad." "Bob, help us understand—what · do you think makes you bored?" I inquired. Bob responded, "I don't know, I just always had a difficult time in groups. At my other program I just stopped going to groups at the end." "What made you stop going to groups?" "Well, actually, I wasn't allowed to attend groups because I talked so much." "So the group leader would just ask you to leave when you started interrupting people?" "Pretty much, yeah—that's what happened." "Bob, I don't want you to leave the group, I want you learn how to use the group—how to help others and to get help for yourself." Denise jumped in, "I don't think we should ask anybody to leave or anything. I think we should ask them how come they are not paying attention." "That's an excellent idea. What do the others think?" Steve, Donald, and Mike thought it would be a good idea. "So let's try—what was going on for you, Bob, when you started talking to Mike?" "I really don't know." I asked, "What do you all think might be the reasons you would be talking, not listening, and not trying to be of help to Susan?" Loretta responded, "I don't know about Bob and Mike, but I know that it is hard for me to talk in groups, especially when we're talking about stuff like Susan was bringing up." Mike added, "Yeah, I mean, I'm having a hard time here too, and I don't know if I like talking about it." Denise replies, "But talking about it is good; that's why we're here. I'm sick of playing games and all that other shit we do here. We need a group like this—to help each other and not run away from each other." Bob responded, "I'm sorry, I'm just not used to talking about personal stuff in a group." I asked, "Can we talk about what makes it difficult to talk about personal stuff in this group?" The group responds by saying yes or nodding their heads. "Okay, let's start by talking about what 'stuff' means and what kind of 'stuff' is difficult to talk about."

Some group members feel too vulnerable to listen to painful life issues. Side talk avoids dealing with pain. Other group members are more ready to become engaged and risk getting close to other group members and to their life struggles. The social work intern engages the group in examination of the group obstacle. She realizes that it is not her problem to solve, but it is the group's work. Paradoxically, by helping the members to examine what is making it difficult for them to get engaged with each other, she helps them to begin to become engaged with each other.

For another example, a student formed a task group of elderly members, with an interest in horticulture, to consider uses of a newly built greenhouse (Lo, 2005). Commonality existed in their love of growing things. Because the agency wanted the greenhouse to serve as a showcase, the staff consistently increased their expectations, assigning the group primary responsibility for its development and care. The intern was also pressured by her field instructor, who emphasized task accomplishment over process. Even though group members felt increasingly overwhelmed and withdrawn, she found it more comfortable and safer to ignore the static underlying group discussions. On her field instructor's advice, she planned a series of horticultural workshops. After the second workshop, she realized she would have to change her approach and invite the members to explain their apparent weariness and disinterest.[3]

SOCIAL WORK INTERN:	That was a long workshop—you seem pretty tired.
FAY:	Well, it was very interesting, but maybe next time we don't need to have slides.
SOCIAL WORK INTERN:	You feel the meeting was too long.
DANIEL:	(Interrupting) Slides are better, they are infinitely better than listening to people.
MARY:	(Blurted out) Well, maybe I'm just dumb, but these lectures are getting too highfalutin for me, too—what's the word?—technical.
SOCIAL WORK INTERN:	So, the workshops are too technical and boring. Is there anything else about them that you don't like?
GROUP:	(Silence)
LUCY:	Yeah, I'll tell you what's going on. I'm sick and tired of these here experts coming in and telling us what to do. Who needs it! What are they trying to prove, anyhow?
SOCIAL WORK INTERN:	I had a feeling something was wrong, and I'm really glad you shared your reactions with me.
LUCY:	Well, you know, I like to say it like it is.
SOCIAL WORK INTERN:	I like to hear it like it is, so please go on.
LUCY:	We've been knocking ourselves out with all these people coming in to give us these talks. What for? We don't want to be experts.
NANCY:	Yeah, we feel like we are really being pushed around. They tell us the greenhouse is for us, but they want to do it their way.
SARAH:	Nancy's right. We want to have fun, to learn from our mistakes; they want a perfect garden to show off.

The intern's willingness to "hear it like it is" releases the members' mounting frustration and anger and becomes a turning point in the group (Gitterman & Wayne, 2003). She demonstrates courage, risking being perceived as disloyal to the agency. She becomes curious about the members' experience and moves into the unknown, forgoing a clear and comfortable prescribed script.

For another example, earlier in this chapter, we discussed a curriculum-driven group developed for parents of autistic children in a special early childhood center. The curriculum focused on coping with the life challenges of supporting, educating, and caring for a child with pervasive developmental challenges. Group members became relatively passive and subservient to the authority of the curriculum and intern. Members were not involved with each other. In the fourth meeting, a member who had a painful encounter with a teacher stated that she wanted to talk about her disappointment with the school rather than continue with the scheduled presentation. The intern set aside the curriculum and asked the parents if they had similar experiences. The other members agreed with this member, and became involved with each other. As their comfort levels increased, the parents began to share their personal hardships and family turmoil. At the end of the meeting, the intern inquired how the members experienced this particular meeting compared to the previous ones. Members responded enthusiastically, and one parent asked if they could have more meetings like this one: "You know, meetings where we can talk heart to heart." We join the group in the fifth meeting.

Mrs. Patterson and Mrs. Lewis were preparing their coffee. Mrs. Thomas began to laugh. I inquired what she was thinking about. Mrs. Thomas responded, "Oh, I was just thinking about the first time I brought Roslyn here for an assessment. I was so nervous that Roslyn would not be able to control herself and would just cry all the time. Well, she did pretty well the whole day—you know how long those evaluations can be. Anyway, when we were leaving, we must have looked like a mess. I was a nervous wreck. Anyway, we were leaving and Roslyn went flying right down those front steps and landed hard. I never thought I would be able to laugh about it." I then said, "Was she OK? What happened?" "Well, we both ended up leaving the school in an ambulance, and Roslyn was in a full leg cast for the next six months. That's why she can barely walk now. On top of everything else, this had to happen. I cried myself to sleep for the next couple of weeks."

Mrs. Lewis responded, "I can relate. Charlie just insists on not doing the steps. So I carry him, and when the teachers see me carrying him they have a fit." Mrs. Patterson added, "I have Alice at home. She went to this school also. She is now in the second grade and is doing real well, but when she began she was just like Roslyn. She is just beginning to talk now. My husband insists that I start working again, but it is so hard with the two of them." I said, "You all have a tremendous amount to deal with—Mrs. Patterson, have you spoken to your husband about why it is so hard for you to go back to work now?" "Of course I have, but I mean there is the reality of the rent and all the other expenses. That doesn't go away just because you have these problems. I know he is right, but then again he doesn't have to be around them all the time. I don't think he really knows what it is like." Mrs. Patterson took a deep breath, then added, "I mean, I have to do this all by myself." The other group members nodded. I said, "You all are nodding. . . ." Mrs. Thomas jumped in, "The same thing goes on in my home. My husband works very hard to support us, but when I get done taking care of the kids and then taking care of him, well, I just collapse. I can't tell you the last time we went out to-gether, I mean just him and me. I am so exhausted each day, I just can't even think about working." I asked, "What do you think your husbands would say if you told him about your exhaustion?" Mrs. Thomas replied, "These days he doesn't say much. Sometimes I feel as though I am talk-ing to the wall. I don't know what to say to him. I am just so tired."

Mrs. Lewis took Mrs. Thomas's hand and held it. Mrs. Thomas ex-claimed, "I thought life would be different, do you know what I mean?" Mrs. Patterson agreed, "I always thought life would be better than this." "So did I, there is no way to be prepared for what we have had to go through," stated Mrs. Lewis. She continued, "But it feels great to talk about—to know that I am not the only one that feels this way—that I have to always act strong." I added, "You all carry a heavy load and burden, and you all have this amazing strength, but I worry that you are trying to do it alone—try to be super-mom, super-wife, and super-everything. We need to find where you can get the support you all need. Maybe the group can provide some of it." Mrs. Lewis replied, "You're right. When Charlie is on a school vacation and I find myself spending days on end with no other company than Charlie, by the end of the day, I feel like I am going nuts. I mean I haven't had an intelligent conversation all day. I would not give up Charlie for anything, but some-times I would give up everything for a simple adult conversation." "Wow! That's exactly how I feel," added Mrs. Patterson. Mrs. Thomas sug-gested, "Why don't we exchange phone numbers?"

Group members become involved with each other. They rise above their passivity and risk mutual engagement. The intern, to her credit, makes the decision to become emotionally involved with the members and takes the risk of setting aside the security blanket of the prescribed curriculum. By sharing their grief, daily challenges, and emotional and social isolation and loneliness, group members begin to make a deep connection. Occasionally, the intern becomes overwhelmed by the members' pain and offers a prema-ture suggestion (e.g., "Mrs. Patterson, have you spoken to your husband?"). However, by and large, the intern stays out of the members' way and allows them to take greater control over "their" group (and their lives).

Often, however, a single invitation is insufficient to break through the group's (and the worker's) resistance to relinquishing an established and comfortable pattern. As the pattern repeats itself, the worker can reflect on prior transactions ("OK, here we go again, it's happening right now"). For example, in a prior illustration, the social worker could have commented, "Dick, you just started in on Bill when we began talking about your being discharged from the hospital." The worker could also encourage members to give up a pattern, even if slowly, by suggesting, "Come on, let's not start on Bill. Dick, are you worried about going home?" or, to examine the pattern directly, "Let's talk about what's happening right now."

Often group members cannot or do not accept a worker's identification of a dysfunctional transactional pattern. Giving up entrenched processes is far from easy: avoiding conflict, painful material, intimacy, or threatening changes, or escaping into an "illusion of work," may initially be an easier and understandable maneuver. For the group to progress, however, the worker has to attend to dysfunctional patterns and hold members to their agreed on focus. To illustrate, a social worker formed a group of pregnant adolescents. The group's purpose was for members to help one another with the effects of pregnancy on their relationships with boyfriends, parents, relatives, friends, and institutions. The group members struggled to avoid dealing with common concerns.

The worker inquired about the "boyfriend situation":

Sally began talking about her boyfriend at great length. I allowed her to continue for a while, and then said, "Have any of you had similar difficulties with your boyfriends?" Sally stopped for a second, but proceeded with her story. I waited for a minute again, unsure of how to deal with the other members' lack of involvement, and asked Linda, "Did your boyfriend react the same way as Sally's?" Linda sighed and said nothing. I waited for her to respond, but immediately Karen started saying, "My boyfriend is wonderful; he started out as a shit, but I blew him away." She then told the group all the fun things they had done together. I returned to Linda and asked, "What are you thinking?" Linda began to say, "Well, he doesn't even call me anymore." Sally, Susan, and Karen started a private conversation about their male conquests. (At this moment, I overidentified with Linda instead of reaching underneath the bravado for the common fear.) I turned my attention to the trio and stated firmly, possibly harshly, "Let's give Linda a chance, and then you'll have your chance to share your experiences. It's only fair to give everybody a chance to talk." Sally ignored me, saying, "Oh, but listen to this," and continued with her upbeat story.

I put myself in their shoes and realized they were attempting to evade and avoid their pain. I commented, "I know talking about some of the difficulties related to being pregnant can really be uncomfortable and hard to talk about." Sally broke in, "I know, but listen to this," and continued her recital of partying, staying up all night, and so on. After a couple of minutes (in which I was thinking how to deal with the collective avoidance), I said, "I really feel bad. You girls have so much pain, and you could help each other so much with things going on in your life, but you are choosing to act as if you aren't pregnant, as if life is wonderful, when you and I know it ain't no fun."

Karen began to relate how her mother hassles her; Sally and Susan immediately began to talk and to laugh. I was moved by the intensity of their resistance, their fear of dealing with such an overwhelming and powerful reality, and said, "I am sure you have noticed that every time one of you begins to talk about being pregnant and its consequences, you find something else more cheerful to talk about." Silence. "I know you are feeling badly inside; can you try to share what's happened since you and others found out that you were pregnant?" Linda started to cry. Susan said, "It's OK, Linda, I cry a lot. My father thinks I am a slut (tears came to her eyes)." Sally added, "It's no big deal, yeah, I cry too." I broke in and said, "Sally, what's happening to you right now?" Sally blurted out with rage in her voice, "OK, you wanna know, I'll tell you—my mother kicked me out of the apartment, she wants nothing to do with me." As I put my arm around her, she began to cry, sobbing hysterically.

Challenging dysfunctional patterns can induce a momentary crisis or explosion, which loosens entrenched processes and structures, allowing communication and relational patterns to improve. Anger and open conflict in a formed or natural group are particularly difficult for many beginning practitioners. They experience anxiety, feel powerless, and fear members' anger and their own reactions. To cope with their own feelings, they detach themselves from the conflict and thus are unable to help members deal with the interfering interpersonal processes.

Workers must deal with their feelings toward a group member or risk the member withdrawing, intervening preemptively, or acting out. An intern, for example, was assigned to a predischarge group in a mental hospital. After several meetings, a new member was added. She refused to accept the client role: instead, she assumed the role of helper, which threatened the intern.

SOCIAL WORK INTERN:	Mrs. Palmer is joining our group today, and I told her this morning what the group was about.
MRS. PALMER:	(Interrupting) I'm quite aware of the purpose of a discharge group. I was in one last year, and I contributed all I could. I finally resigned because I felt a less fortunate person should have a chance to be in it.
SOCIAL WORK INTERN:	What about yourself, Mrs. Palmer: do you think you can also be helped by being in the group?
MRS. PALMER:	(Smiling) I do not think so, I have no problems, but I will be able to help other members.

By attempting to get Mrs. Palmer to say that she could be helped in the group, the intern focused on the most frightening area for her—leaving the hospital. Mrs. Palmer might have been asked instead to describe her previous group experience. Other members could have been asked to describe the current group. Together, they might have searched for connections in order to ease her entry. The intern's confrontation with Mrs. Palmer in subsequent sessions continued:

SOCIAL WORK INTERN:	It's so quiet today; why do you think that is?
MRS. GREENBERG:	Yes, we have been talking about some of the things that are scary about leaving here.
MRS. PALMER:	I am sure you are afraid. You are always in a daze—you can't go anywhere. (Mrs. Jackson turned to Mrs. Palmer and made a face.)
MRS. GREENBERG:	(After a brief pause) I don't need a spokesman to talk for me.
MRS. PALMER:	Well, I think you do—you certainly don't say anything on your own.
MRS. GREENBERG:	She knows everything, doesn't she?

After this remark, there was another long silence. Ms. Phillips broke it by suggesting that Mrs. Palmer can be helpful to the group because she has been in a predischarge group before. She asked specifically about proprietary homes. Mrs. Palmer said negative things about the homes. Members' faces registered confusion and sadness. My anger was ready to burst through, and I said, "Mrs. Palmer is making you all a little uncomfortable." Mrs. Greenberg said, "Well, there is a lot of truth in what she is saying." And Mrs. Bergio added, "Yeah, I'd better get an apartment." I asked, "How else are you feeling about what Mrs. Palmer said?" There was no response, and the meeting ended in silence.

The intern was immobilized by anger and withdrew from the interaction. While he struggles with his feelings, the group members feel abandoned. Finally, Ms. Phillips searches for connections between the new member and the group. The group needed to examine the specific content of Mrs. Palmer's comments. But the intern's fear that he had lost control of the group inhibited him. The group members sense that he wants them to take on Mrs. Palmer for him. They shy away.

Mrs. Palmer dominated the next two meetings. Her anxiety about leaving the hospital trapped not only her but also the group and the intern. The intern felt he had lost the group. He became less active, and the group floundered.

SOCIAL WORK INTERN:	Lately, it has been difficult for all of you to talk in the group.
MRS. PALMER:	It's not difficult—I have been talking.
SOCIAL WORK INTERN:	For the last two weeks, you have taken us off the group focus and onto topics that have little to do with concerns about discharge.
MRS. PALMER:	Oh, no! You are so wrong. I think I have been right on the point.

This particular meeting ended on a bitter note:

SOCIAL WORK INTERN: Mrs. Palmer, I think it must be hard for you as a new member in this group.

MRS. PALMER: It isn't difficult for me at all.

SOCIAL WORK INTERN: I think it is hard; every week you talk about anything but what we are supposed to be working on. How do you feel about being a new member in the group?

MRS. PALMER: I am not new. I know everyone; we live on the ward. You are new! And besides, I have been through this already in the other group.

The intern responded to the provocations as though he were a group member (Gitterman, 2003c). He located the problem in the client and her psychological difficulties, and his vacillation between withdrawal and confrontation resulted in a welter of maladaptive communications. Before work could begin on the group's structure and interpersonal processes, the intern had to recognize and accept his fears and vulnerability. In the next meeting, he acknowledged his mistakes and succeeded in placing the interpersonal issue on the group's agenda:

SOCIAL WORK INTERN: I have been thinking about something that Ms. Jackson said about taking a trip. I think it's a good idea. What do the rest of you think?

MRS. PALMER: I think it's a very good idea. I said so when she first mentioned it.

SOCIAL WORK INTERN: Mrs. Palmer, when Ms. Jackson made the suggestion, I was so angry and hurt by you that I didn't even respond to it or to your support for the idea—I'm sorry. (She smiled, but said nothing.)

MS. JACKSON: I think trips would be fine. Like I said, it will give us some practice in leaving. (Mrs. Greenberg began to speak, but was immediately cut off by Mrs. Palmer and withdrew.)

SOCIAL WORK INTERN: Mrs. Greenberg, you wanted to say something, but I think you got a little frightened by Mrs. Palmer. I can understand that—sometimes I am a little scared of her—but I don't think she means to come on that strong.

MRS. BERGIO: (Lifted herself out of her chair) You, you are afraid, you are afraid of her also—it's not because we are crazy?

SOCIAL WORK INTERN: (Smiling) Yes, I think we are all a little afraid of her—and I think she is a little afraid of us—we each handle being afraid differently. (Mrs. Palmer returned my smile.)

The intern, by expressing his concerns and feelings instead of acting them out, lifts a heavy burden from the group. Their fears are legitimized, and their energies released for work.

When anger is unexpressed, denied, or avoided, members and worker often develop a reservoir of negative feelings, which block communications. Thus, it is essential for the worker to elicit these feelings and the associated content. By inviting the expression of feelings, workers convey care and respect for the group members and faith in their ability to communicate and to work on interpersonal issues. When group members act out their anger and frustrations, workers must explore what underlies the interpersonal process rather than negatively judge the behavior or protecting weaker members.

I have observed members' rejection of certain men in my group at the nursing home. The more active members show a dislike of the less lucid men. Occasionally, a member will point to an individual who appears to be out of contact and say, "Look at the vegetable. You wonder why there's no action on this ward. Look at him, he doesn't even know where he is." The lack of response by the victim of these attacks increases the vehemence of the attacker and elicits open or silent approval of the attack by other members. Initially, I attempted to eliminate the hostility by defending the frailer member. But the behavior continued. The next time, I asked the attacking member what he saw when he looked at the other man. He responded, "The hospital staff think we are all like that. They think we have no feelings, nothing to say about anything. Like we are a bunch of cattle, a bunch of bums." As he said this, other members expressed their discomforts: "Yeah, bums, like we didn't work all our lives, liked we lived off Social Security and welfare all our lives. We worked until we couldn't anymore." One member pointed at the disoriented man and said, "Even him, don't you think he worked hard? He can't help what happened to him."

The men's fears of being identified with the more impaired patients—their feelings of impotence, confusion, and anger—would have remained latent, sustaining the dysfunctional interpersonal patterns and interfering with the group's tasks had the worker continued to defend the symbolic scapegoats and herself. She moved beyond her initial preemptive interventions and examined the fears underlying the scapegoating. This helped the members move ahead on their tasks related to transitional and environmental issues.

Exchanges among members provide the means by which the group can examine its communication and relationship patterns. The social worker encourages each member's participation in the discussion of discrepant perceptions, disagreements, and conflicts. This requires a secure atmosphere in which differences can be examined without threat or recrimination. Thus, the worker has to establish protective ground rules, which facilitate rather than subvert open and direct communication. Explicit rules barring physical violence, threats, or negative sanctions against the expression of feelings, opinions, or facts are set forth. These provide structural and normative supports for weaker, lower ranking members. The social worker encourages the group to abide by the agreed-on conditions to avoid situations in which the weaker member has to be protected or rescued.

A social worker developed a group service for five girls, ages nine to eleven, in a school for learning-disabled youngsters. There are forty-two students in the school, only ten of which are girls. Maintaining control and managing frustration are difficult for several of the girls. In the first meeting, the worker emphasized that she would not permit fighting, nor would she let anyone get hurt. Several dyads developed in the group. Since Carmen was the newest student, the youngest group member, and the least able to express herself verbally and control her frustration, she attempted to pair herself with the worker. She constantly sought the worker's attention and assistance. She kept her chair close to the worker or leaned on her when they sat on the floor. In contrast, Jean is more self-assured, but highly provocative. She also has low tolerance for frustration. In two consecutive meetings, the two girls got into fights with each other. Carmen is Puerto Rican and Jean is African American. Carmen uses Spanish for teasing and name-calling. Jean is the only group member who doesn't understand Spanish. This gives Carmen power over her and makes the insults even worse. Early in the first meeting, Carmen and Jean started their first fight. The worker had selected an activity to help members get to know each other.

Jean stated, "I know Barbara and her (pointing at Carmen)." She continued to look at me and said angrily, "You know what she does. . . . [S]he gives out candy and then takes it back." Carmen pushed her chair back from the circle and put her hands in her pockets. She looked extremely threatened. I said, "It looks like you are really mad at Carmen right now. Why don't you tell her about it?" Jean repeated her complaint. Carmen tried to defend herself but became tongue-tied. To my total amazement, Carmen jumped up and hit Jean. They began to wrestle. I pulled them apart and said loudly, "OK, stop it, sit down!" Members started talking loudly among themselves. I remained standing to get their attention and said, "You two aren't getting along right now. Maybe you can use the group to learn to get along better. This is a good time for us to talk about group rules." Sitting down, I asked the members to develop some rules. Terry volunteered, "No fighting." I said, "That's a good rule—we will not fight in this group. We can talk to each other without hitting." Jean shouted that she was going to hurt Carmen's face. Carmen muttered something back. I interrupted them and said, "Nobody will be allowed to hurt anyone here anymore!" Carmen slid her chair close to mine and held my hand. I repeated, "I am not going to let you hurt each other."

The worker's initial intervention primarily focused on Jean's concerns. She thought the youngster was asking for help with an interpersonal conflict. She addressed the conflict from Jean's perspective by encouraging her to tell Carmen how she felt. In doing this, the worker neglected Carmen's fears of being attacked. When the worker directed the interaction between Jean and Carmen, she neglected the other group members, inadvertently set up a fight, and provided an audience. Had she made the issue more group relevant, members might have participated rather than just watching the fight. However, the worker's firm explanation that she would not permit fighting or let anyone get hurt related to all the members' concerns. The worker's use of the situation to develop "ground rules" was responsive to the needs of the group, but it was not well timed.

The establishment of protective norms is essential to a group's ability to develop their common purpose and pursue the associated goals. A group composed of poorly functioning members immediately requires structure and guidelines. Loose structure and lack of guidelines encourage loss of control. In school, youngsters are used to classroom structure and clearly defined rules. The unstructured atmosphere in this first meeting was probably too much change for these girls. Learning-disabled children often react to any small change in their environment or routine with confusion, disorganization, and loss of control.

Even with protective "ground rules" in place, conflict between Carmen and Jean resurfaced near the beginning of the fourth meeting, when Carmen said something about a retarded boy liking Barbara.

I began by asking what everyone thought retarded meant, but Jean interrupted and accused Carmen of being the retarded one. Terry joined in and agreed with Jean. They both shouted that Carmen was retarded because she takes medication (Ritalin for hyperactivity). I tried to explain that being retarded and taking medication were two different things. Jean and Carmen were standing, yelling and insulting each other. Carmen insulted Jean in Spanish. Both seemed to be saying that the other was crazy. From the start the group supported Jean in the argument, possibly because Carmen attacked Barbara, the most popular member.

When I raised my voice and said, "Stop! Time out!" they did not respond. I stood between the two girls to keep them from hitting each other. Terry said, "Oh. She's mad. You're going to get in trouble. She's going to tell our teacher." I said, "I am getting mad because this fighting messes up the group and gets in the way of your being able to help each other, but I am not going to tell your teacher. What happens here is between us." I put one hand on each girl's shoulder to separate her and said, "I am not going to let you hurt each other." The girls seated themselves on the floor. As I took my seat I asked someone to sit between Jean and Carmen so they would be separated. Barbara volunteered to sit between them. I said, "We can see that Carmen and Jean aren't getting along too well. The same thing happened in our first meeting." Before I could lead them into a group discussion about fighting, Jean said, "I'm sorry. I didn't mean nothing." I suggested she directly tell Carmen. Jean turned to Carmen and reluctantly repeated her apology. Carmen did not reply. I said, "Carmen, what do you think about what Jean just said?" Carmen muttered that she was going to deck Jean, and something else in Spanish, which made Jean mad all over again. Barbara translated the insult. Before I knew it, Jean picked up a chair and was moving toward Carmen with it. The other members chorused, "She said she was sorry, Carmen." I stood up again, took the chair out of Jean's hands, separated them, and pointed to separate corners of the room where each would have to sit. I asked the other group members what they thought was going on and what we could do about it. The members began to express how annoyed they were becoming with these disruptions and suggested that in the future the provoker should be asked to leave that particular meeting. With both Jean and Carmen participating, the group developed several consecutive steps in dealing with group disruptions (i.e., initial warning by the worker, group intervention, and member asked to leave).

By the fourth meeting the worker was prepared for the conflict and made the incident group relevant. She identified fighting as a group issue, asked members to sit between the fighting members, and engaged the youngsters in developing ways to solve the problem. While she moved too quickly for reciprocal apologies rather than exploring common hurts and vulnerabilities, she clearly established rules and their enforcement as group issues. She was prepared to help them, but not to accept the policing function by herself. It was a shared issue.

A natural friendship adolescent girls' group valued interpersonal loyalty. One member, Gladys, violated this by flirting with and kissing another member's boyfriend. The group issue was exacerbated by the worker's tendency to shy away from conflict and anger. She used a theoretical orientation to explain and to rationalize her passivity while being too frightened to deal with the intensity of the members' emotions and her own. In an extremely difficult meeting, she ventured new ways of coping and managing group conflict:

Gladys was first to arrive, followed by several others. When Rita arrived, she said hello, slugged Gladys hard on the side of her face, and continued walking to an empty chair, casually greeting everyone on the way. At first, there was no response or acknowledgment of the action by anyone (this was the first time a member physically attacked another). The girls (except Gladys) began planning for an upcoming party as though nothing had happened. I was stunned. Soon a few members began to giggle. I said, "Hey what's going on? What just happened?" Rita responded that it was a personal matter between her and Gladys, and continued to plan the party.

I put my hand on Rita's arm and asked again more firmly what happened between her and Gladys. She said, "Nothing, it's all settled now; everything is over." I said, "Bullshit! Everything is not over! Gladys is very upset and so are you!" Rita said she was not upset. I was determined not to withdraw and replied, "Come on, Rita, you're still furious; what happened?" Rita began to rant at Gladys, bawling her out for kissing her boyfriend, Reggie, at a party over the weekend. Everyone else joined the attack. It seemed Rita's boyfriend flirtatiously asked Gladys for a kiss and she kissed him, twice. Rita continued her angry tirade as Gladys attempted first to deny and then to excuse her behavior. The other girls began to rant at Gladys. When I asked for their reactions, Sue responded that she was telling Gladys for her own good that she better leave other people's boyfriends alone. She said there had been an incident with her own boyfriend, which she had found out about, and Gladys was lucky she hadn't said anything about it. There was a tense silence followed by Rita talking to everyone, with Gladys sitting quietly.

After a few minutes, I said, "I can't stand this atmosphere! You and Gladys are not talking to each other." Rita responded, "Everything is settled—it was settled when I did what I did." I said she was still fuming, and I was still upset about what had happened. This started a second and calmer round. I asked Gladys what she thought of what Rita was saying. Gladys replied, "I didn't kiss Reggie twice, and Rita should tell Reggie not to mess with me again." I suggested she tell this to Rita. Rita said, looking at me, "All the boys play around like that." I suggested she tell this to Gladys, which she did. I asked Rita if she was saying she wouldn't say anything to Reggie about messing around with Gladys. Rita said, "No, I will take care of Reggie later on, but Gladys could not expect boys to not mess around." I said, "So when the boys play around, Gladys should . . . ?" Rita and Sue said, "She should say, 'No! Leave me alone!'" I asked Gladys, and she said, "I said, 'No, come on, Reggie.'" (The *no* was very soft.) I asked the girls, "What would you think if you were the boys messing around with Gladys and she said that?" Sue said she'd push Gladys right into the bedroom. I said, "So Gladys doesn't say it like she means it, doesn't say it firmly—right?" They agreed.

The girls role-played with Gladys different situations and how they should be handled. The discussion ended with some criticism of Rita's slugging Gladys. Rita said it was a spontaneous thing—she just walked in and let Gladys have it; and anyway, Gladys should have said something to her first. Gladys said she had been going to but she hadn't had a chance.

I said as mad as they were at each other, the important thing was they were able to talk about it. It was hard to do, and they did well.

The worker facilitated the group's work on successfully managing interpersonal conflict. She held the members to the work, and did not allow them to avoid the painful encounter. She communicates faith in the process by demanding they work and by investing herself in the process. She risked her emotions, trusting that she can use her anger rather than act it out. To her credit, she risked personal spontaneity. She confronted the complexities and challenges rather than retreating behind a personal and professional mask. Her firmness and persistence conveyed a strength and genuine concern, which in turn released members' energies to confront the dysfunctional process. She used her own feelings to reflect the group members' anger, and she invited each member's perceptions of the situation. After pulling together the facts, she directed members to talk to one another rather than through her and to examine the situation in a new way. As members considered their differences, the worker listened carefully for possible common definitions and perceptions.

Staying with conflict and searching for common ground require open and direct communication. Group members need support and credit for their willingness to struggle and risk themselves. There is, however, a subtle distinction between rewarding members' efforts to deal with difficult issues and praising them for meeting the worker's values and expectations. The first is responsive to members' needs; the second reflects an imposition of the worker's own needs. Members need social workers' support, but not the burden of pleasing them. In helping groups with dysfunctional interpersonal processes, the worker often assumes an active and directive role.

This is illustrated by the author's experience with a group of disadvantaged older African American adolescent boys who were consistently unable to plan or engage in problem solving in a simple, focused discussion.[4] A member's comment would be immediately punctuated by another member's slur or epithet about a girlfriend, mother, and so on (Wayne & Gitterman, 2004). Chaos invariably followed.

As I struggled to help the group with these dysfunctional processes, I drew on certain concepts. The concept of social structure was particularly significant. This group's structure was too loose, with ill-defined roles and undifferentiated communication patterns. I attempted to tighten the group's structure by assigning specific roles and responsibilities. This met with limited success and was rarely transferred from one activity to another. I then redefined the issue, focused on the group's interpersonal obstacles, and invited members to examine their communication difficulties rather than continue my attempts to orchestrate a more integrated structure. When disruptions took place, I "froze" their interactions and asked the members to examine their exchanges. Unfortunately, this approach further intensified their difficulties and our mounting frustration.

During our first basketball game, I realized the issue was incorrectly defined. To them, basketball is a game of one-on-one moves: a pass is an alien concept, and arguments and fights disrupted the game. The game dramatically enlarged my own vision. The issue was not so much a loose social structure or dysfunctional interpersonal processes as it was a gap in learning the value and skill of teamwork. How could they be expected to collaborate in planning and decision making?

I related my observations to the members and proposed a sequence of steps we could use in planning programs or making decisions: (1) each member silently thinks through specific suggestions; (2) in round-robin fashion, each member presents one idea at a time, which is then recorded on a master list (during this step, no comments or alternative suggestions are allowed, in order to prevent premature closure and unfair criticisms); (3) discussion of each alternative is limited to clarification and identification of potential negative outcomes; and (4) after duplicate ideas are eliminated and impractical alternatives voluntarily withdrawn, the group votes for the preferred decision and plan. These steps provided a structure for collaboration and eliminated disabling criticism. The positive results reinforced interest; motivation to cooperate and collaborative activity were gradually internalized. After several months, the boys voted to eliminate the schema as no longer needed.

This experience shows once again that different definitions of dysfunctional processes lead to correspondingly different interventions. Being open to one's practice experiences, instead of blocking them out, requires keeping oneself from holding to rigid definitions. Many practice experiences fall between or outside anticipated definitions. One must tolerate ambiguities and uncertainties while acting with optimism and confidence. In the above illustration, guiding was used to replace chaos with order, and conflictual, parasitic behaviors with collaborative, mutually supportive behaviors. The guiding method is also important in work with withdrawn, passive, and apathetic members (Gitterman, 2001b).

A social worker was struck by how the environment reinforced the sense of helplessness among an inpatient group of depressed members. Hospital research staff regularly recruited patients for research protocols: at a time convenient to the staff, the patient is tested. The patient is given no prior notice regarding the type or timing of the testing. The lack of prior notice creates anxiety and inconvenience for the patient. The worker felt the group needed to learn how to deal with the outside world. She used desensitization exercises and assertiveness training techniques to teach members the interpersonal skills essential to gain mastery of their environment. As their external reality was accepted, respected, and dealt with seriously, members increasingly shared their experiences and invested themselves in the discussions.

MRS. KING:	(Rushing into the room out of breath and exasperated) I'm sorry I'm late—the research people asked me if I would be willing to take more tests, so I was upstairs—AGAIN!
MRS. SIMMONS:	They really upset me. Last Friday—Good Friday—actually it ended up being BAD FRIDAY—those research people asked me to do a few studies. They kept me over two hours. In the meantime, my friend Gloria came to accompany me to Good Friday Mass. I can't get out of this place without a chaperone. She left after an hour, and I missed Mass.
SOCIAL WORKER:	Ouch—is this testing mandatory?
MRS. KING:	Well, it helps them with research that might help someone else someday.
SOCIAL WORKER:	How is it actually helping you?
MRS. THOMAS:	It isn't helping me; it's just easier to go along with it than put up a stink.
SOCIAL WORKER:	Mrs. King, is that the way you also experience it?
MRS. KING:	Yes.
MRS. MARTIN:	Well, I don't think we should go along with it!
SOCIAL WORKER:	OK—how could you respond differently to them?
MRS. MARTIN:	Oh, gosh, I don't know, but we shouldn't let people test us if we don't want to.
MRS. FRANKOS:	I can't even say "no" to my two year old; how am I going to say "no" to a doctor?
MRS. SIMMONS:	You too? Wait until they're fifteen and you still can't refuse them!
SOCIAL WORKER:	I think we have a theme song, ladies: "I'm Just a Girl Who Can't Say No"! (We all laughed, and Mrs. Martin went on to complete the second line, "I'm in a terrible fix.")

The worker's gentle tone, manner, and sense of humor encouraged members to share their experiences. She invited members to prepare for future encounters with research staff and to rehearse alternative responses. Using an assertiveness sequence (describe behavior, express associated feelings, request specified change, and identify positive consequences), she guided members in how to complain effectively. Group members showed dramatic improvement in communication skills. Mrs. King, however, continued to find it difficult. After four more sessions, she once again raised her concern.

Our discussion led us to identify outside forces to which they acquiesced. Mrs. King voiced concern about resuming her outside therapy with her psychiatrist.

MRS. KING:	I'm a little afraid of my contact with my doctor. I know so much more now about my illness and my medication thanks to you helping me ask the questions. I don't agree with the

	way he prescribes new medication, a hundred pills at a time. Then if I have any side effects and we have to change the medication, I have all these pills left and wasted money.
MRS. SIMMONS:	Why don't you just ask him to prescribe smaller doses?
MRS. THOMAS:	He'd probably tell her he was the doctor and knew best.
SOCIAL WORKER:	Is that how you think he would respond? (Mrs. King was unsure what the doctor would say. I asked how she thought she might approach him about this.)
MRS. KING:	Well, I'd tell him (she looked down), "No." I'd ask him (she looked at me and smiled), "No." I'd tell him (she was looking down again), "I'd rather you give me fewer pills at one time so if they had side effects it won't end up costing me so much money."
SOCIAL WORKER:	Could you close your eyes and visualize your doctor's office—how he would look, and how you would feel saying those words to him?
MRS. KING:	(She looked down for a long time silently, then looked up.) "Please rewrite the prescription with fewer pills so if they have side effects it won't end up costing me so much money." (Everyone applauded and laughed, and Mrs. Simmons congratulated her and Mrs. Martin began to sing, "We're Just the Girls Who CAN Say No.")

Role-play helps members develop greater interpersonal empathy (role reversal), verbalize pain (role soliloquy), or dramatize a particular incident (role enactment) (Duffy, 1990). Social workers can also provide group members with cognitive tools to examine their communication and relational patterns. Between sessions, behavioral assignments or tasks such as shared activities or monitoring behavior can improve interpersonal patterns. Activities and program skills provide another means for changing maladaptive processes.

For example, a member of a developmentally challenged young adult group was isolated and occasionally scapegoated. The worker's creative use of dance was an effective step in integrating the member into the group's life (Schwartz, 1978):

While the others were dancing, I noted a spark in Barbara's eyes, especially when Sheila danced with her boyfriend. I sat down next to Barbara and asked if she knew how to dance. She was quiet. I asked if she enjoyed dancing, but still she didn't respond. I said maybe she felt that she couldn't dance as well as Sheila. She nodded and said, "And I don't feel like it." I commented that her eyes said she wanted to dance. She smiled. After we watched together for a while, I took her hand to see if she would like to dance. She responded and joined the group briefly.

She danced rather stiffly, standing in place and moving her arms around. She seemed pleased, and after a while sat down. I said, "You like to dance," and she nodded.

In a subsequent meeting, Barbara brought her own records, but she wouldn't leave her seat. The worker did not pressure her, but let her know that she was available to dance with her whenever she would like.

In a later meeting, I noticed Barbara watched me dance with others. I danced her step, precisely as I could, and told the group that I was doing Barbara's step. She smiled in response. In a circle dance, I continued to dance her step and reached for her hand to join me. She did, saying that her step didn't fit this dance so she couldn't do it right. I made an adaptation of her step, and she said she still couldn't do it. I held her hand and did it over and over again. She tried and got it. She joined the circle dance, smiling at me. I said enthusiastically, "You're doing great!" Together we taught "the Barbara" to the group, and she tried some steps the others were doing.

During the next meeting, she danced spontaneously with Earl. After the meeting, I credited her progress. She laughed, obviously happy with herself.

Barbara is on the way to being integrated into the group and to participating in its activities and relationships. By differential use of various techniques—which require activity, engagement, and involvement—social workers can help group members to view a situation or a process in new ways and develop relationships and communications that support development and adaptive functioning.

Groups are a powerful healing force for people who share common needs, concerns, and aspirations (Greif, 2005). For this potential to be realized, social workers must help groups deal with dysfunctional interpersonal processes that might emerge at any point in a group's life course. Similar maladaptive interpersonal processes can appear between workers and members. These maladaptive processes impede communications and the formation of trusting relationships. Hence, the next chapter takes up dysfunctional patterns that develop between workers and those who are served.

ELEVEN

REDUCING INTERPERSONAL STRESS
BETWEEN WORKER AND CLIENT

Dysfunctional patterns similar to those in families and groups arise between service recipients and social workers.

Interpersonal Processes between Worker and Client as Life Stressors

Resistance grows out of strains in the encounter between service recipient, worker, and agency and their respective efforts to maximize their own control over the situation and the process.[1] Agencies may try to control worker–client encounters with rigid policies and procedures. Workers may try to control the encounter through premature reassurance and interpretation, imposition of values and solutions, impatience with process, avoidance of relevant content and feelings, or inadequate exploration. Service recipients may try to control the content and focus of the interview and the worker by (1) active behaviors such as provocation, intellectualization, interruption, projection, verbosity, and seductiveness; (2) passive withdrawal, compliance, martyrdom, and nonverbalness; (3) flight behaviors such as instant recovery, canceled appointments, and precipitous termination; and (4) avoidance behaviors such as changing the subject, withholding data, minimizing concerns, and forgetting appointments.

Numerous diverse and interrelated factors account for dysfunctional interpersonal patterns. These factors need to be understood as they pose difficult challenges and painful experiences for both clients and social workers.

Agency Authority and Sanction Structures

Agency authority and sanctions form the context and role-defining frame-work for client–worker relationships. The agency expects practitioners to carry out its mission and mandates. In chapter 6, distinctions were drawn among services sought, offered, or mandated. Each can be associated with difficulties due to agency authority, sanctions, policies, or procedures. Such agency operations can adversely affect clients and workers and their rela-tionship. For example, Mrs. Chambers's children were removed from her home two years ago, following the detection of gonorrhea in her five-year-old daughter and the discovery of physical abuse inflicted on her two sons, ages fourteen and seven. Her boyfriend was the suspected perpetrator. She was referred by the court to agency services as a condition for the return of her children. For the past two years, Mrs. Chambers has denied that her chil-dren had been abused and resisted all court referrals. When it became clear to her that completing the court-mandated counseling program was the only way to regain custody, she reluctantly came to the agency. After miss-ing her first four appointments, she arrived thirty minutes late, nonchalantly entered the office, and threw herself into a chair.

MRS. CHAMBERS:	(Momentarily stopped snapping her gum to say, in a monoto-nous voice) Hi.
WORKER:	(After remaining silent for a few moments to see if anything else was forthcoming) I am sorry that we won't have much time.
MRS. CHAMBERS:	(Irritated) I'm late 'cause my bus was late!
WORKER:	(After a minute's silence as she stared out the window) I understand you're without your children?
MRS. CHAMBERS:	Ya.
WORKER:	Tell me about the situation.
MRS. CHAMBERS:	What's to tell—they took my children away from me. They said my daughter had "gonorrhea."
WORKER:	(After a brief silence) You sound pretty upset. . . .
MRS. CHAMBERS:	(Interrupting) You're damned right I'm upset!
WORKER:	Do you believe your daughter had gonorrhea?
MRS. CHAMBERS:	(In a calmer tone) No, I don't think she had it; at least I know she didn't get it from my boyfriend like they're saying, because I tested negative. Now, if he gave it to her, he'd have it, and so would I.
WORKER:	Does your boyfriend still live with you?
MRS. CHAMBERS:	(Again looking toward the window) I can't say. Somebody told me not to say anything.

Since time was up, I decided not to challenge her, and instead we negoti-ated our next appointment time. Before she left, I asked her what she thought about coming to the agency. She responded, "I think you people are really nosy, that's what I think" (she laughed nervously).

Mrs. Chambers is angry at the mandate and angry at her loss of autonomy. Her past experiences with social agencies were negative, and, understandably, she conveys suspicion, mistrust, and rage. The social worker personalizes Mrs. Chambers's resistance and opens the interview with a hostile question, "I understand you're without your children?" She has internalized institutional stereotypes and biases and lacks empathy. To Mrs. Chambers, the worker is yet another threatening representative of an oppressive system.

In unwanted mandated services rife with ambiguity, conflict, and pain, workers must fulfill several simultaneous roles: (1) as an organizational representative accountable to agency mission and mandate, (2) as a colleague aware of peer perceptions and definitions, (3) as a professional identified with the profession's values and ethics, and (4) as a staff member legally or institutionally responsible for supervising and reporting on the client's progress or lack thereof. Unless these various roles are managed well, they create dysfunctional interpersonal processes that could be intractable. Managing these organizational and professional roles well requires empathic skills to hear the client's voice.

A residential treatment center required children awaiting adoption to prepare a "life book" as emotional preparation for this critical transition. Writing and illustrating their life stories were expected to help children develop a sense of continuity and positive self-concept.

A social worker was assigned to help fourteen-year-old Pedro, who was being adopted by a member of the child care staff. His biological parents relinquished parental rights a few years ago. The case was assigned with the hope that the social worker could help Pedro work on abandonment issues and behavioral outbursts. Pedro didn't want to meet still another social worker, but the service was mandated. While seeking agreement on focus and plans, the worker was unable to arouse his interest or energy. But the "life book" did engage his interest. However, he was unaware of the agency and worker's hidden intent to discuss his feelings of abandonment and loss. He expected the book to be a photograph album of his loved ones and his accomplishments. He didn't want "bad stuff" in his book, and he excluded his biological family. The agency and worker rationalized their unethical paternalism as fear that Pedro would not agree to the project. However, such professional dishonesty is a violation of professional ethics.

During their first meeting, the worker mentioned his "other family." He stopped her in midsentence with "I never will discuss that with you." He was defensive, stern, and seemingly practiced in setting this limit with past social workers. After a few sessions in which Pedro developed a "life book" that excluded his biological parents, the social worker brought in a picture of his parents to include in the book. Pedro jumped up, started going through her desk drawers, ripped up some papers, and ran out of the room. After the "life book" failed, the worker suggested a trip to his old neighborhood. Pedro looked up at the ceiling and turned his back to her. When she persisted, Pedro shouted, "NO! I don't want to talk about them, I don't want to go there," and stormed out of the office. That night, he went AWOL.

The worker felt pressure from the agency's demand to carry out its new policy. Pedro's pain was drowned out and intimidated by the agency's "voice." In yielding, however, she alienated Pedro and added to his distrust of social workers.

For another example, a social work student was placed in a psychiatric hospital's subacute unit composed of eleven boys between the ages of eleven and fifteen. A twelve-year-old patient, Julio, had numerous psychiatric hospitalizations throughout his childhood. His parents physically abused and neglected him, and their parental rights were terminated. His mother's cousin, Mrs. Rodriguez, adopted him at a young age. While Julio had been in the hospital, Mrs. Rodriguez had cancelled over half of her family therapy sessions and visiting times on the weekend. On a recent home visit, in opposition of the team's instructions, Mrs. Rodriguez took Julio to visit his biological mother (in prior visits Julio's biological mother made numerous promises to him, only to change her mind.) Team members were frustrated with Mrs. Rodriguez's noncompliance and instructed the intern to confront her. As their interview begins, the intern questions whether the biological mother made any false promises to Julio.

MRS. RODRIGUEZ: No. Like I said, he was with me the whole time and she knows she isn't supposed to say anything like that to him. She really has come a long way with her therapy. He said to me he really wanted to see her and I talked to him about what has happened with her in the past. Julio said to me that he realizes that she is his mom, but that I am his mom who he is going to live with and that he knows that he can count on me because no matter what happens, I will always love him.

SOCIAL WORK INTERN: When things happen that prevent you from coming to sessions or visits, we see the way Julio acts.

MRS. RODRIGUEZ: It is really hard for me to get here because of the distance. I have diabetes, and sometimes it is hard for me to see at night.

SOCIAL WORK INTERN: Hold on a second. I understand that there may be reasons sometimes for not making it, but for example, when it was too windy for you to drive up for the holiday luncheon, we saw Julio sitting at the luncheon looking around at all the other parents and crying, "I want my mommy."

MRS. RODRIGUEZ: What was I supposed to do, drive and get into an accident, and then not be here at all for him? I tried to call a parent and get a ride up here for that day, but she couldn't do it. I look around at some of the biological parents and see how they are. I didn't get the department involved because of something that I was doing. I called to get some help for Julio and me. I adopted him.

SOCIAL WORK INTERN: I think that what you did by adopting him was a good thing. Nobody is blaming you for what kind of kid he is. Everyone realizes that he is a sick kid and that he is very difficult, but there is the question of you coming up for appointments.

MRS. RODRIGUEZ: It's not like I'm just not coming. I can't help it when I'm not here. I have legitimate reasons.

SOCIAL WORK INTERN: When you look at your attendance for scheduled appointments on a piece of paper, it doesn't look that good. Some people may even look at it and think that you are not very committed to coming.

MRS. RODRIGUEZ: I'm very committed to Julio. I have missed work and have taken him into my home. I can't believe that anyone would say that I'm not committed. It is things like that that make me think that I want to get him out of the hospital right now.

SOCIAL WORK INTERN: I can see that you are very upset by this and even getting a little defensive, but let's talk a little about your options and what can happen.

MRS. RODRIGUEZ: You know, people tried to warn me about getting DCFS (Department of Children and Family Services) involved. They told me that DCFS was going to try to take away my custody. It really makes me mad to hear that people are saying that I am not committed to him. I'm doing the best I can for him. Maybe you think that I'm being defensive, but I'm really upset by this and by you. I can't handle this kind of stress with my diabetes (begins to cry).

SOCIAL WORK INTERN: I understand that this is very stressful and I am telling you things you don't like to hear, but I want to be clear that nobody is saying that they want to take custody away from you. Let's look at some options. The other week you were asking why Julio couldn't come home rather than going to residential. DCFS asked the same question, and the hospital had to write them with a recommendation. A

	lot of the reasoning behind him going to residential was based on your attendance to visits and family therapy sessions. In order for him to be considered for discharge to home with wraparound services, we need to know that you will be at all the scheduled appointments.
MRS. RODRIGUEZ:	That's not fair! You people need to look at the reasons for my canceling. When he was home before, I didn't have problems with him. It was when he was at school that he was having all his problems. He kept getting into trouble at school, then he would go to the hospital. He would keep bouncing back and forth. I got DCFS involved because I wanted to stop the bouncing around, not because I was having problems handling him—I don't need family therapy!
SOCIAL WORK INTERN:	OK, but part of him being able to function at home means functioning in other settings safely, like school and in the community.
MRS. RODRIGUEZ:	Well, I don't know what control I can have over him while he is at school. They are a special school.
SOCIAL WORK INTERN:	The wraparound services will help you. If you really want him going home instead of residential, let's see what happens over the next couple of months. In family sessions we can discuss what needs to be different this time around, and make sure that we keep any appointments that we make. You need to know that he can also go to residential from here, and I want you to keep in mind that he may be placed as far or even further away.

The social work intern loses her professional mediating function by completely siding with the team at the expense of exploring Mrs. Rodriguez' narrative. The intern feels pressure to fulfill the team's agenda. This pressure fuels the intern's frustration and annoyance, which, in turn, interfere with her being curious and concerned about the mother's experiences.

Worker Authority and Power

The worker's authority and power are potential sources of interpersonal obstacles. As organizational representatives, workers are vested with authority. They embody the organization and people have to test which side workers are on, mistrusting them if they are totally aligned with the agency. As a representative of a profession, the worker has additional authority apart from the organization. Professional status lends an aura of expertise and competence. Over time, people test the extent to which the status is deserved and merits respect. If the worker personalizes such testing and responds inappropriately, a dysfunctional pattern becomes entrenched.

Twenty-eight-year-old Mrs. Taub sought services from a family agency. She could not decide whether to seek marital counseling or a divorce. Ambivalence and consequent immobilization propelled her to seek help. Ambivalence toward her husband was transferred to the worker. She immediately questioned the social worker's competence, sincerity, and depth of understanding. A new and youthful practitioner was threatened by the testing in the first interview.

MRS. TAUB: I am not really sure how much therapy is going to do for me. I mean, I've been through this before—about six months' worth of therapy—and I really don't think I got much better.

WORKER: Well, I certainly do hope that our work together will be more beneficial to you. (I started to get a sinking feeling in my stomach.)

MRS. TAUB: I don't know, maybe I just don't trust the whole therapeutic process. I mean, here you have a stranger meeting another stranger, a perfectly artificial meeting. One person doesn't really give a damn about the other, and one person is supposed to help the other. I mean, it really seems absurd and cold to me.

WORKER: I can understand how you'd feel that way, but even in this situation some real change can happen. (I wish I said this with more confidence.)

Because the worker is threatened, she doesn't respond to Mrs. Taub's core concern: "Do you really care about me as much as I need to be cared for?" Mrs. Taub missed the second appointment without calling. In response to the worker's telephone call, she attended the next session and introduced a further test.

MRS. TAUB: (Looking away from me) I'm sorry I missed last week's appointment.

WORKER: What happened?

MRS. TAUB: I felt really ill (stated in a matter-of-fact way).

WORKER: Why didn't you call to cancel?

MRS. TAUB: I just felt too ill. Are you going to charge me for the visit?

WORKER: I'm afraid that's our policy.

MRS. TAUB: I feel that if you cared about me—which I really don't understand how you can—I mean, you've only seen me for a total of two hours. But anyway, if you really cared about me you'd be more concerned about my health than about the dumb fee.

WORKER: Mrs. Taub, I am concerned about your health, but we also have a contract that we will meet weekly and that if one of us needs to cancel, we'll call twenty-four hours in advance.

Mrs. Taub tests the worker's caring and competence, and the worker reacts with frustration and a bureaucratic explanation. By focusing on organizational policy, the worker distances herself from a direct conversation about the meaning of Mrs. Taub's behavior (Gitterman, 1983, 1989a).

In the fourth interview, Mrs. Taub talks of the pain of her older brother's suicide. She uses this to pose another test.

MRS. TAUB:	I'm not really sure you can understand how much I really loved Ted. Our love was really special. There was something almost spiritual about our relationship.
WORKER:	Tell me what was special about the relationship.
MRS. TAUB:	I don't know if I can really describe our relationship. And I am not sure you'd really understand it.
WORKER:	Mrs. Taub, I get upset when you make comments, which suggest that I don't have the capacity to understand you. What makes you distrust me?
MRS. TAUB:	(Pauses and responds defensively) Well, maybe I am saying something like that. I mean, how are you supposed to understand how much Ted and I shared? I don't know anything about you. I don't even know if you ever had a relationship, let alone been in love.
WORKER:	It sounds as though you don't trust me.
MRS. TAUB:	Why should I trust you?
WORKER:	What would it take for you to trust me?
MRS. TAUB:	Well, I guess I want you to tell me a bit about your life. Have you ever suffered losses? Have you ever loved anyone? Have you ever felt pain?
WORKER:	The answer is yes to all your questions, but how will this help you to trust me?

Mrs. Taub continues to challenge the worker, becoming more explicit about her concerns. The social worker is threatened, defensive, and unable to deal with or use what was triggering her disconnected, unempathic responses. Interestingly, how a social worker deals with the testing behavior is a significant measure of professional competence.

Professional Socialization

Like other professionals, social workers are socialized to their profession. We take on preferred philosophical and theoretical assumptions about the behaviors and situations of those we serve. Such assumptions provide a frame of reference and a sense of order and predictability. Favorite theories and assumptions may become overly cherished so one is tempted to fit people into them. A need for certainty, constancy, and stability can compromise professional curiosity about a person's uniqueness and distinctiveness. Professional socialization can formalize the work and stiffen one's approach. Ambiguity threatens when it ought to challenge us. We then might become cautious, avoid risks, develop rigid and mechanical responses, and seek comfort in prescriptions and symmetries. The result can be our detachment from those we serve (Gitterman, 1991).

Workers' assumptions, whether accurate or inaccurate, may color client–worker relationships. We may unwittingly select and hear those communications that confirm our assumptions. Elements of the communications that do not fit our assumptions may elude us. For example, social workers committed to advocacy practice may primarily direct people to environmental issues, fracturing life transitional and environmental stressors. A social worker committed to clinical practice may direct people to life transitional issues, fracturing environmental and life transitional stressors. In response to the worker's subtle or unabashed efforts to influence and direct, the service recipient has the choice of satisfying or resisting the worker's preoccupations. When people resist being fit into the practitioner's assumptions, they are often labeled as "unmotivated," "nonverbal," or "resistant." Rigid belief systems may blind us to the ordinary details and realities of people's lives and their aspirations, anxieties, and daily hassles.

Differences

Conflicting expectations are associated with mutual dissatisfaction. Poor clients need help with immediate and current life issues, but a worker might concentrate on past experiences to uncover underlying problems. A client may seek advice and direction, while a worker may seek psychodynamic explanations and insights. Similarly, poor clients may view themselves as being "in charge" and competent, while a worker views them as reactive and as burdened by recurring troubles, underlying handicaps, and limited potential for change. Differences in race, social class, gender, sexual orientation, age, religion, and physical and mental functioning may also affect worker–client interaction by giving rise to incongruent perceptions and expectations. When clients' lifestyles, adaptive patterns, values, and perspectives are not respected, client testing and resistance become methods of coping.

Mrs. Cooper, a thirty-two-year-old African American woman, placed her eleven-year-old son, James, in a residential treatment center. He is truant, constantly fights, and frequently insults his teachers. The white worker felt that Mrs. Cooper was not a good mother, and wanted to teach her to be a better mother. Mrs. Cooper and the worker had been discussing the fact that James is telling lies, and Mrs. Cooper attributes it to his father's example.

MRS. COOPER: It seems pretty obvious to me! It's his father. He just keeps calling up James and promising him all these things and never comes through with them. James sees his father lying and getting away with it and figures he can do the same thing!

WORKER: Mrs. Cooper, how does it make you feel when Jimmy lies?

Mrs. Cooper wanted the worker to know her intense anger toward her husband: she had told of how he broke up the family, physically abused her, and neglected their children. After the first few years of marriage, he began using and selling drugs. He gradually sold their possessions, and ultimately they had to leave their apartment. He pushed her down the stairs in view of the children. Her leg was broken, and she left him. She couldn't provide for her son and left him for periods of time with her husband. Because of serious neglect, she brought him back to live with her. The worker wanted to focus on her son and his problems, not on her and her life stressors and issues. She wanted to use the interview to begin to teach her to be a better mother. After the first session, Mrs. Cooper canceled the next four appointments. With each cancellation, the worker's negative feelings toward Mrs. Cooper's concern for her son intensified: "if she didn't care enough to come to sessions, then how much could she care about her son?" In spite of the worker's objection, the treatment team sent James home for a week as a ploy to engage Mrs. Cooper. The following excerpt is taken from the second interview, which occurred three months after the first. The worker continued with her agenda of teaching Mrs. Cooper.

WORKER: What would Jimmy say about his father?

MRS. COOPER: Jimmy would say that he loved his father.

WORKER: Uh-huh. So, if you love somebody, do you think you can say you don't want to see or talk to him or her even if she or he hurt you or even if it's obvious to others that he or she may be doing something wrong?

MRS. COOPER: No—I guess not.

WORKER: Yes, you're right. I think that as adults it's important for us, in order to understand children, to try standing in their shoes once in a while to see how it feels.

MRS. COOPER: I know I have to understand Jimmy, but my shoes have a whole lot of stuff that come with them.

WORKER: What do you mean by "stuff"?

MRS. COOPER: Oh, you know all that bullshit I went through with Jimmy's father.

WORKER: I understand how angry you are at Jimmy's father, but I think it's important, if we're to understand and help Jimmy, that we try to keep your anger toward his father separated from Jimmy.

An important practice principle is to relate to the person one is with rather than to an absent third person. For example, Mrs. Cooper has pain she wants to share with the worker. Ironically, the worker who wants to teach Mrs. Cooper to listen more to Jimmy is not listening to Mrs. Cooper. The social worker ignores the life circumstances of an African American low-income woman who has spent much of her life struggling to survive. Mrs. Cooper pleads for empathy—"My shoes have a whole lot of stuff that come with them"—but the worker, insensitive to racial and class themes, ignores her moving plea.

An inexperienced young student began working in a nursing home with an "experienced" elderly resident who had feelings about receiving help from a much younger person.

MRS. GOLD:	How is it going? How do you like your new job?
SOCIAL WORK INTERN:	I was concerned when you canceled our appointment last week. Let's talk about it.
MRS. GOLD:	So tell me, what are your days like here?
SOCIAL WORK INTERN:	Rather than doing that, why don't we look at how I can be helpful to you?

This pattern continued for several sessions. At a later meeting, Mrs. Gold introduced the age factor.

MRS. GOLD:	You youngsters look at things differently.
SOCIAL WORK INTERN:	Does my being young affect our working together?
MRS. GOLD:	Well, for example, Mr. Hall (another new worker), who runs our meetings here—everyone likes him, but they feel he is young. All the residents like new workers and students, but feel they haven't experienced many things.
SOCIAL WORK INTERN:	How do you feel about my being young and new?
MRS. GOLD:	To tell you the truth, I think of you as being young. I feel that you haven't had many of the experiences, which I've had.
SOCIAL WORK INTERN:	Do you think it would be more helpful for you to see one of the older and more experienced social workers?
MRS. GOLD:	(Silence)

While the student invites discussion about the age difference, she is unable to struggle with the difference. In an institutional setting, a resident's struggle for self-dignity and autonomy is particularly poignant. This student, however, is threatened by Mrs. Gold's effort to decrease their status differences. She becomes defensive and refers the "uncooperative" Mrs. Gold to a more experienced worker.

Interpersonal Control

Struggles for interpersonal control can also lead to interpersonal issues between worker and client. Workers possess needed information, concrete resources, and procedures for referrals. They gain further influence from such personal qualities as friendliness, articulateness, assertiveness, and gentleness. People may become dependent upon approval and sensitive to subtle disapproval or judgmental statements. Whatever the source of workers' interpersonal influence, those served are likely to experience ambivalence and anxiety about gaining or losing interpersonal control within the relationship.

Clients too have means of interpersonal influence. They may try to control the focus and content of the interview or the relationship by various active, passive, flight, or avoidance behaviors. They can overwhelm social workers by the magnitude of life stressors and demands, creating in workers a parallel sense of vulnerability and impotence. This can result in expressions of impatience, inadequate exploration of client perceptions and experiences, or premature interpretation and reassurance.

Mrs. Charles, age twenty-three, married with two young children, had been hospitalized three times within the last two months for ovarian cysts and treatment complications. Her hospitalizations resulted in the removal of a large cyst, one ovary, and, finally, a hysterectomy and salpingo-oophorectomy (removal of the cyst, ovary, and fallopian tube). At the end of her medical ordeal, she commented, "I have nothing left inside me to cause these problems again." The family was unable to cope with the medical expenses and her lost salary. The social work intern helped her apply for public assistance, food stamps, and Medicaid for catastrophic coverage. She was approved for catastrophic coverage, but was responsible for $6,000 of her medical expenses. In dealing with the social work intern and other professionals, her frustration and bitterness were manifested in a combative and unappreciative style. While this helped her to exert more situational and emotional control, it decreased the motivation of the student and other professionals to help. During her second hospitalization, Mrs. Charles asked a nurse to notify the social work department that she wanted to see a social worker. The receptionist notified the intern that Mrs. Charles was highly agitated and sounded "nasty." When the intern entered Mrs. Charles's room, her "stare was strong and cold." The student was cut off in midsentence:

MRS. CHARLES:	I'm glad you're finally here. I called your office just a few minutes ago to be sure someone was coming up.
SOCIAL WORK INTERN:	Yes, Mrs. Charles, your nurse phoned the office about a half hour ago, but we were in a meeting so I didn't get the message until the meeting was over. Is there something I can help you with? (I immediately felt on the defensive and found myself somewhat annoyed.)
MRS. CHARLES:	I wouldn't have called you if there weren't something I needed. I can't pay my hospital bill. I have two small children at home. My husband is between jobs and working at night. He hardly makes enough money to support us, and the bills are out of sight. I've applied to

MEDICAID, and I don't know where I stand. Those people over there are so stupid; they don't know what's going on.

SOCIAL WORK INTERN: How can I help you with Medicaid? (I found myself reacting to her anger rather than her desperation. She almost hissed as she spoke. I snapped back the above response.)

MRS. CHARLES: You're a social worker, don't you deal with them?

SOCIAL WORK INTERN: Well, the accounts department handles billing problems, so they are the ones to contact Medicaid to get your number. But, if you'd like me to give them a call to check on the status of your case, I'd be glad to. I'll get back to you in an hour or so. (My backup: I became preoccupied with regaining control and being in charge. She slumped on the bed and practically whispered for me to do what I could.)

Throughout the brief session, the intern was overwhelmed by Mrs. Charles's intense feelings, and was unable to see beyond her tone of voice, glaring look, and combative style. The intern became caught up in an emotional power struggle, fueling the confrontation rather than reaching beneath the anger and connecting to the despair. The next session came after a subsequent hospitalization. The intern saw Mrs. Charles's name on the admissions chart, and went to see her.

MRS. CHARLES: (In a panicky voice) My husband received a letter from Medicaid saying we're responsible for $6,000 of my hospital costs. I just can't believe I'll have to pay it. I can't do it. I'll go crazy.

SOCIAL WORK INTERN: God, Mrs. Charles, I'm also beginning to feel overwhelmed. Let's slow down. I need to get this clearly.

Throughout this session, Mrs. Charles wanted to ventilate and the student wanted to gather facts. They had discrepant agendas: Mrs. Charles wanted a sympathetic and patient ear, and the student wanted to prepare for her conversation with Medicaid. Mrs. Charles became increasingly agitated, and the student became increasingly frustrated. Within two hours, Mrs. Charles called the office twice asking for her. When the student called back, the following exchange took place:

MRS. CHARLES: (In a sweet, apologetic tone of voice) Hi, did you talk to the worker?

SOCIAL WORK INTERN: (In an abrupt and matter-of-fact voice) Yes, she told me that since you and your husband are employed and will be earning $30,000, Medicaid policy states you are responsible for all medical expenses up to $6,000, or approximately 25 percent of your annual income. There seems to be no way around it. (This was my worst intervention. I reacted to her as a terrible pain in the neck. She took up a great deal of time; she annoys everyone in the office and the nurses on the floor. In turn, they are on my back, constantly complaining about her. Moreover, I didn't think I could help her. She and the whole situation made me feel incompetent.)

MRS. CHARLES: (Began to sob) Then I'll quit my job and my husband will have to quit his. . . . (She continued to sob.)

SOCIAL WORK INTERN: Listen, sorry about this whole thing—I'll be right up.

MRS. CHARLES: I'm sorry about our telephone conversation. I didn't mean to cry. You didn't have to run up.

SOCIAL WORK INTERN: I wanted to come up. I know you are very fed up and upset with this; I really would like to try to help.

When Mrs. Charles began to cry, the student felt less threatened and defensive. She felt more empathic and, simultaneously, in greater control of the interview and the interpersonal relationship. If a worker personalizes a client's struggle for control, the result is passive and aggressive behaviors and becoming caught in a power struggle. Interpersonal obstacles simmer as the worker concentrates on self-justification. Depersonalizing tensions and recognizing that they are rooted in a reciprocal struggle for control comprise the first step in meeting the challenge and converting threat into opportunity.

Transference and Countertransference

In professional relationships, workers may reenact parental and sibling experiences, transferring impulses, thoughts, and feelings to the client (Hafkenscheid, 2005; Horowitz, 2000, 2002; Malawista, 2004; Morris, 2002; Phillips, 2003; Pope, Sonne, & Greene, 2006a; Sarasohn, 2005; Stampley & Slaght, 2004; Zilberfein & Hurwitz, 2003). Inexperienced social workers, like other professionals, are affected by client personalities and behaviors and might respond poorly to some. Their own personalities also have an impact upon clients. Lack of self-awareness and not managing this reality encourages and intensifies interpersonal barriers. Counterfeelings and responses give rise to power struggles in which client and worker both feel misunderstood and put upon. But when social workers carefully monitor their own reactions, they are more likely to respond appropriately.

In this example, Greta, age fifty, sought help from an outpatient mental health clinic because of feeling "extremely sad, hopeless, and powerless about my marriage." Greta described her inability to assert her needs and wants to Steven, her husband, and to her twenty-seven-year-old daughter; prolonged sleeping in the middle of the day during weekends; alcohol abuse; and uncontrolled verbal outbursts. Greta repeatedly described her helplessness, despair, and anger, as well as her views of others as tyrants, oppressors, and abusers, and herself as a powerless victim. The social work intern, Michael, became frustrated and panicked. He felt that somehow he should have immediate solutions. His experience mirrored Greta's: both felt vulnerable and out of control. Unfortunately, he acted out his feelings by confrontation, impatience, and anger. Exchanges from the eleventh interview illustrate the dysfunctional interpersonal pattern:

GRETA: Steven did go to Pennsylvania with me. He was in an awful mood most of the time. He behaved even worse with his parents, abusing and torturing me in front of them. You know when he does this in front of his parents, I'm tempted to defend myself and explain to them that his complaints about me aren't true. But I stopped myself. I couldn't stand there and fight in front of his parents. One day I wanted to go to the movies and Steven jumped up from his seat and started screaming, "What! You say you are going to the movies and screw me, right?" He jumped up and grabbed the car keys. There was nothing I could do. There was no other way but to go over and kick or hit him or do anything. So I did nothing.

MICHAEL: Why didn't you say anything?

GRETA: It's always been the same. It's always feeling powerless. It's absurd. You end up in the same situation and say, "I don't deserve this." And yet you end up with the same situation. There is always a bizarre order to Steven's behavior. So why should I get upset any longer?

MICHAEL: You need to learn to assert yourself.

GRETA: With Steven there is no assertion. I'm in the car on the road, and I get abused. Or I say I want to go to the movies and he takes the car keys away, which I can only retrieve by physical force, causing a major fight. There's nothing I can do!

MICHAEL: Why didn't you ask him for the car keys?

GRETA: Because he wouldn't give them to me!

MICHAEL: But it sounds like you gave in to him as soon as he started yelling.

GRETA: I would be a fool to insist on something that would bring about a battle, especially in front of his parents. I can't do that, Mike.

MICHAEL: But he shouldn't be allowed to act like a child.

GRETA: But he is. That's the way it is. What should I do? I better not get so upset that I say, "Give me the keys, or else" because it would be "or else." There's nothing you can do, and I know that most people don't believe me.

MICHAEL: (In exasperation) What is it that keeps you in this marriage?

Greta seeks the student social worker's affirmation and understanding of her difficult, stressful, and painful experience. She lacked the support and strength to deal with the overwhelming misery that fills her life. She needs support and encouragement to cope with an abusive relationship. She needs help in sorting out priorities so that the issues become less overwhelming and more manageable for her. She needs to learn the steps in problem solving. Issues should be reframed in a way that points to possible changes. Instead, Michael approached her with disbelief and confrontation. In evaluating his intervention he realized that interpersonal conflict between Greta and him was triggered by her life issues, which called up pain he had known in his own family during the prolonged, conflictual divorce of his parents. His mother occupied a similar role to Greta's, and when he asked why Greta stayed in the marriage, it might have been a question for his mother. He wrote that "my impatience and frustration with Greta's passivity were in part coming from my own unresolved anger at my mother, who was unable to protect herself and her children from an abusive father and husband." For this student, Greta was a powerful teacher.

Taboo Content

Taboo areas such as sexuality, incest, violence, and death and dying—and practitioners' difficulties with such material—are significant sources of interpersonal stress (Pope, Sonne, & Greene, 2006b, 2006c). Many beginning workers find it difficult to invite people to tell their story and to explore and clarify particular details. A tendency to avoid direct discussion of intimate or painful material is understandable. The content easily triggers suppressed personal experiences and associated feelings. The pain inherent in the content may overwhelm social work beginners, generating anxiety and fear of losing control of the interview.

Seventy-four-year-old Mrs. Plante's husband recently died, and she was discharged from a psychiatric hospital after treatment of reactive depression. Following discharge she moved into protective and supportive housing for the elderly. A social worker, skilled in case management, was assigned at her daughter's request. The worker and Mrs. Plante agreed to the goal of successful transition in the new living arrangement. The social worker focused on connecting Mrs. Plante to supports in her new environment, applying for Social Security Insurance/Medicare, joining the local senior center, becoming acquainted with the new community and its offerings, and the like. While the worker was comfortable and competent in case management functions, she was uncomfortable with and awkward in responding to Mrs. Plante's need to express the grief and pain of her loss. When Mrs. Plante introduced this taboo area, the worker was uncomfortable and mechanical in her responses. She lacked confidence in helping with difficult life transitions and the associated intense stress. Several exchanges follow:

MRS. PLANTE:	The move here has been difficult, but I know that being around people will be good for me.
WORKER:	So your initial response to moving here has been a positive one?
MRS. PLANTE:	Oh, yes, everyone has been really nice. (Pauses.) You know, Janice, one of the reasons I was brought here by my daughter was because I just couldn't accept that my husband's time had come. Even when he collapsed at home and had to be taken to the hospital by ambulance, I kept insisting that he would come back home again. My denial that he was dying was so strong.
WORKER:	You must have loved your husband very much, and I hope you will get to like it here. . . .
MRS. PLANTE:	I am relieved to be living here, I really am. It's just that it takes time getting used to. It takes time. . . . (Her voice trailed off.)
WORKER:	You mean it takes time getting used to living in a new apartment and in a new community?
MRS. PLANTE:	It takes time getting used to being alone. It was fifty-five years of my life with my husband, taking care of him many of those years. You know, Janice, it's just not the same being alone in this world without your husband.
WORKER:	That's one of the reasons we are meeting together, to help you feel less alone.

Mrs. Plante describes her inability to deal with her husband's death. The worker tries to keep Mrs. Plante from expressing her devastating pain at the loss of her husband. The worker can't allow herself to hear this pain, and instead hopes that she "will get to like it here." Mrs. Plante's grief is so profound that it overwhelms the worker, who is experienced in environmental work, but inexperienced in work with powerful emotions. She felt the intensity of Mrs. Plante's sadness, pain, and fear, but was unable to accept these feelings in herself. A worker's emotional response is a critical barometer of the client's feelings, and investing oneself in a painful experience requires trusting and using one's own thoughts and feelings. Clients are quick to forgive genuine and caring mistakes, but playing it safe and being mechanical cannot move the work forward.

Client Defenses

Initial denial or negation, for example, can aid coping with painful experiences and therefore is adaptive until it becomes an obstacle to growth and change. Practitioners find it difficult to assess and respond to unconscious denial or conscious negation. Some are fearful and join the denial or the negation. Others seek to break down the defense, thinking that this will resolve the problem. Either response is dysfunctional, distancing the service recipient from the worker and creating a serious communication barrier. The social worker then has to struggle to reverse this pattern and engage the coping dimensions of the denial or negation. A person is more likely to examine and relinquish a contradictory reality when she feels the worker's effort is motivated by genuine concern, warmth, and care than when she feels it is motivated by frustration, impatience, or annoyance.

For example, Mr. Wallace, a sixty-year-old, married white man, was recently admitted to Jefferson Hospital due to a diagnosis of acute mylogeneous leukemia (AML).[2] Due to the severity of his illness, Mr. Wallace had to remain in isolation for a minimum of thirty days. Despite this rigorous treatment, the death rate for AML is 95 percent. Mr. Wallace's oncologist requested that a social worker be assigned to help him process his diagnosis and prognosis, as well as to offer support to his wife and two adult children.

In offering social work services to Mr. Wallace, the social work intern assumed that he would be as accepting of her effort to help him with the diagnosis as were her other patients. However, when after four sessions Mr. Wallace continued to avoid discussing his cancer diagnosis, the intern attempted to pressure him to talk about it. When he continued to avoid the conversation, she became frustrated and annoyed. Prior to their fifth session, Mr. Wallace's physician informed him that his treatments were not working; however, the treatments would be continued with the hope that his blood cell count would begin to change. He was also informed that he would become more physically ill as his body battled with the disease. The nurse informed the social work intern that Mr. Wallace was not showing any signs of being upset or concerned over his poor prognosis. The intern thought that the latest setback would motivate Mr. Wallace to "open up and connect to his feelings about the recent information he had received." She met with Mr. Wallace a few minutes after the physician left his room. (The intern had developed a rapport with Mr. Wallace through the use of humor.)

MR. WALLACE:	So yeah, you really need to tell your brother that mechanical engineers had it easy in college. The real engineers are the electrical engineers like me, and the nuclear engineers.
SOCIAL WORK INTERN:	Well, I will mention it and see what he says, although I think he would disagree. I can imagine, Mr. Wallace, that being here for such a long time, and receiving all the treatments you are, must be very difficult for you since your life is changing.
MR. WALLACE:	Oh, I'm fine. I am going to beat this, and hey, I'm doing great with these treatments. This is just a temporary issue, and then I'll be back at work. I haven't been sick, and I have been up and around making sure I get my

exercise. I'm going to beat this. You know, you might want to tell your brother that he should consider getting an MBA. I have one, you know. I've owned my own business for several years, and I own five houses. I've been able to be really successful once I got my MBA. Of course, I feel that I have always been successful.

SOCIAL WORK INTERN: I certainly notice that you have good color, and that's really awesome that you feel well. Mr. Wallace, do you worry at all that your treatment isn't working?

MR. WALLACE: Nahh. I'll be back in no time. This is just a temporary set-back. Did I ever tell you that I also studied medicine? I went to med school and took some classes at the University of North Carolina to learn about Chinese medicine. That's why I'm into special diets and all that. Natural medicine and Chinese remedies. It's kept me very healthy.

SOCIAL WORK INTERN: I think you did mention that you did some studying of different medicines in the past. In terms of your health, Mr. Wallace, right now—you are really sick. (Authoritative tone) How is that impacting you?

MR. WALLACE: (Closed affect) Like I said, I'm fine. The doctor was just here and we talked about how I'm feeling. I've still been able to get up and move around on my own. I even go down to the library to check my e-mail, mask and all. (He points to the IV.)

SOCIAL WORK INTERN: I've actually seen you heading down to the library. I admire your strength on being able to still get around. What is the doctor's assessment of how well you are doing?

MR. WALLACE: Oh, you know doctors. They have a whole lot to say and sometimes never say anything. He talked about my blood cell count and all of that medical terminology about what my body is doing.

SOCIAL WORK INTERN: Can you remember any of what he said? I may be able to decipher some of it for you.

MR. WALLACE: Well, like I said, he talked about my blood cell count and the treatments I have been getting. A lot of doctor talk.

SOCIAL WORK INTERN: How is your blood cell count?

MR. WALLACE: Well, it's pretty much the same since I was admitted. But you know, this is the first round of treatment that I've had, so I figure it's par for the course, you know. So we do it again and then retest. The good thing is I haven't been sick yet, just a little night sweats but I can manage that. So we do it again.

SOCIAL WORK INTERN: Are you worried at all about what the doctor shared?

MR. WALLACE: Hey, one thing you need to learn is that engineers never worry. (Laughs.) We're very factual people and like to have proof. The doctor showed me the results. I have proof that he is right. We just keep going. I'm pretty confident the treatments will begin to work because I'm not supposed to be feeling so well. Like I said, I feel really great, so I think it will just take a little more time than they originally thought.

SOCIAL WORK INTERN: I am glad that you are feeling so well. You really do have good color. Is there anything that you feel you need some help with?

MR. WALLACE: Nahh. I'm all right. Actually, I am pretty tired right now and should probably rest, so thanks for stopping by and I'll see you again later. (He waves his hand at me, shooing me away.)

SOCIAL WORK INTERN: (Very passive voice) Oh, OK. Well, thanks for letting me take so much of your time. It was great to talk to you. I'll see you in a few days. Bye.

Mr. Wallace wants the intern to be aware of his professional status and successes, and be aware that there is much more to him than being a cancer patient in a hospital gown with an IV. In turn, the social work intern feels inadequate and overwhelmed. She insightfully wrote, "When I am with him I feel very self-conscious and inept. . . . He maintains a wall of defense, which results in my wall of defense going up, and we face each other stone face and stone walled." The intern expects Mr. Wallace to share his weakness, pain, and despair over his potential dying and death. She expects him to be humbled by his disease, to cry, and to bargain for life. In contrast, Mr. Wallace desperately struggles to maintain control over his emotional, physical, and interpersonal life. Both intern and client are scared of showing and sharing their softness and vulnerability. Their fears are intermingled. In order to help Mr. Wallace, the intern will have to find the courage to openly and honestly share her concerns and feelings.

Table 11.1 summarizes the sources of interpersonal obstacles.

Table 11.1
Sources of Interpersonal Obstacles

- Agency authority and sanctions
- Practitioner authority and power
- Professional socialization
- Differences in social class, race, ethnicity, gender, age, physical and mental status, and sexual orientation
- Attempts to control
- Taboo content
- Client defenses

Social Work Functions, Modalities, Methods, and Skills

When dysfunctional client–worker interpersonal processes interfere with the ability to help, the social worker invites open and direct communications, establishes common stressor definitions, and develops greater mutuality and reciprocity in relationships. Practitioners rely on the methods of enabling, exploring, mobilizing, guiding, facilitating, and mediating to achieve these aims. Social workers must take a transactional view of the interpersonal issue and be willing to examine their contribution. Taking responsibility for engagement with, and easing barriers to, the relationship (often mislabeled "resistance") is an essential professional function.

Professional Methods and Skills, and Practice Illustrations

Social workers must examine the source of interpersonal obstacles and acknowledge their own contributions. Unless we do this, we will be unable to reverse a dysfunctional pattern of communicating and relating. If the pattern continues, the client is likely to intensify resistance and testing behaviors or to precipitously terminate service. When obstacles appear, as they invariably do, ecological thinking about the obstacle is essential. Workers and students who struggle to resolve the troubling issues noted in several vignettes show ecological thinking:

I am struggling with Mrs. Charles's open anger, frustration, and bitterness in regard to my ability or inability to understand and work through her strong feelings about the hospitalizations and mounting financial burdens. The feelings are manifest in a combative style. Her tone of voice is accusatory. Her annoying persistence in repeatedly contacting the social work department, nurses, department of welfare, and doctors—and expecting immediate service—has taken its toll. The medical and social service staffs view her negatively. She is frequently described as having an "attitude problem" and being a "pain in the neck." From Mrs. Charles's perspective, she might describe our interpersonal difficulties as "I cannot pay these bills—there's just no way. And you are just part of the big system that keeps making me feel like scum asking for help, and then, after it's all over and I do everything you ask, you screw me again. I'm not asking for much, and I'm furious that I have to go through all this for a little help." In fact, Mrs. Charles does exactly what needs to be done in going through the system. She keeps appointments, gives information and documents requested of her, answers questions, and tries to obey rules and guidelines. In return, Mrs. Charles expects to get what she is asking for—immediately. When she is made to wait or is inconvenienced by the system, she is quick to show her anger. Her displays turn people against her.

My view of our exchanges is that her anger, frustration, and bitterness make it difficult for me to WANT to help her. I do not want to be made a representative of the system that screwed her, nor do I wish to be thrown into that category so arbitrarily. She has not even inquired to see how I am different and how I might be able to help her negotiate the systems she confronts. I react to being blamed, and become angry and unsympathetic. I become overwhelmed, self-doubting, and defensive. It's like a mechanism gets triggered—I get ready for battle, for self-defense. And when I react (actually, overreact), I later feel terrible about my lack of empathy and occasional insensitivity. She makes me feel incompetent and guilty. I am struggling not to act out these feelings.

This student's self-esteem is threatened by Mrs. Charles's efforts to cope. She feels misunderstood and challenged, and responds with antagonism. Belatedly, the student takes the critical first step in reversing this dysfunctional pattern by examining her contribution to the interpersonal problem.

In much the same way, Michael reflected on his work with Greta:

When Greta started to talk about her helplessness, despair, and anger and cast herself as the victim, I became frustrated. I thought I should have immediate solutions, and I felt powerless. I turned off the feeling and latent content of her statements and many times only responded to the manifest and cognitive aspects of her message. I was accusatory about her allowing her husband to verbally abuse her. During other exchanges, I changed the subject and tried to uncover historical data, or I made ill-timed interpretations of what she was feeling and experiencing now as connected to what she had felt and experienced in the past. All this only served to intensify her feelings of anger, sadness, and helplessness. She looked as if she would explode. Her voice, though low, was intense and desperate. Other times, when I confronted her in an impatient and irritated tone, she became compliant and in a low, sad voice said she would try to do whatever it was I wanted her to do. Sometimes she became silent and withdrawn, sighed heavily, and exclaimed that her situation with her husband was hopeless.

From Greta's perspective, she perhaps felt that I as a much younger inexperienced student could not understand her many stressors, much less help her cope effectively with them. I think it was clear to Greta that I was not "hearing" her desperation and plea for help and that I was becoming increasingly impatient and frustrated. She may have thought that I believed things were not as bad as she thought them to be or sensed that I too was overwhelmed by her misery. Toward the end of our work together, I think she experienced me as another uncaring, insensitive man who was not only unable to care for her but also angry at her pain, over which she felt she had no control. My behavior was just another example of how nobody understood her struggle to live. She may have taken my responses to mean that her worst fears of being beyond help were true.

The interpersonal problem between us intensified. The more she presented herself as incompetent and helpless, the more impatient and confrontational I became. She in turn became angrier (and, I believe, felt more helpless) and more insistent as a victim who was oppressed and abused not only by her husband, daughter, and sister but also by the agency and me. Unfortunately, I fell in with all the others and became abusing. It is hard for me to believe how I fell into the oppressor role.

Greta's life story is reenacted in the helping process. She seeks help with abusive relationships, and the student's "help" is still another such relationship. Inexperienced, overwhelmed, and threatened by a client's stressors and coping patterns, a social worker may unwittingly blame a client for being difficult. The beginning professional must view the helping encounter as a microcosm of the client's own interpersonal issues. The encounter provides firsthand data regarding people's interpersonal relational and communication style, while the worker's own reactions yield data regarding clients' reactions to them. The professional tasks are to use one's reactions rather than act them out, to be self-monitoring and self-critical, and to learn from one's errors. These tasks replace any tendency toward using theoretical and personal rationales to justify practice disconnections. Greta was a powerful teacher for this student. He examined his own reactions and will be better prepared to empathize:

If I had another opportunity, I would make a new agreement with Greta on the most pressing concerns she wanted to work on. From there, I would help her set priorities to make the stressors more manageable. We would then discuss our expectations of what the work would look like. I would explore how she envisions our work together and reach mutual understanding. I would point out that people often want and even may expect quick, simple answers to complex, difficult troubles. Some can be quickly and easily eliminated; others take longer. I would also explore her reactions to our gender and age differences. I would explain that many people wonder about their social worker's level of experience, and gender and age (and ethnic and racial, when appropriate) differences, and we can talk about that too.

In the case of Pedro, the agency subscribes to the philosophy that many children are not properly emotionally prepared for the transition to adoption, causing disruption and possible disintegration of the adoptive placement; therefore, preparation is an integral part of the adoption process.

While I agree with this philosophy, the agency does not deal with the reality that our services are mandated. My progress with Pedro on the "life book" was reviewed every three months at team conferences, and I felt a tremendous pressure from the agency to focus on the "outcome" of our work rather than the "process." This external pressure from the agency compromised my effectiveness. At times, I forced the issue and did not work from Pedro's felt need and sense of timing, which led to his refusal to continue the project.

Pedro's view of our interpersonal difficulty was that I continually bothered him with painful topics, which he had never agreed to work on. When he did bring up his anxiety or his unclear feelings, he wanted me to "make it all better" quickly. He did not want to sit with his painful feelings, nor explore and clarify them; he wanted concrete solutions to what he viewed as environmental issues. For example, Pedro would be angry with his adoptive parents and would come to me to request another family. He would speak of nothing but his concrete plan of action to escape the situation. He would become angry with those who chose not to relieve his feelings. Therefore, I was constantly disappointing him because I could not make the pain go away.

Often, I complied with his request for immediate relief, thus maintaining an alliance built on avoidance and the fantasy that the avoidance will wash away the past. Initially, my perception of the problem was clear: Pedro was uncooperative in a therapeutic relationship and I had no recourse but to continually attempt to engage him. I blamed him as he blamed me. As I reviewed my work, I began to realize that each of us had a significant part to play in the dysfunction. In addition to the agency's implicit pressure to confront Pedro no matter how ineffective that intervention might be, I found powerful forces within myself that affected my interventions.

Viewing Pedro as a survivor of an emotionally abusive childhood, I desired to help him maintain his "fortress" rather than risk breaking it down, being unsure of what I would do with the pieces. I identified with Pedro's avoidance of hurt and disappointment, in that it reminded me of my own early self-protective avoidance. Within my internal desire to protect Pedro is my desire to protect myself. Our time together was in large part spent in our mutual avoidance of his feelings about either family. When my initiating these painful topics disrupted the balance, a period of intense discomfort or conflict followed, which then led us back to the safety of avoidance.

Specifically, I have observed two distinct dysfunctional transactional patterns. First, I would initiate the subject of Pedro's feelings about either his biological family or his adoptive family and talk to him in an uncharacteristically cold, calm, and serious way. Discomfort in discussing his loss contributed to my fear of his inevitable reaction. When I confronted him, he would immediately disengage with exasperation and no response to questions or react by aggressively disrupting my desk, cursing, or leaving the room. Pedro frequently told me he would never cooperate, and I was wasting my time by trying. I would then change the subject. Once the balance was regained, exchanges became smooth. The less frequent second pattern is reflected in my inability to explore Pedro's feelings. A painful event would happen in Pedro's life, and he would come into my office and express his anxiety by crying or by pleading for my immediate solution. I felt his pain intensely but was paralyzed with anxiety at the responsibility he was giving me, so I responded to his emotions and expectations with rational explanations. I tried to be empathic, but I falsely reassured him that everything would turn out all right one day, and gave him no tools to cope with the immediate issue. Although my emotions overwhelmed me, my external affect became logical and rational. My patterned reaction was to ask him factual, closed-ended questions and slowly refocus the interview on concrete, less threatening topics. Thus, we colluded to avoid emotional issues.

Discrepant views of the situation and focus often lead to chronic challenges and resistance. After a while patterns are set and the chance for engagement becomes increasingly difficult. To help with client–worker dysfunctional patterns, the worker takes responsibility for reversing them by disengaging from power struggles and reaching beyond the static. Table 11.2 summarizes how social workers prepare themselves for work with dysfunctional interpersonal patterns.

Barry, a young adult diagnosed with schizophrenia and recently released from a mental hospital, moved into a halfway house. He chose a low-demand day hospital program. After three months, agency policy required that he take another step toward his goal of full-time employment. This meant doing something more demanding in addition to or instead of the day hospital. Shortly after he received this information, staff and residents noticed that

Table 11.2
Professional Preparatory Tasks

- Develop the transactional perspective, and define the interpersonal obstacle.
- Examine potential sources of the interpersonal obstacle.
- Acknowledge own contribution to the obstacle.
- Accept professional responsibility for dealing with and reversing dysfunctional patterns.
- Take responsibility for disengaging from power struggles.
- Tune in to own feelings and use them rather than act them out.
- Tune in to client's perceptions of self and situation.
- Develop empathy for client suffering.

Barry spent increasing time away from the halfway house and seldom slept there at night. Because regular attendance at various house functions was a requirement, his absences were seriously jeopardizing residency. The social worker was instructed by the team to confront Barry about his almost total absence.

BARRY:	(Looking at the floor, head down, shoulders sagging) What is it you wanted to talk to me about?
WORKER:	You didn't make your coffee hours last week.
BARRY:	Yeah, I suppose I didn't.
WORKER:	One of the conditions for living here, Barry, is that you attend coffee hours. (I handed him a copy of this rule.)
BARRY:	(Glancing at what I handed him) Well, I'll try to make them next week.
WORKER:	Actually, that isn't all. The house counselors said that at rounds this week, it looked like you hadn't slept in your bed, and quite a few residents are saying they haven't seen you around much lately.
BARRY:	That's MY business! I've been seeing the folks a lot.
WORKER:	Is there trouble at home?
BARRY:	Yeah. Quite a bit.
WORKER:	What's been happening?
BARRY:	Dad went on one of his drinking binges—God, I swear they are getting worse—and took a bunch of pills. Scared the hell out of Mom. I've been trying to help out over there. My Dad is OK, but he is pretty shaky.
WORKER:	This has been a real rough week for you.

The worker begins the interview in a confrontational mode. Organizational pressures can intimidate workers and cause them to incorporate them into their professional approach rather than mediating to improve the fit between agency demands and service recipient needs. This practitioner was able to reverse gears, place herself in Barry's shoes, and invite his perceptions and life issues ("Is there trouble at home?"). This avoided a power struggle that both would have lost. She engaged Barry in productive work on the debilitating crossfire of pressures emanating from home and agency.

Workers may overidentify with clients, their concerns, and their perceptions. Social workers are sometimes caught between clients' needs and the needs experienced by significant people in clients' lives.

Mr. French, a forty-five-year-old, single, white, Protestant male, was admitted to a psychiatric hospital a month after suffering from decompensation (the loss of appropriate psychological defenses). He had been evicted from his boardinghouse after neighbors, employees, and relatives reported his bizarre behavior. Mrs. Houghton, his sister, helped him move out of the boardinghouse and brought him to the hospital. After six weeks, the treatment plan focused on encouraging his return to the community, his return to his job, independent living, and outpatient treatment. The worker met twice with Mrs. Houghton to engage her in the discharge plan. In the first meeting, she met alone with Mr. and Mrs. Houghton and Mr. French; in the second meeting, the psychiatrist joined them. Mobilizing coping resources for Mr. French was discussed, and Mrs. Houghton expressed her feelings evoked by the responsibility for her brother. The more the worker and psychiatrist pushed, the more she resisted. By the third interview, the worker was more attentive to her concerns and anxieties:

MRS. HOUGHTON:	I hope your plan works; otherwise, you and Dr. Knight will have to think of something else for my brother. He's YOUR patient!
SOCIAL WORKER:	Mr. French was not able to go to Byetown, and perhaps it was an overwhelming initial task. We are still working on the plan as discussed. We should also think about the possibility of your accompanying him to town to look for an apartment.
MRS. HOUGHTON:	I won't do it. I have leg trouble. I also don't like to drive that far. I finally have my kids out of the house, my own job, and my own money from that job. I'm at the point in my life that I only want to take care of my husband and myself.
SOCIAL WORKER:	I can appreciate the fact that you should have less responsibility for others and not more. Do you think we can explore ways that you can help your brother and still set limits on your responsibility for him?
MRS. HOUGHTON:	I'm concerned about my own mental health, and I need to take care of myself (in the prior session, she discussed her previous psychiatric outpatient treatment for depression).
SOCIAL WORKER:	Although Mr. French is our patient, I am also concerned about your well-being. I realize you are currently under great pressure due to your brother's hospitalization.
MRS. HOUGHTON:	Thank you for your concern. I really do appreciate it. I am under a lot of pressure, and it concerns me.
SOCIAL WORKER:	Do you think you would feel comfortable seeking help if you felt you needed it?
MRS. HOUGHTON:	Yes. I will contact someone if I feel I need it, because I know it can help. I have the names of several psychiatrists. And I may have to do it if I let my brother deplete me.
SOCIAL WORKER:	How do you see your role in regard to your brother? That is, ideally, how do you envision it?
MRS. HOUGHTON:	I would like to invite him for holidays and occasional weekends to my home, but I don't want to go see him and have to check on him. If it comes to that, I would want him to go to one of the halfway homes that my cousin operates in Florida.
SOCIAL WORKER:	That is an alternative, but the fact is that Mr. French has invested most of his life in Byetown and his job, which was

MRS. HOUGHTON:	meaningful to him. To remove him from what he knows might not be the most helpful option.
MRS. HOUGHTON:	I see what you mean, but we will have to see if this plan works and if he can find an apartment.
SOCIAL WORKER:	You are absolutely right. Let's see how the next couple of weeks go and plan to meet again with your brother.

In this session, as in the prior ones, Mrs. Houghton is letting the worker know that she feels overwhelmed by responsibility for her brother's care. Initially, the worker ignores Mrs. Houghton's message and perpetuates the pattern of trying to convince her and "sell" the agency's treatment plan. While family members can become an effective extension of the clinical team, they must want to be included in the aftercare and must know what to do and how to do it. To move beyond the emerging interpersonal obstacle, the worker had to become attentive to Mrs. Houghton's needs by inviting her to talk of her pain, anger, and associated guilt. In pursuing a desired task or outcome, family members' feelings and perceptions must be obtained and not bypassed. When social workers empathize with and respect family members' autonomy and separate their needs from the patient's needs, the power struggle subsides.

For example, a social worker was assigned to fourteen-year-old Denise in her third month of pregnancy. Two weeks before discovering her pregnancy, she was placed in foster care after reporting her mother for child abuse. Denise views her pregnancy through the rosy perceptions of an adolescent. She envisions her baby as perfect and doll-like, who will provide her with all the love and affection she has been denied. She has no realistic plan for herself or her child. She merely hopes that a solution will magically appear, allowing her to live happily ever after. She provides herself with a companion who will need her love and love her, rather than face loneliness. "Adoption" is a provocative word, met with negation and obstinacy. She is determined to keep her child. The worker, a recent graduate, is concerned about Denise's unrealistic planning: neither her natural nor foster mother will accept the infant into their homes. The worker tries to collect sufficient data in order to convince Denise that her plans are unrealistic.

DENISE:	(Shouting) I don't know what people are telling you about me. But I ain't going to listen to you either. Nobody is going to tell me what to do!
SOCIAL WORKER:	I have no intention of forcing my opinion on you. Whether you decide to keep your baby, abort it, or place it for adoption is entirely up to you. My purpose is to help you make the decision that is best for you. I want to listen, and help and support you.
DENISE:	(Looking at me skeptically) Why?
SOCIAL WORKER:	I realize what a difficult decision you're facing, and it could be helpful to have someone to talk to and listen to your ideas.

DENISE:	I guess so.
SOCIAL WORKER:	When did you discover you were pregnant?
DENISE:	About three weeks ago.
SOCIAL WORKER:	How did you feel then?
DENISE:	Very happy.
SOCIAL WORKER:	Were you surprised?
DENISE:	No.
SOCIAL WORKER:	Why didn't you use contraception?
DENISE:	My boyfriend said that men could control themselves.
SOCIAL WORKER:	Have you been dating him for a while?
DENISE:	I've dated Marvin for a couple of years on and off.
SOCIAL WORKER:	How did he view your pregnancy?
DENISE:	He was upset at first, but now he is happy.
SOCIAL WORKER:	Do you feel he will be supportive throughout your pregnancy?
DENISE:	He'll be a good father.
SOCIAL WORKER:	Have you given any thought to what your decision might be regarding the baby?
DENISE:	I'm going to have my baby and keep it.
SOCIAL WORKER:	Are you certain this is the right decision for you and the baby?
DENISE:	(Yelling) I AM GOING TO KEEP THE BABY!
SOCIAL WORKER:	Are you planning to continue school when the baby begins to show?
DENISE:	I'll stay in school until I deliver.

Denise's message is loud and clear:

If you are just another person who is going to tell me what to do with my baby, I want no part of it! This is my decision. All my life I've been pushed around, and things are going to be different now! This is my baby! Finally something that is all mine! I have a chance to be happy, to have love! You can't brainwash me, lady—I know what I want! I'm tough, I can do it—oh, but God I'm scared!

While the social worker relates to some of Denise's concerns, she limits herself to a superficial level. She struggles not to impose her agenda; yet she feels that Denise's plans are totally unrealistic. These conflicting pressures ("How can I support her decision, when I know adoption is probably the best thing for Denise and the baby? But if I don't support her, she will reject my help. She has rights too") immobilize the worker and block her natural empathy. Her own battle absorbs the worker's energies ("the fog around me was growing so thick that it nearly engulfed me") and prevents her from responding to Denise's latent messages. She vacillates between trying to convince Denise that her plans are unrealistic and focusing on safe concrete items. And the work is at a stalemate.

DENISE:	My baby will be born in November. I can't wait!
SOCIAL WORKER:	Having a baby would dramatically change your whole life.
DENISE:	I know it won't be easy, but it'll be fun.
SOCIAL WORKER:	When all your friends are going to parties or movies, you'll be home warming bottles and changing diapers.
DENISE:	I don't go for that kid stuff anyway. Besides, I stay home at night a lot with my younger brothers and sisters.
SOCIAL WORKER:	It will be a different ballgame when you're caring for an infant who is totally your responsibility.
DENISE:	I said I could handle it.
SOCIAL WORKER:	People often don't realize how demanding a baby is until they have one of their own.
DENISE:	I know babies are a lot of work, but as long as I have my baby I'm going to be happy.
SOCIAL WORKER:	There will surely be times when you'll be pleased and proud, but I am also certain there will be times you will long for peace and quiet and freedom. Babies are extremely self-centered. All they understand is "I'm hungry! I'm wet! I'm tired and I want to be held!"
DENISE:	(Weakly) I guess so.
SOCIAL WORKER:	The baby will not be capable of understanding that Mommy also has needs. Sometimes you will get to a point where you will give anything for sleep. And the baby will keep crying and crying.
DENISE:	I'm sure that happens to some people, but my baby will be well behaved.
SOCIAL WORKER:	Why do you feel your baby will be different?
DENISE:	I was a quiet baby, so my child will be well behaved also.
SOCIAL WORKER:	I hope you're right, but it doesn't always work that way. No baby can be a perfect angel.

Denise expresses an overwhelming desire to fill the void in her empty, unfulfilled life. She longs to have a role, a place, and a purpose. She associates power and meaning with motherhood. Despite the social worker's efforts to change her mind, Denise holds firm, essentially saying, "I can handle anything that comes my way—this baby is my salvation!" The worker confronts the youngster's denial and negation. Without a relationship, however, Denise is unprepared to listen to the worker's version of reality and determines that she cannot or will not be helpful. Practitioners must not attack a person's defenses. They must demonstrate an understanding and appreciation of the client's perception of reality before the client can explore an alternative reality.

Social workers have to earn a person's trust; empathy is essential to earning trust. With people who face painful life stressors, trust and relationship are often released by mobilizing environmental resources. Denise's social worker identified and assessed the interpersonal obstacle to the work, and committed herself to connecting to Denise more effectively. After several missed appointments and subsequent phone calls, Denise arrived quite agitated:

DENISE: Mrs. Peterson (her foster mother) and Mrs. Thomas (foster care worker) are planning to send me to Isaac House (a home for unwed mothers). I won't go there! If they make me go, I'll run away for good!

SOCIAL WORKER: What bothers you about Isaac House?

DENISE: I don't want to talk about it, but I'm not going there.

SOCIAL WORKER: If you don't want to go to Isaac House, you have to develop an alternative plan. You'll need a place to live and a means of supporting your baby.

DENISE: I agree. Will you help me?

SOCIAL WORKER: Let's deal with one task at a time. First, let's find a place for you and your baby to live. Can you think of any place where you might stay?

DENISE: I haven't thought about it.

SOCIAL WORKER: Will your foster mother allow you to remain if you decide to keep the baby?

DENISE: Mrs. Peterson told me I could stay until the baby is born. After that I will no longer be welcome.

SOCIAL WORKER: Are there any possibilities for you to stay with your grandparents, father, aunts, uncles, or cousins?

DENISE: I've never met my father or anyone on his side of the family; my mother was the black sheep of my family and I'm not on speaking terms with any relatives. I don't trust any of them.

SOCIAL WORKER: Would you ever consider moving back in with your mother?

DENISE: I might if she agrees to counseling.

SOCIAL WORKER: Are you scared your mother might abuse your baby, the way she abused you?

DENISE: This is the main reason why I will not go home unless I have no other option. I feel I can handle being abused myself, but I can't have my own child abused.

SOCIAL WORKER: I can understand your feeling this way, and having a bottom line. Let's examine other possible options. How about your boyfriend's family?

DENISE: That's a great idea! Marvin's parents love me and will want their grandchild.

SOCIAL WORKER: Have they ever discussed the possibility of your moving in?

DENISE: It'll be all right with them.
SOCIAL WORKER: Let's discuss how you might ask them.

The social worker should have explored the youngster's intense negative reactions to being sent to a home for unwed mothers. The worker did not explore possible fears and objections. However, in contrast to previous exchanges, she did focus on Denise's agenda and tried to be responsive. Beginning with the client's definition of the issue and perception of the situation is essential to establishing mutuality and rapport.

Focusing on the client's definition and perceptions of the stressor and the situation is sometimes enough to reverse a dysfunctional pattern. At other times, the worker needs to invite the client to examine the barriers. The social worker must persist in exploring and inviting discussion of the tensions between them. This communicates faith in the helping process and demonstrates caring.

Some workers are able to defuse client–worker tensions with appropriate, timely humor. In certain instances, a light touch can relieve anxiety and expedite the work.

Mr. Kennedy, a sixty-two-year-old Irish-American widower, was forced to retire on complete disability because of severe diabetes. One leg was broken in a fall at a local city hospital when he tried to get off an examining table where he had been left unattended. Mr. Kennedy was then placed at a welfare hotel after a fire destroyed most of his home and all of his clothing. He was in the hotel two weeks when the welfare worker informed him that in another week he would have to attend a hearing to determine whether he would receive an extension. She found him abrasive and uncooperative: he was angry, cursed, and yelled that he didn't intend to go to any hearing. He screamed, "You better let me stay in the hotel. I've worked hard all my life, paid my taxes." He also threatened to "bash in the hotel manager's head with one of my crutches." After this outburst, he asked if the hotel had "a social worker woman like there was at the hospital." He wanted to see her and see what she could do to "help me with all these damned people."

Since he was on crutches and unable to look for an apartment, the social worker, also Irish American, agreed to help Mr. Kennedy to stay at the hotel. She agreed it must be hard to go up and down the stairs on crutches and told him that she would call the hearing office to request a hearing at the hotel because of Mr. Kennedy's physical condition. They agreed to conduct the hearing in an office located on the same street as the hotel. She called and gave Mr. Kennedy the time and date. Three days before the hearing, the hearing officer called to say that he had to move the hearing ahead one day. Because the worker couldn't reach Mr. Kennedy by phone, she left a note in his mailbox telling him of the new date. When the day came, Mr. Kennedy did not arrive. She called him, but there was no answer. The following morning, Mr. Kennedy arrived at the worker's office for the first scheduled interview. She recorded:

When I asked why he had not come the previous day, he looked puzzled, pulled out a calendar with the date circled, and told me he was sure I had told him Friday. I explained about the change to Thursday, my effort to reach him by phone, and the note I left. I asked him if he received my note. He said he had gotten some paper in his box, but didn't know what it was about. I asked if he had read it. He said he didn't have his glasses with him that morning. I kept asking if he had read the note later that day.

Mr. Kennedy became fidgety and looked quite uncomfortable. His face was red, he looked angry, and started yelling, "I am sick and tired of this bullshit. You are just like all the others, asking me to do things I can't do for myself." Thinking that he was referring to arranging the hearing, I pointed out that I had found an easier way for him, and all I asked him to do was to get himself to the hearing on the right day. Mr. Kennedy grabbed his crutches, stood up, glared at me, and blurted, "Look, you dumb S.O.B., I've been trying to tell you—I can't READ!" As he walked out he yelled back, "I don't give a shit about the hearing—you can all go to hell!"

The worker was angry with Mr. Kennedy for making her look bad. She assumed he was refusing to take minimal responsibility for his life. Moreover, as she struggled to control her anger, she became preoccupied with her own feelings, stifling her ability to be curious and to listen. Consequently, she was unable to pick up Mr. Kennedy's clues about his illiteracy. Mr. Kennedy's frustration and anger are understandable: he was being held accountable for taking charge of his life, when he could not read a simple note. From this interview, the worker became aware that Mr. Kennedy's difficulties with agency personnel are not due to temper or hostility but to his frustration, insecurity, and feelings of inadequacy. He used bravado to cover his insecurities.

The social worker realized Mr. Kennedy probably would not come back to see her. She wondered how to recover the contact and restart the dialogue, and what point of entry would mobilize his resistance the least. She remembered from their first contact that he had made numerous references to being Irish, and she decided their common ethnic background might provide a necessary bridge.

When he asked who it was in response to my knock, I told him my name and that I wanted to talk to him. He yelled, "Go back to your office before you freeze out there." I asked if he could hear me, and he didn't respond. I said, "Look, Billy, there's a Mick on the outside of this door who can be just as stubborn as the one on the inside. So, you better open the door before the two of us make a holy show of ourselves."

With that, the door opened wide and Mr. Kennedy stood there laughing. "Well now," he said, "I guess there's still a little of the old sod in you after all." "Well now," I said, mimicking him, "I guess you are not the only Irishman who kissed the Blarney Stone either." We both laughed, and he invited me to sit down and have a "good cup of tea." As we drank the tea, both of us were quiet. I broke the silence by saying, "I am sorry about the other day, sorry that I didn't listen to you and hear what you were saying, and sorry that I was angry at you without understanding how things really are for you. I really want to try to help you and hope you will give me another chance." He immediately answered that if anyone should be sorry, it should be him with his "trashy mouth and rotten temper." He apologized for cursing at me and explained he was so upset because it is hard for him to let anyone know that he can't read. He told me he is very ashamed and feels like a "dummy."

The worker effectively uses their common ethnicity as a point of entry into their interpersonal obstacle. Humor eased the tension and provided a boost to their working relationship. By apologizing to Mr. Kennedy for her insensitivity, she conveys a willingness to risk further rejection. A transactional obstacle is best engaged when the interaction is between real people who have strengths and weaknesses, and struggle to come to grips with them and with each other. With Mr. Kennedy, the encounter led to a major breakthrough in the quality and the depth of their ongoing work.

Mr. Kennedy spoke of having lost everything last year. I asked if he was referring to his wife's death. He said when she died he had nothing more to live for . . . he wanted to die too . . . he felt he couldn't go on living without her. I asked him what got him through the worst days. He said he really didn't know how he managed, but he just went through the motions of living, taking his insulin, preparing his meals, and trying to rest as the doctor ordered. He did all the same things he did when she was with him. At first, she seemed to still be in the house and he found that as the days went on he gradually realized she wasn't there. Then he hit on the idea that if he didn't talk about it, and didn't mention her name, it would seem like nothing had happened, that he could somehow keep her with him. He refused to talk to anyone about his wife, or about the circumstances of her death, or anything concerning her. I remarked that never talking about the one person who was uppermost in his thoughts must have been extremely difficult for him. He looked very dejected, his head sunk low, and he cried softly, "I can't keep her with me, no matter how I try. She is gone. She is never coming back from the grocery store.

I can't make her come back." I answered softly, "No, you can't Billy, but maybe you can begin to talk about her."

(Later in the interview) When I asked him if he had ever tried to learn to read when he got older, he told me his wife was the only one who knew, and he was too ashamed to tell anyone else who might help. He told me that all his life, he had been afraid to take a chance. When he was a child, he never knew where the next meal was coming from or whether there would be a next meal. He thought this had made him cautious about everything until now, when he had lost his wife and everything he owned. He had nothing else to lose. I asked, if he had nothing to lose, would he take a chance with me? I would like to help him learn to read. At first he was cautious, even resistant: "I don't think you can teach me to read—I mean, it's not your job, and what would you know about how to go about it?" Sensing his tension, I said that I had a sense he was about to call me a dumb S.O.B. again. We both laughed, and that relieved the tension. I told him he was right, it takes special skills, and I knew a teacher with remarkable talent in teaching adults how to read. Before I could finish, he said he didn't want a teacher treating him like he was a six year old and teaching him to read. I explained to him who this person was (a retired teacher who had taught reading and English to immigrants applying to become citizens). "You mean she could teach those foreigners who didn't know anything?" I added, "And she didn't treat them like six year olds." He agreed to give the idea some thought.

The next time I saw him, we talked about housing. As we ended, I asked if he had given any more thought to my suggestion about his learning to read. He grinned at me and said, "Well you better call that old lady before we both get too old for her to teach me to read."

With the social worker's support, Mr. Kennedy took lessons and quickly progressed to a fourth-grade reading level. He seemed increasingly self-confident, smiling easily, getting along with his landlord, traveling independently, and trying new foods. Clearly, being able to read has opened a new world and imparted a sense of mastery. The social worker's progress with Mr. Kennedy is associated with her ecological thinking, an astute definition of the interpersonal obstacle, and total empathy. Without this perspective, Mr. Kennedy might have been dismissed as "resistant" and "unmotivated." With ecological thinking, the worker defined the obstacle as being within her professional function. She owned her contribution to the obstacle, apologized, used humor to reduce tensions, and pursued Mr. Kennedy's stake in working on his long-standing life issue. Table 11.3 summarizes the skills of dealing with interpersonal obstacles.

When client and social worker work effectively on their dysfunctional interpersonal patterns, they grow in confidence and mutual trust. Hence,

Table 11.3
Skills of Dealing with Interpersonal Obstacles

- Reach beneath manifest behaviors and verbalizations.
- Invite and explore perceptions, content, and related feelings.
- Engage coping aspects of defenses.
- Demonstrate genuine concern, warmth, and caring.
- Demonstrate understanding of client's perceptions of self and situation.
- Identify tension and obstacles in relationship and communication.
- Invite perceptions of client–worker relationship and communication patterns.
- Acknowledge potential discomfort in work on tensions and obstacles.
- Make supportive and persistent demands that issues in the work be addressed.
- Use appropriate and timely humor to defuse tensions.
- Demonstrate own stake in the work and in the relationship.
- Pursue client's stake in the work and in the relationship.

practitioners need to view such obstacles as inherent in the helping process and struggle against discouragement and self-blame. The work together gives the opportunity for both participants to meet and master a difficult challenge with creativity.

ENDINGS

Settings, Modalities, Methods, and Skills

The decision to end can occur in several ways. Too often, the client prematurely drops out of services (Williams, Ketring, & Salts, 2005). Brogan, Prochaska, and Prochaska (1999) found that premature terminators were more likely to be oriented toward changing their environment than themselves. More effective anticipatory empathy, contracting, case focus and direction, reminders of appointment, and development of a therapeutic alliance can lessen premature termination (Hatchett, 2004; McCabe, 2002; Ogrodniczuk, Joyce, & Piper, 2005).

The decision to end could also be made jointly by the client and worker (Fortune, Pearlingi, & Rochelle, 1991); it could be imposed by the nature of the setting, as at the end of the school year or at the end of hospitalization (Zuckerman & Mitchell, 2004); or it might have been settled in advance, as in planned short-term service. Occasionally, the decision to end comes about through an unexpected event involving either worker or client, such as illness, a move, or a job change. However the decision is made, termination represents an important transition and role exit, and makes specific demands of both worker and client (Baum, 2005). These include (1) managing feelings aroused by the ending; (2) reviewing accomplishments and what remains to be achieved; (3) planning for the future, including, where indicated, transfer to another worker or referral to another agency; and (4) evaluating the service provided. Like the preparation, initial, and ongoing phases of practice, the ending phase requires social workers' sensitivity, knowledge, careful planning, and range of skills.

Preparation

Separation is painful; even the termination of a brief relationship or one that was fraught with ambivalence can reawaken distressing feelings connected to earlier losses. The termination of a professional relationship can have a similar impact. If the experience of termination and its meaning to the particular client are ignored or mishandled, any gains achieved in the work together can be lost. Future involvement with social work services could also be jeopardized. When the ending phase is handled well, however, termination results in growth for both client and worker.

Ending is a mutual experience. The client needs to separate from the worker and the agency; the worker needs to separate from the client. In preparing to help individuals, families, and groups move through termination, social workers consider organizational, temporal, and relational factors and anticipate their likely impact on the client and on themselves.

Organizational, Temporal, and Modality Factors

The agency itself influences the content and process of ending, particularly in respect to temporal features. Organizations differ in how they structure and use time. A public school, for example, has a natural temporal structure that fits well with both temporary separations and permanent endings. During holidays and vacation periods, temporary separations reflect natural pauses: the building is closed, family and friends may be more accessible, and time is available for other activities. A temporary separation is less likely to stimulate feelings of abandonment and rejection than separation in other organizational contexts. Similarly, completion of the academic year carries intimations of graduation. A permanent ending at this time meshes with the temporal structure. It may be readily connected to a sense of progress and achievement, minimizing the sense of loss.

Long-term treatment facilities for the chronically ill, the elderly, and children provide different temporal structures. Holidays and worker vacations are painful for these clients, who already feel isolated and abandoned. The social work intern's absence could intensify that sense of desertion and arouse depressed feelings. No natural point of "graduation" coincides with ending. Client or worker might leave at any time. The client may be suddenly transferred or discharged, and the worker finds the bed empty. Workers may leave or be transferred. These aspects also characterize short-term institutional facilities, making endings difficult. They require careful attention in preparing for termination.

The agency's definition of the status of the social work student has consequences for termination. Agencies must not present social work interns to their clientele as regular staff. This practice violates the *Code of Ethics* (NASW, 1999) and forces students to devise reasons for their departure. They fear being found out, and suffer discomfort and self-consciousness throughout the ending phase. The client, in turn, senses the lack of authenticity, and may begin to question the student's credibility, caring, and commitment.

Agencies should be open and direct about their training function and present their students as supervised interns. Clients should be informed of the intern's departure at the end of the academic year. Termination and transfer are likely to be viewed as legitimate (though some people do "forget" they were told at the start). Some clients are pleased to know that they contributed to student learning in return for a valued service. In settlement house programs, members often joke about "breaking in" another student. In university-affiliated hospitals, patients are keenly aware of the rotation of medical interns, residents, nursing students, and social work students, and accept the arrangement as natural. This is not to say that termination may not be distressing in these settings, but only that honesty about the student status from the outset decreases unnecessary guilt on the part of the student and unnecessary resentment on the part of the client. Ethical practice demands no less.

The temporal nature of the service itself also affects the ending phase. By definition, open-ended services carry no time limit or ending date. The relationship intensifies over time, perhaps even carrying a freight of ambivalence and dysfunctional dependency along with positive feelings. In long-term services, much time and energy are invested in maintaining and sustaining the therapeutic relationship. When the worker introduces termination for whatever reason, some people may experience shock and disbelief and perceive the ending as a personal rejection.

Planned short-term services have a specified duration with an ending date clearly stated at the outset. The dynamics of termination in planned short-term services are therefore very different from those of open-ended services. When planned short-term services are based on clinical decisions rather than arbitrary managed care time limits, clients are more likely to perceive the ending as an integral aspect of the service. Both client and intern mobilize their energies to accomplish specific objectives within the designated time period, and termination is an expected and therefore neutral event. In contrast, when planned short-term services are solely determined by managed care's shortsightedness, "mismanaged care," or "lack of care," both client and intern will negatively experience termination (Wachtel, 2002).

The modality (individual, family, group, and community) of service influences the ending phase in important ways. For the individual, termination can mean a loss that has both realistic and unrealistic features (Fortune, Pearlingi, & Rochelle, 1992). The person may experience anger, sadness, and perhaps a resurgence of helplessness. Such feelings are especially intense among those who are most dependent upon their environment because of age and physical factors that affect their competence and self-direction—children, elders, and disabled or chronically ill people.

In families and groups that remain intact, members will have one another as a mutual aid or support system. Less intensity exists in the relationship with the social worker, especially when the work opens communication channels and strengthens relationships. Termination of the professional relationship may therefore be less stressful for a collectivity than for an individual (Hopper, 2005; Walsh & Harrigan, 2003a, 2003b). If, however, the family or group faces separation from one another along with separation from the worker, as in a divorce or a move away from the family, or the breakup of a graduating school or camp group, the combined losses may be even more painful and difficult to manage (Shulman, 2006; Toseland & Rivas, 2005).

Relational Factors

A social worker had been working with ten-year-old Carlos in residential treatment. The youngster avoided discussing the termination by talking to himself, singing in rhymes, and jumping up and down in his chair. The sheer energy required of the worker simply to stay with the youngster was a severe drain. Carlos maintained control during this time by not responding to questions or participating in conversation. When the social worker attempted to gently break through the negation by reminding him how many sessions remained, he withdrew into rhymes. The worker responded to his regression by assuring him of her affection and caring for him. However, promises of affection had accompanied abandonment and betrayal by all the other "mothers" he had loved. Carlos's response was to withdraw and protect himself from yet another loss. The social worker, like the youngster, felt powerless. Her responses were often triggered by intense feelings of guilt for abandoning him. She attempted to take herself out of the line of fire by stressing that it was not her wish to leave. Her responses made it even more difficult for Carlos to express his anger at her.

The vignette illustrates that the intense emotions associated with ending depend on earlier experiences with relationship and loss and the meaning attached to the relationship with the worker (Greenberg, 2002). Children and adolescents seen by social workers may have experienced the loss of parents and other loved ones, losses they have not had the opportunity to process adequately. Facing the loss of their social worker could activate deeply buried pain (Bembry & Ericson, 1999). The more sudden and unexpected the loss, the more difficult is the management of realities and feelings of sadness, abandonment, or anger. Without adequate opportunity to work together on ending, the experience can be devastating. Consequently, work on termination must start at the first session and be a theme in every session. Termination then provides an opportunity to deepen the work on life losses.

Social workers prepare for the ending phase by reviewing what is known about the person's previous experiences with loss and means of coping with it. Through anticipatory empathy, the practitioner considers the potential impact of termination of this relationship on this person, and anticipates likely responses. With families and groups, potential reactions of each member must be considered as well as the likely collective response. For example:

> I had been working with a youth group in a group home, helping the members prepare for discharge and independent living. In trying to anticipate their possible reactions to my own departure, I immediately thought of the deprivations, losses, and separations in their lives. I felt that I would be one more in a series of females who had left or abandoned them. The experience may be more difficult because of life transitional tasks involved in their impending separation from the group home. I anticipated some regression and tried to imagine how each member might deal with my leaving. Bill might reject me; Tony will probably show how much he needs me; Sam will most likely withdraw. I thought the group itself might avoid the idea at first, and then become disruptive. This might be followed in later meetings by absences or lateness. I planned to deal with avoidance of my leaving by persistently presenting the reality, impede flight by "chasing" absent or withdrawn members, and help regulate depression and anger by inviting and empathically acknowledging the intense feelings.

Social workers, too, are subject to painful feelings and reactions (Siebold, 1991). We must therefore examine our own feelings about separating from a particular person, family, or group and our own patterns of coping with the stress of loss. We must especially consider the potential for guilt about leaving and the consequent difficulty in letting the client go. Without such examination, workers might deny the experience themselves. One worker might postpone announcing the ending date so there is no time left for being helpful. Another might express ambivalence toward the relationship through indirect communications, double messages, or repeated postponements of the ending date. The social worker in the preceding example continues:

> I didn't have to go far within myself to touch my own feelings. I am aware that I don't cope with separations or endings easily. I know I tend to postpone the inevitable and to become detached. With these youngsters, I feel guilty about leaving them just when they are already confronting a major separation. I find myself wanting to avoid the issue, even blaming the agency, and needing to falsely reassure the group. Nevertheless, now that I am aware of these possible therapeutic errors, I am determined to invite the boys to express their feelings. I hope that if I do become defensive, I can still reverse myself and allow them to explore and express possible feelings of sadness, disappointment, and anger.

By being in touch with their own pattern of coping with loss, social workers are better prepared to deal with their own feelings and will therefore be freer to help clients deal with theirs. Table 12.1 summarizes the factors that influence the termination process.

Phases in Separation

While responses to termination are unique, most of us seem to go through recognizable phases in ending a relationship. However individual styles and pacing may vary, it is useful to consider four phases that might be involved in ending. The phases are analogous to those observed in dealing with death, though obviously they are not of the same quality or degree. Kübler-Ross (1975) awakened the profession to understanding and teaching about the processes of death and dying. However, her fixed, sequential, universal stages of dying do not accurately describe these processes. We do not all die alike or mourn alike in predictable, uniform, separable stages, but uniquely as a consequence of many interacting factors, which appear, recede, and come to the fore again and again. Death and mourning follow unique pathways and trajectories (Dane, 2005). In general, the phases of termination are *negation and avoidance, negative feelings, sadness,* and *release*. Each phase has its own tasks, although not everyone goes through every phase or in the so-called order. Some people may not experience any of these phases.

Preparation for ending the work involves anticipating which coping demands require exploration and support. The social worker must be responsive to coping processes and resources involved in termination by providing the time needed for their development. Time is critical. In an abrupt ending, no time is available for the expression of feelings, the review of meaning, or planning ahead. Before a client can engage in coping with the tasks, the reality of the ending must be presented. Even when the ending date was agreed on at the outset in planned short-term service, or mentioned at stated intervals in open-ended service, the actual presentation of the ending date is often met by negation.

Negation and Avoidance

The more satisfactory the relationship, the more likely people are to ward off separation anxiety by negating and avoiding its reality. Initially, some

Table 12.1
Factors Influencing Reactions to Termination

- Agency context
- Professional status
- Temporal nature of service
- Modality of service
- Relational factors

people "forget" that termination was mentioned earlier and try to avoid discussing it by changing the subject, engaging in excessive activity, or regressing. Avoidance can be adaptive when it provides time to absorb the meaning of the imminent loss and to develop means of coping with it. Similarly, the more satisfactory the relationship for the social worker, the more likely she or he will have difficulty with the reality of termination. Some workers can also "forget" to mention termination until the last couple of sessions, leaving no time for people to process it.

A social worker in a mental hospital had been working with Mrs. Miller, a deaf patient in medical isolation because of suspected tuberculosis. He was the first person to engage her in a long while. She became dependent on him for concrete assistance, and now that he is leaving, she is unable to accept the reality of his departure. For a month she did not "hear" his statements about leaving or about his interest in helping her to become more self-reliant and to use other resources.

Mrs. Miller greeted me with "Where's my toothpaste?" I wrote a note reminding her we had agreed she would ask an aide for this. After pouting, she said she liked having me help her more than anyone else. I wrote, "Because I'm leaving, it is very important for you to learn to use others, and I know how difficult that is to do. I want to help you with it." She then placed a dollar on the table and asked me to buy her a Sunday paper on Monday. She was holding on, struggling to keep our relationship intact. I wrote suggesting she ask the nurse to buy the paper, because I will soon be leaving, and she must get used to dealing with other staff. She began to pout again. I wrote, "I like you, and this isn't easy for me either, but I know you can do this for yourself." She looked at me with a smile, and said she will ask the nurse. I wrote, "Maybe you can ask her on Sunday night?" She said she would ask her on Saturday so that she can have the paper on Sunday. I credited the idea, and suddenly she began to cry.

The worker's persistence and assurance of caring helped Mrs. Miller begin to cope with the stress of an inevitable ending. His ability to do this rested on his empathy and his awareness of his own difficulty in leaving her with so many helping tasks still undone.

By contrast, a social work intern, placed in a state psychiatric hospital, was assigned to Carl, a fifteen-year-old who was admitted for exhibiting self-abusive, aggressive, and suicidal behaviors that were unable to be managed at his residential placement. The Department of Children and Families' Services (DCFS) obtained custody of Carl and his siblings on the basis of severe abuse and neglect. Carl was a difficult youngster to reach, with a history of a high level of distrust and poor attachments. However, this particular social work intern was able to develop a close therapeutic alliance with him. She was identified with and committed to this youngster, and found herself avoiding discussing termination with him. Four weeks before the end of the semester, the intern's field instructor brought to her attention that she had not introduced termination since the initial session. The field instructor discovered this when she playfully teased Carl about "just wait until I'm your social worker." Carl responded with surprise, concern, and a lot of questions rather than the lighthearted banter she had expected. During a session later in the day, Carl initiated the discussion of termination in a very direct manner.

CARL:	You didn't tell me that you were leaving. Phyllis says that you're (pauses as he struggles with the unfamiliar word) an intern? And you're leaving. That's true?
SOCIAL WORK INTERN:	Yes, Carl. That's true. I will be leaving in a month.
CARL:	But (pause) you're the best social worker I've ever had. I hate this.
SOCIAL WORK INTERN:	I'm sorry, Carl. I hate this also.
CARL:	I have to work with someone else now? Can't somebody just help me get discharged without having another social worker? Please don't tell me I have Susan?
SOCIAL WORK INTERN:	When I leave, you will have Phyllis. I know you like her, and you know that she really cares about you. Phyllis is my supervisor and is aware of everything that's been happening with you, and she understands everything about your discharge plans. She will take good care of you.
CARL:	Yeah, but Phyllis is really busy. She's not gonna have that much time. And she's . . . (He stops.)
SOCIAL WORK INTERN:	She's what, Carl?
CARL:	I don't know. You never told me you were leaving. What is an intern anyway?
SOCIAL WORK INTERN:	Remember when we first met and in the first family session with your dad too, I explained what an intern is and when I would be leaving?
CARL:	(Shrugs his shoulders.) I don't know. I don't think you ever told me. Maybe my dad knows, but you never told me. If you did, I don't remember. That was a long time ago. I thought you would be here until I leave—that I would leave first.
SOCIAL WORK INTERN:	You know, Carl, you are right. It was a long time ago. It's not fair that I let all this time go by without talking about it again. I'm really sorry. That's my fault. I think I was hoping so much that I'd get to be here when you leave that I pushed back that I was leaving too.

CARL:	It's not your fault. I probably spaced or wasn't paying attention or something.
SOCIAL WORK INTERN:	No, Carl. Maybe fault isn't the best word. It's my responsibility to be honest with you, and part of doing that is making sure you understand important things like when I'm leaving. It doesn't matter whether you spaced or not. It's my responsibility, not yours.
CARL:	Well, whatever. It's OK. So when exactly are you leaving?
SOCIAL WORK INTERN:	The first week of May.
CARL:	(Pauses) So that's only three weeks away! What are you gonna do after the first week of May? Can't you stay until the end of May?
SOCIAL WORK INTERN:	Carl I'd love to be able to stay with you until the end of May or as long as it takes until you are discharged. An internship is when a graduate school student gets to work in a place as the kind of person they are studying to be. When the school ends in May, the internship ends. I don't have a choice.
CARL:	(Thinks silently for a minute) So this was part of school? Like you come here instead of going to class? I feel like a guinea pig or an experiment or something. Like I'm just somebody to use to see if you do good or not.
SOCIAL WORK INTERN:	Carl, you are not "just somebody" to me. You are very special to me. You're a great kid, and I really care about you. All the progress you've made is because of how hard you've worked, not because of me trying to do well in school.
CARL:	(Silent for a minute or two, and suddenly his energy shifted.) OK, then, I can help you. You do everything really good, except when you get too serious about stuff and won't let it go. Like "I'm still concerned about . . ." (He proceeds to imitate me—gestures, tone, and all—and he does a great job.)
SOCIAL WORK INTERN:	(I let out a loud laugh.) Yeah. I do that—wow, you really got me good. How do you experience it?
CARL:	(Without hesitation) Frustrated! It's annoying.
SOCIAL WORK INTERN:	Hmm. Thanks, Carl. That is very helpful. I will be mindful of that. Maybe you could let me know when you catch me doing that again. You know, Carl, this is a great example of how observant you are. Not every kid would be able or willing to help their social worker and also to let the social worker help him. Thank you.

Finding out from another worker that his worker is unexpectedly leaving places Carl in double jeopardy. First, he fears that his discharge plan would be jeopardized. Second, he experiences yet another abandonment of an adult he depended on. Yet, through his resiliency, Carl teaches the intern about the importance of directness in the termination process.

Another worker, in a long-term chronic care facility, was unable to help her group with termination because she could not handle her own guilt feelings. She had successfully engaged a group of elderly, brain-damaged, socially isolated men with one another and with her. When she decided to leave the hospital, she could not tell her group.

My plan for this meeting was to begin with my leaving, and we got onto the subject of loss. It would have been natural for me to introduce termination, but I didn't—I couldn't. Mr. Jones was verbally rambling and suddenly brought out his pipe, which was broken in two pieces, and sadly said, "Look at that—that's my only pleasure." It took a while to establish that what was upsetting him was that no one could help him get a new pipe, though he had asked several aides. He exclaimed, "It isn't too much for a man to ask, to have a smoke; there's not much else." After we established that I would help him get a pipe after the meeting, I asked if Mr. Kley and Mr. Dobbs had similar feelings about something they had lost and were sad about. They didn't respond. I said that one thing that they all had in common was that they had lost part of their health. There was much nodding. Mr. Kley agreed, "Yeah—we all got sick." I added they all live in the hospital as home. Mr. Jones said they were all together in this, like neighbors. I noted that the men hadn't known each other, even after many years—not even each other's names sometimes. Mr. Kley said, "Everyone has his own problems." Mr. Jones said he and the others couldn't remember. I asked why they thought we were getting together. Mr. Jones grinned and said, "The neighbors get together." We all laughed.

Literally and symbolically, the worker moved back to the initial phase of agreement on help—to the beginning instead of the ending. Immobilized by her own feelings, she avoided introducing and dealing with termination. She tried again the next week, but, still unaware of her own feelings, she failed to anticipate individual and group responses to her announcement.

I said that by the middle of next month I wouldn't be able to meet with the group anymore as I am leaving the hospital. There were nods. Everyone looked at me blankly. I said we talked last week about having things we like break or taken away. I asked if they remembered. No one responded. After several efforts, there still were no responses. I said this is hard to talk about, or at least I find it hard. More nods, but the men just looked at me. I asked if it were on their minds that I will be leaving.

There was still no response. I asked Mr. Jones if it is on his mind. He smiled and said, "That's nice." I was getting uptight. I asked if the men would like to continue meeting with another worker after I leave. They remained expressionless. I asked if they wanted to close the meeting, and they nodded affirmatively.

The worker's avoidance of the meaning of the relationship evoked a reciprocal avoidance in the group members. They withdraw not only from her but from one another as well. To be helpful the worker must refer to her own feelings about ending a significant relationship. This enables the worker to persist in the reality of termination, as the worker did with Mrs. Miller.

Frequent reminders are often necessary so that the painful reality remains on the agenda. With children, a calendar is helpful, crossing out each completed session and specifying the remaining number. But whatever the means, the worker needs to focus on the issue, risk confrontation with pain, and elicit expressions of negative feelings. This process of working through negation is illustrated in a practice vignette from a twelve-session school group of eighth-grade African American and Hispanic girls.

Keika reminded the group that next week was the last time we were going to meet before the holiday and asked if we could have a party during the last half of the meeting. I agreed that it would be fun and pointed out that today marks the halfway mark for the group. Perhaps they would like to spend some time at the beginning of the next session to take stock and decide the focus for the remaining meetings. Within a few seconds, the entire ambiance completely changed. Although a few registered no visible reactions, most seemed puzzled as they glanced around the room. Alice, Helen, and Maria, who were seldom at a loss for words, looked absolutely thunderstruck. All were quiet. I waited several minutes, and then observed that they were awfully quiet all of a sudden, and I was wondering if my comment about having only five more sessions had taken them off-guard.

The silence just got louder. For a few minutes, I had the sinking feeling that the session might end in silence. Finally, Ivory found her voice and demanded to know why I was cutting the group short when they hadn't done anything "nasty." Then she looked more closely at me and reminded me that I had said I was going to be here until May, so what was the problem? Matilda chirped in a "told you so" tone of voice that I just did not like them—that was the problem. I became flustered and defensive. I mentioned that in individual interviews and at the first meeting, I had emphasized the group would meet for twelve weeks. Ivory retorted that when I had first talked to their class, I had said the group would meet for the entire school year, just like last year's group.

Inez shook her head and corrected her by pointing out that it had been changed to twelve weeks because too many girls signed up. Ivory indignantly declared this was the first she had heard of it. But even if that was the case, why couldn't I just have a second group for the other class? I explained that if they remembered, I had informed them right away that my schedule did not allow me to have two groups, and the agency could not assign another worker. Dramatically, Ivory looked around the group and said in exaggerated disbelief that "I just want to get this straight . . . you are going to give our group to those bimbos?" I responded this was very hard for all of us. There was a tense lull, and finally Maria said quietly that it seemed like we had just started and now we only had a short time left. I agreed, saying that we had come such a long way in such a short time and it's hard to make peace with only five more meetings. Keika responded that she was upset, but if I had taken the other group first, she would expect them to finish on time so her group would have a turn. Alice was animated again and informed me I was going to need a bigger room to have a group with "those ho's" because the only way they know how to talk is when they are lying down.

Persistence and assurance of caring help the group members begin to accept the reality that it will end after five more sessions. By demanding that they confront the reality of termination, the worker helps the group to move into the next phase, expression of negative feelings.

Negative Feelings

Negation and avoidance gradually give way to the reality of the ending through the social worker's empathic support. Still, a period of intense reaction may follow. People express their hurt in many different ways, some through direct anger at the worker.

Walking back from the bus I noticed again what had been happening lately; the girls were very busy talking to themselves and teasing each other. Although it looked as if we were together, I was quite obviously apart. At one point, they actually walked in front of me, laughing over some joke, while I walked alone and behind them.

Once again, I felt isolated. It made me sad, which must have reflected in my face, for suddenly Judy noticed I was walking alone, and came and took my arm condescendingly. Tata's response was, "Shit on her." She and Judy, Carmen, and Kathy laughed hysterically. I said I thought they seemed unhappy with me lately and asked if they wanted to talk about it. Kathy said they weren't unhappy about anything. I asked, "Even about my leaving in the summer?" Tata jumped up and shouted, "Nobody gives a shit about your leaving. Go ahead and leave now if you want to." There were tears in her eyes as she spoke. (Irizarry & Appel, 2005, p. 194)

Some people express anger in a subtler, more symbolic manner. For instance, a physically challenged social work intern had seen John, who is seriously addicted, for nine months. They worked hard and achieved much. In her office she has a footstool she uses to help ease the discomfort of her disability. John usually sits down and hooks the footstool around so he can use it too. The sharing of the stool symbolized the kind of shared work they did together. However, in the session in which the student began termination work with John, he kept the footstool all to himself. The student commented on that, and it led to an exploration of his feelings about ending their work.

Others turn their feelings inward and experience the ending as a reflection of their unworthiness or the worker's disappointment with them. They may also develop physical symptoms or engage in self-destructive behavior. For Phyllis, a twice-divorced, depressed, battered woman, the social worker's impending departure triggered unresolved grief related to other losses, particularly the recent death of a close girlfriend from AIDS. Phyllis developed pneumonia. The worker records her session with Phyllis in the hospital.

Phyllis began the session about being distressed over her forgetfulness and asked if her medication could be causing it. I asked what she meant, and she said she knew I had told her, but she couldn't remember why I was leaving. I reminded her of our previous conversations. Then I asked, "What ran through your mind when you tried to remember the reasons I was leaving the agency?" She said she had thought that once in a while, staff decides to switch cases. I asked how come she thought that. She said, "If it wasn't working out." I asked what she meant. Phyllis said if staff gets tired of working with a person, if the person isn't making enough progress, they let someone else try. I asked if she is concerned that I am tired of working with her and feel she had made insufficient progress. She said, "Yes, I think I was assigned to you with the expectation that I'd be cured in a certain amount of time." I suggested it sounded like she thought she was "just another case" to me, an assignment, and maybe she wondered if I really cared about her. She replied she wasn't sure at all. I responded, "Phyllis, ending with you is also very hard for me. Our relationship has meant a great deal to me also." She said that she had learned a lot from me and would miss me. I said I had learned a lot from her also—about a person's courage to deal with grief and pain, to raise children without the help of a husband, to not allow men to batter her anymore. She said from our work together she felt "like a fog has been lifted from me."

Some people may try to reintroduce needs or tasks that had been resolved or completed. They may regress, become excessively dependent, or in other ways attempt to demonstrate their need for continued service. Still others turn their feelings outward and experience the ending as a reflection of the worker's incompetence and lack of commitment. They may confront the social worker directly with accusations of lack of concern, or indirectly with silence, repeated tardiness, or absence.

The intended message is "I'll leave you before you leave me." The behavior attempts to lessen the pain of the perceived abandonment and, simultaneously, to provoke responses from the worker that will further justify the distancing.

CARLOS:	Do you remember when I brought a snowball in here?
WORKER:	How can I forget? You and I got into a pretty big fight that day.
CARLOS:	(Running around the room, looking up, avoiding eye contact, yelling) I'm bringing the snowball back in here. I'm gonna throw it all over your office! And I'm gonna hurt you real bad. (Smiles)
WORKER:	I know you want to hurt me 'cause I hurt you by leaving you in three weeks. You're real mad at me because I'm leaving.
CARLOS:	(Moving to the furthest corner in the room and yelling) YOU! NEVER! I couldn't give a shit about you. You don't mean anything to me. I'm mad at you, but not 'cause you're leaving. I'm angry 'cause you're a bad social worker and I'm bored. Can I go now? I'm never coming back even if you come trying to find me. I want a new social worker—one that's nice. Would you come looking for me if I didn't show up? Because I'm warning you, I'll run away!
WORKER:	You bet I will. I'm not letting you slip out of my life so quickly. (I smiled at him.) I won't give up on you even if you think I am a terrible social worker. You have every right to be angry with me. If you want, you can yell at me for the next few weeks. But I won't let you just not show up. I care too much about you.

Carlos wants to hurt the worker where she is most vulnerable—her professional competence. He wants to reject her before she can reject him. His anger has an important coping function: he is fighting back rather than giving up in despair. Anger is a form of engagement, a ticket into termination work.

When such angry and rejecting responses occur, the ending phase is difficult for both worker and client. Social workers must be both empathic and sufficiently detached. That is, we must maintain sufficient identification with our clients to understand the feelings that have been aroused and, at the same time, we must be free to invite and pursue the expression of negative ideas and feelings about the service and ourselves. Feelings must be accepted as real for the person. Inappropriate reassurance by sugarcoating the feelings must be avoided.

In families and groups, the social worker must be sensitive to individual perceptions and experiences, which create disparate behaviors and responses to termination. A session with a group of older adolescent residents of a group home illustrates the complexities involved.

I said it was hard to talk about my leaving. John said he was tired. He arranged three chairs together and lay down across them. He talked of how close he is to his siblings, and said they are the most important people to him since his mother died. Nobody else matters. He described how hard growing up had been for him, and he emphasized his ability to make it by himself. Bill was watchful and restless, and I asked what he was feeling. He said nothing but got up and left the room. Sam cursed at me and followed Bill out. I went after them, and they returned. I said it's difficult for us to talk about my leaving, but we have worked too hard to run away from each other. Sam screamed that I had a nerve to "open us up" and then leave. Bill yelled that he always knew I didn't care. "We are just a job." I'm just like all the other social workers they knew—"phony." I said I knew how much they're hurting, and I'm hurting, too.

In lying down, John expressed his fatigue and depression; in talking of important memories in his life, he attempted to negate the worker's importance. In contrast, Bill withdrew, and Sam acted out. The worker stayed with them, pursued Sam and Bill, and helped the members explore their shared feelings of resentment. In these ways, she demonstrated her caring about them and her faith in their ability to work together despite their negative reactions. Endings often call for the social worker to reestablish credibility, skill, and commitment. A common error is a too early expression of one's own sense of loss, which can shut off the expression of members' negative reactions.

Sadness

As the reality of ending and resentment about it are successfully confronted, clients and workers are freed to experience shared feelings of sadness at separating. Social workers encourage and support client expressions and respond to them by sharing their own sense of intimacy and loss. They now can disclose the personal meaning of the experience and invite clients to do the same. People have varying capacities for such expression; and for some, the practitioner's recognition of their unexpressed feeling may be relief enough. Some clients (mostly males) express their intense sadness over the loss of intimacy by sexualizing the therapeutic relationship. For example, during termination a young adult client, Alvin, informed his female worker,

"I guess I love you." When I pointed out that caring and love could easily become confused when two people work hard together, Alvin said he must be oversexed and is ashamed for fantasizing about me. I examined his feelings of love, and he then identified "gratitude, respect, honesty, and affection." He explained, "I never let a woman get so close to me before. Jesus, we've never even shaken hands, and yet I feel we are so close." "Yes," I replied, "our minds have touched, our hearts have touched, and even our souls have touched; that's made our work very special."

Many clients will not feel anything as intense as sadness but only a mild regret, perhaps that the relationship is ending. The worker must guard against the projection that results in overemphasis and overintensity. At the same time, the worker must be aware of attempts to cover up feelings and to avoid the embarrassment often associated with the expression of positive affect.

Both client and worker may attempt to escape into happy activities. Camp staffs, aware of the intensity of relationships that develop, structure end-of-the-season rituals that help assuage the pain of separation: special campfires and other traditional ceremonies that serve to review achievements and to reaffirm the ties of comradeship. By contrast, an emphasis on farewell parties alone may interfere with the campers' experiencing the reality of separating. Alone on the bus, or back at home, the full measure of their grief spills out, to the dismay of parents.

The worker with the group of elderly men in the chronic care facility helped the group experience together the sadness of leaving, instead of continuing to withdraw from one another and from her:

As I reintroduced my leaving, Mr. Dobbs burst into tears. He looked at me, then down, and shook his head. I reached across the table and put my hand on his; he continued to weep. I said I knew this is rough. He wept harder, and Mr. Lawrence reached across the table and patted his arm. Mr. Andrews, immobile, watched with a blank expression. Mr. Jones's eyes filled, and he said, "There'll be nobody left for us. Men will watch television." I asked, "Are you worried that there would be no more activities?" He said, "Yes, ma'am, that's what I mean. You need to get up from sitting in front of that thing. You need to do things." Mr. Andrews and Mr. Kley nodded. As I mentioned the plans for another worker, Mr. Dobbs began to weep again, and couldn't talk. I said, "Mr. Dobbs, we got close this year, didn't we?" He nodded. I said I knew he and the others would miss me very much, just as I would miss them. They all nodded. I continued that sometimes when people have to say goodbye, like us, they feel very much alone. Mr. Dobbs said, "Yeah," and pointed to himself. I said I hoped they won't shut each other out. They learned to care for each other, and they still have that. They looked at each other and nodded. I looked at Mr. Dobbs, and he responded clearly, "I understand; I'm with you."

The worker recognized with the members how difficult the subject of her leaving is. She responded to their feelings verbally and with the intimacy of physical contact, which is as important to the elderly as it is to children. She disclosed her own feelings of sadness. Together, members and worker feel the sadness and the closeness, and the members struggle to identify what the group experience has meant to them. The worker locates the strength in their situation: they have each other.

Moving past negative feelings to sadness requires time. In the same way, moving through sadness to letting go of the relationship, to acceptance, also requires time. The worker with the group of preadolescent girls described earlier provided them with ample time for them to deal with separation. Without that time, it is doubtful they could have reached the degree of acceptance demonstrated in the following excerpts.

As soon as I mentioned my leaving, Nilda turned away and started looking at pictures on the bulletin board. She asked, "Who's Joanne?" I reminded her Joanne is the social worker who will be taking my place. Nilda turned from the board, insisting, "We don't talk about her!"

For several weeks, the girls refused to refer to the new worker by name, and they avoided any discussion of her coming. But their curiosity and beginning acceptance finally generated some discussion.

Lydia said she was wondering what would happen when I leave. I said Joanne is coming in to take my place. Lydia said, "But I may not like her." I nodded, and she went on to say that if she doesn't like her, she won't come back to the club. I thought most of the girls feel this way but they will have time to see what they think of her. I reminded them they hadn't been too sure of me in the beginning, either; they hadn't liked to talk with me much and whispered together instead. Lydia roared with laughter.

With acceptance growing, more open curiosity appeared the next week.

Suddenly, Tata blurted out, "When is that other girl coming, anyway?" I said she would arrive in the beginning of August. She shouted, "We are going to kick her ass!" I said that didn't surprise me. She added, "Well, you'd better tell her about us!" Nilda asked me if I had seen her and talked to her. I said I'd seen her a few times. Tata asked if I'd told her about them. Kathy said immediately, "Of course! What do you think they talk about?" I agreed, saying Joanne had asked me about them, and I'd said they might feel like kicking her ass at first but this didn't mean they wouldn't get to like her. Everyone laughed and I said I was serious, that this was just what I had told her. Judy asked me how tall Joanne is, and I said she was a little taller than me. Nilda exclaimed, "My God, another tall one," and asked if she is older than me. I said, "No, younger." Tata said she'd be too young to take care of them. (Irizarry & Appel, 2005, pp. 195–196)

Little by little, over time, the new worker became a real person, with personal attributes and an interest in knowing the members. Table 12.2 summarizes the helping skills of dealing with the phases of avoidance and negation, negative feelings, and feelings of sadness.

Release

Having faced and shared the pain of separating, worker and client may now feel that the tasks of termination are completed. Yet, the most important ones lie ahead, for it is the next set of coping tasks that provides the client

Table 12.2
Phases of Separation: Negation and Avoidance, Negative Feelings, and Sadness

• *Helping with negation and avoidance:*	Sort out own feelings.
	Provide sufficient time to allow for period of avoidance.
	Offer frequent and persistent reminders.
	Refer to one's own feelings.
	Use visual aids such as a calendar.
	Provide support and assurance of caring.
• *Helping with negative feelings:*	Sort out own feelings.
	Invite and pursue negative feelings.
	Accept expression of negative feelings.
	Sustain expression of client anger.
	Avoid premature reassurance and power struggle.
	Connect client behaviors and actions to unexpressed feelings.
	Convey faith in the client and the professional relationship.
• *Helping with feelings of sadness:*	Sort out own feelings.
	Encourage and support expression of sadness and regret.
	Share own sadness and regret.
	Avoid escape into happy activities.

with the opportunity to integrate the whole of her experience, and to find the meaning in it. The three tasks are (1) recognizing gains and specifying remaining work; (2) developing plans for the future such as transfer, referral, or self-directed tasks; and (3) final goodbyes, disengaging, and evaluation.

Earlier phases of separation, if completed successfully, stimulate renewed energy for the sequence in release. Where this is not so, however, the worker can provide energy by initiating and focusing the discussion. A starting point might be a joint consideration of where the agreed upon goals and action now stand. "Let's examine together what has and has not been accomplished." Throughout the discussion, the worker not only emphasizes the client's strengths and the gains made, but also elicits discussion of any areas of remaining difficulty. Mrs. Felstein, a seventy-five-year-old resident in a nursing home, had severe difficulty in adapting to institutional life. A social work intern met with her for thirty weeks and helped her to cope with the stress of unresolved life transitions and to make new environmental connections. In the next-to-last session, they reviewed their work together:

SOCIAL WORK INTERN:	What were some of the things you found most helpful?
MRS. FELSTEIN:	You've helped me a great deal. I used to think you were too young and only a student, but I feel differently now.
SOCIAL WORK INTERN:	I think it will be helpful to review our work together.
MRS. FELSTEIN:	We've talked about so many things, and I've come so far since the beginning.
SOCIAL WORK INTERN:	When we first started, you talked a lot about your sister's death and your guilt feelings.
MRS. FELSTEIN:	Yes, I still feel badly about that, but I no longer have that terrible feeling of it being my fault.
SOCIAL WORK INTERN:	At that time, you also felt pretty bad about the situation with your friend Dora.
MRS. FELSTEIN:	(Quickly boasting) You know, she doesn't mean a darn thing to me now. I see her, and she doesn't affect me at all.
SOCIAL WORK INTERN:	I also remember how you felt you made the wrong choice in coming into the home.
MRS. FELSTEIN:	(Disappointed voice) I realize now I have to be here. It's just not what I expected it to be, but I guess I expected too much.
SOCIAL WORK INTERN:	I remember we talked a lot about this, and that most recently, we talked about your role here, and your trying to find a more comfortable role.
MRS. FELSTEIN:	I don't know if I can ever fully adjust to being in a home. I try to read more, watch the news, and do things I like. It will be very hard for me to get along without you. You've been a great help to me.

SOCIAL WORK INTERN:	I know it will be hard because we have become very close.
MRS. FELSTEIN:	Did I tell you about the community social worker who had originally developed the plan for me to come here? At first I thought the girl wouldn't be able to help me because she was so young—I thought she'd never understand my problems, but then she turned out to be very dedicated.
SOCIAL WORK INTERN:	You thought of her in the same way you initially thought about me.
MRS. FELSTEIN:	(Smiling) Yes.
SOCIAL WORK INTERN:	(Taking her hand) I am sure you will feel the same way about the new intern.
MRS. FELSTEIN:	I sure will if they give me another young one.

We ended our conversation about how my supervisor will be available to her in the summer and will help her with the transition to the new social work intern. I asked if she has some ideas of what she would like to work on in the fall. She said she has been thinking about getting involved with the senior center across the street and would like help in getting connected.

Plans for carrying on with the work, encouragement in the tasks, and the expression of confidence in the client's ability to cope with life stressors can be combined with conveying the agency's availability for future services as needed.

In a situation of a worker leaving an agency, a group of five adolescent girls lived in the same cottage in a residential treatment center and had met with the worker for over a year and in individual and family sessions as well. The following excerpt is from the group meeting that took place three days after it was announced in the cottage that the social worker would be leaving the agency in several months. Three girls came in together and seemed in a happy mood. They said they'd had a good week in school. Beth arrived singing, "Everything is Beautiful." She took her seat and was laughing with everyone.

WORKER:	Hey, it's great to see everybody in such a good mood and I hate to be a party pooper, but you know that I'm leaving and a lot of things between you and me will be drawing to an end.
MARGIE:	You have a hell of a nerve.
WORKER:	You mean about my leaving?
MARGIE:	Yeah, that and a whole lot of things.
WORKER:	OK, let's hear them. I am sure that my leaving and the ending of the group have caused a lot of reactions in all of you. (No one picked up on that.)
MARGIE:	Are we going to have a group next year?

GIRLS:	Yeah, we want to have another group next year.
BETH:	Let's have a party in honor of your leaving. (She began talking about a party that they had been to, and all of a sudden turned to me.) You're leaving, you God-damn fink. (Everybody stopped and looked at me.)
WORKER:	I'm leaving, and that makes me a fink.
GIRLS:	Why are you leaving? Why do you have to leave us? Why can't you stay?
JILL:	Why are you leaving?
WORKER:	I don't know if it's the reason that really matters; it's more how you feel knowing that I'm leaving, for whatever the reason.
GIRLS:	No, no, we want to hear the reasons; we don't understand.
WORKER:	OK, let me try to explain. I'm leaving because I've been here for a number of years. Working here has meant a lot to me, and you have all meant a lot to me. Yet a combination of things, the long traveling and working nights, has become hard for me, and I want to work nearer to where I live. That's pretty much the reason. If there's anything you don't understand, ask me and I'll try to explain more.
BETH:	(Crying) You can't leave. We need you.
WORKER:	You mean you won't be able to make it without me?
MARGIE:	You're the best social worker I ever had. I won't be able to talk to anybody else.
WORKER:	We've all been real close, and I guess the thought of starting over with somebody else is scary. What do you think it was about me that made it easier to talk to me?
BETH:	It's because you cared about us. We knew that even when you were mad at us, you were really sticking up for us, and you were really with us.
DONNA:	Yeah, but if you cared so much you wouldn't be leaving.
WORKER:	That's the thing, isn't it? How could I leave you if I really care for you?
GLADYS:	We know you care for us. We know you're leaving because you really feel that you have to.
WORKER:	But the words don't help very much, huh? They don't take away the bad feeling.
BETH:	That's right; what good does it do me to know that you care if you're not here?
JILL:	Yeah, you've been my social worker for a whole year. I don't want anybody else.
WORKER:	You're upset with me, you have a right to be, but it's also hard for me to leave you.
BETH:	If it's hard for you to leave us, then you wouldn't leave us.

MARGIE:	No, Beth, that's just not the truth. It was hard for me to leave home. (Gladys put her head down and began to cry, and one of the kids hollered, "Oh, cut it out. This hurts us as much as it hurts you.")
WORKER:	Maybe it hurts each of you in a different way, and this is how Gladys is reacting.
GLADYS:	Oh, leave me alone. None of you care about me.
MARGIE:	Yes we do. You don't want help. You just want to feel sorry for yourself.
WORKER:	You're all getting angry with Gladys, yet she's acting out how you feel. Is it that you hurt so much that you don't have room for anybody else's hurt?
JILL:	She cries all the time. Who gives a damn about her?
DONNA:	I care about her, but I don't know what to do.
BETH:	(To Gladys, who was sitting alone) Gladys, why don't you come over here? (Gladys just shrugged, and one of the other kids said, "Aw, leave her alone." There was an uncomfortable quiet in the room.)
WORKER:	I don't think that you feel right leaving her alone.
BETH:	Well, what can we do?
WORKER:	What do you feel like doing?
BETH:	(Walked over to Gladys and put her arms around her) You're scared, right? (Gladys nodded.)
DONNA:	We're all in that situation, too. Not only you.
BETH:	But maybe it is different for Gladys.
GLADYS:	You have a mother and father. Every one of you has at least a mother or a father. Who do I have?
BETH:	You have foster parents.
GLADYS:	Big deal. They don't want me.
BETH:	I think I know how it feels. I think I know how bad it feels. And if you want to cry, that's OK, but you gotta live. You got to pick yourself up. You gotta face it.
GLADYS:	No, I can't.
DONNA:	Even when you're alone, you have to trust yourself.
MARGIE:	That's pretty hard to do.
BETH:	But you're not all alone, Gladys; you have us. We'll help you, and sometimes you'll help us.
MARGIE:	You gotta have confidence in yourself.
WORKER:	How do you do that, Margie? Can you tell her?
MARGIE:	You gotta think of the things that you do right, not only the bad things. Even when people leave you, you gotta think of what you did have with them, and all that was good. And then you got to believe that you're going to have somebody else, too.

BETH:	You gotta learn to stand on your own feet. You gotta learn how to make friends.
JILL:	You gotta take responsibility for what you do, even when it's hard.
WORKER:	It sounds like you feel that Gladys can do these things, even though now she doesn't think that she can.
BETH:	That's right, and I mean it even coming from me. Lots of times I hate her, but other times I really like her and I remember when she was nice to me, and when she helped me, and I do believe in her, and I believe she can pick herself up.
GLADYS:	I feel real, real bad. Miss S's leaving hurts me more than anybody can know, but you've helped me and I want to thank you.
WORKER:	This is what it's about. This beautiful thing that you can do in helping each other, and you've got that now. You own that. And no matter who leaves, no matter how much it hurts, you can't lose that.
BETH:	I hate you for leaving, but I know what you mean. I know you're right.
WORKER:	Go ahead, Margie: what do you want to say?
MARGIE:	I know what Beth means, and I want to feel that I can go on also, and we can even have a group without you and we can keep helping each other just like we do in the group. I'm scared.
WORKER:	Sure, it's a scary thing. Can you talk a little more about what you're scared about?
MARGIE:	I'm scared that we won't be able to do it alone, that we need you to help us.
BETH:	Well, maybe we'll have somebody else who can help us.
DONNA:	And maybe we'll have to help ourselves.
GLADYS:	I know what you mean. I know that in the end, I do have to help myself.
BETH:	We'll help you, too. Just like we did here this morning.
WORKER:	Wow, you kids are fantastic. (They all kind of laughed and somebody said, "Maybe we'll become social workers, too," and that broke the tension.) (Adapted from Nadelman, 2005, pp. 242–243)

The social worker helped the members to express their feelings, and she accepted the legitimacy of their resentment. As members and worker experienced their sadness together, energy was released to reach out to Gladys. The worker supported their sense of mutual aid and enabled them to reaffirm their affection and need for each other. They could then contemplate a future without the worker but with one another. They expressed their appreciation and devotion by identifying with her.

In work with children and elders, or when agreements are more implicit than explicit, the social worker helps people find release by recalling together their shared experiences. This helps clarify where client and practitioner were when they started, where they are now, and even what new goals might be considered for the future. Work on release helps to consolidate gains, complete any unfinished work, and make plans for the future. It is also the time when people are helped to see the personal resources they have rediscovered for coping with the environment, managing life stresses, and making decisions about the use of community resources and other important areas of life. In the case of the group in the chronic care facility, the worker wrote:

We began to discuss the things the group had done, reliving their activities together—bingo and horseshoes. I asked what they liked and hadn't liked about each activity. As they did this, I pointed to something positive each had accomplished in the group. "Mr. Jones, remember how hard horseshoes was in the beginning?" He nodded. "You got so good at it you made the highest points last time we played." He grinned. I remembered with Mr. Dobbs how he had struggled to stand up in his wheelchair to play horseshoes, and now he was really good at it. He and several others nodded excitedly. I remembered how Mr. Kley had given us the idea to make collages, how Mr. Calagieri became so good at puzzles that he could help everyone else, and so on with each one. Each time there was pleased acknowledgment.

The social worker helped the men credit their strengths and achievements. The directive approach to eliciting their shared memories was appropriate in light of their mental disabilities.

Reminiscing and evaluating progress might result in the identification of uncompleted work. If the work is significant and cannot be accomplished in the remaining time, the social worker identifies the area for future work either with another worker or with the client's own personal and environmental resources. However, if the work is significant and can be accomplished in the remaining time, the social worker develops an agreement with the client to work on the circumscribed area of concern. For example, a social work intern was terminating with a nursing home resident, Mrs. Jacobson, with a history of hospitalizations for depression. She experienced intense difficulties in transitioning into the nursing home. In reviewing the admissions record, the intern learned that Mrs. Jacobson's son had been in a "tragic home accident." During their work together on other life losses (death of parents, health, and independence), the death of her son was not discussed until only three weeks remained in the intern's placement. In the beginning of the work, when the intern inquired about her son, Mrs. Jacobson would grimace and say something like "He's been gone a long time now," or "Talking about him doesn't change anything." If the intern pursued her obviously unresolved grief, Mrs. Jacobson retreated into silence or proceeded with a rush of complaints about the quality of food and the staff. After a couple of months, the intern stopped mentioning Mrs. Jacobson's son, deciding that she had held on to her sorrow for eighteen years since her son's death and that her coping efforts should be respected. In the third-to-last session, Mrs. Jacobson bitterly and repetitively complained about the nursing home staff. The intern connected Mrs. Jacobson's anger to her leaving the nursing home. The following exchange occurred:

MRS. JACOBSON:	(In a whisper) Why have you never asked me about my son?
SOCIAL WORK INTERN:	You are right. I never pushed you to tell me about him. Please do.
MRS. JACOBSON:	He'd be sixty-two years old now. He was my firstborn. I had a cesarean. (She starts to shake with a tearless cry.)
SOCIAL WORK INTERN:	(Reaches for Mrs. Jacobson's hand. Mrs. Jacobson responds by tightly grasping her hand, and then holds on.)
MRS. JACOBSON:	(In a choking voice) Why didn't you ask me? Maybe I would have talked about it earlier.
SOCIAL WORK INTERN:	(Said very quietly and gently) I wasn't sure you wanted to, but I should have given you more chances. You are right. I am sorry.
MRS. JACOBSON:	I can't even cry. (As tears well into her eyes)
SOCIAL WORK INTERN:	You have held your feelings in for such a long time. You don't have to any longer.
MRS. JACOBSON:	(Starts to cry) I've never talked to anyone about this before. I can't talk to anyone like I can talk to you.
SOCIAL WORK INTERN:	Let's talk about your son, and you won't have to feel so alone with your grief. What was his name?
MRS. JACOBSON:	And maybe I won't feel so angry all the time. (In a whisper) Larry.
SOCIAL WORK INTERN:	Please tell me about Larry.
MRS. JACOBSON:	But you are leaving next week.
SOCIAL WORK INTERN:	I will be leaving in two weeks. Would you like to meet twice a week over the next two weeks so that we can talk about Larry?
MRS. JACOBSON:	Yes, please.
SOCIAL WORK INTERN:	How would it be easiest for me to get to know Larry? Looking at pictures together might help. Do you have any pictures of Larry that we could look at together?

MRS. JACOBSON: Yes, I would like that.

SOCIAL WORK INTERN: OK—next time we meet—let's use the pictures for me to learn about your and Larry's lives together.

Before the intern leaves, Mrs. Jacobson tests whether the intern had the ability to create a safe climate for her to explore her deepest and most buried hurt. While being perpetually angry at the world has helped her to deflect the sorrow, nevertheless, for eighteen years the grief has consumed her life. The imminent loss of the intern brings the pain to the surface. As the intern arrives for the next session, she notices Mrs. Jacobson holding a large picture album.

SOCIAL WORK INTERN: Last session talking about Larry was very emotional for you. How have the last few days been for you?

MRS. JACOBSON: I have been thinking about him all the time. I want you to know that he committed suicide. No one outside the family knows. I've held this secret in for a long time.

SOCIAL WORK INTERN: Please tell me what happened.

Before sharing the album, Mrs. Jacobson has to unburden herself of the family secret. Mrs. Jacobson goes into a very long monologue in minute detail about the suicide of her son, including how she found the body. She required minimal encouragement to speak and simply unburdened herself from eighteen years of fortressing her feelings. She spontaneously began to leaf through the picture album. She introduced the intern to Larry as a baby, bar mitzvah, and so on. She explained her remembrances, cried a great deal, and talked about his being special and her love of him.

The worker also helps clients consider options: transfer to another worker, referral to another agency, or termination. If the decision is to terminate service, practitioner and client plan the phasing out of their work together. They may decrease the frequency and duration of sessions to every two weeks and then to once a month. They may arrange for a follow-up and review after a few months. Whatever the arrangement, the social worker prepares the client to continue to work on any remaining tasks, and to cope with expected and unexpected life events.

When transfer is accepted or mandated, the social worker involves the client in planning the meeting with the new worker. Together they may decide to have the new worker observe one session, followed by another in which they summarize their work and specify future objectives. In the final transitional session, the new worker may assume primary responsibility. Gradual transition helps minimize the discouragement in having to begin again.

When needed referral to another agency is accepted or mandated, the worker helps the client plan for the initial contact with the selected service. If clients are to initiate contact, workers prepare them to deal with procedures and to anticipate complications. If workers are to initiate contact, they establish client eligibility and agency receptivity. When both client and agency accept referral, the worker prepares the new agency worker to receive the client. One helps the client to think about presenting his needs and priorities to the new worker. The social worker may even participate in the first meeting, but, in any case, it is imperative that the social worker follow up to make sure linkage is successfully joined.

When planning is completed, client and worker are ready for disengagement. Some clients may show appreciation through a gift to the worker. This natural interest needs to be respected and handled with sensitivity. In our judgment, there are no hard-and-fast rules for handling this interest, although some agencies prohibit the acceptance of gifts. Certainly, some gifts are inappropriate such as money or a tip for rendered services, a romantic bouquet of flowers, or a suggestive undergarment. These types of gifts have to be returned as they blur the professional role. Similarly, at times, the worker might want to provide the client with a symbolic gift (e.g., a group picture, a special event, a sturdy plant, or a poem about resilience). For example, in the case of Carl, the youngster awaiting discharge from a psychiatric hospital, the social work intern offers to take him to a "special" movie.

CARL:	(Swiveling back and forth in the chair at my desk, looking at the calendar on the wall behind him) Ya know what? (He doesn't pause for an answer.) I can't believe it! Your last day is the same day that *Star Wars* opens!
SOCIAL WORK INTERN:	Wow, it's finally coming out! (I smile big because I know how much *Star Wars* means to him.) You have been tracking this movie for months. What does it mean to you that the movie and my last day are the same?
CARL:	Nothing, really. It's just weird that two sort of important things are happening on the same day. Like a . . . what's the word? Coin . . .
SOCIAL WORK INTERN:	A coincidence.
CARL:	Yeah, like a coincidence, but weird like it was supposed to happen that way or something. You were supposed to leave here (he points to the previous, two-week-earlier termination date that was changed so that I could help him with discharge), and then you changed it and now the movie is coming out. You know what I mean? I don't know. It doesn't matter.
SOCIAL WORK INTERN:	It doesn't matter? (We have been working on that his thoughts and feelings do matter.)
CARL:	I know. I'm not supposed to say, "It doesn't matter." But this time maybe it really doesn't.
SOCIAL WORK INTERN:	It does to me.
CARL:	Uugh! (He makes an exasperated sigh, but he's smiling.)

SOCIAL WORK INTERN:	Seriously, Carl, when that kind of "too weird to be a coincidence" stuff happens in my life, I pay attention to it and try to figure out what it means to me. Like if there's a message or a lesson or something I should do. What do you think?
CARL:	I think you're doing that thing you do again. (He's smiling as he says this and very quickly makes the next statement, still smiling.) No. No, I'm only kidding. OK. Let's see. (He gestures like he is thinking very seriously and hard.) Maybe the message is that you should take me to see the movie.
SOCIAL WORK INTERN:	Maybe it is. I've been trying to think of an ending activity. You know. A way to celebrate all the progress you have made. Maybe we should plan to go.
CARL:	You're serious! I was only kidding. Can we really go? Man, that's cool! I'll get to see it before my brother. I bet we're not going to be able to get tickets. You know it's going to be really, really crowded that day. Maybe you can try to get the tickets ahead of time on the phone or the Internet. If we can't, we will have to get there really early to stand in line. This is really cool, but you know it's going to take the whole day, Maybe I should wait for Dad to take me.
SOCIAL WORK INTERN:	It's OK if you prefer to go with your dad and brother. There are lots of other things we can do.
CARL:	I'd go see it again with them. Actually, I'd rather be able to tell my brother that I got to see it first. (He seems confused and hesitant.)
SOCIAL WORK INTERN:	Carl, what's the matter?
CARL:	You know how you came in on a Friday once when I had a discharge interview?
SOCIAL WORK INTERN:	Yes. (I am confused—I don't know where he is going with this.)
CARL:	Well, I was thinking that maybe if you could come for a little while on Friday, then we could still go to see the movie on Thursday. But you don't have to if you don't want to. I had just thought it would be better.
SOCIAL WORK INTERN:	Ohh, I get it. You don't want to mix a happy thing like *Star Wars* with a sad thing like my last day.
CARL:	Yeah.
SOCIAL WORK INTERN:	You are absolutely right—I'll come in on Friday. That way we can go see *Star Wars* and still have some time to talk and say goodbye to each other.
CARL:	OK! (He smiles and starts to write "Star Wars" on the calendar.)

SOCIAL WORK INTERN: You know, Carl, maybe the message in the coincidence was about how to handle happy things and sad things when they happen at the same time.

Sometimes clients are smarter and ahead of their workers. Carl does not want his last session to be an escape into fun and games. He struggles to separate his happy and sad feelings or, possibly, to keep them separate. The social work intern deserves tremendous credit for all her helping efforts as well as for offering the perfect termination gift—to take Carl to the *Star Wars* movie.

Some clients may ask that the relationship continue on a personal basis. Others may ask for the worker's telephone number or for a promise to correspond. This natural interest needs to be respected and handled with sensitivity. One's own human need for appreciation and continued involvement in the life of another should play no part in worker responses. Most people want to give as well as to receive, wish to continue a rewarding human relationship, and hope for some assurance they will not be forgotten. These needs are not to be regarded as problematic, but should be responded to with an understanding of their meaning for each individual. However, in most situations it is unhelpful for the social worker to agree to further contact. More often than not it interferes with the client's involvement with future social workers, and commitments are not fulfilled. The following excerpt illustrates the pressures for continued involvement as a school social worker attempts to help a young girl achieve release and a readiness to move on to new relationships.

Sandy, age seventeen, lost both parents the year before. Her mother died of cirrhosis of the liver, and her father of spinal cancer. She now lives in the home of relatives, who are heavy drinkers. Sandy and the social worker worked together on Sandy's anger, guilt, and grief over her losses; her conflicts with her relatives; the stormy relationship with her boyfriend and his subsequent rejection; and her own future plans. Sandy knew from the beginning the social work intern would leave at the end of the school year. Nevertheless, when the subject was introduced six weeks in advance, Sandy was devastated. Although unable to express her feelings about ending, she did use the remaining time to work productively on other areas of her life. The social work intern and Sandy decided on a noon picnic for their last meeting.

Sandy got into my car, and I immediately sensed she was in an uncharacteristically "up" mood. She spoke animatedly of a recent humorous incident. We both laughed and then became suddenly quiet. Then we began to chat in a casual way. Finally, I said that it was pretty hard to talk about this being our last day together. Sandy said, "Yeah, but I really don't feel bad because I know I can see you again. I know you will be living in Center City, and you can become my friend. I don't care what you say—I can take a train there to visit you. I can also get your number and call you, so I don't really think of this as goodbye." I knew it was not helpful to leave Sandy with these fantasies. I acknowledged that her wishes reveal her caring. And then, to help her face reality, I said, "You know, Sandy, this really is the end. We won't meet every week like we did; things can't be the same." Understandably, Sandy countered, "You talk like you don't want to see me or hear from me." Gently, I said, "I guess it sounds as if I don't care, but that isn't so. I care for you very much. We shared a great deal this year and have talked about so many important things. Now that it's time to say goodbye, it's especially hard." She quietly agreed.

Sandy had found it hard to express anger and loss, so I said, "Sandy, I think I would be pretty upset if people close to me were splitting." She gritted her teeth, "Yeah, everybody, and I don't have a fucking thing to do with it. My mother, she had no excuse. She didn't have to drink. My father couldn't help it. It's not fair." I said softly, "It does seem very unfair, Sandy." She responded, "You're fucking right, and now you. You know, you keep asking me if I'm upset with you and what do I think? I'm thinking that you really don't care. You just saw me each week because you had to, that's all. You don't care, because if you did, you would see me again."

I told her, "You know it's easy to think that people—your parents, your boyfriend, your former social worker—come and go, and you have no control over it." She added quickly, "Yes, you're right. What would you do if I telephoned you? Hang up?" I said, "No, I would feel torn also. I would be pleased and happy to hear from you, but I also know it is hard to say goodbye. That's what's hard to face, isn't it?" She agreed. I said, "So, even though deep inside we know we won't see a person again, we say, 'Oh, I'll see you.' It makes it easier for the moment." Sandy remarked that was true. I then reminded her how she felt when the former intern left. She hadn't wanted to meet with me at first. But then she made a choice, and in spite of her sorrow last year, she tried again. We talked of how much she accomplished this year and what starting with a new social work intern would be like. Now that I am leaving, there isn't much either of us can do. I gently told her that she might not see me again. But what we had together and what she learned were something she would always have with her. No one can take away her special feeling and the accomplishments.

As we drove back to school, we both sat very still and quiet. Finally, I said, "Sandy, I don't want you to leave until you have a chance to tell me what you are thinking. Try to say it now, rather than saying to yourself later, 'I should have told her.'" Sandy turned to me and said, "I'm going to miss you a lot. I just don't know what it will be like not seeing you every week. I really liked you a lot." She held back her tears. I said I felt the same way about her and added, "I know it's hard for you. We'll both feel very sad later as you go back to school and I go back to my office, and we think about each other." Sandy said, "I know," and we hugged each other. Then she left.

As Sandy attempts to avoid the permanence of ending, the worker helps her to confront the reality. She affirms Sandy's feelings of abandonment and anger, and responds without defensiveness and with sensitively to questions about the genuineness of her caring. She helps Sandy evaluate her accomplishments and prepare for a new social worker. Her final invitation, "Try to say it now," enables Sandy to express her affection and to disengage with a sense of shared intimacy. Table 12.3 summarizes the skills of helping clients to release.

Evaluating the Provided Service

Endings are especially valuable in building professional knowledge and refining skill. Joint assessment of outcomes with clients, identifying what was helpful and what was not, and why, can be gradually generalized to practice principles. Much of what is considered intuition in a gifted worker is actually practice expertise and wisdom, seldom raised to an explicit practice principle. As experience expands, one notes patterns of responses across cases and tests one's hypotheses of what works with particular groups of people, needs, or situations.

Most agencies require workers to complete statistical forms for use by the agency, regulatory bodies, or funding sources. The client's responses to questions concerning quality yield a measure of worker accountability. Accountability is not complete, however, until those served have the opportunity to evaluate their experiences with the agency and social worker during the ending phase. When practitioner and agency take evaluation seriously, practice becomes more effective, services more responsive to need, and accountability to those served more assured.

Table 12.3
Skills of Helping Client to Release

- Invite review of work together.
- Emphasize strengths and gains.
- Elicit discussion of remaining areas of difficulty.
- Review work and experience.
- Consider next steps: transfer, referral, or termination.
- Develop plans to carry out next step:
  For transfer, connect to new worker.
  For referral, find and link to new resource.
  For termination, phase out work.
- Provide opportunity for final goodbye.

Creating a climate that permits people to be candid in assessing service is a measure of worker skill. Many workers and agencies, however, go beyond the ending phase in order to assure accountability. Hospital social service departments are usually included in the hospital's questionnaire about total patient care. Many social agencies use questionnaires mailed after termination to tap client responses to the service. These are valuable as they can reveal attitudes and responses that the person hesitated to share with the worker. Workers themselves often follow up some time after termination to ascertain the individual's or group's current situation and to determine if gains continue. Even though some suggest that this creates or prolongs dependency, we strongly believe that follow-up demonstrates the continuing interest and goodwill of the agency and its concern for quality service.

PART THREE

LIFE-MODELED PRACTICE AT COMMUNITY, ORGANIZATION, AND POLITICAL LEVELS

Part 3 examines life-modeled practice designed to influence the quality of community life through engaging residents, to advocate for needed policy and program changes in human service organizations, and to use political methods and skills to advance the cause of social justice. Porter Lee, in his 1929 presidential address to the National Conference of Social Work (Lee, 1929b), noted that social work was moving away from a concern with a cause (social reform) and was assuming the character of a function (direct services). In Lee's view, both cause and function are valuable and essential for social welfare: a cause once won depends on organization, methods, and skills for its implementation. But a tendency to become overly preoccupied with organizational maintenance and professional prerogatives can lead to a blunting of commitment. Lee (1929b) envisioned a synthesis in which social work would develop its service as a function of well-organized community life without sacrificing its capacity to inspire enthusiasm for a cause.

Unfortunately, direct practitioners have shied away from "cause" practice, identifying it as the province of community organizers, administrators, and policy practitioners: for community organizers to mobilize and organize communities to improve community life; for social work administrators to change service delivery and accountability structures; and for policy practitioners to create new legislation, improve existing ones, or defeat the policy initiatives of other groups. These community, organizational, and policy "specialists" engage a system on behalf of a class of clients. These macro specialists are essential to carrying out the profession's social justice mandate. However, for the profession to fully fulfill its social justice commitment, community, agency, and policy practice must be carried out by generalist practitioners in their day-to-day activities as well as by advanced specialists. In order for social workers to help oppressed and disadvantaged populations, both generalists and specialists must engage in community, organizational, and legislative practice.

In helping individuals, families, and groups with their life stressors and issues, social work practitioners daily encounter the lack of fit between people's needs and the resources available in communities, organizations, and broader society. Thus, the life-modeled generalist practitioner must assume professional responsibility for mobilizing community resources to influence quality of life in the community, for influencing unresponsive organizations to develop responsive policies and services, and for influencing local, state, and federal legislation and regulations to improve the lives of their clients. Part 3 of this book deals with the expansion of direct practice activities from helping individual, families, and groups deal with life stressors to influencing community and neighborhood life (chapter 13); employing organizations (chapter 14); and legislation, regulations, and electoral politics (chapter 15).

THIRTEEN

INFLUENCING COMMUNITY
AND NEIGHBORHOOD LIFE

The lack of community resources, problems in the coordination of community resources, or people's difficulty in gaining access to available resources may cause or exacerbate life stressors. To enhance the quality of community and neighborhood life, all social workers in life-modeled practice must acquire certain knowledge and skills of community work. Generally, the social worker in life-modeled practice moves to the community modality because a significant community issue has arisen during work with an individual, family, or group and affects other community residents as well. Occasionally, the community modality is used when the social worker recognizes a need and canvasses the neighborhood or community to determine if the members agree about the seriousness of the need. When the service recipient and other residents believe that change is needed to improve the quality of community life, the practitioner helps them to achieve their objective.

Community and Neighborhood

The community is most often defined as a geographically bounded locale recognizable by its location, such as its natural boundaries; social, economic, and demographic patterns; and social history (Ohmner & Korr, 2006). A community performs certain necessary functions for its residents. These include the production, distribution, and consumption of goods and services; the transmission of prevailing knowledge, social values, customs, and behavior patterns that contribute to the socialization of individual residents; social control to maintain conformity to community norms; and social participation through formal and informal groups. A wide range of public and private organizations and informal networks of individuals, families, and groups carry out these functions.

The community is the main conduit through which resources, formal and informal systems, and political, social, and economic forces exert major influences on individuals, families, and neighborhoods. The distinctive elements of any community's influence on the development and functioning of residents consist of its demographic characteristics; mobility patterns; systems of transportation, sanitation, and fire and police protection; and formal and informal networks, and the accessibility, equity, and quality of its health, educational, and social services.

Nonlocale communities are groups of people with a common interest and/or reference who do not necessarily live in the same area. These include, for example, gay and lesbian communities, nonlocale ethnic communities, professional communities, arts communities, and religious communities.

Neighborhoods are smaller geographic components of a larger community. A neighborhood's size is subjective. A neighborhood-based social agency might define it as consisting of several thousand people. Residents might define it spatially, depending on whether one can walk from end to end, which could depend on age and physical capacity. If one is able to walk past only a few buildings on either side of one's home, the neighborhood is apt to be defined as small indeed. The immediate neighborhood is a potential site for intimate personal interchanges and informal support systems. These informal support systems are a source of mutual aid through the exchange of instrumental and expressive resources. They also influence behaviors, attitudes, and norms (e.g., pregnancy and childrearing).

Essentially, a neighborhood is more than its geography or its numbers. Some definitions of neighborhood refer to even smaller units termed social blocks, with interaction more prominent at the block level. How many social blocks constitute a neighborhood depends again on how size is defined. Also, some residents may live in congregate units such as housing projects, single-room-occupancy hotels, residential treatment centers, nursing homes, group homes, and the like. Congregates are frequently viewed by their own residents and by neighbors as separate "communities" that are not part of the surrounding neighborhood.

Contemporary Community and Neighborhood Stressors

Poverty and discrimination are major community and neighborhood stressors and embed other stressors. Poverty and discrimination create an unsafe habitat for residents and a preponderance of stigmatized niches, which undermine community and neighborhood formal and informal structures and the health, emotional well-being, and social functioning of residents.

In some neighborhoods, residents have little or no contact with their neighbors because of pervasive violence. Many poor people, young and old, are less mobile than wealthier people, who find a satisfying social life outside their neighborhood or community. Some poor people live in a cohesive, eth-nically homogeneous neighborhood that provides social integration. But others have no way out of what is a noncohesive neighborhood despite their constant and realistic fear of neighbors and of neighborhood conflict and violence. Many low-income community residents feel powerless and alienated.

> Women, children, and the elderly, especially those living in poor communities, are at highest risk of victimization by crime. They simply are easier prey! Perpetrators tend to be caught in a cycle of family poverty, illiteracy, drugs, racism, child abuse, and family violence. When they are incarcerated, they usually return to their community further damaged, hardened, and embittered. They often become socialized to a lifetime of crime and intermittent incarceration. In poor communities, both the victim and the perpetrator are trapped in a mire of despair. (Gitterman, 2001b, pp. 3–4)

Life stressors afflicting a poor community include a shortage of affordable, safe housing; hospital closings; underfunded school systems; business and factory closings, or moves of businesses out of the community; asbestos and lead paint contamination in schools and dwellings; hazardous waste dumps and toxic emanations from workplaces; drug trafficking and associated violence; growing prevalence of AIDS and other chronic illnesses; inadequate systems of public sanitation and transportation (especially in rural communities); inadequate health and mental health care; and unresponsive public and corporate bureaucracies, which generate other life stressors. Corporate relocation, zoning, banking and realty trends, and availability and accessibility of public services conspire to create demographic changes. Some communities and neighborhoods are subject to periodic traumatic natural catastrophes, including hurricanes, earthquakes, floods, and fires.

Schools in poor communities of color, for example, are underfunded and overcrowded, starving the minds of poor children and blighting their futures. Because of inequitable financing, the poorer the community, the less money is expended for each child, whereas the more affluent the community, the greater that expenditure. Consequently, children of color in poor communities and neighborhoods receive inadequate education; consequently, they have fewer opportunities for employment. Lack of employment opportunities institutionalizes poverty with resulting physical, psychological, and social consequences. Among poor families of color, morbidity and mortality rates are strikingly higher than among those of sufficient economic means. Poverty also creates the conditions for crime and violence (Gitterman, 2001b).

Social workers can help impoverished and vulnerable neighborhoods or communities to meliorate some of these effects. But the responsibility for their ultimate elimination rests with society itself. This reality underlies our emphasis on community, organizational, and political advocacy to influence social legislation in conjunction with life-modeled practice.

Social Work Function, Modality, Methods, and Skills

The Social Worker and Life-Modeled Community Practice

The lack of essential and desired community and neighborhood resources in poor communities provides the life-modeled social worker with the social purpose of helping to influence the quality of community and neighborhood life of residents. The purpose is fulfilled by (1) helping community and neighborhood residents to undertake action to improve the fit between available and desired formal and informal resources, (2) developing community programs and services to meet residents' needs, (3) building informal community support systems of relatedness, and (4) improving the coordination of community services. In all areas of community work, the social worker also provides formal and informal consultation to community-based service providers, other professionals, and community members.

Professional Methods and Skills for Helping Community and Neighborhood Residents Undertake Action

Engaging impoverished and vulnerable neighborhood or community residents in a collective effort to empower themselves and to achieve their desire for social change is a significant professional goal for the life-modeled social worker. Community and neighborhood social action aims at assisting an impoverished community, or an oppressed segment of its population, to demand and secure needed resources or services (Brooks, 2001; Germain, 1985a, 1985b; Mondros & Wilson, 1994; Rothman, 1996; Shepard, 2005; Weil, 2005). Taking action to improve the quality of community and neighborhood life is essential to collective and individual mental health.

In engaging community and neighborhood residents to undertake action on their own behalf, the social worker carries out several tasks. Community and neighborhood residents are more likely to become involved and take action when they have identified an issue of immediate concern and importance to them. Thus, a fundamental principle of life-modeled community practice is that issues must arise from community and neighborhood residents (including their interest in a social worker's proposal).

To this end, the social worker undertakes a community or neighborhood needs assessment (equally important for developing new programs and support systems of relatedness). The practitioner must learn about the physical layout of the community and neighborhood, as well as its demographic composition, discontents and intergroup tensions, formal and informal leaders, organizations and services, values and norms, political structure, financial and other resources, and history. All this and more are gathered by studying pertinent documents, talking to key community and neighborhood "gatekeepers," and conducting a formal survey. By developing an initial understanding of community and neighborhood dynamics, the social worker gains information on critical existing and potential issues, turf boundaries, demographic trends and characteristics, key governmental and private institutions, informal organizations, and powerful actors in community life (Netting, Kettner, & McMurtry, 2004; Rubin & Rubin, 2001).

A social worker (and her colleagues as well) employed by a hospital's methadone maintenance treatment program was concerned about the lack of community acceptance, the negative attitudes, and the discrimination experienced by methadone maintenance clients. While methadone maintenance helped most of her clients to maintain steady employment and establish meaningful relationships, they consistently felt misunderstood, stigmatized, and discriminated. For example, in a mutual aid recovery group led by her, many group members shared their experiences of attending Alcohol Anonymous (AA) and Narcotics Anonymous (NA) meetings in which they were verbally berated for being on methadone. They also expressed fears about their employer discovering that they were methadone clients and losing their jobs. Accumulating these informal data prompted the social worker to conduct an informal survey. Twenty-one (out of thirty) hospital methadone clients responded to the following questions:

1. Are you employed? (If "no," go to question 4.)
    18 out of 21 (86 percent): yes, employed.
    3 out of 21 (14 percent): no, not employed.
2. Does your employer know you are taking methadone?
    12 out of 18 (67 percent): employer does NOT know.
    5 out of 18 (28 percent): employer DOES know.
    1 out of 18 (6 percent): N/A (self-employed).
3. Do you fear losing your job if your employer found out you were taking methadone?
    10 out of 12 (83 percent) fear losing job.
    2 out of 12 (17 percent) do not fear losing job.
4. Have you or someone you know had difficulty finding employment as a result of being on methadone?
    9 out of 21 (43 percent) had or know someone.
    12 out of 21 (57 percent) did not have or do not know someone.
5. Are you reluctant to share information with health professionals regarding your methadone maintenance?
    14 out of 21 (67 percent) do not share.
    7 out of 21 (33 percent) do share.
6. In general, do you feel there are negative attitudes in your community about taking methadone?
    15 out of 21 (71 percent) do feel.
    6 out of 21 (29 percent) do not feel.
7. Do you know someone who is fearful about receiving methadone treatment because of community negative attitudes toward methadone?
    11 out of 21 (54 percent) know someone.
    10 out of 21 (46 percent) do not know someone.

Survey results documented members' fears of losing their jobs (83 percent among those whose employers did not know they were receiving methadone treatment), experience of discrimination in seeking employment (43 percent of the full sample), reluctance to share methadone treatment with health professionals (67 percent), encounters with negative community attitudes (71 percent), and knowledge of people fearful of receiving treatment because of negative community attitudes (54 percent). Clearly, the majority of clients were affected by perceived negative community attitudes, and these perceived attitudes affect the decisions and choices they make in their lives.

In order to assess the actual or perceived negative community attitudes toward methadone maintenance, the social worker set out to collect various community data. One source entailed a review of the local newspaper. She found the following headlines:

> "Neighborhood Tenants Say They Are Unhappy about the Proposal for a Methadone Clinic Nearby Because It Would Add to Drug Traffic in the Area"
>
> "Neighbors, Parents Protest Rehab Center"
>
> "Despite Several Attempts to Open the Clinic in Downtown, Neighborhood Rejection of Two Proposed Facilities Forced the Middletown Hospital to House It in the Hospital"
>
> "Lots of Reasons Were Given for the Opposition, but It Essentially Came Down to Support for the Idea of a Clinic Somewhere Else, Not Here"

These represent just a few of the many headlines and article quotations from the community newspaper.

Employer attitudes were also assessed. Ten merchants located at the community's major mall were given the following survey:

1. Do you perform drug screening prior to and/or during someone's employment?

    1 out of 10 (10 percent) perform drug screening.

2. If yes, does the screening include methadone?

    0 out of 10 (0 percent) perform methadone screening.

3. Would you be hesitant to hire someone if you knew he or she was on methadone?

    6 out of 10 (60 percent) would be hesitant to hire.

    4 out of 10 (40 percent) would not be hesitant to hire.

4. If you had to choose, whom would you prefer to hire: a recovering alcoholic or a recovering heroin addict who is taking methadone?

    5 out of 10 (50 percent) chose recovering alcoholic.

    1 out of 10 (10 percent) chose person on methadone.

    4 out of 10 (40 percent) gave no response.

5. In general, do you think there is a negative attitude on the part of employers in your community toward taking methadone?

    5 out of 10 (50 percent): yes, there is a negative attitude.

    1 out of 10 (10 percent): there is no negative attitude.

    4 out of 10 (50 percent) gave no response.

The data collected from the small sample of community merchants substantiates client fears of employment discrimination. If the four nonresponders are removed from the sample, 83 percent of the employers think there is a negative attitude on the part of employers in the community toward methadone treatment. They would choose a recovering alcoholic over a person on methadone. If these employers are representative of community employers, the data are compelling.

The social worker also collected data from members of AA and NA. Among questions these members were asked, one was particularly informative:

1. In general, do you feel there is a negative attitude toward people taking methadone in the AA/NA community?

    11 out of 13 (85 percent): yes, there is a negative attitude.

    2 out of 13 (15 percent): there is no negative attitude.

These data suggest a lack of support for methadone clients in the 12-step community. The data are further supported by an examination of organizations' literature. Narcotics Anonymous' literature considers methadone patients to be on a substance and, therefore, discourages them from using NA as a support system. In recognition of these associations' perspectives, the National Alliance of Methadone Advocates (1999, p. 10) warned:

> If clients feel that the 12-Step concept would be beneficial to their recovery, they must decide whether to expose themselves and risk being ostracized or keep their methadone use a secret so they can participate. Neither of these solutions is compatible with rehabilitation.

Interviews with long-term community residents and with organizational and political leaders generated additional data. They identified the impact of significant historical community events. For example, the closing of a residential treatment program drastically affected the chemically dependent population. Many of these patients became homeless with limited resources and assistance available to them. The residential treatment program's closing increased the community's homelessness and prevalence of drug use, which, in turn, negatively affected community attitudes toward drug addiction.

The closing of a factory, a major community employer, represented another significant historical event. Its closing created a large loss of jobs and marked the beginning of an economic shift for the community. Unemployment increased, housing values decreased, and a sense of hopelessness and despair became pervasive. Several long-term residents associated a significant increase in substance abuse to the closing of the factory.

Anecdotal as well as survey- and interview-generated data indicate the lack of community acceptance of methadone treatment and the serious ramifications this lack of acceptance has on methadone clients and their need for comprehensive services. In this particular community, several leaders were identified as being potentially helpful in alleviating the negative stigma and increasing community acceptance of methadone treatment. For example, the city's mayor has fully supported the need for the methadone treatment clinic. He stated to a newspaper reporter, "I am confident we will be able to allay the fears and concerns people have about the methadone program." Similarly, the chief executive officer of the hospital has also been a vocal supporter. He advocated for the clinic to be based in the hospital when a community site could not be determined. In a community newsletter, he was quoted as stating, "We are proud to have this opportunity to prove to the residents of the community that a methadone clinic can be blended into our community without causing any upheavals in our daily operations."

In addition to these and other community leaders, two national organizations are significant resources—the National Alliance of Methadone Advocates (NAMA) and Advocates for Recovery through Medicine (ARM). One of NAMA's primary goals is to help establish 12-step programs for methadone clients in affected communities, calling this network of support "Methadone Is Recovery." ARM uses educational, media, and political arenas to increase awareness and acceptance of methadone as an effective treatment for opiate dependence. Outside of the immediate community, the National Institute of Health, the Institute of Medicine, the American Psychiatric Association, and the American Medical Association endorse methadone treatment. The support of these organizations can also be utilized.

After completing an initial community assessment, the social worker develops a list of residents and institutional representatives who might be interested in taking action in regard to this or a different issue and selects the most effective recruitment method. In identifying a pool of potential members, Mondros and Wilson (1994, pp. 43–49) suggest three characteristics of effective recruitment: (1) natural networks, (2) representativeness, and (3) special individual attributes. Tapping into natural networks is an expedient method for recruiting community and neighborhood residents. A social worker might consult with a key resident, who then contacts or introduces the worker to relatives, friends, and neighbors. Or a social worker might reach out to local churches, synagogues, or mosques. For many people, the trust, familiarity, and support provided by natural networks help them to become involved. However, the social worker must not settle for a convenient homogeneous pool of residents at the expense of excluding or alienating potentially significant contributors.

If a diverse constituency is required for successful action, representatives of each element of the community's heterogeneity are desirable. In this situation, the social worker purposively recruits members who represent diverse formal and informal community systems: the broader the representation, the greater the chance for legitimacy and influence. While heterogeneously composed groups have more power, they are much more difficult to keep together and remain focused.

In some situations, a community action group could be composed on the basis of special personal attributes. Residents with special leadership abilities or with an intense commitment to an issue (such as the need for child care, or services for developmentally challenged children) could be more effective than action groups composed of natural networks or representatives of different constituencies. Social workers must avoid a common error of recruiting potential leaders solely on the basis of their articulateness. While they may be articulate, their neighbors, for example, may actively dislike them. Failure to carefully evaluate their actual commitment to the issues and how other members view them could lead to chronic lack of participation by neighborhood or community residents.

The next important task for the social worker in life-modeled practice is to gain community residents' initial willingness to participate in undertaking action on their own behalf. Brager, Specht, and Torczyner (1987, p. 63) define participation as "the means by which people who are not elected or appointed officials of agencies and of government influence decisions about programs and policies that affect their lives." Participation educates residents and increases their competence, increases organizational and/or political responsiveness, and influences decisions that affect their daily lives. This view of participation turns the issue around in an important way. Instead of asking, "Why don't the poor participate like those others [middle- and upper-income participants]?" the question becomes "How do the poor participate, and how can their participation be made of greatest use to them?" The issue, then, is not merely how to get the poor to participate more actively, but how to make their already active and nonvoluntary participation more beneficial and meaningful to them (Brager et al., 1987, p. 67).

In our view, both questions are equally important: how to recruit and engage community residents to undertake action on their own behalf, and how to make their participation beneficial to them. The practitioner's initial contact with community residents often determines whether they decide to become involved and the extent of their involvement. The social worker must give careful consideration and preparation to what will be said to potential recruits, and their possible reactions. The social worker must anticipate, invite, and explore initial distrust, fear, reluctance, and ambivalence. The social worker's clarity in explaining purpose and role is critical to obtaining effective community participation. The statement should be clear, direct, and responsive to the interests and motivations of potential members.

The opening statement should be responsive to the following questions: "What do we want to say in this message?" "What's in it for the joiner?" "What can the recruit contribute?" "What can I say the efforts will produce?" (Mondros & Wilson, 1994, p. 50). The quality of the first contacts is important in ensuring participation.

In the first meeting, the social worker identifies a common focus and interests and explores fears, doubts, and hesitations. The worker must avoid slipping into "selling" rather than inviting, exploring, and developing mutual focus. Practitioners "incorrectly . . . prepare themselves to discuss only the issues and desired ends. Consequently they may fail to detect cues about the secondary expressive concerns of members. . . . New recruits may shrink from the overly eager approach" (Mondros & Berman-Rossi, 1991, p. 204).

Successful recruitment and effective description of purpose and the professional role generate initial interest in dealing with a community issue. Refreshments, social meetings or events, and icebreakers at meetings also support active participation and help participants to feel more at ease with one another. The next professional task is gaining commitment to a membership structure and to democratic participation in its activities. For community residents to sustain structured participation, they must feel that the process is democratic (i.e., rules for their participation are explicit and fairly applied). In a large group, a structure of officers and specification of responsibilities integrate membership (Ephross & Vassil, 2005). When membership and group roles are new to community residents, the social worker is more active in guiding structured participation and decision-making processes.

For example, a social worker found that severe interpersonal stress being experienced by families in a large housing project was generated at the stairwell level. Each high-rise building had a number of stairwells. Twelve families shared each stairwell. The social worker hypothesized that positive change at stairwell levels could produce positive change in the building and ultimately in the total project-as-community. Stairwell meetings were used to deal with conflicts among the stairwell families and to elicit their shared concerns about their social and physical environments. All stairwell members were encouraged to identify their common stressors and environmental needs, and plan for and take action to achieve goals such as improving maintenance, developing recreational facilities, improving relations with the school, and the like. These stairwell meetings laid the base for what became a tenants' association that later worked on the shared life issues of the total "project-as-community." Association members addressed the power structure (the housing authority) about required improvements with confidence and competence (Glaser, 1972).

Participants will often need a social worker's guidance and consultation in learning to conduct their own meetings, to engage in democratic group decision making, to reach out and build constituencies, to deal with differences, and to build a consensus. The development of these skills becomes a source of constituency power in later, more complex efforts.

Conflict management is an indispensable skill in forming groups, developing and sustaining mutual support, and dealing with internal and external conflict (Keefe & Koch, 1999; Secemsky, Ahlman, & Robbins, 1999). Conflict between members of a constituency or between the community and the power structure often arises. Conflict is neither bad nor good in itself: engaging and successfully resolving conflict are what are important, whether it is conflict among community or neighborhood subgroups of constituents or between the constituency and a decision-making body.

The social worker must expect that in most groups, legitimate instrumental and expressive differences, competition for power among natural leaders, and testing whether the worker's willingness to share power is genuine are likely to emerge. Members may tend to avoid or control differences. But if difference and conflict are submerged, positions harden, and the conflict persists or is driven underground only to reappear and drain group energy. Premature consensus should be challenged, and difference and conflict welcomed and invited. The social worker supports and guides the group's leaders to recognize conflict early and to invite members to discuss it. The social worker must model comfort with difference as well as comfort with conflict, and convey a faith in the democratic processes to achieve conflict resolution. Resolving internal differences strengthens the group structure and members' ability and willingness to engage with external conflict.

Community residents may find themselves in conflict with institutional power structures. When constituencies from poor and oppressed communities organize, the threat to the status quo may mobilize the opposing forces. Although dominant groups and power structures can be expected to resist efforts at social change, the community residents and social worker are not limited to conflict-oriented interventions. Other methods need to be tried first.

For example, a building superintendent referred Mrs. Rosen, a sixty-nine-year-old, mentally frail woman living in a small apartment in a poor and crime-ridden community, to a community-based social agency because of her disruptive behavior. A direct service student was assigned. The city's public housing authority ran the building, housing forty elderly people. Mrs. Rosen complained to the student of feeling friendless and fearful because the emergency alarm system, intercom, and front-door buzzer had been broken for almost a year and the housing authority had not responded despite the high crime rate in the neighborhood.

During her weekly visits to Mrs. Rosen, the social work intern observed that the tenants came together only while they waited in the lobby for the mail delivery, with little or no social interchange. While continuing to help Mrs. Rosen with her individual life issues, the social work intern involved herself in the larger community issues. For several weeks, she made a point of introducing herself to those in the lobby, and many told her of loneliness and fears similar to those of Mrs. Rosen. Some expressed a wish for social activities in the building's lounge, "which is hardly ever used."

Most despaired of ever having their requests met by the housing authority. She came to view the residents as a "community," a congregate whose members had common needs and concerns. Her brief initial assessment of the building-as-a-community included the following:

1. *Strengths.* The super, who is also frustrated with the housing authority's red tape, is a potential ally. Also, one resident is a natural helper who has given holiday parties for the other residents, is active in community affairs, and is knowledgeable about resources.
2. *Obstacles.* The obstacles include an unresponsive bureaucracy, the physical and mental impairment of many of the elderly tenants, and the lack of a cohesive, organized group structure.

She inquired into their interest in meeting together. Some were interested in social gatherings, others desired informational meetings, and several thought they should work together to influence the housing authority. Next, the worker canvassed the group for volunteers to plan the first meeting.

Several tenants prepared announcements of meeting dates and topics. The first two meetings were given over to socializing, information gathered by several tenants on comparative drug prices in neighborhood pharmacies, and an outside speaker on elder health. The group decided next to hold a planning session to discuss needed repairs. Twelve residents attended. Plans were worked out, an agenda developed, and individual presentations rehearsed. An invitation to attend was sent by the planning group to the authority's director, and that meeting drew thirty residents. The director was unable to attend, but he sent three representatives. The agenda was followed, and the residents' presentations were clearly and firmly stated. The group then formally requested that the needed repairs be started within two weeks. The three representatives stated that they would need a few months to initiate the repairs. Members were prepared to negotiate and settled on a six-week period. The members scheduled a follow-up session with the representatives in two months to evaluate the results of their efforts and to plan next steps. The repairs actually began before the end of the month.

At the end of her placement, the student concluded:

The educational programs and social activities the tenants requested facilitated their active engagement with one another. This, in turn, led to increased social skills, enhanced confidence and self-esteem, and a beginning development of a social network. This was possible because of residents' growing interest in organizing themselves as a cohesive group to do something about the serious problems in their shared physical and social environment.

This vignette reveals what can happen when a practitioner helps community residents achieve their desired goals. The student's personal contacts with the elderly residents engaged their interest and resulted in active participation. In this situation, mild confrontation was sufficient to achieve housing repairs. These impoverished elderly residents also developed a new sense of themselves as a social congregate within their surrounding neighborhood. They became more self-directed with an increased sense of competence in dealing with common life issues generated by their shared environment, an increased sense of collective empowerment, enhanced self-esteem, and beginning relatedness to one another.

In reviewing their successful organizing action, the intern underscored the members' new skills and capacities for self-directed efforts, including the presence of self-maintaining structures for continued problem solving. The natural helper and one other tenant were further encouraged and prepared to serve as indigenous tenant leaders in planning and carrying out their desired social, educational, and advocacy activities. In community or neighborhood groups, members might decide on a formal structure with responsibilities for group tasks spread among elected officers and voluntary committees. A self-maintaining structure should be firmly in place. Table 13.1 summarizes the professional tasks and skills associated with helping community and neighborhood residents engage in efforts at social change.

Professional Methods and Skills for Developing Community and Neighborhood Programs and Services

Successful engagement of neighborhood or community residents in developing and implementing new programs to meet collective needs simultaneously improves the fit between available and desired resources and is potentially empowering (de-Beer & Marais, 2005; Descamp, Flux, McClelland, & Sieppert, 2005; Laverack, 2006). Programs involve planning, funding, staffing, physical facilities, and support for needed new services. Most new programs require financial resources, staffing, and physical facilities.

We limit our discussion to developing programs to (1) improve community social conditions, and (2) promote physical and mental health for all community residents or selected subgroups. Development of both types of community programming requires assessing needs, gaining residents' involvement and participation, guiding group process, and managing conflict. For example, identification and assessment of need include recognizing a pattern in one's own caseload of unmet need, checking with colleagues whether a pattern is evident in their caseloads, determining who is served by community agencies and through what type of services, determining gaps in the service delivery systems found by other staff, engaging community groups and natural helpers in discussions of needs and priorities, and developing a more formal needs survey. The data-gathering and assessment process in itself also heightens institutional and community awareness of the need. As in community and neighborhood social change activity, community program development includes the active participation of the constituency in identifying need and planning and carrying out programs.

Table 13.1
Professional Tasks and Skills of Helping Community and Neighborhood Residents to Undertake Social Change

• *Construct a community or neighborhood needs assessment in order to identify residents' immediate concerns:*	Study pertinent documents. "Hang out." Talk to key community or neighborhood "gatekeepers." Conduct formal surveys.
• *Select most effective membership recruitment method:*	Tap into natural networks. Recruit representatives of diverse constituencies. Recruit on basis of personal characteristics.
• *Gain initial willingness of community or neighborhood residents to participate in undertaking social change on their own behalf by:*	Anticipatory preparation. Clear and direct statement that is responsive to potential members' interests and motivations. Inviting and exploring reactions, including doubts, hesitations, ambivalence, and fears. Developing shared focus.
• *Develop commitment to a membership structure and democratic participation in activities by:*	Developing explicit rules for membership and their even application. In large groups, developing structure of officers and responsibilities. Active initial role in guiding structured participation and decision making.
• *Develop and sustain mutual membership support by:*	Challenging premature consensus. Welcoming and inviting differences and conflict.
• *Help manage internal membership conflict by:*	Modeling comfort with difference. Conveying faith in democratic process.
• *Help members to manage external conflict with dominant groups and power structures.*	
• *Evaluate social change experiences, including successes and failures by:*	Underscoring members' new skills and capacities for self-directed efforts in dealing with any changes in group leadership. Planning next steps.

Improving Community Social Conditions.   Using the needs assessment, social workers help community residents improve social conditions by developing needed programs or services. To improve community social conditions, local leadership and organizational structure have to be established, and residents' participation and involvement sustained (Longest, 2006). For example, an experienced work-study student at a northeastern state welfare department who served individuals and families in several rural counties provided this vignette of her life-modeled practice with a community of some 2,600 residents.

This rural town had one of the highest percentages of low-income and TANF families in its county, one of the highest referral rates for child abuse and neglect, and the highest rate of teenage pregnancy. Yet no support services were available except for a monthly well-child clinic conducted by the Visiting Nurse Association (VNA). All other formal services were twenty miles away in the nearest small city, but the lack of transportation was a formidable barrier. The social worker and her social work and nursing colleagues on the interdisciplinary Suspected Child Abuse and Neglect (SCAN) team decided to work on mobilizing and strengthening natural or informal helping systems. Interested members of SCAN formed an independent task force, the Rural Community Resources Group (RCRG), to begin a community process of developing its own informal resources (Germain, 1985b).

Data were gathered to assess the support and participation of influential members of the community and for seeking grant assistance. The social worker familiarized herself with the physical layout of the community as well as its social structure, demographic composition, and norms and values. She called on prominent residents, spoke at meetings, and met regularly with the mothers' group and with other members of the RCRG. She also obtained data pertaining to teenage pregnancy, child abuse, and neglect. Almost all town residents participated in the needs assessment, which was carried out by volunteer mothers in door-to-door canvassing of residents' responses to the proposed project and their ideas for it.

Ten mothers, including some from the Visiting Nurse Association group, and some protective service clients met weekly with the RCRG during May and June. There was immediate agreement on the goal: a drop-in parent–child center, perhaps a cooperative, where children could be cared for a few hours a day or week and where mothers could seek information and find a sympathetic ear. Both respite and improved parental functioning were seen as desired outcomes.

The mothers and other residents canvassed all residents door to door, using a questionnaire. Additional questionnaires were left at the two grocery stores, the free swimming pool, and the physician's office. The mothers made and distributed posters, and a news article was written and published in the local free newspaper. The overall aim was to plan with the community residents, not for them, and to identify and support natural leaders.

The town's director of Community Development assisted us in locating four vacant sites. We hoped to make final arrangements on a visible and accessible site by September so that the program could begin. We undertook a search for seed money. Various community residents were helping with this task, some approaching the trustees of a local trust fund, others approaching the officers of the local bank, businesses, and civic clubs for donations. I approached the State

> Welfare Division, which has a new grant for direct services in rural areas, and administrators agreed to accept a proposal from us. (Germain, 1985b, p. 132)

The center for mothers and their preschool children opened in September and was located in the fellowship hall of a local church. A grant of $25,000 from the governor's comprehensive children's and youth project supported this center and one in another rural town. Both centers were open one morning a week, providing self-planned programs and discussions for parents, child care, and transportation services. The programs were later extended to two mornings a week as interest grew.

An inevitable question is "How can an already overburdened social worker spare the time that program development in a community requires?"

> The first problem I encountered was how to convince my immediate superiors that any time involved would eventually be worthwhile for our clients. There has only been intervention on one level, after the fact of abuse or neglect, and preventive services are nonexistent. The Department of Welfare has never hired a community worker nor moved into group services, and any deviation in traditional services would require a series of administrative approvals. However, my student status, requiring new learning experiences, won the day. (Germain, 1985b, p. 134)

Many agencies now view the community modality as part of their practitioners' responsibilities. In an agency that has not yet embraced this view, however, it is important that life-modeled practitioners gain the approval of the person to whom they are accountable for time spent in community work. The knowledge and skills involved in influencing one's agency and its decision makers in such matters are discussed in the next chapter.

Promoting Physical and Mental Health for All Community Residents or Selected Subgroups.   Dubos (1965) pointed out that the ancient Chinese paid their personal physicians to keep them healthy. The really good doctors were believed to be not those who treated the sick, but rather those who instructed people on how to not become ill. This is a position analogous to life-modeled social workers' interest in developing programs to promote community physical and mental health for all residents or for a selected subpopulation.

Common life issues such as expectable life transitions, the assumption of new or altered social statuses and roles, and interpersonal processes in family, work, and community life are the major arenas in which human development and adaptive functioning take place. Therefore, programs in these three areas can forestall difficulties that some people might experience because of life circumstances or because of demands that exceed their coping resources.

Developing community programs that promote physical and mental health requires the participation of community residents in planning and carrying out such programs. If community- and neighborhood-based programs are to be successful, the residents or their representatives must participate in identifying areas of mental, physical, or social functioning that are important to them. Drawing on the practitioner's consultation, as needed, community members specify the need that is not being met, set priorities and program goals, plan the program and strategies, carry out the program, and evaluate its effectiveness. "Graduates" of former programs often become conveners, coaches, leaders, or trainers in subsequent rounds of the program.

Community programs are developed for the general public and for defined populations such as teenage mothers, in which young mothers learn about infant and child development. As in all life-modeled practice, emphasis from the beginning is on strengths, not on deficits.

Varied types of potential community programs can promote physical and mental health. One type of program builds *resistance* to life stress by teaching residents to cope effectively with common, expectable life issues people experience or are about to experience (Diaz, Peake, Surko, & Bhandarkar, 2004; Ng et al., 2006). This requires the identification of the skills, capacities, and information needed to deal with the particular life issue. Learning and emotional growth experiences, anticipatory guidance, and environmental supports are required to enhance capacities and skills. Community programs for populations facing new statuses and new role demands, for example, include groups for new and expectant parents, adoptive parents, foster parents, solo fathers or mothers, people approaching retirement, and newly separated, divorced, or remarried people. They also include drug, alcohol, and tobacco education, and programs to increase understanding and acceptance of human and cultural diversity.

Another type of program attempts to *prevent or diminish* stress and *strengthen* coping responses from unexpected, severe, and unavoidable stressors. Such programs range from inviting young children awaiting hospitalization to visit the hospital, view the equipment, and meet the staff, to groups for the newly unemployed, or for family members caring for patients with severe chronic illness. In grave emergencies such as a fatal school bus accident, a neighborhood murder, or a cluster of adolescent suicides, school and social agency support programs are designed to help children, youth, and adults to cope effectively with the associated stress, grief, and fear.

In some instances, programs attempt to help people to *avoid anticipated life stressors* by promoting competence, a strong self-concept, and preventive behaviors (Bullock & McGraw, 2006; Hatchett & Duran, 2002; Hurdle, 2001). These programs, for example, may emphasize racial, ethnic, gender, and sexual orientation identity; rites of passage; and so on. Group activities are used to promote self-esteem and health- and mental health–promotional behaviors. Table 13.2 summarizes the types of programs that promote physical and mental health of community residents.

Table 13.2
Types of Community Programs That Promote Physical and Mental Health of Community Residents

• *Build resistance to potential stressors:*	Programs build resistance to potential stress associated with expectable life stressors by identifying and imparting the skills, capacities, and information needed to deal effectively with the life stressor.
• *Prevent or diminish stress and improve coping:*	Programs lead to management of severe life stressors by organizing informational, anticipatory, or guidance activities or group experience to prevent or diminish difficult stress responses and replace them with positive behaviors that will strengthen coping with unanticipated, unavoidable stressors.
• *Avoid anticipated life stressors:*	Programs help people to avoid anticipated life stressors by promoting competence, a strong self-concept, and preventive behaviors.

When these overlapping types of community physical and mental health promotion programs are effective, they promote and enhance the competence, relatedness, self-esteem, and self-direction of the participants.

> A "health promotion" strategy attempts to improve the quality of life and foster optimal health in the population. It focuses on "wellness" and maintaining health rather than mitigating "sickness" and restoring health. Services based upon a developmental scheme emphasize access to education, recreation, socialization, and cultural resources. These programs attempt to engage social competence, cognitive and emotional coping, and achievement. (Gitterman, 1987, p. 9)

Professional Methods and Skills for Building Informal Community Support Systems

Informal systems are built by establishing relationships with individual natural helpers and validating the importance of natural helping in the community; helping to establish self-help groups; and recruiting, training, and supervising volunteers.

Shaped in part by the neighborhood, community, or congregate in which they are embedded, informal support systems of relatedness in turn help shape the community and its collective life. They are important bases of empowerment through which individuals and communities take greater control of their own and the community's destiny by joint decision making, action, and social and emotional supports. These informal systems contribute to community pride and facilitate residents' meaningful participation in their larger community and the society.

Natural Helpers.   Natural helpers who function well in their own lives and whose life circumstances are similar to those of their neighbors are often known in the neighborhood for their resourcefulness and their ability to give advice, provide information and empathic support, and connect others to needed informal and formal resources (Gumpert, Saltman, & Sauer-Jones, 2000; Kinney & Trent, 2003; Lewis & Suarez, 1995; Patterson & Marsiglia, 2000). They may or may not know those who come to them for help or advice. In addition to urban communities and neighborhoods, natural helpers are found in congregates such as housing projects, some workplaces, and churches, and they are usually strong in rural areas. Even some children and teenagers are natural helpers to their peers.

Other natural helpers include beauticians, bartenders, storekeepers, pharmacists, building superintendents, waitresses, and restaurant operators who are alert to the well-being of their elderly, physically challenged, mentally impaired, or depressed and anxious customers. They listen, empathize, and offer concrete advice and reassurance. At times, an unlikely person serves in the role of a natural helper. For example, a postmistress in a neighborhood post office weighed babies on her postal scale. Many young mothers stopped by to see this grandmotherly woman and received her support and advice (Swenson, 1981).

The presence of natural helpers represents a neighborhood and/or community strength that could be extended to others in the community who lack such resources. Social workers can readily engage the interest and help of a known natural helper in an individual or family situation, always with the individual's or family's agreement and interest. Natural helpers enlisted in this way serve as consultants and resource people as needed. The worker can also affirm their helpfulness and their value and offer them encouragement and realistic praise. Neighborhood-oriented social workers interested in drawing on or strengthening sources of natural helping can locate natural helpers by talking with colleagues, school personnel, clergy, physicians, shopkeepers, and members of voluntary associations in the neighborhood. Natural helpers could be encouraged to talk about their helping activities and be asked if they are interested in having contact with individuals or families who lack helpful friends and relatives in the face of difficult situations and wish for such a relationship.

Linking individuals to enlisted natural helpers requires the motivation, interest, and agreement of both parties. The social worker follows up on the referral and evaluates the level of fit. Helpers should be evaluated on the basis of how helpful they are, not on whether their values and attitudes are congruent with professional ones. Ethnic, racial, or religious matches may be desirable depending on the needs and circumstances.

Establishing a Self-Help Group.   Life-modeled social workers can also help initiate (and serve as consultant to) a community self-help group. Mutual aid through self-help groups (face-to-face, or via telephone or computer networks) has taken on the character of a fast-growing social movement over the past several decades. Groups of people facing a shared need or condition band together to give and receive emotional and social support and to learn effective means of managing the shared concern. It is believed that millions of Canadians and Americans are members of rapidly growing numbers of such mutual aid systems (Gitterman & Shulman, 2005; Gumpert et al., 2000; Mesec & Mesec, 2004; Mok, 2004; Morris & Yates, 2002; Salzer, Rappaport, & Segre, 1999; Wituk, Shepherd, Slavich, Warren, & Meissen, 2000).[1]

Developing a self-help group requires assessing and identifying an unmet need in a community and neighborhood; obtaining information about similar groups in other communities; contacting community leaders, natural helpers, and agency staff about need and methods for reaching potential members; speaking to potential members and engaging their interest; publicizing the proposed self-help group through social agency, health, education, and religious bulletin boards, community newsletters, flyers, and newspapers; leading the first meeting with an emphasis on focus and ground rules; and beginning development of group leader roles (Ben-Ari, 2002; Wituk, Tiemeyer, Commer, Warren, & Meissen, 2003).

Self-help groups and mutual aid systems not only fit the worldview of various cultural groups in multicultural North American society but also are a significant force for empowering impoverished or devalued communities. No matter what the groups may later accomplish, most start from a powerless position. They lack needed resources, social respect, or an opportunity to be in control of their situations. Through group processes, members gradually empower themselves as they gain information, develop some control over their need or condition, and rediscover their own capacities. As the self-help group is empowered, the community itself gains in power in an upward spiral of adaptive exchanges, a reversal of the disempowerment generated by a downward cycle of community–family–individual maladaptive exchanges (Mok, 2005).

Recruiting, Training, and Supervising Role-Related Volunteers. All the informal helpers so far discussed here and in chapter 8 are actually volunteers. They receive no pay, although some may receive reciprocal help when needed. However, we confine our discussion here to role-related volunteers, those who are formally attached to social work services as collaborators, service extenders, or supervised assistants. For example, social workers in a large private voluntary hospital recruit, train, and supervise volunteers in several different services. One group visits lonely elderly patients while they are in the hospital and continues the visiting (and outings, if feasible) after discharge, with ongoing access to the social worker supervisor for consultation, affirmation, and encouragement.

Increased child abuse and neglect, for another example, have spurred the development of volunteer parent aide programs of varied types to supplement and complement the professional services of child welfare and family agencies. One such program is built on principles of natural friendship and informal helping. The aide is committed to at least a year of service, visits the family regularly, and is available by telephone. She (90 percent of the aides in this program are women) models life skills and provides practical assistance in managing household and childrearing tasks. Thus, the aide's function with the family is very different from the function of the social worker. Such programs benefit the family served, the trained volunteer, the social worker, the agency, and the community. Experience so far suggests that past and current parent aides form a cadre of community people whose talents and goodwill have been expanded and who become available as "specialists" to serve many people in their community in areas of family functioning, parenting, and child abuse and neglect. Aides acquire broadened knowledge of the community's formal systems and can connect people to formal resources when needed.

Volunteers are growing in numbers and providing diverse services. People volunteer in programs for the elderly, child welfare, intimate partner abuse, hospice care, the homeless and the hungry, and AIDS patients (Corcoran, Stephenson, Perryman, & Allen, 2001; Etkin, Prochaska, Harris, Latham, & Jette, 2006; Kovacs & Black, 1999). Factors accounting for the growth in volunteers include the increasing numbers of elderly who are able and eager to perform volunteer services, the ethos of caring among some segments of the population, and a response to cutbacks in social and health care services (Sherr & Straughan, 2005; Wilson, 2005). However, danger lies in any assumption that voluntary activities are cost-cutting substitutes for public responsibility. The need is greater than ever for professional services and adequately supported health, education, and social welfare programs, especially in areas where informal help is missing and cannot be generated.

The most successful volunteer programs are those that provide opportunities for giving service that is useful, respected by the staff, and personally rewarding, and that in some instances could lead to skills acquisition pertinent to a future career goal (Nelson, Hooker, DeHart, Edwards, & Lanning, 2003). When the work is real and the volunteers are respected and appreciated, they are likely to improve in their own functioning as well as in helping others (Jirovec, 2005; Jirovec & Hyduk, 1998; Larkin, Sadler, & Mahler, 2005) Essential to success are training, professional supervision, and a collegial, reciprocally respectful relationship. Yet few programs of social work education provide content on voluntarism, its history and significance, the nature of social worker–volunteer relationships and activities, and how to make use of trained volunteer service wisely and well. Interestingly, social workers actively and generously volunteer in professional associations, social agencies, political contests, community action and advocacy activities, and disaster work (Gitterman & Malekoff, 2002; Heitkamp, 1999). Table 13.3 summarizes some characteristics of building informal community systems of relatedness.

Improving the Coordination of Community Services.   Improving service coordination is an important objective in community practice. Service coordination refers to collaborative planning among agencies, joint fundraising, and other general social welfare activities. At the direct practice level, however, community-based case management is an example of responsive service coordination (Frankel & Gelman, 2004; Rothman, 1994).

The growth of community systems of care was largely sparked by the deinstitutionalization of chronically mentally ill people that began in the

Table 13.3
Characteristics of Informal Community Systems of Relatedness

• *Characteristics of natural helpers:*	Function well in their own lives.
	Life circumstances similar to those of their neighbors whom they help.
	Known in the neighborhood for resourcefulness and ability to give advice, provide information and empathic support, and connect others to needed informal and formal resources found in workplaces, housing projects, churches, and certain occupations such as beauticians and barbers, bartenders, storekeepers, building superintendents, and waitresses.
	May or may not know those who come for help or advice.
	Usually not trained.
	Some schoolchildren and teenagers are natural helpers to their peers.
• *Characteristics of community self-help groups:*	People band together to give and receive emotional and social support.
	Members gain information, develop some control over their need or condition, and rediscover their own capacities.
	Empower impoverished or devalued communities.
• *Characteristics of role-related volunteers:*	Formally attached to social work services in social agencies and hospitals as collaborators, service extenders, and supervised assistants.
	Recruited, trained, and supervised by staff social workers.
	The social worker–volunteer relationship is collegial and mutually respectful.
	Successful programs provide opportunities for giving service that is useful, respected by staff, and personally rewarding, and in some instances leads to skills acquisition pertinent to future career goals.

1970s following the development of drugs that help control symptoms. The movement assumed that communities would provide a less restrictive, more humane environment. Since many if not most communities were (and still are) unable to furnish group housing to people with serious chronic mental disorders, many former patients ended up on the streets or in board-and-care homes or homeless shelters.

In the 1990s and into the twenty-first century, case management is a rapidly growing system of community-based care for defined populations who suffer profound, long-term, or permanent challenges or for populations who are at risk and require protection. The chronically mentally challenged are the largest population served, followed by the physically and developmentally challenged (Anthony, Cohen, Farkas, & Cohen, 2000; Bigby, Ozanne, & Gordon, 2002; Moxley, 2002).[2] A growing population of older people who are unable to provide adequately for their health, social, and economic needs without in-home services are also maintained in the community through public and private case management agencies staffed by social workers (Ferry & Abramson, 2005; Hyduk, 2002; Wodarski & Williams-Hayes, 2002). Similarly, physically challenged and physically ill people in the community who require multiple social and health services in order to maintain independent living are served by case managers attached to rehabilitation agencies or provided by case management and community-based agencies (Parrish, Burry, & Pabst, 2003). Families and youths at risk also receive case management services (Anderson, 2001; Lightfoot & LaLiberte, 2006; Sangalang, Barth, & Pointer, 2006; Zlotnick, Kronstadt, & Klee, 1999).

Case managers serve individual clients and the community in a special way. The community is always part of the case manager's direct responsibility in addition to being an influential environment in which all resident individuals and collectivities are embedded. For example, the case manager is expected to participate in community needs assessment, organizing communities, and developing community resources. Furthermore, the case manager is expected to document needs and resource limitations and present these data to political and community leaders and agency executives (National Association of Social Workers, 1992, p. 16).

Providing Social Work Consultation

Social workers are frequently called on to provide formal or informal social work consultation to community-based service providers, other professionals, and community residents. For many decades, interprofessional consultation was mainly a one-way process, with social workers receiving consultation from psychiatrists, physicians, and, to a lesser extent, lawyers. Psychiatric consultation often took on the character of supervision, as though social work knowledge, skill, and experience were inferior to those of the psychiatrist in spite of differences in professional function. As the social work profession matured, its practitioners themselves became consultants, not only to other social workers but also, increasingly, to other professionals in the community including teachers, nurses, administrators, and, less extensively, lawyers, psychiatrists, physicians, ministers, and judges; and to paraprofessional or nonprofessional personnel such as institutional child care staffs, law enforcement personnel, group home operators, nursing home and day care staffs, and other community caregivers (Bassett & Johnson, 2004; Goldman, Botkin, Tokunaga, & Kuklinski, 1997; Kaplan, Turner, Norman, & Stillson, 1996; Miller & Fewell, 2002).

Social work consultants may be locally recognized experts in a field of practice, a community agency, or a BSW or MSW educational program; they may hold positions as consultants in public health, mental health, and other community facilities; or they become known through their work in the community. School social work practitioners and students often provide individual consultation to teachers pertinent to a classroom situation or the behavior of particular children. They also provide group consultation in the form of workshops on such topics as children with chronic illness or working with parents. In family and child welfare agencies, social workers provide consultation to natural helpers, foster parents, and parent aides. Rural social workers, because of lack of services, almost inevitably serve as consultants on a range of community concerns.

Shulman (1987) distinguishes between formal case consultation, program consultation, and a blend of the two. Case consultation is client focused: a particular individual, family, group, or community being served with the intent of helping the worker solve problematic elements in the situation. Program consultation might focus on the design of new services or on needed staff development such as introducing the use of group services in a family agency. The blended type of consultation usually starts with case consultation to agency staff and subsequently moves to organizational issues that are revealed in the case situations and that affect the quality of services adversely or increase the difficulties faced by the social work staff. It is designed to help resolve problematic issues in organizational functioning and might include line, supervisory, and administrative staff.

In working with community residents, consultation tends to be less formal and more egalitarian. Community residents are experts about their community; the social worker is expert about professional practice in the community. Community residents might provide consultation to a social worker about various community resources such as natural leaders, natural helpers, and historical benchmarks. In turn, a social worker might provide consultation to community residents about community assessment tools, procedures and processes for conducting a meeting, and finding resources.

In programmatic and organizational consultation, consultants must determine if they have knowledge and skills needed in the situation, and sanction by administration if the invitation did not come from administration, and time to learn as much as possible about the consultee and the particular setting before consultation begins. They must also assess the reality of including consultee expectations, objectives, respective roles, and evaluation of effectiveness. In the case of external organizations, the same clarity and contracting are carried out with the agency's administrator as well, including confidentiality regarding the consultee's statements.

In offering advice to other professionals or to paraprofessionals, volunteers, and community leaders, the social worker must avoid creating an image as a superior expert who has instant answers to a problem that the consultee (such as a teacher, nurse, or community caregiver) has struggled with for some time. Instead, it is usually better to suggest a second session to continue the discussion, adding that the consultant will give further thought to what has been said in the light of past experience with similar situations. When the consultant is ready to present several alternative ideas—even in the initial session, if that is to be the only one—the ideas should be presented as possibilities to consider. The emphasis is on assisting the consultee to describe the situation, consider associated or contributing factors, and examine alternate solutions and their consequences. In formal and informal consulting, presenting one's view as the right solution must be avoided in order to support the ultimate goal: to increase consultees' capacity for clear thinking, problem solving, and decision making in their own realm.

If the social worker is white and the consultees are persons of color, Gibbs (1980) suggested that an interpersonal orientation in the consultation relationship is more useful than an instrumental one. An interpersonal orientation emphasizes mutual rapport and trust in the beginning phase of community consultation. Different perceptions of values, role expectations, resource and reward allocation, and feelings about the control of dependency are apt to exist during the early phase. In consulting, the social worker must be knowledgeable about cultural differences and social class variations. According to the author, African Americans, for example, typically evaluate professional interactions in terms of the interpersonal skills demonstrated in early encounters, while whites typically evaluate the interactions in terms of instrumental skills. Gibbs (1980) believes that this interpersonal orientation can be generalized to other racial minority groups, "particularly those who share with Black people a relatively disadvantaged position in American society and have developed adaptive strategies to cope with their lower status" (p. 205).

Specifically, Gibbs's model for understanding African American responses to consultation includes the following phases: (1) "sizing up" the consultant for personal authenticity; (2) investigation or "checking out" how the consultant relates to people of different educational, social, and cultural backgrounds; (3) involvement (if the consultant checked out favorably and was familiar with African American culture, symbolic behaviors, attitudes, and values); (4) commitment to program (based on evaluation of consultant's empathic skills, demonstrated comprehension of the institution's problems and complexities, and support and nonjudgmental attitudes when consultees expressed personal conflicts or professional frustrations); and (5) engage-ment (based on evaluation of the consultant's instrumental competence). Phases 4 and 5 overlap: "While black persons will make this commitment as a result of their evaluation of the consultant's interpersonal competence in the first four [phases], white persons will make this commitment in terms of the instrumental competence shown by the consultant up to this time" (Gibbs, 1980, p. 200).

Kelley, McKay, and Nelson (1985) provide an example of culturally con-gruent consultation activity with Canadian Indians in northern Ontario. The setting was an Indian-staffed crisis house, and the authors (as practitio-ners, researchers, and consultants) were faculty of the Lakehead University Department of Social Work. The goal was agency development, and the consultants conceived their role as facilitators and mentors, particularly since the agency's Indian administrator called them her "elders." The desig-nation was apt, as they provided information and instrumental and emo-tional support, shared experiences with staff, and modeled problem-solving behavior without imposing solutions. The role was carried out through the use of four practice principles: mutuality in relationships, maximizing un-derstanding of cultural differences, empowerment, and a structural ap-proach.

Early contacts were at the Indian agency, where staff would feel safe in their own territory. Later sessions were held at the university, the first such experience for the staff, who delighted in viewing themselves as "university students." The consultants emphasized their own personal values rather than their professional selves, as Indian staff members differentiate very lit-tle between personal and work activities. Hence, the consultants were more person oriented than task oriented.

Cultural differences were brought to the surface and explored to maxi-mize mutual understanding and self-awareness of both staff and consultants and to minimize cultural barriers in the helping process. The authors de-scribe common value differences between Indians and non-Indians in eight dimensions, and they suggest that mutual trust and understanding are best generated by immediately acknowledging the limited ground shared by In-dian consultees and non-Indian consultants.

Avoiding the expert role, validating the competence and self-directedness of the staff, and implementing the transfer of power from consultants to staff minimized the power differential.

> At the beginning the agency staff, at all levels, felt inadequate and powerless in their relationships to each other and with the external environment. Rather than directly mediating conflicts, solving problems, or advocating on behalf of the agency, the consultants assumed a nondirective position and saw their primary task as helping agency staff act on its own behalf. (Kelley, McKay, & Nelson 1985, p. 599)

A primary focus was on the structural aspects of the agency's internal and external transactions. "Some of these structures are accountability and information-gathering methods, records, job descriptions, and agency policies and procedures" (p. 600). For example, the Indian resident counselors viewed themselves as house maintenance workers, while the administrator wanted to help them realize that their helping role included responding to client needs affectively and not just instrumentally. Transactions between clients and counselors were modified by new structures (e.g., a case management perspective and daily log recording) developed jointly by the Indian workers and the consultants.

> This recording format facilitated client assessment for staff and provided intervention guidelines. It also required staff to deal with clients differently. The new demands on staff for increased knowledge and skill led to staff requests for more staff development in the areas of assessment, goal-setting, and intervention. (p. 601)

The authors emphasize that a structural approach can only be successful when used in combination with the other three principles—mutuality, maximizing understanding of differences, and empowerment. If a structural instrument is developed by consultants and imposed on staff, their self-direction, competence, and motivation are undermined.

The common ultimate goal of all life-modeled community practice is that the community or neighborhood becomes more competent and self-directed, begins to be laced with systems of relatedness, and experiences a growing sense of community pride. These community attributes are developed or enhanced by the participants as they work together toward their avowed objectives with the guidance of the social worker, as needed. In the process, the constituents' personal competence, self-direction, relatedness, and self-esteem are regained or enhanced. Table 13.4 summarizes skills of community consultation.

Table 13.4
Some Skills of Community Consultation

- Ask for specific information about issues: what has been done, and how is it similar to or different from usual experiences.
- Assess associated or contributing factors.
- Examine alternative solutions and their consequences.
- Present possible strategies for consideration.
- Emphasize mutual rapport and trust.

FOURTEEN

INFLUENCING THE
PRACTITIONER'S ORGANIZATION

The life model broadens the conception of professional function to include influencing the worker's own organization to improve services, correct dysfunctional processes, and increase responsiveness to the needs of the population it serves or is expected to serve. Within this expanded function, social workers must take account of their employing organization's presence in the lives of all actual and potential clients and always seek to improve the fit between needs and services.[1] The broader function requires practitioners to move beyond prescribed organizational roles.

Societal, Professional, and Bureaucratic Forces

Social needs and injustices are often brought to public attention through the vision and zeal of social reformers who make the problems more visible; support is mobilized, and public or private monies are made available. In attempting to carry out its mission, the organization, or a department within it, confronts its own structural or functional imperatives as well as various societal and professional forces affecting its practices (Burke, 2002; Gibson, Ivancevich, & Donnelly, 2000).

External Organizational Stressors

While society makes financial assistance and services available to poor clients in need, the historic ideological distinction between worthy and unworthy poor, as well as the current public reaction to the tax burden, have led to stigmatizing and stereotyping recipients. Financial aid is provided in a punitive, demeaning manner, demonstrated by inadequate allowances, time limits, deteriorated and uncomfortable physical facilities, long waiting lines, and negative attitudes and behavior of some personnel in many urban welfare offices. Such conditions attest to the impact on service delivery of budget stringencies that are supported by societal values and norms. Political and economic pressures place significant constraints on human service organizations, compromising their ability to fulfill social mandates (Austin & Prince, 2003).

Depending upon public and private support, organizations are shaped by funding trends, managed care, and other regulatory and accountability mechanisms. Funding becomes available, and agencies respond with new programs that replace other programs. Some services receive as much or more than is required; others receive less than is required. A hospital patient in one department receives excellent care, while a patient in another department of the same hospital receives substandard care. The needs of rural areas receive less than proportionate attention in comparison to those of urban areas. From time to time, certain problems and needs receive national attention, while others are overlooked. When one problem increases in visibility and another recedes in the public's attention, financing shifts. Some agencies, unable to initiate new programs, hold on desperately to familiar services and processes. Others, unable to define a clear function, change with each new trend in financing.

Human service organizations are confronted by an increasing emphasis on accountability, encouraging confusion about what efficiency and effectiveness are in human service organizations as compared to other organizations (Claiborne & Fortune, 2005). In hospitals, for example, financial accountability demands rapid discharge, which raises a question for social workers of whose interests are being served (Moody, 2004). "Timely" assessment and "timely" discharge planning have become central tasks for social workers assigned to medical or surgical services. As Gitterman and Miller (1989, p. 152) point out:

> The word "timely" however is the official euphemism in reimbursement regulations. It does not mean the right or the opportune time, but often foretells hurried and inadequate assessment and premature discharge. Because failure to conform with regulations would imperil the already strained financial position of the organization, we accept and condone actions, which are not necessarily in the best interest of the client.

Similarly, mental health and child welfare workers are bombarded with statistical forms that have become ends in themselves.

Internal Organizational Stressors

Organizations require a chain of command or levels of authority to coordinate the various subunits and personnel, to specify responsibility and accountability, and to provide leadership in decision making. While the authority structure serves these and other functions, it also can produce contradictions and problems; decisions may be made with distorted information. Different positions in the hierarchy develop different priorities and have different interest groups to please, which can create tensions and turf struggles. The social worker may have limited ascribed authority, insufficient information, and inadequate structural opportunities to influence organizational processes. Rigid authority structures further intensify the disadvantage and stifle initiative and creativity, while ambiguous authority structures discourage coordination and accountability (Schmid, 2004).

Organizations also require a division of labor to integrate service activities. However, specialized role assignments encourage preoccupation with developing and maintaining one's turf. Organizational and client needs are often held hostage to turf interests.

As knowledge and technology proliferate and specialized competence is required to perform complex tasks, professional services are essential. Organizations that employ professionals benefit from both their competence and the associated status. But professionals can also generate problems for the organization and clients. Professionals require autonomy and may resist bureaucratic processes. Similarly, professional interests do not always match client interests. To achieve their interests, professionals and organizational administrators institute certain trade-offs. Low salaries, for example, may be accepted in exchange for flexible work schedules; or, undesirable work conditions and practice requirements may be accepted for high salaries or job security. These tacit agreements often lead to identification with the organization, its practices, and its procedures. Socialization of the social work student within a tutorial pattern of master–apprentice field instruction, where power and authority are vested in one person, may encourage organizational docility and discourage risk taking. Bureaucratic structures and trade-offs preserve the status quo. As a consequence, client interests are too often ignored.

In one family agency, intake records revealed that 75 percent of outreach clients had more than a significant wait for intake, while 90 percent of clients seeking services were seen quickly. Further analysis showed that a high proportion of the outreach clients were people of color. The second group of clients received services; the first group were in effect denied service. Those 25 percent who did endure the significant delay were frequently defined at intake as mistrustful. Barriers to service produce a pool of "preferred" clients, who are able to wait, whose lives are not in crisis, and whose employment and child care responsibilities are manageable. The remaining applicants are then defined as "unmotivated" and "resistant" to service. Not only are they denied service, but also to justify their exclusion we blame them. Agency and professional contributions to resistance and lack of motivation remain unnoticed. Such labels are self-fulfilling and provide a rationale for administrators' and practitioners' neglect. Examinations of organizational and professional interests are avoided.[2]

In attempting to cope with practice ambiguities and clients' overwhelming life stressors, social workers may try to fit people and their situations into comfortable belief systems or preferred categories. The need to fit people into a preferred orientation hinders professional curiosity about which theory or concept best facilitates our understanding and ability to help an individual, family, group, or community in a particular situation at a particular time. Some embrace a deterministic view of human behavior in which either psychic or environmental forces are thought to be outside people's control. Clients are then perceived to be adrift in a turbulent sea where survival is dependent upon the velocity of the wind, the power of the waves, and the design of the ship. Other social workers incorporate a phenomenological, existential view of human behavior in which life forces are considered to be within people's control. Clients are then perceived to be steering a craft in a turbulent sea where survival is dependent upon their will, motivation, and skill. Social workers hear those dimensions of a client's experience that confirm their beliefs and ignore those that do not.

Finally, agency and professional definitions of social work purpose also have a strong impact on clients. When an agency is characterized by divergent professional orientations, clients may be held hostage to competitive interests, struggles, and discrepant practices. Yet, when an agency adheres to a single orientation, clients are often expected to fit that approach.

Organizational Issues and Problems in Service Provision

Societal, professional, and bureaucratic forces can create practices that serve societal, professional, or organizational interests at the expense of client interests. In general, organizational problems for users of services grow out of three interrelated areas: the agency's definition of its purposes and services, the structures and procedures used to coordinate and integrate organizational operations, and service arrangements.

If agencies define a client's life issue as located in the person (e.g., anger management), external forces are likely to receive insufficient attention. In such agencies, the definition of social work purpose reflects professional preferences and results in service definitions and styles that are unresponsive to client needs. When agencies rigidly define their purpose and services, people may become lost in the service network. When agencies' purposes and services are ambiguous, people may fall between the cracks because no agency appears responsive to their particular situation.

To cope with community and bureaucratic pressures and forces, an agency develops structures and procedures to coordinate and integrate the varied activities of its participants. Such procedures sometimes create unintended difficulties for clients. An authority structure, for example, may discourage staff differentiation and specialization (Tropman & Shaefer, 2004). Hence, it stifles initiative and creative programming.

- In the Ridgeway Settlement House, the director is unable or unwilling to delegate tasks and responsibilities to staff. He is involved in so many activities and projects that he cannot handle them all properly. At the same time, staff has inadequate information for performing their function and requires approval for every detail. Settlement members are affected by the agency's general inertia and the staff's diminished investment in the program.

In contrast, an authority structure may delegate too much, providing staff with limited leadership and accountability. Services remain uncoordinated, and each worker practices privately. In this pattern, professional role definitions and expectations are either specialized and narrow and encourage isolation, or are ambiguous and overlapping and encourage competition.

Similarly, agency policies and procedures may be overformalized or underformalized. Outdated rules may be imposed in new situations. Rules favorable to client needs may be systematically ignored. Service arrangements may be inadequate or inaccessible because of the agency's definition of its purpose and service and its related internal structures:

- In the Eastern Community Mental Health Center, adaptive tasks required by day patients' transition from hospitalization to community reintegration are ignored. They fit into neither the inpatient nor outpatient departments. What is needed in the catchment area is a transitional service or a day hospital program for recently released hospital patients.

In other instances, services might be available, but methods and style of delivery discourage their use:

- Jackson Adolescent Health Center experiences a 44 percent no-show rate for applicants scheduled for intake interviews. No systematic attempt is made to "capture" this applicant pool, although an informal follow-up procedure based on professional judgment is conducted on a case-by-case basis. The procedure is largely limited to informing a referral source that an applicant did not appear for an intake and is directed to an estimated 1 percent of applicants.
- Longshore Community Services, a sectarian family agency, limits its intake to self-referrals. The agency does not attempt to make itself visible or accessible to the community. Since the agency offers no outreach services, many clients who would make use of the agency's services do not know it exists.

When organizational processes and structural arrangements place additional stress on users of services, social work function broadens to include tasks of influencing the agency to change.

Social Work Functions, Modalities, Methods, and Skills

The Social Worker and Life-Modeled Organizational Practice

Some social workers maintain a distance from their organization as if they are in private practice. They see clients, and that's it. Such isolation fails to serve client interests. Other workers identify completely with their organization. Their overidentification also fails to serve clients' interests. And yet others identify consistently with the client, as if the agency were their mutual enemy. While circumstances sometimes justify this stance, it is sustained at the risk of dismissal. In this way, clients again lose. We propose that social workers must identify simultaneously with their organization, their clients, and the profession, in a three-way mediation among clients' needs, organizational requirements, and professional purpose (Schwartz, 1976).

Social workers must maintain a vigilant stance toward organizational processes that bear on client services. When such processes become problematic, ethical practice seeks modification of the maladaptive practices, procedures, or programs.

Next, we discuss and illustrate the methods and skills of influencing employing organizations through preparation, initial organizational analysis, entry, engagement, implementation, and institutionalization.

Preparation Phase

Preparation for influencing the practitioner's organization begins with the identification of a problem. Users of service are the primary point of reference. Workers obtain data about problematic organizational arrangements and practices through careful attention to clients' direct and indirect expressions, review of records, and other data. They are open to potential organizational issues reflected in clients' troubles. Colleagues are another resource. By attentive listening in staff meetings, in-service training programs, group supervision, and informal conversations, the worker learns of problematic patterns. Specification and documentation of where and how the problem manifests itself are achieved through systematic observation, formal data collection, and informal conversations. Practitioners then assess the problem's salience and relevance to client service. Once the problem is identified and documented, alternative solutions or objectives and the specific means for achieving them are considered. Advantages, potential consequences, and feasibility of each potential solution are carefully examined. Based on the initial appraisal, a tentative objective and specific means for achieving it are determined. The following vignettes illustrate the preparation phase.

---

1. *Medical hospital—surgical floor*

Problem: definition of social work function: Social work practice is limited to discharge planning. All other patients, regardless of their need for social work services, are overlooked.

Documentation: One woman, distraught over a planned amputation, was not referred because the family could take her home after surgery. Another woman in the terminal stages of cancer and severely depressed was not referred because her sons were making discharge arrangements.

Desired outcome: Expand the social work function to include high-risk situations.

Means of implementation: Try to broaden the content of team meetings to include identifying high-risk patients.

2. *Halfway house*

Problem: coordination and integration of structures and procedures: Insufficient coordination among staff.

Documentation: Residents constantly complain about lateness, service and quality of meals, inequities in house assignments, inadequate protection from residents who steal or are physically abusive, and hostile and demeaning behavior by staff. Staff complaints include residents' failure to cooperate, administration's insensitivity to staff needs, and ineffective coordination of services. Lack of enforcement of house rules and regulations is also a staff complaint. The director, on the other hand, locates the problem in the lack of staff initiative, creativity, and assertiveness in carrying out programs and policies.

Desired outcome: Improve internal operations of the house and communications among the three groups.

Means for implementation: My initial and tentative plan is to obtain commitment to and approval for creating an advisory staff group to the director. Once the advisory group is in place, I will try to have residents added and redefine the group as a house council.

The means for implementation in this instance is a feasible structural innovation, which can lead to permanent change. The worker defined the problem as lack of structure and procedures for coordination, and devised a means for integrating the various parts of the house system. If the director's problem definition remained in place, the worker might then have sought improved staff performance through in-service training. But when problems generated by missing structures and procedures are located in the staff and call for in-service training, the dysfunctional structures and procedures escape attention. They continue to affect service adversely.

---

3. *Hospital adolescent health clinic*

Problem: services provided: Clinic's intake practices discourage many adolescent applicants from using services.

Documentation: Review of the intake log over a six-month period was conducted. Monthly data were compiled that demonstrated actual numbers of intakes scheduled and no-shows. No-shows were further analyzed for the number of rescheduled appointments. In the six-month period, 465 adolescents had intake appointments and 208 (45 percent) failed to appear. For the first rescheduled intake appointment, 133 (28 percent) failed to appear. Only 38 (8 percent) called to cancel or reschedule their appointments. They will not be part of the targeted change, which focuses on applicants who make no attempt to communicate on their own.

Desired outcome: The objective is to increase professional staff involvement with applicants with the goal of increasing the number of applicants who become clients (Alcabes & Jones, 1985).

Means for implementation: Professional staff will be involved by initiating a call to remind the applicant of his or her appointment and a follow-up call to each no-show applicant (if self-referred) or to the applicant's referral source. Such phone calls may provide a bridge into the clinic.

4. *Union setting*

Problem: services arrangements: The social program for retired members is poorly planned and carried out.

Documentation: Members complain that programs are canceled, guest speakers do not arrive for announced lectures, and most activities are dull. My observations are similar. The program is losing members and is not attracting new ones.

Desired outcome: Improve the quality of the social program.

Means for implementation: Obtain approval for and organize a steering committee of retirees, union program personnel, and myself to plan programs.

In this setting, a steering committee is congruent with organizational norms. It is not a radical innovation, and it invites a broad representation of participants, particularly the lower ranking retirees. As union members, the retirees are entitled to services: when they become involved, their potential power will assure accountability to their interests. The new arrangement is likely to have a permanent impact.

---

5. *Community social services*

Problem: services provided: The agency's intake practices discourage many applicants from using services.

Documentation: Telephone calls to a small random sample of people who had failed to show up for their appointments, or refused to make an appointment after intake, yielded initial data. Complaints included lack of evening hours, lapse of several weeks between intake and assignment to a social worker, demand to fill out numerous research forms, and adolescents' discomfort with the psychiatrist's detailed questions concerning sexuality.

Desired outcome: Increase responsiveness and relevance of intake service to client needs.

Means for implementation: An ad hoc committee to study the high dropout rate.

Table 14.1
Preparation Skills

Obtain data to identify and document the organizational problem from
- clients' direct and indirect expressions.
- a review of agency records.
- informal conversations with colleagues.
- formal participation in staff meetings.
- systematic data collection.

Examine alternative solutions, specify desired outcome, and identify tentative means for desired outcome while
- avoiding mobilizing the organization's defenses.
- identifying staff's self-interest.

Ad hoc committees are important structures for revising agency practices and programs. A direct assault on the agency's intake services can generate resistance. The agency prides itself on its scientific approach and has a full-time researcher, so the proposed research committee is consistent with formal and informal norms. Composition of the ad hoc committee will be important if change is to occur. Committee members must enjoy sufficient flexibility to entertain proposed changes in intake arrangements and sufficient respect to influence their colleagues. Table 14.1 summarizes preparation skills used to influence an organization.

Initial Organizational Analysis

Having tentatively identified and documented an organizational problem and selected an objective and means for achieving it, the worker now undertakes a formal organizational analysis. Lewin (1952) characterized the status quo in any social system as the balanced result of countervailing forces toward and against change. A force-field analysis helps the practitioner to identify and visualize the specific forces promoting and resisting change. The worker assesses which environmental, organizational, and interpersonal forces are apt to support the proposed change and which are apt to resist change (Brager & Holloway, 1992).

Environmental Forces. The social worker must evaluate features in the environment that may support and those that may frustrate the change effort, such as societal trends and available funding. Even fiscal constraints can induce and promote creative organizational change (Gibson & Barsade, 2003). A financially troubled agency, for example, may be receptive to changes in intake policies and procedures that reduce costs or expand the fee base even though such changes are contrary to its ideological orientations.

The extent to which community groups hold the agency accountable for services and practices is also important. Such groups include the board of directors, other organizations on which the agency depends for referrals and evaluation, and public and private standard-setting bodies. Even the agency's location, condition, and size affect its relations with its neighborhood. Data on environmental forces are collected from written materials, informal conversations, and focused observations. From the data, the social worker develops preliminary indicators of environmental forces likely to promote or inhibit the proposed change.

Organizational Forces. Internal characteristics of the agency also affect change processes (Freund, 2005). Complex organizations with a number of professional disciplines and staff with advanced training are thought to have a higher rate of innovation. Such agencies are characterized by diversity, openness to new methods and technologies, and competing interest groups. Organizations that are highly centralized with power located in a few elites, or are highly formalized with a large number of codified rules, are thought to demonstrate lower rates of innovation. Knowledge of such organizational properties is used as gross predictors for determining a feasible objective and the means for achieving it (Holloway, 1987). Figure 14.1 portrays the combined impact of organizational complexity and formalization on receptivity to change.

In agencies characterized by a low degree of complexity and a high degree of formalization (Figure 14.1, section C), the worker has to formulate limited objectives, often limiting desired outcomes to procedural changes such as enforcement of existing rules favorable to clients or suggestions of new procedures to replace outdated ones. Modification of organizational purpose or basic programs is quite unlikely in a department of welfare, department of children's services, or Social Security office. In contrast, a worker employed by a highly complex and informal agency (B) may aspire to greater functional, structural, or programmatic changes. In community mental

	Complexity	
	Low	High
Low	− + (A)	+ + (B)
Formalization		
High	− − (C)	+ − (D)

Figure 14.1 Impact of Organizational Complexity and Formalization upon Change

(+) = Property increasing feasibility; (−) = Property decreasing feasibility.

health centers, the worker can often undertake more ambitious influence efforts. While a particular organization may have overall features of high complexity and low formalization, a department within it may not share those characteristics. For this reason, the organizational analysis must include the subsystem and its relation to the larger system.

Less definitive statements can be made about agencies characterized by low complexity and low formalization (A) or by high complexity and high formalization (D). In a relatively undifferentiated community agency, for example, services may suffer from a lack of staff diversity and narrow ideological commitments. While the worker may be unable directly to influence the purpose and program of an organization that is low on complexity, he or she may have sufficient support and resources for indirect influence. A family or group consultant, for example, might be used to expose staff to new knowledge and technology. Determining whether sufficient organizational supports and resources are available for the change effort requires an assessment of the staff's status-role system, norms, and interests.

Interpersonal Forces. Practitioners need to identify key participants who will affect and be affected by the proposed change. They then estimate each participant's likely response to the proposed change and evaluate its probable impact on their job performance and satisfaction. If the desired outcome and means support participants' self-interest by increasing their prestige, autonomy, influence, or authority, their support is more likely. Conversely, if the desired outcome and means threaten participant self-interest, then resistance may be anticipated (Brager & Holloway, 1978; Holloway, 1987). Although people usually act in their own self-interest with fairly predictable responses, the complexities, subtleties, and idiosyncrasies of human behavior require careful attention and preparation for the unexpected. Such attention includes observation of behaviors during formal and informal contacts with key participants—looking at patterns (e.g., risk taking, conformists, and "closet" advocates), norms (e.g., work group pressures, individual and collective values), activities (e.g., job responsibilities, outside interests), and motivation (e.g., what constitutes satisfaction and stress for each person).

Worker Influence. Social workers next evaluate their own position in the organization and their structural and personal resources for influence. Their structural location may or may not provide opportunities for interacting with key participants and obtaining essential data. Doctoral students, for example, quickly learn the importance of developing a relationship with the department secretary, who controls access to a critical faculty member. To most students and staff social workers, the agency secretary represents a source of influence to be cultivated. While a baccalaureate or master's of social work student has a relatively limited structural position in the agency, access to influential people and opportunities to experiment may be given just because of student status.

Social workers interested in social change must also assess how others view them in the organization. In developing organizational self-awareness, practitioners must try to see themselves as others do rather than how they would like to be seen. They need to evaluate the extent to which they are viewed as competent, valuable colleagues whose advice and favor are sought and whose committee work is respected. Finally, workers must consider their time and energy: for the tasks involved in seeking change, time and energy are essential.

Through analysis of organizational forces, one can then evaluate feasibility, that is, the potential for success. When support is strong and opposition is weak, feasibility is high. When support is weak and opposition is strong, feasibility is low. Often, a change in the means for attaining the desired outcome increases feasibility without compromising the objective. In the earlier example of the union's inadequate retiree program, the worker initially had intended to have a professional hired. The analysis, however, revealed powerful constraints, which mobilized resistance by the department. The less threatening strategy of a steering committee diminished resistance and heightened feasibility. When supports and opposition are both weak, an open situation exists suggesting that supportive elements have to be mobilized. And finally, strong support and strong opposition indicate potential conflict. The outcome is unpredictable, and a low-keyed approach is indicated. Table 14.2 presents an organizational analysis of a branch office of a sectarian family agency where intake was limited to self-referral. The worker wants to reach out to the community.

The overall pattern and direction reflect strong supports and moderate-to-weak opposition. This suggests feasibility and points to entry actions to mobilize supports and decrease resistance. This outreach program can also be readily connected to agency financial pressures. Table 14.3 summarizes the initial organizational analysis skills.

Entry Phase

After determining feasibility, the next step is to develop a receptive organizational climate. For instance, in the sectarian family agency, the social worker observes:

I was aware of staff concerns about declining intakes and their fears of cutbacks in funding and staff cutbacks. During my informal discussions with staff members, I encouraged conversation on the decline in intakes and the effect on the agency. I felt out their attitudes and thinking on the subject and their possible reactions to alternative solutions. Where appropriate, I dropped hints about possible outreach to the community. I mentioned a suggestion made by a respected administrator at a central office meeting to offer premarital counseling groups. I also invited their thinking about active case finding and collaborative projects to increase the agency's visibility in the community.

Table 14.2
Organizational Analysis

- *Agency:* Branch office, sectarian family agency
- *Problem:* Intake limited to self-referral, excluding many potential clients from service
- *Desired outcome:* To reach more clients
- *Means for implementation:* Community outreach demonstration

Supports	Environmental Forces		Opposition
	Intensity	Intensity	
Coordinating agency's threat of funding loss	High	Low	Coordinating agency's loss of some control over accountability
Threat to staff's job security	High	Low	Undeveloped community relationships
Interest and availability of religiously affiliated community agencies for collaboration	High	Moderate	Present collaboration arrangements (e.g., co-leadership, fee splitting)

	Organizational Forces		
	Intensity	Intensity	
Complexity: employs variety of professionals, historically has been somewhat unorthodox	High	High	Decentralization and formalization: staff given wide latitude, with limited accountability
Decentralized: in competition with other branches	High		
Formalization: modest number of rules, but not rigidly enforced, often left ambiguous (e.g., job descriptions not defined, leaving opportunity for community work)	High		

Interpersonal Forces

	Intensity	Intensity	
Administrator is experiencing environmental pressures, is liberal in views, and active	High	Low	Administrator sometimes doesn't follow up
Psychologist is service-minded, concerned about decline in number of clients served	Moderate	Moderate	Psychologist is inactive in decision-making process
The social workers are quite liberal and client-oriented	High	Moderate	The social workers have relatively low status, limited influence
Psychiatrist is relatively uninvolved, follows administrator	Moderate	Low	Psychiatrist may be threatened by outreach
Educational consultant is invested only in school collaboration and will not restrain my efforts	Low	Low	Educational consultant may be threatened; however, he has the lowest organizational status
Total work group: high identification with branch, and perception of themselves as innovative, creative, and committed to serving their population	High	High	Total work group: outreach could potentially mean more work, travel, uncertainties, and contact with less motivated clients

Worker Influence

	Intensity	Intensity	
Supervised by administrator, therefore has easy accessibility to critical participants	High	Low	New-worker status limits right to undertake a new project
Recent-graduate status provides legitimacy to experiment	Moderate	Low	Motivation might be suspect
Personal positioning includes excellent informal relationships, and is perceived as a highly motivated worker; on several occasions has demonstrated competence in community contacts	High		
Highly motivated and has time and energy to undertake this influence	High		

Table 14.3
Initial Organizational Analysis Skills

• *Assess environmental forces likely to support or constrain proposed change:*	Examine impact of societal, technological, legislative, community, and physical contexts.
• *Assess organizational forces likely to support or constrain proposed change:*	Examine extent of complexity, centralization, and formalization of total organization or specific department.
	Evaluate combined effect of organizational forces.
• *Assess interpersonal forces likely to support or constrain proposed change:*	Identify key participants.
	Evaluate effect of proposed change on key participants' job performance and satisfaction (prestige, self-esteem, autonomy, and influence).
	Evaluate key participants' interactional patterns and organizational activities.
• *Assess elements of worker influence likely to support or constrain proposed change:*	Evaluate one's formal position in the organization.
	Evaluate one's personal position in the organization.
	Evaluate one's resources of time and energy.
• *Assess feasibility and potential for success:*	Strong supports and weak opposition suggest high feasibility.
	Weak supports and strong opposition suggest low feasibility.
	Weak supports and weak opposition suggest an open situation.
	Strong support and strong opposition suggest potential conflict.

The worker begins informal discussions with organizational friends, testing out possible reactions and inviting their ideas in collaborative problem solving.

In contrast, an attempt by a social worker at a psychiatric impatient service to have patients decide on their own passes failed at the outset. Without informal scouting or positioning in advance, this practitioner raised the issue at a general staff meeting.

At the conclusion of the discussion, I brought up the issue of patients' passes. The nurses immediately voiced their disagreement. The floor doctor identified the multidisciplinary conference structure as the appropriate mechanism. The meeting ended without any support for my idea.

The worker took premature action in the formal system. Resistance was mobilized and precipitated immediate rejection. Support for proposed innovation or change must be developed and cultivated before going public.

Brager and Holloway (1978) suggest three methods of preparing a system: personal positioning, structural positioning, and management of stress. *Personal positioning* is essential for the social work practitioner. Since practitioners usually have limited formal authority, their organizational effectiveness depends upon achieving influence by other legitimate means. Professional competence is a major resource and "immediately precludes or mitigates easy dismissal of one's ideas and opinions" (Gitterman & Miller, 1989, p. 160). The first positioning task is illustrated by a social worker's effort to achieve visibility:

I had been prompt and attentive in doing weekly intakes for several months. I involved Mr. Phillips, the director of intake, whenever I had a question about procedure. I recently completed an intake on behalf of the husband of a client in treatment with an experienced worker. I consulted with her to gain a better understanding and assessment of the case. She complimented my work and apparently discussed it with the director of intake and the agency director.

Being competent is not enough in itself; competence must be visible. Recognized knowledge and expertise gain respect, credibility, and influence. An effective presence in the agency's informal system is indispensable to professional influence (Holloway & Brager, 1985). The social worker who is an insider, who is attentive to colleagues' interests and concerns, and who possesses interpersonal skills will acquire a support system and organizational allies. An isolated practitioner who deviates from informal norms will have limited resources for influencing organizational practice.

In evaluating group composition, the worker considers the driving and restraining forces represented by people, jurisdictional factors, and decision-making patterns. After selecting the appropriate *structure*, the social worker considers which formal and informal processes may facilitate or retard movement and then settles on the most effective person—oneself or another—to introduce the idea. The practitioner is quite prepared to give up any claims to ownership of the idea.

Involvement of service users is critical. Their evaluative feedback and anecdotal material are vital data for both personal and structural positioning. Segments of the actual or potential clientele may welcome opportunities to be involved in efforts at change. Their opinions can be secured through questionnaires. A social worker in a child guidance clinic was interested in working with adolescents. She soon discovered, however, that few adolescents or parents sought services, perhaps because of the agency's name, a lack of publicity and outreach, and the reluctance of staff to get involved with "difficult teenagers." Her first step in influencing her agency to live up to its objective was to interest the director in forging links to the local junior high school as a way of increasing agency income. With his permission, she approached the principal and guidance counselor with an offer of group services to interested students. Together they designed a questionnaire, which was distributed to the students in their social science class. Responses were almost totally positive. Armed with these data, the worker and the clinic director planned staff involvement, collaboration with school personnel, and parental permission. Their objective was to provide group services in the school and eventually to provide individual youth services as an integral part of the agency.

Hospital social service departments often ask patients and families to evaluate the service received. These data are important sources of support for change efforts. In addition, the process communicates to clients that their opinions are valued and used. In some instances, clients are involved in later steps of a change process. For example, a children's developmental disability clinic was threatened with closing when a new director changed the hospital's fiscal and service priorities. The clinic had been providing group services to parents of disabled children, and each group was eager to contribute to staff efforts to sustain the clinic. Members mobilized a telephone and mail campaign among their friends and neighbors, and they interested a local radio station and a neighborhood newspaper in their plight. Staff drew up proposals for funding. The administrator agreed to withdraw his plan to dismantle the clinic. Services to the needy children and their parents were safeguarded. In addition, these parents felt empowered, having gained actual power to bring about a significant change in their lives.

A family agency social worker was concerned that no evening hours were offered by the agency. She obtained the director's permission to invite several interested clients to a staff meeting and, later, to a board meeting. In such instances, clients' own presentation of their needs may be more effective in influencing staff and policy makers than the worker's presentation. Similarly, a child welfare agency that had been reluctant to offer group meetings to foster parents was influenced to do so by a worker's carefully thought out proposal of content for the meetings and her mobilization of the eager support of many foster parents who then called and wrote to the director about their interest.

Users of the service must be fully informed of all that is at stake in their active participation, or even in their passive support of an influencing effort. The positives inherent in successful influencing are easy to identify and share. Possible negative consequences for clients must nevertheless be considered and shared with them, so they may make an informed decision to participate or not.

Organizations can erect elaborate defenses by which the problem is rationalized, minimized, avoided, or denied. Before there can be motivation to examine and modify dysfunctional practices and procedures, some *stress* has to be experienced by organizational participants. An important positioning task is to bring the problem to the participants' consciousness by increasing its visibility and consequences. A worker in a union setting recorded:

I made sure the director knew about the problems all staff were having with the scheduling of psychiatric consultations. I dramatized a recent experience I had with a member who waited two hours and then wasn't seen. The director was disturbed by this incident.

I also exchanged experiences with other staff members, and this created and maintained anxiety about the issue. Before long, several workers asked that the issue be placed on the agenda for a staff meeting.

In informal contacts, the worker listens to others' dissatisfaction and encourages conversations about the problem. Heightened stress is often an impetus to action.

At times, data are sufficiently compelling to create organizational discomfort. In the adolescent health clinic in which intake practices discourage many adolescent applicants from using services, the worker analyzed the 45 percent no-show data by referral source. Self-referred applicants had the highest (69 percent) and community agencies the lowest (32 percent) no-show rates for the initial appointment. Self-referral usually implies recognition of a problem and motivation to seek help. Why this subgroup should have the highest no-show rate requires the agency to examine its intake structures and processes. These data created stress for agency administrators and staff, and prompted an examination of factors involved.

If stress is excessive, an agency or department staff could be overwhelmed by conflict or hopelessness. The stress itself is a constraining force. The worker needs to specify the problems and help staff mobilize. A hospital team, for example, was locked in battle, and the hostility immobilized them from working on common goals. The worker attempted to reduce stress by suggesting that the source of the problem was organizational rather than interpersonal. She began with nonmedical staff, the most despairing group, affirming their value to the team and strengthening their respect for their professional and organizational roles. Three excerpts from the worker's log are presented:

We were sitting around shooting the breeze when Phyllis asked me what I thought of the new batch of residents. I said they weren't so new anymore but, like everyone else, I missed the old ones. Jean agreed wholeheartedly and added that the new ones "don't seem to care what anyone else has to say. Half the time they don't know what's going on with their patients." I asked if that's why she stopped coming to rounds. Phyllis replied that there's no point in going. Jean added that no one wants to hear what she has to say. I said it was a sad state of affairs when staff didn't communicate with one another because "how else would I have known that Mrs. S. was thinking about signing out because she was worried about her kids and needed help, if you hadn't told me? You know more about patients in some ways than we do because you spend the most time with them." Jean responded, "You know that, but they [residents] don't." I said not coming to rounds isn't the answer because then no one can talk to each other, and patients will suffer. Phyllis said that was the pity of it all.

Alice seemed quite despondent. She said her impression is that no one is interested in occupational therapy, and she questions the value of her program to patients. I said her feelings had changed dramatically in the last three months. She described how the residents ignore her and de-value her program. I praised her program and skills, offering specific examples of the impact she had made. I also pointed out that she isn't the only one feeling this way. It seems that all disciplines are questioning their value in rounds, citing social work as a case in point. Alice thought about this and agreed there did seem to be a general problem; no one talks except the residents.

Jackie suggested that people's anger with one another had developed into personality clashes, which are better left alone. I responded that while this was the result, it seemed to me the problem was basically one of communication among the team members. Jackie asked me to spell it out further. I said things are not going to get better unless we talk about the problem. "I understand staff not wanting to discuss personality con-flicts, which would get us no place. Perhaps there is another way to ap-proach it, through improving communication in rounds—that really is the problem." Jackie thought about this and then said that this approach certainly might defuse the problem, and it was worth a try.

As staff depersonalized the struggle, they began to function with greater energy and resourcefulness. The positioning task was to reduce the stress so that the overwhelming problem could be confronted. In the process of rede-fining the problem, the social worker gained important allies in dealing with the organizational problem. Table 14.4 outlines skills used in the entry phase.

Engagement

After establishing a receptive organizational climate for the formal intro-duction of the identified issue and the proposed solution, the worker must decide on methods from among the following: demonstrating, collaborat-ing, persuading, and creating conflict (Brager & Holloway, 1978). The ac-tion taken depends on the type of issue, the degree of goal consensus between worker and critical participants, and the worker's resources for influence.

Table 14.4
Entry-Phase Skills

• *Create receptive organizational climate:*	Informally discuss the problem with friends in the organization.
	Develop informal support for problem identification.
• *Achieve influence through personal positioning:*	Demonstrate professional competence.
	Actively participate in interpersonal networks.
• *Achieve influence through structural positioning:*	Actively participate in formal organizational structures.
	Engage service users.
• *Bring the problem to the awareness of organizational participants:*	Increase visibility of the problem and its consequences.
	Decrease excessive stress by specifying the problem.
	Help staff to mobilize.

Demonstrating is especially effective with issues associated with professional practice and program gaps. Broadening the conception of an agency or department's social work function or introducing a new modality, for example, is best achieved by demonstrating. By persistently and skillfully showing through action the value of group services, a social worker with limited organizational resources (rank) but sufficient personal resources (competence and energy) may neutralize rather than mobilize.

A recent graduate began professional employment in Rainbow House, a residential facility serving twenty adolescents. Its objective is to prepare the residents for independent living at age eighteen, when they are no longer eligible for substitute care. The residents have spent most of their lives in foster care. Like many of their peers, residents of Rainbow House are cynical and resentful of having been bounced from foster home to foster home and from group home to residential treatment institution. Rainbow House reinforces their sense of powerlessness by excluding them from decision making. Although the agency emphasizes "empowerment," it limits this to individual treatment of early narcissistic injuries, separation, and loss. Being denied a voice in decision making replicates a life pattern of institutionalized helplessness and dependency, and sabotages the agency goal of preparation for independent living. A frequently heard statement, "I just want to do what I got to do and get out of this place," conceals the terror of residents of final discharge and independent living. When they do complain about unfair practices such as too many or inconsistent structures, policies, and processes, they focus on the issue at hand, and not on the fact that staff makes all decisions. Professional staff attributes many of residents' complaints to their narcissistic wounds and other pathologies ("Regrettably, his defenses are too primitive for him to make mature governance decisions"; or "We do not want to set them up to fail"). Child care staff attributes complaints to general immaturity and a distorted sense of entitlement.

> False assumptions, taken-for-granted beliefs, unquestioned operating rules, and numerous other premises and practices can combine to create self-contained views of the world that provide both a resource for and a constraint on organized action. While they create a way of seeing, and suggest a way of acting, they also tend to create ways of not seeing, and eliminate the possibility of actions associated with alternative views of the world. (Morgan, 1986, p. 202)

The worker's desired outcome was to develop a youth council of residents to plan programs and discuss concerns with staff. As a new worker, she cautiously broached the idea with a few influential staff. Their response was unenthusiastic. However, within a few months Rainbow House experienced several traumatic events that seriously threatened the program. A staff member's increased disability from AIDS prevented his continued employment. A skillful senior child care worker was provoked into a fight with a resident, and his employment was terminated. A resident charged an administrator with sexual abuse. A respected professional staff member left for a new position. These changes were devastating to staff and residents. The social worker used the organizational crisis to gain staff and resident approval for weekly meetings of the youth council as a six-month demonstration. He designated six months to reassure the director that the members would act responsibly. He carefully listened to the director's concern: "The one saving grace of our residents is that they never act in concert with each other. The day they stage a coup d'état is the day I retire." Staff and residents found a common ground: all parties expected the project to fail. Staff lacked confidence in residents' ability to act responsibly; residents lacked trust in staff's willingness to listen to them.

The worker acted quickly to hold Rainbow House's first resident election of members to the youth council. Of the eight elected, two missed the first three meetings, and the residents selected two additional members to replace them. The social worker invited a high-status child care worker to co-lead the council. This ensured child care staff cooperation with the project. The weekly house meeting structure was used to present their issues and concerns to the staff. The worker carefully prepared members to present and discuss selected issues, guiding them in how to prepare and keep to an agenda, gain maximum participation, divide up tasks and responsibilities, and keep other residents involved. The youth council also worked on rules to govern its operation. For example, after two residents asked to join the council, the members decided that nonelected members could become members with approval of two-thirds of the council. The director and child care staff were impressed by the members' articulateness and seriousness. The director increased his support by providing the council with a small budget.

When invited, he attends meetings. The youth council has effected new policies and procedures, and has promoted a greater sense of community. The worker proved the youth council's value to the organization by devoting equal attention to organizational as well as council processes and to disciplined completion of tasks. After the initial six months, the youth council was an integral part of Rainbow House.

Collaborating is effective in relatively open organizations where goal consensus exists and there is either equitable resource distribution or the presence of close interpersonal relationships (Brager & Holloway, 1978). The social worker engages key participants in collaborative problem solving through a shared search for data, possible solutions, and resources. Activity is limited to providing relevant information and mild persuasion, without attempts to convince another or to change another's position. For instance, a worker in a children's residential treatment center was concerned about poor handling of the children's bedtime. Children were ordered to bed by child care staff, and some were assigned early bedtimes as punishment for misdeeds. At the same time, the worker had a genuine appreciation for staff's concerns such as management issues, low pay, overwork, and lack of appreciation. Because of good relationships with staff and a similar organizational status, the social worker selected the method of collaborating.

---

1. *Psychiatrist*: During a recent treatment conference, I encouraged a parent to discuss her daughter's complaint about being put to bed early. The psychiatrist agreed to look into the matter. At a subsequent clinical meeting, I presented my observations and concerns and received a commitment that the issue will be placed on a staff meeting agenda.

2. *Child care supervisor*: I shared my concerns and engaged him in thinking of ways to resolve the problem. He welcomed knowledge about the uses and effects of punishment. For example, since children are punished with an early bedtime for infractions that occurred in the morning or on previous days, I brought in behavioral studies on the lack of effectiveness of delayed responses to misbehavior. I made no suggestions about this material.

3. *Child care staff*: In informal conversations, I defined bedtime as a troubling time for them to manage since many of the children were particularly difficult during this period, and I encouraged them to seek solutions to the problem.

As a result of these collaborative efforts, the supervisor raised the concern in the child care staff meeting. A respected staff member, with whom I had developed a close relationship, said that whenever she had time to tuck some of the children into bed, their management was easier. A second staff member stated that telling stories was sometimes calming. They all complained about little time for these activities. The supervisor suggested they bring unmanageable children to him. Staff was pleased with this structural change and, in turn, agreed to tuck the children in. At the next meeting of the clinical and child care staff, my supervisor inquired about a particular child. A child care staff member reported that the child was sent twice to the supervisor at bedtime, and this had calmed her as well as the other children. I suggested we spend a few minutes on additional suggestions for easing the problem further. One child care staff person suggested that the recreation department could be useful in storytelling or singing before bedtime. The child care supervisors and other staff agreed, and a meeting was arranged with the head of the recreation department. A program for this was developed. At this same meeting, the psychiatrist referred to the use of early bedtimes as punishment and to the research I had provided him. The staff was asked to consider alternatives for discussion next week, and I agreed to inquire how other institutions handle punishment.

Here the worker used facilitating and guiding methods to engage key participants in collaborative evaluation, goal consensus, and problem solving.

Persuading is effective in situations characterized by goal dissent and disparate power. The existence of a problem must be brought home to key participants, who then must be persuaded that solving the problem is necessary and feasible. To influence the opinions and ideas of others, the worker requires specific skills in developing and presenting the case for change and participating in debate.

The burden of proof is on the worker as a proponent for change. Issue definition is the important first task. To a large extent, how a problem and proposed solution are defined determines the grounds on which arguments will be based. The social worker has to develop arguments that demonstrate the existence of the problem, its seriousness, and the effectiveness of the plan to deal with it.

Problem definition must be clear and supported by facts, illustrative material, and, if possible, testimony of colleagues and clients. If a problem remains unrecognized, key participants will easily defeat or simply ignore the argument. A social worker student in a union setting, for example, attempted to persuade an administrator of a union local to change procedures because retirees were not informed about the termination of their medical insurance. She reflected on her mistakes:

First, I assumed Mr. Johnson knew what I was talking about when I referred to "Senior Care." I failed to review briefly the terms of this insurance coverage and to connect it to the union's responsibility for informing members of changed coverage.

Second, I failed to discuss the clients' situation adequately. I did not take advantage of the administrator's commitment to the service ethic by presenting large medical bills, describing complications in applying for Medicaid, or relating relatives' threats to sue the local.

Third, I failed to provide convincing statistics such as the percentage of all eligible members who have Senior Care and the negligible cost of my proposal.

At the end of my presentation Mr. Johnson said, "Although this seems like a worthwhile proposal, it may be a luxury, and we really can't be responsible for the members' not reading their newsletter." As I began to object, he thanked me for my interest, and we were dismissed. I tried to present my plan to get insurance information to the members, but I didn't take the first step in the persuasion process: establish the need for the change.

Forces committed to the status quo attack the problem by either denying its existence or minimizing its seriousness. The worker must possess supporting data to establish need.

When the problem is documented, argued, and established, opposition may turn on the proposed solution and potential negative consequences. The worker must be prepared to manage such attacks. If resistance is anticipated, the two-sided argument (one's own and the probable counterposition) can to some extent dissipate opposition (Hample, 2005; Karlins & Abelson, 1970; Poggi, 2005). Humor and role-play are effective in deflecting expected resistance or rebuttal. Also, the worker should describe the proposal "in language that is compatible with the values of the audience . . . and that will address their major concerns" (Frey, 1990, p. 145). If a positive response is expected, however, a one-sided argument is more effective since a reference to counterperspectives could create doubts and resistance. The one-sided argument should appeal to the self-interests and value systems of key participants. If anxiety needs to be aroused about the consequences of failure to act, it is done so out of concern, loyalty, and identification with the organization, not out of dissent.

Throughout the persuasion process, practitioners must assess reactions, and determine which positions are fixed and which are flexible. They may need to change the problem definition, proposed solutions, or the content and method of presentation in response to their continuing appraisal. They may, for example, broaden the proposed solution to encompass the interests of neutral participants. Conversely, they may narrow the proposal in order to eliminate the objections of a powerful participant. Implicit in effective persuasion is skillful negotiation and bargaining.

Smithdale High School is situated in one of the poorest cities in the state and suffers a high incidence of adolescent pregnancy and excessive rates of school truancy and dropout. Violent encounters among students have increased significantly in the past three years. In response, the superintendent of schools created a task force to study the problem and make recommendations. Sharply divergent perspectives developed among the task force members. The school social worker argued against a proposed program that focused on punishment and advocated involving students in problem identification and resolution. She explained that without student involvement, any intervention would be sabotaged. Other members disagreed. After considerable debate, the task force recommended and the principal implemented a discipline management program of unilateral, nonnegotiable interventions with students who engage in violent conflict. Administrators dictate the terms of conflict resolution, and students are expected to comply.

The social worker viewed violence in part as a response to powerlessness and oppression. As the lone voice representing the rich social work tradition of citizen participation and self-determination, she believed that the authoritarian program would not address the problem and might even increase the violence.

Education has its own traditions and mandates. Its institutions often preach democratic principles and values, but practice autocracy. Students are alienated by the discrepancy between philosophy and practice. As the social worker anticipated, the emphasis on unilateral decision making and punishment led to the program's failure. The program instructed students about unacceptable activities and behaviors and the consequences for noncompliance, but it did not provide alternate means for dealing with conflict. Even the teachers were frustrated and ceased to carry out the program.

Ironically, the program's deficits increased the social worker's stature. She was asked to chair a committee to explore other alternatives and was given permission to invite the president of student government to attend. After extensive review, the committee selected a program with two important components: (1) teachers will be trained to resolve conflicts in the classroom and to incorporate a conflict resolution curriculum into regular lessons, and (2) teachers will be taught group process skills and undertake self-exploration to expand awareness of their own conflict resolution styles. Students are to observe teachers instructing and modeling alternate conflict resolution strategies. Other high schools have reported dramatic success in decreasing the incidence of school violence through this comprehensive program involving new curriculum content and increased ease and skills experienced by teachers.

The superintendent, the principal, the teacher's union, and the student government approved the committee's recommendations. The superintendent secured private funding for the training program. However, before the program could be implemented, an unrelated controversy erupted. A group of teachers was concerned about severe depressive symptoms affecting a Latina colleague. Her depression had a negative impact on the students. These teachers could no longer ignore the problem and asked the principal, a Latino male, to furnish a medical leave of absence. The principal denied the request. Some teachers wanted to appeal to the superintendent, a non-Latino. At this point, the teachers split along ethnic and racial lines. The Latino and African American teachers refused to go over the principal's head and warned the white teachers not to do so. A severe rift ensued when the white teachers met with the superintendent. Racial polarization replaced a cooperative faculty climate.

In many school districts, administrators and teachers determine the function and roles social workers have in the educational setting, but in this instance, the social worker maintained a proactive stance in the school system. Although aware of her professional status as a "resident guest" in a host setting (Dane & Simon, 1991), she persisted in urging the racially divided factions to deal with their conflict for the sake of the students. After much pleading and informal networking, agreement was reached to use this discord as a case example for training in conflict resolution. In preparing to undertake the teacher-training program, the social worker contacted the trainers to alert them to the specific issues confronting the school's faculty. In her final report, she noted, "I hope a collective concern for the student body will sustain the training effort—now all I can do is hope."

Conflict is a method rarely used by low-ranking participants in dealing with organizational problems. The low-ranking practitioner is vulnerable to reprisals, and caution is necessary. At the same time, certain situations, such as violations of clients' rights, do require more adversarial actions, especially in the face of marked dissent over goals and methods. Before engaging in organizational conflict, however, practitioners must evaluate possible responses and their own resources. If either their job or personal credibility is at stake, only severe injustices and unethical practices should require such risks and sacrifices. If ambiguity about organizational response or worker resources exists, accommodation is only achieved through a test of respective strengths (Fisher, 1994).

In undertaking individual adversarial action, the worker holds to a stance of organizational loyalty rather than one of moral indignation. Polite, respectful disobedience can be highly effective. For example, a family agency required workers to submit confidential data to the state department of social services. After several unsuccessful efforts by a practitioner to have the policy changed, the supervisor demanded her confidential data. The social worker politely refused the request, citing the ethical principle of client confidentiality. The worker also expressed concern about the negative impact on the agency and its reputation, "should the practice become public." The agency retreated and renegotiated the arrangement with the department of social services. Had this practitioner escalated the issue, an unnecessary crisis would have been precipitated. Calling attention to negative consequences was successful because it provided leverage for testing relative power.

Group action can diminish the risk of reprisal. Collective positions, manifestos, petitions, or demonstrations are effective methods in dealing with powerful harmful practices and organizational participants. The alliance or coalition must be firmly unified and committed. If members are intimidated and become mutually exploitative, a long period of powerlessness and despair will result. In undertaking collective action, workers must first be sure each member is publicly committed to the cause in order to avoid finding him or herself with a group of "closet advocates" whose barks are ferocious but whose bites are mild. Methods and skills of the engagement phase are listed in Table 14.5.

Implementation and Institutionalization

After a desired outcome is adopted, it needs to be put into action. Initial acceptance does not ensure implementation. For the practitioner, much work and frustration may still lie ahead. An adopted change can be negated by a delay in execution. It can be distorted, undermined, or scaled down by executive participants, organizational processes, or personnel responsible for the change (Holloway, 1987).

Executive staff uncommitted or opposed to the adopted change may interfere with implementation. They might simply be preoccupied with other issues, or they may pay insufficient attention to necessary follow-up, postpone implementation, or provide inadequate personnel and financial resources.

In the implementation phase, informal and formal structures can be used to reduce stress associated with the change. To maintain administrators' cooperation, the innovation has to be experienced as being in their self-interest. After a worker influenced a union local to establish a steering committee to improve retiree programs, the local's director changed the meeting time to discourage attendance. His ambivalence was evident. The worker came to this conclusion:

I realized our failure to take the interests of the director into account. To repair the damage, I invited him out for lunch and discovered he had long been interested in holding a reunion of the local's membership. I asked him to bring his idea to the steering committee, and I guaranteed my support. At the next meeting, I backed his suggestion for a reunion. The steering committee agreed to do the work, collect necessary data, send out invitations, etc. He was pleased, participated throughout the meeting, and agreed to distribute our minutes to the membership.

The steering committee as an innovative structure was responsive to the director's interests. His stress was decreased, and his involvement and commitment were increased. Acquiring and maintaining the commitment of key

Table 14.5
Engagement Methods and Skills

• *Select appropriate engagement method:*	Demonstrating method is responsive to problems associated with professional function and program gaps.
	Collaborating method is responsive in open organizations where goal consensus exists and there is either equity in resource distribution or presence of close interpersonal relationships.
	Persuading method is responsive in organizations characterized by goal dissent and disparity of power.
	Creating conflict method is used only in situations where a more extreme form of pressure is required, as in violations of client rights.
• *Demonstrate through action and proposed change:*	Persistent and skillful doing.
• *Collaborate with colleagues in identifying problem and effective solution:*	Invite common search for data, possible solutions, and resources.
• *Persuade colleagues of problem and solution:*	Clearly define problem.
	Illustrate the problem's seriousness with facts, case material, and testimony of colleagues and/or clients.
	Present case of the effectiveness of the plan for solution.
	Provide evidence for feasibility and desirability of proposed solution.
	Use two-sided argument when resistance is anticipated.
	Use one-sided argument when positive response is expected.
	Use humor and role-play to deflect resistance.
	Use language compatible with the values of the audience.
	Arouse anxiety out of concern, loyalty, and identification with organization.
	Propose alternative solutions and involve staff in process.
	Prepare extreme solution and pursue a reasonable compromise.
• *Engage in conflict to resolve problem:*	Evaluate potential organization responses and personal/structural resources.
	Assume stance of organizational loyalty rather than moral indignation.
	Reduce individual risk through collective action.
	Develop public commitment for each member.

participants are always essential. Their support provides the context and sets the tone for other participants' cooperation.

The social worker seeks to keep the agreed-on change in people's minds and on the organizational agenda by assigning specific tasks to participants. If possible, a feedback system is built into the proposal such as regular progress reports to staff to provide monitoring and accountability.

Some organizational structures are incompatible with particular innovations. Even organizational features that promote acceptance of innovation can nevertheless hinder its implementation. Organizations of low formality, for example, tend to encourage innovation but also tend to hinder its institutionalization. In changing from a traditional to an open classroom approach, for example, a school maintained its rigid temporal schedules and grading system. These structures undermined the desired change. While some structures are too rigid, others are too flexible to support and integrate the innovation. Therefore, even before an adopted change is implemented, the worker attempts to modify existing structures to increase the chance of success.

As a new format for team meetings was adopted, I realized that the time structure could cause frustration. At the first meeting under our new plan, I wondered aloud if there would be sufficient time to discuss patients scheduled for presentation at the end of the meeting. Staff agreed to extend rounds another fifteen minutes.

The staff found the additional time beneficial. It eliminated the potential for stress arising from many designated tasks competing for time. Now each would receive sufficient attention.

Staff assigned to carry out the innovation represents another potential obstacle to implementation. Expectations may be unclear, or the staff may unwittingly distort the objective. Participants may lack knowledge and skills for performing the required tasks. Others may lack sufficient motivation to commit themselves to the new way of doing things. Also, the additional demands and competing time pressures may overwhelm others. From the outset, social workers must concern themselves with organizational participants assigned responsibility for implementation. They are sensitive to and empathic with the anxiety aroused by changes in role expectations. They must provide a clear conception of role requirements, building into the implementation in-service training, consultation, and ongoing support necessary to ensure interest, motivation, and skilled task performance.

Throughout the implementation phase, the worker must pay careful attention to task performers and needs for approval and recognition. After a designated time, implementation is evaluated to determine whether the desired objective is being achieved and whether unexpected negative consequences have appeared. If modifications are needed, they are instituted before the innovation is standardized and formalized (Pressman & Wildavsky, 1973).

Once an innovation is in place, it is important to evaluate the extent to which the problem has been ameliorated. If the innovation has been successful, the "final task is to stabilize it to ensure its permanence in the system" (Holloway, 1987, p. 734). When the change in an organization's purpose, structure, and procedures or services arrangements is no longer perceived as a change but as an integral part of its ongoing activities, the innovation is institutionalized. An innovation remaining essentially the same even though some initial participants are no longer involved serves as proof that an innovation is integrated into the organization's structure. To assure continuity, the worker lodges the innovation with a person who has staying power or occupies a stable status.

Every six months, team composition changes with the rotation of residents. In addition, a new chief resident means that a new personality and work style are introduced. The head nurse is key to maintaining stability, so the structural change was lodged with her. She orients new team members to the workings of the floor—the routines, procedures, etc.—and will see that the change is continued.

Other linking devices may be developed to ensure stability, such as inviting new staff to observe existing processes and procedures, or preparing a manual to formalize staff responsibilities. Whatever the method, the worker continues to monitor the institutionalization of the innovation.

FIFTEEN

INFLUENCING LEGISLATION, REGULATIONS, AND ELECTORAL POLITICS

Social work's commitment to social justice through political activity originated a century ago in the practice of settlement workers such as Jane Addams. Contemporary life-modeled practice actively embraces the commitment to a just society through the participation of practitioners in policy advocacy. The purpose of policy advocacy is to improve opportunities and resources for the poor and other vulnerable populations by attaining more effective legislative and regulatory responses to human needs. Social work policy advocacy attempts to accomplish various policy reforms, including the following (Jansson, 2007):

Rights-conferring policies protect people from discrimination (e.g., civil rights and grievance procedures).

Needs-meeting policies provide essential economic and health benefits to vulnerable populations.

Opportunity-enhancing policies provide education and training opportunities (e.g., Head Start) in order to "level the playing field."

Equity-enhancing policies target resources and services to especially vulnerable populations (e.g., Medicaid and TANF).

Public improvement policies help all people (e.g., public transportation, highways, and parks).

Economic development policies promote economic growth (e.g., empowerment zones and small business loans).

Asset accumulation policies mostly assist advantaged citizens but can also help the less advantaged (e.g., mortgage tax deduction and earned income tax credit).

Regulations protect the public from corporate, business, and landlord abuses (e.g., regarding pollution, prescription drugs, false advertising, and rent control).

Social services help vulnerable populations with life transitional and environmental stressors (e.g., child welfare, health and mental health, and school).

Social workers are involved in all these areas of policy advocacy.

Policy advocacy is practiced across local, state, provincial, and federal levels of government, and requires knowledge about policy development, legislative and regulatory processes, and electoral politics. In its simplest form, policy advocacy includes telephoning and writing letters to the decision makers and persuading others to do the same. In its more complex forms, policy advocacy includes lobbying, coalition building, testifying, demonstrating, rallying public support, and working with the press and other media on behalf of desired legislation.

Political advocacy by social workers consists of the following:

1. Influencing legislative policies by lobbying for or against new statutes and social policies or those being considered for modification. This requires knowledge of legislative process, existing law and policy, and methods and skills to influence policy development.
2. Influencing official regulations that control how statutes and policies are carried out by lobbying the people who write the regulations. This requires knowledge of the regulatory process, existing regulations that bear on the particular concern, and methods and skills used to modify regulations that go beyond statutory authority or the spirit of the law.
3. Influencing the electoral process through work in the political campaigns of candidates for elective office who support the advancement of social justice.

Influencing Legislation

The Legislative Process

In the U.S. federal government and in most states, the legislative process by which a bill becomes a law begins with a legislator introducing it.[1] Legislators often introduce specific legislation at the request of specialized advocacy groups as well as individual constituents. Social workers can influence legislation through participation in special interest groups or in their role as a constituent of a legislator. Constituent social workers who work for the election or reelection of a legislator may have additional influence.

After a legislator(s) introduces a bill, it is assigned to a committee. Committee members have several options: reject the bill by taking no action, refer the bill to another committee, or refer the bill to a subcommittee for research. If rejected by the subcommittee, the bill dies. If approved, the bill then goes to the full committee for debate and amendment. If rejected by the full committee, the bill dies. If approved by the full committee, the bill is forwarded for a public hearing. After the public hearing, the committee decides whether to defeat the bill or forward the bill to the full membership.

If the latter decision is made, the bill proceeds to the full membership of the lower chamber for further debate and amendment. If rejected by the lower chamber, the bill dies. If approved, it proceeds to the higher chamber, where it undergoes the same process.

When both bodies pass very or slightly different legislation, the differences must be reconciled. The bill is forwarded to a conference committee. If the conference committee works out the differences and reaches an agreement, a report is forwarded to both chambers. If both chambers accept the report, the bill is forwarded to the president or governor.

If the bill is passed in both chambers without change in language, it is sent to the president or governor, who has a certain number of days to sign or veto the bill. If the bill is signed, it becomes law. If the president or governor vetoes the bill, it may still become law if the legislature overrides the veto by a two-thirds vote in both chambers. During this process, many legislators spend countless hours with lobbyist and citizen groups.

Since the legislative process is messy and extremely time and effort consuming, legislators are selective regarding which bills they will place on the legislative agenda.[2]

> It takes time and effort to consider even simple pieces of legislation. In each chamber of Congress . . . subcommittees need to consider the policies, forward them for further debate and votes to the full legislative committee, which forward them to the full chamber for floor debates and votes. Then, they may have to be sent to [a] conference committee composed of members of both chambers if each chamber has enacted a different version, and then sent to the president for his signature. Moreover, during this process, many legislators must spend endless hours with lobbyist[s] and other citizens. It is no wonder[,] then, that leaders of legislature decide not to put most measures on the legislative agenda, thus reserving their scarce time for those pieces of legislation that they want to concentrate on. (Jansson, 1999, p. 125)

Acquiring support and favor with their constituents, gaining media attention, and chances for success are some of the factors that influence legislators whether to sponsor a bill. Social work policy advocates must be aware of these contextual factors. The context must be assessed for opportunities as well as constraints.

Social Work Lobbying

Successful social work lobbying requires information gathering, building an agenda, engaging legislators and influential officials, networking, coalition building, and testifying.

Information Gathering.   The policy advocate attempts to ascertain the viewpoints of key officials by studying their positions on similar issues in the past. Jansson (2007) emphasizes the importance of learning about the prior positions of the chief executive, important legislators (e.g., influential role in caucuses, official positions, and own district), key members of the government bureaucracy, public polls, and media coverage.

Researching bills is the base for effective lobbying, whether bills propose a new statute or seek to amend, revise, supplement, or delete an existing one. In influencing the passage or defeat of a particular bill, the social worker needs to undertake both substantive research on the contents of the bill as well as procedural research on its history.

Substantive research rests on a review of the existing laws that the bill seeks to change. Writing a position statement follows this type of review (especially important in testifying). The position statement includes the following:

1. An analysis of the modifications or additions to the present law as proposed by the bill, including strengths and weaknesses of the bill, new problems that the bill may create, and needed amendments to the bill (Kleinkauf, 1981).
2. Facts that support or negate key points in the bill.
3. Costs of implementing the bill, source of funding, and new positions required to carry out the legislation. This information is usually contained in the financial impact statement prepared by the legislative staff or the relevant governmental agency.
4. Positions held on the bill by relevant governmental agencies and other groups. Their positions yield information on points made for and against the bill, and on potential allies or opponents.

In procedural research, the social worker must determine the following:

1. Identify which committee originally referred the bill, where it is now, and where it has yet to go.
2. If a similar bill exists in the other chamber of the legislature and, if so, the committees to which the bill has been referred.
3. If the bill has already been amended and, if so, where, when, why, and how this was done. This information gives clues regarding what in the original bill was objectionable or unworkable and whether the bill has the support of key legislators.
4. Identify the sponsors of the bill and their motive in introducing it.
5. Review the legislature's rules of procedures for conducting legislative business. Copies are available from committee staff.

Analyzing the committee and its members is as important as analyzing the bill (Kleinkauf, 1981, 1989). Data needed include the following:

1. Details about each committee member such as background, constituencies, and interests. Other influences are personal philosophy, political consequences of the vote, party affiliation, and issues on which the member

campaigned. From such information, the social worker can construct a committee profile useful in lobbying and preparing testimony.

2. Voting records of committee members, although care should be exercised in generalizing from them to a likely vote on the bill.

3. Information on committee practices, special procedures, and the protocol followed in the committee's hearings can be obtained from committee staff and by observing the committee in action.

In this and other research, the staff of legislative committees, the staff assistant of a friendly legislator, or a lobbyist from NASW (or one of its chapters) or the League of Women Voters can be of assistance, and it is well worth taking the time to become acquainted with helpful people who are available (Kleinkauf, 1981).

Building an Agenda. After gathering relevant information, the social work policy advocate develops strategies to have an important decision maker(s) place the issue on the agenda of other decision makers in the legislative setting. Jansson (2007) suggests that the initial strategies emphasize creating favorable conditions, interest, and support for policy and regulatory reform. To accomplish these tasks, the policy advocate has to assess the constraints and opportunities created by the context. Having assessed the context, "policy advocates must soften it; that is[,] they must make it more amenable to specific policy initiatives" (Jansson, 1999, p. 128).

Timing of the initiative is an important consideration. The policy advocate searches for a window of opportunity. For example, a dramatic incident of child abuse or neglect or the death of a homeless person may raise the public's awareness and receptivity to a legislative initiative. The policy advocate "seizes the moment" and has the proposed legislation placed on the agenda. In presenting data on the magnitude of the problem, the policy advocate presents rates (percentages of people), incidences (ratios), and prevalence (ratios to total population). In relation to availability of services, the policy advocate presents data on "felt" need (people's beliefs), "expressed" need (people's actual search for services), "expert" need (estimates of severity of need), and "comparative" need (comparison of services offered in different areas to measure unmet need) (Jansson, 2007).

Engaging Legislators and Influential Officials. The social worker seeking to influence legislation needs to develop personal relationships with legislators and initiate frequent contact with them (Mathews, 1982, p. 625). From these contacts, the social worker attempts to ascertain the viewpoints and positions of important legislative "actors," including government or chief executives, legislators from one's own district as well as other important ones, key members of the government bureaucracy, and lobbyists and interest groups (Jansson, 2007).

Legislators are likely to be influenced by the most active segments of their constituencies. Interest groups and individuals (including lobbyist social workers) who are the most influential maintain frequent contact with legislators and provide them with technical and political information. Reputation, professionalism, and the ability to influence constituents appear to be more important in legislators' assessment of lobbyists than party affiliation or ideology. The social worker should stay involved and keep communicating to establish and maintain visibility, credibility, and identity (Mathews, 1982, p. 627).

The social worker can set up an interview with a legislator through the legislator's secretary. Copies of the proposed bill and a typed position statement for the legislator should be left with the secretary in advance of the appointment. Such interviews are usually very brief. "Generally, the legislators' first (and maybe only) question is 'Who is against it?' They want to know who they'll offend if they support it. You have to give an honest answer, else you lose credibility" (Dempsey, 1988, p. 25). Occasionally, social workers have a chance to describe the merits of a bill they favor or the disadvantages of a bill they oppose. "But most often legislators plan to go along with the recommendation of the committee the bill came out of or to vote along party lines" (Dempsey, 1988, pp. 25–26). In any event, an interview is likely to reveal the legislator's position on a bill.

On the state level, the support of the governor is essential in light of the governor's veto privilege. In order to influence his or her view of the proposed bill, it is wise to engage people close to the governor in arranging an interview (and perhaps a photo opportunity) to briefly present the proposed bill, other endorsements, and support of the relevant agency. If an interview is not possible, a brief letter can be left with the governor's executive assistant, together with copies of the proposed bill and the social worker's position on the bill. Administrators of relevant state agencies can be important sources of support because legislators listen seriously to agencies' representatives. Agency-requested legislation generally has a significantly better chance of passage than legislation without such a request.

Networking. Networking with other social workers is an important potential resource of the lobbyist social worker. Such networks might include practitioners who live in a legislator's district, those active in their party, social agencies with legislators on their board, and social worker politicians. "Clearing the bill" is part of networking. It might include negotiating with state agencies and other groups that will be affected by a bill in order to gain their support. Clearing a bill also might include reaching compromises so that all parties are satisfied. When several state agencies are involved, however, satisfactory compromises are difficult to attain.

Networking also includes establishing working relations with legislative staff. Social work lobbyists have access to legislative staff, who serve as the links between their legislator and lobbyists (Kleinkauf, 1989). For example, a social work professor and his students met with the staff aides of a U.S. senator and a member of Congress. Both meetings centered on AIDS. In discussion with the senator's staff aide on the issue of testing for HIV, a student described the agonizing dilemma of rape victims who do not know whether the rapist was infected. Given the civil liberties and privacy concerns involved, serious questions can arise for any social worker. The staff aide had not thought about the issue from this perspective. In the meeting with the Congress member's staff aide, another student described her frustration at not being able to find and provide services to infants who may be infected, and how this lack of services was a strong deterrent to finding and retaining foster parents. Again, the issue was entirely new to this staff aide. The social work professor commented,

> I tell students in class that social workers are uniquely situated to "witness" the effects of social policies on the lives of the people they serve and try to help.
>
> In both instances, I was struck by the truth and importance [of being thus situated] that came from the mouths of students who were simply reporting difficulties which they and clients face as a result of policies designed and organized by others. (Rosen, 1988)

Networking among supporters is also carried out by groups of social workers in politically oriented task forces or committees. Group actions include sending out newsletters and legislative alerts, and establishing telephone "trees" for calling legislators when a vote on a bill is imminent. Policy advocacy sometimes requires the group to garner more widespread public support for a proposed bill from voters, prominent individuals, and organizations. Networking strategies include the following (Bonilla-Santiago, 1989; Van Gheluwe & Barber, 1986):

- Gather information to justify the need for a bill's passage or defeat.
- Use the collected information in awareness and educational campaigns directed toward the public, professional groups, and legislators.
- Solicit written endorsements from professional groups or prominent individuals and signed petitions from voters.
- Send news releases to newspapers and organization newsletters.
- Offer presentations to groups and organizations on the issues.
- Prepare and broadcast radio spots.

Coalition Building.   Coalitions in the political arena are formed for a limited purpose and are usually temporary. When a coalition achieves its objective, the members may decide to dissolve it or to take advantage of the linkages that were developed and build a new coalition to address a new issue. Coalitions of organizations and social workers, other professionals, and interested community members can and do influence legislation and policy making, and they advocate for social change more effectively than separate and competing interest groups. Especially in a time of economic stringency, competition among agencies for limited resources heightens. It can be destructive of services, agency budgets, and interagency relationships, and is apt to be ineffective. Human services coalitions for legislative influencing have grown in number and size in response to severe cuts in services and programs sorely needed by vulnerable families and individuals.

Agencies and other groups that decide to band together in a coalition can benefit from pooling their resources and working cooperatively to "educate" and influence political decision makers. Also, a broad-based, unified voice is more apt to be heard than is the cacophony of competing voices.

If an issue is specific and time-bound, then organizations with conflicting interests are more willing to overlook their differences and form a coalition for a more powerful impact. But if an issue is wide in scope, it is more likely to highlight differences that, in turn, could reinforce self-interest, discourage organizational cooperation, and promote narrow interest politics.

Hearings, Preparing Testimony, and Testifying. The policy advocate assembles and enlists supporters to place their names on, or "sponsor," a legislative proposal. Jansson (1999, p. 137) suggests that the chances to pass legislation are much greater if powerful politicians with an array of perspectives sponsor it than if the proposed legislation lacks the support of powerful and diverse politicians. Essentially, multiple sponsors make the proposed legislation more visible. The multiple sponsors increase the power that will push the bill past legislative obstacles. They can press for a hearing, make necessary compromises and trade-offs to move the bill out of committee, push to get it scheduled by the rules committee, get it out of the rules committee and onto the floor of the legislature, and apply pressure to get it passed by both houses (Dear & Patti, 1982).

Committee chairs and committee members (looked to by other members because of their expertise in particular areas) are influential. When a bill touches on a concern of a legislator's constituency, active sponsorship is likely. Hence, the social worker's awareness of potential effects on a lawmaker's constituency is crucial in determining a legislator's position since the effects on the constituency are often the basis of the legislator's vote (Kleinkauf, 1989). In controversial legislation, legislators with secure electoral margins are more likely to be responsive to interest groups and to support unpopular causes (Dear & Patti, 1982).

Hearings draw media and public attention to a proposed bill, although they also run the risk of expanding public opposition. The social work policy advocate should press for open committee hearings. When such hearings are held, the social worker then attempts to arrange for testimony on behalf of the bill by expert witnesses, especially staff members of relevant governmental agencies. Depending on the nature of the bill, former or potential clients, practitioners, community leaders, representatives of special interest groups, and independent professionals can also be effective. Presentations based on research or on intimate familiarities with the subject (case vignettes) are persuasive to legislators (Dear & Patti, 1982).

Substantive and procedural research, described in the first section of this chapter, is basic to effective testimony. Prior to the hearing, the social work policy advocate develops a position paper on the topic, setting forth a general philosophy of what is to be achieved (which is approved by the social worker's organization). Next, written testimony is developed from the major points made in the position paper. Written testimony should not be read but spoken from an outline in order to maintain eye contact with committee members and sustain their interest.

Oral testimony should briefly describe the issue addressed by the bill and the position taken. Attention should be called to what the bill will and will not accomplish: objectivity enhances the credibility of testimony. Professional terminology and arguments based on values instead of facts should be avoided (Kleinkauf, 1981, p. 300).

The social worker must be prepared to answer questions from the committee and to furnish additional information and comments on particular points of the bill. Copies of the position paper and the written testimony should be distributed to committee members beforehand, and copies should also be available at the hearing.

An Illustration of Influencing Legislation

This example illustrates some of the various methods of legislative lobbying that were used to gain passage of the Limited Medically Needy Bill in Mississippi despite difficult economic conditions. The proposed bill provided (1) prenatal and delivery services for pregnant women who are married but are as poor as solo-parent recipients of Medicaid, and (1) outpatient services for children from intact families who are as poor as families on welfare whose children receive those services. Need for the new law arose from a Mississippi Medicaid regulation that required recipients to be aged, blind, disabled, or living in families in which one parent had deserted, was disabled, or had died. Congress had passed an act in 1981 that addressed such budget constraints by allowing individual states to cover married poor people with partial rather than full Medicaid benefits. Partial benefits had to include prenatal and delivery services and outpatient health care for the children of eligible recipients.

Policy health care advocates saw this enabling act as a cost-effective way to provide desperately needed services in the face of the state's high infant mortality rate, low per capita income, and growing unemployment. The Coalition for Mothers and Babies and other supporters of the idea of the Limited Medically Needed Program formed a task force for the bill's passage. It was composed of the following Mississippi state organizations: the Health Care Commission, the Conference on Social Welfare, the Department of Health, NASW chapter, and the Children's Defense Fund office. Strategy meetings were open to all. Strategies included information gathering, awareness and education, advocating and soliciting support, networking, and monitoring.

In *gathering information*, data were compiled that would justify the need for the program. Reports on costs and numbers served were obtained from other states, and Mississippi statistics were analyzed. Information gathered was used in awareness and educational campaigns directed toward the public, professional groups, and legislators.

In addition to networking activities mentioned in the earlier section, the task force developed a slide tape show and distributed it statewide. Public *awareness* packets were sent to the press and legislators. Information booths were set up at fairs and other activities around the state. These local functions received television coverage, as did a legislative rally held in the state capitol. The latter included a press conference by parents in need of the proposed program.

Over fifty organizations statewide gave written endorsements of the bill. Hundreds of petitions were signed. Key legislators were identified and lobbied by the NASW and other groups to work actively for passage.

In the *networking* process, supporters received continuously updated information through legislative alerts and a newsletter from the Coalition for Mothers and Babies. Through an extensive telephone tree, nine calls allowed over 400 people statewide to be given updated news about the bill's progress. At the point when a negative decision about the bill was about to be made, the tree was activated and within an hour over 100 calls were made to the capitol in support of the bill. The vote that followed was in favor of the bill.

Task force members constantly *monitored* subcommittee, committee, and floor actions that dealt with the bill. All discussion and voting on the bill were observed by one or more supporters to monitor legislators' voting patterns. This facilitated (1) passing on pertinent information to legislators who were supporting the bill, (2) soliciting statewide support at crucial times, (3) forwarding accurate information on the bill's progress to supporters around the state, and (4) securing an accurate count of who voted for and against the bill.

The bill passed both houses and was signed by the governor. During the subsequent legislative session, however, severe revenue problems led to reducing many state-funded programs. A bill was passed to delay implementation for two years. In light of the economic situation, program supporters agreed to a one-year delay and were successful in persuading the legislators to accept the change. Subsequently, funding was secured for the program. Table 15.1 summarizes lobbying skills.

The Regulatory Process

Regulatory Context

All publicly funded social welfare programs are carried out within a regulatory context.[3] When social welfare legislation is enacted, the authority to

Table 15.1
Lobbying Skills of the Political Advocacy Method

• *Gather substantive information:*	Review existing laws.
	Study strengths and weaknesses of proposed bill.
	Learn facts that support or negate key points.
	Study implementation costs.
	Research positions held on the bill by key actors.
• *Gather procedural information:*	Review committee route for bill.
	Explore current status.
	Assess sponsors and their interests.
	Learn legislature's rules and procedures.
• *Engage legislators and influential officials:*	Study legislator's background (e.g., voting record, constituencies, interests).
	Develop personal relationships.
	Maintain frequent contacts.
	Develop and maintain contacts with persons close to the governor.
	Gain support of administrators of relevant state agencies.
• *Influence legislative processes:*	Seek multiple legislative sponsors.
	Seek support of majority party.
	Seek support of influential legislators.
	Use amending process for promoting favorable outcome.
• *Develop networks:*	Find others to support (e.g., social work politicians, social workers living in a legislator's district).
	Clear bill with other groups.
	Find people to bear witness regarding need.
	Send out newsletters and legislative alerts.
• *Build coalitions:*	Join organizational and personnel resources.
	Educate and influence political decision makers.

implement the law is delegated to a governmental administrative agency that was created by the legislation or empowered by it to carry out the law. The agency develops regulations and rules about how service providers are to operate their programs that fall within the purview of the statute. The regulations must stay within the limits of the intent and policy goals of the legislation. At the federal and state levels, judicial review "tests whether the agency has exceeded its constitutional or statutory authority, has properly interpreted the applicable law, has conducted a fair hearing, and has not acted capriciously and unreasonably" (Robinson & Gelhorn, 1972, p. 33, cited by Albert, 1983).

An administrative agency develops three kinds of regulations:

1. Procedural rules (methods of operation) are usually authorized by the statute and are binding on the administrative agency. For example, if a regulated unit such as a social agency can show that the administrative agency did not comply with its own rules, the administrative agency's decision can be reversed.
2. Interpretive rules are issued as a guide for the administrative agency's staff and regulated parties of how the agency will interpret its legislative mandate. Policy statements announced through a press release are subject to public scrutiny for the purpose of influencing the regulatory environment in which a social agency operates.
3. Substantive rules are actually administrative laws through which administrators exercise their constitutional administrative powers. Notice and hearing usually must precede issuance of a substantive rule.

Publishing regulations in the *Federal Register* (or, in the case of a state statute, in a state register) prior to implementation fulfill requirements for notice to the public and allow sufficient time for public comment. Such comment may be written or, in some instances, offered at a public hearing. Following the comment period, comments are analyzed, and public influence, if any, has an effect. Final regulations are then adopted and published.

Influencing the Regulatory Process

As in the legislative context, a policy social work advocate gains influence in the regulatory context through effective lobbying for or against particular regulations.

> Effective social work advocacy in the regulatory process will, as a practical matter, depend on [workers'] ability to analyze the regulations, properly organize written comments and testimony for hearings, and engage in pre- and post-notice activities to maximize their input. (Albert, 1983, p. 477)

Analyzing the Regulations. Social workers must understand the statutory authority for the regulation before they can argue whether it is within the scope of the statute upon which it is based. In order to assess the validity of the statutory authority for the regulation, the following questions for social workers to ask themselves are suggested (Statsky, 1975, p. 140, cited by Albert, 1983):

- Is there some statute in existence that gives the agency authority to pass regulations on the general subject matter of the regulations before you?
- Is there a statute that is the authority for the particular regulation before you?
- Is the agency's interpretation of its own regulation consistent with the statute upon which it is based?
- Is your interpretation of the regulation consistent with the statute upon which it is based?

Organizing for Hearings.   The comment period is an opportunity for social workers to influence the scope and type of the final rules. Social work administrators and supervisors, for example, will understand a regulation's likely impact on social services. A carefully drafted written response to the agency or a well-structured presentation at a public hearing could be influential. And successful coalition building might increase the number of people who write comments or provide testimony at the hearing. Hearings as formal settings require a more structured response than a written comment:

- Identify yourself and your agency's interest in the matter.
- Explain the regulation's impact on the people served, and describe your agency's unique expertise.
- Provide the reasons for your agency's conclusions regarding the impact on those served.
- Recognize the legitimacy of other views, but refute them when necessary.
- Provide clear documentation (e.g., data and case examples) to support your agency's position and its long connection with the regulatory topic.

Pre- and Postnotice Activities.   These activities can help to connect the analysis to the written comments or to hearing testimony. They emphasize mutual education, information sharing, and constituency building to strengthen communication between the administrative agency and the social worker advocate. Both parties have an interest in the potential impact of the regulation; that fact can be used to facilitate negotiation on points of difference. Prenotice activities include the following:

- Learn about the administrative agency's structure, decision-making hierarchy, jurisdiction, and policy statements.
- Become acquainted with the administrative agency's staff to identify sources of support or opposition.
- Share views so they will understand your professional interests and the extent to which they reflect the interests of other service providers.
- Identify staff within the administrative agency who have expert knowledge in the pertinent substantive areas.
- Research the administrative agency position to predict potential decisions and to identify interest groups that seem to dominate agency decision making.

Postnotice activities following participation in the hearings include the following:

- Maintain communications with other affected service providers and sympathetic staff of the administrative agency in order to keep in touch with developments.
- Monitor the relevant regulations and their subsequent hearings for actual or potential implementation problems.

- Share relevant new information with your agency's staff, and mobilize support among other service providers.
- Stand ready to organize service providers against a proposed or final regulation.

The philosophy underlying these pre- and postnotice activities in regard to administrative regulations and rules is congruent with the life-modeled practice emphasis on the exchanges between people and their environment and its efforts to improve the level of fit. Social worker advocate participation in the regulatory process is significant because many social services fall within some administrative agency's jurisdiction.

After those who are interested in or affected by the regulations have been given an opportunity to be heard, final regulations are issued.

A Case Study

Torczyner (1991) and Cotler and Torczyner (1988) provide an illustration of discriminatory actions against welfare recipients that went beyond any existing regulations in Quebec's welfare administration.

> [In 1986, a newly elected] Quebec Minister of Manpower and Income Security announced a new program whereby his department would spend $9 million to hire special investigators to weed out fraud among welfare recipients. He claimed that 20 percent of welfare recipients were frauds or cheats and that these actions would recoup some $80 million annually. (Torczyner, 1991, p. 123)

No public hearings were held as the investigations were introduced as administrative changes that required no change either in law or in regulations. The investigators had no legal authority, but they had extraordinary discretionary power:

> A 30-page instruction book detailed how to conduct the inspections to determine almost every aspect of a recipient's financial, personal, and private circumstances: searching for signs of men's clothing, checking bank transactions, looking for signs of concealed employment such as a sewing machine, estimating the value of furniture and books, and examining birth certificates to verify that the correct children were in residence.
>
> Through a media campaign and a court challenge by community social workers and human rights advocates, the investigations were declared unconstitutional by the Quebec Human Rights Commission, a quasi-judicial body empowered to investigate and adjudicate allegations of discrimination that violate the Quebec Charter of Human Rights. (Torczyner, 1991, pp. 123–124)

Courtroom and media attention focused on the case of Mrs. Nguyan before the Quebec Human Rights Commission. Mrs. Nguyan was a welfare recipient, single, and a refugee from Southeast Asia living in Montreal. She spoke no

English or French, and had no relatives living in Canada. The case documented 100 violations of her rights during the time a welfare investigator sought to coerce her into implicating another welfare recipient in fraud. The commission based its ruling on the Nguyan case. In June 1988, the commission ruled that the investigations represented systematic violations of the rights of poor people. The ruling restored the fundamental human rights of all welfare recipients in the province and eliminated the investigations program.

Electoral Politics

Work in Political Campaigns

Many social workers serve as volunteers or as paid organizers in the political campaigns of candidates whom they favor, or whom the NASW supports by raising and contributing campaign funds through Political Action for Candidate Election (PACE). Whether social workers occupy formal or informal leadership roles in a campaign, they can make a unique contribution to maintaining morale during the strains of campaigning. Through group process, team building, and networking, social workers can help campaign staff and volunteers coordinate their work and extend support and encouragement to them. Such approaches help avoid common campaign problems of competitiveness and conflict.

Social Workers in Electoral Politics

Some social workers run for elective office, and increasing numbers are elected. According to the National Association of Social Workers (2007), over 170 social workers have been elected to national, state, and local offices, including two U.S. senators (Barbara Mikulski, D–Maryland, and Debbie Stabenow, D–Minnesota) and four U.S. representatives (Representative Ciro D. Rodriguez, D–Texas; Representative Barbara Lee, D–California; Representative Ed Towns, D–New York; and Representative Susan Davis, D–California).

Many social workers serve as state legislators. For informational purposes, they include the following:

Alaska: Betty Davis (D)
Arizona: Jorge Luis Garcia (D), Kyrsten Sinema (D), and Rebecca Rios (D)
Arkansas: Jim Medley (R)
California: Patty Berg (D)
Colorado: K. Jerry Franga, Gwyn Green, and Anne McGihon (D)
Connecticut: Christopher Donovan, Toni Edmunds-Walker, Kenneth Green, and Edith Prague (D)
Florida: Edward Bullard (D), Mandy Dawson (D), and John Legg (R)
Hawaii: Ryan Yaman (D)
Illinois: Christine Radogno (R), Kenneth Dunkin (D), and Joe Micon (D)

Iowa: Mark Smith (D), Romaine Foege (D), Geri Huser (D), and Maggie
   Tinsman (R)
Kentucky: Jim Wayne and Susan Westrom (D)
Maine: Joseph Brannigan, Lynn Bromley, and Michael Brennan (D)
Maryland: Salima Siler Marriott and Melony Griffith (D)
Massachusetts: Vincent Pedrone and Doug Peterson (D)
Michigan: Sheldon Johnson and Lawrence Hosch (D)
Missouri: Margaret Donnelly and Beth Low (D)
Montana: Rosalie Buzzas (D)
Nebraska: Gwen Howard (D)
New Hampshire: Barbara Richardson and James MacKay (D)
New Jersey: Sheila Oliver (D)
New Mexico: Mary Jane Garcia (D)
New York: Earlene Hill Hooper, Vito Lopez, Patricia Eddington (D)
North Dakota: Tim Mathern and Kari Conrad (D)
Ohio: Barbara Sykes (D)
Oregon: Carolyn Tomei and William Shields (D)
Rhode Island: Roger Picard (D)
South Carolina: Gilda Cobb-Hunter (D)
Tennesse: Tommie Brown (D)
Texas: Elliott Naishtat and Vilma Luna (D)
Virginia: Janet Ancel, James Leddy, Ann Pugh, and Michael Fisher (D)
Washington: Mary Lou Dickerson, Eric Pettigrew, and Pat Thibaudeau (D)
West Virginia: Donna Reid Renner and Jon Blair Hunter (D)
Wisconsin: Tamara Grigsby (D)

Others are elected to county or borough, city or municipal, and school
boards. Still others serve as staff assistants or as consultants to state legislators or members of Congress, and still others fill appointed positions that
carry political power, such as commissioners or directors of local, state, or
federal agencies. In a quite different mode, many social workers are engaged
in paid or volunteer work in political campaigns of candidates who support
social welfare issues.

A Study of Social Work Influence

Increasingly, social workers are undertaking political activity and social
agencies are employing social work policy advocates. These policy advocates
are committed to working politically to improve the quality of life of the
populations they serve. Yet given the many professional responsibilities already carried by social workers, why should we take on such a difficult additional task as political influencing? The answer:

> Because there is a chance that by our "going out on a limb," we will begin a pro-
> cess of change that in the short run may benefit our clients and in the long run
> may really have an impact on the fabric of our country. . . . The profession will

be seen both by clients and decision-makers as a professional resource for social planning and change. (Kinoy, 1984, p. 9)

Furthermore, in times of fiscal constraint and political conservatism, effective political advocacy by social workers could mean that social welfare programs will not be ignored in the competition for available funds.

The social work profession is changing in the process of responding to traditional and new needs, knowledge, and skills, and has incorporated new aspirations and goals to meet new social and cultural conditions. Clinical methods and skills must be connected structurally to the advocacy and political processes. Most social workers are committed to the poor and oppressed. They serve the chronically mentally ill, the abused and misused, the homeless, those suffering from AIDS, newly arrived immigrants and refugees, poor people in hospital emergency rooms and rural clinics, frail and poor elderly living alone or in institutions, tenants in public housing, children in ghetto schools and their parents, the chronically physically ill, the physically challenged and their families, prisoners, parolees, and probationers.

Social work's professional purpose in society is more necessary and more complex than ever. Practice and education for practice must be consonant with new knowledge, new needs, new social conditions, cultural diversity, and the search for an end to oppression. The profession has always shown the courage and the will to move in new ways in response to social problems and societal failures. We believe that life-modeled practice, through its values and practice principles derived from the ecological perspective, is well-suited to the social conditions of today's world. Life-modeled practice seeks to elevate the fit between people's needs and their environmental resources. In mediating the exchanges between people and their environments, social workers bear witness against social inequalities and injustice by mobilizing community resources to improve community life, influencing unresponsive organizations to develop responsive policies and services, and politically influencing local, state, and federal legislation and regulations to support social justice.

Life-modeled practice is committed to responding constructively to changes within the profession and in pertinent new theory and research findings, and to increases in human and environmental diversity. It will continue its quest for ever-broadening understanding of, and respect for, the endless variety of human strengths, exemplified in the lives of all those whom social work serves.

This chapter concludes the journey that readers and the authors together have taken through the realms of life-modeled practice. We believe that the evolving nature of life-modeled practice with its openness to new theory makes it especially suitable for understanding and helping people as they confront new and old life stressors generated by new and emerging social conditions and increasingly difficult national and global issues.

INDIVIDUAL, FAMILY, AND
GROUP ASSESSMENTS

Individual Assessment: Mrs. Ross

Background data. Mrs. Ross, a sixty-five-year-old Catholic of Italian and Scottish descent, was receiving daily homemaker service. A Medicaid patient, she was also periodically visited by a public heath nurse. Because of Mrs. Ross's increasing withdrawal and apathy, and with her consent, the nurse called the senior service division of a family agency, requesting social work service. After three home visits, the social worker (a first-year student) prepared a tentative formal assessment for a case conference.

Mrs. Ross had accepted the offer of service and supplied her background. Her mother died when Mrs. Ross was four months old and her father placed her in a Catholic institution, where she lived until her adoption at age six. She remembers her adoptive mother as loving and compassionate, but she died six years later after a long illness. A year later, her adoptive father married a young woman four years older than Mrs. Ross. At age seventeen, Mrs. Ross was engaged to a man who burned to death in a car accident. A year later she married a man who was a "gentleman" until the day of their wedding, when he turned into a monster overnight. Several years into the marriage a son, Jack, was born, and five years later a daughter, Janice, was born. Her husband beat her almost daily, and he also beat both children.

One day, Mrs. Ross found Jack with a shotgun; he said he was going to kill his father. She took the children and walked out of the marriage. She moved to another town and worked at two jobs in order to support herself and the children. Some twenty years ago she married a "good man." Six months later he died of a heart attack, and since then she has lived alone. Her daughter is married and lives across the continent, and they occasionally visit by telephone. Her son lived a few blocks away from his mother, with his wife and two children. He visited often. Six months ago he was hospitalized for minor surgery, suffered a stroke, and died. Mrs. Ross did not visit him in the hospital, nor did she attend his funeral, as she had no way to travel. She loves his two children, but she never felt close to her son's wife and was uncomfortable whenever she visited their home.

Fifteen years ago, Mrs. Ross developed Crohn's disease, a painful, debilitating intestinal disorder. She had to stop working and has since been housebound.

1. Definition of Life Stressors

Initially, Mrs. Ross requested help with emotionally charged life issues. "Losing my son, Jack, is the latest and most dreadful of the losses in my life. When he died, I couldn't stand the pain. I wanted to say the hell with it all, but five months later I'm still alive and the pain is still unbearable. I just can't handle it on my own anymore." Mrs. Ross and I agreed on twelve weekly home visits, framed by my impending departure from the agency and the agency's waiting list. During three home visits, other painful life issues emerged. Clearly, some are interrelated, unresolved earlier transitions and losses reactivated by the son's death. All are now intensified by Mrs. Ross's worsening physical condition, her grief, and her social and emotional isolation. Her increasing disability and dependency are additional current stressors. Her loneliness is connected to the great geographic distance between her and her daughter, to her dislike of her daughter-in-law despite the latter's frequent invitations to Mrs. Ross to visit her and her grandchildren, and to the lack of friends. Another stressor is living on the second floor and being unable to negotiate two flights of stairs. She cannot leave the apartment by herself; the ambulette attendants who drive her to medical appointments carry her down. Mrs. Ross says she cannot afford a move to the ground floor. Mrs. Ross needs and wants help in coping with these difficult life issues and her feelings of depression and helplessness.

2. Client Expectations of the Agency and Worker

Mrs. Ross expects me to provide her an opportunity to talk about her life losses and her suffering. Since she is not used to sharing and exposing her innermost thoughts and feelings, she will be sensitive to my reactions.

3. Client's Strengths and Limitations

When Mrs. Ross's life situation was presented to the agency's utilization review committee, several members suggested that Mrs. Ross is quite disturbed and deals in a pathological way with her stress (e.g., not getting up from her bed for three months). I believe that this assumption ignores the magnitude of her loss, gives insufficient attention to the physical disability caused by Crohn's disease and severe arthritis, and underrates Mrs. Ross's strengths and her coping efforts.

Strengths. Mrs. Ross demonstrates numerous strengths in coping with her losses. Her religious faith is a major strength. She finds comfort in prayer and in her belief in a life hereafter. Her God is close and personal, and she often talks to God. Several times since Jack's death, religious beliefs have deterred suicidal thoughts: "It would come into my mind that I didn't want to live anymore, but I couldn't do that—it is a sin." Her sense of humor is another strength. After Jack's death, in despair, she questioned the meaning of life. She called her church and asked to talk to a priest. When she was told, "Sorry, but they are all at bingo," she was able to laugh at life's ironies. She also finds pleasure in small things so that in the midst of her grief, she still enjoys looking at flowers or reading a letter from an overseas relative. Mrs. Ross remembers her adoptive mother telling her to "stand straight and hold your head high." Mrs. Ross has lived by her interpretation of this message: "I rely on myself and keep going no matter what happens to me." Courage, self-reliance, and ability to blunt emotional pain have sustained Mrs. Ross through many traumatic life events and have supported her through physical pain and emotional suffering. She is a survivor, finding ways and reasons to go on with the tasks of living. She deals competently with various organizations and bureaucracies, initiating contacts as needed and following through on commitments.

Limitations. Self-reliance seems to mean self-control to Mrs. Ross. As she speaks of her losses, she conceals the hurt and buries the pain. The emphasis on self-reliance may have cost her dearly in the past in terms of poor health and currently in terms of isolation from her son's family. Inhibiting the grieving process, while it may help her to survive, seems to be a maladaptive coping pattern. Her stoicism in the face of trauma may be related to the belief that traumatic events are expressions of God's will. Mrs. Ross's increasing immobility poses another serious limitation.

4. Environmental Supports and Obstacles

The social and physical environments have profound effects on Mrs. Ross's functioning.

Social environment. Mrs. Ross's contacts with complex organizations are generally favorable. Representatives from Social Security and Medicare are responsive to her needs. She has experienced little difficulty in maintaining daily homemaker services and the attention and responsiveness of health care systems, especially the public health nurses. In contrast, her informal network is severely depleted. She was accustomed to contacts with friends, but in the ten years since she became homebound they faded away. In spite of having lived in her apartment for nineteen years, she apparently is not involved with other residents. She says she feels close to her daughter and four grandchildren 3,000 miles away and they talk by phone every week. But she has not seen them in seven years. No other relatives are within reach. However, a deacon from her church visits weekly; her homemaker has been with her for four years; and her doctor, her physical therapist, her nurse, and now I are also supportive professional resources. She has a cat, acquired as a kitten just before Jack's death. It is a pleasurable companion. Her daughter-in-law occasionally telephones, but she and her young children have not visited since Jack's death. Mrs. Ross says she doesn't understand why, but she has neither asked why nor invited them to visit. So far, she resists my offer to work with her on finding ways to connect with her daughter-in-law and grandchildren. It is hard for her to even discuss or share her feelings about this relationship, beyond insisting she is rejected rather than rejecting. She is apparently willing to risk estrangement from her grandchildren rather than negotiate a truce with their mother. Opportunities for making new social contacts are severely curtailed, and Mrs. Ross doesn't "send out invitations." Thus her isolation is partly of her own making, perhaps because of her emotional vulnerability and her sensitivity concerning her physical disablement. For instance, she describes herself as "ugly" and "crippled."

Physical environment. Mrs. Ross is isolated in her second-floor apartment, accessible only by a narrow flight of stairs. The apartment is sparsely furnished but spotlessly clean. Rugs and doors are missing in order to allow easy access for the wheelchair. She is only able to leave her apartment to go to the hospital or the doctor.

5. Level of Fit

The lack of family involvement is a major limitation. The services provided by my agency, other agencies, and the church attempt to meet this void. While these services are essential to her life, they cannot meet the needs for caring provided for by one's family. Clearly, this needs to be a focus of my helping efforts.

6. Plans

A. More information is needed about Mrs. Ross's relationship with family members, from their perspective as well as hers. I will need to engage her more fully in her or my reaching out to her daughter and daughter-in-law. They need to become more involved in her life.

B. Because it takes time to build a trusting relationship, and given Mrs. Ross's severely stressful situation and my limited time with the agency, I recommend an increase to two home visits a week for the nine weeks remaining of the twelve that we agreed on.

A carefully planned termination is crucial so that Mrs. Ross has some control over the loss it will represent. I believe she is likely to be receptive to transfer to another worker. I am not sure what the agency's response will be, but I will advocate.

Family Assessment: Mr. and Mrs. Carter

Background data. Family Services of Hartown is a multiservice mental health setting. It has early morning, evening, and Saturday appointments in order to accommodate the community. The downtown location on a major bus route makes the agency accessible by both pubic and private transportation. Intake response is timely and efficient; waiting lists are resolved within a week. A crisis is seen immediately.

Denise Carter, age thirty-five, and Melvin Carter, age forty-seven, are an African American couple living in a suburb with Denise's two adolescent daughters. They are nonpracticing Protestants. Mr. Carter is a recovering alcoholic, sober six years; Mrs. Carter is a daily beer drinker. The couple married eighteen months ago after living together for two years. Both have been married before. Mr. Carter has three grown children from his first marriage; they all live out of state. After their marriage, their arguments about Mrs. Carter and her family members' drinking turned to screaming matches. Last May, after Mr. Carter lost his job (he charged the employer with racial discrimination), the constant verbal arguments escalated. Mr. Carter became violent, and Mrs. Carter called the police. In September, Mrs. Carter became violent, and Mr. Carter left home for three weeks. Mrs. Carter initiated counseling two weeks ago, alarmed that the relative calm following Mr. Carter's return is now replaced by days and nights of constant verbal fighting.

1. Definition of Life Stressors

The couple and the social work intern contracted to meet for eight sessions to deal with their dysfunctional communication and relationship patterns. At the end of the period, we are to consider whether they want to continue to work on their relationship or whether they want help in separating.

The focus of our work was clear and mutual. However, I should have also discussed what the work would look like—for example, both could not speak at the same time and I was not a referee. In other words, the content of our work was specified, but the process was left undefined.

They have trouble listening to each other; their communication styles vacillate between explosions and withdrawal.

2. Family Patterns

Both Mrs. and Mr. Carter come from large families. Mrs. Carter has six siblings, all living in her neighborhood. There is a history of alcoholism in her maternal grandmother's family, and two of her brothers abuse drugs and alcohol. Mr. Carter's siblings live out of state. His father, who died twenty years ago, had been a recovering alcoholic for the last fifteen years of his life. Mr. Carter and one of his brothers are also recovering alcoholics. Six years ago Mr. Carter entered a one-month alcohol rehabilitation program; subsequently, he lived for six months in a drug and alcohol rehabilitation halfway house. He has remained sober since then. His determination to stay sober results in a militant anti-alcohol stance. When Mr. Carter met Mrs. Carter, she was not working and, by both accounts, was living a partying lifestyle. Both Carters attribute Mrs. Carter's change in habits—cutting down on beer drinking, maintaining more regular sleep patterns, and finding and holding a clerical job—to Mr. Carter's encouragement and support.

Mrs. Carter grew up in a family with fluid boundaries. Today, family members and friends sleep and eat at each other's apartments with no prior arrangement and, according to Mr. Carter, with little respect for individual or marital privacy. Individuals seldom own problems; the group works on them together. This lack of unit boundaries is a crucial issue in the Carters' marriage. Mr. Carter resents Mrs. Carter's siblings walking into their bedroom at 11 P.M.; he also resents the time she spends at her mother's and sister's homes. He describes his family of origin as fairly formal. Visitors to his extended family were by invitation, and friends never blended easily into family situations. He rarely interacts with his own family; his interactions with Mrs. Carter's family are mostly limited to breaking up their drinking parties in his apartment and telling them to leave.

Communication between Mrs. Carter and Mr. Carter is vituperative, driven at present by Mr. Carter's increasingly toxic reaction to Mrs. Carter's drinking. They are so intensely reactive to each other that they have difficulty sustaining any nonvolatile exchange. They alternate between heated fighting and withdrawal—Mr. Carter into silence and television, and Mrs. Carter into her family, her friends, and beer. Although both appear to understand the role that environmental factors (unemployment, job, and financial pressures) play in their verbal and physical violence, their animosity is so great that their focus is on blaming each other.

The Carters are also currently experiencing the effects of breadwinner role reversal, a reversal painful to Mr. Carter and somewhat confusing to Mrs. Carter. Just at the time Mr. Carter was fired, Mrs. Carter received a promotion. Mr. Carter spends his days driving Mrs. Carter to and from her job and looking for work. The isolation of Mr. Carter's days is not alleviated by contact with peers. Mr. Carter and Mrs. Carter developed friendship patterns as alike as their family relationship patterns are different. They cultivated drinking buddies, people who drifted in and out of their lives, people brought together by their interest in partying. Mrs. Carter still has these buddies. Mr. Carter, encouraged by his association with AA, avoids his onetime buddies and is estranged from people he and Mrs. Carter had in common.

Mr. Carter tends to assume the role of "pursuer," and Mrs. Carter that of "distancer," in areas of maintaining stable routines, regulating partying, and balancing time spent with each other versus time spent with people outside the relationship. Mr. Carter often goes after Mrs. Carter to bring her home from local drinking spots. She pursues him only when she has been drinking. Then she will call him, tell him that she loves him, and sexually approach him. He repulses these attempts at intimacy.

3. Level of Fit

The fit between Mr. and Mrs. Carter is poor, as is the fit between the Carters and their social environment. Mrs. Carter's drinking and Mr. Carter's struggle to maintain sobriety are at the core of their interpersonal and environmental lack of fit. They are simply at different places. The role that alcohol plays in each of their lives dominates their marriage. The drinking is the major stressor in the marriage and will require priority in the marital sessions.

4. Plans

(Practice with this family was discussed and illustrated in chapter 9, "Helping with Dysfunctional Family Processes.")

Group Assessment: Bereavement Group

Background data. The bereavement support group met from 6:00 to 7:30 in the evening once a week for six consecutive weeks at a hospice hospital. All members had recently suffered the loss of a loved one. The purpose of the group was to provide a safe and supportive environment for members to help each other deal with their loss; deal with feelings of loneliness, sadness, isolation, and anger; incorporate the loss in one's life; and reach out to available supports. The group met in a large, well-lit, clean, and attractively decorated room.

1. Temporal Arrangement, Group Size, and Space

Members responded well to the planned short-term six sessions. The time limit kept the work focused, and termination was experienced neutrally. The fact that all members began and ended together fostered a sense of group identity. The fact that many members made connections outside of the group facilitated the mutual aid processes. The one-and-a-half-hour period seemed also to work well. Members had energy for work. The 6:00 P.M. beginning time worked well for all but three members, who had very long commutes. They were consistently five to ten minutes late due to heavy traffic. Since the group could not begin earlier and did not want to begin later, these three members' geographic distances were discussed in the first session, and their lateness accepted by other members. Interestingly, the group saved the "tougher" discussions for after the arrival of these three members.

The bereavement group began with sixteen members. Two members withdrew after the second session. Initially, the group felt quite large, and members seemed intimidated by it. However, by the second session, group members participated regularly and freely. Only two members seemed to hold back. While they attended every session and were involved, possibly a smaller group would have made it easier for them to participate. Large groups of ten or more may decrease participation, with less verbal and assertive members being intimidated by the group's size (Gitterman, 2005; Sundel, Glasser, Sarri, & Vinter, 1985). However, the intensity of the common bond seemed to overcome the potential constraints of the large number of members. Only two members did not participate regularly, but (as mentioned above) they did attend all the sessions. Whether their lack of verbal participation was a result of the large group size, their level of grief, their younger age, or the fact that they were both present with a parent is unclear. The two members who left the group after the second session had recently lost their husbands. For both, talking about their losses seemed too difficult. They needed more time to process the loss. They did participate in our next six-session group.

For the first two meetings, the group sat at a long rectangular table, with two group co-leaders sitting at the head of the table. At the end of the second meeting, I shared with the group that the long table seemed to create a barrier to interaction and that the positioning of the co-leaders ascribed to them much authority—like teachers rather than co-facilitators. The members agreed, and in the third meeting the tables were removed and chairs were set up in a circle. Members were pleased with the new arrangement as they could see and hear each other much better.

2. Compositional Balance

The fourteen group members were the following:

Diane: An African American woman in her early fifties whose husband died last month of lung cancer. She had a difficult time accepting his death in light of the fact that he never smoked. In the first three meetings, she expressed a wish to join her husband; however, by the end of the group, she talked about moving on with her life.

Betty: A Jewish woman in her mid-fifties whose husband died eight months ago of metastasized lung cancer. She was a very talkative and supportive member.

Rebecca: A Jewish woman in her late fifties. Her husband died five months ago of liver cancer. She was supportive of other members, but had difficulty sharing her own pain.

Mary: A white Catholic woman in her early twenties. Her father died of bone cancer two months ago. She hardly spoke in the group, fighting back tears and staying in the shadow of her sister, Stacy, and mother, Barbara.

Stacy: A white Catholic woman in her early thirties. While she actively participated, it was rarely about her grief. She focused on her anger at the medical system and recruited other members to write letters of complaint to hospital administrators.

Barbara: Mary and Stacy's mother, in her early sixties, rarely spoke in the group. When she did speak, her voice was very quiet and difficult to hear.

Margaret: An African American woman of Baptist faith in her early forties whose husband died two months ago of pancreatic cancer. She actively and supportively participated, easily sharing her feelings.

Jennifer: An African American woman of Baptist faith in her early fifties whose mother died of stomach cancer a month before the group began. In the first two meetings, she cried and could not talk. By the third meeting, she began to participate actively.

Jackie: An African American woman of Baptist faith in her early fifties whose mother died five months ago of lung cancer. Since her mother's death, Jackie has retreated from her friends and church. Previously, religion had played a significant role in her life. She could not face her friends asking her how she was doing since her mother's death. While not active in discussions, her nonverbal (i.e., eye contact and body language) communications were accepting, empathic, and warm.

Ted: An African American man in his early fifties. He is Jackie's husband and came to the group to help his wife grieve.

Allen: A Jewish man in his early seventies whose wife died six month ago of breast cancer, having lived with the disease for twenty years. He was having trouble functioning without his wife. He tended to monopolize discussions.

Louise: A Jewish woman in her late fifties whose husband died a few months ago of bone cancer after a long and painful battle with the disease. She had a very supportive and soothing style.

Sheila: Louise's daughter, in her mid-twenties. She did not speak much and seemed shaken and sad most of the time.

Gladys: A white Catholic woman in her mid-fifties. Her husband died three months ago of bone cancer, which had metastasized to the brain. While she was an active and supportive group participant, she tended to minimize her emotions.

This group is obviously quite heterogeneous in terms of race, religion, gender, and age. Also, some have experienced the death of a spouse, while others that of a parent. In contrast, the group is highly homogeneous in that everyone has experienced the death of a loved one to cancer. The common bond of suffering a profound loss makes the background differences among members relatively inconsequential. In fact, these differences deepened the quality of exchanges and problem solving (Gitterman, 2005).

3. Mutual Agreement

The purpose of the bereavement group was bringing together people who were struggling and feeling alone with their grief and helping them to help each other deal with their losses together. As co-facilitators, we defined our roles as aiding them in communicating with and listening to one another as well as helping them to heal one another. We reached for their feedback to make sure that the purpose met their expectations. Members were clear about the group's purpose. The level of mutuality about focus and role expectations was very good, as evidenced by the members' immediate focus on their grief. While one member had wanted more of a social action group focus, we were able to accommodate her concerns and effectively integrate her with other group members.

4. Interaction, Friendship, and Role Patterns

Louise appeared to be the indigenous leader of the group. This came as a surprise to me because, initially, Louise seemed reserved and unassuming. However, her relaxed manner had a calming effect on the group. She often set the tone for the group sessions. She would often be the first to speak when we opened the group and spoke about how the week preceding the group meeting had gone. After a couple of weeks, it became the norm that Louise would speak first and then the others would follow her lead. Her initiation was welcomed and broke the ice. She also set the tone for being honest in the expression of emotions—not glossing over her and other members' feelings. For example, in one group meeting, Allen expressed a painful emotion and Rebecca's response was "You should not feel that way." Louise responded, "But he does, and I do too sometimes." This comment refocused the group to the difficult emotions Allen was experiencing and made it possible to continue the work. Interestingly enough, after the first two meetings other members, following Louise's lead, ceased cutting off other members' feelings. For another example, the co-leader and I developed problems between us. When our behavior, either verbal or nonverbal, cut off the work, Louise was able to move in and transition the focus off the leaders and back on to the work. In many ways, she was the third co-leader—her role was pivotal in moving the work forward.

Betty, Rebecca, Margaret, and Sheila assumed the role of supporters. They were naturally empathic, and group members began to look forward to their supportive statements and expressions. Stacy gave voice to anger at the hospital and its medical representatives. Interestingly, while members gave her support in the expression of her complaints, they also made sure that it did not replace the focus on their grief. An implicit agreement was negotiated that allotted Stacy approximately ten minutes at each meeting to give voice to her as well as the group's anger; however, the primary focus remained on their dealing with the loss of a loved one.

Allen was the group's monopolist. Since his rambling was related to the group's focus rather than tangential, he was fully accepted. Members would build on his ideas or gently take the "floor" from him. His despair and loneliness generated much sympathy and acceptance from group members.

5. Normative and Sanctioning Patterns

As previously discussed, two related group norms evolved: Louise would break the ice and initiate the work, and expression of painful emotions was accepted and preferred. Group members also began to have contact before and after the group meetings. For example, Louise would have dinner with her daughter in the hospital cafeteria. The first two weeks, they ate alone. However, by the third week, Diane and Margaret had joined them, and by the last session so had Rebecca, Betty, and Allen. Other members who were unable to arrive early enough to have dinner would arrive ten to fifteen minutes early to the group to have cookies and coffee with the "dinner crowd." Similarly, some members lingered together after the meeting, exchanged phone numbers, and gave each other support in between group sessions. These group "rituals" were established early in the group and were adhered to by members throughout the group's life.

Another group norm that evolved and was not known until it was broken was a prohibition against interjecting humor into group discussions to deflect from pain. For example, when Stacy made a joke about her feelings, I normalized her feelings, but Louise and other members were not responsive to the joking nature of the comment and moved the work back to where it had begun. The members placed a high value on working on grief, bereavement, and the healing process. Louise embodied this group norm—hence, she was the group's indigenous leader.

6. Phases of Group Development

The group did not struggle long, if at all, with the first phase of authority or with the power and control phase (Berman-Rossi, 1993; Garland, Jones, & Kolodny, 1976). Perhaps dealing with such powerful and connecting issues of grief and bereavement immediately propelled the group toward the intimacy phase. Perhaps the fact that it was a primarily female group accounted for the preoccupation with intimacy rather than testing the leaders' authority (Schiller, 1995, 1997).

7. Transactions with Its Environment

The group was supportive of Stacy's petition focused on improving hospital services. Group members also helped each other with dealing with unresponsive family members. However, in the foreground was always the life transition of dealing with loss and expressing their pain. The group became a support system where they could express their sadness and not be told to "move on" with their lives.

8. Next Helping Steps

The life stressor of the group members' grief and bereavement was not solved during the six weeks. This would have been an impossible expectation since grief and bereavement require a process. There was a noticeable difference between the first group meeting, when the focus was on the pain of the loss and the strong need to repeatedly tell the story of the illness and death, and the last couple of meetings, when the focus was on the need to go on with life and establish new identities without the deceased while remaining connected to the person. If the group had not ended, my next helping steps would have been focused on the emerging themes of rediscovering the self and going on with a new life while holding on to the memories of the deceased.

PRACTICE MONITORING:
RECORDS OF SERVICE

Sample Record of Service (Summarized): Ms. H.

Student/Worker Name: Joe Jackson
Agency: Bridgetown Hospital
Time Period: October—4 sessions
Check Modality:
Individual _X_ Family ____ Group ____ Community ____
Professional Helping Area (Indicate Focus):
Initial Phase ____; Life Transitional Stressor ____; Environmental Stressor _X_;
Interpersonal Stressor (Family ____, Group ____, or Client:Worker ____);
Ending Phase ____.

1. Brief Introduction

Ms. H. is a fifty-year-old black woman. She was admitted to the rehabilita-tion center seven months ago, inebriated, after being hit by a car while crossing the street. The accident broke her legs and left them permanently weakened. . . .

2. Level of Mutuality about Focus and Role Expectations

Ms. H and I agreed to work on the difficulties she experienced within the rehabilitation center, and ultimately on needs at discharge, including appro-priate housing.

3. Identify the Life Stressor

The particular life stressor I am examining is an environmental one. The orthopedic medical staff neglects to remove Ms. H's casts, and she is reluctant to discuss her concerns with them. . . . The environmental life stressor first came to my attention in the second interview. Ms. H. told me that the orthopedist had seen her a couple of days ago, but hadn't removed her casts. She felt she couldn't ask him why he had not done so.

4. Personal (or Collective) and Environmental Strengths and Limitations

Various personality, situational, and organizational factors produce and sustain the environmental life stressor. . . . Ms. H. copes with stress through withdrawal and avoidance. . . . By neglecting Ms. H., the orthopedist gains time for treating the more disabled patients. . . .

5. Present and Analyze Selected Consecutive Transactions

These illustrate your practice over the specified time. For each transaction:

  A. Conceptualize your intervention.
  B. Provide the actual transaction—the client's statement and your response. The client's statement always comes first.
  C. Place yourself in the client's shoes and in the first person describe what he, she, or they are thinking, feeling, and trying to communicate to you.
  D. Place yourself in the client's shoes and in the first person describe the extent to which your (the worker's) intervention did or did not connect to what the client was trying to communicate.
  E. In the first person describe what you were thinking and feeling at the moment and how your thoughts and feelings affected your interventions.
  F. Another try: based on the client's message and using what you were thinking and feeling at the moment, how would you now intervene differently?
  G. Name your new skill and share your rationale for this new choice.

Interview #2.   Ms. H. told me that the orthopedist came to see her and said that the casts should come off. Several days passed, and he had not removed them. (Casts were periodically removed to check the progress of healing.) First cluster (group of relevant transactions):

MS. H:	Dr. James (orthopedist) came to see me and said that the casts should come off. (Looking down on her cast) This was two days ago. (Casts were periodically removed to check the healing.)
WORKER:	*Ms. H., have you thought of asking the doctor about this?* (1)
MS. H:	(Shrugging her shoulders in a childish manner) I didn't

think I could do that. I don't think I could understand
what he says. Would you do it for me?

WORKER: *Yes, I will.* (2)

A. *Conceptualize intervention*: I reached for information.

B. *Provide actual transaction*:

MS. H: Dr. James (orthopedist) came to see me and said that
                        the casts should come off. (Looking down on her cast)
                        This was two days ago. (Casts were periodically
                        removed to check the healing.)

WORKER: *Ms. H., have you thought of asking the doctor about this?* (1)

C. *Place self in client's shoes*: "I want to talk about my anger at the doctor and
my concern that there might be something wrong with my legs."

D. *Evaluate from client's shoes*: "You don't hear my concerns and make me even
more anxious by suggesting that I speak to the doctor."

E. *What I am thinking and feeling*: "I feel pressure to solve the problem—I feel
out of control in the face of ambiguity and begin to rush. What do I do if
he forgot about her?"

F. *Another try*: "Are you worried that he forgot about you?"

G. *New skill*: Reaching for her underlying concern.

A. *Label intervention*: I assumed responsibility for the task.

B. *Provide actual transaction*:

MS. H: (Shrugging her shoulders in a childish manner) I didn't
                        think I could do that. I don't think I could understand
                        what he says. Would you do it for me?

WORKER: *Yes, I will.* (2)

C. *Place self in client's shoes*: "I can't talk to the doctor—he hardly speaks
English, he rushes in and out of the room, he makes me feel helpless.
Please help me."

D. *Evaluate from client's shoes*: "I appreciate your willingness to do it for me,
but I wish you would ask me more questions—to find out what I am
concerned about."

E. *What I am thinking and feeling*: "'Doing for' is comfortable for me—I have
always been the one that takes care of things. I feel more in control, more
competent. However, I realize that I am making her more dependent. I
don't even ask her what exactly the doctor said, or if she had tried to speak
to him. I must have communicated a lack of faith in her ability to follow
through. I am feeling out of control and I can't stand it."

F. *Another try*: "'Can you tell me what the doctor said about returning?' If the
doctor was ambiguous, I could have followed with 'Did you get a chance to
ask him when he would remove your cast?' And if my follow-up was
required, I should have invited her to plan with me, discussing the comparative advantages and disadvantages of her or my talking to the doctor
or our talking to him together."

G. *New skill*: Reaching for facts, and engaging client in problem solving.

Interview #3.   I arranged a meeting with Dr. James. *Second cluster:* (group of relevant transactions)

DR. JAMES:	Please, come into the office.
WORKER:	*Dr. James, is there some reason that Ms. H.'s casts are still on and have not been checked by you?* (3)
DR. JAMES:	(He seemed taken aback, and then said) I have been very busy, but will take care of it right away.
WORKER:	*(I thanked him and left.)* (4)

A. *Label intervention*: I advocated client's position directly with the doctor.
B. *Provide actual transaction*:

DR. JAMES:	Please, come into the office.
WORKER:	*Dr. James, is there some reason that Ms. H.'s casts are still on and have not been checked by you?* (3)

C. *Place self in doctor's shoes*: "I wonder what she has on her mind."
D. *Evaluate from doctor's shoes*: "What a self-righteous jerk—who does she think she is! I have been negligent, so I better not retaliate."
E. *What I am thinking and feeling*: "I am furious at this doctor—he doesn't care about Ms. H. I want to deliver for her. I know you will want to know how come I am so angry, what is being triggered. Well, a similar thing happened to me when I was a patient—I can't believe how passive I was. I became overidentified with the 'helpless' client and marched into battle. My advocacy did not represent an assessment-based intervention, but rather an expression of my own experiences and feelings. In retrospect, my initial intervention should not have been adversarial since I had never met the doctor and had no evidence that he would be antagonistic."
F. *Another try*: "Ms. H. is concerned about the delay in the removal of her casts. She had wanted to ask you about the delay, but I remember when I had surgery it is very difficult to ask a question—everything happens so fast."
G. *New skill*: I clarified the situation.

A. *Label intervention*: I shared my appreciation.
B. *Provide actual transaction*:

DR. JAMES:	(He seemed taken aback, and then said) I have been very busy, but will take care of it right away.
WORKER:	*(I thanked him and left.)* (4)

C. *Place self in doctor's shoes*: "I resent your tone of voice. I am the doctor and you are the social worker. But I better do it because I have not followed up. I will get even with her at another time."
D. *Evaluate from doctor's shoes*: "That's better—at least she thanked me, but I still don't like her tone."
E. *What I am thinking and feeling*: "Oh! Oh! I hope he doesn't report me to my field instructor. My anger threw him, but it also scared me. I realize that I

have a 'slush fund' of anger at men with power. They have a way of making me feel small and incompetent."

F. *Another try*: "Dr. James, I want to apologize for my tone. Ms. H.'s situation reminded me when I was in the hospital and felt too intimidated to ask questions. I realize we have never even met—could we start over?"

G. *New skill*: I demonstrated congruence and humility.

6. Where Things Stand Now

As soon as I gave Ms. H. support and began through role-play to stimulate her latent interest in participating, she made progress in "trying on" a bit of assertiveness with the doctor. She became less depressed . . .

7. Next Helping Steps (Hypothetical if No Longer Working with Client)

I plan to continue involving her in acting on her social environment. She had found role-play helpful in preparing for and dealing with the physician and other staff. . . .

8. Apply Theory and Research Findings

A review of relevant literature brought the environmental obstacle into clearer focus. For example, Berman-Rossi, T. (2001). Older persons in need of long-term care. In A. Gitterman (Ed.), *Handbook of social work practice with vulnerable and resilient populations* (2nd ed., pp. 715–768). New York: Columbia University Press. The author describes . . .

PRACTICE MONITORING:
CRITICAL INCIDENTS

1. Summarized Sample Critical Incident (Analysis of Individual Transactions)

Student/Worker Name: Angela Sampogna
Agency: York Mental Health Clinic
Time Period: Twelve weeks
Check Modality:
Individual _____ Family _____ Group _X_ Community _____ Organization _____
Professional Helping Area (Indicate Focus):
Initial Phase _____; Life Transitional Stressor _____; Environmental Stressor
_____; Interpersonal Stressor (Family _____, Group _____, or Client:Worker _____);
Ending Phase _X_.

1. Group Formation

Twenty eighth-grade girls were interested. They were divided into two groups, each to meet for twelve weeks. When one group ended, I began the second group. Each group had ten members. All the members had been in the same class for at least two years, and several had been together since kindergarten. They all lived in low-income public housing in a neighborhood where drug trafficking and associated violence were part of everyday life. The homogeneity in backgrounds and geography provided a common frame of reference that enhanced cohesion and promoted mutual aid. Half the girls were Puerto Rican, and half were black. However, friendships were not based on racial and ethnic backgrounds. These youngsters knew each other for so long that the building they lived in was more defining than race. The girls identified themselves as a single entity in terms of their income level, neighborhood, school, class, and group.

We met in a small alcove in the library. Since the library was not open in the morning, the space provided the group with essential privacy.

2. Agency Context

Group services were offered to all eighth-grade students in my school. They were divided into two groups. These groups were assigned to two interns from an outside agency. There were some rough spots in the development of the group services, many of which could have been avoided had we taken the initiative to involve the principal in the service creation. We had not realized the importance of developing vertical as well as horizontal organizational sanctions and supports (Gitterman, 2005). We had worked out with the guidance counselor that groups' memberships would be voluntary with a focus on the youngsters helping each other to work on common life issues. It had never occurred to us that the principal had a different perspective. He wanted the focus to be on changing disruptive and undesirable behaviors in students who had been identified as problems, and wanted the group to be mandated for them. There were four children who had not signed up for the group who he strongly felt needed to be in it. The compromise we worked out was that these four children would receive intensive individual help and the groups would continue in the direction charted by the interns and guidance counselor.

3. Level of Mutuality in Focus and Role Expectations

When we met individually with each girl and again in the first group meeting, we explained that the group was a place where the girls could help each other with things going on their lives that they would like some help with—things going on at school, at home, and with boys, other girls, and their bodies. That is all the invitation the girls needed. They had been waiting six months for this group, and they took off. They were on task, knowing that the group would end in twelve weeks.

4. Define Life Stressor

The focus of this critical incident is my effort to help the girls with termination. In spite of the fact that these girls had been friends and classmates for a long time and would still be together after the group ended, they had developed newfound intimacy, trust, and mutual aid. When the issue of termination came to the fore in the seventh meeting, I was totally unprepared (which was my fault, as I was in my own denial) for the intensity of members' reactions. The predetermined number of meetings had been discussed in the individual meetings as well as the first group meeting, and I had naïvely assumed they were aware of the number of meetings left. The ending date also had been mentioned "in passing" during earlier sessions without evoking visible reactions. Yet, in the seventh session, I found myself confronted with much greater anger than I had anticipated. In retrospect, I realize that termination triggered many countertransferential issues and I was in just as much avoidance and denial as the youngsters. I have my own issues about abandonment, which make endings and separation very difficult for me.

5. Social and Normative Structures, Phases of Group Development, Relationship to Its Social and Physical Environments, and Level of Fit

Alice and Inez assumed the roles of the group's indigenous leaders. Because of her competent, take-charge manner, Inez emerged as the task leader. Alice emerged as the "socioemotional" leader in that she was most attuned to what other members were feeling and able to help them verbalize it. Nora had the role of work deflector, and Maria the role of scapegoat. Both members, with the group's assistance, do their jobs really well when group discussions get intense. . . .

A very strong group norm is that fathers are not to be mentioned. Although I tried to point out the omission on a few occasions, the group members creatively sidestepped the issue or remained silent. Interestingly, during termination a few members talked about losing their fathers to the competing needs of stepfamilies. The loss of the formal group triggered discussion about other losses in life. . . .

Developmentally, the group moved very quickly through the first stage, "pre-affiliation," because the members knew each other so well (Garland, Jones, & Kolodny, 1976). In the "power and control" stage, the members tested me by having Inez sit in my seat in the first meeting. I passed the test by pulling my chair next to her and leaving her with a more prominent position while, at the same time, conveying that I was the adult professional who would make the experience safe and productive. . . .

6. Critical Incident

Context for the incident: This was the seventh meeting, and it had been going very well. The discussion had centered on the girls' frustration and anger with their mothers' "lack of trust" as demonstrated by their "unreasonable and overprotective" attitudes about boys, parties, and curfews. The highlight of the discussion came when the members agreed to do a role reversal and become a group of their mothers who, in turn, discussed their fears and aspirations for their daughters. We had much fun with the role reversal; the group members were very animated and "hammy," yet insightful, at times, and poignant as they bounced back and forth between roles.

> Keika reminded the group that next week was the last time we were going to meet before the holiday and asked if we could have a party during the last half of the meeting. *I agreed that it would be fun and pointed out that today marks the half-*

way mark for the group. (1a) *Perhaps they would like to spend some time at the begin-ning of the next session to take stock and decide the focus for the remaining meetings.* (1b) Within a few seconds, the entire ambiance completely changed. Although a few registered no visible reactions, most seemed puzzled as they glanced around the room. Alice, Helen, and Maria, who were seldom at a loss for words, looked absolutely thunderstruck. All were quiet. *I waited several minutes,* (2a) *and then observed that they were awfully quiet all of a sudden, and I was wondering if my com-ment about having only five more sessions had taken them off-guard.* (2b)

The silence just got louder. For a few minutes, I had the sinking feeling that the session might end in silence. Finally, Ivory found her voice and demanded to know why I was cutting the group short when they hadn't done anything "nasty." Then she looked more closely at me and reminded me that I had said I was going to be here until May, so what was the problem? Matilda chirped in a "told you so" tone of voice that I just did not like them—that was the problem. I became flustered and defensive. *I mentioned that in individual interviews and at the first meeting I had emphasized the group would meet for twelve weeks.* (3) Ivory re-torted that when I had first talked to their class, I had said the group would meet for the entire school year, just like last year's group.

Inez shook her head and corrected her by pointing out that it had been changed to twelve weeks because too many people signed up. Ivory indignantly declared this was the first she had heard of it. But even if that was the case, why couldn't I just have a second group for the other class? *I explained that if they re-membered, I had informed them right away that my schedule did not allow me to have two groups, and the agency could not assign another worker.* (4) Dramatically, Ivory looked around the group and said in exaggerated disbelief that "I just want to get this straight . . . you are going to give our group to those bimbos?" *I re-sponded this was very hard for all of us.* (5) There was a tense lull, and finally Maria said quietly that it seemed like we had just started and now we only had a short time left. I agreed, saying that we had come such a long way in such a short time and it's hard to make peace with only five more meetings. Keika responded that she was upset, but if I had taken the other group first, she would expect them to finish on time so her group would have a turn. Alice was animated again and informed me I was going to need a bigger room to have a group with "those ho's" because the only way they know how to talk is when they are lying down.

7. Practice Analysis (Individual Transactions)

1. Keika reminded the group that next week was the last time we were going to meet before the holiday and asked if we could have a party during the last half of the meeting. *I agreed that it would be fun and pointed out that today marks the halfway mark for the group.* (1a) *Perhaps they would like to spend some time at the beginning of the next session to take stock and decide the focus for the remaining meetings.* (1b)

A. *What is your present understanding of what the group members are trying to communicate to you (in the members' voices)?*

KEIKA'S VOICE: "I want to communicate the good feelings and sense of closeness that are evolving in the group. I am invested in what we talk about—that is why I am suggesting only a half hour be devoted to the party."

GROUP'S VOICE: "We love the idea of celebrating our closeness."

B. *What was the purpose or intention behind your response (or silence)?*

My response began as reinforcement of those good feelings and to support the notion of the importance of having fun as well as our work. I was especially pleased at the moment that this session had been a landmark point where a deeper level of intimacy and mutual aid had been achieved. I found myself thinking that it was such a shame to have to terminate at this point in the group's life. My thinking found its way into my tongue. I cannot say that it was a deliberate intervention.

C. *How did the group members experience and evaluate your intervention(s) (in the members' voices)?*

> GROUP: "What is she talking about—this group is not ending in a few weeks. Something must be wrong. Her timing sucks—we are planning a party, and she drops a bomb."

D. *If your interventions were inconsistent with the members' messages and/or your intentions, examine what interfered with your ability to respond to the members' messages (in your voice).*

Although the halfway point is theoretically an optimal time to take stock and to remind members that our time together is precious, my abrupt "doorknob" comment was a reflection of my own separation anxiety. I had a sinking feeling—it suddenly hit me how much I was going to miss these kids and that this wonderful group was going to have to end.

E. *Based on what you know, how would you respond differently? (Be specific.)*

If I could do this intervention over, I would raise termination at the beginning of the meeting rather than at the end. "I know this is going to be hard to talk about and part of me would prefer not to have to think about it, but we do need to talk about that after today's meeting, we only have five meetings left." This puts it out in a real way and invites work.

2. Within a few seconds, the entire ambiance completely changed. Although a few registered no visible reactions, most seemed puzzled as they glanced around the room. Alice, Helen, and Maria, who were seldom at a loss for words, looked absolutely thunderstruck. All were quiet. *I waited several minutes, (2a) and then observed that they were awfully quiet all of a sudden, and I was wondering if my comment about having only five more sessions had taken them off-guard. (2b)*

A. *What is your present understanding of what the group members are trying to communicate to you (in the members' voices)?*

> GROUP: "What is she talking about? The group has a long time to go. We can't be half over. She must be leaving us—another adult abandoning us."

B. *What was the purpose or intention behind your response (or silence)?*

I let the silence linger for a while because I sensed that they were experiencing the same anxiety that I had felt a few seconds earlier. However, they were stunned. I wanted to verbalize that my observation took them off-guard. I wanted to reach inside the silence and check out my perceptions.

C. *How did the group members experience and evaluate your intervention(s) (in the members' voices)?*

> GROUP: "I am having trouble breathing. She just took my breath away. Why is she being so quiet, and what is she talking about?"

D. *If your interventions were inconsistent with the members' messages and/or your intentions, examine what interfered with your ability to respond to the members' messages (in your voice).*
Same as previous one.

E. *Based on what you know, how would you respond differently? (Be specific)*
I would skip the silence—it only made them more anxious.

3. The silence just got louder. For a few minutes, I had the sinking feeling that the session might end in silence. Finally, Ivory found her voice and demanded to know why I was cutting the group short when they hadn't done anything "nasty." Then she looked more closely at me and reminded me that I had said I was going to be here until May, so what was the problem? Matilda chirped in a "told you so" tone of voice that I just did not like them—that was the problem. I became flustered and defensive. *I mentioned that in individual interviews and at the first meeting, I had emphasized the group would meet for twelve weeks.* (3)

A. *What is your present understanding of what the group members are trying to communicate to you (in the members' voices)?*

INEZ: "I am shocked and furious. I love Angela. There must be some explanation."

GROUP: "Did we do something wrong? Does she not care about us? Is it beyond her control?"

B. *What was the purpose or intention behind your response (or silence)?*
I wanted to provide important information.

C. *How did the group members experience and evaluate your intervention(s) (in the members' voices)?*

GROUP: "What is it—why are you leaving us—we have to find out! You're withholding from us."

D. *If your interventions were inconsistent with the members' messages and/or your intentions, examine what interfered with your ability to respond to the members' messages (in your voice).*
I became defensive—the information was to defend myself, and not to help them.

E. *Based on what you know, how would you respond differently? (Be specific.)*
I would remind them, but in a much softer and less defensive manner.

4. Inez shook her head and corrected her by pointing out that it had been changed to twelve weeks because too many people signed up. Ivory indignantly declared this was the first she had heard of it. But even if that was the case, why couldn't I just have a second group for the other class? *I explained that if they remembered, I had informed them right away that my schedule did not allow me to have two groups, and the agency could not assign another worker.* (4)

A. *What is your present understanding of what the group members are trying to communicate to you (in the members' voices)?*

INEZ: "I got to take some heat off Angela. I hope they don't get mad at me. But I do remember our conversations."

IVORY: "I have no recollection of what she says—we are supposed to be meeting the entire school year."

> GROUP: "We are very upset—yeah, we remember the
>   conversations, but so what? We love this group."

B. *What was the purpose or intention behind your response (or silence)?*
Just feeling defensive and defending myself.

C. *How did the group members experience and evaluate your intervention(s) (in the members' voices)?*

> GROUP: "Oh—oh—she is getting mad. She sounds like a
>   lawyer. What happened to Angela? She is not
>   connected to us."

D. *If your interventions were inconsistent with the members' messages and/or your intentions, examine what interfered with your ability to respond to the members' messages (in your voice).*
Help! I am drowning in guilt. I feel like a child again, having to defend myself. I didn't lie—please love me. A flash of anger for being wronged too often follows the guilt. It is happening at the moment. I am missing the point. It is irrelevant who said what to whom in what time frame. We are all very upset that the group will be ending in five weeks, and we need to take that reality in. I need to be seen as "a good guy." I hurt to the core when I feel falsely accused—again, like a little child being scolded by my parents. I really love these kids, and to be perceived as insensitive, uncaring, hard-nosed—it hurts—I feel raw.

E. *Based on what you know, how would you respond differently? (Be specific.)*
I would say, "I know you feel that I am backing out, and I feel terrible about this."

5. Dramatically, Ivory looked around the group and said in exaggerated disbelief that "I just want to get this straight . . . you are going to give our group to those bimbos?" I responded this was very hard for all of us. (5)

A. *What is your present understanding of what the group members are trying to communicate to you (in the members' voices)?*

> IVORY: "You are picking those other kids over us—you gotta
>   be kidding."
> GROUP: "It is not fair!"

B. *What was the purpose or intention behind your response (or silence)?*
To verbalize the common feeling!

C. *How did the group members experience and evaluate your intervention(s) (in the members' voices)?*

> GROUP: "She finally seems interested in what we are feeling."
> IVORY: "That's exactly what I am feeling—just don't give me
>   any bullshit excuses."

D. *If your interventions were inconsistent with the members' messages and/or your intentions, examine what interfered with your ability to respond to the members' messages (in your voice).*
I feel I am getting closer and beginning to reverse my self-defensiveness. I am beginning to relax.

E. *Based on what you know, how would you respond differently? (Be specific)*
I would say, "We all are upset that the group will be ending in five weeks— what are the other members' reactions?"

8. Present Status of Life Stressor

In the analyzed incident, the group and I experienced all the phases of termination. We avoided and denied the ending, and expressed anger and sadness, and the group began trying it out for size by envisioning themselves being back in Spanish class. In the next meeting, about half the girls were absent from school. The group decided just to eat their refreshment and have no discussions because of the absent members. In the first meeting after the Christmas holidays, all the members were present and got into a discussion of family members who had left them in their lives. The discussion was poignant in itself and even more so related to the group's termination. A few members insightfully shared how they learned to leave people first before they left them so that they would not be hurt. I connected this insight to the poor attendance at the prior meeting. While they were not ready for that connection, they began to reminisce about the group and recount their favorite expressions and uses of speech coming from me (e.g., "I am going to bite your nose"). They were giving me a beautiful gift, and I appreciatively accepted. When they finished, I offered my list of favorites of their expressions. We roared with laughter and tears in our eyes.

9. Next Helping Steps

I would like to prepare members for life after the group. I plan to use the third-to-last meeting to help them to meet together without me. These kids can really help each other. In the next-to-last meeting, I would like, for at least part of the meeting, for them to meet as if I were not there. And then for us to evaluate what was done well, could be done better, and so on. I am unsure about the last meeting—will involve the group in deciding.

10. Theoretical Concepts and Research Findings That Support and/ or Challenge Practice Analyses and Next Helping Steps

The conceptual and empirical readings related to termination. . . .

2. Summarized Sample Critical Incident (Analysis of *Total Incident*)

Student/Worker Name: Alicia Parker
Agency: Metropolitan Emergency Psychiatric Services
Time Period: Twelve weeks
Check Modality:
Individual _X_ Family ____ Group ____ Community ____ Organization ____
Professional Helping Area (Indicate Focus):
Initial Phase ____; Life Transitional Stressor _X_; Environmental Stressor
____; Interpersonal Stressor (Family ____, Group ____, or Client:Worker ____);
Ending Phase ____.

1. Case Summary

Maria, a nine-year-old Latina girl, temporarily lives with her great-aunt, great-uncle, and eighteen- and five-year-old third cousins in an urban area. She is learning disabled and has repeated the second grade twice. Maria moved from Mississippi about four months ago, where she lived with her biological mother and a younger brother and sister. Her father was in jail for grand larceny. Maria and her great-aunt reported that she was moved because her mother could not take care of her anymore. The great-aunt received temporary custody.

2. Agency Context

The agency is Metropolitan Emergency Psychiatric Services (EMPS). The agency serves children 4–18 years of age. EMPS responds to calls for children and adolescents who have suicidal or homicidal ideation or other crises. Once an assessment has been completed, the agency provides the youngster and her or his family with in-home counseling. The agency was contacted by Maria's school due to her repeated outbursts and suspensions. She frequently initiated verbal and physical fights with peers and teachers. Maria also disclosed to the school social worker that she wished she were dead.

3. Level of Mutuality in Focus and Role Expectations

I met with Maria and her great-aunt at the school. I explained that I was a social work intern working in an agency that worked with children and adolescents who were not feeling good about themselves and were overwhelmed with tough life experiences and their current situations. As a way of expressing that hurt, these kids wound up hurting themselves and others. I further explained that the school contacted me because Maria had had many verbal and physical fights with other kids and teachers and let it be known that she wished that she were dead. I explained to both that I did not work for the school and that I would not be informing them about what we had talked about. I was here to help Maria and her great-aunt with their pain and not to represent the school. I wanted them to know that they could refuse my offer of service—that it was not required and that it was their choice. If they were interested, we could meet for six to twelve weeks either at the school or at their home. I commented on how sad Maria looked and asked for her reactions to what I stated. Maria agreed that she was sad, angry, and alone—that no one listened to her and that she needed someone to talk with. I said that we could work together to understand how she felt and how it was connected to her life circumstances, like living away from her mother, brother, and sister. She agreed to meet with me. I also offered to meet with her great-aunt about her concerns, and she also accepted.

4. Define Life Stressor

Maria is dealing with simultaneous and cumulative life transitions. First, she recently moved from Mississippi. During this move, she was separated from her mother, siblings, friends, and familiar physical environments (home, neighborhoods, and school). At the same time, she moved into a new neighborhood, school, and house, and was living with various family members she had not even met in the past. She lives in a high-crime neighborhood that is full of violence. This prevents her from being allowed to go outside to play (she played outside every day in Mississippi).

5. Level of Fit Between Personal Strengths and Limitations and Environmental Resources and Gaps

Maria and her great-aunt accepted services offered by EMPS and have continued to be highly motivated and involved in the services. This is a major strength. For example, Maria consistently implements tasks agreed on (such as talking to a teacher about a concern or reaching out to a peer). The great-aunt is open to my suggestions and actively involved in family counseling. Maria has made friends, and they have become part of a new support system. In reaching out to her father's family, they also have been responsive and have expressed their love. Maria has found great comfort in her extended family and new friends. I am very pleased with this highly improved level of fit. What strains the fit is that Maria has pronounced learning difficulties, and it will be difficult to sustain her learning motivation as well as the school's commitment to her. Her mother remains verbally abusive and is a negative force in Maria's life. Maria's father being in jail also represents a significant gap in her life. There are frequent battles between the two families, and Maria feels the pressure to choose which family she loves more. Maria's neighborhood is also an important constraint. These limitations and resource gaps strain the current level of fit that has been achieved. It clearly indicates that without an outside agency, Maria is at serious risk. I am currently working on a referral to a community agency.

6. Critical Incident

Context for incident: Over a period of five weeks and biweekly meetings leading to this critical incident, Maria and I have been discussing all the changes that have occurred in her life. We traced the progression and course of her sadness and feelings that her mother did not love her anymore, culminating in her being sent away to be "someone else's problem." She pieced together all the people in her life and how they all saw her as a problem. She felt "ugly and stupid." Her mother repeatedly told her that she was not as cute as her younger sister. I am presenting an incident from our sixth meeting. She had been suspended that day from school for swearing at the teacher. As punishment, her great-aunt stated that she could not go to her paternal grandparents' house for the weekend, as had been planned. Maria is extremely angry and crying.

MARIA: I hate her (great-aunt). She never lets me do anything (angry and crying).

WORKER: *(Holding her hands) I feel really badly for you* (1a)—*you feel like you have no control over your own life.* (1b)

MARIA: Yeah . . . how can she keep me from my dad's family? It's like she wants to find every reason to keep me away.

WORKER: *You must feel like you are stuck in the middle sometimes.* (2a) *Your dad's family is important to you.* (2b)

MARIA: (Sobbing) I am going to have to explain why I can't see them and they'll get mad, and I can't even explain because (screaming) SHE WON'T LET ME TALK TO THEM ON THE PHONE!!!

WORKER: *I understand how upset and angry you are.* (3a) *They mean a lot to you, and you feel their support and you don't want to lose them.* (3b)

MARIA: (Crying) Well . . . yes! What difference does it make what I do? I get in trouble for everything. She is trying to have my dad's family push me away too.

WORKER: *I understand your worrying about losing them. You have experienced many losses—much too much for someone your age.* (4)

MARIA: (Crying) I'm not perfect.

WORKER: *Are you afraid that if people do not feel you are perfect, they will not care about you?* (5)

MARIA: (Crying) Yes. They want me to be perfect, or else.

WORKER: *You don't have to be perfect for me.* (6a) *I care about you and understand that you are living in a lot of pain right now.* (6b)

MARIA: It's a mess. I have no one. Mom didn't want me (starts crying again).

WORKER: *I can see that you feel no one cares about you. You feel that there are many people swirling around you, yet no one is paying attention to you.* (7)

MARIA: (Crying and yelling) THAT'S BECAUSE THEY DON'T CARE!!! Look at your face—I can tell you feel sorry for me, like I'm broken.

WORKER: *I am concerned about you, but I do know that you are strong and a survivor and that you can get through this.* (8)

MARIA: I can't even go outside. I can't go anywhere. I can't do anything, like I'm in prison.

WORKER: *Do you think if your Dad were around, things would be different?* (9)

MARIA: Yeah . . . then I could stay with him and my grandparents. It would be better. Now I have to sit here all weekend. I can't even call my mother until I'm off punishment.

WORKER: *How would your dad make things different?* (10)
MARIA: He never would be so mad at me all the time. He wouldn't
            expect me to be perfect 'cause he isn't, 'cause he is in jail.
WORKER: *You want to live in a place where you felt loved and people paid*
            attention to the good parts of you too. (11)
MARIA: Yeah, I can be good sometimes.
WORKER: *I know you can—that is the part I mostly see.* (12)

7. Practice Analysis (Total Incident)

A. *What is your present understanding of what the client is trying to communicate to*
   you (in the client's voice)?
Maria is saying to me, "No one cares about me. Even my own mother doesn't
care about me. Why should anyone else care about me, including you? Why
should I care about myself? My great-aunt wants to control me—not love me. I
am trapped and I HAVE NO CONTROL OVER MY LIFE."
B. *What was the purpose or intention behind your response (or silences)?*
I wanted to help Maria to verbalize her underlying feelings and to legitimize her
pain. I also wanted her to reflect on the meaning of her experiences.
C. *How did the client experience and evaluate your interventions (in the client's*
   voice)?

MARIA: "The worker is mostly connected with my feelings of
            anger, loss of control, and hopelessness. She gets how I
            am feeling, but she doesn't understand the depth of my
            pain. She could have conveyed a greater empathy for
            my despair. She gives me some glib reassurance rather
            than deal with the part of me that feels like a broken
            doll, hopeless, helpless, and trapped. Why is she talking
            so much about my dad?"

D. *If your interventions were inconsistent with the client's messages and/or your*
   intentions, examine what interfered with your ability to respond to the client's
   message (in your voice).
Although many of my interventions were connected to the client, when I place
myself back into the moment I remember feeling some disappointment with
Maria for getting suspended. We had worked very hard, and she had been showing marked improvement in school. I am struggling not to have my disappointment affect my interventions. On the one hand, I realize that I should not feel
that Maria let me down, yet on the other hand, there is part of me that feels let
down. I am struggling with my narcissism—that the school staff will see the
suspension as a reflection of my practice. I am also struggling with much anger
at Maria's great-aunt. Denying her contact with both her dad's family and her
mother seems overly punitive. Maria's anger and resentment became my anger
and resentment. I am overwhelmed by the chaos in Maria's life. I totally miss
her feelings of being broken in transaction #8. I know the feeling of feeling
unloved, the despair of feeling that there must be something wrong with me—I
know that feeling much too well.
E. Based on what you know, how would you respond differently? (Be specific.)
Based on getting closer to my experiences at the moment, I would have shared

that as a child I too felt a similar despair. She read my face as one of pity for her—it was pity for myself. I needed to be much more real with Maria. I am fighting against myself—so worried about my own feeling spilling into the work that I remove them all and keep a distance from Maria. In transaction #8, I could have said, "I too had trouble with my mom when I was your age—I know how hopeless life can feel without a mother's love and support. But I made it, and I want to help you make it." That is much closer than telling her that she is strong and a survivor when she feels so weak and victimized.

8. Present Status of Life Stressor

In relation to the life transitional stressors, I have helped Maria to mourn, mourn some more, and even mourn some more. Over time, the festering wound began to be less raw and heal a little. While working on her losses, we also worked hard on improving Maria's relationship with her great-aunt. Maria and I worked on it, the great-aunt and I worked on it, and all three of us worked on it. Slowly, the great-aunt is becoming the stable life force Maria never had. The great-aunt has learned to provide love and support alongside the discipline and consequences. When I praised the great-aunt's efforts, she responded, "It's a Latin thing—love, support, and lots of family." And Maria has responded extremely well to the great-aunt's support and involvement of other family members.

Maria also suffered from being labeled as a "troublemaker" in school. Over the years she internalized the label. I worked with her teachers and administrators to see her differently, as a child hungry—starved—for love, support, and praise. Slowly, the transactions between Maria and school personnel began to change. Currently, she is being tested for a clear picture of her learning disabilities and will obtain additional learning services. Maria and I also worked on getting her connected in the community. She loves to play baseball, and I got her connected to a girls' Little League team. She turns out to be a very good player, and her coach has been very supportive and attentive. From this experience, she has begun to make new friends.

9. Next Helping Steps

Termination and referral will be the focus of my future work. . . .

10. Theoretical Concepts and Research Findings That Support and/ or Challenge Practice Analyses and Next Helping Steps

The current research on abandonment trauma . . .

NOTES

1. Social Work Practice and Its Historical Traditions

1. American historian Richard Hofstadter (1948) formulated the term "social Darwinism" to describe the nineteenth- and twentieth-century philosophy of "survival of the fittest" developed by Herbert Spencer (1851). The theories of evolution were applied to nations competing for survival in a competitive and hostile world.

2. I am indebted to Professor Nancy Humphreys for this insight.

3. The settlement leaders were the first to understand the importance of community geography. Their maps and surveys incorporated data on the geographic features of the community. Only recently is geography being included in social planning through the advent of geographic information systems.

4. Jane Addams was also a founding leader of the American Recreation Association, the Women's International for Peace and Freedom, and the League of Women Voters.

5. Carlton-LaNey (1999) suggests that the mutual aid tradition was perfected during the enslavement of African Americans.

6. Mexico sold the Southwest Territory to the United States for $15 million.

7. The country's long-standing racism was ever so evident when, after Japan attacked Pearl Harbor in World War II, many Japanese citizens were sent to internment camps at the very same time that whites marched in support of Germany in the Yorkville neighborhood of New York.

8. Flexner was a physician who had recently completed an assessment of the professional status of the medical profession, which he judged to be high. NCCC leaders most likely expected Flexner to pronounce that social work was also a profession.

9. Reynolds struggled to combine Marx and Freud's theories. She argued that she was a Marxist-psychoanalyst.

10. "The punishment, stigmatization, and regulation of the lives of single women are especially true in the case of adolescent women who get pregnant and choose to parent children, especially those who are of color. These policies constitute a form of

not-so-latent racism. Since it is no longer acceptable in polite society to be openly racist and critical, it is nevertheless quite possible to discriminate and stigmatize those on welfare, which everyone (mistakenly) 'knows are mostly black'" (personal communication from Professor Nancy Humphreys, 2006).

11. My friend and colleague, Professor Lawrence Shulman, has had similar experiences in his classrooms, workshops, seminars, and consultations.

2. The Ecological Perspective

1. We thank Professor Susan Kemp for her suggestion of a nonevent or a thwarted event as a life stressor.

2. The ecological view of resilience does not accept the Horatio Alger myth: the mistaken and propagandistic view that anyone can succeed in our society if he or she simply works hard.

3. The Life Model of Social Work Practice: An Overview

1. For the NASW's *Code of Ethics* (1999), see http://www.socialworkers.org/pubs/code/code.asp; and for the Canadian Association of Social Workers' *Code of Ethics and Guidelines for Ethical Practice* (2005), see http://www.casw-acts.ca. Also see the International Federation of Social Workers' *Ethics in Social Work Statement of Principles*, http://www.ifsw.org/en/p38000252.html, and its *Universal Declaration of Human Rights*, http:/www.unchr.ch.udhr/lang/eng.htm. The Association for the Advancement of Social work with Groups (2006) Standards for the Practice of Social Work with Groups is available in English and Spanish at http://www.aaswg.org/Standards/standards.htm.

2. The author expresses appreciation to Professor Lawrence Shulman for this practice illustration.

3. The author expresses appreciation to Professor Lawrence Shulman for this practice illustration.

4. This discussion is drawn from Gitterman (2003b).

4. Assessment, Practice Monitoring, and Practice Evaluation

1. I wish to acknowledge the contributions of Professor William Schwartz to the formulation of these ideas.

2. I wish to acknowledge the contributions of Professor William Schwartz in the early development of these instruments.

3. Feminists have extended the constructivist tradition by embracing ideologically oriented application—*critical theory and research*. The approach focuses research on oppression by the powerful over those without power. The desired outcomes of the research are social criticism and social justice. The critical researchers reject the notion of a disinterested science, emphasizing rather the connection between people and subjective meanings of social contexts (Brown & Stega, 2005; Morris, 2006).

4. I wish to express my appreciation to Professor Martha Dore for sharing her ideas and materials related to goal attainment scaling.

5. Preparation: Settings, Modalities, Methods, and Skills

1. Discussion about forming a group is adapted from the author's prior publications (Gitterman, 1982, 2005).

6. Beginnings: Settings, Modalities, Methods, and Skills

1. For an excellent discussion of motivational interviewing, the process of change, and the helping process, see Hanson and El-Bassel (2004).

2. Rarely do human beings progress through linear, sequential stages. We prefer the concepts of phases, which suggest overlap and multidirectionality. People move in spiral form, back and forth, between the phases of change rather than in a linear progression.

7. Helping Individuals, Families, and Groups with Stressful Life Transitions and Traumatic Events

1. This practice illustration and discussion are presented in and adapted from Gitterman (2004).

10. Helping with Dysfunctional Group Processes

1. Recent advances in measurement have made it possible to assess engagement in groups. Macgowan developed the Group Engagement Measure (GEM) (Macgowan, 2003; Macgowan & Newman, 2005).

2. The discussion and illustration is drawn from Gitterman (1989b).

3. The discussion and illustration is drawn from Gitterman (1991).

4. The discussion and illustration is drawn from Gitterman (1991).

11. Reducing Interpersonal Stress Between Worker and Client

1. This discussion draws from Gitterman (1983, 1989a).

2. This illness affects the white blood cell count of an individual, and requires several blood transfusions as well as numerous rounds of chemotherapy.

13. Influencing Community and Neighborhood Life

1. Although started informally on a community level, many self-help groups have developed into large, formalized, powerful, national advocacy or research organizations. The question for groups that develop into formal organizations is how to simultaneously meet the needs of new members for support and mutual aid and of long-term members for services such as fundraising, research, and advocacy. Some organizations try to continue informal mutual aid at the local level.

2. Developmental disabilities, as defined by the Developmental Disabilities Assistance and Bill of Rights Act of 1990 (P.L. 101-496), are severe, chronic conditions that are attributable to mental or physical impairments or a combination of both, are manifested before age twenty-two, are likely to continue indefinitely, result in substantial limitations in three or more major activity areas (self-care, receptive and expressive language, learning, mobility, self-direction, capacity for independent living, and economic self-sufficiency), and require a combination and sequence of special, interdisciplinary, or generic care, treatment, or other services that are of extended or lifelong duration and are individually planned and coordinated (Freedman, 1995).

14. Influencing the Practitioner's Organization

1. We continue to be grateful to the late Dean Emeritus George Brager and Dean Emeritus Stephan Holloway for referring us to the literature and generously sharing their ideas while we wrote the first edition of this work (Germain & Gitterman, 1980).

2. This illustration and discussion is drawn from Gitterman and Miller (1989).

15. Influencing Legislation, Regulations, and Electoral Politics

1. In describing the legislative process and the relationship between the legislative and executive branches, a typical legislative process is being described. Please note that states vary in their legislative processes; therefore, the social worker must research the particular state's processes.

2. Professor Nancy Humphreys familiarized the author with an old saying: "There are two things you do not want to see made—sausage and legislation."

3. This section draws in part on Albert (1983).

REFERENCES

Abbott, D. A., Berry, M., & Meredith, W. H. (1990). Religious beliefs and practice: A potential asset in helping families. *Family Relations, 39*(4), 443–448.

Abraham, K., & Weiler, P. (1994). Enterprise medical liability and the evolution of the American health care system. *Harvard Law Review, 108,* 381–436.

Abramowitz, M. (2005). The largely untold story of welfare reform and human services. *Social Work, 50*(2), 175–186.

Abramson, M. (1985). The autonomy-paternalism dilemma in social work practice. *Social Casework, 66*(7), 387–393.

Abramson, M. (1989). Autonomy vs. paternalistic beneficence: Practice strategies. *Social Casework, 70*(2), 101–105.

Abramson, M. (1996). Reflections on knowing oneself ethically: Toward a working framework for social work practice. *Families in Society, 77*(4), 195–202.

Adams, R. G., & Blieszner, R. (1993). Resources for friendship interventions. *Journal of Sociology and Social Welfare, 28*(4), 159–175.

Addams, J. (1910). *Twenty years at Hull House.* New York: Macmillan.

Addams, J. (1930). *The second twenty years at Hull House.* New York: Macmillan.

Alaggia, R., & Kirshenbaum, S. (2005). Speaking the unspeakable: Examining the impact of family dynamics on child sexual abuse disclosures. *Families in Society, 86*(2), 227–234.

Albert, R. (1983). Social work advocacy in the regulatory process. *Social Casework, 64*(10), 473–481.

Albert, V. (2000). Reducing welfare benefits: Consequences for adequacy of and eligibility for benefits. *Social Work, 45*(4), 300–311.

Alcabes, A., & Jones, J. (1985). Structural determinants of "clienthood." *Social Work, 30*(1), 49–53.

Almack, K. (2005). Children born within lesbian-parent families. *Sexualities, 8*(2), 239–254.

Altman, I. (1975). *Environment and social behavior.* Monterey, CA: Brooks/Cole.

Altman, L. K. (2002). When peer review produces unsound science. *New York Times*, January 11, pp. 1, 12.

American Cancer Society. (2007). *Cancer facts & figures, 2007*. Atlanta, GA: Author.

American Psychiatric Association (APA). (1994). *Diagnostic and statistical manual of mental disorders* (4th ed.). Washington, DC: Author.

Anderson, R., Kochanek, K., & Murphy, S. (1998). Report of final mortality statistics, 1995. *Monthly Vital Statistics Report, 45*(11, Suppl. 2) (August).

Anderson, S. G. (2001). Welfare recipient views about caseworker performance: Lessons for developing TANF case management practices. *Families in Society, 82*(2), 165–174.

Andrews, H. B. (2000). The myth of the scientist-practitioner: A reply to R. King (1998) and N. King and Ollendick (1998). *Australian Psychologist, 35*(1), 60–63.

Andrews, J., & Reisch, M. (1997). The legacy of McCarthyism on social group work: An historical analysis. *Journal of Sociology & Social Welfare, 24*(3), 211–235.

Anthony, W. A., Cohen, M., Farkas, M., & Cohen, B. F. (2000). Clinical care update: The chronically mentally ill: Case management—more than a response to a dysfunctional system. *Community Mental Health Journal, 36*(1), 97–106.

Antognoli-Toland, P. L. (2001). Parent–child relationship, family structure, and loneliness among adolescents. *Adolescent & Family Health, 2*(1), 20–26.

Antsey, M. (1982). Scapegoating in groups: Some theoretical perspectives and case record of intervention. *Social Work with Groups, 5*(3), 51–63.

Arkin, N. (1999). Culturally sensitive student supervision: Difficulties and challenges. *The Clinical Supervisor, 18*(2), 1–16.

Armelius, K., & Armelius, B. (2000). Group personality, task and group culture. In M. Pines (Ed.), *Bion and group psychotherapy* (pp. 255–273). Philadelphia: Jessica Kingsley.

Armstrong, B. (2001). Adolescent pregnancy. In A. Gitterman (Ed.), *Handbook of social work practice with vulnerable and resilient populations* (2nd ed., pp. 305–341). New York: Columbia University Press.

Arvay, M. J. (2002). Putting the heart back into constructivist research. In J. D. Raskin & S. K. Bridges (Eds.), *Exploring constructivist psychology* (pp. 201–224). New York: Pace University Press.

Association for the Advancement of Social Work with Groups, an International Professional Organization, Inc. (2006). *Standards for social work practice with groups, second edition*. Retrieved March 21, 2007, from http://www.aaswg.org/Standards/standards.htm.

Atkinson, D. R., Morton, G., & Sue, D. W. (1998). *Counseling American minorities* (5th ed.). Boston: McGraw-Hill.

Auslander, G., Dobrof, J., & Epstein, I. (2001). Comparing social work's role in renal dialysis in Israel and the United States: The practice-based research potential of available clinical information. *Social Work in Health Care, 33*(3/4), 129–151.

Auslander, G., & Levin, H. (1987). The parameters of network intervention: A social work application. *Social Service Review, 61*(June), 305–318.

Austin, A. M., Macgowan, M., & Wagner, E. F. (2005). Effective family-based interventions for adolescents with substance use problems: A systematic review. *Research on Social Work Practice, 15*(2), 67–83.

Austin, D. M. (2000). Social work and social welfare administration: A historical perspective. In R. Patti (Ed.), *The handbook of social welfare movement* (pp. 27–54). Thousand Oaks, CA: Sage.

Austin, M. J., & Prince, J. (2003). The implications of managed care and welfare reform for the integration of health and welfare services. *Journal of Health and Social Policy, 18*(2), 1–19.

Bandler, B. (1963). The concept of ego-supportive psychotherapy. In H. Parad & R. Miller (Eds.), *Ego-oriented casework: Problems and perspectives* (pp. 27–44). New York: Family Service Association of America.

Barlett, P. F. (Ed.). (2005). *Urban place: Reconnecting with the natural world.* Cambridge, MA: MIT Press.

Barlow, D., & Hersen, M. (1973). Single case experimental designs: Uses in applied clinical research. *Archives of General Psychiatry, 29*(3), 319–325.

Barnard, C. P. (1994). Resiliency: Shift in our perception? *American Journal of Family Therapy, 22*(2), 15–144.

Bartlett, H. M. (1970). *The common base of social work practice.* Washington, DC: National Association of Social Workers.

Basic Behavioral Task Force of the National Advisory Mental Health Council. (1996). Basic behavioral science research for mental health: Vulnerability and resilience. *American Psychologist, 51*(1), 22–28.

Bassett, J. D., & Johnson, J. A. (2004). The role of clinical consultation in child protection investigations. *Smith College Studies in Social Work, 74*(3), 489–504.

Baum, N. (2005). Correlates of clients' emotional and behavioral responses to treatment termination. *Clinical Social Work Journal, 33*(3), 309–326.

Baures, M. (1994). *Undaunted spirits: Portraits of recovery from trauma.* Philadelphia: Charles Press.

Becket, J. O., & Dungee-Anderson, D. (1996). A framework for agency-based multicultural training and supervision. *Journal of Multicultural Social Work, 4*(4), 27–48.

Bell, T. R., Sr., & Bell, J. L. (1999). Help-seeking in the black church: An important connection for social work to make. *Social Work and Christianity, 26*(10), 144–154.

Bembry, J. X., & Ericson, C. (1999). Therapeutic termination with the early adolescent who has experienced multiple losses. *Child & Adolescent Social Work Journal, 16*(3), 177–189.

Ben-Ari, A. T. (2002). Dimensions and predictions of professional involvement in self-help groups: A view from within. *Health and Social Work, 27*(2), 95–103.

Bent-Goodley, T. (2001). Ida B. Wells-Barnett: An uncompromising style. In I. B. Carlton-LaNey (Ed.), *African American leadership* (pp. 87–98). Washington, DC: National Association of Social Workers.

Benway, C. B., Hamrin, V., & McMahon, T. J. (2003). Initial appointment nonattendance in child and family mental health clinics. *American Journal of Orthopsychiatry, 73,* 419–428.

Berger, R. (2001). Gay stepfamilies: A triple-stigmatized group. In J. M. Lehmann (Ed.), *The gay & lesbian marriage & family reader: Analysis of problems and prospects for the 21st century* (pp. 171–194). Lincoln, NE: Gordian Knot.

Bergeron, L. R., & Gray, B. (2003). Ethical dilemmas of reporting suspected elder abuse. *Social Work, 48*(1), 96–105.

Berkman, C., & Zinberg, G. (1997). Homophobia and heterosexism in social workers. *Social Work, 42*(4), 319–332.

Berkman, L. F. (2000). Social support, social networks, social cohesion and health. *Social Work in Health Care, 31*(2), 3–14.

Berlin, R., & Davis, R. (1989). Children from alcoholic families: Vulnerability and resilience. In T. F. Dugan & R. Coles (Eds.), *The child in our times: Studies in the development of resiliency* (pp. 81–105). New York: Brunner/Mazel.

Berman-Rossi, T. (1992). Empowering groups through understanding stages of group development. *Social Work with Groups, 15*(2/3), 239–255.

Berman-Rossi, T. (1993). The tasks and skills of the social worker across stages of group development. *Social Work with Groups, 16*(1/2), 69–92.

Berman-Rossi, T. (2001). Older persons in need of long-term care. In A. Gitterman (Ed.), *Handbook of social work practice with vulnerable and resilient populations* (2nd ed., pp. 715–768). New York: Columbia University Press.

Berman-Rossi, T. (2005). The fight against hopelessness and despair: Institutionalized aged. In A. Gitterman & L. Shulman (Eds.), *Mutual aid groups, vulnerable and resilient populations, and the life cycle* (3rd ed., pp. 493–535). New York: Columbia University Press.

Berman-Rossi, T., & Miller, I. (1994). African-Americans and the settlements during the late nineteenth and early twentieth centuries. *Social Work with Groups, 17*(3), 77–95.

Berman-Rossi, T., & Rossi, P. (1990). Confidentiality and informed consent in school social work. *Social Work in Education, 26*(2), 195–207.

Berry, M. C. (1956). Current concepts in community organization. In National Conference on Social Welfare, *Group work and community organization*. Chicago: University of Chicago Press.

Besthorn, F. H. (2002). Natural environment and the practice of psychotherapy. *Annals of the American Psychotherapy Association, 5*(5), 19–20.

Besthorn, F. H., & McMillen, D. P. (2002). The oppression of women and nature: Ecofeminism as a framework for an expanded ecological social work. *Families in Society, 83*(3), 221–232.

Bidart, C., & Degenne, A. (2005). Introduction: The dynamics of personal networks. *Social Networks, 27*(4), 283–287.

Biegel, D. E., Tracy, E. M., & Corvo, K. N. (1994). Strengthening social networks: Intervention strategies for mental health case managers. *Health and Social Work, 19*(3), 206–216.

Bigby, C., Ozanne, E., & Gordon, M. (2002). Facilitating transition: Elements of successful case management practice for older parents of adults with intellectual disability. *Journal of Gerontological Social Work, 37*(3/4), 25–43.

Birnbaum, M. L., & Auerbach C. (1994). Group work in graduate social work education: The price of neglect. *Journal of Social Work Education, 30*(3), 325–335.

Birnbaum, M. L., & Wayne, J. (2000). Group work in foundation generalist education: The necessity for curriculum change. *Journal of Social Work Education, 36*(2), 347–356.

Blacher, M. (2005). A response to Heather Fraser "Doing Narrative Research." *Qualitative Social Work, 4*(1), 99–104.

Bloch, J., Weinstein, J., & Seitz, M. (2005). Families journey toward equilibrium: Children with developmental disabilities. In A. Gitterman & L. Shulman (Eds.), *Mutual aid groups, vulnerable and resilient populations, and the life cycle* (3rd ed., pp. 400–422). New York: Columbia University Press.

Blythe, B., & Tripodi, T. (1989). *Measurement in direct practice*. Newbury Park, CA: Sage.

Boehm, W. (1959). *Objectives for the social work curriculum of the future* (Vol. 1). New York: Council on Social Work Education.

Bogard, M. (1984). Family systems approaches to wife battering: A feminist critique. *American Journal of Orthopsychiatry, 54*(October), 558–568.

Bogdanoff, M., & Elbaum, P. L. (1978). Role lock: Dealing with monopolizers, mistrusters, isolates, helpful Hannahs and other assorted characters in group psychotherapy. *International Journal of Group Psychotherapy, 28*(2), 247–262.

Bond, R. (2005). Group size and conformity. *Group Processes & Intergroup Relations, 8*(4), 331–354.

Bonilla-Santiago, G. (1989). Legislating progress for Hispanic women in New Jersey. *Social Work, 34*(3), 270–272.

Brager, G., & Holloway, S. (1978). *Changing human service organizations: Politics and practice*. New York: Free Press.

Brager, G., & Holloway, S. (1992). Assessing prospects for organizational change. *Administration in Social Work, 16*(3/4), 15–28.

Brager, G., & Specht, H. (1973). *Community organizing*. New York: Columbia University Press.

Brager, G., Specht, H., & Torczyner, J. (1987). *Community organizing.* New York: Columbia University Press.

Breckinridge, S. (1927). *Public welfare administration in the United States.* Chicago: University of Chicago Press.

Breton, M. (1994). On the meaning of empowerment and empowerment-oriented social work practice. *Social Work with Groups, 17*(3), 5–22.

Breton, M. (1998). Empowerment practice in a post-empowerment era. In W. Shera & L. M. Wells (Eds.), *Empowerment practice in social work: Developing richer conceptual foundations* (pp. 201–229). Toronto: Canadian Scholars' Press.

Brewer, P. R., & Wilcox, C. (2005). Trends: Same-sex marriage and civil unions. *Public Opinion Quarterly, 69*(4), 599–616.

Brickel, C. (1986). Pet-facilitated therapies: A review of the literature and clinical implementation considerations. *Clinical Gerontologist, 5*(2), 309–332.

Brogan, M. M., Prochaska, J. O., & Prochaska, J. M. (1999). Predicting termination and continuation status in psychotherapy using the transtheoretical model. *Psychotherapy: Theory, Research, Practice, Training, 36*(2), 105–113.

Bronfenbrenner, U. (1977). Toward an experimental ecology of human development. *American Psychologist, 32*(4), 513–531.

Bronfenbrenner, U. (1995). Developmental ecology through space and time: A future perspective. In P. Moen, G. H. Elder, & K. Luscher (Eds.), *Examining lives in context* (pp. 619–647). Washington, DC: American Psychological Association.

Bronfenbrenner, U. (Ed.). (2005). *Making human beings human.* Thousand Oaks, CA: Sage.

Brooks, F. (2001). Innovative organizing practices: ACORN's campaign in Los Angeles organizing workfare workers. *Journal of Community Practice, 9*(4), 65–85.

Brown, A., & Mistry, T. (1994). Group work with "mixed membership" groups: Issues of race and gender. *Social Work with Groups, 17*(3), 5–21.

Brown, L. B., & Stega, S. (2005). *Research as resistance.* Toronto: Canadian Scholars' Press.

Bruner, J. (1966). *Toward a theory of instruction.* Cambridge, MA: Harvard University Press.

Bulham, H. A. (1985). *Frantz Fanon and the psychology of oppression.* New York: Plenum Press.

Bullis, R. K. (Ed.). (1996). *Spirituality in social work practice.* Philadelphia: Taylor & Francis.

Bullock, K., & McGraw, S. A. (2006). A community capacity-enhancement approach to breast and cervical cancer screening among older women of color. *Health and Social Work, 31*(1), 16–25.

Burke, W. W. (2002). *Organizational change: Theory and practice.* Thousand Oaks, CA: Sage.

Burwell, N. Y. (1995). Shifting the historical lens: Early economic empowerment among African Americans. *Journal of Baccalaureate Social Work, 1*(1), 25–37.

Burwell, N. Y. (2001). Lawrence A. Oxley: Defining state public welfare among African Americans. In I. B. Carlton-LaNey (Ed.), *African American leadership* (pp. 99–110). Washington, DC: National Association of Social Workers.

Bussey, M. & Wise, J. B. (2007). *Trauma transformed.* New York: Columbia University Press.

Cain, D. S., & Combs-Orme, T. (2005). Family structure effects on parenting stress and practices in the African American family. *Journal of Sociology & Social Welfare, 32*(2), 19–40.

Callahan, J., & Turnbull, J. E. (2001). Depression. In A. Gitterman (Ed.), *Handbook of social work practice with vulnerable and resilient populations* (2nd ed., pp. 163–204). New York: Columbia University Press.

Canadian Association of Social Workers. (2005). *Code of ethics and guidelines for ethical practice*. Retrieved October 19, 2007, from http://www.casw-acts.ca.

Canda, E. (2002). The significance of spirituality for resilient response to chronic illness: A qualitative study for adults with cystic fibrosis. In D. Saleebey (Ed.), *The strengths perspective in social work practice* (pp. 63–79). Boston: Allyn & Bacon.

Caplan, T., & Thomas, H. (2004). "If we are all in the same canoe, why are we using different paddles?" The effective use of common themes in diverse group situations. *Social Work with Groups, 27*(1), 53–73.

Capra, F. (1996). *The web of life*. New York: Anchor Books.

Carlassare, E. (1999). Socialist and cultural ecofeminism: Allies in resistance. *Ethics and the Environment, 5*(1), 89–106.

Carlton-LaNey, I. B. (1999). African American social work pioneers' response to need. *Social Work, 44*(4), 311–321.

Carlton-LaNey, I. B. (2001a). George Edmund Haynes and Elizabeth Ross Haynes: Empowerment practice among African Americans social welfare pioneers. In I. B. Carlton-LaNey (Ed.), *African American leadership* (pp. 111–122). Washington, DC: National Association of Social Workers.

Carlton-LaNey, I. B. (2001b). Birdye Henrietta Haynes: A pioneer settlement house worker. In I. B. Carlton-LaNey (Ed.), *African American leadership* (pp. 35–53). Washington, DC: National Association of Social Workers.

Caron, S. L., & Ulin, M. (1997). Closeting and the quality of lesbian relationships. *Families in Society, 78*(4), 413–419.

Carter, G. W. (1958). Practice theory in community organization. *Social Work, 2*(2), 49–57.

Castelli, P., Hart, L. A., & Zasloff, R. L. (2001). Companion cats and the social support system of men with AIDS. *Psychological Reports, 89*(1), 177–187.

Castonguay, L. R., Goldfried, M. R., Wiser, S., Raue, P. J., & Hayes, A. M. (1996). Predicting the effect of cognitive therapy for depression: A study of unique and common factors. *Journal of Consulting and Clinical Psychology, 64*(3), 497–504.

Catlin, P. (1998). Developmental disabilities and horticultural therapy practice. In S. P. Simson & M. C. Straus (Eds.), *Horticulture as therapy: Principles and practice* (pp. 131–156). Binghamton, NY: Food Products Press/Haworth Press.

Chandler, S. K. (2001). E. Franklin Frazier and social work: Unity and conflict. In I. B. Carlton-LaNey (Ed.), *African American leadership* (pp. 189–201). Washington, DC: National Association of Social Workers.

Chang, C. Y., Hays, D. G., & Shoffner, M. F. (2003). A developmental approach for white supervisors working with supervisees of color. *Clinical Supervisor, 22*(2), 121–138.

Christ, G. H., Sormanti, M., & Francoeur, R. B. (2001). Chronic physical illness and disability. In A. Gitterman (Ed.), *Handbook of social work practice with vulnerable and resilient populations* (2nd ed., pp. 124–162). New York: Columbia University Press.

Cingolani, J. (1984). Social conflict perspective on work with involuntary clients. *Social Work, 29*(5), 442–446.

Ciro, D., & Nembhard, M. (2005). Collaborative data-mining in an adolescent mental health service: Clinicians speak of their experiences. In K. Peake, I. Epstein, & D. Medeiros (Eds.), *Clinical and research uses of an adolescent mental health intake questionnaire: What kids need to talk about* (pp. 305–318). Binghamton, NY: Haworth Press.

Claiborne, N., & Fortune, A. (2005). Preparing students for practice in a managed care environment. *Journal of Teaching in Social Work, 25*(3/4), 177–195.

Clayton, S., & Opotow, S. (Eds.). (2003). *Identity and the natural environment: The psychological significance of nature*. Cambridge, MA: MIT Press.

Cleak, H., & Howe, J. L. (2003). Social networks and use of social supports of minority elders in East Harlem. *Social Work in Health Care, 38*(1), 19–38.

Clemans, S. E. (2004). Life changing: The experience of rape-crisis work. *AFFILIA*, *19*(2), 146–159.

Cnaan, R. A., & Boddie, S. C. (2002). Charitable choice and faith-based welfare: A call for social work. *Social Work*, *47*(3), 224–235.

Cohen, B. D., & Schermer, V. I. (2002). On scapegoating in therapy groups: A social constructivist and intersubjective outlook. *International Journal of Group Psychotherapy*, *52*(1), 89–109.

Cohen, J. A. (2003). Managed care and the evolving role of the clinical social worker in mental health. *Social Work*, *48*(1), 34–43.

Cohen, M. (2001). Homeless people. In A. Gitterman (Ed.), *Handbook of social work practice with vulnerable and resilient populations* (2nd ed., pp. 628–650). New York: Columbia University Press.

Cohen, M. B., & Mullender, A. (1999). The personal in the political: Exploring the group work continuum from individual to social change goals. *Social Work with Groups*, *22*(1), 13–31.

Cohen, S., & Horm-Wingerd, D. (1993). Children and the environment: Ecological awareness among preschool children. *Environment and Behavior*, *25*(1), 103–120.

Coleman, D. (1991). Non-verbal cues are easy to misinterpret. *New York Times*, September 17, pp. C1, C9.

Collins, B. G. (1986). Defining feminist social work. *Social Work*, *31*(3), 214–219.

Congress, E. P. (1994). The use of culturgrams to assess and empower culturally diverse families. *Families in Society*, *75*(9), 531–540.

Congress, E. P., & Lyons, B. B. (1992). Cultural differences in health beliefs: Implications for social work practice in health care settings. *Social Work in Health Care*, *17*(3), 81–96.

Connors, G. J., Donovan, D. M., & DiClemente, C. C. (2001). *Substance abuse treatment and the stages of change: Selecting and planning interventions.* New York: Guilford Press.

Cook, S. W. (2001). Mary Church Terrell and her mission: Giving decades of quiet service. In I. B. Carlton-LaNey (Ed.), *African American leadership* (pp. 153–162). Washington, DC: National Association of Social Workers.

Cooley, R. (1998). Wilderness therapy can help troubled adolescents. *International Journal of Wilderness*, *4*(3), 18–20.

Corcoran, J., Stephenson, M., Perryman, D., & Allen, S. (2001). Perceptions and utilization of a police–social work crisis intervention approach to domestic violence. *Families in Society*, *82*(4), 393–398.

Cordero, A. (2004). When family reunification works: Data-mining foster care records. *Families in Society*, *85*(4), 571–580.

Cordero, A., & Epstein, I. (2005). Refining the practice of family reunification: "Mining" successful foster care case records of substance abusing families. In G. Mallon & P. Hess (Eds.), *A handbook of children, youth and family services* (pp. 392–404). New York: Columbia University Press.

Coren, S. (1996). Accidental death and the shift to daylight savings time. *Perceptual and Motor Skills*, *83*(3, Pt. 1), 921–922.

Cotler, I., & Torczyner, J. (1988). *Complainant's reply* (Dossier No. 8606004542--0001-0). Montreal, Quebec: Commission des Droits de la Personne.

Coulmont, B. (2005). Do the rite thing: Religious civil unions in Vermont. *Social Compass*, *52*(2), 225–239.

Coyle, G. L. (1947). *Group experience and democratic values.* New York: Women's Press.

Coyle, G. L. (1948). *Group work with American youth.* New York: Harper & Brothers.

Cusicanqui, M., & Salmon, R. (2004). Seniors, small fry, and song: A group work libretto. In R. Salmon & R. Graziano (Eds.), *Group work and aging: Issues in practice, research, and education* (pp. 189–222). Binghamton, NY: Haworth Press.

Cutler, L. J., Kane, R. A., & Degenholtz, H. B. (2006). Assessing and comparing physical environments for nursing home residents: Using new tools for greater research specificity. *The Gerontologist, 46*(1), 42–51.

Dalrynmple, D. (2003). Professional advocacy as a force for resistance in child welfare. *British Journal of Social Work, 33*(4), 1043–1060.

Dalzell, H. J. (2000). Whispers: The role of family secrets in eating disorders. *Eating Disorders: The Journal of Treatment & Prevention, 8*(1), 43–61.

Dane, B., & Simon, B. (1991). Resident guests: Social workers in host settings. *Social Work, 36*(3), 208–213.

Dane, B. O. (2005). Death of a child. In A. Gitterman (Ed.), *Handbook of social work practice with vulnerable and resilient populations* (2nd ed., pp. 455–480). New York: Columbia University Press.

Daniels, R. (1962). *The politics of prejudice: The anti-Japanese movement in California and the struggle for Japanese exclusion.* Berkeley: University of California Press.

Danzinger, S. (1997). America unequal: The economy, the labor market and family incomes. Special plenary, Council on Social Work Education annual program meeting, March 7.

Darwin, C. (1874). *The descent of man, and selection in relation to sex.* New York: A. L. Burt.

Darwin, C. (1988). *Origin of species 1859.* New York: New York University Press.

D'Augelli, A. R., Grossman, A. H., Hershberger, S. L., & O'Connell, T. S. (2001). Aspects of mental health among older lesbian, gay, and bisexual adults. *Aging and Mental Health, 5*(2), 149–158.

D'Augelli, A. R., Hershberger, S. L., & Pilkington, N. W. (1998). Lesbian, gay and bisexual youth and their families: Disclosure of sexual orientation and its consequences. *American Journal of Orthopsychiatry, 68*(3), 361–371.

Davidson, J. R., & Davidson, T. (1996). Confidentiality and managed care: Ethical and legal concerns. *Health and Social Work, 21*(3), 208–215.

Davis, E. C., & Friel, L. V. (2001). Adolescent sexuality: Disentangling the effects of family structure and family context. *Journal of Marriage & the Family, 63*(3), 669–681.

Dean, R. G., & Rhodes, M. (1992). Ethical-clinical tensions in clinical practice. *Social Work, 37*(2), 128–132.

Dear, R. B., & Patti, R. J. (1982). Legislative advocacy: Seven effective tactics. *Social Work, 27*(4), 289–296.

de-Beer, F., & Marais, M. (2005). Rural communities, the natural environment and development: Some challenges, some successes. *Community Development Journal, 40*(1), 50–61.

De Jong, P., & Berg, I. K. (2001). Co-constructing cooperation with mandated clients. *Social Work, 46*(4), 361–376.

De Jong, P., & Miller, S. D. (1995). How to interview for client's strengths. *Social Work, 40*(6), 729–736.

Delgado, M. (1988). Groups in Puerto Rican spiritism: Implications for clinicians. In C. Jacobs & D. H. Bowles (Eds.), *Ethnicity and race: critical concepts in social work* (pp. 34–47). Silver Spring, MD: National Association of Social Workers.

Delgado, M., & Humm-Delgado, D. (1982). Natural support systems: Source of strength in Hispanic communities. *Social Work, 27*(1), 83–90.

Dempsey, D. (1988). Interview with legislator. *Practice Digest, 3*(3), 25–28.

Denby, R., & Alford, K. (1996). Understanding African American discipline style: Suggestions for effective social work interventions. *Journal of Multicultural Social Work, 4*(3), 81–98.

DeParle, J. (1998). Shrinking welfare rolls leave record high share of minorities. *New York Times,* July 27, pp. A1, A12.

Department of Health and Human Services, Administration on Aging. (2003). Retrieved November 6, 2007, from http://www.aoa.gov/prof/Statistics/2003.

Descamp, E., Flux, D., McClelland, R., & Sieppert, J. (2005). Community development with older adults in their neighborhoods: The elderly friendly communities program. *Families in Society, 86*(3), 401–410.

Devlin, A. (1992). Psychiatric ward renovation: Staff perception and patient behavior. *Environment and Behavior, 24*(1), 66–84.

Devore, W., & Schlesinger, E. (1995). *Ethnic-sensitive social work practice* (4th ed.). Boston: Allyn & Bacon.

Dewey, J. (1916). *Democracy and education.* New York: Macmillan.

Dewey, J. (1930). *Democracy and education* (2nd ed.). New York: Macmillan.

Dewey, J. (1938). *The theory of inquiry.* New York: Holt, Rinehart and Winston.

Diaz, A., Peake, K., Surko, M., & Bhandarkar, K. (2004). Including at-risk adolescents in their own health and mental health care: A youth development perspective. *Social Work in Mental Health, 3*(1/2), 3–22.

Dickerson, J. G. (2001). Margaret Murray Washington: Organizer of rural African American women. In I. B. Carlton-LaNey (Ed.), *African American leadership* (pp. 55–73). Washington, DC: National Association of Social Workers.

DiClemente, C. C., & Prochaska, J. O. (1998). Toward a comprehensive, transtheoretical model of change: Stages of change and addictive behaviors. In W. R. Miller & N. Heather (Eds.), *Treating addictive behaviors* (2nd ed., pp. 3–24). New York: Plenum Press.

Dinwiddie, C. (1921). *Community responsibility: A review of the Cincinnati Social Unit Experiment.* New York: New York School of Social Work.

Docherty, D., & McColl, M. A. (2003). Illness stories: Themes emerging through narrative. *Social Work in Health Care, 37*(1), 19–39.

Dolgoff, R., & Skolnik, L. (1996). Ethical decision-making in social work with groups: An empirical study. *Social Work with Groups, 19*(2), 49–65.

Dominguez, S., & Watkins, C. (2003). Creating networks for survival and mobility: Social capital among African-American and Latin-American low-income mothers. *Social Problems, 50*(1), 111–133.

Dore, M. (1990). Functional theory: Its history and influence on contemporary practice. *Social Service Review, 64,* 358–374.

Dore, M., & Dumois, A. (1990). Cultural differences in the meaning of adolescent pregnancy. *Families in Society, 71*(February), 93–101.

Drachman, D., Kwon-Ahn, Y., & Paulino, A. (1996). Migration and resettlement experiences of Dominican and Korean families. *Families in Society, 77*(10), 626–638.

Drachman, D., & Paulino, A. (2004). Introduction: Thinking beyond United States' borders. In D. Drachman & A. Paulino (Eds.), *Immigrants and social work: Thinking beyond the United States borders* (pp. 1–10). Binghamton, NY: Haworth Social Work Practice Press.

Drachman, D., & Ryan, A. (2001). Immigrants and refugees. In A. Gitterman (Ed.), *Handbook of social work practice with vulnerable and resilient populations* (2nd ed., pp. 651–686). New York: Columbia University Press.

Dubos, R. (1965). *Man adapting.* New Haven, CT: Yale University Press.

Dubos, R. (1968). *So human an animal.* New York: Scribner's.

Duehn, W., & Proctor, E. (1977). Initial clinical interventions and premature discontinuance in treatment. *American Journal of Orthopsychiatry, 47*(2), 284–290.

Duffy, T. (1990). Psychodrama in beginning recovery: An illustration of goals and methods. *Alcoholism Treatment Quarterly, 7*(2), 97–109.

Dufrechou, J. P. (2004). We are one: Grief, weeping, and other deep emotions in response to nature as a path toward wholeness. *Humanistic Psychologist, 32*(4), 357–378.

Duncan, B. (2001). The future of psychotherapy. *Psychotherapy Networker, 25*(4), 24–33, 52–53.

Duncan-Ricks, E. N. (1992). Adolescent sexuality and peer pressure. *Child and Adolescent Social Work Journal, 9*(4), 319–327.

Dyche, L., & Zayas, L. H. (2001). Cross-cultural empathy and training the contemporary psychotherapist. *Clinical Social Work Journal, 29*(3), 245–258.

Early, T. J., & GlenMaye, L. F. (2000). Valuing families: Social work practice with families from a strengths perspective. *Social Work, 45*(2), 118–129.

Eckholm, E. (2006). Plight deepens for black men, studies warn. *New York Times,* March 20, pp. A1, 18.

Edelstein, M. R. (2002). Contamination: The invisible built environment. In R. B. Bechtel & A. Churchman (Eds.), *Handbook of environmental psychology* (pp. 559–588). Hoboken, NJ: Wiley.

Edgette, J. S. (1999). Getting real. *Family Therapy Networker, 23*(5), 36–41.

Edwards, R. (2002). Creating "stability" for children in step-families: Time and substance in parenting. *Children & Society, 16*(3), 154–167.

Efron, D., & Moir, R. (1996). Short term co-led intensive group work with adult children of alcoholics. *Social Work with Groups, 19*(3/4), 117–129.

Elkin, I., Parloff, M., Hadley, S., & Autry, J. (1985). NIMH treatment of depression collaborative research program. *Archives of General Psychiatry, 42*(March), 305–316.

Ephross, P., & Vassil, T. (2005). *Groups that work* (2nd ed.). New York: Columbia University Press.

Epstein, I. (1996). Promoting reflective social work practice: Research strategies and consulting principles. In E. J. Mullen & P. Hess (Eds.), *Practitioner-researcher partnerships: Building knowledge from, in, and for practice* (pp. 83–102). Washington, DC: NASW Press.

Epstein, I. (2001). Using available clinical information in practice-based research: Mining for silver while dreaming of gold. *Social Work in Health Care, 33*(3/4), 15–32.

Etkin, C. D., Prochaska, T. R., Harris, B. A., Latham, N., & Jette, A. (2006). Feasibility of implementing the Strong for Life Program in community settings. *The Gerontologist, 46*(2), 284–292.

Evans, G. W. (2006). Child development and the physical environment. *Annual Review of Psychology, 47,* 423–451.

Evans, S. (1997). *Born for liberty: A history of women in America.* New York: Free Press Paperbacks.

Federal Interagency Forum on Child and Family Statistics. (1997). *America's children: Key national indicators of well-being.* Washington, DC: Author. Retrieved October 1998 from http://www.fedstats.gov/index20.html.

Fein, A. J., Plotnikoff, R. C., & Wild, T. C. (2005). An examination of adolescents' perceptions of the school physical environment related to physical activity. *International Journal of Sport and Exercise Psychology, 3*(2), 179–195.

Feinauer, L., & Stuart, D. (1996). Blame and resilience in women sexually abused as children. *American Journal of Family Therapy, 24*(1), 31–40.

Ferry, J. L., & Abramson, J. S. (2005). Toward understanding the clinical aspects of geriatric case management. *Social Work in Health Care, 42*(1), 35–56.

Figueira-McDonough, J. (1993). Policy practice: The neglected side of social work intervention. *Social Work, 38*(2), 179–188.

Finkelhor, D., & Browne, A. (1985). The traumatic impact of child sexual abuse: A conceptualization. *American Journal of Orthopsychiatry, 55*(4), 530–541.

Finkelhor, D., Hotaling, G., Lewis, I. A., & Smith, C. (1990). Sexual abuse in a national survey of adult men and women: Prevalence, characteristics, and risk factors. *Child Abuse and Neglect, 14*(1), 19–28.

Finn, J. (1995). Computer-based self-help groups: A new resource to supplement support groups. *Social Work with Groups, 18*(1), 109–117.

Finn, J. (1996). Computer-based self-help groups: On-line recovery for addictions. *Computers in Human Services, 13*(1), 21–41.

Fischer, F., & Siriani, C. (Eds.). (1994). *Critical studies in organization and bureaucracy.* Philadelphia: Temple University Press.

Fisher, J. (1993). Empirically-based practice: The end of ideology? *Social Service Research, 18*(1), 19–64.

Fisher, R. (1994). *Beyond Machiavelli: Tools for coping with conflict.* Cambridge, MA: Harvard University Press.

Flexner, A. (1915). Is social work a profession? In National Conference on Social Work, *Proceedings* (pp. 576–590). Chicago: University of Chicago Press.

Fluhr, T. (2004). Transcending differences: Using concrete subject-matter in heterogeneous groups. *Social Work with Groups, 27*(2/3), 35–54.

Follett, M. P. (1924). *Creative experience.* New York: Longmans, Green.

Follett, M. P. (1941). *Dynamic administration: The collected papers of Mary Parker Follett* (Ed. Henry C. Metcalf & L. Urwick). New York: Harper.

Follett, M. P. (1950). *Creative group experience.* New York: Longmans, Green.

Fong, M. L., & Lease, S. H. (1997). Cross-cultural issues for the white supervisor. In D. B. Pope-Davis & H. L. K. Coleman (Eds.), *Multicultural counseling competencies: Assessment, education and training, and supervision* (pp. 387–405). Thousand Oaks, CA: Sage.

Ford, K., & Jones, A. (1987). *Student supervision.* London: Macmillan Education.

Fortune, A., Pearlingi, E., & Rochelle, C. D. (1991). Criteria for terminating treatment. *Families in Society, 72*(6), 366–370.

Fortune, A., Pearlingi, E., & Rochelle, C. D. (1992). Reactions to termination of individual treatment. *Social Work, 37*(2), 171–178.

Foster, A. L (2006). Technology: Safeguarding networks is priority no. 1. *Chronicle of Higher Education,* January 6, p. A11.

Frankel, A. J., & Gelman, S. R. (2004). *Case management: An introduction to concepts and skills.* Chicago: Lyceum.

Frankl, V. (1963). *Man's search for meaning: An introduction to logotherapy.* Boston: Beacon Press.

Fraser, M. (Ed.). (2004). *Risk and resilience in childhood: An ecological perspective.* Washington, DC: NASW Press.

Fraser, M. W., Richman, J. M., & Galinsky, M. J. (1999). Risk, protection and resilience: Toward a conceptual framework for social work practice. *Social Work Research, 23*(3), 131–143.

Frazier, E. F. (1939). *The Negro family in the United States.* Chicago: University of Chicago Press.

Frazier, E. F. (1957). *The Negro in the United States.* New York: Macmillan.

Freddolino, P. P., Moxley, D. P., & Hyduk, C. A. (2004). A differential model of advocacy in social work practice. *Families in Society, 85*(1), 119–128.

Freedman, R. I. (1995). Developmental disabilities and direct practice. In R. L. Edwards (Ed.), *The encyclopedia of social work* (19th ed., pp. 721–729). Silver Spring, MD: National Association of Social Workers.

Freeman, E. (1984). Multiple losses in the elderly: An ecological approach. *Social Casework, 65*(5), 287–296.

Freeman, E. (2001). *Substance abuse intervention, prevention, rehabilitation, and systems change strategies: Helping individuals, families, and groups to empower themselves.* New York: Columbia University Press.

French, R., Reardon, M., & Smith, P. (2003). Engaging with a mental health service: perspectives of at-risk youth. *Child and Adolescent Social Work Journal, 20*(6), 529–548.

Freund, A. (2005). Work attitudes of social workers across three sectors of welfare organizations: Public, for-profit, and third sector. *Journal of Social Service Research, 31*(3), 69–92.

Frey, G. (1990). A framework for promoting organizational change. *Families in Society*, *71*(3), 142–147.

Friedrich, W. (1990). *Psychotherapy of sexually abused children and their families*. New York: Norton.

Fukuyama, M. A., & Ferguson, A. D. (2000). Lesbian, gay, and bisexual people of color: Understanding cultural complexity and managing multiple oppressions. In R. M. Perez, K. A. DeBord, & K. J. Bieschke (Eds.), *Handbook of counseling and psychotherapy with lesbian, gay and bisexual clients* (pp. 81–105). Washington, DC: American Psychological Association.

Furman, R., & Langer, C. L. (2006). Managed care and the care of the soul. *Journal of Social Work Values and Ethics*, *3*(2). Retrieved November 6, 2007, from http://www.socialworker.com/jswve/content/blogcategory/13/46/.

Gale, J. (2003). The natural environment as an element in a therapeutic community treatment programme. *International Journal for Therapeutic and Supportive Organizations*, *24*(3), 205–215.

Galinsky, M. J., & Schopler, J. (1985). Patterns of entry and exit in open-ended groups. *Social Work with Groups*, *8*(2), 67–80.

Galinsky, M. J., & Schopler, J. (1989). Developmental patterns in open-ended groups. *Social Work with Groups*, *12*(2), 99–114.

Galinsky, M. J., Schopler, J. H., & Abell, M. D. (1997). Connecting group members through telephone and computer groups. *Health and Social Work*, *22*(2), 181–188.

Galinsky, M. J., Terzian, M. A., & Fraser, M. W. (2006). The art of group work practice with manualized curricula. *Social Work with Groups*, *29*(1), 11–26.

Gambrill, E. (1992). *Critical thinking in clinical practice: Improving the accuracy of judgments and decisions about clients*. San Francisco: Jossey-Bass.

Gambrill, E. (1999). Evidence-based practice: An alternative to authority-based practice. *Families in Society*, *80*(4), 341–350.

Gambrill, E. (2006). *Social work practice: A critical thinker's guide* (2nd ed.). New York: Oxford University Press.

Garland, J., Jones, H., & Kolodny, R. (1976). A model of stages of group development in social work groups. In S. Bernstein (Ed.), *Explorations in group work* (pp. 17–71). Boston: Charles River.

Garvin, C. (1974). Task-centered group-work. *Social Service Review*, *48*, 494–507.

Garvin, C. (1992). A task centered group approach to work with the chronically mentally ill. *Social Work with Groups*, *15*(2/3), 67–80.

Geller, J. L. (1996). Mental health services of the future: Managed care, unmanaged care, mismanaged care. *Smith College Studies*, *66*(2), 223–239.

Gelman, S. R., Pollack, D., & Weiner, A. (1999). Confidentiality of social work records in the computer. *Social Work*, *44*(3), 243–252.

Germain, C. B. (1970). Casework and science: A historical encounter. In R. W. Roberts & R. H. Nee (Eds.), *Theories of social casework* (pp. 3–32). Chicago: University of Chicago Press.

Germain, C. B. (1973a). Social casework. In H. B. Trecker (Ed.), *Goals for social welfare, 1973–1993*. New York: Association Press.

Germain, C. B. (1973b). An ecological perspective in casework. *Social Casework*, *54*(6), 323–330.

Germain, C. B. (1976). Time: An ecological variable in social work practice. *Social Casework*, *57*(7), 419–426.

Germain, C. B. (1978a). General systems theory and ego psychology: An ecological perspective. *Social Service Review*, *52*(4), 535–550.

Germain, C. B. (1978b). Space, an ecological variable in social work practice. *Social Casework*, *59*(9), 515–522.

Germain, C. B. (Ed.). (1979). *Social work practice: People and environments.* New York: Columbia University Press.

Germain, C. B. (1983). Using social and physical environments. In A. Rosenblatt & D. Waldfogel (Eds.), *Handbook of clinical social work* (pp. 110–134). San Francisco: Jossey-Bass.

Germain, C. B. (1985a). The place of community work within an ecological approach to social work practice. In S. H. Taylor & R. W. Roberts (Eds.), *Theory and practice of community social work* (pp. 30–55). New York: Columbia University Press.

Germain, C. B. (1985b). Understanding and changing communities and organizations in the practice of child welfare. In J. Laird & A. Hartman (Eds.), *A handbook of child welfare: Context, knowledge, and practice* (pp. 122–148). New York: Free Press.

Germain, C. B. (1990). Life forces and the anatomy of practice. *Smith College Studies in Social Work, 60*(March), 138–152.

Germain, C. B. (1994). Using an ecological perspective. In J. Rothman (Ed.), *Practice with highly vulnerable clients: Case management and community based service* (pp. 39–55). Englewood Cliffs, NJ: Prentice Hall.

Germain, C. B., & Bloom, M. (1999). *Human behavior in the social environment: An ecological view* (2nd ed.). New York: Columbia University Press.

Germain, C. B., & Gitterman, A. (1979). The life model of social work practice. In F. Turner (Ed.), *Social work treatment* (pp. 361–384). New York: Free Press.

Germain, C. B., & Gitterman, A. (1980). *The life model of social work practice.* New York: Columbia University Press.

Germain, C. B., & Gitterman, A. (1987). Ecological perspective. In A. Minahan (Ed.), *The encyclopedia of social work* (18th ed., pp. 488–499). Silver Spring, MD: National Association of Social Workers.

Germain, C. B., & Gitterman, A. (1995). Ecological perspective. In R. L. Edwards (Ed.), *The encyclopedia of social work* (19th ed., pp. 816–824). Silver Spring, MD: National Association of Social Workers.

Getzel, G., & Mahony, K. (1993). Confronting human finitude: Group work with people with AIDS. *Social Work with Groups, 16*(1/2), 27–42.

Getzel, G. S. (2005). No one is alone: Groups during the AIDS pandemic. In A. Gitterman & L. Shulman (Eds.), *Mutual aid groups, vulnerable and resilient populations, and the life cycle* (3rd ed., pp. 249–265). New York: Columbia University Press.

Getzel, G. S., & Willroth, S. W. (2001). Acquired immune deficiency syndrome (AIDS). In A. Gitterman (Ed.), *Handbook of social work practice with vulnerable and resilient populations* (2nd ed., pp. 39–63). New York: Columbia University Press.

Gewirth, A. (2001). Confidentiality in child-welfare practice. *Social Service Review, 75*(3), 479–489.

Gibbs, J. T. (1980). The interpersonal orientation in mental health consultation: Toward a model of ethnic variations in consultation. *Journal of Community Psychology, 8*(3), 195–207.

Gibbs, L., & Gambrill, E. (2002). Evidenced-based practice: Counterarguments to objections. *Research on Social Work Practice, 12*(3), 452–476.

Gibelman, M., & Shervish, P. H. (1996). The private practice of social work: Current trends and projected scenarios in a managed care environment. *Clinical Social Work Journal, 24*(4), 323–338.

Gibson, D. E., & Barsade, S. G. (2003). Managing organizational culture change: The case of long-term care. *Journal of Social Work in Long-Term Care, 2*(1/2), 11–34.

Gibson, J. L., Ivancevich, J. M., & Donnelly, J. H., Jr. (2000). *Organizations: Behavior, structure, processes.* Boston: Irwin/McGraw-Hill.

Gilbert, M. C., & Beidler, A. E. (2001). Using the narrative approach in groups for chemically dependent mothers. *Social Work with Groups, 24*(3/4), 101–115.

Gill, David G. (1998). *Confronting injustice and oppression*. New York: Columbia University Press.

Gilligan, C. (1982). *In a different voice: Psychological theory and women's development*. Cambridge, MA: Harvard University Press.

Gingerich, W., Kleczewski, M., & Kirk, S. (1982). Name calling in social work. *Social Service Review, 56*(3), 366–374.

Gitterman, A. (1971). Group work in the public schools. In W. Schwartz & S. Zelba (Eds.), *The practice of group work* (pp. 45–72). New York: Columbia University Press.

Gitterman, A. (1977). Social work in the public schools. *Social Casework, 58*(2), 111–118.

Gitterman, A. (1979). Group work content in an integrated method curriculum. In S. Abels & P. Abels (Eds.), *Social work with groups: Proceedings 1979 symposium* (pp. 66–81). Louisville, KY: Committee for the Advancement of Social Work with Groups.

Gitterman, A. (1982). The uses of groups in health settings. In A. Lurie, G. Rosenberg, & S. Pinskey (Eds.), *Social work with groups in health settings* (pp. 6–21). New York: Prodist.

Gitterman, A. (1983). Uses of resistance: A transactional view. *Social Work, 28*(2), 127–131.

Gitterman, A. (1987). Social work looks forward. In G. St. Denis (Ed.), *Implementing a forward plan: A public health social work challenge* (pp. 3–16). Pittsburgh, PA: University of Pittsburgh Press.

Gitterman, A. (1988). The social worker as educator. In *Health care practice today: The social worker as educator* (pp. 13–22). New York: Columbia University School of Social Work.

Gitterman, A. (1989a). Testing professional authority and boundaries. *Social Casework, 70*(2), 165–171.

Gitterman, A. (1989b). Building mutual support in groups. *Social Work in Groups, 12*(2), 5–22.

Gitterman, A. (1991). Creative connections between theory and practice. In M. Weil, K. Chau, & D. Southerland (Eds.), *Theory and practice in social group work: Creative connections* (pp. 13–28). Binghamton, NY: Haworth Press.

Gitterman, A. (1996). Advances in the life model of social work practice. In F. Turner (Ed.), *Social work treatment: Interlocking theoretical perspectives* (pp. 389–408). New York: Free Press.

Gitterman, A. (1999). Vulnerability, resilience, and social work practice. In *Monograph: The fourth annual Dr. Ephaim T. Lisansky lecture*. College Park: University of Maryland School of Social Work.

Gitterman, A. (2001a). Vulnerability, resilience, and social work with groups. In T. Berman-Rossi, T. Kelly, & S. Palombo (Eds.), *Strengthening resiliency through group work* (pp. 19–34). Binghamton, NY: Haworth Press.

Gitterman, A. (2001b). Social work practice with vulnerable and resilient populations. In A. Gitterman (Ed.), *Handbook of social work practice with vulnerable and resilient populations* (2nd ed., pp. 1–38). New York: Columbia University Press.

Gitterman, A. (2003a). The uses of humor in social work practice. *Reflections: Narratives of Professional Helping, 9*(2), 79–84.

Gitterman, A. (2003b). The meaning, scope, and context of the concept of social justice in social work with groups. In N. E. Sullivan, E. S. Mesbur, N. C. Lang, D. Goodman, & L. Mitchell (Eds.), *Social work with groups: Social justice through personal, community, and societal change* (pp. 25–34). Binghamton, NY: Haworth Press.

Gitterman, A. (2003c). Dealing with group members' testing of authority. *Social Work with Groups, 25*(1/2), 185–192.

Gitterman, A. (2004). The mutual aid model. In C. Garvin, L. Gutierrez, & M. Galinsky (Eds.), *Handbook of social work with groups* (pp. 93–110). New York: Guilford Press.

Gitterman, A. (2005). Group formation: Tasks, methods and skills. In A. Gitterman & L. Shulman (Eds.), *Mutual aid groups, vulnerable and resilient populations, and the life cycle* (3rd ed., pp. 73–110). New York: Columbia University Press.

Gitterman, A. (2006). Building mutual support in groups. *Social Work with Groups, 28*(3/4), 91–106. (Reprinted as a classic.)

Gitterman, A., & Germain, C. B. (1976). Social work practice: A life model. *Social Service Review, 50*(December), 601–610.

Gitterman, A., & Malekoff, A. (Eds.). (2002). September 11 memorial issue. *Reflections: Narratives of Professional Helping, 8*(3).

Gitterman, A., & Miller, I. (1989). The influence of the organization on clinical practice. *Clinical Social Work Journal, 17*(2), 151–164.

Gitterman, A., & Miller, I. (1992). Should part of social workers' salaries be contingent on the outcomes they achieve with their clients? NO. In E. Gambrill & R. Pruger (Eds.), *Controversial issues in social work* (pp. 279–287). Boston: Allyn & Bacon.

Gitterman, A., & Nadelman, A. (1999). The white professional and the black client revisited. *Reflections: Narrative of Professional Helping, 5*(2), 67–79.

Gitterman, A., & Schaeffer, A. (1972). The white professional and the black client. *Social Casework, 53*(2), 280–291.

Gitterman, A., & Shulman, L. (2005). The life model, oppression, vulnerability and resilience, mutual aid, and the mediating function. In A. Gitterman & L. Shulman (Eds.), *Mutual aid groups, vulnerable and resilient populations, and the life cycle* (3rd ed., pp. 3–37). New York: Columbia University Press.

Gitterman, A., & Wayne, J. (2003). Turning points in group life: Using high tension moments to promote group purpose and mutual aid. *Families in Society, 84*(3), 433–440.

Givelber, D. J., Bowers, W. J., & Blitch, C. L. (1984). Tarasoff, myth and reality: An empirical study of private law in action. *Wisconsin Law Review, 2*, 443–497.

Glaser, J. S. (1972). The stairwell society of public housing: From small groups to social organizations. *Small Group Behavior, 3*(August), 159–173.

Glassman, U., & Kates, L. (1993). Feedback, role rehearsal, and programming enactments: Cycles in the group's middle phase. *Social Work with Groups, 16*(1/2), 127–136.

Goff, K. (2004). Senior to senior: Living lessons. *Educational Gerontology, 30*(3), 205–217.

Gold, N. (1990). Motivation: The crucial but unexplored component of social work practice. *Social Work, 35*(1), 49–56.

Goldman, R. K., Botkin, M. J., Tokunaga, H., & Kuklinski, M. (1997). Teacher consultation: Impact on teachers' effectiveness and students' cognitive competence and achievement. *American Journal of Orthopsychiatry, 67*(3), 374–384.

Goldstein, E. G. (1997). To tell or not to tell: The disclosure of events in the therapist's life to the patient. *Clinical Social Work Journal, 25*(1), 41–58.

Goldstein, H. (1973). *Social work practice: An unitary approach*. Columbia: University of South Carolina Press.

Gomberg, R. (1943). Function as a psychological concept in casework theory. *The Family, 24*, 58–64.

Gonchar, N., & Adams, J. R. (2000). Living in cyberspace: Recognizing the importance of the virtual world in social work assessments. *Journal of Social Work Education, 36*(3), 587–596.

Gordon, D. R. (1998). Humor in African-American discourse: Speaking of oppression. *Journal of Black Studies, 29*(2), 254–276.

Gordon, W. E. (1969). Basic constructs for an integrative and generative conception of social work. In G. Hearn (Ed.), *The general systems approach: Contributions toward a holistic conception of social work*. New York: Council on Social Work Education.

Granello, D. H. (1996). Gender and power in the supervisory dyad. *The Clinical Supervisor, 14*(2), 53–67.

Gray, J. N., Lyons, P. M., & Melton, G. B. (1995). *Ethical and legal issues in AIDS research*. Baltimore: Johns Hopkins University Press.

Green, R. J. (1996). Why ask, why tell? Teaching and learning about lesbians and gays in family therapy. *Family Process, 35*(3), 389–400.

Greenberg, L. S. (2002). Termination of experiential therapy. *Journal of Psychotherapy Integration, 12*(3), 358–363.

Greenebaum, J. (2004). It's a dog's life: Elevating status from pet to "fur baby" at yappy hour. *Society & Animals, 12*(2), 117–135.

Greif, G. L. (Ed.). (2005). *Group work with populations at risk* (2nd ed.). New York: Oxford University Press.

Grosser, C. (1965). Community development programs serving urban poor. *Social Work, 10*(3), 15–21.

Grosser, C. (1973). *New directions in community organizing*. New York: Praeger.

Grotstein, J. (1995). Orphans of the real: Some modern and postmodern perspectives on the neurobiological and psychosocial dimensions of psychosis and other primitive mental disorders. *Bulletin of the Menninger Clinic, 59*(3), 287–307.

Guelzow, J. W., Cornett, P. F., & Dougherty, T. M. (2002). Child sexual abuse victims' perception of paternal support as a significant predictor of coping style and global self-worth. *Journal of Child Sexual Abuse, 11*(4), 53–72.

Gummer, B. (1995). Go team go! The growing importance of teamwork in organizational life. *Administration in Social Work, 19*(4), 85–100.

Gumpert, J., Saltman, J. E., & Sauer-Jones, D. (2000). Toward identifying the unique characteristics of social work practice in rural areas: From the voices of practitioners. *Journal of Baccalaureate Social Work, 6*(1), 19–35.

Gutierrez, L. M. (1990). Working with women of color: An empowerment perspective. *Social Work, 35*(2), 149–154.

Gutierrez, L. M., & Lewis, B. A. (1999). *Empowering women of color*. New York: Columbia University Press.

Haas, K., Simson, S. P., & Stevenson, N. C. (1998). Older persons and horticultural therapy practice. In S. P. Simson & M. C. Straus (Eds.), *Horticulture as therapy: Principles and practice* (pp. 231–255). Binghamton, NY: Food Products Press/Haworth Press.

Hack, T. F., Osachuk, T. A. G., & De Luca, R. V. (1994). Group treatment for sexually abused preadolescent boys. *Families in Society, 75*(4), 217–228.

Hafkenscheid, A. (2005). Event countertransference and vicarious traumatization: Theoretically valid and clinically useful concepts? *European Journal of Psychotherapy, Counselling and Health, 7*(3), 159–168.

Håkansson, E. J. (2006). Empathy and viewing the other as a subject. *Scandinavian Journal of Psychology, 47*(5), 399–409.

Håkansson, E. J., & Montgomery, H. (2002). The role of action in empathy from the perspective of the empathizer and the target. *Current Research in Social Psychology, 8*(4), 50–62.

Håkansson, E. J., & Montgomery, H. (2003). Empathy as an interpersonal phenomenon. *Journal of Social and Personal Relationships, 20*(3), 267–284.

Hall, M. J., Ng, A., & Ursano, R. J. (2004). Psychological impact of the animal-human bond in disaster preparedness and response. *Journal of Psychiatric Practice, 10*(6), 368–374.

Halleck, S. (1963). The impact of professional dishonesty on behavior of disturbed adolescents. *Social Work, 8*(April), 48–65.

Halperin, D. (2001). The play's the thing: How social group work and theatre transformed a group into a community. *Social Work with Groups, 24*(2), 27–46.

Hamilton, G. (1940). *Theory and practice of social casework.* New York: Columbia University Press.

Hample, D. (2005). *Arguing: Exchanging reasons face to face.* Mahwah, NJ: Lawrence Erlbaum.

Hanson, M. (1998). The transition group: Linking clients with alcohol problems in outpatient care. *Journal of Chemical Dependency Treatment, 7*(1/2), 21–36.

Hanson, M. (2001). Alcoholism and other drug addictions. In A. Gitterman (Ed.), *Handbook of social work practice with resilient and vulnerable populations* (2nd ed., pp. 64–96). New York: Columbia University Press.

Hanson, M., & El-Bassel, N. (2004). Motivating substance-abusing clients through the helping process. In S. L. A. Straussner (Ed.), *Clinical work with substance-abusing clients* (pp. 39–63). New York: Guilford Press.

Hardman, K. (1997). A social work group for prostituted women with children. *Social Work with Groups, 20*(1), 19–32.

Hareven, T. K. (1982). The life course and aging in historical perspective. In T. K. Hareven & K. J. Adams (Eds.), *Aging and the life course transitions: An interdisciplinary perspective* (pp. 1–26). New York: Guilford Press.

Harper, E. B., & Dunham, A. (Eds.). (1959). *Community organization in action.* New York: Association Press.

Hartford, M. E. (Ed.). (1964). *Working papers toward a frame of reference for social group work.* New York: National Association of Social Workers.

Hartford, M. E., & Lawton, S. (1997). Groups for the socialization to old age. In J. K. Parry (Ed.), *From prevention to wellness through group work* (pp. 33–45). Binghamton, NY: Haworth Press.

Hartman, A. (1970). To think about the unthinkable. *Social Casework, 51*(October), 467–474.

Hartman, A. (1978). Diagnostic assessment of family relationships. *Social Casework, 59*(October), 465–476.

Hartman, A. (1979). *Finding families: An ecological approach to family assessment in adoption.* Beverly Hills, CA: Sage.

Hartman, A., & Laird, J. (1983). *Family centered social work practice.* New York: Free Press.

Hartman, A., & Laird, J. (1998). Moral and ethical issues in working with lesbians and gay men. *Families in Society, 79*(3), 263–276.

Hatchett, B., & Duran, D. A. (2002). An approach to community outreach practice in the 21st century. *Journal of Community Practice, 10*(2), 37–52.

Hatchett, G. T. (2004). Reducing premature termination in university counseling centers. *Journal of College Student Psychotherapy, 19*(2), 13–27.

Hawley, D. (2000). Clinical implications of family resilience. *American Journal of Family Therapy, 28*(2), 101–117.

Healy, T. C. (2003). Ethical decision making: Pressure and uncertainty as complicating factors. *Social Work, 4*(November), 293–301.

Hearn, G. (Ed.). (1969). *The general systems approach: Contributions toward a holistic conception of social work.* New York: Council on Social Work Education.

Heitkamp, T. (1999). Treading water: A social worker's personal narrative. *Reflections, 5*(3), 33–42.

Herman, J. (1992). *Trauma and recovery.* New York: Basic Books.

Hess, P. & Howard, T. (1981). An ecological model for assessing psychosocial difficulties in children. *Child Welfare, 60*(8), 499–518.

Hodge, D. R. (2001). Spiritual assessment: A review of major qualitative methods and a new framework for assessing spirituality. *Social Work, 46*(3), 203–214.

Hodge, D. R. (2004). Spirituality and people with mental illness: Developing spiritual competency in assessment and intervention. *Families in Society*, *85*(1), 36–44.

Hodge, D. R. (2005). Developing a spiritual assessment toolbox: A discussion of the strengths and limitations of five different assessment methods. *Health and Social Work*, *10*(4), 314–323.

Hoffman, L. (2002). *Family therapy: An intimate history*. New York: Norton.

Hofstadter, R. (1948). *The American political tradition and the men who made it*. New York: Knopf.

Hollis, E. V., & Taylor, A. L. (1951). *Social work education in the U.S.* New York: Columbia University Press.

Hollis, F. (1964). *Casework: A psychosocial therapy*. New York: Random House.

Hollis, F. (1968). *Typology of casework treatment*. New York: Family Service Association of America. (Four articles reprinted from *Social Casework*.)

Hollis, F. (1972). *Casework: A psychosocial therapy* (2nd ed.). New York: Random House.

Holloway, S. (1987). Staff initiated organizational change. In A. Minahan (Ed.), *The encyclopedia of social work* (18th ed., pp. 729–736). Silver Spring, MD: National Association of Social Workers.

Holloway, S., & Brager, G. (1985). Implicit negotiations and organizational practice. *Administration on Social Work*, *9*(2), 15–24.

Hooker, C. (1976). Learned helplessness. *Social Work*, *21*(3), 194–199.

Hopper, S. (2005). Commentary on "therapist-initiated termination." *International Journal of Group Psychotherapy*, *55*(2), 305–309.

Horowitz, L. (2000). Resisting amnesia in the countertransference: A clinical strategy for working with lesbian patients. *Clinical Social Work Journal*, *28*(1), 55–70.

Horowitz, R. (2002). Psychotherapy and schizophrenia: The mirror of countertransference. *Clinical Social Work Journal*, *30*(3), 235–244.

Hough, E. S., Magnan, M. A., & Templin, T. (2005). Social network structure and social support in HIV-positive inner city mothers. *Journal of the Association of Nurses in AIDS Care*, *16*(4), 14–24.

Humphreys, N. (2006). Comments on Alex's book. Personal communication, October 1.

Hurd, E. P, Moore, C., & Rogers, R. (1995). Quite success: Parenting strengths among African Americans. *Families in Society*, *76*(7), 434–443.

Hurdle, D. E. (2001). Social support: A critical factor in women's health and health promotion. *Health and Social Work*, *26*(2), 72–79.

Hutchison, E. (1987). Use of authority in direct social work practice with mandated clients. *Social Service Review*, *61*(4), 81–98.

Hyduk, C. A. (2002). Community-based long-term care case management models for older adults. *Journal of Gerontological Social Work*, *37*(1), 19–47.

Iglehart, A. P., & Becerra, R. M. (2000). *Social services and the ethnic community*. Long Grove, IL: Waveland Press.

International Federation of Social Workers. (N.d.). *Ethics in social work statement of principles*. Retrieved October 19, 2007, from http://www.ifsw.org/en/p38000252 .html.

International Federation of Social Workers. (N.d.). *Universal declaration of human rights*. Retrieved October 19, 2007, from http:/www.unchr.ch.udhr/lang/eng.htm.

Iris, V-Y., Rafaeli, A., & Yaacov, C. S. (2005). Instrumentality, aesthetics, and symbolism of office design. *Environment and Behavior*, *37*(4), 533–551.

Irizarry, C., & Appel, Y. H. (2005). Preteens in double jeopardy: Supporting developmental growth through a natural friendship group. In A. Gitterman & L. Shulman (Eds.), *Mutual aid groups, vulnerable and resilient populations, and the life cycle* (3rd ed., pp. 165–202). New York: Columbia University Press.

Ivanoff, A., Blythe, B. J., & Briar, S. (1987). The empirical clinical practice debate. *Social Casework*, *68*(5), 290–298.

Jackson, P. (1978). Black charity in progressive era Chicago. *Social Service Review, 5*(3), 400–417.

Jacobson, S. W., & Jacobson, J. L. (2000). *Teratogenic insult and neurobehavioral function in infancy and childhood.* Mahwah, NJ: Lawrence Erlbaum.

Jaffee v Redmond, 116 S. Court 1923 (1996).

Jagendorf, J., & Malekoff, A. (2000). Groups-on-the-go: Spontaneously formed mutual aid groups for adolescents in distress. *Social Work with Groups, 22*(4), 15–32.

Jansson, B. S. (1984). *Theory and practice of social welfare policy: Analysis, process, and current issues.* Belmont, CA: Wadsworth.

Jansson, B. S. (1990). *Social welfare policy: From theory to practice.* Belmont, CA: Wadsworth.

Jansson, B. S. (1999). *Becoming an effective policy advocate: From policy practice to social justice* (3rd ed.). Pacific Grove, CA: Brooks/Cole.

Jansson, B. S. (2007). *Becoming an effective policy advocate: From policy practice to social justice* (5th ed.). Belmont, CA: Wadsworth.

Jaskyte, K., & Dressler, W. W. (2005). Organizational culture and innovation in nonprofit human service organizations. *Administration in Social Work, 29*(2), 23–41.

Jayarante, S., & Levy, R. (1979). *Empirical clinical practice.* New York: Columbia University Press.

Jirovec, R. L. (2005). Differences in family functioning and health between older adult volunteers and non-volunteers. *Journal of Gerontological Social Work, 46*(2), 23–35.

Jirovec, R. L., & Hyduk, C. A. (1998). Type of volunteer experience and health among older adult volunteers. *Journal of Gerontological Social Work, 30*(3/4), 29–42.

Johnson, D. C. (2006). Corporate wealth shares rises for top-income Americans. *New York Times*, January 29, p. 22.

Johnson, K. D., Whitbeck, L. B., & Hoyt, D. R. (2005). Predictors of social network composition among homeless and runaway adolescents. *Journal of Adolescence, 28*(2), 231–248.

Jones, A. C. (2004). Transforming the story: Narrative applications to a stepmother support group. *Families in Society, 85*(1), 129–138.

Jones, M. A., & Gabriel, M. A. (1999). Utilization of psychotherapy by lesbians, gay men, and bisexuals: Findings from a nationwide survey. *American Journal of Orthopsychiatry, 69*(2), 209–219.

Jonson-Reid, M. (2000). Understanding confidentiality in school-based interagency projects. *Social Work in Education, 22*(1), 33–45.

Jordon, J. V. (1991). Empathy and self-boundaries. In J. V. Jordon, A. G. Kaplan, J. B. Miller, I. Stiver, & J. L. Surrey (Eds.), *Women's growth in connection: Writings from the Stone Center* (pp. 67–80). New York: Guilford Press.

Joseph, V. (1985). A model for ethical decision making in clinical practice. In C. Germain (Ed.), *Advances in clinical social work* (pp. 207–217). Silver Spring, MD: National Association of Social Workers.

Kadushin, A. (1983). *The social work interview.* New York: Columbia University Press.

Kahn, M., & Scher, S. (2002). Infusing content on the physical environment into the BSW curriculum. *Journal of Baccalaureate Social Work, 7*(2), 1–14.

Kahn, P. H., & Kellert, S. R. (2002). *Children and nature: Psychological, sociocultural, and evolutionary investigations.* Cambridge, MA: MIT Press.

Kalish, Y., & Robins, G. (2006). Psychological predispositions and network structure: The relationship between individual predispositions, structural holes and network closure. *Social Networks, 28*(1), 56–84.

Kaplan, C. P., Turner, S., Norman, E., & Stillson, K. (1996). Promoting resilience strategies: A modified consultation model. *Social Work in Education, 18*(3), 158–168.

Karlins, M., & Abelson, H. (1970). *Persuasion: How opinions and attitudes are changed.* New York: Springer.

Karls, J. M., Lowery, C. T., Mattaini, M. A., & Wandrei, K. E. (1997). The use of the

PIE (Person-in-Environment) system in social work education. *Journal of Social Work Education*, *33*(1), 49–58.

Karls, J. M., & Wandrei, K. E. (1992). PIE: A new language for social work. *Social Work*, *37*(10), 80–85.

Karls, J. M., & Wandrei, K. E. (Eds). (1994). *The P.I.E. classification system for social functioning problems*. Washington, DC: NASW Press.

Karls, J. M., & Wandrei, K. E. (1995). Person-in-environment. In R. L. Edwards (Ed.), *The encyclopedia of social work* (19th ed., pp. 1818–1827). Silver Spring, MD: National Association of Social Workers.

Katz, J. M. (2003). Tales of a therapist: Unexpected self-disclosure in couple therapy. *Journal of Couple and Relationship Therapy*, *2*(1), 43–60.

Kavanagh, J. (1998). Outdoor space and adaptive gardening: Design, techniques, and tools. In S. P. Simson & M. C. Straus (Eds.), *Horticulture as therapy: Principles and practice* (pp. 287–316). Binghamton, NY: Food Products Press/Haworth Press.

Keefe, T., & Koch, S. J. (1999). Teaching conflict management in social work. *Journal of Teaching in Social Work*, *18*(1/2), 33–52.

Kelley, M. L., McKay, S. & Nelson, C. H. (1985). Indian agency development: An ecological practice approach. *Social Casework*, *66*(10), 594–602.

Kelley, P. (2002). A narrative therapy approach to brief treatment. *Journal of Brief Therapy*, *1*(2), 91–100.

Kelly, T. B. (2005). Accumulated risk: Mutual aid groups for elderly persons with a mental illness. In A. Gitterman & L. Shulman (Eds.), *Mutual aid groups, vulnerable and resilient populations, and the life cycle* (3rd ed., pp. 536–569). New York: Columbia University Press.

Kelly, T. B., & Berman-Rossi, T. (1999). Advancing stages of group development theory: The case of institutionalized older persons. *Social Work with Groups*, *22*(2/3), 119–138.

Kemnitzer, L. (1978). Native Americans. In K. Chandras (Ed.), *Racial discrimination against neither-white-nor-black American minorities* (pp. 5–18). San Francisco: R & E Research Associates.

Kilpatrick, W. H. (1940). *Group education for a democracy*. New York: Association Press.

Kim, R. Y. (2001). Welfare reform and "ineligibles": Issue of constitutionality and recent court rulings. *Social Work*, *46*(4), 315–323.

King, Y. (1983). Toward an ecological feminism and a feminist ecology. In J. Rothschild (Ed.), *Machina ex Dea* (pp. 118–129). New York: Pergamon.

Kinney, J., & Trent, M. (2003). Walking our talk in the neighborhoods: Building professional/natural helper partnerships. *Family Preservation Journal*, *7*(1), 57–77.

Kinoy, S. K. (1984). Advocacy: A potent antidote to burnout. *NASW News* (November), 9.

Kiresuk, T., Smith, A., & Cardillo, J. (Eds.). (1994). *Goal attainment scaling theory, measurement, and applications*. Hillsdale, NJ: Lawrence Erlbaum.

Kirk, S., & Kutchins, H. (1994). The myth of the reliability of DSM. *Journal of Mind and Behavior*, *15*(1/2), 71–86.

Kirk, S., Wakefield, J., Hsieh, D., & Pottick, K. (1999). Social context and social workers' judgement of mental disorder. *Social Service Review*, *73*(1), 82–104.

Klein, W. C., & Bloom, M. (1994). Is there an ethical responsibility to use practice methods with the best empirical evidence of effectiveness? Yes. In W. W. Hudson & P. S. Nurius (Eds.), *Controversial issues in social work practice* (pp. 106–111). Boston: Allyn & Bacon.

Kleinkauf, C. (1981). A guide to giving legislative testimony. *Social Work*, *26*(4), 297–303.

Kleinkauf, C. (1989). Analyzing social welfare legislation. *Social Work*, *34*(2), 179–181.

Knei-Paz, C., & Ribner, D. S. (2000). A narrative perspective on "doing" for multi-problem families. *Families in Society, 81*(5), 475–482.

Knight, C. (2005a). From victim to survivor: Group work with men and women who were sexually abused. In A. Gitterman & L. Shulman (Eds.), *Mutual aid groups, vulnerable and resilient populations, and the life cycle* (3rd ed., pp. 320–351). New York: Columbia University Press.

Knight, C. (2005b). Healing hearts: Bereavement groups for children. In A. Gitterman & L. Shulman (Eds.), *Mutual aid groups, vulnerable and resilient populations, and the life cycle* (3rd ed., pp. 113–128). New York: Columbia University Press.

Konopka, G. (1949). *Therapeutic group work with children.* Minneapolis: University of Minnesota Press.

Konopka, G. (1954). *Group work in institutions.* New York: Association Press.

Kopels, S., & Kagle, J. D. (1993). Do social workers have a duty to warn? *Social Service Review, 67*(1), 101–126.

Kopels, S. & Kagle, J. D. (1994). Teaching confidentiality breaches as a forum of discrimination. *Arete, 19*(1), 1–9.

Kosoff, S. (2003). Single session groups: Applications and areas of expertise. *Social Work with Groups, 26*(1), 29–45.

Kovacs, P. J., & Black, B. (1999). Volunteerism and older adults: Implications for social work practice. *Journal of Gerontological Social Work, 32*(4), 25–39.

Krieger, L. M. (2006). "Internet addiction" a growing problem, study finds. *Journal News,* October 22, p. 9B.

Kübler-Ross, E. (1975). *Death: The final stages of life.* Englewood Cliffs, NJ: Prentice-Hall.

Kuechler, C. F. (1997). Psychoeducational groups: A model for recovery and celebration of the self. In J. K. Parry (Ed.), *From prevention to wellness through group work* (pp. 47–59). Binghamton, NY: Haworth Press.

Kurdek, L. A. (2003). Differences between gay and lesbian cohabiting couples. *Journal of Social and Personal Relationships, 20*(4), 411–436.

Kurland, R., & Salmon, R. (1992). Group work vs. casework in a group: Principles and implications for teaching and practice. *Social Work with Groups, 15*(4), 3–14.

Kurland, R., & Salmon, R. (1998). Purpose: A misunderstood and misused keystone of group work practice. *Social Work with Groups, 21*(3), 5–17.

Kurland, R., & Salmon, R. (2002). Caught in the doorway between education and practice: Group work's battle for survival. In *Plenary presentation at the 24th annual symposium of the Association for the Advancement of Social Work with Groups,* Brooklyn, NY.

Kutchins, H. (1991). The fiduciary relationship: The legal basis of social workers' relationships to clients. *Social Work, 36*(2), 106–113.

Kutchins, H., & Kirk, S. (1987). DSM-III and social work malpractice. *Social Work, 32*(May/June), 205–212.

Kutchins, H., & Kirk, S. (1988). The business of diagnosis: DSM-III and clinical social work. *Social Work, 33*(May/June), 215–220.

Laird, J. (1989). Women and stories: Restoring women's self-constructions. In M. McGoldrick, F. Walsh, & C. Anderson (Eds.), *Women in families* (pp. 420–450). New York: Norton.

Laird, J. (1996). Family-centered practice with lesbian and gay families. *Families in Society,* 77(9), 559–572.

Laird, J. (1998). Invisible ties: Lesbians and their families of origin. In C. Patterson & A. D'Augelli (Eds.), *Lesbian, gay, and bisexual identities in families: Psychological perspectives* (pp. 197–228). New York: Oxford University Press.

Lamison-White, L. (1998). *Poverty in the United States: 1996* (U.S. Bureau of the Census, Current Population Reports, Series P60-198). Washington, DC: Government

Printing Office. Retrieved August 1998 from http://www.census.gov/pub/prod/3/97pubs/p60-198.pdf.

Lancaster, E., & Lumb, J. (1999). Bridging the gap: Feminist theory and practice reality in work with the perpetrators of child sexual abuse. *Child and Family Social Work, 4*(2), 119–129.

Landon, P. S. (1995). Generalist and advanced generalist practice. In R. L. Edwards (Ed.), *The encyclopedia of social work* (19th ed., pp. 1101–1108). Washington, DC: NASW Press.

Lane, R. P. (1939). The field of community organization. In National Conference on Social Welfare, *Proceedings*. Chicago: University of Chicago Press.

Lang, N. C. (1972). A broad-range model of practice in social work group. *Social Service Review, 46*(1), 76–89.

Larder, J. (1998). Deadly disparities: Americans' widening gap in incomes may be narrowing our life spans. *Washington Post*, August 16, p. C1.

Larkin, E., Sadler, S. E., & Mahler, J. (2005). Benefits of volunteering for older adults mentoring at-risk youth. *Journal of Gerontological Social Work, 44*(3/4), 23–37.

Larner, A. J. (2005). Gardening and dementia. *International Journal of Geriatric Psychiatry, 20*(8), 796–799.

Laverack, G. (2006). Using a "domains" approach to build community empowerment. *Community Development Journal, 41*(1), 4–12.

Lazarus, R. (1980). The stress and coping paradigm. In L. Bond & J. Rosen (Eds.), *Competence and coping during adulthood* (pp. 28–74). Hanover, NH: University Press of New England.

Lazarus, R., & Folkman, S. (1984). *Stress, appraisal, and coping.* New York: Springer.

Lazarus, R. S., & Lazarus, B. N. (2006). *Coping with aging.* New York: Oxford University Press.

Leahy, D. (2004). How and why movement works: A movement workshop for adults with schizophrenic disorders. *Social Work with Groups, 27*(2/3), 113–127.

Lee, J. A. B. (1992). Personal communication, June 15.

Lee, J. A. B. (1994). *The empowerment approach to social work practice.* New York: Columbia University Press.

Lee, J. A. B. (2001). *The empowerment approach to social work practice: Building the beloved community* (2nd ed.). New York: Columbia University Press.

Lee, J. A. B. (2005). No place to go: Homeless women and children. In A. Gitterman & L. Shulman (Eds.), *Mutual aid groups, vulnerable and resilient populations, and the life cycle* (3rd ed., pp. 373–399). New York: Columbia University Press.

Lee, J. A. B., & Swenson, C. R. (2005). The concept of mutual aid. In A. Gitterman & Lawrence Shulman (Eds.), *Mutual aid groups, vulnerable and resilient populations and the life cycle* (3rd ed., pp. 573–596). New York: Columbia University Press.

Lee, P. (1929a). *Social casework, generic and specific, an outline: A report of the Milford Conference.* New York: American Association of Social Work.

Lee, P. (1929b). Social work as cause and function. In *Social work as cause and function and other papers: Selected papers of Porter R. Lee* (pp. 3–24). New York: Columbia University Press.

Lens, V. (2000). Protecting the confidentiality of the therapeutic relationship: *Jaffee v. Redmond. Social Work, 45*(3), 273–276.

Lens, V. (2002). Managed care and the judicial system: Another avenue for reform? *Health and Social Work, 27*(1), 27–35.

Lens, V. (2004). Principled negotiation: A new tool for case advocacy. *Social Work, 49*(3), 506–513.

Lens, V. (2005). Advocacy and argumentation in the public arena: A guide for social workers. *Social Work, 50*(3), 231–238.

Lerner, R. M. (2005). Foreword. In U. Bronfenbrenner (Ed.), *Making human beings human: Bioecological perspective on human development* (pp. ix–xxvi). Thousand Oaks, CA: Sage.

Levine, K., & Lightburn, A. (1989). Belief systems and social work practice. *Social Casework, 70*(March), 139–145.

Levinsky, L., & McAleer, K. (2005). Listen to us! Young adolescents in urban schools. In A. Gitterman & L. Shulman (Eds.), *Mutual aid groups, vulnerable and resilient populations and the life cycle* (3rd ed., pp. 203–219). New York: Columbia University Press.

Lewin, K. (1952). Group decisions and social change. In E. Maccoby, T. Newcomb, & E. Hartley (Eds.), *Readings in social psychology* (pp. 207–111). New York: Holt, Rinehart & Winston.

Lewis, E., & Suarez, Z. E. (1995). Natural helping networks. In R. L. Edwards (Ed.), *The encyclopedia of social work* (19th ed., pp. 1765–1772). Silver Spring, MD: National Association of Social Workers.

Lewis, M. (2005). The child and its family: The social network model. *Human Development, 48*(1–2), 8–27.

Li, H., Edwards, D., & Morrow-Howell, N. (2004). Informal caregiving networks and use of formal services by inner-city African American elderly with dementia. *Families in Society, 85*(1), 55–62.

Licoppe, C., & Smoreda, Z. (2005). Are social networks technologically embedded? How networks are changing today with changes in communication technology. *Social Networks, 27*(4), 317–335.

Lide, P. (1966). Dynamic mental representation: An analysis of the empathic process. *Social Casework, 47*(2), 146–151.

Lightfoot, E. B., & LaLiberte, T. L. (2006). Approaches to child protection case management for cases involving people with disabilities. *Child Abuse and Neglect, 30*(4), 381–391.

Lin, N., Ye, X., & Ensel, W. M. (1999). Social support and depressed mood: A structural analysis. *Journal of Health and Social Behavior, 40*(4), 344–359.

Lind, B. (1982). Mental patient status, work, and income: An examination of the effects of a psychiatric label. *American Sociological Review, 47*(April), 202–215.

Lindeman, E. (1924). *Social discovery: An approach to the study of functional groups.* New York: Republic.

Lindeman, E. (1926). *The meaning of adult education.* New York: New Republic.

Lindholm, G. (1995). Schoolyards: The significance of place properties to outdoor activities in schools. *Environment and Behavior, 27*(3), 259–293.

Linzer, N. (1999). *Resolving ethical dilemmas in social work practice.* Boston: Allyn & Bacon.

Lo, T. W. (2005). Task-centered groupwork: Reflections on practice. *International Social Work, 48*(4), 455–465.

Loewenberg, F., Dolgoff, R., & Harrington, D. (2000). *Ethical decisions for social work practice* (6th ed.). Itasca, IL: F. E. Peacock.

Longest, B. B., Jr. (2006). The community development potential of large health services organizations. *Community Development Journal, 41*(1), 89–103.

Lovett, B. B. (2004). Child sexual abuse disclosure: Maternal response and other variables impacting the victim. *Child and Adolescent Social Work Journal, 21*(4), 355–371.

Lubove, R. (1965). *The professional altruist.* Cambridge, MA: Harvard University Press.

Lucco, A. (1991). Assessment of the school-aged child. *Families in Society, 72*(7), 394–407.

Luckey, I. (1994). African American elders: The support network of generational kin. *Families in Society, 75*(2), 82–89.

Lukens, E. (2001). Schizophrenia. In A. Gitterman (Ed.), *Handbook of social work practice with vulnerable and resilient populations* (2nd ed., pp. 275–302). New York: Columbia University Press.

Lum, D. (2004). *Social work practice and people of color: A process-stage approach* (5th ed.). Belmont, CA: Brooks/Cole.

Lynn, M., & Nisivoccia, D. (1995). Activity-oriented group work with the mentally ill: Enhancing socialization. *Social Work with Groups, 18*(2/3), 33–52.

MacDonald v. Clinger, 84 A.D.2d 482, 446 N.Y.S.2d 801 (4th Dep't) (1982).

Mack-Canty, C. (2004). Third-wave feminism and the need to reweave the nature/culture duality. *NWSA Journal, 16*(3), 154–179.

Macgowan, M. J. (2003). Increasing engagement in groups: A measurement based approach. *Social Work with Groups, 26*(1), 5–28.

Macgowan, M. J., & Newman, F. L. (2005). Factor structure of the Group Engagement Measure. *Social Work Research, 29*(2), 107–118.

Malawista, K. L. (2004). Rescue fantasies in child therapy: Countertransference/transference enactments. *Child and Adolescent Social Work Journal, 21*(4), 373–386.

Malekoff, A. (1994). A guideline for group work with adolescents. *Social Work with Groups, 17*(1/2), 5–19.

Malekoff, A. (2004). *Group work with adolescents: Principles and practice* (2nd ed.). New York: Guilford Press.

Malgady, R. G., & Zayas, L. H. (2001). Cultural and linguistic considerations in psychodiagnosis with Hispanics: The need for an empirically informed process model. *Social Work, 46*(1), 39–49.

Mallon, G. P. (1994). Cow as co-therapist: Utilization of farm animals as therapeutic aides with children in residential treatment. *Child and Adolescent Social Work Journal, 11*(6), 455–474.

Marcos, L. R. (1994). The psychiatric examination of Hispanics across the language barrier. In R. G. Malgady & O. Rodriguez (Eds.), *Theoretical and conceptual issues in Hispanics' mental health* (pp. 143–154). Melbourne, FL: Krieger.

Margison, F. (2001). Practice-based evidence in psychotherapy. In C. Mace, S. Moorey, & B. Roberts (Eds.), *Evidence in the psychological therapies: A critical guide for practitioners* (pp. 174–198). Philadelphia: Taylor & Francis.

Martin, E. P., & Martin, J. M. (1995). *Social work and the black experience*. Washington, DC: National Association of Social Workers.

Maseko, M. (2003). A young parent's anxieties in raising her infant in a non-traditional family structure. *Journal of Child and Adolescent Mental Health, 15*(2), 77–80.

Mathews, G. (1982). Social workers and political influence. *Social Service Review, 56*(4), 616–628.

Mattaini, M. (1993a). *More than a thousand words: Graphics for clinical practice*. Washington, DC: NASW Press.

Mattaini, M. (1993b). *The visual ecoscan for clinical practice*. Washington, DC: NASW Press.

Mattaini, M., & Kirk, S. (1993). Misdiagnosing assessment. *Social Work, 38*(2), 231–232.

Mattison, M. (2003). Ethical decision making: The person in the process. *Social Work, 45*(3), 201–212.

May, J. C. (2005). Family attachment narrative therapy: Healing the experience of early childhood maltreatment. *Journal of Marital and Family Therapy, 31*(3), 221–237.

Mayer, F. S., & Frantz, C. M. (2004). The connectedness to nature scale: A measure of individuals' feeling in community with nature. *Journal of Environmental Psychology, 24*(4), 503–515.

Mbiti, J. (1970). *African religions and philosophy*. Garden City, NY: Anchor Books.

McCabe, K. M. (2002). Factors that predict premature termination among Mexican-

American children in outpatient psychotherapy. *Journal of Child and Family Studies*, *11*(3), 347–359.

McCarty, D., & Clancy, C. (2002). Telehealth: Implications for social work practice. *Social Work*, *47*(2), 153–161.

McCoy, J. M. (2005). Linking the physical work environment to creative context. *Journal of Creative Behavior*, *39*(3), 169–191.

McCoy, V. H., & Vila, C. K. (2002). Tech knowledge: Introducing computers for co-ordinated care. *Health and Social Work*, *27*(1), 71–74.

McFerran-Skewes, K. (2004). Using songs with groups of teenagers: How does it work? *Social Work with Groups*, *27*(2/3), 143–157.

McGowan, M. L. (1997). Thinking outside the box: The role of adventure in spiritual and ethical development. *Journal of Experiential Education*, *20*(1), 14–21.

McMillen, J. C. (1999). Better for it: How people benefit from adversity. *Social Work*, *44*(5), 455–466.

McMullin, P., & Gross, A. (1983). Sex differences, sex roles, and health-related help-seeking. In B. DePaulo, A. Nadler, & J. Fisher (Eds.), *New directions in helping* (Vol. 2). New York: Academic Press.

McNeil, J. (1995). Bereavement and loss. In R. L. Edwards (Ed.), *The encyclopedia of social work* (19th ed., pp. 7–15). Silver Spring, MD: National Association of Social Workers.

Merin, Y. (2002). *Equality for same-sex couples: The legal recognition of gay partnerships in Europe and the United States*. Chicago: University of Chicago Press.

Mesec, B., & Mesec, M. (2004). Conceptualization of the new methods of self-help appearing on the Internet. *European Journal of Social Work*, *7*(2), 181–194.

Meyer, C. H. (1970). *Social work practice: A response to the urban crises*. New York: Free Press.

Meyer, C. H. (1976). *Social work practice: The changing landscape* (2nd ed.). New York: Free Press.

Meyer, C. H. (1993). *Assessment in social work practice*. New York: Columbia University Press.

Meyer, C. H. (1996). My son the scientist. *Social Work Research*, *20*(1), 101–104.

Mickelson, J. S. (1995). Advocacy. In R. L. Edwards (Ed.), *The encyclopedia of Social Work* (19th ed., pp. 95–101). Washington, DC: NASW Press.

Middleman, R. (1980). The use of program. *Social Work with Groups*, *3*(3), 5–23.

Middleman, R., & Goldberg, G. (1974). *Social service delivery: A structural approach to social work practice*. New York: Columbia University Press.

Miller, A. L. (2005). *Observing children in their natural worlds: A methodological primer* (2nd ed.). Mahwah, NJ: Lawrence Erlbaum.

Miller, D., & Turnbull, W. (1986). Expectancies and interpersonal processes. *Annual Review of Psychology*, *37*, 233–256.

Miller, D. C., & Fewell, C. H. (2002). Social workers helping social workers: Self-help and peer consultation—a dialogue. *Journal of Social Work Practice in the Addictions*, *2*(1), 93–104.

Miller, J., & Donner, J. (2000). More than just talk: The use of racial dialogue. *Social Work with Groups*, *23*(1), 31–53.

Miller, W., & Rollnick, S. (2002). *Motivational interviewing: Preparing people to change addictive behavior* (2nd ed.). New York: Guilford Press.

Miller, W. R. (1983). Motivational interviewing with problem drinkers. *Behavioral Psychotherapy*, *11*, 142–147.

Millstein, K. (2000). Confidentiality in direct social work practice: Inevitable challenges and ethical dilemmas. *Families in Society*, *81*(3), 270–282.

Minami, H., & Tanaka, K. (1995). Social and environmental psychology: Transaction between physical space and group-dynamics processes. *Environment and Behavior*, *27*(1), 43–55.

Mirabito, D. M. (2001). Mining treatment termination data in an adolescent mental health service: A quantitative study. *Social Work in Health Care, 33*(3/4), 71–90.

Mishna, F., Antle, B. J., & Regehr, C. (2002). Social work with clients contemplating suicide: Complexity and ambiguity in the clinical, ethical, and legal considerations. *Clinical Social Work Journal, 30*(Fall), 265–280.

Mok, B. H. (2004). Self-help group participation and empowerment in Hong Kong. *Journal of Sociology and Social-Welfare, 31*(3), 153–168.

Mok, B. H. (2005). Organizing self-help groups for empowerment and social change: Findings and insights from an empirical study in Hong Kong. *Journal of Community Practice, 13*(1), 49–67.

Mondros, J., & Berman-Rossi, T. (1991). The relevance of stages of group development theory to community organization practice. *Social Work with Groups, 14*(3/4), 203–221.

Mondros, J., & Wilson, S. (1994). *Organizing for power and empowerment.* New York: Columbia University Press.

Moody, H. R. (2004). Hospital discharge planning: Carrying out orders. *Journal of Gerontological Social Work, 43*(1), 107–118.

Moore, B. C. (2005). Empirically supported family and peer interventions for dual disorders. *Research on Social Work Practice, 15*(4), 231–245.

Moreno, C. (2001). Developmental disabilities. In A. Gitterman (Ed.), *Handbook of social work practice with vulnerable and resilient populations* (2nd ed., pp. 205–223). New York: Columbia University Press.

Morgan, G. (1986). *Images of organizations.* Beverly Hills, CA: Sage.

Morris, K. B. (2002). Countertransference: One person's experience in working with the elderly. *Reflections, 8*(4), 3–10.

Morris, S. E., & Yates, R. (2002). Community energies under-evaluated: Drug initiatives on the margins. *Drug and Alcohol Professional, 2*(1), 36–41.

Morris, T. (2006). *Social work research methods: Four alternative paradigms.* Thousand Oaks, CA: Sage.

Morrison, J. (1991). The black church as a support system for the elderly. *Social Work with Groups, 17*(1/2), 105–120.

Morrow, D. F. (1993). Social work with gay and lesbian adolescents. *Social Work, 38*(6), 655–660.

Mota, J., Almeida, M., & Santos, P. (2005). Perceived neighborhood environments and physical activity in adolescents. *Preventive Medicine: An International Journal Devoted to Practice and Theory, 41*(5/6), 834–836.

Moxley, D. P. (2002). The emergence and attributes of second-generation community support systems for persons with serious mental illness: Implications for case management. *Journal of Social Work in Disability and Rehabilitation, 1*(2), 25–52.

Munetz, M. R., & Freese, F. (2001). Getting ready for recovery. *Psychiatric Rehabilitation Journal, 25*(1), 1–10.

Nadelman, A. (2005). Sharing the hurt: Adolescents in a residential setting. In A. Gitterman & L. Shulman (Eds.), *Mutual aid groups, vulnerable and resilient populations, and the life cycle* (3rd ed., pp. 220–245). New York: Columbia University Press.

Naderi, S., Miklósi, Á., & Dóka, A. (2001). Co-operative interactions between blind persons and their dogs. *Applied Animal Behaviour Science, 74*(1), 59–80.

Naess, A. (1989). *Ecology, community, and lifestyle: Outline of an ecosophy* (Trans. David Rothenberg). Cambridge: Cambridge University Press.

National Alliance of Methadone Advocates. (1999). *Starting a 12 step group.* New York: Alliance of Methadone Advocates.

National Association of Social Workers. (1992). *NASW standards for social work case management.* Washington, DC: Author.

National Association of Social Workers. (1999). *Code of ethics of the National Association of Social Workers.* Washington, DC: Author. Retrieved October 9, 2007, from http://www.socialworkers.org/pubs/code/code.asp.

National Association of Social Workers. (2007). Social work profession. May 17. Retrieved March 21, 2007, from https://www.socialworkers.org/pressroom/features/general/profession.asp.

Needleman, H. L., Schell, A., Bellinger, D., Leviton, A., & Allred, E. N. (1990). The long-term effects of exposure to low doses of lead in childhood. *New England Journal of Medicine, 322,* 83–88.

Nelsen, J. (1981). Issues in single-subject research for nonbehaviorists. *Social Work Research and Abstracts, 17*(Summer), 31–37.

Nelsen, J. (1985). Verifying the independent variable in single-subject research. *Social Work Research and Abstracts, 21*(Summer), 3–8.

Nelsen, J. (1988). Single-subject research. In R. Grinnell Jr. (Ed.), *Social work research and evaluation* (pp. 362–399). Itasca, IL: F. E. Peacock.

Nelson, H. W., Hooker, K., DeHart, K. N., Edwards, J. A., & Lanning, K. (2003). Factors important to success in the volunteer long-term care ombudsman role. *The Gerontologist, 44*(1), 116–120.

Netting, F. E., Kettner, P. M., & McMurtry, S. L. (2004). *Macro practice* (3rd ed.). Boston: Allyn & Bacon.

Neugarten, B. (1969). Time, age, and the life cycle. *American Journal of Psychiatry, 136*(7), 121–130.

Newman, B. S., Dannenfelser, P. L., & Benishek, L. (2002). Assessing beginning social work and counseling students' acceptance of lesbians and gay men. *Journal of Social Work Education, 38*(2), 273–288.

Newstetter, W. I. (1947). The social inter-group work process. In National Conference on Social Welfare, *Proceedings* (pp. 205–217). Chicago: University of Chicago Press.

Ng, S. M., Chan, T. H.Y., Chan, C. L. W., Lee, A. M., Yau, J. K. Y., Chan., C. H. Y., & Lau, J. (2006). Group debriefing for people with chronic diseases during the SARS pandemic: Strength-Focused and Meaning-Oriented Approach for Resilience and Transformation (SMART). *Community Mental Health Journal, 42*(1), 53–63.

Nichols, M. P., with Schwartz, R. C. (2004). *Family therapy: Concepts and methods.* Boston: Allyn & Bacon.

Nicotera, N. (2005). The child's view of neighborhood: Assessing a neglected element in direct social work practice. *Journal of Human Behavior in the Social Environment, 11*(3/4), 105–133.

Noble, C. (1997). *Welfare as we know it: A political history of the American welfare state.* New York: Oxford University Press.

Norman, J. (2000). Constructive narrative in arresting the impact of post-traumatic stress disorder. *Clinical Social Work Journal, 28*(3), 303–319.

Nosko, A., & Wallace, R. (1997). Female/male co-leadership in groups. *Social Work with Groups, 20*(2), 3–16.

Ogrodniczuk, J. S., Joyce, A. S., & Piper, W. E. (2005). Strategies for reducing patient-initiated premature termination of psychotherapy. *Harvard Review of Psychiatry, 13*(2), 57–70.

Ohlemacher, S. (2006). Illegal immigrants increase to 12 million. *Journal News,* March 8, p. 3B.

Ohmner, M. L., & Korr, W. S. (2006). The effectiveness of community practice interventions: A review of the literature. *Research in Social Work Practice, 16*(2), 132–145.

Ohtsubo, Y., & Masuchi, A. (2004). Effects of status difference and group size in group decision making. *Group Processes & Intergroup Relations, 7*(2), 161–172.

Orme, J. (2002). Social work: Gender, care and justice. *British Journal of Social Work, 32*(6), 799–814.

Orr, A. (2005). Dealing with the death of a member: Visually impaired elderly in the community. In A. Gitterman & L. Shulman (Eds.), *Mutual aid groups, vulnerable and resilient populations, and the life cycle* (3rd ed., pp. 471–492). New York: Columbia University Press.

Oswald, R. (2000). Family and friendship relationships after young women come out as bisexual or lesbian. *Journal of Homosexuality, 38*(3), 65–83.

Oswald, R. F. (2002). Inclusion and belonging in the family rituals of gay and lesbian people. *Journal of Family Psychology, 16*(4), 428–436.

Padilla, Y. C. (1997). Immigration policy: Issues for social work practice. *Social Work, 45*(6), 595–606.

Papell, C., & Rothman, B. (1966). Social group work models: Possession and heritage. *Journal of Education for Social Work, 2*(1), 66–77.

Parad, H. (Ed.). (1965). *Crisis intervention: Selected readings.* New York: Family Service Association of America.

Parrish, M., Burry, C., & Pabst, M. S. (2003). Providing comprehensive case management services to urban women with HIV/AIDS and their families. *AFFILIA, 18*(3), 302–315.

Passell, P. (1998). Benefits dwindle along with wages for the unskilled. *New York Times,* June 14, pp. 1, 28.

Patrick, J., & Rich, C. (2004). Anger management taught to adolescents with an experiential object relations approach. *Child and Adolescent Social Work Journal, 21*(1), 85–100.

Patterson, C. J. (2000). Family relationships of lesbians and gay men. *Journal of Marriage and the Family, 62*(4), 1052–1069.

Patterson, S., Memmott, J., Germain, C. B., & Brennan, E. (1992). Patterns of natural helping in rural areas: Social work research implications. *Social Work Research and Abstracts, 28*(3), 22–28.

Patterson, S. L., Germain, C. B., Brennan, E. M., & Memmott, J. (1988). Effectiveness of rural natural helpers. *Social Casework, 69*(5), 272–279.

Patterson, S. L., & Marsiglia, F. F. (2000). "Mi casa es su casa": Beginning exploration of Mexican Americans' natural helping. *Families in Society, 81*(1), 22–31.

Patti, R., & Resnick, H. (1972). Changing the agency from within, *Social Work, 17*(4), 48–57.

Paulino, A. (1995). Spiritism, Santería, Brujería, and Voodism: A comparative view of indigenous healing systems. *Journal of Teaching and Social Work, 12*(1/2), 105–124.

Peake, K., Surko, M., Epstein, I., & Medeiros, D. (2005). Data-mining client concerns in adolescent mental health services: Clinical and program implications. In K. Peake, I. Epstein, & D. Medeiros (Eds.), *Clinical and research uses of an adolescent mental health intake questionnaire: What kids need to talk about* (pp. 287–304). Binghamton, NY: Haworth Press.

Peeble-Wilkens, W., & Francis, E. A. (1990). Two outstanding black women in social welfare history: Mary Church Terrell and Ida B. Wells-Barnett. *AFFILIA, 5*(4), 87–100.

Perkins, K., & Tice, C. (1995). A strengths perspective in practice: Older people and mental health challenges. *Journal of Gerontological Social Work, 23*(3/4), 83–97.

Perlman, H. H. (1957). *Social casework: A problem-solving process.* Chicago: University of Chicago Press.

Phillips, A. (2006). A mind is a terrible thing to measure. *New York Times,* February 26, pp. 4, 13.

Phillips, D. G. (2003). Dangers of boundary violations in the treatment of borderline patients. *Clinical Social Work Journal, 31*(3), 315–326.

Phillips, H. (1951). *Essentials of social group work skill.* New York: Association Press.

Pierce, D. (1984). *Policy for the social work practitioner.* New York: Longman.

Pietsch, U. K. (2002). Facilitating post-divorce transition using narrative therapy. *Journal of Couple and Relationship Therapy, 1*(1), 65–81.

Pincus, A., & Minehan, A. (1973). *Social work practice: Model and method*. Itasca, IL: F. E. Peacock.

Pinderhughes, E. (1982). Black genealogy: Self-liberator and therapeutic tool. *Smith College Studies in Social Work, 59*(1), 93–106.

Pinderhughes, E. (1983). Empowerment for our clients and for ourselves. *Social Casework, 64*(6), 331–338.

Pinderhughes, E. (1989). *Understanding race, ethnicity, and power*. New York: Free Press.

Poggi, I. (2005). The goals of persuasion. *Pragmatics & Cognition, 13*(2), 297–336.

Polack, R. J. (2004). Social justice and the global economy: New challenges for social work in the 21st century. *Social Work, 49*(2), 281–290.

Pope, K. S., Sonne, J. L., & Greene, B. (2006a). Therapists' sexual arousals, attractions, and fantasies: An example of a topic that isn't there. In K. S. Pope, J. L. Sonne, & B. Greene (Eds.), *What therapists don't talk about and why: Understanding taboos that hurt us and our clients* (pp. 27–41). Washington, DC: American Psychological Association.

Pope, K. S., Sonne, J. L., & Greene, B. (2006b). Questioning myths, taboos, secrets, and uncomfortable topics. In K. S. Pope, J. L. Sonne, & B. Greene (Eds.), *What therapists don't talk about and why: Understanding taboos that hurt us and our clients* (pp. 3–26). Washington, DC: American Psychological Association.

Pope, K. S., Sonne, J. L., & Greene, B. (2006c). Possible clues to taboo topics and uncomfortable feelings. In K. S. Pope, J. L. Sonne, & B. Greene (Eds.), *What therapists don't talk about and why: Understanding taboos that hurt us and our clients* (pp. 65–83). Washington, DC: American Psychological Association.

Porter, E. (2006). Stretched to the limit, women stall march for work. *New York Times*, March 2, pp. A1, C2.

Pottick, K., Wakefield, J., & Kirk, S. (2003). Influence of social workers' characteristics on the perception of mental disorder in youth. *Social Service Review, 77*(3), 431–454.

Prato-Previde, E., Fallani, G., & Valsecchi, P. (2006). Gender differences in owners interacting with pet dogs: An observational study. *Ethology, 112*(1), 64–73.

Pressman, J., & Wildavsky, A. (1973). *Implementation*. Berkeley: University of California Press.

Price, P. C., Smith, A. R., & Lench, H. C. (2006). The effect of target group size on risk judgments and comparative optimism: The more, the riskier. *Journal of Personality and Social Psychology, 90*(3), 382–398.

Prochaska, J. O., & DiClemente, C. C. (1982). Transtheoretical therapy: Toward a more integrative model of change. *Psychotherapy: Theory, Research, and Practice, 19*(3), 276–288.

Prochaska, J. O., & DiClemente, C. C. (2005). The transtheoretical approach. In J. C. Norcross & M. R. Goldfried (Eds.), *Handbook of psychotherapy integration* (2nd ed., pp. 147–171). New York: Oxford University Press.

Prochaska, J. O., DiClemente, C. C., & Norcross, J. C. (1992). In search for how people change: Applications to addictive behaviors. *American Psychologist, 47*(9), 1102–1114.

Proshansky, H., Ittelson, W., & Revlin, L. (1976). *Environmental psychology: People and their settings*. New York: Holt, Rinehart & Winston.

Pruchno, R., Dempsey, N., Carder, N., & Koropeckyj-Cox, T. (1993). Multigenerational households of caregiving families: Negotiating shared space. *Environment and Behavior, 25*(3), 349–366.

Raines, J. C. (1990). Empathy in clinical social work. *Clinical Social Work Journal, 18*(1), 57–72.

Raines, J. C. (1996). Self-disclosure in clinical social work. *Clinical Social Work Journal*, *24*(4), 357–375.

Raines, J. C. (2004). To tell or not to tell: Ethical issues regarding confidentiality. *School Social Work Journal*, *28*(2), 61–78.

Rank, M. R., Yoon, H., & Hirschl, T. A. (2003). American poverty as a structural failing: Evidence and arguments. *Journal of Sociology and Social Welfare*, *30*(4), 3–29.

Reagh, R. E. (1994). What's wrong with prevention research? In J. A. Fickling (Ed.), *Social problems with health consequences: Program design, implementation, and evaluation* (pp. 89–96). Columbia: Proceedings of the Bi-Regional Conference for Public Health Social Workers in Regions IV and VI, University of South Carolina College of Social Work.

Reamer, F. (1990). *Ethical dilemmas in social service*. New York: Columbia University Press.

Reamer, F. (1995a). Ethics and values. In R. L. Edwards (Ed.), *The encyclopedia of social work* (19th ed., pp. 893–902). Washington, DC: NASW Press.

Reamer, F. (1995b). Malpractice claims against social workers: First facts. *Social Work*, *40*(4), 595–601.

Reamer, F. (1997). Managing ethics under managed care. *Families in Society*, *78*(1), 96–101.

Reamer, F. (2003). Boundary issues in social work: Managing dual relationships. *Social Work*, *48*(1), 121–133.

Reamer, F. (2005). Ethical and legal standards in social work: Consistency and conflict. *Families in Society*, *86*(2), 163–169.

Reamer, F. (2006). *Social work values and ethics* (3rd ed.). New York: Columbia University Press.

Redfer, L., & Goodman, J. (1989). Brief report: Pet facilitated therapy with autistic children. *Journal of Autism and Developmental Disorder*, *19*(3), 461–467.

Reed, P., & Rothenberg, D. (1993). *Wisdom in the air: The Norwegian roots of deep ecology*. Minneapolis: University of Minneapolis Press.

Reese, D. J., & Sontag, M. A. (2001). Successful interprofessional collaboration on the hospice team. *Health and Social Work*, *26*(3), 167–175.

Regan, S. (1992). A mutual aid based group role play: Its use as an educational tool. *Social Work with Groups*, *15*(4), 73–87.

Regehr, C., & Antle, B. (1997). Coercive influence: Informed consent in court-mandated social work. *Social Work*, *42*(3), 300–306.

Reid, K., Mathews, G., & Liss, P. (1995). My partner is hurting: Group work with male partners of adult survivors of sexual abuse. *Social Work with Groups*, *18*(1), 81–87.

Reid, W. (1992). *Task strategies: An empirical approach to clinical social work*. New York: Columbia University Press.

Reid, W. J. (2002). Knowledge for direct social work practice: An analysis of trends. *Social Service Review*, *76*(1), 6–33.

Reiss, D. (1981). *The family's construction of reality*. Cambridge, MA: Harvard University Press.

Reitan, T. C. (1998). Theories of interorganizational relations in the human services. *Social Service Review*, *72*(3), 285–309.

Reitzel, L. R., Stellrecht, N. E., & Gordon, K. H. (2006). Does time between application and case assignment predict therapy attendance or premature termination in outpatients? *Psychological Services*, *3*(1), 51–60.

Resnick, H., & Jaffee, B. (1982). The physical environment and social welfare. *Social Casework*, *63*(6), 354–362.

Reynolds, B. (1942). *Learning and teaching in the practice of social work*. New York: Farrar and Rinehart.

Reynolds, B. C. (1934/1982). Between client and community: A study in responsibility in social casework. *Smith College Studies in Social Work*, 5(1, Entire Issue). Republished as *Between client and community: A study in responsibility in social casework*. Silver Spring, MD: National Association of Social Workers.

Reynolds, B. C. (1951). *Social work and social living; explorations in philosophy and practice.* New York: Citadel Press.

Reynolds, B. C. (1964). The social casework of an unchartered journey. *Social Work*, 9(4), 13–17.

Rhodes, M. L. (1992). Social work challenges: The boundaries of ethics. *Families in Society*, 73(1), 40–47.

Richardson, G., Neiger, B., Jensen, S., & Kumpfer, K. (1990). The resiliency model. *Health Education*, 21(6), 33–39.

Richmond, M. E. (1917). *Social diagnosis.* New York: Russell Sage.

Riessman, C. K., & Quinney, L. (2005). Narrative in social work: A critical review. *Qualitative Social Work*, 4(4), 391–412.

Riley, M. W. (1985). Women, men, and the lengthening of the life course. In A. S. Rossi (Ed.), *Aging and the life course* (pp. 333–347). New York: Aldine.

Roberts, S. (2007). New demographic racial gap emerges. *New York Times*, May 17, p. A21.

Robinson, G., & Gelhorn, O. (1972). *The administrative process.* Saint Paul, MN: West.

Robinson, V. (1930). *A changing psychology in social casework.* Chapel Hill: University of North Carolina Press.

Rock, B., & Congress, E. (1999). The new confidentiality for the 21st century in a managed care environment. *Social Work*, 44(3), 253–262.

Rodgers, K. B., & Rose, H. A. (2002). Risk and resiliency factors among adolescents who experience marital transitions. *Journal of Marriage and the Family*, 64(4), 1024–1037.

Rodwell, M., & Blankebaker, A. (1992). Strategies for developing cross-cultural sensitivity: Wounding as a metaphor. *Journal of Social Work Education*, 28(2), 153–165.

Roer-Strier, D., & Rosenthal, M. K. (2001). Socialization in changing cultural contexts: A search for images of the "adaptive adult." *Social Work*, 46(3), 215–228.

Rogers, C. (1961). The characteristics of a helping relationship. In C. Rogers (Ed.), *On becoming a person* (pp. 33–58). Boston: Houghton Mifflin.

Rooney, R. H. (1992). *Strategies for work with involuntary clients.* New York: Columbia University Press.

Rooney, R. H., & Bibus, A. A., III. (1996). Multiple lenses: Ethnically sensitive practice with involuntary clients who are having difficulties with drugs or alcohol. *Journal of Multicultural Social Work*, 4(2), 59–73.

Rose, S. D., Duby, P., Olenick, C., & Weston, T. (1996). Integrating family, group and residential treatment: A cognitive-behavioral approach. *Social Work with Groups*, 19(2), 35–48.

Rosen, S. M. (1988). Memorandum. New York: Columbia University School of Social Work (unpublished).

Rosenbloom, M. (1995). Implications of the Holocaust for social work. *Families in Society*, 76(9), 567–576.

Ross, M. G. (1955). *Community organization: Theory and principles.* New York: Harper & Brothers.

Rothman, J. (1994). *Social work with highly vulnerable populations: Case management and community-based service.* Englewood Cliffs, NJ: Prentice-Hall.

Rothman, J. (1995). Approaches to community intervention. In J. Rothman, J. Erlich, & J. Tropman (Eds.), *Strategies of community interventions: Macro practice* (5th ed., pp. 27–64). Itasca, IL: F. E. Peacock.

Rothman, J. (1996). The interweaving of community intervention approaches. *Journal of Community Practice, 3*(3/4), 69–99.

Rounds, K. A., & Galinsky, M. J. (1991). Linking people with AIDS in rural communities: The telephone group. *Social Work, 36*(1), 13–18.

Roy, M. M., & Christenfeld, N. J. S. (2004). Do dogs resemble their owners? *Psychological Science, 15*(5), 361–363.

Rubin, H. J., & Rubin, I. S. (2001). *Community organizing and development* (3rd ed.). Boston: Allyn & Bacon.

Russell, G. M., & Greenhouse, E. M. (1997). Homophobia in the supervisory relationship: An invisible intruder. *Psychoanalytic Review, 84*(1), 27–42.

Rutter, M. (1987). Psychosocial resilience and protective mechanisms. *American Journal of Orthopsychiatry, 57*(3), 316–331.

Ryan, A. S., & Hendricks, C. O. (1989). Culture and communication: Supervising the Asian and Hispanic social worker. *The Clinical Supervisor, 7*(1), 27–40.

Ryan, S. D. (2000). Examining social workers' placement recommendations of children with gay and lesbian adoptive parents. *Families in Society, 81*(5), 517–528.

Sackett, D. L., Richardson, W. S., Rosenberg, W., & Haynes, R. B. (1997). *Evidence-based medicine: How to practice and teach evidence-based medicine.* New York: Churchill Livingstone.

Sackett, D. L., Rosenberg, W. M. C., Muir Gray, J. A., Haynes, R. B., & Richardson, W. S. (1996). Evidence-based medicine: What it is and what it isn't. *British Medical Journal, 312,* 71–72.

Saino, M. (2003). A new language for groups: Multilingual and multiethnic groupwork. *Social Work with Groups, 26*(1), 69–82.

Saleebey, D. (2004). "The power of place": Another look at the environment. *Families in Society, 85*(1), 7–16.

Saleebey, D. (Ed.). (2006). *The strengths perspective in social work practice* (4th ed.). Boston: Pearson/Allyn & Bacon.

Salzer, M. S., Rappaport, J., & Segre, L. (1999). Professional appraisal of professionally led and self-help groups. *American Journal of Orthopsychiatry, 69*(4), 536–540.

Sanders, C. R. (2000). The impact of guide dogs on the identity of people with visual impairments. *Anthrozoos, 13*(3), 131–139.

Sands, R. G. (1996). The elusiveness of identity in social work practice with women: A postmodern feminist perspective. *Clinical Social Work Journal, 24*(2), 167–186.

Sangalang, B. B., Barth, R. P., & Pointer, J. S. (2006). First-birth outcomes and timing of second births: A statewide case management program for adolescent mothers. *Health and Social Work, 31*(1), 54–63.

Sarasohn, M. K. (2005). The use of shame and dread in the countertransference. *Clinical Social Work Journal, 33*(4), 445–453.

Sarno, M. T., & Chambers, N. (1997). A horticultural therapy program for individuals with acquired aphasia. *Activities, Adaptation & Aging, 22*(1/2), 81–91.

Sarri, R. C. (1974). Behavioral theory and group work. In P. Glasser, R. Sari, & R. Vinter (Eds.), *Individual change through small groups* (pp. 50–79). New York: Free Press.

Saucier, D. A., & Cawman, A. J. (2004). Civil unions in Vermont: Political attitudes, religious fundamentalism and sexual prejudice. *Journal of Homosexuality, 48*(1), 1–18.

Saulnier, C. F. (2000). Incorporating feminist theory into social work practice: Group work examples. *Social Work with Groups, 23*(1), 5–29.

Schamess, G. (1998). Corporate values and managed mental health care. In G. Schamess & A. Lightburn (Eds.), *Humane managed care?* (pp. 23–35). Washington, DC: NASW Press.

Schatz, H. A. (1970). *Social work administration: A resource book.* New York: Council on Social Work Education.

Schiele, J. H. (1996). Afrocentricity: An emerging paradigm in social work practice. *Social Work*, *41*(3), 284–294.

Schiller, L. Y. (1995). Stages of development in women's groups: A relational model. In R. Kurland & R. Salmon (Eds.), *Group work practice in a troubled society* (pp. 117–138). Binghamton, NY: Haworth Press.

Schiller, L. Y. (1997). Rethinking stages of group development in women's groups. *Social Work with Groups*, *20*(3), 3–19.

Schiller, L. Y., & Zimmer, B. (2005). Sharing the secrets: The power of women's groups for sexual abuse survivors. In A. Gitterman & L. Shulman (Eds.), *Mutual aid groups, vulnerable and resilient populations, and the life cycle* (3rd ed., pp. 290–319). New York: Columbia University Press.

Schilling, R. (1987). Limitations of social support. *Social Service Review*, *61*(March), 19–31.

Schloemer, F. (2000). The role of self-disclosure in helping and healing between gay clients and therapists. *Reflections*, *6*(4), 50–57.

Schlutsmeyer, M. W., & Pike, N. E. (2002). Owning research: The appropriation of psychological data. In J. D. Raskin & S. K. Bridges (Eds.), *Exploring constructivist psychology* (pp. 181–200). New York: Pace University Press.

Schmid, H. (2004). Organization-environment relationships: Theory for management practice in human service organizations. *Administration in Social Work*, *28*(1), 97–113.

Schmid, R. E. (2006). Report: U.S. not good for Hispanics' health. *Journal News*, March 2, p. 8B.

Schon, D. A. (1987). *Educating the reflective practitioner.* San Francisco: Jossey-Bass.

Schopler, J. H., Abell, M. D., & Galinsky, M. J. (1998). Technology-based groups: A review and conceptual framework for practice. *Social Work*, *43*(3), 254–266.

Schopler, J. H., & Galinsky, M. (1984). Meeting practice needs: Conceptualizing the open-ended group. *Social Work with Groups*, *7*(2), 3–21.

Schopler, J., Galinsky, M., & Abell, M. (1997). Creating community through telephone and computer groups: Theoretical and practice perspectives. *Social Work with Groups*, *20*(4), 19–34.

Schorr, A. (1985). Professional practice as policy. *Social Service Review*, *59*(2), 178–196.

Schwartz, W. (1959). Group work and the social scene. In A. J. Kahn (Ed.), *Issues in American work.* New York: Columbia University Press.

Schwartz, W. (1961). The social worker in the group. In *The social welfare forum* (pp. 146–177). New York: Columbia University Press.

Schwartz, W. (1962). Toward a strategy of group work practice. *Social Service Review*, *36*(3), 268–279.

Schwartz, W. (1969). Private troubles and public issues: One social work job or two? In *The social welfare forum 1969* (pp. 22–43). New York: Columbia University Press.

Schwartz, W. (1971). On the use of groups in social work practice. In W. Schwartz & S. Zelba (Eds.), *The practice of group work* (pp. 32–24). New York: Columbia University Press.

Schwartz, W. (1976). Between client and system: The mediating function. In R. Roberts & H. Northern (Eds.), *Theories of social work with groups* (pp. 171–197). New York: Columbia University Press.

Schwartz, W. (1978). Rosalie. *Social Work with Groups*, *1*(3), 265–278.

Seabury, B. (1971). Arrangements of physical space in social work settings. *Social Work*, *16*(8), 43–49.

Sebba, R. (1990). The landscapes of childhood: The reflections of childhood's environment in adult memories and in children's attitudes. *Environment and Behavior*, *22*(July), 395–422.

Secemsky, V. O., Ahlman, C., & Robbins, J. (1999). Managing group conflict: The development of comfort among social group workers. *Social Work with Groups, 21*(4), 35–48.

Seligman, M. (1980). *Human helplessness.* New York: Academic Press.

Shapiro, B. A., & Kaplan, M. J. (1998). Mental illness and horticultural therapy practice. In S. P. Simson & M. C. Straus (Eds.), *Horticulture as therapy: Principles and practice* (pp. 157–197). Binghamton, NY: Food Products Press/Haworth Press.

Shepard, B. (2005). Play, creativity, and the new community organizing. *Journal of Progressive Human-Services, 16*(2), 47–69.

Sherr, M. E., & Straughan, H. H. (2005). Volunteerism, social work, and the church: A historic overview and look into the future. *Social Work and Christianity, 32*(2), 97–115.

Shippy, R. A., & Karpiak, S. E. (2005). The aging HIV/AIDS population: Fragile social networks. *Aging & Mental Health, 9*(3), 246–254.

Shore, E. R. (2005). Returning a recently adopted companion animal: Adopters' reasons for and reactions to the failed adoption experience. *Journal of Applied Animal Welfare Science, 8*(3), 187–198.

Shulman, L. (1967). Scapegoats, group workers, and pre-emptive interventions. *Social Work, 12*(2), 37–43.

Shulman, L. (1978). A study of practice skills. *Social Work, 23*(4), 274–281.

Shulman, L. (1979). *The skills of helping: Individuals and groups.* Itasca, IL: F. E. Peacock.

Shulman, L. (1981). *Identifying, measuring, and teaching helping skills.* New York: Council on Social Work Education and the Canadian Association of Schools of Social Work.

Shulman, L. (1986). The dynamic of mutual aid. In A. Gitterman & L. Shulman (Eds.), *The legacy of William Schwartz: Group practice as shared interaction* (pp. 51–60). Binghamton, NY: Haworth Press.

Shulman, L. (1987). Consultation. In A. Minahan (Ed.), *The encyclopedia of social work* (18th ed., pp. 326–331). Silver Spring, MD: National Association of Social Workers.

Shulman, L. (1991). *Interactional social work practice: Toward an empirical theory.* Itasca, IL: F. E. Peacock.

Shulman, L. (2005). Persons with AIDS in substance-abusing recovery: Managing the interaction between the two. In A. Gitterman & L. Shulman (Eds.), *Mutual aid groups, vulnerable and resilient populations, and the life cycle* (3rd ed., pp. 266–289). New York: Columbia University Press.

Shulman, L. (2006). *The skills of helping individuals, families, groups and communities* (5th ed.). Belmont, CA: Thomson Higher Education.

Siebold, C. (1991). Termination: When the therapist leaves. *Clinical Social Work Journal, 19*(2), 191–204.

Simmons, T., & O'Neill, G. (2001). *Households and families: 2000.* Retrieved July 26, 2006, from http://www.census.gov/population/www/cen2000/briefs.html.

Simon, B. L. (1994). *The empowerment tradition in American social work: A history.* New York: Columbia University Press.

Siporin, M. (1984). Have you heard the one about social work humor? *Social Casework, 65*(8), 459–464.

Sloane, C. (2003). How did we get here? The importance of sharing with members the reasons for a group's formation and the history of its development. *Social Work with Groups, 26*(2), 35–49.

Smith, A. (1981). Goal attainment scaling: A method for evaluating the outcome of mental health treatment. In P. McReynolds (Ed.), *Advances in psychological assessment* (Vol. 5, pp. 424–459). San Francisco: Jossey-Bass.

Smith, A. (1997). Cultural diversity and the coming-out process: Implications for clinical practice. In B. Greene (Ed.), *Ethnic and cultural diversity among lesbians and gay men* (pp. 279–301). Thousand Oaks, CA: Sage.

Smith, C., & Carlson, B. (1997). Stress, coping and resilience in children and youth. *Social Service Review, 71*(2), 231–256.

Smith, D. (1987). The limits of positivism in social work research. *British Journal of Social Work, 17*, 401–416.

Smith, L. L., Smith, J. N., & Beckner, B. M. (1994). An anger-management workshop for women inmates. *Families in Society, 75*(3), 172–175.

Smith, R. L., & Montilla, R. E. (2004). *Counseling and family therapy with Latino populations: Strategies that work.* New York: Brunner-Routledge.

Smith, T. L., Toseland, R. W., Rizzo, V. M., & Zinoman, M. A. (2004). Telephone caregivers support groups. In R. Salmon & R. Graziano (Eds.), *Group work and aging: Issues in practice, research and education* (pp. 151–172). Binghamton, NY: Haworth Press.

Solomon, B. B. (1976). *Black empowerment: Social work in minority communities.* New York: Columbia University Press.

Solomon, B. B. (1982). Social work values and skills to empower women. In A. Weick & S. T. Vandiver (Eds.), *Women, power, and change* (pp. 206–214). Washington, DC: National Association of Social Workers.

Specht, H. (1986). Social support, social network, social exchange, and the social work practice. *Social Service Review, 60*(2), 218–232.

Specht , H., & Specht, R. (1986). Social work assessment: route to clienthood—Part I. *Social Casework: The Journal of Contemporary Social Work, 67*(9), 525–532.

Speer, P. W., & Zippay, A. (2005). Participatory decision-making among community coalitions: An analysis of task group meetings. *Administration in Social Work, 29*(3), 61–77.

Spencer, H. (1851). *Social statics, or the conditions essential to happiness specified, and the first of them developed.* London: John Chapman.

Sperry, D. M., & Gilbert, B. O. (2005). Child peer sexual abuse: Preliminary data on outcomes and disclosure experiences. *Child Abuse and Neglect, 29*(8), 889–904.

Sperry, L. (Ed.). (2004). *Assessment of couples and families: Contemporary and cutting-edge strategies.* New York: Brunner-Routledge.

Spira, J. L., & Reed, G. M. (2003). Group structure and content. In J. Spira, L. James, & G. M. Reed (Eds.), *Group psychotherapy for women with breast cancer* (pp. 34–70). Washington, DC: American Psychological Association.

Stampley, C., & Slaght, E. (2004). Cultural countertransference as a clinical obstacle. *Smith College Studies in Social Work, 74*(2), 333–347.

Statsky, W. P. (1975). *Legislative analysis: How to use statutes and regulations.* St. Paul, MN: West.

Stein, L., Rothman, B., & Nakanishi, M. (1993). The telephone group: Accessing group services to the homebound. *Social Work with Groups, 16*(1/2), 203–215.

Steinberg, D. M. (1999). The impact of time and place on mutual-aid practice with short-term groups. *Social Work with Groups, 22*(2/3), 101–118.

Steinberg, D. S. (1997). *The mutual-aid approach to working with groups: Helping people to help each other.* Northvale, NJ: Jason Aronson.

Stokes, N., & Gillis, J. (1995). Effective treatment strategies with adult incest survivors: Utilizing therapeutic group work methods within the context of an immediate family. In R. Kurland & R. Salmon (Eds.), *Group work practice in a troubled society* (pp. 189–201). New York: Haworth Press.

Stone, G. L. (1997). Multiculturalism as a context for supervision: Perspectives, limitations, and implications. In D. B. Pope-Davis & H. L. K. Coleman (Eds.), *Multicultural counseling competencies: Assessment, education and training, and supervision* (pp. 263–289). Thousand Oaks, CA: Sage.

Strauss, D., & Gabaldo, M. (1998). Traumatic brain injury and horticultural therapy practice. In S. P. Simson & M. C. Straus (Eds.), *Horticulture as therapy: Principles and practice* (pp. 105–129). Binghamton, NY: Food Products Press/Haworth Press.

Straussner, S. (1998). Group treatment with substance abusing clients: A model of treatment during the early phases of outpatient group therapy. *Journal of Chemical Dependency Treatment, 7*(1/2), 67–80.

Strom-Gottfried, K. (2003). Understanding adjudication: Origins, targets, and outcomes of ethics complaints. *Social Work, 48*(1), 85–95.

Strom-Gottfried, K., & Corcoran, K. (1998). Confronting ethical dilemmas in managed care: Guidelines for students and faculty. *Journal of Social Work Education, 34*(1), 109–120.

Strommen, E. F. (1993). "You're a what?" Family member reactions to the disclosure of homosexuality. In L. D. Garnets & D. C. Kimmel (Eds.), *Psychological perspectives on lesbian and gay male experiences* (pp. 248–266). New York: Columbia University Press.

Sturgeon, N. (1997). *Ecofeminist natures: Race, gender, feminist theory and political action.* New York: Routledge.

Sue, D. W. (2006). *Multicultural social work practice.* New York: Wiley.

Sue, D. W., Carter, R. T., Casas, J. M., Fouad, N. A., Ivey, A. E., Jensen, M., LaFromboise, T., Manese, J. F., Ponterotto, J. G., & Vazquez-Nutall, E. (1998). *Multicultural counseling competencies: Individual and organizational development.* Thousand Oaks, CA: Sage.

Sulman, J., Savage, D., & Way, S. (2001). Retooling social work practice for high volume, short stay. *Social Work in Health Care, 34*(3/4), 315–332.

Sundel, M., Glasser, P., Sarri, R., & Vinter, R. (1985). *Individual change through small groups* (2nd ed.). New York: Free Press.

Swenson, C. (1979). Networks, mutual aid, and the life model. In C. B. Germain (Ed.), *Social work practice: People and environments* (pp. 213–238). New York: Columbia University Press.

Swenson, C. (1981). Using natural helping networks to promote competence. In A. Maluccio (Ed.), *Promoting competence in clients* (pp. 103–125). New York: Free Press.

Swigonski, M. E. (1996). Challenging privilege through Afrocentric social work practice. *Social Work, 41*(2), 153–161.

Szent-Gyorgyi, A. (1967). *Collected papers 1913–31, 1949–54.* Bethesda, MD: National Library of Medicine.

Taft, J. (1937). The relation of function to process in social casework. *Journal of Social Work Process, 1*(1), 1–18.

Takahashi, K. (2005). Toward a life span theory of close relationships: The affective relationships model. *Human Development, 48*(1/2), 48–66.

Tannen, D. (2004). Talking the dog: Framing pets as interactional resources in family discourse. *Research on Language and Social Interaction, 37*(4), 399–420.

Tarasoff v. Regents of University of California, 17 Cal. 3d 425, 551 P.2d 334, 131 Cal. Rptr. 14 (Cal. 1976).

Taylor, U. (1998). The historical evolution of black feminist theory and praxis. *Journal of Black Studies, 29*(2), 234–253.

Terkelsen, K. G. (1980). Toward a theory of the family life cycle. In E. A. Carter & M. McGoldrick (Eds.), *The family life cycle: A framework for family therapy* (pp. 21–52). New York: Gardner.

Terrell, M. (1940/2005). *A colored women in a white world.* Washington, DC: Ransdell. Reprint, Amherst, NY: Humanity Books.

Thomas, H., & Caplan, T. (1999). Spinning the group process wheel: Effective facilitation techniques for motivating involuntary client groups. *Social Work with Groups, 21*(4), 3–21.

Tillyn, N., & Caye, J. (2004). Using writing and poetry to achieve focus and depth in a group of women parenting sexually abused children. *Social Work with Groups*, 27(2/3), 129–142.

Tolman, R. M., & Molidor, C. E. (1994). A decade of social group work research: Trends in methodology, theory, and program development. *Research on Social Work Practice*, 4(2), 142–159.

Torczyner, J. (1991). Discretion, judgment, and informed consent: Ethical and practice issues in social action. *Social Work*, 36(2), 97–192.

Toseland, R. W., & Rivas, R. F. (2005). *An introduction to group work practice* (5th ed.). Boston: Allyn & Bacon.

Toseland, R. W., & Rizzo, V. M. (2004). What's different about working with older people in groups? In R. Salmon & R. Graziano (Eds.), *Group work and aging* (pp. 5–24). Binghamton, NY: Haworth Press.

Tracy, E. M. (1993). Teaching about social networks and social support: A social network mapping exercise. *Journal of Teaching in Social Work*, 7(2), 37–46.

Trecker, H. B. (Ed.). (1955). *Group work foundations*. New York: Whitened, William Morrow.

Trecker, H. B. (Ed.). (1956). *Group work in the psychiatric setting*. New York: Whitened, William Morrow.

Trecker, H. B. (1961). *New understanding of administration*. New York: Association Press.

Trimble, D. (2005). Confronting responsibility: Men who batter their wives. In A. Gitterman & L. Shulman (Eds.), *Mutual aid groups, vulnerable and resilient populations, and the life cycle* (3rd ed., pp. 352–372). New York: Columbia University Press.

Tropman, J. E., & Shaefer, H. L. (2004). Flameout at the top: Executive calamity in the nonprofit sector: Its precursors and sequelae. *Administration in Social Work*, 28(3/4), 161–182.

Tropp, E. (1971). Social group work: The developmental approach. In *The encyclopedia of social work* (pp. 1246–1252). New York: National Association of Social Workers.

Truax, C., & Carkhoff, R. (1967). *Toward effective counseling and psychotherapy*. Chicago: Atherton.

Tufts, J. (1923). *Education and training for social work*. New York: Russell Sage Foundation.

Tully, C. T. (2000). *Lesbians, gays and the empowerment perspective*. New York: Columbia University Press.

Turner, S. G. (2001). Resilience and social work practice: Three case studies. *Families in Society*, 82(5), 441–448.

Tyler, T. R., Boeckman, R. J., Smith, H. J., & Huo, Y. J. (1997). *Social justice in a diverse society*. Boulder, CO: Westview Press.

Uchino, B. N. (2004). *Social support and physical health: Understanding the health consequences of relationships*. New Haven, CT: Yale University Press.

Unger, M. (2002). A deeper, more social ecological social work practice. *Social Service Review*, 76(3), 480–497.

U.S. Bureau of the Census. (1996). *Marital status and living arrangements* (U.S. Department of Commerce, Economics and Statistics Administration, Series P20-496, March). Retrieved August 1998 from http://www.census.gov/population/www.socdemo/ms-la.html.

U.S. Bureau of the Census. (1997). *Press release*. Washington, DC: U.S. Department of Commerce, Economics and Statistics Administration. http://www.census.gov/Press-Release/cb97-162.html.

U.S. Bureau of the Census. (2003). *Health insurance coverage: 2002* (Current Population Reports, Series P60-223). Washington, DC: Government Printing Office.

U.S. Bureau of the Census. (2005). *Poverty in the United States*. http://www.census.gov/hhes/www/poverty/poverty05/pov05hi.html.

U.S. House of Representatives, Committee on Ways and Means. (1996). *Green book.* Washington, DC: Government Printing Office.

Valentine, D. P., Kiddoo, M., & Lafleur, B. (1993). Psychosocial implications of service dog ownership for people who have mobility or gearing impairments. *Social Work in Health Care, 19*(1), 109–125.

VanBergeikj, E., & McGowan, B. (2001). Children in foster care. In A. Gitterman (Ed.), *Handbook of social work practice with vulnerable and resilient populations* (2nd ed., pp. 399–434). New York: Columbia University Press.

Van Den Bergh, N., & Cooper, L. B. (Eds.). (1986). *Feminist visions for social work.* Silver Spring, MD: National Association of Social Workers.

Van Gheluwe, B., & Barber, J. K. (1986). Legislative advocacy in action. *Social Work, 31*(5), 393–395.

Van Voorhis, R., & McClain, L. (1997). Accepting a lesbian mother. *Families in Society, 78*(6), 642–650.

Vera, M., Alegria, M., Pattatucci-Aragon, A. M., & Pena, M. (2005). Childhood sexual abuse and drug use among low-income urban Puerto Rican women. *Journal of Social Work Practice in the Addictions, 5*(1/2), 45–68.

Vinter, R. D. (1959). Group work's perspectives and prospects. In *Social work with groups.* New York: National Association of Social Workers.

Vinter, R. D. (Ed.). (1966). *Readings in group work practice.* Ann Arbor, MI: Campus Publishers.

Wachtel, P. L. (2002). Termination of therapy: An effort at integration. *Journal of Psychotherapy Integration, 12*(3), 373–383.

Wade, J. C. (1994). African American fathers and sons: Social, historical, and psychological considerations. *Families in Society, 75*(9), 561–570.

Waites, C. (2001). Victoria Earle Matthews: Residence and reform. In I. B. Carlton-LaNey (Ed.), *African American leadership* (pp. 1–16). Washington, DC: National Association of Social Workers.

Wakefield, J. C. (1988). Psychotherapy, distributive justice, and social work. Part I: Distributive justice as a conceptual framework for social work. *Social Service Review, 62*(2), 187–210.

Wald, L. (1915). *The house on Henry Street.* New York: Holt.

Walden, T., Wolock, I., & Demone, H. W., Jr. (1990). Ethical decision making in human services: A comparative study. *Families in Society, 71*(1), 67–75.

Wall, J. C. (2001). Trauma and the clinician: Therapeutic implications in clinical work with clients. *Clinical Social Work Journal, 29*(2), 133–145.

Walsh, F. (2002). A family resilience framework: Innovative practice applications. *Family Relations, 51*(2), 130–137.

Walsh, J., & Harrigan, M. (2003a). The termination stage in Bowen's family systems theory. *Clinical Social Work Journal, 31*(4), 383–394.

Walsh, J., & Harrigan, M. (2003b). The termination phase in structural family intervention. *Family Therapy, 30*(1), 13–26.

Wampold, B. E., & Bhati, K. S. (2004). Attending to the omissions: A historical examination of evidenced-based practice movements. *Professional Psychology: Research and Practice, 35*(6), 563–570.

Ward, K. (2002). Confidentiality in substance abuse counseling. *Journal of Social Work Practice in the Addictions, 2*(2), 39–52.

Warner, A. G. (1894). *American charities: A study of philanthropy and economics.* New York: Thomas Y. Crowell.

Wasco, S. M. (2003). Conceptualizing the harm done by rape: Applications of trauma theory to experiences of sexual assault. *Trauma, Violence, & Abuse, 4*(4), 309–322.

Wax, J. (1968). Developing social work power in a medical setting. *Social Work, 13*(5), 62–71.

Wayne, J., & Cohen, C. S. (2001). *Group work education in the field*. Alexandria, VA: Council on Social Work Education.

Wayne, J., & Gitterman, A. (2004). Offensive behaviors in groups: Challenges and opportunities. *Social Work with Groups, 26*(2), 23–34.

Webb, S. A. (2001). Some consideration on the validity of evidence-based practice. *British Journal of Social Work, 31*, 57–79.

Weil, M. O. (2005). Introduction: Contexts and challenges for the 21st century. In M. O. Weil (Ed.), *The handbook of community practice* (pp. 3–33). Thousand Oaks, CA: Sage.

Weisner, T. S. (2005). Attachment as a cultural and ecological problem with pluralistic solutions. *Human Development, 48*(1/2), 89–94.

Weiss, R. (1973). The nature of loneliness. In R. Weiss (Ed.), *Loneliness: The experience of emotional and social isolation* (pp. 9–29). Cambridge, MA: MIT Press.

Weiss, R. (1982). Attachment in adult life. In C. Parkes & J. Stevenson-Hinde (Eds.), *The place of attachment in adult life* (pp. 171–183). New York: Basic Books.

Wellman, B., & Haythornthwaite, C. A. (Eds.). (2002). *The Internet in everyday life*. Malden, MA: Blackwell.

Wells, R. (1982). *Planned short-term treatment*. New York: Free Press.

Werner, C., Altman, I., Oxley, D., & Haggard, L. (1987). People, place, and time: A transactional analysis of neighborhoods. In W. Jones & D. Perlman (Eds.), *Advances in personal relationships* (pp. 243–275). New York: JAI Press.

Wichrowski, M., Chambers, N. K., & Ciccantelli, L. M. (1998). Stroke, spinal cord, and physical disabilities, and horticultural therapy practice. In S. P. Simson & M. C. Straus (Eds.), *Horticulture as therapy: Principles and practice* (pp. 71–104). Binghamton, NY: Food Products Press/Haworth Press.

Wierzbicki, M., & Pekarik, G. (1993). A meta-analysis of psychotherapy dropout. *Professional Psychology: Research and Practice, 24*, 190–195.

Wigle, T. (2003). *Child health and the environment*. New York: Oxford University Press.

Williams, S. L., Ketring, S. A., & Salts, C. J. (2005). Premature termination as a function of intake data based on ethnicity, gender, socioeconomic status, and income. *Contemporary Family Therapy: An International Journal, 27*(2), 213–231.

Wilson, A. M. (2005). Trained volunteers as mental health counselors: addressing the enormous shortage of trained counselors. *AFFILIA, 20*(4), 476–484.

Wilson, E. O. (2001). Nature matters. *American Journal of Preventive Medicine, 20*(3), 241–242.

Wise, J. B. (2005). *Empowerment practice with families in distress*. New York: Columbia University Press.

Wituk, S., Shepherd, M. D., Slavich, S., Warren, M. L., & Meissen, G. (2000). A topography of self-help groups: An empirical analysis. *Social Work, 45*(2), 157–165.

Wituk, S. A., Tiemeyer, S., Commer, A., Warren, M., & Meissen, G. (2003). Starting self-help groups: Empowering roles for social workers. *Social Work with Groups, 26*(1), 83–92.

Wodarski, J. S., & Williams-Hayes, M. M. (2002). Utilizing case management to maintain the elderly in the community. *Journal of Gerontological Social Work, 39*(4), 19–38.

Wood, G. G., & Frey, A. (2003). Helping children cope: A narrative approach to the Life Space Interview. *School Social Work Journal, 27*(2), 57–78.

Wright, W. (1999). The use of purpose in on-going activity groups: A framework for maximizing the therapeutic impact. *Social Work with Groups, 22*(2/3), 31–54.

Wyers, N. L. (1991). Policy practice in social work: Models and issues. *Journal of Social Work Education, 27*(3), 241–250.

Yalom, I., & Leszcz, M. (2005). *The theory and practice of group psychotherapy* (5th ed.). New York: Basic Books.

Zilberfein, F., & Hurwitz, E. (2003). Clinical social work practice at the end of life. *Smith College Studies in Social Work, 73*(3), 299–324.

Zilberfein, F., Hutson, C., Snyder, S., & Epstein, I. (2001). Social work practice with pre– and post–liver transplant patients: A retrospective self study. *Social Work in Health Care, 33*(3/4), 91–104.

Zlotnick, C., Kronstadt, D., & Klee, L. (1999). Essential case management services for young children in foster care. *Community Mental Health Journal, 35*(5), 421–430.

Zuckerman, A., & Mitchell, G. L. (2004). Psychology interns' perspectives on the forced termination of psychotherapy. *Clinical Supervisor, 23*(1), 55–70.

INDEX

Note: Page numbers in *italics* indicate tables or figures.